# The Infinite Dream
## THE OPENING OF THE GREAT AMERICAN WEST

# Allan W. Eckert
January 30, 1931 - July 7, 2011

Allan W. Eckert, historian, naturalist, novelist, poet, screenwriter, and playwright, was nominated for a Pulitzer Prize on seven separate occasions. Allan died on July 7, 2011, shortly before the publication of *The Infinite Dream*, his forty-first major book.

◆

*To all of us who love American history and love any master teacher-writer who can sharply illuminate and clarify the specific details of our short but dramatic and complex story, Allan has been a national treasure. I personally owe far more to him for my humble knowledge of the 18th- and 19th-century settling of the American wilderness than I do to any other historian, and I suspect that legions and legions of my fellow citizens are similarly indebted to him.*

*We will miss Allan and always be in his debt.*

—Thayle Anderson
Professor Emeritus
Murray State University

# The Infinite Dream
## THE OPENING OF THE GREAT AMERICAN WEST

by
Allan W. Eckert

JESSE STUART
FOUNDATION
Ashland, Kentucky
2011

Copyright © 2011 by Allan W. Eckert

FIRST EDITION

All rights reserved. Printed in the United States of America. No part of this publication may be reproduced in whole or in part, or utilized in any form or by any means, electronic or mechancial, including photocopying, recording, or by any information or retrieval system, without written permission of the publisher.

ISBN: 978-1-931672-75-7

Illustrations by
Jim Marsh and Thom Marsh

Published by
Jesse Stuart Foundation
1645 Winchester Avenue
Ashland, Kentucky 41101
(606) 326-1667
jsfbooks.com

# Prologue

◆

*[September 21, 1834 · Sunday]*

Standing at the steamship rail with a throng of other passengers, the man in the rumpled dark suit attracted no particular attention. His gaze was fixed on the bustling activity of this waterfront city they were approaching on the shoreline of the turbid Mississippi River. This was St. Louis and though from all he'd heard, he rather expected a good-sized town, he was quite taken by how big it actually was, and how busy.

Half a dozen steamships loading and unloading cargo were moored at the many wharves lining the shore. Next to the scarred wooden platforms stood dozens of essentially windowless buildings that were undoubtedly warehouses, while scores of workmen—stevedores, merchants, slaves, messengers and crewmen—mingled with crowds of travelers laden with baggage, some ready to board for other destinations, some newly arrived and moving generally into the city that sprawled up the bluffs and into an impressive, more level expanse beyond.

John Sutter smiled slightly. This was it. Here his new life would begin; the place where he might sink permanent roots if circumstances seemed right; but equally it could be the place from which he would launch himself into some unknown destiny. Whatever that destiny might be, he felt that it had to be a life better than that through which he had plodded for the past three decades.

At thirty-one, Johann August Sutter had thus far walked beneath a stormy cloud of failure in virtually every undertaking. There had even been a tremendous snowstorm on the night he was born, February 15, 1803, in the tiny hamlet of Kandern, nestled in the mountains of northern Switzerland near the German border.[1]

# The Infinite Dream

The entire countryside was in turmoil throughout his childhood as Germany clashed with Napoleon's army and numerous troops bivouacked at Kandern. When he was ten, the allied leaders opposed to Napoleon—King Frederick Wilhelm of Prussia, Emperor Joseph II of Austria and the Russian Czar Alexander—established their campaign headquarters in Basel. Their troops, led by officers in dashing uniforms, forced Napoleon, after the Battle of Leipzig, westward out of Germany and across the Rhine River into France. All this made a lasting impression on young Sutter, who envisioned himself in dashing uniform and fearlessly leading such troops.

Sutter's mother, Frau Clara, was the educated daughter of a clergyman and schooled Johann and his brothers well—they, much more attentive than he—until they were old enough to attend French and Latin classes at Kandern's public school. Latin was of little interest to Johann, but he quickly became fluent in French, which he already knew to some degree. For an interval following this they were tutored in a private school at Neuchatel, Switzerland. Johann did poorly and was frequently disciplined for disruptive conduct. At age seventeen he apprenticed to a well-established printer, Emanuel Thurneysen, but he was restless and unreliable and finally, after four disruptive years, was fired.

In the town of Aarberg, ten miles northwest of Berne, he found a new job selling drapery materials and it was here that he met Annette Dubeld.[2] She was not attractive but her widowed mother was reasonably wealthy and Annette was available. She fell in love with him and he fell in lust with her. She had little difficulty convincing him to quit his draperies job and move to her home town of Burgdorf, a dozen miles northeast of Berne, so they could be together more frequently. There he found a job as a butcher's assistant.

When Annette conceived a child, Sutter showed no inclination to marry, despite her entreaties which soon evolved into threats. He changed his mind, however, when he was visited by two husky men—the Revered Samuel Jaggi, an elder of Annette's church, and the reverend's friend, a lawyer named Carl Schnell—who made it quite clear that marry her, Sutter must. And so he did, on October 24, 1826—a scant two months before the birth of their son, Johann Augustus Sutter.

It came as no surprise when Sutter failed miserably as butcher's aide but with glib charm and guile that was one of his greatest assets, he managed to convince his mother-in-law to provide financial backing for him to open a dry goods establishment in Burgdorf. For a while he appeared to be doing well but appearances are deceptive; he had, in fact, gravely overextended by buying too much stock, by badly botching his bookkeeping, by blandly trusting an unproven assistant who stole the store's funds, and by impulsively taking to heart and acting upon all manner of suspect business advice. Nor was his personal life any better: While he and Annette argued incessantly, it did not prevent her from churning out offspring on a regular basis. As Sutter constantly fell deeper into debt, by the end of 1833 four more children were born.[3]

With bankruptcy only a hairsbreadth away, Sutter surreptitiously sold off much of his remaining stock at prices well under cost to finance what he was planning. Through the help of some shady friends he acquired a bogus passport and without a word to anyone—Annette in particular—he left Burgdorf and went first to Basel, then on to France's busiest seaport, Le Havre. He quickly located a ship preparing to embark for America and, with that same charm and glibness that had served his purposes so well with his mother-in-law, secured a job as cabin-boy.

On the very day that Sutter set sail for the New World a brief notice appeared in Berne and was widely distributed elsewhere in Switzerland:

### Berne. June 12. 1834

*Johann A. Sutter, merchant of Burgdorf, Canton of Berne, has secretly liquefied his assets and is believed to be on his way to America. He owes the sum of 6,000 francs. The police are hereby notified to arrest him on sight and notify the authorities at Berne immediately.*

It was not until Sutter had found himself temporary quarters in New York City that he wrote to Annette, apologizing for leaving her in such manner but that, under the circumstances, he'd had no other choice. He added that he knew Annette's mother would take her and the children into her comfortable household where they would be better provided for. He closed by saying that when he earned enough money he would return to Burgdorf and care for her in a manner that would suit her custom. He did not tell her that he had altered his given name to John upon reaching America, nor did the envelope in which he sealed her letter bear a return address.

He had worked in New York just long enough to earn the requisite amount to purchase a meager wardrobe and essentials. Then, utilizing the money he had earned as cabin boy, he made his way to Pittsburgh where he bought passage aboard a steamboat heading down the 1,000-mile stretch of the Ohio River to its mouth, then upstream on the Mississippi another 250 miles.

Now standing at the rail with St. Louis looming before him and watching the gap steadily closing between ship and Missouri shore, John Sutter's smile broadened. Somehow, some way, everything would work out.

He knew it would.

*[August 15, 1836 • Monday]*

Henry Bigler was a young man who was not outstanding in any respect. Average was particularly suitable to him: Average height and build; average features; neither brilliant nor dull but just average; living in what he viewed as an average household and, as a student, he had never been deemed as anything better than average.

He had been born on his parents' farm only a short distance from the village of Shinnston, Harrison County, in western Virginia and that was where he had been raised and still lived.[4]

Bigler was not customarily given to philosophical contemplation and even less to introspection. Nor was he, despite his upbringing in a Mennonite family, particularly inclined toward Godly endeavors. He often viewed with amused distaste those who strode through life carrying Him on their shoulders and regularly spouting Biblical rhetoric. Evangelists were anathema to him—those who proclaimed themselves to be the chosen disciples bestowed with divine latitude to be interpreters of God's word and the instruments of His discipline; those who were convinced they were invested with the power to damn to Hell all who did not believe; those who condemned all who did not comport themselves in strict conformance to the tenets and strictures they uttered and which they devoutly claimed to be orders received directly from the Almighty.

Henry Bigler believed in God, yes, and always had, so far as he could remember, but hardly as an avenging overseer constantly sitting in judgment; more, in fact, as a benevolent semi-presence in his life who took on the aspect of a conscience that gently approved or disapproved of the choices he made and provided a sort of tenuous standard of morals that guided behavior and molded character.

Now, quite suddenly, his entire religious outlook had been changed.

Last week two well-dressed gentlemen riding in a black carriage en route to New York City had tarried for a day in Harrison County, having previously made two-day stops in Huntington, Charleston and Clarksburg. This stop in Shinnston had not been part of their itinerary but had become necessary when one of their carriage wheels required repair. Henry and his father had come to town that day from their nearby farm, the farm where Henry had been born and where he had always lived, riding. Father and son had made this trip to town in their dilapidated wagon pulled by their equally dilapidated mare, Tillie. Their errand had been to buy a few supplies at Hampton's General Store and that was where they had encountered the pair. Henry, intent on visiting a friend who lived in town, had excused himself and gone on, but Jacob had engaged in lengthy conversation with them. When Henry rejoined his father two hours later and they headed home with supplies, Jacob spoke of the two men. They were, he said, Mormons—elders of the Church of Jesus Christ of Latter-day Saints—and he had become intrigued with what they had to say about the faith and its founder, Joseph Smith.[5] That the pair had made an extraordinary impact was clear to Henry; his father, never quickly nor easily swayed about anything new, was so taken with what the Mormon elders had said that he was returning home with two books they had sold him at a price the Bigler family could ill afford. These books were *The Book of Mormon*, published three years ago, and *Doctrine and Covenants*, which had been published only last year.

Oddly enough during the subsequent week, Jacob Bigler, apparently chagrined at his impulsive purchase, had not even opened them, but Henry had. Books were a precious commodity in the Bigler household and their own meager library had been read repeatedly by every member of the family. Any new book that became a part of that little hoard, irrespective of content, would be regarded initially as a first rate experience and afterwards as a household treasure to be read and reread as time passed. And so, more out of curiosity than anything else, this past week Henry Bigler had read both.

The two volumes changed his life. He had thought of little else since reading them; the more he considered their content, the more convinced he became that *The Book of Mormon* was a divine record and Joseph Smith himself divinely inspired. And though he had yet taken no official vows nor had even attended a Mormon service, today he made the fervent and absolute vow to himself that hereafter the faith of the Mormons was his own faith, to which he would adhere for so long as he lived.

It was perhaps significant that today was Henry W. Bigler's twenty-first birthday.[6]

*[June 6, 1837 • Tuesday]*

John Sutter continued to stare at the door for a long moment after Father Rene Beaulieu left the store and disappeared from view, the French-Canadian priest's words still echoing in his mind. The fundamental pattern of Sutter's life had not changed; once again he had experienced the bitter taste of failure and once again he had become buoyed by an exciting new possibility for his future.

Over the nearly three years since he had first arrived in St. Louis, Sutter had felt sure in his own heart that he would make his mark quickly in this new land, but that hadn't happened. Immediately upon having disembarked from the steamship that had brought him to Missouri, he had made his way to the Hotel Schwyzerland, recommended to him by a fellow passenger as a place operated by and habituated by Germans, both locals and travelers. He took lodging there and, in his usual charming way, made acquaintances easily. He quickly became a favorite as he mingled with the groups who played card games or chess or held lengthy discussions about politics, literature, art and, most particularly, the American frontier. When questioned about his own background in Europe, he glibly made up a tale that he had been a captain in the Swiss Guard of Charles X but that he had been forced to flee for his life from France when the 1830 revolution had broken out.

The associations Sutter made with German and French merchants handily paved the way for his finding backing among them to open a trade of sorts among the rather large population of German immigrants who had settled in a broad semicircle around St. Louis and he did rather well at it. By the following spring he had earned enough not only to repay his backers but to begin to set aside funds for a new project that had begun to interest him. Among the many people he met were merchants who regularly plied the trade route from the Missouri River at the far western border of Missouri, through the arid Indian Territory to Santa Fe, where the large Spanish population was hungry for whatever goods were brought. After accompanying one of the trading caravans that went there, and seeing the huge profits, Sutter was confident he could do equally well, if not better. He returned to St. Louis and continued working through the ensuing fall and winter to earn a stake large enough for him to procure the wagons and goods needed to launch his own Santa Fe trading enterprise.

The idea was good, but there were two important factors Sutter neglected taking into consideration; a competition among the traders that was much more fierce and cut-throat than anticipated, and the horrendous taxes levied against American traders by Spanish authorities. Instead of returning with a healthy profit, he lost his entire investment, including his wagons. He was too ashamed to return to St. Louis and so depressed over this latest failure that for a while he actually contemplated suicide.

Eventually, however, Sutter drifted into western Missouri, used by the fur brigades as a staging area for their operations. Mingling with them he learned something of what the mysterious West promised for those hardy enough to survive its perils. For the first time he began contemplating going there himself. However he was destitute—again. He would need a stake and toward this end he soon found a job as clerk in a mercantile house in the nearby settlement appropriately called Westport and gradually built up a new reserve of funds.[7]

It was at this juncture that Sutter's tenuous idea of going to the West became more focused. He had first heard of California from a trader at Santa Fe whose description of that Spanish territory had sparked his interest. Now it had abruptly become a distinct destination. This change occurred when Father Beaulieu stopped by the store. He was heading eastward with Quebec his goal, having just completed an extended stay in California and Sutter, whose curiosity about that territory had already been piqued, plied him with questions. They talked for several hours and the Franciscan priest told him details of the beautiful land that lay westward of the Sierras; a land of consistently moderate temperatures, fertile valleys of great dimension, a lengthy growing season; vast forests of virgin timber and millions of acres of land ideal for raising cattle, sheep and horses. It was, Father Beaulieu told him, little short of paradise. Best of all, it was so sparsely populated—with virtually all of the existing non-Indian population living in a mere handful of communities along the Pacific Coast. Better yet, Spanish authorities welcomed foreigners and much of the journey westward could be accomplished by following the already well-proven Oregon Trail. A responsible man with good credentials and finances, he added, might well expect to receive a grant of land in the thousands of acres, simply by applying to the governor of the territory.

There was, in California, Father Beaulieu continued, an abundance of game as well as a great many sparkling rivers teeming with salmon, trout and sturgeon; but the greatest of these—the river that formed the drainage for the entire northern and central regions as well as the Sierras to the east—was the mighty Sacramento, which had not yet been explored beyond some thirty or forty miles up from its mouth. Its broad valley could easily become, for a strong and enterprising individual, the seat of a vast empire of cattle and agriculture.

At last the priest departed to continue his journey eastward, but the seed he had unwittingly left behind had quickly taken root in John Sutter's imagination and he was already considering the steps he would have to take to reach this paradise called California—the place where he was suddenly quite certain he was destined to establish a Sutter empire.

*[November 30, 1837 • Thursday]*

At twenty-nine, Lieutenant Mariano Guadalupe Vallejo was already one of the wealthiest men in all of California and now the promotion he had just received was helping him to become the most powerful. On his grant, called Petaluma, roamed some 10,000 head of cattle, thousands of sheep, and more than 6,000 horses. His ranch house, always referred to as La Hacienda, was the place he most liked to be—a retreat where he could occasionally escape the restrictions and responsibilities imposed by his official position—but more often, as now, he would be found at his desk in the baronial headquarters facing the plaza in the small town of Sonoma.[8]

He glanced through the broadly arched window at the troops already beginning to assemble on the parade ground for his inspection and smiled faintly, reflecting on the long road that had brought him finally to this place and position. Such a wonderful land California was and how foolish mother Spain had been to so shamefully neglect it, to treat it as an afterthought, and of little consequence. Vallejo's smile evolved into a vague frown as his recurrent fear returned that one of these days some foreign power would wrest away this poorly defended territory.

That such an event had not occurred more than half a century earlier when the Russians first came, was a wonderment. Luckily for Spain, the intruders were more interested in peltry than conquest. Their sole reason for encroaching along California's rugged coast was to tap the rich resource of furs—fur seals, sea lions and, most of all, the sea otter, whose coat was second in quality only to Russian sable. Though Alta California, with the exception of San Diego in its southwestern corner, was populated only by a multitude of unallied Indian tribes at that time, Spain had nevertheless become alarmed at their incursions.[9] In order to more firmly substantiate the Spanish claim and to exhibit the ready willingness of Carlos III to defend this remote region of his empire, the viceroy of New Spain—José del Galvez—ordered that a string of presidios, missions and pueblos be established along the coast northward from San Diego. It then had fallen upon Lieutenant Colonel Juan Bautista de Anza, Captain of the province of Sonora's Royal Presidio of Tubac, to execute that order. In the autumn and winter of 1775 he did so. His entire force, numbering 240 individuals included a small army comprised of three officers—Vallejo's father, Don José Juan Vallejo, being one of them—and twenty seasoned soldiers, many with families, along with thirty mule handlers, plus three Franciscan missionaries and twenty destitute civilian families from Sinaloa in Sonora who were to begin the colonization. These became the first Europeans to enter California by land, successfully crossing treacherous deserts and mountains, establishing the Spanish Trail.

The Spanish colonizers had established their first little pueblos along the California coast during the early months of 1776 and finally, in mid-June, they reached a great headland where they built a more substantial pueblo. De Anza named it Monterey and declared it to be the capital of Alta California.[10] The move north continued to an even greater headland, with the Pacific to the west and the gigantic natural harbor of San Francisco Bay to the east. Here at its heart was established the Mission Dolores and three miles northwest, at the commanding uppermost point of land overlooking the entry to San Francisco Bay, de Anza established the Presidio of San Francisco. Not long after, he established a mission even farther north, naming it the Mission San Francisco Solano. In the ensuing years, more California missions sprang up and large numbers of Spanish families came from Mexico to settle, forming sprawling communities in the area surrounding the twenty-one missions that had been established at Santa Catalina, San Gabriel

# The Infinite Dream

[Los Angeles], San Buenaventura, San Fernando, Santa Barbara, San Luis Obispo, San José and other locations.

This string of Franciscan missions had served the Spanish communities along the coast well enough but, unlike their Jesuit counterparts far to the east in the St. Lawrence Valley and the region of the Great Lakes, they developed little influence over the vast populations of native tribes inland. At most, only some 30,000 Indians were proselytized, which was a scant ten per cent of the 300,000 known to be living in California, and troubles with these Indians remained a problem for Lieutenant Vallejo. It was, he reflected, a problem his own people had brought upon themselves with their bestial treatment of the Indians. Early on almost all the Spanish families had Indian slaves; many still did. These were acquired easily enough by Spanish vaqueros who rode into the wilderness to the east and entered Indian villages, driving out the children before them and casually killing any parents who tried to intervene. These children, ideally from five to twelve years old—and girls more desirable than boys—were herded to Spanish settlements and sold at auction, usually bringing between $50 and $100 each. The captives quickly learned to take over such chores as cooking, housecleaning, gardening, washing, ironing and nurse-maiding. Little wonder the interior tribes remained hostile and a continuing problem that Vallejo was now shouldering.

The Russians—having established their headquarters on Sitka Island in the Aleutian archipelago of Alaska, which they claimed as their territory—were still interested in California only as a source of peltry. When they petitioned Spain for permission to use an expanse of land fronting on the safe harbor of Bodega Bay fifty miles north of the Presidio of San Francisco, that boon was granted. During 1811 the Russians built there a strong fortification named Fort Ross. It became the center of a relatively small farming community called Port Romanov and the core of their California fur trade operations; a dangerous toehold to give to a foreign power within Spanish territory but, again, conquest was not the Russian objective at this point.

Vallejo himself had been born only three years earlier in Monterey, on July 7, 1808, to a family both wealthy and influential. He had received an excellent education and his term as military cadet prepared him well for his present role in Alta California. His father at Monterey and grandfather, Don Ygnacio Vallejo, at San Luis Obispo, had been visionary enough to build great systems of aqueducts to bring in fresh water. They also helped their communities overcome the menace posed by the great numbers of wild horses that competed for pasturage with domestic cattle, horses and sheep. In 1801 some 7,000 such wild horses were deliberately driven into the sea and drowned at Santa Barbara and nine years later another 8,000 were similarly slain at Monterey.

Vallejo was concerned that California might eventually be ruined or usurped by foreigners who were arriving in ever increasing numbers. He was more than a little appalled by, and strongly opposed to, the current government policy that not only welcomed foreigners but often even gave them grants of land. The influx had begun slowly: The first foreigner to permanently settle in California was James Gilroy, a Scottish sailor who had arrived in 1814 and, with government approval, established a rancho. Two years later Thomas W. Doak became the first American to settle here permanently. And then came others—Bill Gulnac, J.A. Forbes, Harry Bee, J.W. Weeks, John Burton and Matthew Fellom being among the earliest.

When only a boy of eleven, Vallejo was outraged that mother Spain, in an 1819 deal that defied his comprehension, ceded to the United States all claims to the lands north of forty-two degrees North Latitude—a parcel called the Oregon Territory; a deal disputed by the British, who averred it was theirs to begin with. That the ongoing argument over it between the United States and Great Britain might ultimately result in a war seemed to young Vallejo a reasonable likelihood that could only further jeopardize California itself. Others, including many Mexican individuals of great influence, remaining incensed over the cession, became outspoken in their long-held belief that Mexico should declare independence from Spain. It was a matter of great satisfaction to Vallejo when, two years later, on February 24, 1821, Mexico did exactly that, at the same time claiming independence from Spain for both Texas and California.

Spain did not dispute the act and the Mexicans immediately crowned thirty-eight-year-old Augustin de Iturbide as temporary emperor pending selection of a new ruler the next year. When that time came, however, Iturbide was retained as emperor. Designations were changing and to differentiate between them, the Spaniards who had taken up permanent residency in Mexico continued to be called Mexicans, while those in Texas were called Texans or, by the Americans living there, Texicans, and those in California were referred to as Californios. The governor of this Mexican California was an elderly, much respected politician named Ygnacio Sola.

The influx of foreigners to California continued, with commerce as the impetus. Ships arrived ever more often and from varied ports. Many were trading vessels out of Boston that had made the long voyage down the Atlantic and around Cape Horn at the southern tip of South America. From there they sailed northward on the Pacific to the California coast where they bartered for a wide variety of fruits and vegetables in the southern ports, tallow and hides in the middle ports and peltry—particularly sea otter, which were selling from $4 - 6 per pound, and beaver, which brought about half as much—in the north.[11] During the early 1820s a disturbing number of both American and British hunters and fur trappers began drifting into California by land, most of them associated either with John Jacob Astor's fur empire or the Hudson's Bay Company. While the latter faction came and left rather quickly, numbers of the Americans stayed on. Some courted and married the daughters of wealthy Spanish ranchers and then, through their in-laws' influence, obtained sizeable land grants.

In 1824, Vallejo, then 16, entered the Mexican military as a cadet in the Monterey Company. Discipline was strict but lessons in soldiering were well taught. In Vallejo's class were his nephew, Juan Bautista Alvarado, and fiery-tempered friend, José Castro. All three were eager to learn more of their world, but the books available in the academy were primarily of a spiritually uplifting nature or religious tomes; other books were considered heretical and strictly banned. Governor Sola, however, who had taken a special interest in boys, aided in procuring a few volumes of a more secular aspect. Vallejo's first promotion came on July 30, 1827 when he was nineteen and elevated to the rank of *alferez*, equivalent to an ensign; at the same time he became a member of the Territorial Deputation.

In 1830, at age twenty-two, Vallejo was reassigned from the Monterey Company to the San Francisco Company at the Presidio and the following year he was made commandant of the San Francisco Company of the Mexican Army, in which capacity he led several successful campaigns against hostile Indians in California's interior, especially those who had been attacking settlers along the Contra Costa River.[12] It was on his return from one of these forays that he met and fell in love with the most attractive woman he had ever encountered—Francisca Benecia Carrillo—and she with him. She was the loveliest of the beautiful daughters of Don Joaquín Carrillo and his wife, Maria Ignacia López, and the pair were married in the Mission Dolores on March 6, 1831.

In 1832 the commandant of the Presidio of San Francisco, Captain Ygnacio Martínez, died and Vallejo, now twenty-four, succeeded him in command, a signal honor for one so young. The Presidio at this time had a population of near 250, including the wives and children of the soldiers. Vallejo was elated at his appointment and soon became particularly interested in the establishment of a port to serve the increasing number of vessels entering San Francisco Bay where not one port yet existed. Locating the proper site had already been an issue under consideration by one of the foreigners living near the Presidio, an English sea captain named William A. Richardson, who commanded a trading vessel operating down the Pacific Coast as far south as Valparaiso, Chile, and whose wife was the daughter of the late Captain Martínez. In addition to his own ship, Richardson was presently in charge of a schooner owned by the Mission Santa Clara and several belonging to the Mission Dolores. He owned the Sausalito Rancho directly opposite The Presidio on the north side of the entry to San Francisco Bay and his neighbors with adjoining ranches included another Englishman who was an otter hunter, Tim Murphy, and a Scot named James Black. All were as interested as Vallejo in establishing a port and discussed the matter at length. Because of his maritime experience, Richardson was requested to locate the best possible site.

All this occurred while Mexico was falling ever deeper in debt. Most of those who worked for the government—military officers in particular—had not been paid in a very long time. Some resigned but others stayed on and maintained their duties at their own expense, which was a costly matter for those such as Vallejo, who were in command positions. It became the practice, for those who had suffered this onus to a critical point on behalf of the government, military and civilians alike, to submit a request for a land grant. This was the one way in which reparation could be made that was a relatively satisfactory substitute. On such grants the Californios could then raise stock and recoup their lost wages in the process of selling beef, cowhides and sheep tallow. Despite this sop, many of the presidios, unable to be maintained, were abandoned.

Vallejo was surprised and pleased when, in 1834, he was richly rewarded for his excellence in military command, for his services in quelling Indian attacks and mollifying various chiefs, and for his personal expenses in maintaining The Presidio of San Francisco. His reward was a grant of land that he immediately named Petaluma Rancho—a grant of ten square leagues, to which Vallejo added five more by purchase. The total area of his new property amounted to 66,000 acres and he began at once, with a portion of the funds he had remaining, to build a grand estate he would call La Hacienda, and to buy large numbers of sheep, horses and cattle to run free over the land and procreate.

During the following spring, Vallejo was as thunderstruck as most other Californios when an official proclamation was circulated announcing the secularization of all the missions in California. It was totally unexpected and inexplicable to most, but Vallejo was among those with a keen enough grasp of the situation to understand why the missionaries were being sent home and their missions deactivated as religious sites. It had been no secret to the Mexican government that during the sixty years of their existence, the twenty-one missions that had been established had not only proselytized 30,000 Indians, they had also accumulated 60,000 horses, 400,000 head of cattle and 300,000 sheep. Just the annual butchering of 200,000 beeves alone produced an income of $1 million for the church, and that was but one aspect of their total annual earnings.

The Mexican politicians were appalled that such vast funds being collected each year were never seen by them—or, as an afterthought, by the government—and political greed came to the forefront. The reasoning was that if the mission priests were sent packing and if the missions themselves were converted into Indian pueblos, the income that had previously been going to the church would instead come to the government or, more pertinently, to pad the pockets of the governor and other select government figures. But without the stabilizing influence of the priests, most of the Christianized Indians fled and reverted to their previous lives of barbarism. As a result, the secularized missions largely became abandoned shells and what incipient income remained went mainly into the pockets of Governors Flores and Alvarado and a few other high-placed officials.

While Vallejo was, by duty, required to play a role in this sweeping, ill-conceived transition, he neither received nor desired to receive any of the subsequent booty, and his role in the great scenario was not only minor, it was as honorable as he could enable it to be. The advisory had come appointing him director of colonization in the North and ordering him to go as commissioner to secularize the Mission San Francisco Solano and lay out a pueblo there. He was also authorized to bestow land grants to Californios to thwart any notion the Russians at Bodega Bay might entertain to extend their land occupation eastward. He had done exactly as directed and more, laboring much to lay out the pueblo, including his headquarters, which he named Sonoma—Valley of the Moon—after the Indian name for the river valley. He then convinced a number of Californio families to take up residence in the new town.

No longer able to maintain The Presidio of San Francisco out of his own personal funds, Vallejo ordered it abandoned and transferred his entire San Francisco Company to Sonoma. In addition, from the still hovering Christianized Indians in the area he recruited a force of fifty as supernumerary to his company and drilled them in the manual of arms. With no funds likely to be coming from the government, he supported the whole new operation out of his own pocket. Finally, he confronted Count Alexander Rotchev, commander of Fort Ross and governor of Port Romanov, the Russian community at Bodega Bay.

"I must remind you, sir," he said in his firm, dignified manner, "that you and your people are on California soil and that while your use of the Bodega Bay area is being tolerated, should you permit foreigners to land here and enter the country in defiance of our laws, you must not be surprised if you find Mexican troops stationed here."

Rotchev, who only the day before had received word of a strong likelihood existing that Czar Nicholas I would, in the not too distant future, order the abandonment of Fort Ross, smiled pleasantly. "And I, sir," he replied, "can only assure you with the greatest of sincerity that we here are deeply indebted to the Mexican government for its past generosity and the thought of betraying that kindness has not once entered our minds."

Vallejo, though well versed in the deceits of high station, nevertheless believed Rotchev and returned to Sonoma with his concerns about the Russian situation in satisfactory abeyance. Upon arriving at his new headquarters on June 22, he was deeply gratified to learn of his promotion to the rank of lieutenant.

Immediately afterward, Vallejo met with Captain William

Richardson and inspected the site the seaman thought best for establishing a port in San Francisco Bay. No place along the northern shore of the headland from sea to bay lent itself to any kind of feasible mooring, but by following the south shoreline eastward and then southward along the west side of the bay, Richardson had found a slight but extensive indentation, a little cove that had potential, just to the south of a prominent knoll called Loma Alto. The water was deep enough that even the largest of vessels could anchor close to shore, while the shoreline itself seemed near ideal for future waterfront development. The site was only a mile from Mission Dolores where a population of some 2,000 Indians still lingered, not knowing where else to go after having lived here for so many years. A fair number had been educated at the Mission and were now fairly well skilled as carpenters, tailors, blacksmiths and shipwrights, with many more unskilled but available for all manner of menial labor; a ready work force that would be of considerable benefit in development of the new port.

Vallejo nodded in approval. "Does this place have a name?"

Richardson grunted. "It's called Yerba Buena Cove—means Good Grass…Good Pasture. Good enough name for the port, Yerba Buena."[13]

Vallejo immediately performed what preliminary steps were requisite for establishment of a civil government for the Port of Yerba Buena. Reasonably enough, William Richardson was appointed harbormaster and received instructions that any ships of foreign registry that arrived for any purpose other than trade were first required to stop at the Port of Monterey to be granted official government permission. The ship captain had soon erected the first dwelling in the town. The trading tent, as he termed it, wasn't much: four redwood posts sunk upright into the ground with a large piece of canvas stretched over it, tacked into place and the whole covered with a piece of ship's sail large enough to almost reach the ground on three sides.

Not until eleven months later, however, in May, 1836, did the first permanent structure rise. It occurred when American trader Jacob Leese, who had been living in the Los Angeles pueblo, came north and conferred with his partners, Nathan Spear and William S. Hinckley, in Monterey, and then with the governor. He came away with written instructions for the *alcalde* at Yerba Buena to grant Mr. Leese and his partners a land allotment sufficient to his requirements.[14] Upon his arrival at Yerba Buena, he announced his intention of establishing a mercantile house on the site and was granted a plot of ground measuring 100 *vara* just south of Richardson's tent, some 250 yards from the water's edge.[15] With the assistance of Indian carpenters hired from the Mission Dolores, Leese then set about erecting a quite substantial frame building which was completed by July 4.

Since the beginning of 1836, political interest was manifest in California, with many of the Californios protesting "the corrupt practices of Governor Gutierrez flagrantly feathering his own pockets through secularization of the missions." Prominent among the protestors were two of Lieutenant Vallejo's former cadet classmates—the fiery-tempered José Castro and Vallejo's own nephew, Juan Bautista Alvarado. When the latter mounted a campaign to unseat Gutierrez and install himself as California governor, Vallejo at first supported him fully.

Popular and handsome, Alvarado was, in fact, successful in supplanting Gutierrez as governor but now, a year later, Vallejo's support had waned. It had become clear to the lieutenant that his hedonistic nephew was filling his own pockets. Alvarado was enjoying far too much the lavish luxuries to which his office gave him access, while at the same time sorely neglecting his administrative duties and mainly leaving the affairs of government to the horde of political sycophants constantly in attendance. His nepotism was clearly evident and favoritism toward friends was making severe inroads into government funds. Worst of all, he had begun bestowing an excessive number of land grants, primarily to friends but also to foreigners. Even though California had lands galore to grant at governmental whim, Vallejo could not help but feel that the practice, as being carried out by his nephew, could only ultimately be to the detriment of all Californios.

Lieutenant Mariano Guadalupe Vallejo also suspected that he had inadvertently become a part of Alverado's nepotism with the notification he had just received of his significant promotion: His rank remained the same but he was appointed Military Commander of the Northern Frontier, making him one of the most powerful military figures in all California.

Now, while still uncomfortable with the suspicion that nepotism had played a hand in his appointment, at the same time he knew he deserved the office and vowed to fulfill his duties with utmost fairness and with the benefit of the citizens of California always a foremost consideration.

*[November 30, 1838 • Friday]*

Henry Bigler did not fully understand the antipathy that had sprung up against Mormons gathered here in the westernmost reaches of Missouri, not only evident in the citizenry but in the highest echelons of state government. Joseph Smith had loudly declared the town of Far West in Jackson County to be the Zion of the Mormons; Bigler, along with thousands of others who had embraced the theology and doctrines of the Church of Jesus Christ of the Latter-day Saints, had come here not only to be at the heart of the church but to be close to its charismatic founder and leader. All were eager to aid in the erection of a great temple that Smith had announced God had directed be built on this site. A cornerstone was laid last July 4, but that was where the work had stopped because of sharply increased persecution of the Saints.

There were four primary causes, along with a host of minor ones, for the widespread and growing hatred of the Mormons. First of all, both the strength of the Mormons and their greatest weakness lay in their unity. It was part of what Joseph Smith had ordained as the *Law of Consecration and Stewardship*; a system under which communicants were required to consecrate all they possessed to the church. In return they received stewardship, which meant a home in the church, the requisite resources to practice their trade or profession and, of course, acceptance into the true family of God. It was a congregation with enormous power. The church itself termed it the *United Order* and it was, in essence, a practical, working form of theocratic communism. To the uneducated, it was equivalent to the single-mindedness of a large and rapidly-growing nest of ants.

Secondly, they wielded undeniable grassroots political power. When election time came, they voted as one in whatever direction the church deemed appropriate and, with thousands of controlled votes, this created a political bloc that could, and often did, alter the balance of power. Politicians recognized this strength and the various political parties, including even the most prominent—Whigs and Democrats—actively sought their support; but as much as they sought it, so too they feared it.

A third factor involved the matter of economics. The Mormons used their strong, united influence to control finances, trade and real estate values throughout whatever region in which they chose to settle. That caused anger to rise among bankers, frustration among realtors, bitterness among traders and unparalleled envy among ordinary citizens.

Finally, and perhaps the most frequently cited reason for such hatred, the church permitted the practice of polygamy. At first they were relatively open about it but because of the strong opposition of outsiders, over the past five years they had become more discreet in this pursuit. However, the secrecy was not absolute and periodic news stories fanned the flames of disgust and horror. Polygamy was unquestionably an abomination in the eyes of a society that generally deemed monogamy as an important foundation stone in religious institution.

A strong factor underlying all the other causes for the hatred were declarations by virtually all Mormons that they were the chosen of God and that whatever they did was done at His bidding; they did nothing to allay the impression that they possessed a God-given monopoly on truth and righteousness. Their mantle of smug conviction that they would very quickly dominate the entire world was more than irritating to the adherents of other faiths; adherents whom the Mormons regarded as misguided and faiths they deemed little short of meaningless.

Those were the fundamental reasons for the prevailing distrust and aversion non-Saints felt for the people who proclaimed themselves to be the *only* Saints. Yet, by far the majority of these Saints were similar to Henry Bigler—simple, gentle, generous, hard-working people who had found in Mormonism a faith and a *unity* that expelled selfishness in favor of what was good of all.

Bigler was aware that persecution had followed the Mormons— or generated around them—wherever they happened to be; first in New England, then in Ohio; now, even more pointedly, here in western Missouri, especially in the counties of Caldwell, Carroll, Clay, Daviess and Jackson.

Last June, when Bigler had first come here to the proclaimed Zion, he was elated at being able to see Joseph Smith, The Prophet, himself. He immediately threw his energies into the work that was relegated to him, cutting and stockpiling lumber at a sawmill. A fortnight later he witnessed the laying of the cornerstone of the planned temple, but the affair was somewhat sullied by the threatening aspect of non-Mormons— gentiles—who hovered about. In August, when elections were occurring in Daviess County, a loose mob of Missourians attempted to prevent the Mormons from voting, at which time a general fight broke out and the Saints, refusing to be bullied, ousted the aggressors. That incident caused a stir that spread statewide and inspired outrage, belligerence and a general outcry that the Mormons should be evicted from the state. Abruptly, western Missouri was in turmoil as night riders commenced acts of terrorism against the Mormons and Mormon reprisal was no less deadly; along with several beatings and acts of arson, there were murders.

With the situation showing no sign of abating, Governor Lillburn Boggs finally stepped in. That the governor had no love for Mormons became clear when, in October, motivated by what he had heard, of which only a small portion was true, he called up the 6,000 troops of state militia and gave their commander, General William Lucas, what was now referred to by Bigler and others of the Saints as "the Extermination Order." Boggs' written orders to General Lucas were brutally to the point:

> ...The Mormons must be treated as enemies and must be Exterminated or driven from the State if necessary for the public peace—their outrages are beyond description.

Lucas marched his force at once. Included in his army were six militia regiments formed into a brigade under command of Colonel Alexander Doniphan, a prominent Clay County attorney and member of the State Legislature, who was not at all pleased with the way matters were progressing.[16] They reached the vicinity of Far West on October 30.[17] The Mormons initially thought they were being advanced upon by a mob, since previously a mob led by one Jacob Rogers attacked the Mormon settlement at thirty-mile-distant Hauns Mill, where at least eighteen Saints were slain after throwing down their arms and begging for quarter. With Far West swiftly surrounded, the Mormons braced themselves for an all-out battle in the morning, until word came that this was not a mob but rather State Militia ordered out by Governor Boggs. Upon learning that, the Mormons surrendered. While no gunfire was exchanged, Bigler deplored the fact that, apparently as a manifestation of their anger at being thwarted in a fight eagerly anticipated, the militiamen shot many of the Mormons' livestock.

Immediately after the surrender, Joseph Smith and his brother, Hyrum, along with several other Mormon leaders, were taken into custody and tried at once by court-martial on charges of treason. Sitting in judgment was one of Lucas's militia officers, Sterling Price, a renowned Mormon-hater, along with several other officers of like mind and seventeen religious leaders of various denominations. In a remarkably short trial they found all the prisoners guilty and sentenced them to be marched into the Far West public square and shot in the presence of their families. General Lucas sent an order to Colonel Doniphan to carry out the execution.

"I will be god-damned if I or my men will have anything to do with that honor," Doniphan bristled. In a terse note sent back immediately to General Lucas he wrote:

> ...It is cold-blooded murder. I will not obey your order. My brigade shall march for Liberty tomorrow morning at 8 o'clock and if you execute these men I will hold you responsible before an earthly tribunal, so help me God.[18]

With no further word exchanged between them, Doniphan marched his brigade in the morning as promised. General Lucas thereupon overrode the decision of the court-martial and ordered the prisoners be placed in the custody of Missouri civil authority.[19] Bigler and fellow Mormons vowed they would never forget the kindness and courage of Alexander Doniphan.

The Saints who remained gravitated toward Clay County, but the atmosphere there was no better. Harassment increased substantially and now, at last, an order was being circulated from the high council of the church that greatly pleased Henry Bigler and the others: All the Mormons were to pack up and leave Missouri at once. They were to make their way eastward to the Mississippi and cross into Illinois. Some fifty miles upstream from Quincy on the Illinois side they were to converge at the new headquarters of the Church of Jesus Christ of Latter-day Saints, at the site the church now owned, a community that had previously gone by the name of Commerce but which, henceforth, would be called Nauvoo—meaning Beautiful Place.

*[December 15, 1838 • Saturday]*

John Sutter's plan to request a land grant from Mexican authorities in California had taken a strange twist. He chuckled as he glanced from the small balcony at the palm trees rising above lush greenery and deeply inhaled the scent of jasmine that permeated the air: Who could have envisioned, he mused, that his journey to California would first take him here to Honolulu in the Sandwich Islands, or that this would become so fortuitous a circumstance? Certainly he had no conception of it when he joined that party of trappers last April.

He'd heard about the trappers from a traveler who'd stopped at the store in Westport. Sutter went at once to their camp a few miles away along the Missouri River. They were a party under Captain David Tripps, working for the American Fur Company and preparing to head west to a rendezvous in the Wind River Valley and from there to their western headquarters, Astoria, in the Oregon Territory at the mouth of the Columbia River. Tripps was reluctant when Sutter first asked to be able to travel with them, not wanting to care for a novice, but gave in when Sutter explained he'd spent two seasons in the Santa Fe trade and was accustomed to trail hardships, as was his aide, a young German fellow who had been assisting him.[20]

Sutter lost no time in quitting his job at the Westport store and preparing for the trip. On the appointed day he and his aide arrived on horseback with two packhorses in tow loaded with supplies. They started off at once, a party of seven, and followed the faint trail that traced the course of the Platte River and the North Platte, turning due north at Jedediah Smith's South Pass and reaching the Wind River rendezvous in the Wyoming Country without difficulty except for physical exhaustion.

Scores of mountain men, trappers, traders and quite a few Indians had assembled for the combination of picnic, rodeo and reunion. Liquor flowed freely and there was a great deal of bartering. A sense of camaraderie prevailed and there were innumerable contests of frontier skills in which Sutter and his aide did not compete but enjoyed watching. In the evenings, rings of men sitting shoulder to shoulder gathered around campfires and swapped tales of where they had been and what they had seen and what they had done since the rendezvous of the previous year, grousing about fur prices and trapping conditions, trade restrictions, Indian matters and broken-down horses. And quite frequently, in their cups, they became excessively maudlin over lost companions.

Sutter joined in the trading only to a degree, dealing mainly with one of the mountain men who hardly fit what he had initially pictured as requisite for such an occupation—a skinny, freckled, former Kentuckian of about thirty with an unruly mop of red hair. His name was Christopher

Carson, although he favored being called Kit. It was from this man that Sutter purchased an Oregon Indian youth whom Carson had rescued from a hostile war party which had taken him prisoner and now no longer wished to be burdened with him. On impulse, Sutter also purchased from a Canadian trapper $100 worth of prime beaver pelts, bought on credit and payable in due course to any agent of the Hudson's Bay Company in their several posts stretching from here to Fort Vancouver.[21]

After the rendezvous, Sutter, his German aide and the Indian youth traveled with six different trappers the remaining distance to Fort Vancouver. It was a much more difficult journey, but they moved on steadily and the only stop made of any consequence was where they reached the Snake River at the Hudson's Bay Company post called Fort Hall in the Idaho country.[22] Here they paused to rest, relax and refresh their horses for several days. When they took to the trail again they followed the Snake to the Columbia, then downriver to the mission at The Dalles. After a two-day rest, they left on October 22 and from there the journey to Fort Vancouver, Pacific headquarters of the Hudson's Bay Company—which normally took the traveler seventeen days—was accomplished by Sutter and his trapper companions in just one week. The trappers, who had enjoyed Sutter's companionship during their long overland journey, now invited him to remain the winter with them, but with other matters much more pressing, he declined with thanks.

High on Sutter's agenda was becoming acquainted with the head man—called the factor—of the fur trading post. This was Sir James Douglas, who was a fine gentleman, fluent in French, which delighted Sutter since he was himself far more comfortable and skilled conversing in French than in English. On the second day of November the pair engaged in a long conversation that was of uncommon interest to Sutter. First and foremost, of course, was discussion of his eagerness to push southward to California but Sir James quickly quashed that notion.

"With the season this advanced," he said, shaking his head, "no guide would be insane enough to try to lead you over the mountains. It is November now and there is much snow at the higher elevations and the passes are already closed. You'd never make it."

They talked about California at length and what Sir James told him confirmed what he had heard of it before leaving Westport and what the trappers had told him, both at the rendezvous and en route to here. All described it as a beautiful and fertile paradise with incomparable climate, simply awaiting the man who had the vision, strength and finances to bring a dream to fruition. That Sutter made no secret of wanting to be just such a person who would raise wheat and other crops, plus great herds of livestock in the Sacramento Valley was of interest to Sir James.

"The Sacramento," he said, "is a mighty river with many tributaries, each with its own tributaries in an enormous natural drainage system. The borders of all of those streams," he added, his eyes taking on a rather speculative gleam, "are alive with fur bearers – beaver, mainly, but otter, too, as well as mink and ermine. There's a fortune to be made in furs alone." As he continued, it became more as if he were talking to himself than to Sutter, expounding on a theme that had long been present in his own thinking. "One of the largest of those tributaries is the American River, which enters the Sacramento from the east. The junction of these two streams is in very fertile, relatively level country that would be ideal for a base of operations, a headquarters that could well command the whole system."

"It does indeed sound ideal," Sutter agreed, then pressed on, "Since going overland is out for now, what about going by sea? Aren't there ships that go down the coast from here? Why couldn't I take passage on one of them?"

"There are no ships from here making that run," Sir James replied. "But if you're set on going as quickly as possible, there is one alternative I can suggest. We do have ships—the *Columbia* is one—that go to the Sandwich Islands; from there you can find ships that sail to California. Indeed, it might be your best course to go to Honolulu first for other reasons. Men of great influence and wealth are there who might take interest in backing your venture for this little empire you are intent upon establishing. I would be delighted to provide you with letters of introduction." He nodded and reiterated, "My advice to you, Monsieur, is to sail on the *Columbia*. She leaves for the Islands in a short time."

Thanking Sir James for his hospitality, for his advice and for the letters of introduction and recommendation, Sutter made arrangements for passage for himself, his German aide and the Indian youth, but just prior to embarking he chanced to meet a former French officer who had for sale an elegant, well decorated French captain's uniform. He was looking to purchase a fine beaver skin and since Sutter had just such an item from the rendezvous, they made an even trade. Sutter's mind was already racing with plans for using the uniform.

During the crossing his aide made a few alterations in the uniform and, when Sutter strode down the gangplank, he wore the gold-braided garment and presented an impressive mien to the onlookers. Without delay he made three formal calls: to Mr. George Pelly, the British consul, John C. Jones, the American representative to the Islands, and to the Islands' most prosperous merchant, William French. Reverting to a variation of the story he had concocted years before, Sutter smoothly passed himself off as former captain of the Swiss Guard in Paris but now on a mission at the direction of his backers—whose identity he was not at liberty to divulge—to establish both a new colony and an agriculture and livestock-raising empire in California. The letters of introduction and recommendation he presented from Sir James Douglas added significantly to the impression he was making and he was accorded the respect due an important French dignitary.

Now, standing on his small balcony and reveling in the freshness and aroma of this lovely new morning, Sutter knew with an utmost assurance never before so strongly experienced that he was on the threshold of a future beyond his wildest expectations. Doors to the pinnacle of Island society were opening widely to him and tomorrow he would have audience with none other than King Kamehameha III himself.

*[August 8, 1839 • Thursday]*

Henry Bigler was more than a little stunned when he finally laid eyes on Nauvoo. To be sure, it was a beautiful place situated on the Mississippi. An attractive expanse of marshland with graceful emerald reeds wafting in the breeze rimmed the water's edge to the west, and great rocky bluffs rose majestically to the east, with the broad level expanse of Nauvoo in between. What surprised him most, however, was the large number of fellow Mormons already gathered here and more coming all the time.

His own arrival had been delayed. Last February, after crossing the Mississippi into western Illinois, he had found its citizens friendly and helpful, willingly giving assistance to the Mormon refugees streaming away from the persecution they had faced in Missouri. Bigler was one of those and, like some, he remained for a time in the city of Quincy, employed as a handyman at a boarding house, for which he was paid

# The Infinite Dream

$12 per month. As May began, he accepted the offer of a better-paying job; $25 per month and found to act as watchman aboard a steamboat moored at the Quincy wharf.

About the time the steamboat was ready to sail again, near the end of June, Bigler fell sick and the paddle-wheeler left without him. He remained in Quincy until his illness faded and then helped in the harvest of a wheat crop at a dollar a day. When that work was finished, he set off afoot for Nauvoo, about which he had been hearing a great deal, much of which he didn't believe because it seemed so preposterous.

Nauvoo, in less than half a year, had become one of the largest cities in Illinois, with a population of 10,000 and with more Saints constantly converging on this place that Joseph Smith was calling The City of the Lord God Jehova, King of Kings. Hundreds of new houses had already been built and hundreds more were under construction in a beehive of activity. Henry Bigler was proud to be a part of it all, the more so when informed he was being elevated to the rank of elder. Since then he had spent most of his time in a nearby quarry, excavating the limestone that was being used for the construction of the great temple that had been denied them in western Missouri. For the first time, the Mormons seemed to have found a true home.

There were whisperings, however, that all was not so idyllic. Using its political power to promise various state legislators unanimous support in the elections to come, the Mormons had easily won a city charter for Nauvoo, but what they had established was considerably more than that. Governor Thomas Ford was not pleased, making it quite clear that Nauvoo had become a theocracy within the state and that this was incompatible with the established democracy of Illinois.

In his address to the state legislature at Springfield, Ford darkly declared that what the Mormons had established at Nauvoo was "...a government within a government; a legislature with power to pass ordinances at war with the laws of the state; courts to execute them with but little dependence upon the constitutional judiciary; and a military force at their own command."

"A society so structured," he warned, "cannot exist in Illinois without inspiring conflict."

*[August 12, 1839 • Monday]*

The five months spent in the Sandwich Islands in his guise as a

French dignitary had paid off handsomely for this man who had become known to all as Captain John Sutter.

It was his initial meeting with William French that set the tone for his future meetings with this most prosperous of the Sandwich Islands merchants. It also established the pattern he followed, with certain variations, in a series of meetings held with other elite merchants of the business community; meetings that had resulted in his obtaining firm support from several of them, some in the form of goods but most providing financial backing. These were speculators eager to gamble on what they believed to be an investment that would eventually bring a hundredfold return.

In that preliminary meeting with French, Sutter smoothly convinced the merchant of his ownership, in Bergdorf, Switzerland of a large firm that he was in the process of expanding into an international operation, adding almost as an afterthought that the profits of this enterprise had given him the wherewithal to seek other avenues of investment.

In subsequent meetings between the two, Sutter discussed his just concluded investigation into the possibilities that might exist for business investment in the United States, but added that he was disappointed with the existing tariffs and federal restrictions. He had then, he told French, traveled to the New Mexico country and inspected its potential as it involved the Santa Fe trade, but had rejected that possibility because of the arid and treacherous nature of the terrain.

"I should tell you, Monsieur French," he confided, "that since inspecting the Santa Fe potential, I have become especially intrigued with reports received concerning California and its attributes. Sir James himself expounded on the region's fine climate, its remarkable fur-trapping potential, the fertility of the land and the expansive prairies so suitable for raising cattle. I must admit that I'm of a mind to go there—perhaps to where the American River empties into the Sacramento—and establish a Swiss colony. Assuming," he added quickly, "that I can obtain the blessing of Mexican officials."

French was intrigued with the idea and said he thought there was a possibility he might be interested in involving himself in the plan, if Captain Sutter would not object to their doing some business together. John Sutter made it clear he had no such objection.

"I have some excellent contacts there," French went on, "who could likely be of assistance. I take it, Captain, you have not yet made arrangements for passage to California?" At Sutter's negative response he bobbed his head. "Good, good! You see, I have chartered a brig—the *Clementine*—which my people are loading at this moment with goods destined for the store at Yerba Buena, which is the principal port on San Francisco Bay. They will be embarking on the third of May, but *en route* they must drop off a cargo at Sitka. It's a rather roundabout way to get to California but it could be to our advantage—yours and mine."

He then went on to explain that Sutter and his entourage could take passage on the *Clementine* and be in charge of the valuable goods to be sold to the Russians at Sitka. He would, he said, give Sutter letters to Governor Kouprianoff, who was not only manager of the trading post located there but who was also in charge of the Pacific holdings of the Russian-American Fur Company, which included Fort Ross and its small community, Port Romanov, on Bodega Bay. Further, while a Russian settlement, most of its inhabitants, as well as the commander himself, spoke French as fluently as Sutter, so there would be no difficulties in communication. Kouprianoff would no doubt give him letters of introduction and recommendation to deliver to the Fort Ross commander, who also might be of help in Sutter's California plans. Finally, French said he would himself provide Sutter with a commission to purchase goods at Sitka, these to be taken to California and sold there. Was Sutter agreeable to all this?

Successfully masking his churning excitement, Sutter considered for a short time and then nodded agreed. He and William French, who was obviously pleased about the whole matter, shook hands, sealing their deal.

King Kamehameha III, upon learning of the arrangement between Captain John Sutter and William French, without being asked, volunteered to provide Sutter with ten strong, young native men—Kanakas—to accompany him to California. Some would be bringing wives. For their help, Sutter was to pay each man $10 per month. If the venture proved to be anywhere near so good as the captain suggested, the King promised to send many more. As an altogether unexpected bonus, Kamehameha provided Sutter with a strong letter of recommendation to California's Governor Alvarado. In addition to the Kanakas, Sutter hired three white men—two of them German mechanics—to assist in this venture.

During the five years that had passed since he first arrived in

America, John Sutter had given precious little thought to his wife and children in Switzerland and none at all since his arrival in the Islands. Part of the reason was that he certainly had not been chaste after reaching North America, and shortly after his arrival in Honolulu he had met and become smitten with a lovely, well-mannered young lady. She was the daughter of a Kanaka woman, from whom she inherited her shapeliness and long black hair, and the English captain of a whaling ship, from whom she had inherited her blue eyes. Her name was Manawitta—which Sutter quickly shortened to Mana—and though not highly educated, she had attended the Methodist School in Honolulu for three years. She was only sixteen and, so far as Sutter was concerned, had only one fault: She was married. Two years earlier she had wed a muscular but lazy young man whom everyone called Kanaka Harry. The young man was—as incredible as Sutter found it to believe—very pleased that his wife and the famous French officer were attracted to one another. Kanaka Harry boasted of it and actually encouraged them to cohabit, believing that this relationship between his wife and such a distinguished officer enhanced his own standing. To some extent, it did. Sutter was more than a little surprised when he learned that Kanaka Harry was included among the ten young men King Kamehameha had selected to accompany him to California and delighted to learn that the King had given Kanaka Harry permission to take his wife along.

As the day for departure neared, Captain Sutter's portfolio of letters of introduction and recommendation for the Russians and Mexicans grew even larger as he was presented with similar additional documents from American Representative John C. Jones and British Consul George Pelly. The latter also presented him with the gift of a very fine, large fierce-looking English bulldog. Sutter named him Snorts.

Headed for the Aleutian Islands, the *Clementine* left her moorings with the early morning tide of May 3 under command of Captain John Blinn of Glasgow. With fair winds and good seas, the brig reached Sitka on May 22. Sutter was welcomed in a perfunctory manner by Governor Kouprianoff, whom he found to be a bluff, good-natured fellow with an impish sense of humor but also an iron will when it came to matters of trade. However, upon reading the letters Sutter had brought for him, the governor warmed significantly and in a few hours' time it was as if they had always been friends. John Sutter, with his own brand of charm, good humor and always glib tongue, chatted amiably with the men and flattered the women without offense and quickly became popular in the community.

Over the ensuing month, trading was accomplished in a jovial atmosphere and cargoes exchanged to the satisfaction of all involved. Governor Kouprianoff had given Sutter a crude map of the Sacramento River Valley which, he said, had been drawn by a would-be settler named Belcher, who had been driven away by the Indians. The governor had also given Sutter two letters of introduction and praise for him and his plans, directed to the California Governor Alvarado and his own compatriot, Count Alexander Rotchev. The count, he commented, who was governor of the little community of Port Romanov and commander of Fort Ross, was, in mother Russia, a very influential man whose status had been further enhanced by his marriage to Princess Helene de Gagarin, a beloved niece of Czar Romanov. He could be an important friend and ally and Sutter should not fail to visit Fort Ross and spend some time with him. It was from Fort Ross, he added, that Sitka regularly received virtually all its fruits, grains and garden vegetables, as well as some 50,000 gulls harvested annually, which were being devoured as if they were chickens. The furs received from Fort Ross, however, were quickly transshipped to Mother Russia, along with those harvested in Alaska.

The *Clementine* left Sitka on June 20 and, with strong prevailing winds favoring, at first sailed smoothly and swiftly southward along the North American coastline. Soon, however, they encountered a series of severe gales that caused damage to the rigging and hull, but nothing that couldn't be caulked and otherwise repaired as soon as they took up anchorage. Of somewhat more concern was that much of their food supply and most of their barrels of fresh water had been contaminated by sea water and though Sutter was sorely tempted to put in at Port Romanov as they approached Bodega Bay, he reasoned that it was more important to first find anchorage for both repairs and supplies and also to determine what sort of reception he would receive from the Mexican authorities.[23]

Late in the day on July 1 they rounded the headland that was the rugged northern shore of the mile-and-a-quarter gap that formed the entry to San Francisco Bay. Under the skilled hand of Captain Blinn, who had many times negotiated this passage, the storm-battered, double-masted square-rigger sailed diagonally across the cut, limped its way around the southeastern headland and finally, in the gathering dusk, took anchorage in a bit of a cove among several other ships riding at rest. They were a short distance from what Sutter considered a disappointingly insignificant port comprised of a few small wooden structures and several tents. *This* was the Port of Yerba Buena?

They had spent the night aboard, planning to go ashore in the morning but that didn't happen. Shortly after dawn a whaleboat was spied heading toward them, rowed by six men and bearing fifteen soldiers and an officer.[24] A second, smaller boat in which there were several Indians trailed behind. Sutter went below and quickly donned his uniform. When the open boats reached the *Clementine* the officer, courteously but without warmth, asked permission to board. Captain Blinn acquiesced and the officer, followed by his entire squad, clambered aboard and let his glance slide across the seamen and passengers and then settle on the skipper. The officer saluted Captain Blinn and greeted him in Spanish. Blinn, who had little Spanish, smiled faintly. It was Sutter who responded with *"Buenos dias."*

The officer, recognizing the nationality and rank of Sutter's uniform, saluted but continued to address Captain Blinn, demanding to know who they were and what their purpose was in anchoring here, since the official port of entry was Monterey.

"Sir," Blinn replied haltingly, "we have come here from the Sandwich Islands by way of Sitka. My ship has suffered storm damage that requires repair and we are in immediate need of water and food supplies. This gentleman," he gestured, "is Captain John Sutter, who is in charge of a cargo of trade goods consigned to William French's agent here at Yerba Buena and who also carries important documents for Governor Alvarado."

The officer regarded Sutter with increased respect, but shook his head. "Nevertheless, you are forbidden to disembark here without first obtaining permission in Monterey. In light of your situation, you may have two days in which to effect your repairs and take on water and food, but then, since our harbormaster is away, you must go to Monterey for a permit."

They talked a while longer and, after Captain Blinn had instructed his crew in regard to making repairs and obtaining supplies, the officer invited Blinn and Sutter to come ashore and he would guide them on a brief tour of the town. They agreed and followed his boat in the one manned by the Indians.

On shore, the officer showed them through the town, which did not take long. He pointed out the ramshackle little dwelling magnanimously called Casa Grande, which belonged to Harbormaster Captain Richardson, who was presently in Sonoma. Close by was the house owned by trader Jacob Leese, whose little daughter Rosalie, the first child born at Yerba Buena, sat playing on the doorstep.[25] A house owned by A.B. Thompson was next, close to two smaller places Sutter was told had been built by John Fuller. The largest structure was hung with a sign: *General Merchandise*. It was the trading post belonging to William Hinckley and Nathan Spear. The final two structures close by were a wooden house belonging to a Frenchman named Victor Prudon and another used occasionally by Hudson's Bay Company employees.

When Sutter asked their guide about the Sacramento River, which emptied into San Francisco Bay on the east, the officer described it as a powerful, clear stream that had originally been named by Fathers Abella and Fortuni, a pair of priests from the Mission San José, who called it Rio del Santo Sacramento—River of the Holy Sacrament. When Sutter mentioned his intent to settle along it and found his colony, the Mexican officer shook his head. Others, he said, had tried and failed—all for the same reason: Indian troubles. One of the would-be settlers had been a reprobate Russian named Otto von Kotzebue and another was George Simpson, an Englishman who was a Knight of the British Realm. He also mentioned Belcher, whose map of the river valley was presently in Sutter's possession. That all these men had been driven off by Indians did not frighten Sutter, but it gave him food for thought.

Within a day—a much shorter time than anticipated—the repairs to their brig had been finished, the food and water supplies replenished. They weighed anchor without delay and set sail for Monterey, arriving at the California capital late on July 3. Sutter, clad in his uniform, at once arranged his affairs with the Monterey Customs House and then presented himself to Governor Juan Alvarado. The pair spoke together for hours and Sutter made an extremely favorable impression. The letters he bore for the governor were read with much interest. That this man should receive such outstanding recommendations from so wide a variety of important individuals—a British consul, an American representative, a high official of the Hudson's Bay Company, a Russian governor, the most powerful merchant in the Sandwich Islands and even from King Kamehameha himself—was amazing. That this man wished to found a Swiss colony in California was refreshing because, unlike other foreigners who had always applied for land grants in coastal regions, he wished to do so in the essentially unexplored interior of California. The governor warned Sutter of the bellicose nature of the Indians in the interior, especially those in the Sacramento Valley, expecting that this might cool his enthusiasm, but Sutter merely chuckled. Claiming to have had much experience with hostile Indians along the Santa Fe Trail, he assured Alvarado he could handle that matter without difficulty.

When their session concluded, John Sutter was elated. On a provisional basis, he had been granted eleven square leagues of land—almost 49,000 acres—in the Sacramento Valley.[26]

It was provisional because California law forbade bestowing land grants upon any save Mexican citizens. For this to become a permanent grant he would have to apply at once for Mexican citizenship, which could not be granted for a year. His group would be given a general passport and, during that year's interval, Sutter would have to live upon his grant, subdue the hostile Indians, put a portion of land under cultivation, acquire and produce cattle and other livestock, and develop a reasonable foundation to the colony he proposed.

"You have," Governor Alvarado reiterated, "one year in which to accomplish this. At the end of a year you will return here and if you have lived up to all these conditions, the land grant will become permanently yours."

"Sir," Sutter responded, "you can count on my being here one year from now. I am deeply grateful to you and thank you, as well, for giving me permission to land and transact business at Yerba Buena. I will not disappoint you."

Before leaving Monterey, Sutter filled out his application for Mexican citizenship and gave it to the government clerk. Then they returned aboard the brig to Yerba Buena and hired Indians to unload the cargo consigned to William French's agent, after which they reloaded the *Clementine's* hold with a cargo of hides and tallow for the Sandwich Islands. With this completed, Sutter shook hands with Captain Blinn and bade him and his crew farewell.

Eager to be on his way across San Francisco Bay and up the Sacramento, Sutter had to bridle his enthusiasm and plan the operation carefully. His first step was to meet with trader Nathan Spear to buy or lease the boats he was going to need. Spear, as impressed as Alvarado had been with Sutter's numerous letters of recommendation—especially that from William French, who was renowned for his business shrewdness—met with his partner, William Hinckley, and discussed to what extent they should advance Sutter credit. In the end they agreed to stake him to whatever he needed, but all of it payable in one year. Beaver, otter and other peltry would be acceptable as payment, as would deer and bear fat. Exuding an outward confidence but trembling inside, Sutter agreed.

The greatest expenses were for the boats and wages for the individuals—Indians primarily, who would be hired to man them—boats he would need to charter temporarily for transportation of his supplies, gear and company upriver and those he would buy for permanent use. The latter amounted to three smaller boats—grandiosely termed launches—canopied craft with auxiliary sail and, in reality, somewhere between a rowboat and a whaleboat in size. The leased boats were the sister schooners named *Isabella* and *Nicholas*, both under command of the latter's well-experienced skipper, William Heath Davis, with whom Sutter would be riding. Additional charges would be incurred for the large volume of supplies and equipment requisite to initiate this ambitious project; a substantial quantity of various foodstuffs, along with condiments and spices; numerous axes, shovels, picks, saws, awls and other hand tools; knives of several types would be a necessity, plus agricultural needs such as plows, hoes, spades, seeds, ropes, baskets and sacks. They would need additional clothing of wide variety and sizes, bolts of cloth and sewing gear; medications and bandages sufficient for emergencies, as well as a good supply of used rifles or muskets and plentiful ammunition and gunpowder. Finally, what Sutter deemed as absolutely essential and what Nathan Spear would probably not be able to provide; three small cannon along with an ample supply of cannonballs and powder.

There was a hitch, however. Nathan Spear had already contracted to ferry an entire herd of cattle across San Francisco Bay for José Martínez—a project that would require many bay crossings and the better part of a month to accomplish. At Spear's suggestion, Sutter used the delay as a time to familiarize himself with the San Francisco Bay area and visited many of the ranchos around it, his uniform meticulously cleaned by servants each night as he slept and ready again for wear in the morning. He was warmly welcomed and respectfully treated wherever he went, even when he made a special point to pay his respects to the commandant of the Northern Frontier District, Mariano Vallejo, at his headquarters in Sonoma. Despite the commander's cordiality, however, Sutter detected a certain reserve in his manner and attributed it to what Spear had told him was Vallejo's innate distrust of foreigners and his conviction of their potential damage to his beloved California. Sutter had already heard from several of the rancho owners that Vallejo considered it unconscionable for Governor Alvarado to have bestowed on this foreigner a very substantial provisional grant of land along the Sacramento. When they finally parted, Sutter felt it possible that one day this Mexican officer might become a formidable foe.

After leaving Vallejo, Sutter visited Fort Ross, a square bastion three hundred feet to the side, with two imposing octagonal turrets and palisade walls with cannon positioned in portholes every ten feet. Armed guards in fine uniforms were everywhere and an escort of them guided him past extensive, well kept gardens where all manner of fruits and vegetables were growing in abundance. They strolled past arsenals and quarters for officers and soldiers. Here there were several large kitchens, bake-houses and dairy rooms, and there a gristmill, a smithy, stables for half a hundred horses, peltry houses where the furs were fleshed, dried and baled, eight bath houses and a picturesque Greek church with bells that proclaimed the hour.

He was taken to the commander's quarters and here met with Governor Rotchev and his charming wife, Princess Helene. The handsome couple had already heard about Sutter from Governor Kouprianoff and welcomed him as if he were visiting royalty. Gracious, well educated and cultured, the couple escorted him through luxurious rooms whose connecting halls were lined with magnificent tapestries and exquisite Turkish rugs; numerous niches held silver vases containing a variety of fragrant flowers. In the library were comfortable lounges and sofas and, on the rich mahogany shelves, hundreds of fine leather-bound volumes in Russian, Greek, French, English, Latin and German.

Dinner that evening in the formal dining room was memorable: The lace-covered table was adorned with silver candelabras, food elegantly prepared and served, wines in exquisitely hand-cut engraved crystal. Following dinner they retired to a warmly appointed parlor where Princess Helene, at her husband's request, went to the piano and played Beethoven and Mozart, Couperin and Chopin. And after the princess excused herself, Alexander Rotchev and John Sutter lighted pipes and chatted for an hour or so longer.

Following a wonderful night's rest in the most comfortable bed he had ever occupied, Sutter headed again for Yerba Buena, his mind filled with thoughts of the fort he would eventually build on his own grant, a fort he envisioned to be patterned after the elegance of Fort Ross. In every respect his visit there had been a delightful experience and his final private chat with Count Rotchev had turned out to be the icing on the cake. The Russian governor had agreed to sell him, on credit of course, three of the fort's smaller brass cannon and an abundant supply of powder and cannonballs, along with the promise that they would be delivered to him before he left Yerba Buena for the interior. And so they were.

Sutter had signed a one-year promissory note to Hinckley and Spear for all the supplies, equipment and boats that had been advanced to him on credit and prior to their departure he had made numerous inquiries in an effort to locate someone who had ascended the Sacramento River, even if only for a short distance, to act as guide for the party. No such person was available, however, and his only recourse was to refer to the very crude map that had been given to him by Governor Kouprianoff, so inaccurate it was practically useless. Sutter had also bought on credit numerous horses and other livestock from José Martínez but they were still on the Ignacio Martínez Rancho, as it was not practical to bring them along on this initial foray into the unknown. The same held true for the more than 1,000 head of cattle he purchased, also on credit, from rancher Don Antonio Sunol and a similar number of sheep from rancher Don Joaquín Gómez.

When at last Sutter's party headed eastward across the great bay on August 1, they numbered twenty-two, exclusive of the boat handling crews; they included Sutter and his three assistants, ten Kanakas and three of their wives, including Mana, and five white men who had been drifting about in Yerba Buena and had applied to Sutter for work. These men were Louis Morstein, Jack O'Dell, Henry King, Frederick Hugel and Joe Nevins. The five were a disreputable group and Sutter was suspicious of them, but he needed the extra hands. The three smaller boats were handled by Indian crews supplied by Nathan Spear, who directed them to follow the schooner *Nicholas*, in which he and Sutter rode. And, of course, there was Snorts, who had become Sutter's devoted companion.

The boats were well loaded with supplies and equipment, including the three brass cannon that had arrived from Fort Ross as Governor Rotchev had promised. No difficulty was encountered in crossing the bay but a considerable problem followed in trying to locate the mouth of the Sacramento River. Gradually they worked their way northward but there were many pockets and estuaries that confused them and it was days before they finally realized there was a gradual quickening of current, which they followed upstream. As their course became more easterly, the land masses on both sides closed in more, but even then it was some time before they realized that this expanse of water, a mile wide at its narrowest and usually much broader, had to be the river's mouth.

As they continued upstream and the current quickened even more, the schooner had to tack constantly to make headway and so Sutter took to leading the way in one of the smaller boats manned by a crew of six Indian rowers, which was able to take a more direct route and often pulled well out of sight of the others. One of the cannon was positioned in this boat, primed and ready to be fired, if necessary. Occasionally Sutter would put in and explore a little on shore, but the ground was marshy and inappropriate.

Finally, some eighty-to-ninety miles upstream, the character of the land began to change. There were higher stretches of ground and stands of large oak trees. Here and there Indian symbols hung from branches near the water—tufts of feathers, strung shells, strips of fur with the dried skin painted—but whether as warnings or appeasements, no one could say.

At one point, there was an area of dry soil right to the water's edge and Sutter put ashore, accompanied by Snorts. Not until the dog suddenly growled, however, did Sutter realize he had encountered the first wild Indians.[27] At first he saw only a few, their faces and bodies painted in frightening patterns, but more appeared out of the underbrush until there were some 200, the majority armed with bows, clubs or knives, all appearing to Sutter to be hostile.

Two of the natives, naked except for loin cloths, approached, then stopped a dozen feet away. They appeared in no way afraid of the white man but they looked fearfully at the big growling bulldog. One spoke in a tongue Sutter could not understand and he shook his head. The native spoke again, this time in broken Spanish and Sutter could understand him to a degree, but what the painted man said was not encouraging. He was telling Sutter to go away, to go back where he came from.

Sutter moved back and stepped into the bow of the boat. As the whole assemblage of Indians moved closer, he glanced at the cannon, which was pointed forward and tilted upward at an angle of perhaps twenty degrees. He sucked deeply on his pipe several times and with the tobacco glowing in the bowl, touched it to the fuse projecting from the base of the cannon. It sputtered and sparked and then moved swiftly downward and into the firing hole. The resultant blast was horrendous and the ball screamed over the heads of the natives and plunged through the oaks, smashing off leaves and branches, including one substantial limb several inches thick, which fell to the ground with a crash.

The majority of the terrified Indians fled instantly but the two who had approached held their ground, though obviously very much afraid. As Sutter had hoped, these natives had never before seen or heard cannon-fire. Behind him, the recoil had sent the big gun smashing backward, snapping the cords that had anchored it, knocking down one of the crew, breaking the boats middle seat and toppling to one side, nearly falling overboard.

Sutter spoke loudly but slowly in Spanish, telling the two Indians before him that they were fortunate he had been merciful and only shot into the trees, for if he had aimed at them, they would all be dead. He then stepped out of the boat and the two Indians watched his approach fearfully. From pouch and pockets he took out tobacco, a few colored beads, a few strips of smoked meat and offered it to them. Hesitantly they accepted the gifts, their fear diminishing. He talked to them for a long time and while he knew they did not understand all he said, they seemed to get the gist of his remarks.

He told them they must never try to harm him or his friends, including those in the other boats just coming into view, or the big guns would destroy them all. He said he would remain peaceful so long as they did and that he had come to find good ground, with wood close by, a place where another great river joined this great river and that if they would guide him to such a place, he would pay them, and that if any of their people would do work for him, he would pay them as well.

The taller of the pair was their chief. He spoke to Sutter in halting Spanish: His people needed food—roots, fish, insects. His name was Anashe. He would guide them. Sutter told him to return on the morrow; there would be more gifts.

They had come back and Sutter distributed the promised gifts;

food, beads, tiny mirrors that delighted and, for the chiefs, pocket knives greatly treasured. Guided by Anashe, whom they had taken aboard the *Nicholas*, they inspected several other sites, but none was exactly what Sutter sought. At one point, still moving upstream, they passed a substantial Indian village on their left at the mouth of a stream.[28] The natives on shore became alarmed, but Anashe cupped his mouth with his hands and called reassurance to them and there was no trouble. Nevertheless, trouble did threaten when an unexpected problem arose: The five men hired in Yerba Buena had become discontent, complained about how long they had been out, the abundance of mosquitoes, the presence of dangerous Indians. Their mood becoming more irascible, the demeanor of two in particular—Joe Nevins and Jack O'Dell—became downright ugly. Sutter sensed a mutiny brewing and readied himself to take action.

The previous day, August 11, about 100 water miles from where they began, they reached the point where another great river entered the Sacramento from the east and Sutter knew it had to be the American River that Sir James Douglas had told him about. Anashe had directed them to turn upstream on the tributary and a few minutes after they had done so he pointed to the right and indicated they should go ashore. The ground here was low and there was evidence that it was susceptible to flooding, so they turned back and boated downstream from the confluence a mile or so and found a landing place where the ground was higher and dry, where a satisfactory amount of timber was available and deep-drafted vessels could approach to within mere yards of the shore. It seemed ideal and he ordered a temporary camp be made and all goods and equipment offloaded. They strategically set up the three cannon, loaded and ready to fire, with extra balls and powder kegs stacked close to each. Then they built their campfires.

Sutter thanked Anashe for guiding them and gave him a colored glass necklace and two more knives as payment for his services. Anashe nodded as he accepted them and then, for the first time, Sutter saw him smile. The Indian told him he would return when the moon became full—two weeks. Then, turning, he and his man vanished in the heavy brush.

Sutter spent the waning daylight hours exploring the surrounding area. Some distance eastward, adjacent to a small creek that angled northward toward the American River, he found a fine site on a small rise and knew at once that this was what he had been seeking. He returned to where the boats were moored and told Captain Davis that his job was done and that the next morning he could leave with his schooners for Yerba Buena.

Now the new morning had come and with the *Isabella* already underway downstream and the *Nicholas* on the verge of following, Sutter asked Captain Davis to delay his departure, promising he would be back in a moment. Then, rifle in hand, he strode to the separate campfire set up by the five malcontents. They looked up and blanched as they stared into the muzzle of the gun held steadily at waist height.

"On your feet," he ordered. "I will shoot the first man who does not instantly do as I say. Now, all of you, to the *Nicholas*. I said *now!*"

The men scrambled to their feet and moved rapidly to where the schooner was anchored, its gangplank sloped to shore, its surprised skipper peering over the rail. All five hesitated at the bottom.

Sutter's tone was deadly: "Captain Davis will take you back. This is no place for such goddamned dogs! Get up there!"

The men marched meekly up the gangplank to the schooner's deck. The first two, Nevins and O'Dell disappeared from view, but Hugel, King and Morstein paused, then turned back and descended. It was King who spoke earnestly for them: "We'll stay, Cap'n, an' help out, if you want."

Sutter looked at them for a moment and then nodded, keenly aware he needed the manpower. He lowered the rifle and shook the hand of each in turn. "You'll never regret it," he said.

The *Nicholas* departed and, knowing that they were still being observed by hostile Indians in hiding, Sutter ordered a farewell salute of nine shots, three from each cannon, certain that would help insure that the Indians would not try to creep in and attack them during the night. The remainder of the morning was spent in stowing the majority of their goods under protective canvas, making the camp site somewhat more permanent and forming rings of stones for their fires. The Kanakas, for immediate shelter, quickly built three grass-roofed houses on wooden frameworks, while Sutter and the other whites erected small tents.

In the afternoon, following an hour's rest, Sutter led his men, loaded with goods, to the spot he had located yesterday. Here, under his direction, they staked out the dimensions of the fort to be built and the lines along which palisade walls would be erected.

Now in his own tent well after midnight, with Mana lying asleep beside him and Snorts stretched out at his feet, gently wheezing and snuffling, Sutter, propped up on an elbow, wrote in his diary under the light of his lantern:

> *Aug't 12th — Today with the help of ten Kanakas three white men and a bulldog I founded a new colony called New Helvetia.*

### [August 29, 1840 • Saturday]

California Governor Juan Bautista Alvarado was very pleased with the reports he had been receiving for so many months concerning John Sutter and his colony of New Helvetia. That Sutter had managed to bring the Indians under his control and now had a great many of them working for him was a remarkable achievement; these were the very Indians that had previously terrorized or murdered everyone who had penetrated what they claimed to be their territory. Even the campaigns that had been led against them by Alvarado's uncle, Mariano Vallejo, had done little more than send the Indians into hiding until the troops left, after which they reappeared and were just as hostile as previously.

Alvarado had actually expected the same to happen with Sutter and his little nucleus of colonists, but it hadn't. By first demonstrating his power with cannon fire and then plying them with food and gifts, Sutter had more or less won them over. There had been a few flare-ups, but Sutter and his men had quashed those handily and even on those several occasions when the Indians had tried to sneak into the little colony under cover of darkness, they had swiftly been repulsed. Alvarado chuckled as he recalled the report that told of how Sutter's big ugly bulldog had helped by biting the legs of several Indians bold enough to slip into the camp at night and that Sutter claimed his own life had been saved by Snorts on three separate occasions.

While Sutter could be very harsh with the Indians, on the whole his treatment of them had been exemplary and, as ever more of them had come to visit and receive occasional trinkets and the food Sutter gave them in abundance, many had become quite attached to him. He was the only white man they had ever encountered who had made an effort to learn their language and he was now able to converse with them reasonably well. It was relatively easy for him to induce them to stay and make adobe and do much of the other work. The reports Alvarado had received estimated Sutter's Indian employees numbering over 300, with ever more coming in and eager to work a full day for little more than food and several colored glass beads, which he could buy by the barrelful for almost nothing. They tended his cattle—over 500 head purchased from ranchos around San Francisco Bay—; they herded his more than 1,000 sheep; and they brought in to the fort, when he needed them, his drove of fifty horses, half of them brood mares.—They tended his extensive vegetable gardens planted last spring and kept the livestock out of the 300 acres already planted in wheat, maize, barley and flax.

The governor thought it wise of Captain Sutter to have made it a priority to immediately start building his installation. While few outsiders knew that he called his growing little colony New Helvetia, that installation—Sutters Fort, as it was now being called by everyone— had become the talk of California. The main fort building itself was still barely under construction, but the perimeter walls—constructed of oversized adobe bricks, eighteen feet high, three feet thick, and enclosing five acres—were finished. Their projecting bastions rose from northwest and southeast corners, beneath which were prison rooms. With further purchases from Fort Ross, he had fully a dozen cannon mounted on parapets and three other big guns—a field piece and two brass cannon— unmounted and ready to move to wherever they might be needed at a moment's notice. It was the former malcontents, Hugel and King, who had taught the Indians how to make adobe bricks and Sutter's house had already been erected within the walls—the first good tule-covered adobe house, twenty by forty feet, containing a kitchen, a blacksmith shop and Sutter's office and living quarters. There were also more than a dozen temporary tule-roofed skeletal wood-frame shelters that served as storage areas, a smithy, a makeshift kitchen, a tannery and even a saloon of sorts, where wines and liquors were served in wooden or pewter cups directly from tapped kegs and barrels. Among these new structures were quarters not only for his Kanakas but also for the close to fifty whites and scattering of Mexicans that had drifted in sporadically and, being offered employment, had stayed. Many of them—foremost among whom was a Frenchman named Octave Custot—were given supervisory positions over the principal workforce of Indians.

Alvarado had been informed that Sutter was very deeply in debt and continually buying on credit—and with abandon—more food supplies, material goods, equipment and livestock. The man was apparently unconcerned that some of his creditors were becoming agitated over not having been paid, but at least they were aware that he was trying to make good his debts. His trapping efforts had paid off well, thanks to the Indians he had hired to do most of the trapping—they being more interested in the meat, which he let them have, than the peltry—and he had shipped an abundance of baled furs as well as his very good first wheat crop, already harvested, to his two biggest creditors, half to Fort Ross and half to Spear and Hinckley, with the promise of much more to come; satisfying them enough to extend the due dates of his payments.

The reports Governor Alvarado had received described John Sutter as a man constantly on the move, a man who seemed to be everywhere at once and who had the habit of hardly inaugurating one plan before he was off on another. He was sending out various parties to search for ideal sites on his grant to establish a gristmill, tanneries and shearing stations, and he was testing the adaptability of various fruits to different terrain. With the timber resources in the vicinity of Sutters Fort practically depleted already, he was sending parties far up the Sacramento in an effort to locate new timber resources, a site where a good sawmill could eventually be built and the cut lumber economically transported by rafts or wagons to his headquarters. They had already built two decent roads from the fort site, one of them two miles directly westward to the Sacramento River, the other a mile northward to the American River. At both waterfronts the ground was cleared for the construction of preliminary wharves and embarcaderos.

That his initial impression of Sutter as a potential asset to the opening of California's interior was being so well borne out was gratifying to Alvarado, especially in view of the fact that Vallejo had been so opposed to it. Now the governor picked up the ornate letter opener on his desktop and tapped the blade against a saucer-sized brass disk mounted on a small pedestal. It reverberated with a melodious cymbalistic clang and instantly his aide appeared in the doorway.

"You can show Captain Sutter in now, please, Bernardo."

The aide bobbed his head, stepped out of sight and reappeared a moment later with Sutter, clad in rumpled white linen suit. Alvarado stood up and moved a step or two toward him as the aide quietly withdrew. The governor shook Sutter's hand, then leaned back and picked up a crisp white document from his desk. He extended it to his visitor and smiled broadly.

"Congratulations, Captain Sutter," he said. "You have met all the qualifications admirably." He tilted his head toward the document Sutter was now holding and added, "The land grant is permanently yours and you are, as of today, a citizen of Mexico."[29]

# Chapter 1

♦

[*March 14, 1841 • Sunday*]

His name was John Charles Fremont.

He was dashing, adventurous and ambitious. He was also rather charming and spoke with a soft Southern drawl, having been born and raised in Savannah, Georgia. A handsome man of twenty-seven years, his good looks were enhanced by his uniform; a lieutenant in the United States Army. He had already ventured far into the wilderness of the Dakotah Territory as a U.S. Topographical Service engineer in the expedition led by Joseph Nicollet to explore and map the terrain between the upper reaches of the Mississippi and Missouri rivers. He was also self-confident enough to believe he could have done the job himself much more expeditiously than how it was accomplished during 1837 and 1838.

Lieutenant Fremont was intrigued by Thomas Hart Benton, the sixty-year-old Missourian who was one of the most intelligent and powerful leaders in the United States Senate. An expansionist who advocated the acquisition of all territory in the American West, Benton had not only spearheaded Congressional funding for the Nicollet expedition—after all, U.S. Secretary of State Daniel Webster had estimated there to be 50,000 American settlers in that area already—he had also helped push the bill through Congress. That bill gave each family head the right, as soon as these lands would be opened for sale, to buy as much as 160 acres for a mere $200, provided he had built a house on the land and planted crops.[30] So not only was such a goal appealing to Fremont, he also saw in Senator Benton a man who might well be expected to advance the career of a young officer.

The way he chose to bring himself to Senator Benton's attention was not only extreme, it was risky: Here was a man who could as easily destroy Lieutenant John Fremont's career as further it. Benton was noted for high rages when provoked and had not hesitated to engage in a shoot-out when he clashed with the equally fiery-tempered Andrew Jackson during a brawl. Therefore, angering Benton could be perilous. Fremont, however, was noted for his willingness to take risks and, though he hadn't actually planned his move for advancement in rank, that such was a possibility had not escaped him.

With little effort, Lieutenant Fremont had won the heart of Senator Benton's lovely seventeen-year-old daughter, Jessie. So far as the Senator was concerned, she was his special treasure and when the young couple were secretly married, Benton's fury was fearsome. He was poised to squash this brash officer like a bug and would certainly have done so except for the bride's intervention.

When Jessie Benton Fremont confronted her father, it was with an anger that surpassed his own. Without hesitation she lay down two choices: He could take out his fury on her husband and wreck his career, but she would stay with him and never see her father again; or he could accept and support the lieutenant and they could all enjoy a close relationship.

Senator Benton chose not to lose his beloved Jessie.

### [April 4, 1841 • Sunday]

One month ago, in a Washington, D.C. a spectacle had been witnessed by many thousands, despite miserably cold and rainy weather. William Henry Harrison—former Secretary of the Northwest Territory, first Governor of Indiana, former Major General, former U.S. Senator—was inaugurated as the ninth President of the United States, with fellow Virginian John Tyler his vice president. It was a landslide victory with Harrison, a Whig, receiving 234 electoral votes over his Democrat opponent, incumbent Martin Van Buren, who received only sixty.

Extremely popular with the American people, Harrison was the skilled soldier-politician who had defeated the confederated Indians at the Battle of Tippecanoe on November 7, 1811, then the British and their Indian allies under Tecumseh at the Battle of the Thames on October 5, 1813. In the process of doing so, and through subsequent years, he wrested from its Indian inhabitants much of the territory now comprising Ohio, Indiana and Illinois.[31]

Today, on his thirty-first day in office, having contracted pneumonia during the inaugural ceremony, William Henry Harrison died.

*[August 29, 1841 • Sunday]*

Of all the Mexican officials in California, only one seemed at all concerned about both the increasing number of infiltrating foreigners and John Sutter's growing prestige and authority. That one person was Mariano Guadalupe Vallejo—now referred to as General, despite his being a captain; he had received his rank on July 9, 1839 and, during the same ceremony, was named Commandant General of California. The current influx of foreigners he blamed on his nephew, Governor Alvarado, but knew that any complaints lodged with him would have virtually no effect, since they had now become bitter political enemies.

While having had little actual contact with Sutter, Vallejo had heard a great many stories about what he was doing. How else to account for the remarkable success the man had achieved taming the Indians for a 100-mile radius? How else to account for the remarkable growth of his colony?

Now in his own headquarters at Sonoma, Vallejo knew only too well that there were dangers involved in overstepping his authority: For him to go over Governor Alvarado's head was clearly tempting career suicide, but something *had* to be done and if not by him, then by whom? He sighed and looked over what he had already written in the letter begun half an hour ago to the Minister of War in Mexico City. He had strongly expressed his disappointment at the failure of anything occurring in response to his previous request for reform of civil government in California, particularly regarding what he felt were measures necessary for national defense. He had unequivocally given his opinion of the sad state of affairs under Alvarado's rule and his conviction that California was being ruined. He no longer wished to be linked to the travesty of the present civil government of California and formally asked to be relieved of his command. He added that the offices of governor and commandant general should be combined under one person; otherwise there was too much conflict. And where John Sutter was concerned, the man had been given altogether too much leeway: He should not have been allowed to establish an independent colony in the Sacramento Valley or grant passports to foreigners or to usurp for himself numerous other prerogatives.

With another sigh of frustration, General Vallejo dipped his pen and continued writing:

# The Infinite Dream

> ...Sutter, styling his place the Fort of New Helvetia and himself as governor of that fortress, exercises ambition and despotic power, wages war on the natives, forces them to work for him, shoots them without formality or the approval of the governor, receives foreign visitors, no matter whence or how they come, not obliging them to present themselves to the authorities and sometimes not even reporting their arrival, and finally makes seditious threats. With the aid of the Hudson's Bay Company, I believe I can remove Sutter from California. Help must come from Mexico. The civil government in unskilled hands has sworn the destruction of the Military branch. Military companies must be restored. Abuses of every kind are constantly permitted and relief can only come from the national government, the orders of which are presently despised...

At this very moment across San Francisco Bay in Yerba Buena, another individual was busy writing a letter to his home office in London. Sir George Simpson, head of the Hudson's Bay Company, wrote with some degree of smugness that, on behalf of the company, he had just bought out the trading interests and properties of Jacob Leese at Yerba Buena, thus gaining what he considered an important foothold that might, with careful planning, be expanded to the benefit of the Crown. He added that there was, however, one potential danger. Sutter was reportedly thinking in terms of making the embarcadero on the east side of the Sacramento River near his fort into a port providing safe anchorage for seagoing vessels. If successful in such an endeavor, the rapidly growing Sutters Fort community would be in direct competition with Yerba Buena. Further, to the detriment of other trading establishments elsewhere, it would undoubtedly capitalize on its greater proximity to the rich fur resources of the many tributaries of the Sacramento.

As usual, Sir George made no secret of his contempt for the Mexican presence in California:

> ...Nature doing everything and man nothing—that, in a nutshell, is California. The trade of the whole province is in the hands of foreigners, who are almost exclusively of the English race. Of that race, however, the Americans are more numerous than the British. The foreigners are to the Californians as one to ten, while by their over-all monopoly of trade and their command of resources, to say

*nothing of their superior energy and intelligence, they already possess vastly more than their numerical proportion of political influence, exciting not a little jealousy. The population of California has been drawn from the most indolent variety of the most indolent species, being composed of superannuated troops and retired office holders and descendants..*

That California was a ripe plum ready for the plucking seemed quite a reasonable conclusion.

### [September 1, 1841 • Wednesday]

For the past two years Count Alexander Rotchev had heard it whispered about that Czar Romanov had dictated an order that would deeply affect him and everyone else at Fort Ross; an order to abandon the installation. However, when months and then years had passed without such an order being received, most had concluded it was just another of those rumors that mysteriously generate and seem to take on a life of their own.

But then a packet bearing the Romanov imperial seal had arrived a month ago and inside was an edict from the Czar himself that Fort Ross either be sold or abandoned. All military personnel were to report to Sitka for further orders and the Russian civilians in Port Romanov were to be given the option of returning to Russia at government expense or remaining as free agents where they were. As soon as these matters were seen to, Count Rotchev and Princess Helene were to return to the Imperial Court in St. Petersburg.[32]

Since receiving the order, Rotchev had been doing a great deal of traveling. He first visited many of the wealthier rancho owners in the San Francisco Bay region to see if any were interested in purchasing Fort Ross with all its contents except for personal possessions. The asking price was an incredibly low $30,000, which was hardly one-tenth of its replacement value, but that was still much too steep.[33]

Rotchev had then paid a visit to General Vallejo at Sonoma, offering him the same deal, but the California Military Commandant had not the authority to accept and suggested he go to Monterey to see if the governor would entertain the idea of buying it for California. Rotchev, who had already been considering doing just that, went at once to the capital, where he was courteously received and given an audience with

Governor Alvarado. The governor was definitely interested in acquiring, but not in buying. He felt it was incumbent upon the Russians to donate the property and its contents to the Mexican government as a gesture of good will for what he considered to be favors the Russians had previously received from his government. Rotchev declined to do so and returned to Fort Ross. Both Vallejo and Alvarado believed that without a buyer, the Russians would eventually abandon the place, at which time it could be taken over by the Mexican government essentially without cost.

Now with the most likely avenues exhausted for disposing of Fort Ross, one possibility remained. Of all the visitors to the fort over the years, none had been so enthralled by the installation and its accoutrement as John Sutter, but Rotchev had been leery of approaching him. While the New Helvetia founder had repaid almost the entire credit advanced him by the Russian commander, Rotchev had heard the current gossip at Yerba Buena that Sutter was not only almost without operating funds, he was still deeply in debt to a host of creditors and many were beginning to consider him a bad risk.

Yet the fact remained that, in the face of such a burden, Sutter had managed to pay off, as he had promised, almost all of the debts he owed the Russians for credit purchases, a sign on integrity. Knowing full well that the Californios would snap up the place immediately upon its abandonment, Rotchev reasoned it would be better to see Sutter get it and the Russian government benefit to some degree, even if it took a while. Perhaps if only a small amount of down payment were asked, with the remainder payable to the Sitka agent in annual increments, Sutter could manage to take it on.

It was definitely food for thought.

*[December 1, 1841 • Wednesday]*

Captain Mariano Guadalupe Vallejo was becoming convinced that the several letters he had written to the Minister of War in Mexico City were having no effect whatever. He was, in fact, beginning to wonder if they had ever reached their destination.

Could they not see that in California they possessed a country not to be matched for its wonderful potential? So far as Vallejo was concerned, it was nowhere excelled in having such elements for prosperity and growth; an ideal climate, some of the best natural harbors in the world that could be strongly protected with minimal expenditure, great valleys filled with the richest soil, an agricultural paradise which thus far had barely been touched, beautiful rolling grasslands on which great herds of cattle, sheep and horses could prosper and increase.

Despite such potential, California's own population ignored or woefully neglected the land and, instead, imported virtually everything. Why could not the top governmental officials see what a deplorable waste this was and what a great need there was to protect this exceptional country from foreigners who were by no means unaware of its attributes?

So, even though without a single response, Captain Vallejo had continued writing to the Minister of War. His considered recommendations included a rebuilding of The Presidio of San Francisco to protect the great harbor and, at the same time, establishment of a good customs house to regulate the increasing trade. Great numbers of farmers, artisans and skilled laborers should be sent to populate the interior, not just the coastal areas; a Mexican population that would utilize the abundant natural resources lying fallow and, equally, establish a counterbalance to the encroaching foreigners. And, always returning to what he felt was the key to making California an asset rather than a liability, the ousting of the present California governmental hierarchy and the appointment of an energetic and farsighted individual in whom the roles of governor and military commandant would be combined. That he himself might be considered for this role had not escaped him.

Today, at last, dispatches had been received from Mexico City; suddenly the load Vallejo had been carrying for so long was lightened and his smothering depression all but dissolved. Positive steps, he was informed, were being taken to implement *all* of his suggestions. A large number of fine Mexican citizens, eager for the opportunity to have and develop their own lands, were already en route and orders had been dispatched that removed Vallejo's dissolute nephew, Juan Alvarado, from his position as governor. He was to be replaced by an upright individual and a dear old friend, Manuel Micheltorena, in whom the powers of military and civil government were combined.

For Vallejo, it was a great justification. For Alvarado, however, and his cohorts, such as José and Manuel Castro and the brothers Andrés and Pio Pico, it was a bitter pill they might not be able to swallow.

*[December 31, 1841 • Friday]*

Almost everyone in California agreed that this time Captain John

Sutter had bitten off far more than he could possibly chew; yet the New Helvetia founder carried on despite setbacks and discouragements. The majority harbored a deep respect for him, admired his courage in the face of monumental difficulties, and they wished him the greatest success. Some, often envious, had grown to fear and despise him, happily predicting his total failure. But everyone agreed that over the past four months, John Sutter had taken on altogether too much.

It had begun in early September when he had been approached by Count Rotchev with the irresistible offer of Fort Ross and all its possessions for hardly a tenth of its worth. Since his very first visit there, Sutter had coveted the installation. As much as possible he planned for his own fort in the Sacramento Valley to be patterned after it and suddenly he was being given the opportunity to own it. That he had no cash reserves, that he was already considerably in debt, that he would have to gather every asset currently in his storage sheds—peltry, vegetable crops, fruit, grains, tallow, elk hides—just to meet the required down payment of $2,000 in goods or cash, made no difference. He *had* to accept Rotchev's offer.

They had finalized the deal in Yerba Buena, then sealed their bargain with a gala banquet aboard the Russian governor's sleek ship, the *Helena*, anchored before Fort Ross in Bodega Bay. The goods Sutter had offered as down payment had been accepted and the contract he signed bound him to pay the balance of $28,000 over the next three years, payment acceptable in tallow, peltry and grain shipped to the Sitka Colony. The contract also stipulated that Sutters Fort and its environs would serve as collateral put forward to secure the mortgage.

Sutter understood that Rotchev's offer did not include the land upon which Fort Ross and its adjacent community of Port Romanov was located, as this was land that had only been leased from Spain, but he salivated at what was included in the properties, equipment, artwork and furnishings. There were forty well-constructed frame buildings that could be dismantled, the materials transported to Sutters Fort to be used for new construction or the reconstruction of the same buildings. The livestock totaled 1,700 head of cattle, more than 100 milk cows, 900 head of sheep, an unspecified number of goats, several hundred mules and 900 horses—about one-third saddle-broke—plus 1,700 or more brood mares.

There was more, much more. Equipment included tools and conveyances such as a fleet of carts, carriages and deep-bed cargo wagons, plows, threshing tools, scythes, harrows, an abundance of gardening tools, a huge collection of reins, saddles, bits, shoes, and other tack. Furnishings included beautifully finished tables and chairs, bureaus and armoires, chiffoniers, desks and credenzas, footstools, richly brocaded settees and sofas. There were humpbacked storage chests with iron lacings, most containing stores of linens, napery and surplus clothing along with bolts of silks and woolens and other fine materials. There were Turkish rugs and exquisite tapestries and other wall hangings, framed paintings as well as vases and statuary with ornate pedestals. Weaponry included several dozen muskets and old French flintlock rifles and pistols, numerous kegs of gunpowder and lead balls and powder flasks. To Sutter's delight there were forty iron cannon plus several pieces of brass field artillery, a few mortars and howitzers, a variety of crossbows, many daggers and swords—ornamental and functional—with sheaths and scabbards, a dozen pieces or more of ceremonial armor and pole arms.

There were hand-operated flour mills and grinders and numerous varied kitchen implements along with large pots and outdoor ovens. There were four small boats and, perhaps the biggest surprise of all, an excellent twenty-two-ton schooner, called a launch, which could be put into service transporting Sutter, his employees and guests between New Helvetia and Yerba Buena.

Everything would have to be transported, either overland or over water, to Sutters Fort; then Fort Ross itself would have to be dismantled, its valuable lumber transported; all this, Sutter realized, would require at least a year to complete and he immediately commissioned his new clerk, Robert Ridley, to undertake the task. He did not know Ridley well, the man having shown up at Sutters Fort a few weeks ago, as had many others seeking work, and there was something about his character that engendered distrust, but Ridley was educated, a capable worker and he had demonstrated that he could supervise work crews very well.

The armament that had been among the first items transported to Sutters Fort—especially the cannon which were immediately mounted facing in all directions in embrasures and bastions and on wall parapets—caused immediate concern and fear among the Mexican authorities and Sutter had been threatened with dispossession. He had swiftly written to Governor Alvarado and warned that he was now fully capable of defending himself and New Helvetia, that he wished to hear no more talk of dispossession, and that he was prepared to chastise any force that might appear to carry out such threats. Fortunately, Alvarado was soon after relieved of his duties.

John Sutter was no less forceful in dealing with the newly arriving fur trappers and elk hunters. These men were largely of two groups; Britishers in the employ of the Hudson's Bay Company, making their way southward from the still disputed Oregon Territory, or Americans in the employ of the American Fur Company, who were crossing the Sierras from the east. All of them were tapping the rich elk hide and beaver pelt resources of the Sacramento River tributaries—hides and fur that Sutter, overstepping his bounds somewhat, declared were rightfully his and were being stolen. His driving off a number of these parties at gunpoint, however, cooled their ardor and the numbers of intruding parties had diminished significantly.

Sutters Fort had evolved into a focal point, a rendezvous for practically every new person arriving in northern or central California. Sutter, once the matter of the trappers was put to rest, offered a helping hand to all. His reputation as a kind and generous man was quickly becoming widespread, a fact brought startlingly home to him when, in October, a trim schooner flying the American flag coasted to an anchorage at the Sutters Fort embarcadero on the Sacramento. It carried a detachment of fifty soldiers, six officers and a Dr. Pickering. One of the officers, after saluting Sutter respectfully, shook his hand warmly.

"Sir," he said, "I am Lieutenant Robert Ringgold, U.S. Army. We are a detachment of the Wilkes Expedition, which is presently in Oregon. We have merely stopped to pay our respects. Everyone who comes to California wants to meet Captain Sutter and see his fort. You're the most famous man here in California, Sir. In fact, you're famous all over the East."

It was the first Sutter knew that he had acquired any sort of recognition outside of California and, though gratifying, it was disturbing. What were Americans doing here and how could such an armed force be journeying with impunity through Mexican territory? Lieutenant Ringgold explained briefly, but the explanation raised more questions in Sutter's mind than it put to rest. Ringgold said the expedition under Captain John Wilkes had been sent under orders from the U.S. War Department to explore the West; a detachment similar to his was at present exploring overland down the Pacific Coast from Oregon to San Francisco Bay under Lieutenant Thomas Emmons, and his own detachment's mission was to explore and map the entire Sacramento River to its source. He declined with thanks Sutter's invitation to disembark and stay for a while; their mission could not be delayed and they must be off. As they continued upriver, Sutter wondered how it was possible for a foreign armed force, in at least two detachments, to be penetrating, exploring and mapping the lands belonging to Mexico. Why had not General Vallejo's soldiers detained them?

That they had paused here at all, however, was indicative of how important Sutters Fort had become, well beyond its specific sphere of influence. Sutter's own fame, if such it were, had spread. Nevertheless, while it surprised him, it came as no revelation to scores of others who had been drawn here. John Sutter was noted far beyond his ken as being uncommonly liberal in what he gave away, and for his warm hospitality to all who came, whether singly or in large groups. It was not unjustified; if Sutter learned of a party struggling in the wilderness, he immediately had pack mules loaded with supplies and sent to help. Those who were destitute would be given food and shelter and clothing without being asked to sign notes of credit. They seemed to come from everywhere and were of varied backgrounds—hunters, sailors who had jumped ship, trappers, mountain men, adventurers, itinerants. No one who sought employment was ever turned away and wages varied for the whites, depending on skill levels, from $1 to $3 per day in cash and goods. Quite often payments of cash wages were much in arrears, but none seemed to mind so long as they were fed, clothed and housed, which was much preferred to roaming about the countryside hungry.

Many who stayed on at Sutters Fort as employees helped with menial tasks or with the supervision of the hundreds of Indian workers Sutter had more or less tamed. Some of these new white arrivals who had specialized skills were put to work training others in their particular fields: Vaqueros, carpenters, farmers, blacksmiths, gardeners, coopers, shepherds, weavers, hunters, tanners, sawyers, trappers, masons, gunsmiths. Even former soldiers, who had no other professional skills, each evening marched Sutter's new little army of Indians—mainly Miwoks and Nisenans—in close-order drill to the accompaniment of fife and drum and the fort's gate itself was patrolled continuously by uniformed Indians.

New structures were constantly being built adjacent to and in the area surrounding Sutters Fort. A crude hospital shelter was raised for the ill or injured. Huge tannery vats were built for the production of leather, others for the production of tallow that would be exported for the manufacture of soap and candles. A small gristmill was built at which four mules would plod in a circle for four hours at a stretch and then another team would take its place—six such teams working 'round the clock—turning the millstone which ground the wheat into flour, which was then sent to bakeries that were operated day and night to produce the bread consumed daily by more than 300 whites and 500 Indians.[34] A small factory was built for the manufacture of firearms and for the repair of broken weapons. A distillery had been set up and its enlargement was already planned. Sutter's twenty-two-ton launch—rechristened as the *Sacramento*—was put into regular service carrying passengers and goods to Yerba Buena and returning with cargo which included, most importantly, hand sawn redwood lumber from coastal groves for additional construction at the fort—the round trip, depending on weather and water conditions, averaging from three weeks to a month. Including all meals, the one-way passage was $5.

Herding livestock from Fort Ross to New Helvetia had been a major undertaking and required the skills of all the vaqueros as well as most of the trained Indians. The stock animals were driven largely from horseback and though there were many difficulties, crossing the broad Sacramento was by far the most hazardous. The river was up, and about 100 head of cattle drowned during that crossing, but it was not a complete loss since Sutter's men were able to save about half of the drowned animals' hides for the tannery.

Among the many newcomers who presented themselves to Sutter was a well-educated young man named John Bidwell. A Missouri schoolteacher who had been among the thirty-two members of one of the first parties of settlers ever to cross the entire continent by land to California, he had arrived at Sutters Fort with his friend, Charles Weber, and two others. All were seeking work and all were hired.[35] Bidwell was charming and ingenuous and especially skilled with figures. Very taken by his character and education, Sutter put him to work at once as his personal clerk and accountant, taking over those duties previously handled in less than satisfactory manner by Robert Ridley. Within a few weeks it became clear that Ridley was also not entirely satisfactory in the performance of his duties at Fort Ross and so Sutter sent Bidwell there with written orders to take his place as general supervisor.

One of the more lucrative sources of income for Sutter was selling, to those visitors or employees who could afford to buy, plots of land to the northward along the east side of the Sacramento Valley and in the valleys of such tributaries as the American, Feather and Bear rivers, as well as along tributaries of those streams.

He was not meticulous in measuring and recording such plots but when he thought about it at all, he was satisfied that since they were all upon his grant, there could hardly be any boundary problems. Unfortunately, there were also occasions when he sold plots of land that were not located within his grant, even though he thought they were.

As if he were not already bogged down sufficiently with all the

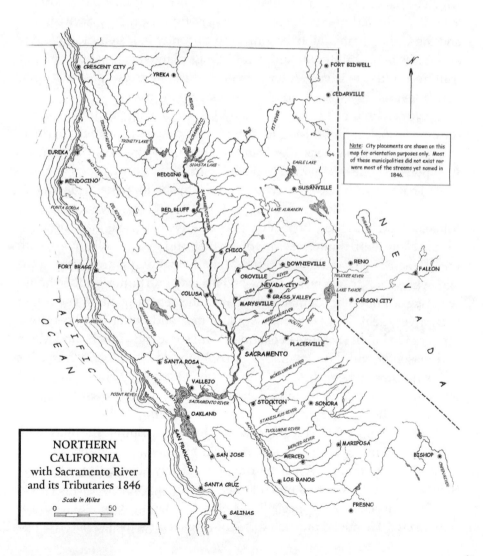

various enterprises he had set into motion, Captain Sutter had, in early October, instituted another that was far more personal and dear to his heart. Some forty miles above the confluence of the American River and the Sacramento—eighteen water miles up the Sacramento to the Feather River and then up the west bank of the Feather another twenty-two miles—he had located an especially lovely area of rolling hills, great oaks well separated from one another, and soil that was a rich black loam in which he believed a hoe handle would take root and grow if thrust in and watered.[36] It was here where he laid out his own private rancho which he named Hock Farm—the title a tribute to the Hock Indians of the area. With the aid of architects and farmers from Germany, Switzerland and the United States, all of whom were currently in his employ, his fine estate was being built, with its surroundings planted in an abundance of fruit trees and extensive gardens, beyond which were lush pastures upon which several thousand head of livestock already grazed.

Now with the old year closing and a new one on the threshold, the future was looking promising for John Sutter despite the weight of debts that hung about his neck like lead weights. Only one real problem—a very personal one—remained to plague him.

That problem was Manawitta and her husband, Kanaka Harry.

Even though Mana was living with Sutter and no longer considered Kanaka Harry as her husband, particularly when he had been so promiscuous with numerous Miwok women and was actually living with one of them, Harry still considered Mana his wife. A couple of months ago, while very drunk, he had smashed his way into Sutter's adobe house wielding a knife and demanding that Mana return to him. There had been a very real danger that he would attack and Sutter had been fully prepared to kill the Sandwich Islander. With some difficulty he and Mana had reasoned with him, managed to cool him down and take him back to his quarters where they lay him on his bed as he passed out. Mana tended, a bit shakily, to laugh off the incident, but Sutter was concerned. He decided he would remain armed and watchful.

Moreover, a few days ago Mana informed Sutter she was with child—his. Although he was still married to Annette, he rarely thought of her in that context. When he did sporadically send letters to her in Switzerland, it was not so much to keep in contact with her as it was to ask about his children, especially his eldest, Johann Augustus, who was now twelve. He hoped one day to see him again after the lad had reached his majority, at which time he would bequeath to his first son this little empire of New Helvetia. But if Johann Augustus came here before that, while he was still very young, might not his mother come with him? And, if she did, what then?

It was a possibility he preferred not to contemplate.

[April 9, 1842 • Saturday]

The guide that had been hired by the government to aid Lieutenant John C. Fremont on this exploratory and cartographic expedition westward did not impress the dapper officer at first glance; he was not big and burly and heavily bearded as Fremont had envisioned the true mountain man to be. This man was clean shaven and decidedly becoming bald and somehow just didn't have that far-visioned aspect of one who could guide an Army detachment into essentially unknown territory.

The man seemed almost disinterested as Lieutenant Fremont explained in detail what the mission, ordered by the U.S. War Department, was to be; to explore, from the community of Independence on the Missouri River westward along what was becoming better known as the Oregon Trail and to carefully map it, locating—in particular for wagon traffic—the streams and springs, the more ideal fording places for river crossings, the best route through difficult terrain, South Pass, the sites of Indian villages and the location of Fort Laramie and any other fur trading posts that might be encountered along the way, as well as the more prominent landmarks to be used as guideposts by future travelers. He was also ordered to locate the confluence of the Raccoon and Des Moines rivers and supervise the building of a fort there to be called Fort Des Moines.

What Fremont did not elaborate upon was how he, a relatively inexperienced lieutenant in the U.S. Topographical Service had landed such a plum assignment as commanding this Congressionally authorized expedition. Nor did he allude to the fact that his father-in-law, Thomas Hart Benton, was one of the most powerful United States senators and who, at his daughter's insistence, got him the appointment. Lieutenant Fremont fully intended doing such an exemplary job that when the next such expedition was planned, he would be chosen to head it; not because of political connection but because of his outstanding leadership on this one.

When he finished his explanation and asked this unlikely guide if he had any questions or doubts about where they were to go, the man merely shook his head and smiled faintly.

"Reckon I'll get you and your soldier-boys wherever you want to go..." he paused and then added, "...and back, too, or my name's not Kit Carson."

*[November 3, 1842 • Thursday]*

Elder Henry Bigler was as devout a member of the Church of Jesus Christ of Latter-day Saints as any of the more than ten thousand saints who had settled here at Nauvoo. Unlike so many of his fellow Mormons, however, who had begun to question the motives and future of the church, he had always followed the dictates of The Prophet and the Council without question. But now, for the first time, he was experiencing more than just vague stirrings of concern for the church, concerns inspired by the increasing and disturbing brandishing of power by its megalomanic leader, The Prophet—Joseph Smith.

Ever since the Mormons had been ousted from Missouri and established themselves here on the east bank of the Mississippi in Hancock County, their western Illinois neighbors had grown ever more alarmed. Nauvoo had become virtually a city-state, self-governing and above the laws of Hancock County or even the State of Illinois—a sanction initially granted in their city charter by state legislators hungry for the Mormon unified vote.

In addition to building his city of Nauvoo, Joseph Smith had built a veritable army, armed and rather ridiculously uniformed, but a dangerous force nonetheless. At 4,000 men it was almost half the size of the entire United States Army, but nowhere near so well disciplined. Its soldiers, officially named the Nauvoo Legion but who called themselves the Sons of Dan, were a congregation of ruffians who, at their commander's direction, delighted in terrorizing non-Mormon neighbors if they refused to sell their lands to the church, and backed up the threats with beatings of those who balked. The army's commander was none other than Joseph Smith, who had bestowed upon himself the rank of lieutenant general, the only person to hold that rank since George Washington. That was in addition to his other titles as Mayor of Nauvoo, Chief Justice of the Nauvoo Municipal Court and Chairman of the Nauvoo City Council.

The Illinois politicians, who had at first curried his favor in the hope of obtaining the Mormon vote, now feared Joseph Smith greatly and what he and his followers could and would do to any who opposed them. Simple crimes, such as counterfeiting United States gold coins, were common. Arson occurred all too frequently and even assassination was not unfamiliar. No one, not even in the highest offices, was safe from the fiery sword of Mormon vengeance. Missouri Governor Lillburn Boggs, who had loosed his entire state militia upon them, discovered that awful truth earlier this year when Mormon O.P. Rockwell severely wounded him with a shot through Boggs' own bedroom window. Neither Rockwell nor the instigator of the assassination attempt, Joseph Smith, could be prosecuted because of Nauvoo's self-governing charter. The fury of Missouri and Illinois residents at this brash obstruction of justice rose to unparalleled heights.

Something needed to be done.

Today, with Joseph Smith's grudging approval, the Nauvoo City Council, which included Smith's right hand man, Brigham Young, drafted an appeal to the United States Congress, asking that body to declare Nauvoo a territory of the federal government and to send in troops to quell the gathering mob's violence.

Henry Bigler felt very sure that the appeal would not be granted and that Nauvoo would ultimately be destroyed. He also feared that Joseph Smith had started a ball rolling which could not be stopped, and that in its momentum, the Church of Jesus Christ of Latter-day Saints itself was in jeopardy.

*[December 31, 1842 • Saturday]*

Sutters Fort was finally nearing completion and while everyone else seemed to view this as an augury in respect to his many enterprises, John Sutter was a worried man.[37]

This had been an unusual year and he admitted, at least to himself, that he had made some unfortunate choices. Chief among those was his support of Manuel Micheltorena, the new California governor and commanding general, who, with an army of 600 men, had been sent by the Mexican home government to succeed Juan Bautista Alvarado and to subdue Sutter, who was now deemed by Mexican authority to have become a possible threat. That it had been more than a possibility was clear in the letter General Vallejo had previously sent by special envoy Victor Prudon to Mexico City:

*...The Swiss upstart intends to make a second Texas out of California*

> and, even worse, to make himself lord and master of all California. We need men and guns to protect ourselves and we need them desperately...

As soon as the change in governors had been announced, Sutter wrote Micheltorena a long letter in French and sent it by special courier William Flugge to meet the general upon his arrival in Los Angeles. The letter conveyed not only a warm welcome and a reiteration of his complete allegiance to Mexican authority, but an explanation of why Mexican officials had become nervous about him. In his own log book, Sutter had written:

> ...At this time, strange to set down, I had full power of life and death over both Indians and white people in my section of Northern California. I officiated personally at all burial and marriages. It was necessary for me to be patriarch, priest, father and judge. Alvarado was well aware that Vallejo and many other native Californians were jealous of my strength here in the outlands. I encouraged American immigration and occupancy of this new land and the Mexicans discouraged it. I sympathized with and respected the Americans who came to this new empire. It was of such men that I planned to build New Helvetia into a sovereign state. But the Mexicans hated all Americans...

So, in an effort to improve his own image with the Mexican government in general and Manuel Micheltorena in particular, in his letter Sutter included an offer to help the new governor in any way it was in his power to do so. It was a very broad commitment.

That was when Sutter decided the work on his fort had been delayed too much and too often and he ordered its completion as a number one priority and virtually everyone pitched in to help—even the Kanakas, whose term of employment had expired but who had decided to stay on, along with another fifty or more of their fellow Sandwich Islanders who had arrived this year. A parallel inner wall was constructed with a roof running from inner to outer wall and the space beneath compartmented into some living quarters and numerous workshops—saddlery, blacksmith, bakery, blanket works, tannery, small flour mill, lime kiln, shoe store, grocery and the expanded distillery.

Now with the year coming to a close, Sutters Fort was close to being finished. Debts still hung heavily on him but he was gradually paying off some of them, even though there had been the failure of an important wheat crop. Trapping had been good and the numerous beaver pelts collected brought in $3 - 4 per pound. The fisheries had been most productive in their harvesting of salmon and sturgeon. Along with quantities of tallow, tanned hides and barrels of brandy made from wild grapes, a significant dent had been made in the more pressing debts.

Dismantling of Fort Ross had continued throughout the year under John Bidwell's supervision, but there was still much to do.[38] The *Sacramento*—the schooner that was part of what Sutter had bought—was kept constantly in service plying between the two ports, at one point even striving to tow the massive wooden wheat-threshing floors from Bodega Bay to Sutters Fort, an effort that had to be abandoned as simply too difficult. There remained yet about a year's work ahead in breaking down and shipping what remained at Fort Ross and Port Romanov, but everything brought thus far to Sutters Fort had been put to good use and most of the heavy work was being done by the Indians Sutter had trained. He even minted his own coin with which to pay them—tin disks stamped with a star die made by the fort's blacksmith; one star equivalent to a day's work, two stars for two days' work and so on. With such coinage the Indians could buy from Sutter's store the items they most wanted—primarily blankets, clothing and food.

There were a few more permanent adobe buildings within the fort now, as well as a tent city surrounding it. Some eighty white men were regularly employed by Sutter, as were 100 Indians, mainly as field hands for the grain crops and the not-yet-producing orchards, and there were fully 200 others dependent on the fort for subsistence and who were on call whenever needed. The fort was now even manufacturing significant quantities of its own guns. Sutter's permanent guard force for the fort was comprised of fifteen strictly trained Indian men who walked their posts and guarded the gate. Throughout the night at half-hour intervals, as a sand glass in the main guard room ran out and was turned over, a bell was struck, at which the guard on duty would call out his "All's well."

Despite having lost through drowning a fair amount of livestock in the process of driving the Fort Ross animals to merge with his own herds purchased on credit from Antonio Sunol, Bob Livermore, Joaquín Gómez, John Marsh and others, Sutter now had in excess of 1,200 head of cattle, more than 10,000 sheep, 1,000 or more hogs and close to 2,000 horses and mules.

A large flour mill was in the planning stages. It was to be built some five miles up the American River from the fort and a half-dozen huge millstones eventually to be installed there had already been ordered from the East. And Sutter was still periodically sending out parties to locate a feasible site for building a sawmill.

John Sutter was viewed by everyone as a very powerful individual and was treated with great respect tinged with an element of awe and fear. His generosity remained unflagging and he was constantly helping new arrivals. Though all appreciated this aid, few indeed ever repaid what he so freely gave, possibly because he was also considered to be very rich. That was a mistake. While Sutter had a flair for increasing his holdings at every turn, it was unfailingly done on credit and, even though some of the creditors received meager payments, his debts continued to mount. If another wheat crop failed or some other problem overtook him, his little empire could fail.

Sutter had always enjoyed imbibing but in recent months he had taken to drinking in excess and was becoming dissolute. It was not uncommon for him to be observed inebriated at almost any time of the day. He harbored notably diminished ideas for new projects and followed through with even fewer. He became curt with friends and a lecher among the Indian women who worked for him, one of whom he bought from Chief Anashe for a string of glass beads. He had become so wholly disinterested in his mistress, Manawitta—and the son she had borne him—that, disgusted, she returned to live with her husband, Kanaka Harry.

Most of the work at the fort was now being handled by the foremen and supervisors Sutter had appointed. Recently he had received a letter from Annette, informing him that his eldest son, Johann, Jr., was looking forward to leaving Bergdorf and coming to America soon to join his father in California and that she was thinking of accompanying him, and that his younger children were all doing well in school. His letter in response was barely cordial:

> "In a year or so I'll send money for your transportation, when the fort is completed, but do not come now. You cannot be comfortable here at the present time, with everything as rough as it is. Moreover,

*we have no schools for the children. I want them to have the best of everything to be a credit to us. They must be educated if they are to succeed in life...*

So, while others at Sutters Fort were complacent, if not distinctly sanguine, about the future, the aspect of a revolution breaking out in California and the potential of New Helvetia's collapse, caused Sutter to experience a pervasive and perpetual fear.

*[March 24, 1844 • Sunday]*
The two men leading the procession of men and horses and heavily laden pack mules that filed out of Sutters Fort today were watched with considerable interest by the inhabitants and no one among them was more thoughtful about their actual purpose than Captain John Sutter.

Eighteen days ago the pair had arrived in deplorable state, their mounts on the verge of collapse, two pack mules in no better condition and the men themselves equally fatigued. One had asked who was in charge here and the pair was directed to Sutter who, surprisingly, was sober and clad in a fresh white linen suit. The two dismounted and approached Sutter and the one who had posed the question saluted the fort's commander and then shook his hand in a firm grip. He was a bearded thirty-year-old whose alert gaze belied the weariness in his aspect.

"My name, Sir," he said, "is Captain John Fremont. This gentleman," he tilted his head toward his companion, "is my friend and guide, Mr. Kit Carson. We are in need of some assistance. We have come west on a mission for our government—a mission to explore the country west of the Rocky Mountains for the United States Topographical Service at Washington, D.C. We have met with difficulties and our party, which we left behind us a day's ride, is on foot and in distress. Can you help us?"

Sutter smiled and nodded. "You may stay here as long as you like," he said. "We will dispatch a party with extra horses to find your men and bring them here. We will endeavor to supply you with food, horses, mules, whatever your needs may be."

As soon as the pair had explained where the remainder of their party was located, Sutter ordered out a rescue party. He then invited Fremont and Carson to his quarters where they were given a good meal and an opportunity to rest.

As the pair ate, Fremont explained to his host that this was the second exploratory expedition he had led into the far west for his government and that they had been on the move in the execution of that mission for nearly a year. They had mapped an enormous expanse of territory and now, with the mission completed, they were eager to return to the United States. Before they could undertake that rigorous journey, however, they would have to be re-equipped with horses and mules to replace those that had been lost, as well as all manner of tack, food supplies, clothing and other essentials. All of which, he added hastily, to be paid for by the United States government. So, then, could Captain Sutter fulfill their needs?

Captain Sutter could. It would take a while, however. A fortnight, at least. Much gratified, Captain Fremont gave the go ahead, remarking that two weeks of delay was certainly better by far than attempting to do without. Everyone in his party needed a good rest and he couldn't imagine a better opportunity.

Sutter immediately put his men into a frenzy of work, rounding up the more than two dozen needed horses, sixty pack mules and a small herd of cattle, setting his blacksmiths to the task of preparing horseshoes and bridle bits, leather-workers to work on reins and bridles, pack saddles and braided rawhide ropes, millers on a 'round-the-clock schedule of grinding flour. All this while Sutter had engaged in lengthy conversations with Fremont and Carson and learned much about the lay of the land in the Sierras and Great Basin to the eastward. At the same time he answered the numerous questions Fremont posed in regard to California, its present state of government, its defenses, its rebellious native Californios, its port, climate and agricultural potential, its fish and game resources. And every evening for an hour or so, Fremont wrote extensively in what he said was the official report of his expedition that he would eventually submit to the United States Congress.

It had taken a bit more than just a couple of weeks to get everything ready, but at last it was done. A short while ago Fremont and his men, rested, fully equipped and ready to go, bade farewell to their highly accommodating host and set off on their return to the United States.

Continuing to watch them go, Sutter remained deeply thoughtful, wondering if a simple mapping expedition was truly the basis for that detachment having come here. There was no way to know for sure, but he felt certain that there was more here than he had been told and that he had just finished entertaining what might well have been unheralded harbingers of momentous changes in California's future.

### [July 11, 1844 • Tuesday]

At twenty-five, Samuel Brannan was best described as dapper. A very handsome, slim young man, he was usually clad in a fine black suit, black derby cocked at a jaunty angle, highly polished shoes, crisp white linen shirt and, as an exclamation point to his character, a flashy cravat. In addition, he was possessed of sharp intellect, a keen sense of humor and an enormous dose of self-confidence. Less obvious at first, he was also very greedy, a confirmed manipulator who was careless of the feelings of others and, whenever possible, subtly but decidedly self-serving.

Born in Saco, Maine, his early years had been essentially uneventful and, to his thinking, entirely boring. He did not particularly care for Maine and yearned for any opportunity to see new places, experience different things, always considering himself on the brink of something momentous that would forever change his life. Though he excelled in school, he was eager to be out in the real world, learning a trade. When his older sister, Mary Ann, married Alexander Badlam of Painesville, Ohio, and she had asked her brother if he would like to come and live with them there, he had leaped at the chance. Alexander had taken up a homestead just outside town and fully anticipated that Samuel would help him with the farming activities. Becoming a farmer was hardly the vocation young Brannan had in mind and it became a constant struggle to get him to share in the workload. After two years of this the Bedlams had more than enough and when an advertisement was posted by the town printer seeking a young man to help him, Samuel was bound out by them as an apprentice.

Young Brannan learned the trade quickly and well. In the process, that wonderfully momentous thing he always thought was about to occur actually happened: When he was instructed to deliver a printing order to a Mr. Smith in the small town of Kirtland, some eight miles to the west, he found a twenty-eight-year-old former Vermonter, founder of some kind of religion called Mormonism, who was presently in the midst of erecting a temple for his followers.

Never before had any kind of religion piqued Samuel's interest, but suddenly this one did—possibly because virtually all outsiders scorned it. Smith—Joseph Smith—seemed to take a shine to the boy and they had a long conversation which wound up with Brannan volunteering to help build the temple. Smith gratefully accepted the offer and after that, whenever possible, young Samuel was on hand helping alongside others. Somehow, Smith always had time to talk with him and, despite the implorings of Mary Ann and Alexander to not let himself be taken in by Smith's doctrine, Samuel became ever more intrigued by what the man told him about his church.

Joseph Smith related how in 1820, when he was fifteen and just an ordinary farmhand, he began to have visions in which it was revealed to him that the Church of Christ had been withdrawn from the earth and that God had selected him to restore it. This continued sporadically until September 22, 1827 when, so Smith said, he was visited by an angel named Moroni who instructed him where to unearth a buried, golden-leaved book printed in hieroglyphics. He was told it was the history of the true church in America and, with the angel Moroni's help, he had translated it—a process that took two and a half years—and published it in Palmyra, New York in 1830 as the 522-page volume called *The Book of Mormon*. In essence, the translation proclaimed that the American Indians were originally Jews who had sailed to this continent from the Near East in the sixth century BC and who had been visited by Jesus following His resurrection. It also, among other tenets, sanctioned polygamous marriage. On April 6 of that year of publication, Smith and his friend, Oliver Cowdery, founded the Church of Jesus Christ of Latter-day Saints in Fayette, New York and had ordained each other as the first elders of the restored church.[39]

Persecution from outsiders had begun almost immediately after the church was established, most often because of public outrage over the polygamy aspect, and as Smith related it to Brannan, had continued to greater or lesser degree over the five years since. Despite such persecution, their membership had grown phenomenally and Smith was confident it would continue to do so. While they had already been driven out of New York and came here to Kirtland in 1831, rumblings against them were growing louder here in northern Ohio and he was sure that sooner or later they would be driven from here as well. Eventually, however, they would find their Zion, where all these Saints who had pledged their faith could finally assemble in peace.

Sixteen-year-old Samuel Brannan was deeply moved by Smith's narration and even more when, on March 7, 1835, he was among the hundred workers who knelt and received Joseph Smith's blessing for their unstinting labor on the Mormon temple. That settled the matter for Samuel and he joined the Church, which made him somewhat less than popular in the Badlam household.

As soon as he was able, Sam Brannan had purchased his remaining time as printer's apprentice and, as journeyman printer, set out to make his own way in the world of commerce. His first stop was Indianapolis, where he hired on to promote a newspaper, but failed. On to New Orleans where he joined his older brother, Thomas, and began publishing a weekly literary paper, but Thomas contracted yellow fever and died, the literary paper contracted lack of reader support and it, too, died. Samuel moved on, this time to New York City, and this time he became a bit more focused.

Brannan had long felt strongly that his church really needed a magazine aimed to interests of the Mormons. He was visited by Joseph Smith's younger brother, William, who concurred in this belief and informed the membership. Then he and Samuel had successively visited the eastern Mormon churches, soliciting their aid for such a project; the periodical, to be published in New York City, was to be called *The Prophet*. Funds were collected to finance the enterprise and publication began.

In the meanwhile, ejected from Ohio as he predicted, Joseph Smith declared western Missouri the new Mormon Zion and Saints from all over converged there, but once again hatreds rose, fighting began and the Mormons, besieged not only by the populace but by the State Militia under orders of Governor Boggs, pulled up stakes and left, turning eastward and settling this time in Illinois at their new headquarters called Nauvoo.

Early last year Brannan, on a visit to Painesville, met a comely young lady named Harriet Hatch. He proposed, she accepted. As it happened, Joseph Smith was visiting Kirtland and he delighted in sealing Hattie and Samuel in matrimony. And in considerably less than nine months they had a daughter whom they named Almira. But Samuel was tired once again; tired of Painesville, tired of Hattie, tired of the infant Almira. With hardly a second thought, he abandoned all three and returned to New York and continued to publish *The Prophet*.

Only a few months later, earlier this year while on a brief visit to Connecticut, Samuel's lust led him into another engagement, this time with Eliza—Anna Eliza Corwin—the attractive daughter of the widow

Fanny Corwin. They married, she in ignorance that he was already married and a father, but since the Church sanctioned polygamy, Samuel saw no real need to reveal anything that didn't really matter anyway, and she returned to New York with him. Then just last week, she had cheerfully announced her pregnancy. Though dismayed and wondering how his meager salary could feed another mouth, he successfully convinced Eliza that he was delighted.[40]

He concentrated on his work with *The Prophet* but refrained from any editorializing or commentary in regard to the schism that had long been simmering among the Mormon leadership and which had lately begun to surface. Sam Brannan's devotion to Joseph Smith remained unwavering, but it was painfully evident that The Prophet's ever-growing power in the Church had instilled a greed within him for even more power on a much broader scale: Last year Smith had announced himself a candidate, in opposition to Henry Clay and James K. Polk, for the Presidency of the United States.[41] He had not won but this past May, Smith actually proposed to the United States Congress that federal legislation be passed authorizing him to construct a whole chain of forts along the Oregon Trail—a chain linking the western limits of the United States to the Pacific Ocean at the mouth of the Columbia River—and that he be further authorized to raise a force of 100,000 volunteers, in no way connected to the U.S. Army, who would have the responsibility of defending all American travelers and interests on the western frontier. This not only dumbfounded many members of Congress, it instilled in as many others a stab of fear that one man and his followers could so casually display such a hideous strength.

Joseph Smith's grandiose idea was matched only by his growing fearful distrust, evidenced in frequent furious outbursts, both of superior Mormon Council members and of subordinates whom he believed were conspiring against him. While not publicized, these matters were becoming apparent not only to Sam Brannan, who had begun to openly oppose The Prophet's decisions and decry his striving for such power, but to other Mormons who had finally allowed their anger to surface, with polygamy as the initial focus.

While there had always been a small element of dissidents in the Church, who railed against the rules and regulations dictated by their leader, now there had arisen a rather sizeable faction—both Mormons and outsiders—that was proclaiming loudly against polygamy. This was a tenet that Smith strongly advocated and about which he was becoming constantly more vocal, despite stern warnings from the Illinois State government against what opponents there termed "such a vile practice." To Governor Thomas Ford and to a great many Illinois congressmen as well, polygamy was the ultimate insult to God, church, home and family. Smith blandly shrugged off their objections, until the dissident Mormons themselves decided to take the issue into their own hands and set up a press right in the heart of Nauvoo in order to print a newspaper to attack Smith publicly. The Prophet's fury was boundless. The one and only issue of the opposition's *Nauvoo Expositor* was actually printed and distributed just five weeks ago, on June 7. Smith's Legion, following The Prophet's orders to the Nauvoo City Council, broke into the building, utterly destroyed the banks of type, smashed the press, then set the newspaper office afire.

The citizens of Illinois could take no more and banded together into an uncontrolled mob. Brutal attacks resulted and continued for days and then weeks, most often occurring at night and with arson being visited regularly upon Nauvoo itself. Scores of buildings were burned, scores of Mormons injured and some killed. The hostilities escalated until Nauvoo itself was almost under siege.

In New York City, far removed from this Illinois mayhem, Sam Brannan felt sure this situation would all resolve itself in time and things would settle back to some degree of normalcy. That's what he thought, that is, until an hour ago when he took his evening stroll and was stunned when he saw the headlines proclaiming that the Mormon Prophet Joseph Smith had been assassinated. Dazed, he bought copies of every newspaper carrying the story and returned with them to his apartment where bit by bit the tragic occurrence came into full focus.

On June 27, while Governor Ford was in Nauvoo investigating charges of counterfeiting against the Mormons, Joseph Smith and his brother, Hyrum, briefly visited the little town of Carthage, seat of Hancock County, some twenty miles east of Nauvoo. In the midst of the afternoon the brothers were unexpectedly arrested and incarcerated in the Carthage jail. Word spread swiftly and soon a vicious mob of Illinois citizens gathered and were demanding the prisoners be turned over to them. Without locking the door, the police chief and jailer slipped away through a back door. Less than ten minutes later, at 5:00 p.m., a portion of the mob, their faces painted with boot-black, surged in. A few moments later a barrage of shots sounded and when the laughing, joking, black-faced mob swept back outside, left behind on the floor of the jail cell were the bloodied bodies of Hyrum and Joseph Smith.

Samuel Brannan had paled while reading the accounts and now he carefully folded the newspapers and set them aside in a neat pile on the corner of his desk. Then he sat quietly in the gathering dusk and pondered three questions for which he had no answers: Who would take over leadership of the Church? What effect would this have on the future of the Church of Jesus Christ of Latter-day Saints? What was his own future in light of all this?

Quite suddenly Samuel Brannan was trembling.

*[August 15, 1844 • Thursday]*

Word of the assassination of The Prophet Joseph Smith and his brother Hyrum took a little longer to reach Elder Henry Bigler, who was on a mission to evangelize in Ripley, Virginia, the seat of Jackson County. As with the majority of Saints everywhere, it struck him a tremendous blow, exacerbated by the additional gloomy intelligence that Nauvoo itself was under attack by the Illinois citizenry.

Bigler was well aware, as virtually all the Mormon elders were, prior to Smith's death, of the growing schism in their church and the various factions and individuals who were striving to gain the seat of power; a struggle in which Joseph Smith would never capitulate; a looming internal conflict that, far more than outside persecution could accomplish, would quite probably destroy the institution. There had been the sure knowledge among them that no greater crises had ever been faced by the Church of Jesus Christ of Latter-day Saints and unless a miracle occurred, Mormonism was doomed.

None of the Saints had anticipated that the Church would, in fact, actually be *saved* by the martyrdom of its Prophet.

The core of the Church abruptly strengthened with the awakening of a dormant will to survive against whatever threat any outside enemies could bring against them and now, while dissension still reigned throughout the institution's hierarchy, it had become a more balanced struggle for control than the lopsided, ultimately destructive battle that would have blossomed had Joseph Smith lived.

Henry Bigler's mission to the eastern states was nearly completed when the tragic news reached him and he immediately canceled the remainder of his schedule and headed for Nauvoo. By the time he arrived and settled in on his father's little farm on the outskirts of Nauvoo, the exterior problems had eased off and were more or less under control, and the internal struggles for leadership had unexpectedly become more clearly defined.

The biggest rift had already occurred. Within a few days of The Prophet's death one of the more prominent Mormon elders, Sidney Rigdon, climbed atop a wagon bed and addressed a large gathering of the Saints. In stentorian tones he proclaimed himself the new Prophet, saying that he had experienced a vision in which he alone was selected as the true guardian of the Church. However, Rigdon was not popular and when he demanded that all who believed in his vision should follow him back to Pennsylvania, which he told them would become the new hub of Mormonism, only a few bewildered Saints clustered under his mantle and headed east.

No less than twenty other leaders in the Church rose to the challenge and just as swiftly faded into oblivion. In a sort of mitosis, three distinct schisms formed and managed to gather significant numbers of converts, then marched away—one heading to Wisconsin, another to Iowa, a third to Arkansas.

About that time one of Joseph Smith's principal lieutenants, who had been diligently working behind the scenes since The Prophet's death and gaining the support of a wide range of important Mormon elders, stepped forward at a mass assembly of the Saints in Nauvoo. Not very tall and somewhat overweight, he was hardly an imposing figure. A native of Vermont, he was forty-three years old and a journeyman painter and glazier. In 1832 he had become converted and baptized into the Mormon faith by Joseph Smith, served for two years as an itinerant missionary for the Church and then, because of his intelligence and keen business sense, became in 1835 a member of the Church's governing body, the Quorum of Twelve Apostles. It was he who had quietly and most effectively directed the settlement of the Mormons at Nauvoo and he had spent two years in England as a missionary. Just last year he had become head of the Quorum of Twelve Apostles and the most important factor in keeping The Prophet's obsession for glory and power under control.

His name was Brigham Young.

Now, as he began his address, a strange silence mantled the assemblage; they became rooted in place, suddenly mesmerized as what they believed they heard was the voice of Joseph Smith emerging from this unlikely personage. A gripping sense swept across them that through some miracle The Prophet had been resurrected and become lodged in the being of Brigham Young. He spoke for an hour or more, calming them, reassuring them of their importance to the stability of the Church, once again instilling in them the courage that had been faltering and the unity that had all but dissolved. Most importantly, he told them that it had become clear that they could no longer remain in Illinois, that they must abandon Nauvoo and, like the Israelites, set off on a journey that would lead them ultimately and finally to their Zion. He admitted that he did not have any idea where that Zion would be but he knew—*he absolutely knew!*—it would be revealed to him.

It would take a vote of the entire membership of some 40,000 Saints worldwide to elect him to that exalted position as the new head of the Church of Jesus Christ of Latter-day Saints. Yet, in the mind and heart of Henry Bigler, as in the minds and hearts of the thousands of Saints here assembled, the Mormon Church already had a new leader and his name was Brigham Young.[42]

*[November 28, 1844 · Thursday]*

Mariano Guadalupe Vallejo, though still being addressed as general by most, had now been elevated to the permanent rank of lieutenant colonel. It was an honor that pleased him but it did not ease the worry that plagued him about what was occurring in California.

As an officer in the Mexican Army, his allegiance had to be to Governor Manuel Micheltorena, yet he was deeply opposed to many of the policies the man planned to inaugurate here. It had been proclaimed that in addition to his army, Micheltorena was bringing with him from Mexico a large number of new settlers for California who were to spread out and not only occupy the existing towns of San Diego, Los Angeles, Santa Barbara and other coastal communities, but equally establish new villages, not only coastally but within California's interior. It was discovered after their arrival, however, that these so-called settlers were actually hundreds of desperadoes called *cholos*—paroled convicts and unconvicted murderers, thieves, low-lives of every description—who had not left their bad habits behind. Murmurings of outrage over this influx of *cholos* quickly evolved into talk of revolution. The Californios were proud of their holdings and ever more resented the rules and regulations imposed against them by the parent government in Mexico, a government in which they had virtually no voice. In particular, the irate residue of Alvarado's ousted government fanned the flames of revolt, declaring in secret meetings that it was time to drive out the undesirable newcomers and their new governor.

Though Vallejo was not truly a part of this revolutionary fervor that was growing among the Californios, he secretly sympathized with it. For Micheltorena to have brought in hundreds of these *cholos* as part of his army and to populate various regions of California was, in Vallejo's opinion, a very serious mistake. Had he not done so, he might have been able to strike a balance of sorts with the Californios, but not now. A die had been cast and was hardening into its final face—outright revolution.

Last June, when Governor Micheltorena summoned him to Monterey, it was to honor him with a gift for his extraordinary services to the Mexican government. There were still no funds available to pay him and his army of men at Sonora for their services, which Vallejo felt was unconscionable, since they were as much a part of Micheltorena's armed forces as the palace guard in Monterey, and it meant that Vallejo would have to continue paying them out of his own pocket. On the other hand, the governor presented him with an extensive land grant called Rancho Nacional Soscol; nowhere near so large as the nearby Petaluma Grant he had received long ago from Governor Alvarado, yet a piece of land certainly not to be scorned.

The gift had placed Vallejo on something of a tightrope. While he had accepted the land with genuine appreciation, he continued to distance himself from the governor so that if and when a hot revolution did break out, the Californios would not consider him an enemy in Micheltorena's pay. It was a position which was, in a way, emphasized by the fact that he and his men had been receiving no financial support from either Micheltorena or the Mexican home government.

Now he was back in Monterey again, more concerned than ever with the intelligence he had received that a revolutionary outbreak of the Californios was imminent and was to be led by José Castro and Pio Pico. This was intelligence that, in light of what he came here to do, he dared not share with the governor. He had decided that he simply could not take any active role against the Mexican government, but neither could he allow Micheltorena to order him to send reinforcements to help defend the hated *cholos*. What he was going to do now was a great gamble.

Shown into the office of the governor, who was studying a document on his desktop, Vallejo stood at stiff attention until Micheltorena slid the paper aside and raised his glance to recognize him.

"Ah, General, how good of you to visit. How may I help you?"

"Governor Micheltorena, it is kind of you to receive me without my having an appointment." The governor nodded and smiled but made no response and Vallejo continued, "Sir, I'm sure you know you are well esteemed by the Californios but it is to your benefit to know that you would be still more highly thought of if you would send away your *cholos*, who have caused the Californios much trouble since their arrival with you."

Micheltorena was shaking his head even before Vallejo finished. "No, no, my friend, that I cannot do. The settlers who accompanied me here—*cholos*, as you call them—are not here at my whim. I was ordered by the Emperor to bring them along and establish them here. I do not have the authority to disobey such an order. The Californios must simply learn to accept what cannot be changed."

Vallejo nodded sadly, having known full well what the response would be. Now it was time for the gamble. "One other thing, sir, if you please. My men and I have received no pay from Mexico for a great while. Is such pay available to be distributed to us now?"

Again the governor shook his head and Vallejo hoped the surge of relief he experienced was not apparent.

"It is not possible at this time, General," Micheltorena said, his manner more brusque now. "That is a matter over which I have no control and, even if I had, there are not funds enough to take care of it. I'm sorry."

It was a dismissal, but Vallejo was not finished. "Then, sir, I regret what I have to tell you. I have paid those troops out of my own pocket for much too long. My funds, too, are depleted and I can no longer support the army at Sonoma at my own expense. As of today, the Northern Army is disbanded."

[*December 2, 1844 • Monday*]

Lieutenant John Charles Fremont was clearly the newest American hero. His two reports on his second exploratory expedition into the West had been published by the Government Printing Office in a single volume entitled *Report of an Exploring Expedition to the Rockies* and practically overnight the volume had become a best seller and Fremont's name was on everyone's tongue.

To a populace eager for excitement and high adventure, this was the real stuff and they devoured it with greater acclaim than was ever accorded a dime novel. After all, this was truth, not fiction. Here was a courageous young officer of the American Army engaged in a variety of thrilling escapades while at the same time providing a great service to his government and to the American people. This was a vicarious journey into a western wilderness few had ever seen and which most believed they would never experience. Yet again, they just might, since Fremont, suddenly broadly characterized as one of the greatest of the great trailblazers, had drawn explicit maps and charted the way, measured the distances and described the landmarks, became navigator of treacherous plains and mountains and deserts where daring, great endurance and determination were the keynotes of survival.

Not since the reports of Lewis and Clark, published four decades earlier, had any publication so gripped the attention of the public. But somehow, Fremont's account was even more exciting, more readable, more interesting than Lewis and Clark's had been, striking at the core of wanderlust and imagination recumbent in each reader. Perhaps this was due to the hand Jessie Fremont supplied in helping her husband write his reports in a fast-paced literary style he could never have managed by himself. Perhaps it was due to the bombastic thundering of his father-in-law, Thomas Hart Benton, making even the rafters of the Senate reverberate with his recounting of tantalizing bits of the exploits of this little-know topographic engineer who had dared to face and survive the perilous wilderness. Perhaps it was because he did not stint in his praise of the two guides who had become his great friends and who had remained so steadfast through it all—Kit Carson and Tom Fitzpatrick—who themselves, to the reader, now typified the singularity, strength and ability of that rare breed; the mountain man. Perhaps it was due to the reader's own yearning to one day be that weary traveler who sees in the wilderness before him that wonderful sanctuary of hope and sustenance and supply that was called Sutters Fort.

And perhaps, when all was said and done, it was due to the small flame that Fremont had ignited in the breast of each who read his account; a small flame that also illuminated a passage into a world that they, too, might actually someday traverse.

*[December 12, 1844 • Thursday]*

Two years ago when Sam Colt introduced his new handgun it

# Infinite Dream

stirred mild interest, although most who heard about it considered it was probably more of a novelty than anything else. Many, in fact, scoffed at the idea of a so-called revolver. How could any gun, and a handgun at that, fire six times without reloading? Hardly a weapon to be taken seriously, it had to be a farce. Before the Colt revolver had even been given a reasonable test, Sam Colt was forced to close his factory due to bad financial management entirely beyond his control.

It took him a while to get production going again but he was finally able to do so and what he had longed for since then was something to occur that would catch the public's attention and show everyone what a superior weapon the revolver truly was.

Today that yearning was fulfilled.

In far-off Texas a little company of fifteen Texas Rangers being led by twenty-seven-year-old Colonel John Coffee Hays, engaged a war party of 300 Comanches.[43] The Rangers were outnumbered twenty to one, but in the fight that ensued they killed 150 of the Indians and intimidated the rest.

The Rangers had been armed with Colt Six-shooters.

No one had any further doubt that here was a weapon that could tame the West.[44]

*[December 25, 1844 • Wednesday]*

John Sutter was in a quandary.

While he had written to Governor Micheltorena, welcoming him to California and offering to assist him in any way possible, he had hoped that offer would be accepted as perfunctorily as it had been made. However much he disapproved of Juan Alvarado's debauchery and nepotism, he was the man who had given Sutter this great grant of land where he had so deeply planted his roots, and this was surely the man to whom he owed loyalty. Yet, Alvarado was now out of power and Manuel Micheltorena was in.

Earlier this year, the revolutionary talk had increased significantly throughout California and those in favor of it had spoken freely in Sutter's presence, reasonably assuming his allegiance was toward his initial benefactor. But then had come a message from Governor Micheltorena requesting Sutter come to Monterey and be his guest at the *Natividad* banquet. Two things were immediately clear: It was a summons and if he did not accept, it would be regarded as an insult; if he did accept it would lead Alvarado and José Castro and others to believe his sympathies and allegiance had changed and he would be regarded as an enemy.

To resolve this dilemma, Sutter let it be known that he had trade business in Monterey, the sole reason for his journey. If then, while in Monterey, he was seen at the governor's festivities, it could be passed off as a courtesy and nothing more; certainly not justification for Alvarado's adherents to conclude he was their enemy.

Leaving Sutters Fort in mid-December, Sutter had ridden out accompanied by his trusted chief assistant, John Bidwell, and one of his foremen, Julio Cavallada, along with a few armed Indian guards and servants. The party had ridden southwest through the Rancho Los Meganos, owned by John Marsh, and stopped overnight in San José where Sutter, bolstering the illusion that this was a business trip, paid a call on the British vice-consul, John Alexander Forbes. The two spoke of trade for a time and then Forbes suddenly became conspiratorial, looking around carefully and lowering his voice to assure they were not overheard. There was, he confided, a matter in the wind of great importance, a real revolution shaping up, led by Carson and Alvarado, who intended to force Micheltorena to return with all his desperadoes to Mexico. He told Sutter there was already a ship waiting in the cove below to transport the governor and his Mexican undesirables back to the Mexican shore.

"We may need your help," Forbes continued. "Micheltorena's not the man for us. Castro and Alvarado have been scouring the countryside getting men to enlist, but it's still all very secret, don't you know. They're bound to succeed, I have no doubt of it, and Micheltorena is doomed."

This confirmed what others had told Sutter along the way and he listened closely as Forbes continued divulging matters he had learned of the coming revolution, which was clearly much more advanced in its preparation than Sutter had realized. They talked well into the night and the following morning Sutter and his little retinue continued their ride into Monterey. When they arrived, noting with a start that the frigate *U.S. Savannah* was riding at anchor in the bay, Sutter immediately went to the home of trader David Spence on Alvarado Street, where he always stayed during his visits to the capital city. The next day, at Spence's invitation, he strolled into the expansive garden behind the house where a *merienda* was taking place. The early luncheon was being attended by many of Monterey's notables, coincidentally including Governor Micheltorena.

Sutter was introduced to the governor, a handsome, dapper man who greeted him effusively, kissed him on both cheeks, addressed him as *amigo mio* and thanked him profusely for accepting his invitation to attend his Natividad celebration the following week. Despite himself, Sutter was thoroughly charmed by the friendly and gracious Micheltorena, who was so sincere in expressing his appreciation for Sutter being one of the few in California who had written to welcome him to his new post. He launched into an enthusiastic explanation of his plans, already being implemented, to end the political corruption prevalent in California for so many years, adding that it was his hope to convince his superiors in Mexico not only of the great beauty of California but equally of its vast potential for development.

"California," he said, "is like a rough gemstone freshly taken from the ground, needing only to be polished to become a precious jewel."

Sutter thought then of Alvarado, a hedonist who was almost constantly drunk, who put his own desires above everything else and to whom California was merely an avenue for filling his own coffers and those of his cronies. The contrast between the former and present governors was stark and it was in that moment that Sutter made his decision.

"Your Excellency," he said softly, "may I have a few words with you in private?"

Micheltorena's expression changed subtly and then he smiled and nodded. "With great pleasure. Please follow me."

They strolled away from the other guests and entered the quiet, tastefully furnished redwood paneled drawing room frequently used by David Spence for private discussions. Several pieces of beautifully executed statuary graced the room and double-thick tucked draperies of deep green velvet framed the portioned, double glass doors that Micheltorena softly closed behind them. The men seated themselves in a pair of brocaded chairs facing one another over a low, elaborately carved and highly polished table. Sutter leaned forward and spoke in a voice not much more than a whisper.

"I have news of utmost importance, Your Excellency. About the revolution. It's underway."

Micheltorena frowned. "Revolution, Capitan? Where?"

"Right here in Monterey."

A faint sigh escaped the governor's lips. "Who is behind it?"

"Juan Alvarado, Excellency, and his old friend, José Castro. They plan to blockade you and your troops here in Monterey. They intend to take you prisoner, declare themselves the new government and ship you and your soldiers back to Mexico. Captain Vioget has already been engaged and his ship is standing by."

The governor nodded, frown deepening. On his arrival here, Alvarado and Castro had welcomed him, expressing friendship, but he had detected a certain wariness behind the words. He shook his head and sighed again. "The Californios have taken a dislike to me, I know." He admitted that thus far he had not been effective in resolving some of the principal problems bothering the Californios—the continuing struggle over whether Los Angeles or Monterey should be the capital, the perpetual problem with the Indians of the interior, the outrages committed against the native Californios by his own troops and the desperadoes brought in for settlement, the ever-present problem of foreigner influx and the pervasive yearning by the Californios for home rule. He slapped his hand down hard on the arm of his chair and his voice became almost plaintive as he concluded. "I have almost no friends here."

Sutter was silent for a long moment, realizing full well that if Alvadado's faction ever really wrested control of California government from Mexico, they would surely oust all foreigners and reclaim their lands and property. He nodded sympathetically, then took the plunge. "It will be an honor for me, Excellency, to assist you in any way possible. Whatever resources I have available at New Helvetia—men, horses, food, rifles, grain, cattle, cannon, whatever—are yours at your need."

Micheltorena's expression softened. "I am in your debt, *amigo*. How may I repay you?"

Sutter hesitated. "I did not come here seeking favor," he said slowly, "but since you ask, there is one thing. My colony is growing rapidly and requires more space. Another grant of land, if possible, would be most appreciated."

"Little enough to ask. Consider it already done."

That was three days ago. The next day Sutter and Micheltorena had signed their agreement and the grant of land was made, larger by far than Sutter could possibly have anticipated. Called the Sobrante Grant, it comprised twenty-two square leagues—96,800 acres—double the size of the grant he already owned. Then, yesterday, Micheltorena had held a council of war with his officers, which Sutter attended, and plans were laid to thwart the uprising. Micheltorena officially bestowed upon Sutter the rank of Capitan in the Mexican Army and lost no time in holding him to his end of the bargain. He ordered Sutter to return at once to New Helvetia and raise as large a force as possible, then hold them in readiness for further orders.

Now it was the evening of Christmas Day and the official Feast of the *Natividad* was finished. Following the lavish banquet, troops had paraded and a huge hot air balloon decorated with long trailers of gaily colored cloth was sent aloft to the cheers of all. Everyone of importance from Monterey and for many miles around had attended, including Alvarado and Castro, who together greeted Governor Micheltorena jovially and with no aspect of enmity apparent. Neither was there any in the greetings they gave Sutter a short while later.

Less than an hour ago, however, David Spence had sought Sutter out with the disturbing news that Castro had issued an order for the *capitan* and his party to be ambushed and taken prisoner as they passed through San Juan on their return. Sutter had instantly made arrangements for his entire party, exclusive of the horses, to be taken to Yerba Buena, where the *Sacramento* was presently situated and which would take them the remaining distance back upstream to Sutters Fort.

Aboard ship in Monterey Bay now, awaiting the outgoing tide, they would weigh anchor at dawn.[45]

*[December 31, 1844 • Tuesday]*

The President-elect of the United States sat alone in the gathering dusk considering what steps he would take as soon as he assumed office in just a bit over three months from now. He was well aware that his even having been nominated for so exalted an office had been remarkable; knew as well that his election was little short of miraculous. There were, he knew, so many others who were greater statesmen by far than he, greater politicians, greater intellects.

At the Democratic National Convention in Baltimore last summer almost everyone expected the Party's nomination would go to Martin Van Buren, despite his being trounced four years ago by the Whig candidate, William Henry Harrison. But the immensely popular Harrison had died a month after taking office and Vice President John Tyler had succeeded him, then soon alienated most Whig supporters by his rejection of a national bank bill. So, with the incumbent President Tyler not considered much of a threat, why not nominate Van Buren, who had a locked-in majority of the Democratic Party's votes? Why not? Because Party leaders were convinced he could not win. This was a different time and circumstances had changed. A strong spirit of expansion was rampant throughout the twenty-seven states. To the Party's dismay, Martin Van Buren had already hamstrung himself to a certain extent with his adamant refusal to support the annexation of Texas. Since that platform would almost surely defeat him, the Democratic Party caucused and, in an unprecedented move to prevent Van Buren's comeback, they changed the rules and unanimously adopted a requirement of two-thirds vote for nomination rather than a simple majority, which effectively pricked the Van Buren balloon.

There were Party members who would surely have been nominated if factionalism had not been so prevalent, but it was. The strongest contenders, John C. Calhoun, General Lewis Cass, Silas Wright and several others were all tightly involved with factions that were seriously disrupting Party solidarity, and the nomination of any one of them was apt to rip the Party asunder. The dilemma was resolved when a powerful nominating committee headed by George Bancroft and including Gideon Pike and Cave Johnson, put up an unexpected name; an individual who had the endorsement of no less a personage than Old Hickory himself, Andrew Jackson. Why Jackson's endorsement? Well, this man was governor of Tennessee and he was a friend and a former associate.

His name was James Knox Polk.

With a bit of arm-twisting here and there, the committee got the delegates on their bandwagon and, for the first time in the history of the United States, what was termed a "dark horse" was nominated and became the Presidential candidate of the Democratic Party.

Nevertheless, the same question was on everyone's lips: Who the devil was James K. Polk?

The answer was provided soon enough: He was a humorless, full-of-himself, dyed-in-the-wool Party Democrat who firmly believed that anybody who wasn't a Democrat wasn't an *American*, either. In the U.S. House of Representatives, he'd been floor leader and then speaker and, hardly as an afterthought, Andy Jackson's legal voice. In his stolid, narrow-minded way he had managed the anti-bank legislation and, of course, there was that gubernatorial thing he'd done. But, as telling as anything else, he was flat-footed solidly an expansionist; he was quite nearly rabid for the annexation of Texas, he wanted the disputed Oregon Territory to be American, not British, he wanted New Mexico and points

# The Infinite Dream

beyond to be American, not Mexican, and he was looking with hungry eyes at that big chunk of real estate on the Pacific Coast called California.

James K. Polk was, in the beginning of the campaign, recognizable to almost no one on a national scale, but he was touched with a vision of future greatness for his country far exceeding the aims of all other candidates; his was a vision of an unlimited future for the United States that his backers referred to proudly—and his opponents disdainfully—as an infinite dream.

As such a champion of an as yet unrealized grasp, he had quickly become the darling of the hundreds of thousands of American voters nationally who were of like mind and who heartily adopted his resounding campaign slogan, "Reoccupation of Oregon, re-annexation of Texas!" The cries of the opposition that Polk was a dreamer whose aims extended wholly beyond his reach did little to squelch the growing enthusiasm he engendered. The public had read the Lewis and Clark reports and, more recently, Fremont's exciting report to Congress that had touched off a renewed interest in the vast, largely unknown West of their continent and instilled a vigorous new spirit of adventure.

The Democrats chortled when the Whigs, as anticipated, nominated as their candidate the incumbent John Tyler. The laughter faded when Tyler, after accepting the nomination, withdrew before the election and the Whigs, hustling for a new candidate, settled on their greatest Party favorite, the renowned Henry Clay. But Clay made a serious error when, after vacillating a bit, he took a stance against the annexation of Texas. The diametrically opposed platforms were in place and Polk's was by far the sturdiest. His "infinite dream" became their own infinite dream, and when November finally rolled around, Clay garnered only 105 electoral votes, sixty-five less than his opponent, and the dark horse James K. Polk was on his way to the White House.

Now only a deeper shadow in the encroaching nightfall, Polk whispered the words aloud for the first time: "Mister President." Two simple words, but they tugged at his soul. What kind of a President would he be? What kind of a legacy would he contribute to the office, to the American people? Did his party yet realize that he couldn't be bullied or cajoled or maneuvered out of doing what he was determined to do, what he felt was just, what he *knew* was the due of the people? Did anyone in this point of time—*anyone*, whether in government or not—have any real inkling that those pre-election campaign declarations about his truly infinite dream of acquiring new territory for the United States were not, at least to some degree, political rhetoric? He thought not. Only he alone knew he meant every word.

The Mexicans had no justifiable claim on Texas, which had separated from Mexican rule and declared itself an independent republic on March 2, 1836. It had paid for its declaration in the blood of fine men at a place called The Alamo and they had made the Mexicans pay for it in the same coin at a place called San Jacinto, where the battle cry was "Remember the Alamo!"

On March 3, 1837, a year and a day after Texas declared its independence, President Andrew Jackson, with the approval of Congress and on his final day in office, recognized the Republic of Texas. He said that Mexico's offenses "would justify, in the eyes of all nations, immediate war." The Texans had appealed to the United States for annexation, yet due to interminable delays concerning slavery and commerce, and Mexico's warning of an outright declaration of war if such annexation were approved, eight years later it still existed unannexed, still an unofficial American protectorate and still engaged in sporadic guerilla warfare with Mexico, which had at first accepted by treaty the Texas independence, only later to arbitrarily repudiate that treaty."[46] But now there were new elements. Great Britain, which had no part in the dispute, had the gall to intervene and persuade Mexico to recognize Texas independence if Texas refused to join the United States. The Texans refused to make any such agreement, but their patience had worn thin and now they were making rumblings about forming an alliance with Great Britain or France and accepting official protectorate status under whichever flag chose them first. *That*, Polk determined, would not, *could not* occur. Texas had to be annexed only by the United States and subsequently be melded into this Union of states.

Polk was no less determined that the Oregon Territory dispute with Great Britain be settled in America's favor since, as he put it, "America's title to it is clear and unquestionable". That territory, originally ceded to the United States by Spain, stretched northward from the northern border of California, but there was no mutually agreed upon northern border for Oregon. Expansionists, including Polk, claimed that American holdings included all of Oregon and that the northern border should be established at the southernmost border of Alaska, at fifty-four degrees forty minutes North Latitude. Polk's ringing campaign slogan of "fifty-four-forty or fight!" had quickly become a catch phrase. The British, on the other hand, said the border was at the forty-second parallel and claimed everything northward by right of occupation and by the establishment of many Hudson's Bay Company fur trading posts over the years. Both British and American compromisers—Henry Clay among them—advocated the forty-nine degree parallel.[47]

The British, early on, were infuriated by the American fur entrepreneur John Jacob Astor's establishment of his principal western headquarters, Astoria, at the mouth of the Columbia River and had erected their own Pacific headquarters, Fort Vancouver, somewhat upriver from there. Two years after the outbreak of the War of 1812, while battles raged in the East between British and American forces, the British underlined their Oregon claim by confiscating Astoria and driving out Astor's men.

With the opening of the Oregon Trail, however, numerous Americans had been making the overland journey westward—a perilous journey during which an average of one out of every ten who attempted it died— and now there were well over a thousand of them settled in the Willamette and lower Columbia valleys. Since there were now many more Americans than British in the territory, Polk determined that the American claim should prevail. His stance was bolstered by reliable intelligence reports that the British themselves had reached the conclusion that too many Americans were now established there than could feasibly be ousted: Contesting ownership of the territory simply was not worth engaging in war to establish. This was intelligence that Polk fully intended to rely upon.

Finally, there were other matters; those concerning the great southwestern area generally termed New Mexico and the great western seaboard territory called California. Both were still possessions of Mexico, the former virtually uninhabited and the latter more populated but at this very moment with a revolution brewing.

President-elect James Polk was unaware of the darkness that had crept into the room. What he was seeing was a grand and glorious vision that answered his own earlier question: What kind of legacy would he contribute to the office, to the American people? He saw this nation not as a collection of states that barely stretched beyond the Mississippi, but as an unbroken collection of united states stretching from the Atlantic to the Pacific and from Canada to Mexico. And he was sure he knew exactly *how* such a vision could become reality:

The key to initiating his infinite dream of the United States lay in the annexation of Texas.

# Chapter 2

♦

[*January 1, 1845 • Wednesday*]
*By the will of God Almighty, I have become Moses!*

The thought struck Brigham Young with such force that he staggered, recovered, then looked around quickly. Had he spoken the words? No, surely not. The sudden realization he was making the most profound decision for the entire membership of the Church of Jesus Christ of Latter-day Saints was unsettling, yet exhilarating. What he was envisioning to happen to the Mormons was tantamount to the Biblical Exodus: He, Brigham Young, was on the threshold of leading his thousands of Saints away from Nauvoo to a far-distant Zion.

He had no clear vision of where this Promised Land would be, except that it lay somewhere to the west. As with the Israelites, they would be facing harsh mountains and searing deserts, the hazards of famine and thirst. He—and he alone—would know it when they found it; he prayed they would not have to wander for forty years to find it. The thought repeated: *I have become Moses!*

All this had come about as a result of the persisting hostilities between Illinois residents and the Mormon population at Nauvoo. The acts of terrorism—burnings and beatings, perpetuated equally by both sides and sprinkled with murders—had continued unabated since the murder of Joseph Smith and his brother Hyrum in the City of Carthage jail last June. Each such act demanded like reprisal and there seemed to be no reasonable solution to it all. The Illinois residents, believing rumors that the Mormons were intent upon massacre, appealed to Governor Ford to call up the militia and exterminate the Saints; the Mormons, believing the Illinois residents meant to wipe them out to the last individual, appealed to Governor Ford for relief.

The governor was wise enough to know that whatever step he took would ultimately please one side and anger the other. In this dilemma he had appointed a special commission to meet with Brigham Young and his counselors. That commission included two of the State's most prominent and unbending politicians—former Congressman John J. Hardin, who was presently competing against Abraham Lincoln for the same Congressional seat, and the man referred to in the press as "the Little Giant," Stephen A. Douglas.

The upshot of their meetings was this: The citizens of Illinois wanted the Mormons out of their state—completely—and Brigham Young's stand on the rights of the Mormons under the United States Constitution and Bill of Rights, while justified, was not realistic under the circumstances. The commissioners stated flatly that if the Mormons did not leave Illinois voluntarily and permanently, there was little doubt they would be exterminated. Therefore, there really was no choice: They had to go. If, however, they would begin immediately to make plans and preparations in this direction, Governor Ford would mollify the Illinois citizenry and simultaneously, so much as it was in his power to do so, he would provide protection for the Mormons until they uprooted themselves and were gone away.

So Brigham Young, on behalf of the Church, accepted the ultimatum and now sent literature throughout the world describing the oppression being visited upon the Saints and asked for donations to support the impending exodus from Illinois. He also dispatched numerous parties of Saints to personally appear before some of the richest and most prominent business and social leaders throughout the United States, earnestly soliciting their help.

Finally, Brigham Young today prepared a statement to be reproduced and a copy of it to go to every Mormon: Nauvoo could no longer be considered the seat of the Church of Jesus Christ of Latter-day Saints; before the end of the year, even though they would continue building their temple here, the evacuation would begin and that he, Brigham Young, would lead the Saints on this exodus to their final destination. It would be a place where they would permanently settle, a place where they would be free of the tyranny and terrorism that had plagued them, a place where they would establish their own government and be accountable to none but God Almighty.

The Promised Land. *Zion!*

*[March 1, 1845 · Sunday]*

The new book about California was an instant success. It was published in Cincinnati by the printing firm of George Conclin and Company, its impact far greater than anticipated. The presses ran ceaselessly, churning out thousands of copies, unable to keep up with the demand. Everyone wanted a copy. It was a book that fueled the small fire ignited by John C. Fremont's account of his expedition to Oregon and California, turning this new book into a beacon that attracted buyers as if they were moths. It downplayed the virtues of Oregon and concentrated on California, described in a manner that made Utopia pale by comparison.

The author of the new book was Lansford W. Hastings, originally of Mount Vernon, Ohio. An enterprising young man, in 1842 he had accompanied an early wagon train to Oregon, a train including more than fifty wagons and 120 individuals. That Hastings had survived the journey was not so much a tribute to his wilderness abilities as it was to the good management and discipline enforced by the party's leader, a thirty-six-year-old physician named Elijah White, whose own reason for going to Oregon was his appointment as Indian Agent for the Northwest.

On their arrival, however, Hastings had not been enamored of Oregon and had moved southward with another party into northern California. As most new arrivals did, he wound up stopping at Sutters Fort and stayed several weeks. He'd been impressed with the colony Sutter was developing and especially with Sutter's sale of lands throughout the expanse of his grant. When Lansford Hastings went back East later in the year and visited the nation's capital, he was sought out by a pair of behind-the-scenes insiders who listened closely to his account of California and especially pricked up their ears in regard to Sutter's New Helvetia Colony. These two were Amos Kendall and A.G. Benson. In subtle ways, they convinced Hastings there was no one of importance in Washington D.C. they did not know, no kind of deal for which they could not find government backing.[48] With what Hastings told them, they sniffed what they conceived could be an unparalleled opportunity for a lucrative wildcat land deal. James Polk was on the eve of entering his Presidency and it was clear he meant to support practically any means possible to encourage American emigration to the West. To do so, government would almost certainly offer land as an impetus to settlement and, while nothing was clear in that respect yet, this pair was sure it soon would be and they meant to be on the ground flood of whatever land proposals were made and later enacted.

Kendall and Benson had readily concocted a scenario in which half of the land ultimately to be granted for settlement would be theirs. They catered to Hastings' ego and it was a tribute to his gullibility that he never questioned the plausibility of such a scheme. The role he was to play in all this would be to combine his limited knowledge of the land with his writing skill and produce a work that would stoke even further the growing flame of public interest in California. Yes, California was the key to it all, rather than Oregon which had already beckoned so many. That Hastings construed their conversation to mean he was being accepted as a full partner in their blooming venture was entirely his own presumptive error.

Now the book had been written and published and was a rousing success. The title page left little to the imagination:

THE
**EMIGRANTS' GUIDE,**
TO
**OREGON AND CALIFORNIA,**
CONTAINING SCENES AND INCIDENTS OF A PARTY OF
OREGON EMIGRANTS:
**A DESCRIPTION OF OREGON;**
SCENES AND INCIDENTS OF A PARTY OF CALIFORNIA
EMIGRANTS;
AND
**A DESCRIPTION OF CALIFORNIA;**
WITH
A DESCRIPTION OF THE DIFFERENT ROUTES TO
THOSE COUNTRIES:
AND
ALL NECESSARY INFORMATION RELATIVE TO THE
EQUIPMENT, SUPPLIES, AND THE METHOD
OF TRAVELING.
**BY LANSFORD W. HASTINGS,**
LEADER OF THE OREGON AND CALIFORNIA EMIGRANTS OF 1842
CINCINNATI:
PUBLISHED BY GEORGE CONCLIN,
STEREOTYPED BY SHEPARD & CO.
1845

What lay inside was even more extravagant.

He wrote that in California perpetual summer was in the midst of unceasing winter.

He wrote that perennial spring and never-failing autumn stood always side by side, as towering snow clad mountains forever looked down upon verdant vegetation.

He declared California was warmer in the winter than most places in the East were in summer and flowers were in full bloom in December but, with all this, an absolute absence of marshy lowlands with their coincident "noxious miasmatic effluvia".

He added that the region was free from all causes of fever, from all sudden changes or variability of climate that could cause catarrh or consumption and even the common cold was unknown.

Moreover, farming was idyllic and the crops magnificent: clover grew to a height of five feet, cloaking the hills with natural hay as far as the eye could see. With such climate and such crops, livestock could be raised without the usual expense of barns or silos or cribs. Like the clover, there were wonderful expanses of wild flax that could produce the finest linen. Oats soared to eight feet tall on stems as thick as one's little finger. There were two wheat crops per year to each field, with most wheat stems supporting seven heads and a single acre of ground producing upwards of 120 bushels—a single bushel of this plump grain easily weighing four pounds more than a bushel of wheat grown anywhere else on earth—and the wheat crop self-seeding so that sowing the following year was unnecessary. Corn grew ears a foot and a half long on stalks twelve feet high and, without tending, a cornfield produced a minimum of sixty bushels per acre. And fruit? Well now, strawberries larger than plums and sweeter than any others anywhere; plums larger than apples; huge grapes in unbelievably large clusters; peach trees that bloomed in January; deep, loamy soil that was perfect for cotton, rice, tobacco, potatoes, peas, squash, practically anything.

Crops, quite simply, never failed.

Thousands of streams, he said, and every one of them alive with salmon up to 100 pounds each and sturgeon topping 300 pounds. Fur animals in amazing abundance. Tens of thousands of wild horses were there for the taking. Gentle winds and regular rains. The California Indians entirely inoffensive.

# The Infinite Dream

And the journey to get there? The one everyone heard was so treacherous? What about that?

Not so, wrote Hastings. Plenty of fuel for campfires all along the entire way. Game animals—deer, antelope, bighorns, grouse—all in abundance for food; buffalo that could be herded like cattle and consumed one after another, as meat was needed. Indians? They weren't a problem, too busy fighting each other to bother emigrants who weren't doing anything except passing through. All the streams to be encountered could be forded with ease, at least to the place where the trail split for Oregon and California. Deserts? A few, but not very extensive and, with a couple of barrels of water along, easily crossed in a day or two. Rocky, narrow trails? Not bad at all until the trail split. If you headed for Oregon at that point, you were in for trouble because traveling got hazardous at once, but the road to California was open and clear. There was even a new route that cut off the necessity of going north to Fort Hall and then back south again; instead, it led straight west from Fort Bridger, past the south end of the big Salt Lake, cutting off 200-300 miles of unnecessary travel. If you decided on Oregon and managed to survive the difficulties of getting there, Hastings warned, you faced five months of constantly leaden skies along with miserably cold rain and sleet before the growing season began again in the spring; California rains, on the other hand, were evenly spaced, gentle warm showers interspersed with glorious crop-inducing sunshine.

Hastings neglected to mention that a death toll of one in ten was not uncommon for those who traversed the overland trail and that he had never even *seen* the alleged cut-off trail that ran westward from Fort Bridger through the Great Salt Desert, one of the most frightful and difficult desert crossings on the continent.

The readers didn't note the omissions or exaggerations or, if they did, didn't care. They wanted to *believe* what Hastings wrote. Fremont had lighted the flame, but it was Hastings who fanned it into a blaze. So what if Fremont's and Hastings' depictions varied? The readers wanted to go to this marvelous place called California.

And, on the basis of *The Emigrants' Guide* by Lansford W. Hastings, many were now planning to do exactly that.

[March 4, 1845 • Tuesday]

"I, James Knox Polk, do solemnly swear that I will faithfully execute the office of President of the United States, and will to the best of my ability, preserve, protect and defend the Constitution of the United States."

With those thirty-eight words, uttered in public ceremony earlier today, James Polk was inaugurated as the eleventh President of the United States and the ball that had been set rolling three days earlier by his predecessor, John Tyler, had now become his responsibility.

It was a ball called Texas.

The question of whether Texas should be annexed by the United States was one that had plagued the nation for nine years, ever since Texas had declared independence from Mexico. Polk, a Democrat, had been elected on his platform of expansionism—The Infinite Dream— and the Whigs realized much too late that the opposition Party had correctly interpreted the pulse of the people as a mandate for both annexation and expansion. They could not now rectify the damage, the Presidency a plum already plucked, but they could regain some stature in the public eye by having President Tyler, in one of his final official acts, make the move that would be historically recorded in their own corner.

American claim to Texas dated from so far back as the explorations of Robert Cavelier de La Salle and though they ceded the claim to Spain in a *faux pas* of statesmanship in 1819, that made little difference now. Texas had declared her own independence as a Republic in 1836 and the result had been their continuing fight with Mexico, which had never recognized that independence. The United States, however, had, and though annexation did not immediately occur as Texans had hoped, Polk's election had assured it.

The abolitionists still screamed with indignation that while annexation might be legally acceptable, it was morally wrong and nothing more than an evil extension of slavery under the guise of the country supposedly attaining its natural boundaries. But such argument had now become moot in view of the will of the masses and the imminent transference of power and so President John Tyler had presented the bill for annexation to Congress. When it failed to get the required two-thirds vote in the Senate, Tyler, with only three days remaining to his administration, had no recourse but to ram it through as a joint resolution.[49]

Hardly had this announcement of the joint resolution been made than the Mexican minister in Washington D.C. demanded his passport and hastily departed for Mexico. In a countermeasure, Polk appointed a statesman friend, John Slidell of Louisiana, as emissary and temporary minister plenipotentiary to Mexico on a two-pronged mission: First, inquire whether Mexico would receive an envoy to engage in negotiations and second, to make it clear that this was diplomacy, not appeasement, and that the contemplated negotiations would in no way be concerned with any actual payment for Texas, stressing that the annexation had been accomplished strictly in accordance with the usages of nations, but that Mexican anger over the annexation could probably be assuaged to some degree by a gratuity.

Texas still had to ratify the annexation but that was simply a procedural matter that would be accomplished in the months ahead; once that was done, the door for Texas statehood would swing wide. It was clear to Polk that Texas would become a State of the Union before the end of the year, but equally clear was the knowledge that Mexico would not recognize the annexation of Texas, nor would she hold still for what would be considered this theft of her territory—in particular with the annexation embracing the boundaries established by the Texans themselves when they declared their independence. Texas had established its southern and western boundary as the Rio Grande. Mexico, on the other hand, declared that if there was a boundary at all, it was the Rio Nueces, 120 miles north of the Rio Grande and that this strip of essentially uninhabited desert terrain was part of the territory comprising its states of Nuevo Leon and Tamaulipas and that Mexico would, if necessary, defend it.

Having embarked this very day on his Presidency, Polk knew that the key to acquiring the so keenly desired southwestern territories as part of his "Infinite Dream" involved more than just the annexation of Texas: It lay in *occupying* that arid belt of land just north of the Rio Grande and, in so doing, forcing Mexico to either defend or back down. He was aware that it was almost inconceivable that Mexico would back away from any occupancy by the United States; threatened, she would take the offensive and attempt to oust the intruders. In so doing, Mexico would be goaded into a war with the United States—a war she could not possibly win. And in winning that war, the United States would win, as well, the West Coast territory called California.

All this was the chain of events that President James Polk was prepared to set into immediate motion as groundwork of the Infinite Dream.

*[April 1, 1845 • Tuesday]*

As the thick adobe walls of Sutters Fort finally loomed before him this afternoon, Captain John Sutter exhaled a deep breath. How many times over these past few months, especially during the past fortnight, had he wondered if he would survive to return? What kind of luck, considering the colossal mistake he had made, had been riding on his shoulder that had enabled him to see these walls once again?

The long-expected revolt of the Californios against Mexican control had finally broken out in earnest last November, when ousted former Governor Juan Alvarado and military leader José Castro took over leadership of the rebel forces and began their attempt to wrest control of California out of the hands of Governor Manuel Micheltorena. It was, Sutter knew, a quarrel that none of California's foreign residents had any business joining, but join they had. Even worse, some had joined with the rebels, others with the Mexican government, choices largely dependent upon their own best interest.

For his own part, Sutter had little choice. Long ago he had given his word to support Micheltorena. The governor had wisely told him to prepare a force and hold it in readiness. For this, Sutter had been given the massive Sobrante Grant lying in conjunction with his original grant for New Helvetia, making the total area of his land holdings in excess of 145,000 acres. He had always hoped, however, that it would not become necessary for him to hold up his end of the bargain. However, within a month of the outbreak, Sutter received an order from Micheltorena to gather all the troops at his command and join the government's army at Monterey.

On January 1, leaving Major Pierson B. Reading behind to man the fort with a small garrison of select Canadians, Frenchmen and Indians, Sutter marched his force southward—100 mounted riflemen, ten artillerymen with five light cannon, and 100 well-trained Indians armed with guns, lances, bows and arrows—vigorously accompanied by the beat of drums and the lively piping of fifers.

Meanwhile, General Castro was assembling his own force at San José, but Sutter's early approach caught him by surprise and instead of standing to fight, Castro hastened his people away to Monterey.

There he gathered together the rebel forces that were blocking General Micheltorena's army and headed them all toward Los Angeles where he could issue a call for help from the populace or coerce them to support him if need be.

Sutter's force joined with Micheltorena's on the Salinas River near Monterey and the combined 600 men set off in pursuit of Castro. They first encountered the enemy in quarters at San Buenaventura and drove them out, but then matters started falling apart for the government. Near Santa Barbara, a large number of Micheltorena's dragoons and California Cavalry deserted to join the rebels and half of Sutter's mounted riflemen did the same. Left with a force of only 350, Micheltorena continued the pursuit, but near the Mission San Fernando they were stymied by a body of more than 1,000 men—many of them American traders—in a well fortified position. The Battle of Cahuenga ensued, the courage of Sutter's men evaporating in the face of such odds, the remainder of his mounted riflemen fleeing, along with the artillerymen. Sutter was captured and taken to Los Angeles, too late aware of the major mistake he had made in underestimating the strength and determination of the Californios and in his siding with the Mexican government.

Several days later, with no food and his remnant army surrounded by Castro's force at Cahuenga Pass near Los Angeles, Micheltorena surrendered. The rebels had been much kinder to him than he had any reason to expect. After the articles of capitulation were signed by both sides, the defeated governor general and his troops were disarmed, escorted to San Pedro and transported by ship to Monterey. There the remainder of Micheltorena's garrison, families and private possessions were taken aboard ship and embarked on their inglorious return to Mexico. Micheltorena's remaining *Cholas* would be driven out or exterminated. For all intents and purposes, the Mexican regime in California had ended and the Californios quickly established a new one with Pio Pico as governor and Castro as commanding general.

John Sutter's fate hung in precarious balance. Pio Pico and Castro were at first very much inclined to have him shot for voluntarily joining Micheltorena to quell the rebellion. Once again Sutter relied on his glibness and imagination and, once again, they served him well. He explained that he had joined the deposed governor not by choice but on direct command, proven by the written orders from Micheltorena that Sutter still had in his dispatches pouch, and that he had had no choice but to obey the orders received from the then legal government. He also lied that he had encouraged the desertion of his riflemen and artillerists so they would not have to be in arms against their own fellow Californios and that this selfless act alone had saved many lives. The tribunal, after brief huddled conference, reached its decision: Captain John Sutter was acquitted, all his rights, rank and property restored and the hope expressed that he would hereafter be as faithful to the new government as he had been to Micheltorena.

So now, just completing his tiring journey, Sutter breathed a sigh of relief and then smiled broadly as a reverberating cannon blast followed by cheers saluted his return. It was good to be home.

*[April 21, 1845 · Monday]*

It had been a long journey for James Wilson Marshall. He'd first heard of Sutters Fort when still east of the Mississippi and somehow the place had become fixed in his mind as a terminal destination.

That journey had begun a dozen years earlier in New Jersey on the east bank of the Delaware River some fifteen miles upstream from Trenton. Marshall had been born only four months after the outbreak of the War of 1812 and there, in Lambertville, was where he had spent his first twenty-one years.[50] His father was a master wagon-maker who elicited from his son, when James was only ten, a promise that he would work at his father's side until he reached his twenty-first birthday, a promise young James had just cause to regret. His father was an austere, serious man who trained him well in the skills of carpentry, metal-working generally, coach and wagon-making specifically, but it had been an essentially cold and joyless upbringing. While young Marshall was glad for the trade being learned, he had ached for the time to come when his obligation would be fulfilled and he could go off on his own—anywhere.

On October 7, 1833, the day after reaching his majority, James Marshall headed westward on foot with never a backward glance.

His first stop was in Pennsylvania, where he hired out as an itinerant carpenter, but he soon became restless and moved on. He worked his way across Ohio and stopped for a few months more in Crawfordsville, Indiana, again working as a carpenter but also doing some metalwork, both as a wheelwright in a carriage shop and as a gear-fitter in the area's gristmills. Warsaw, Illinois, was the next stop but he didn't like it much and after several months moved on to Missouri.

Not until Marshall reached the area just east of Cantonment Leavenworth did he settle himself more firmly, staking out a homestead on the Platte Purchase and taking up farming and trading. A simple, basically unimaginative man, he might have stayed there permanently, but several years later fate took a hand. He came down with mosquito fever, aggravated by ague.[51] He survived the initial onslaught, but was greatly weakened. Over the following six years chronic recurrences of both ailments plagued him and his health gradually deteriorated. Steps had to be taken. A physician gloomily predicted that unless he moved to a drier climate, he probably would not survive more than another year or two, and suggested California where the climate was reportedly the best in the world.

Marshall sold his farm and joined a wagon train that left the Cantonment Leavenworth area on the first day of May last year. Streams were swollen from an unusually rainy late winter and spring, causing interminable delays in their crossings. By the time they reached Fort Hall, the season was well advanced and skins of ice were forming in the water buckets overnight. No longer content to endure the wagon train's slow progress, Marshall joined a party of mounted fur trappers headed for the Columbia River basin. By the time they reached the mouth of the Willamette it was late October and the mountains were snow-covered, balking any travel southward.

Reluctantly, Marshall had wintered in Oregon but as soon as several fur parties began forming in early March, he joined the first one that was heading for the Sacramento Valley. That party of forty horsemen was being led by a pair of experienced mountain men—Green McMahon and Jim Clyman—and despite increased Indian troubles over the past few years, Marshall was assured that if anyone could get him there safely, it was those two.

The passage had been very difficult, exacerbated by frequent arguments among the trappers, each of whom reckoned he knew which of the several possible trails to follow would be best. Several times groups of men split off and headed their own way, but Marshall stayed with Clyman and McMahon as they made their way southward to the valley of the Shasta River and, from there, to the headwaters of the Sacramento. They had experienced no trouble from the Indians—the first party recorded to have enjoyed such immunity—and, some forty miles above Sutters Fort, they made their final camp together at the mouth of Cache Creek. In the morning they had split up into little groups of two or three and struck off on their own. McMahon and Clyman—with Clyman's spaniel, Buck, trotting as usual beside the mountain man's horse—headed overland for the Sonoma area, where Clyman intended to establish a farm, but Marshall continued downriver alone.[52]

A haphazard conglomeration of tents and lean-tos dotted the landscape outside the walls of Sutters Fort and, as Marshall approached, a white-suited man walking with the aid of a cane emerged from the main gate and went to a man who was digging a narrow trench nearby. As they conversed, Marshall approached, oblivious of his own gritty, disheveled appearance and scruffy short beard. He stopped near them and waited until the two had finished and the suited man turned back toward the fort.

"Would you be Cap'n Sutter?"

"I am…," Sutter replied, pausing and facing the stranger, "…and you are…?"

"My name is James Marshall. From New Jersey, originally. I'm looking for work."

Sutter eyed him speculatively. "Skilled or unskilled?"

"Skilled. Carpentry. Wheelwright. Millwork. Some smithy." Marshall looked at him steadily.

Sutter nodded, with a tinge of smile. "A dollar a day till you're proved. If you're good, two dollars a day."

"And if I'm *damned* good?"

The smile broadened. "Two-fifty, but for that you've got to be *goddamned* good!"

For the first time a smile abruptly creased Marshall's lips. "I am."

*[May 23, 1845 · Friday]*

What had prompted Samuel Brannan to act in so disreputable a manner was as much a mystery to him as it was to the Quorum of Twelve Apostles. There was, however, no mistaking the group's anger over what William Smith and Brannan had done or the punishment they meted out.

The whole ugly situation had begun last fall when Smith, younger brother of the assassinated Joseph and Hyrum, visited Brannan in his print shop at Seven Spruce Street in New York City. He had commended Brannan on the job being done with publication of *The Prophet*, but Brannan had to admit that even with the sponsorship and advisory help he was receiving from Apostle Parley P. Pratt, the publication was beginning to falter due to lack of operating funds. Smith, who was visiting New York and New England on a fund-raising mission for the Church, suggested Brannan temporarily discontinue publication of the periodical and solicit financial aid for its continuance by accompanying him to the various Mormon temples. Brannan accepted the invitation.

William Smith, however, possessed considerably less dedication to the Mormon cause than had his murdered brothers. His own interest was more inclined toward self-indulgence, in pursuit of which Brannan happily joined him. When the pair started to canvas the temples for aid, they did so in a desultory and unconvincing manner, their attention more concentrated on the enjoyments they were discovering in the evenings after each day's soliciting activities.

It was their misfortune that Wilford Woodruff, who was a Mormon apostle preparing for a mission to the British Isles, happened to be visiting one of the congregations the pair addressed. A shrewd and highly principled individual, Woodruff, noting their particularly lackluster appeal for funds, became convinced that the minds of this pair were on something else entirely.

Woodruff followed Smith and Brannan and made numerous entries in a little notebook, appalled as they made the rounds of local saloons, drinking and carousing, sporting with ladies of the night and, throughout these forays, proclaiming loudly, drunkenly, their affiliation with the Church of Jesus Christ of Latter-day Saints.

"Who said Mormons never have any fun?" brayed Smith, causing a shrill giggle to erupt from the young woman sitting in his lap as he slid his hand beneath her skirt.

"Not I," came the muffled response from Brannan, whose face was buried between the barely-covered breasts of the woman he was similarly holding.

That was only one of numerous incidents witnessed by William Woodruff and reported to the Quorum in Nauvoo in outraged letters he sent before sailing off. As yet unaware of the charges laid against them, Elders Smith and Brannan had completed their round of visits to the various temples. Smith returned to Nauvoo and Brannan to his New York apartment, where Eliza was caring for their newborn son, Samuel Brannan, Jr.

The Quorum, despite having their hands full with mob activities directed against the Saints and an overriding urgency to complete the construction of the Nauvoo Temple before Brigham Young's ordered evacuation of the Saints should commence, gave high priority to Woodruff's letters and promptly disfellowshipped Smith and Brannan.

Smith didn't seem to care and seemingly drifted off into oblivion, but when the news reached Brannan he was devastated. Without delay he set off for Illinois and today presented himself to the Quorum. His remorse was genuine, his appeal for forgiveness moving, his promise of never again falling so grievously and hereafter devoting himself exclusively to furthering Mormon interests quite convincing.

The Quorum of Twelve deliberated only a short while among themselves and then summoned Brannan once more. He was, they told him, to return at once to New York where, instead of resuming publication of *The Prophet*, he would initiate a new periodical, not generalized and for distribution to Saints worldwide as *The Prophet* had been, but devoted specifically to the Church and its urban Saints in the east, especially concentrating on Boston, New York City, Philadelphia and Baltimore. He would name this new publication *The Messenger*. Last, but hardly least, he was to consider himself reinstated as Elder in the Church of Jesus Christ of Latter-day Saints.

They did not quote John 8:11, but the message was clear.

### [June 22, 1845 • Sunday]

Probably no man in America felt more fulfilled today than Lieutenant John C. Fremont as he stood in the bow of the steamer just now pulling away from the main wharf in St. Louis. Also aboard were sixty U.S. soldiers under his command as well as the mountain man who had become his close friend and associate, Kit Carson.

Fremont had garnered much fame from publication of his report to Congress of the last expedition. That notoriety was much enhanced by the recent, more handsomely bound publication of the same work by popular Washington D.C. publisher, Gales and Seaton. In addition, behind-the-scenes support from his father-in-law, Senator Benton, had seemed to make him a shoo-in for the leadership role in the new expedition recently formulated. Fremont himself had fully expected to be named as commander, but was only too aware that with the military, one learned not to rely on expectations. The niggling concern, however, had proven groundless.

Lieutenant Fremont had no doubt that this third major expedition to the West was by far going to be the most important to his own career, if not historically. His orders directed him to head directly to the central Rocky Mountains and map its watershed. With that accomplished, he was to lead his party to the Great Salt Lake and complete the cartographic work he had begun there during the second expedition. Finally, he was to proceed west into the Sierras and Cascades to obtain information toward improving the existing Oregon Trail or locating a new and easier trail to reduce the difficulties of emigrants through this rigorous terrain. At the same time, the unit was to survey the best possible trail from the Willamette settlements southward to central California.

What the written orders did not convey were the unofficial acts he was to be prepared to perform on a discretionary basis. There were, at this moment, with the steps initially taken by President Polk, intensifying international crises developing in the West. War with Mexico was imminent: If that became a reality, it was imperative for an armed American force to be available in California to take advantage of whatever situation would develop in regard to its newly established and very shaky revolutionary government. Further, the differences Americans and British over Oregon's northern boundary could well degenerate into conflict and an attempt might be made by the British at full occupancy of the territory. Should that occur, it would be equally important to have an armed American force on hand to protect American interests and settlers in the Columbia basin and the Willamette Valley.

To Fremont, the unspoken proviso to these secret orders was implicit: Should the commander of this unit err in exercising proper discretionary judgment, he would be condemned—and his career ruined—for acting outside his official orders and his government would be able to declare itself blameless.

*[October 30, 1845 • Thursday]*

For President James Polk, the eight months following his inauguration had been extremely busy and, with the unnerving prospect of two separate important bills looming, often a trying time.

Reaction to the Congressional joint resolution for the annexation of Texas had been divided throughout the nation, although the consensus seemed to be that it was a good move, long overdue. That it was also goading Mexico toward the point of declaring war was considered more than probable by Whigs and Democrats alike, and debate over the morality or justification raged hotly.

The situation involving British territorial claims in Oregon was equally a topic of controversy, but with an even greater element of trepidation. While Mexico was regarded as weak, disorganized and hardly an enemy to inspire any real fear, Great Britain was a world power with a war machine that twice already had engaged the United States, and fear was mounting that she would not hesitate to engage in a third confrontation.

Polk still wanted the southern boundary of Alaska to be America's northern boundary of Oregon. His campaign slogan of "Fifty-four-forty or fight!" remained a catch phrase for some, but growing numbers thought such a stance to be unrealistic and deemed the forty-ninth parallel a far more appropriate bargaining line; one less likely to provoke the British and nudge them toward war.

British Minister Richard Packenham, a seasoned diplomat, held a different view. Aware that President Polk was placing his country on the brink of war with Mexico, he regarded that as a bargaining chip of no little consequence and not only rejected the Fifty-four-forty proposal out of hand, he now also refused to consider the forty-ninth parallel. Instead, he countered with the mouth of the Columbia River at forty-six degrees sixteen minutes north latitude as the northern limit of the Oregon territorial claim of the United States.

Polk read Packenham only too well and it infuriated him that the Minister thought the President would concede to British demands because of the Mexican crisis. At the same time, however, Polk was disturbed at the reaction of his own Secretary of State James Buchanan to Packenham's ploy. Buchanan was clearly fearful of British might and strongly advised Polk to accept Packenham's counter offer without delay, lest even that be withdrawn and the British claim the whole of Oregon, clear to California, as their own and bring in troops to back it up.

Polk refused to heed Buchanan's appeal and reaffirmed his own position. He would neither give up the Oregon Territory nor would he in the least alter his stance where the Mexican crisis was concerned. "The United States," Polk asserted, "is destined to stretch from coast to coast and no threat, no application of leverage from outside powers, is going to alter that."

Polk's position was not only applauded by the majority of Democratic Party members, it gave birth to a new catch-phrase coined by John O'Sullivan, editor of *The United States Magazine and Democratic Review*. Just then in the midst of preparing the July/August issue of his periodical, O'Sullivan penned a bombastic editorial declaring that the United States' claim to Oregon northward from California to the forty-ninth parallel was entirely justified:

> ...*by right of our* Manifest Destiny *to overspread and to possess the whole of the continent.*

Within days "Manifest Destiny" touched a responsive chord nationwide, emblazoned in the hearts and minds of most Americans as an expression of fundamental belief in their country and its future.

However determined and unbending the basic nature of James Polk, it did not blind him to necessity; in the light of mounting pressure from his own Party, he was at last forced to reassess his stance. However grudgingly, he recognized that claiming the northern border of the United States' Oregon Territory should extend to Fifty-four-forty North latitude was unrealistic in that it blocked the British from having a Canadian west coast, a state of affairs that absolutely would not be tolerated and for which they would unquestionably go to war. Therefore, the forty-ninth parallel was the only logical and reasonable compromise. Both Polk and Pakenham agreed and the matter had at last been placed into the hands of treaty-makers.

With the Texas situation, neither the Americans nor the Mexicans had any intention of either conceding or compromising. War had become inevitable with the issuance on June 4 of a stern proclamation by acting Mexican President José Joaquín Herrera:

### *PROCLAMATION*

*The minister of foreign affairs has communicated to me the following decree: José Joaquín de Herrera, general of division and president ad interim of the Mexican Republic, to the citizens thereof.*

*Be it known: That the general congress has decreed, and the executive sanctioned, the following:*

*The national congress of the Mexican Republic, considering:*

*That the congress of the United States of the North has, by a* decree, which its executive sanctioned, resolved to incorporate the territory of Texas with the American union;

That this manner of appropriating to itself territories upon which other nations have rights, introduces a monstrous novelty, endangering the peace of the world, and violating the sovereignty of nations;

That this usurpation, now consummated to the prejudice of Mexico, has been in insidious preparation for a long time; at the same time that most cordial fellowship was proclaimed, and that on the part of this republic, the existing treaties between it and those states were respected scrupulously and legally;

That the said annexation of Texas to the U. States tramples on the conservative principles of society, attacks all the rights that Mexico has to that territory, is an insult to her dignity as a sovereign nation, and threatens her independence and political existence;

That the law of the United States, in reference to the annexation of Texas to the United States, does in nowise destroy the rights Mexico has, and will enforce, upon that department;

That the United States, having trampled on the principles which served as a basis to the treaties of friendship, commerce and navigation, and more especially to those boundaries fixed with precision, even previous to 1832, they are considered as inviolate by that nation. And finally, the unjust spoliation of which they wish to make the Mexican nation the victim, gives her the right to use all her resources and power to resist to the last moment, said annexation;

### IT IS DECREED

1st. The Mexican nation calls upon all her children to the defence of her national independence, threatened by the usurpation of Texas, which is intended to be realized by the decree of annexation passed by the congress and sanctioned by the president of the United States of the north.

2d. In consequence, the government will call to arms all the forces of the army, according to the authority granted it by the existing laws; and for the preservation of public order, for the support of her institutions, and in case of necessity to serve as the reserve to the army, the government, according to the powers given to it on the 9th December 1844, will raise the corps specified

> *by said decree, under the name of "Defenders of the Independence and the Laws."*
>
> MIGUEL ARTISTAN, President of the Deputies<br>
> FRANCISCO CALDERON, President of the Senate
>
> *Approved, and ordered to be printed and published by*
>
> JOSÉ JOAQUÍN DE HERRERA.<br>
> A.D. LUIS G. CUEVAS<br>
> Palace of the National Government<br>
> City of Mexico, June 4, 1845

In a last-ditch effort to balk Texas annexation by the United States, Mexico offered to recognize Texas independence in a "preliminary to a treaty" being promoted by certain individuals in Texas and Mexico. A proviso, however, was that Texas would remain independent of all nations, including the United States, which Texas refused to accept and the Mexican offer was rejected. Instead, on July 4, one month after the Mexican Proclamation, the Texans, assembled in convention in Austin and accepted the terms of the annexation to the United States.[53]

Shortly afterwards the Mexican government expelled emissary John Slidell and, with that, President Polk issued a series of imperatives. The first was a top secret order dispatched through Secretary of the Navy George Bancroft to Commodore John D. Sloat, commander of the U.S. Pacific Squadron, instructing that should he learn that war had been declared between the United States and Mexico, he was to immediately seize both the Yerba Buena Harbor in San Francisco Bay and Monterey, simultaneously blockading all other California ports. At the same time he was instructed to conciliate the Californios by telling them that this action was being taken not to hamper them, but rather to thwart the Mexican government and whatever other foreign powers might be interested, specifically the British and French.

Because the Santa Fe Trail would surely play an important role in a war between Mexico and the United States, an order was sent to Lieutenant J.W. Abert of the U.S. Topographical Engineers to thoroughly explore and map all areas in proximity to the Santa Fe Trail in northeastern New Mexico and northwestern Texas, those areas having been claimed by Texas at the time it declared its independence from Mexico.

Polk, reluctant to leave matters to chance, directed Secretary of War William Marcy to order his most experienced frontier officer, Colonel

Stephen Watts Kearny, to take five companies of his First Dragoons westward from Cantonment Leavenworth in a show of martial strength, to awe all the Indian tribes in proximity to the Oregon Trail; this to be accomplished as a contingency measure in the event the treaties with Great Britain collapsed and it became necessary for troops to be moved along that route to Oregon.

One of the highest priorities, as soon as Texas annexation was assured, was getting the United States Army, under its most skilled field commander, into position to move swiftly to the attack in the Southwest if it became necessary. Close to 4,000 troops were already being held in readiness at Fort Jesup in Louisiana for this eventuality, but Polk wanted the army to be much closer and primed to move at a moment's notice.

The officer Polk selected as top field commander was Brigadier General Zachary Taylor. A Virginian with a reputation for being determined and resourceful, he was cousin to former President James Madison and had first shown exceptional abilities during the War of 1812: As a captain he had distinguished himself in battle against the Indian allies of the British during their attack on Fort Harrison in the Indiana Territory. For his valor and leadership, he became the first brevet major in the U.S. Army. He had then won further distinction with several significant successes against the allied British and Indian forces at Credit Island, Illinois where his own small force had been outnumbered three to one. That action resulted in his being awarded the permanent rank of major. By 1832 he was a colonel and played a secondary but important role during the short-lived Blackhawk War in Illinois and Wisconsin. In 1837, during the protracted Second Seminole War, he commanded at the Battle of Okeechobee, the single most successful effort of that conflict and for which, the following year, he was brevetted a brigadier general in command of all U.S. forces in Florida. By that time he had been dubbed by his troops as "Old Rough and Ready"—a sobriquet he wore with unmistakable pride.

General Taylor's orders were to march his army to a position at the Nueces River where a bivouac was to be established near the coastal village of Corpus Christi. He was directed to take no aggressive action against the Mexicans unless expressly ordered, and if any Mexican soldiers were encountered, they were to be treated courteously. Other than that, he was to hold his force in readiness. If war was to begin, President Polk cautioned, it would have to be the result of a belligerent action by the Mexicans.

Finally, Lieutenant Archibald H. Gillespie of the United States Marine Corps was selected as special courier and directed to carry secret orders to U.S. Consul Thomas O. Larkin at Monterey. Larkin, who had been a shrewd trader there, had been appointed U.S. Consul as a result of his regular accurate and dependable reports to the Department of State on the developing situation in California. To accomplish his mission, Gillespie would leave Washington on November 3 and travel by road directly to Louisiana, then by ship to Vera Cruz on the Mexican Gulf Coast, continue overland to the Pacific Coast and find transportation to Honolulu and, finally to Monterey, California.

The President's orders to Consul Larkin were ambiguous: Larkin was to mollify the Californios and subtly support their further separation from the parent government in Mexico. A similar dispatch Gillespie carried for Larkin was from Secretary of State Buchanan and while it more or less echoed Polk's remarks, it was more specific: Larkin was to keep actively alert for, and quickly take advantage of, any further revolutionary activities in California that might occur and to help sever any remaining ties that bound that territory to Mexico. At the same time, he was to encourage and guide the Californios toward presenting an official request for annexation to the United States.[54]

With October drawing to a close and Lieutenant Gillespie to depart in a few days, Polk summoned him for a "confidential conversation." Gillespie arrived at the White House promptly at eight o'clock this evening and had a private conference with the President for nearly half an hour. Polk gave him highly secret instructions to be delivered to Brevet Captain John C. Fremont only. Fremont's specific whereabouts were unknown, but Consul Larkin in Monterey would most likely be able to steer him to the captain.[55]

*[November 12, 1845 • Wednesday]*

Over the past five months since his reinstatement Samuel Brannan had been a model Elder. Since first issued on July 5, the new quarto-sized publication, *The Messenger*, had been a striking success among the Saints of the Eastern Seaboard and Brannan considered this more an accolade to his own abilities than to those of the Pratt brothers, Orson and Parley, who had been acting as supervisory co-editors. His hope that the ruling body of the Mormons, the Quorum of Twelve Apostles in Nauvoo, were aware of his dedication was confirmed when a startling order was received from Brigham Young.

Throughout this past summer and fall, Young had made numerous appeals to the federal government that the Mormons be afforded humane treatment, protection and sanctuary. Those appeals had not been refused, merely ignored. All that while, the terrorism occurring in and around Nauvoo not only continued unabated, it increased. It had become clear to Young that, with or without government assistance, the Mormons *had* to leave the United States. He drafted the order that was copied and sent to every Elder and all the Apostles on missions within the nation, directing them to return at once to Nauvoo to aid in the exodus westward until all the Mormons had left the boundary of the United States behind.

The only exception was Samuel Brannan.

In a special letter sent to him by Young, Brannan was ordered to gather together as many of the New York City Mormons who were able to pay for passage, and transport them by sea. To affect this, he was to go to Washington and solicit funds from the government. Should he fail in getting such support, he was to return to New York City and, with funds that would have to be provided by the Saints themselves, charter a sailing vessel that could be refitted for passengers and, as soon as possible, proceed with the evacuation.

Brannan undertook his mission with great energy, knocking on doors of every person who might possibly help and even visiting Secretary of War Marcy and various other members of the President's cabinet. Not unexpectedly, he was rejected by all except the power broker A.G. Benson, who introduced him to his partner, Amos Kendall. They told him that with their enormous political influence they were in a position to help; that they could convince the government to support the emigration, even protect the Mormons on their way west and also give them large tracts of land in California. In exchange for such influence peddling, Brannan was required to sign a contract on behalf of the Church stating that the Mormons would, when they acquired California lands, deed over to Benson and Kendall every alternate section and town lot. It said little for Brannan's otherwise keen intelligence that he allowed himself to be taken in and actually sign the contract drawn up by the pair.[56]

It was while Brannan was in Washington D.C. that Apostle Orson Pratt gave a farewell address to the New York City area Mormons. "We do not," he told them, "want one Saint left in the United States after this time. Let every branch in the east, west, north and south be determined to flee by land or sea." His fierce gaze swept across the congregation as he added, "Any and all of you here who cannot afford to obtain horses and wagons to join with your brethren for the main journey westward by land, I implore you to seek means, in the days and weeks ahead, to earn enough to pay for your passage by ship under the leadership of Elder Samuel Brannan; that ship to take you around Cape Horn to the western coast of America, where you will eventually rejoin those traveling by land. If all want to go, charter a half-dozen or a dozen vessels and fill each with passengers, and the fare among so many will be but a trifle."

When Brannan finally returned from Washington just prior to the departure of the Pratt brothers for Nauvoo, he begged Apostle Orson Pratt to convince The Quorum of Twelve to pay his accumulated debts in New York City and to retain *The Messenger* as the printed voice of the Church. Pratt agreed and wrote to Young:

> ...Brother Brannan thinks it will be difficult to take his printing establishment and go to California, unless he goes away dishonorably without paying debts. He is very anxious to go and is willing to do anything he is counseled. He says the Church perhaps would consider it wisdom to buy his establishment and still keep the paper.[57]

As soon as the Pratt brothers departed, Brannan suspended publication of *The Messenger* and had his press and all printing supplies and equipment crated for transportation to California. He also quickly located a ship available for hire; an old cargo brig commanded by Captain Edward Richardson. This was the 445-ton *Brooklyn*, 125 feet long. It could be chartered for $1,200 per month, with the lessee responsible for all port charges and conversion costs, as well as assumption of all risks. Brannan called for a conference of Mormons in the area and today that meeting was held in American Hall. The place was crowded and Brannan addressed them eloquently for more than an hour.

"The good ship *Brooklyn*," he began, "has been chartered to transport the Eastern Saints to California!" The room resounded with cheers and when the cries faded away, he continued. "It will be an easy and comfortable trip, since at this very moment a crew of carpenters is busy constructing a main cabin and staterooms below deck for your privacy and comfort."

"How much is this going to cost us?" someone shouted.

Brannan grinned. "To ease the financial burden, every effort has been made to keep your initial costs for this great voyage as low as possible. Reservations will be taken today for the cost of $50 per person, plus an additional $25 per person for provisions to be consumed during the trip. Whatever additional charges there might be, which can only be determined by how long the passage takes to complete, will be due on our arrival in California. Our skipper, Captain Richardson, who has made this passage many times, estimates that it will take between five and six months. All who are interested are urged to register before leaving this hall. Our sailing date is scheduled for two months from today—the twelfth of January."

By the time the hall cleared, 235 Mormons had signed up for the voyage by sea to California.

*[November 12, 1845 · Wednesday]*

In California there was a sense of trouble in the air and John Sutter seemed to be at its core.

Ever since the Micheltorena affair had ended so disastrously for him last March, Sutter's relationship with the new government remained shaky. In the Sacramento Valley, Sutters Fort was a commanding presence and there was no doubt that Sutter's control was very strong throughout that entire central and northern California region. More than once during the months that had passed, officials of the new revolutionary government had regretted that they had not executed John Sutter when they'd had sound justification.

Now Sutter and the provisional government were like two strange dogs warily circling and sniffing one another, each ready to defend against the other, understanding that the outcome of struggle was very much in doubt. What bothered Sutter more than anything were the tentative agreements forming between the new government and parent Mexican authorities. Mexico was suddenly taking a much stronger interest in this California country that it had all but ignored for so long. Despite Micheltorena's ouster, Mexico still considered California hers, but realized that to retain it she would have to allow the Californios themselves to have a much greater role in their own destiny. Meetings had been held between officials on both sides and, while the Californios were enjoying the self rule they had won, there was also the recognition that things were occurring in California that demanded the help of the former parent government.

Chief among these matters was the considerable interest of foreigners moving in, especially from the United States. One of the first official acts of the new governor, Pio Pico, was to send Sutter a *banda*—a proclamation—that closed New Helvetia to further immigration from the United States and ordered Sutter to ban all foreigners from entering his lands and fort. He also rescinded, so far as the new Californio government was concerned, the thirty-three-league grant Micheltorena had given Sutter. Nevertheless, foreigners continued showing up in greater numbers all through the summer and converged on Sutters Fort. Sutter, who was required to send in reports on all foreign arrivals, had largely failed in the endeavor, only occasionally sending any of the arrivals to Monterey to apply for passports, as was also mandatory. Worse yet, without government authorization, Sutter continued selling chunks of his land, including large pieces of the Sobrante Grant, to all who wished to buy. Now the lands along the Sacramento and such tributaries as the Yuba, the Feather, the Bear, Cache, Chico and Honcut were peppered with the cabins and small farms of foreigners who had no intention of giving up their properties or conforming to any Mexican—or Californio—authority. In defiance of the restrictions placed against him, Sutter not only continued to welcome and assist new foreigners, he sent out along the main trails several of the mountain men, Caleb Greenwood and Jim Clyman among them, to intercept Oregon-bound emigrants and persuade them to come instead to California.[58]

Thomas Larkin had become Sutter's friend and confidante. Letters between them kept Sutter advised with what was happening regarding the California government, Larkin attuned to what was occurring in Sutter's domain. In early April, shortly after his return to New Helvetia, Sutter informed the consul that he expected about 1,000 new arrivals this year from Oregon alone and perhaps even more from the United States. As he wrote to Larkin:

> *If large numbers of these can be induced to occupy the valley of the San Joaquín, it would be the cheapest way for government to keep the Indians there in check.... I will be sending you more Indian*

> *children as soon as I make another raid on the villages.... I plan to plant 800* fanega *of wheat and this year I will have a good harvest, thank God in Heaven!*[59] *I expect to bring in water from the American Fork for irrigation and mills and expect the Russians will contract for all the grain I will harvest.... Trapping may be profitable this year, although many of my furs are wrongly obtained by others. This year I pay a considerable amount of my debts, the half to the Hudson's Bay Company, a good amount to the Russians, and at least half to Mr. Thompson and others, in furs. One good year more and I shall be clear of debts. Cotton does well in the Valley.*

Unfortunately for Sutter, the elements were against him and his crops failed. He was forced to borrow more, this time from his newest neighbor, William A. Leidesdorff, who had recently established a cattle ranch called Rancho de Los Americanos upstream a few miles on the American River. On July 31 he wrote to Leidesdorff:

> *...the grain crop is poor, the fur trading party has failed and what I need now are people who have the interest of their employer.... As a great favor I would like to ask you for a pound or two of strong cotton thread and a piece of manta or striped cotton or drill, since the boys and girls at the house, a hundred of them, are almost in rags. If you can advance me these goods, I promise not to trouble you again until I have made a good remittance.*

Sutters Fort, with its newly whitewashed walls and adobe structures was also like a beacon in the wilderness, a central depot for a world disconnected from the rest of California. The area immediately surrounding had become so crowded that Sutter hatched plans to establish a new settlement on the Sacramento's left bank, four miles downstream from the fort, on ground well above where the river's flood waters might reach. He decided to name it Suttersville and was convinced the individual lots staked off would be sold quickly.

Continuing largely to ignore the edicts from Pio Pico, Sutter was kept busy aiding new arrivals, hiring as his own employees many of those who came, helping others get established and running the small empire that his holdings had become. Hundreds of thousands of livestock—horses, mules, cattle, sheep and hogs—roamed naturally pastured hills

# The Infinite Dream

and tens of thousands of acres were now under cultivation in wheat, oats, barley and flax, while vast acreages supported vegetable crops and orchards. The establishment of Suttersville itself would be next.

The men Sutter had hired in supervisory, overseer and clerical positions and upon whom he depended heavily—men such as John Bidwell, James Marshall, Pierson Reading, Robert Ridley, Peter Lassen—stayed with him for only two or three years before striking out on their own as ranchers, traders, merchants, farmers, trappers, hunters or fishermen. Bidwell, his chief aide and manager of Hock Farm, had finally left to take up land at a place to the northwest called Chico, Reading did the same even farther north along the Shasta River and Lassen had established his own ranch far up the Sacramento. Among those who stayed, however, Marshall was still foreman over various construction related activities, while Ridley continued to operate the launch *Sacramento* on its regular runs to and from Yerba Buena.

Throughout late summer and early autumn, new arrivals came from the east, the largest being a party of 300 in sixty wagons guided by Bill Sublette. While still in the Sierras, they had serious problems with the passage and ran out of food. Sublette, with fifteen other horsemen, left them and came ahead to Sutters Fort, arriving on September 29, and requested help. As usual, Sutter provided it, making up a large party of men and numerous packhorses loaded with provisions and dispatched to the marooned emigrants. Eight days later they returned, bringing with them all sixty wagons and without a life having been lost.

Sutter was impressed with the respectable character of the party in general and was jubilant at this newest influx of Americans. His enthusiasm and abundant optimism spilled over in the letter he wrote to Larkin:

> ...*I now have a chance to buy plenty of well broken American oxen and wagons from the young men, who prefer horses so they can travel in the country. My establishment will gain a great deal by the immigration. I have employed a good many mechanics, a first rate doctor, Dr. Gildea, will remain here, likewise a clerk. Three new blacksmiths are at work, but I need iron. Twenty splendid plows have been made and I hope to have forty running at once. One of the new men hired is a saddler who is at work on twenty sets of harness. If I have a little luck this next year, people will be astonished at my*

*farming business! I will recommend that owners of land in this valley give a part to new settlers, for it will be our greatest interest and make our lands valuable. Next year in this month we shall have thousands and thousands of emigrants here who should be given land in the Tulares. The newcomers are well armed and will fight like lyons. After the rains a new city will be foundated. V. Prudon is going to leave the court of Sonoma and build a hotel at Suttersville. I have urged him to use his influence with Vallejo to permit entry of cargoes into the Valley free of charge. Prospects for trade are good, but for the cursed custom-house. Several ships are expected and I personally expect some machinery for a steamboat, also a printing press on which I plan to print a paper. I am planning a grist-mill, too. A shorter road to the mountains has been found. There will be a railroad here within five years.*

Three weeks ago, on October 21, more *bandas* arrived, issued by Governor Pico and General Castro. Unconfirmed reports had been received that Mexico and the United States were at war. No further penetration of foreigners into the Sacramento Valley would be tolerated. Any who were discovered would be incarcerated and questioned and, if found to be spies, would be executed.

Sutter swiftly wrote to Larkin, asking him to come to the fort if at all possible to help protect the Americans and other foreigners. He added:

*...If it is not in your power or in the power of the man-of-war to protect them, I will do it. All are protected here, and before I will suffer injustice to be done, I will die first.*

In the meantime, Manawitta was delivered of a baby daughter, falsely claimed as Kanaka Harry's, but Sutter paid the matter little attention. Mana was a closed chapter of his life and he had more important things on his mind. Nor, except for setting laborers to work, did he pay much attention to the loading of close to two hundred bushels of wheat aboard the *Sacramento* for transport to the Russians. Word had just arrived that a combined deputation of officials had been formed at Monterey and would soon head for Sutters Fort accompanied by an escort of thirty mounted soldiers. The party was being led by Californio

# The Infinite Dream

General José Castro and a Mexican officer, Captain Andrés Castillero. Sutter had no idea what this portended but, in view of the war rumors and the number of Americans here, it boded no good. He wondered fleetingly if they were coming to arrest him, perhaps even execute him.

When the party came within view of the fort today, Sutter was alerted and at once had a seven-gun salute fired from the cannon emplaced in the fort's walls. He walked out of the main gate to greet them and felt a wave of relief when he recognized two of the horsemen as old friends—Colonel Victor Prudon of Sonoma and trader Jacob Leese of Yerba Buena. With those two on hand, it was not likely the party had come to do him harm.

As soon as they stopped and dismounted, four separated from the group and approached him. Sutter shook hands first with General Castro, whose expression revealed nothing. Leese shook hands warmly and smiled faintly, and Prudon grasped Sutter's hand in both of his and gave a quick wink. Castro introduced the captain, Don Andrés Castillero, who was not in uniform.

Sutter gave a quick order for the remainder of the party to be refreshed, their horses seen to, then led the way to his quarters. Once seated, they were served brandy by the housekeeper, a plump Indian woman who closed the door as she left.

Captain Castillero did most of the talking, his tone and manner cultured and pleasant. "My military rank, Captain Sutter," he said, "is more honorary than functional. I am a member of the Mexican Senate and, in this instance, an official commissioner of the Mexican government, which has sent me to California to regulate affairs generally, to make peace with the new government," he made a slight bow in Castro's direction, "and to propose to you, Captain Sutter, the purchase of your fort."

Sutter opened his mouth to speak but no words issued and Castillero smiled and continued, "I'm sure that this comes as rather a surprise, but this is not an offer lightly made. In view of present international tensions, of which you are aware, my government has become deeply concerned about the influx of foreigners, specifically immigrants from the United States, to this territory. By purchasing your fort we would be able to garrison it and stem United States immigration."

He paused, still smiling, and took a sip of his brandy. When no one spoke, he tilted his head toward the glass he was holding. "Excellent," he said. "Yours of the making, I presume?"

Sutter nodded.

Castillero's smile faded a bit. He set his glass on an oaken end table. "For this fort and all its appurtenances, Captain Sutter, I am authorized to pay you the sum of $100,000, plus all the land and all the cattle belonging to the Mission San José."

It was a handsome offer—more than three times what he had paid for Fort Ross and all its treasures, and Sutters Fort and its environs came nowhere near measuring up to what Fort Ross had been. He was silent for a long moment, considering how nicely he could pay off all his debts and still live comfortably for the rest of his life. He thought, too, of the hundreds of people presently in the valley who depended upon him, and of the people yet to come, for whom Sutters Fort was more than merely a stopover; it was a goal. He thought of what their lot would be if he pulled out now, the deprivation and persecution they would surely suffer.

At last Sutter spoke. "It is a generous offer, Captain Castillero, and I am tempted. But I'm afraid my answer is no. Sutters Fort is not for sale."

*[November 28, 1845 • Friday]*

Brigham Young still had no firm destination in mind regarding where the new Zion would be established but he did have a general idea. That it would *not* be California, he was sure, even though Elder Samuel Brannan in the East was preparing the Saints there for the long voyage to San Francisco Bay. Young had decided against California primarily because of the continuing unrest and the instability of its government; the Saints had enough problems of their own without deliberately heading into an area that was ripe for more political upheaval. Young had already decided that when Brannan safely arrived there, he would be directed to start his Mormon flock eastward to join the main body, wherever they happened to finally sink their roots.

All appeals for help from the Federal Government continued to be either ignored or rejected and, with the Nauvoo troubles not easing at all, no more time could be wasted in getting these thousands of Saints launched on their newest migration. It was thought, for a time, that by appealing to the British for help, it might inspire the United States Government to take some action simply in an effort to keep the British out of this particular equation. Nor was it an entirely idle measure. A petition was drafted and sent to London, requesting permission for the

Mormons to establish themselves permanently on Vancouver Island. As the memorial pointed out:

> ...*The Government of the United States is doing much to favour the settlement of its territories on the Western Coast, and even to settle territory now in dispute between it and the Republic of Mexico.... Since the United States do manifest such a strong inclination, not only to extend and enlarge their possessions in the West, but also to people them, will not your Majesty look well to British interests in those regions, and adopt timely and precautionary measures to maintain a balance of power in that quarter—which, in the opinion of your memorialists, is destined, at no very distant period, to participate in the China trade.*

Irrespective of whether the memorial was meant to be taken seriously by the Crown or utilized more as a lever to pry the United States into a realization that failing to recognize the Mormon dilemma might have distinctly unfavorable repercussions to itself, neither British nor United States officials responded to the bait. Worse yet, the problems at Nauvoo had suddenly intensified when charges of counterfeiting were lodged against the Saints.

Claims that the Mormons were counterfeiting U.S. gold coins had been bandied about for several years but these new charges stemmed from remarks made last August by Dr. Abiather Williams, who claimed that the Mormon leadership—the Twelve Apostles—had actually "made bogus" at his home in Iowa. Based on this statement, warrants had been issued against all twelve Apostles and when a marshal arrived at nearby Carthage with writs levied against them, Brigham Young had staunchly denied that the Mormons were engaged in any form of counterfeiting. Nevertheless, the twelve had quietly gone into hiding.

That situation was exacerbated when none other than William Smith, the disfellowshipped younger brother of the Church's founder, issued a similar public statement. Still rankled over the action that had been taken against him, Smith had earlier this month publicly charged that the Apostles were greedy thieves preying on their own membership and on the gullibility of Illinois citizens. In a letter from him that was widely reprinted in Illinois newspapers, Smith denounced the Mormon leadership as *"Powerless Rogues Rascals Scoundrels, Counterfeiters, &c &c"*

and that such prominent Saints as Theodore Turley were engaged in criminal activities. Smith went on to say:

> ...more of these truths will appear to light when a Mr. Turley the head Counterfeiter of Nauvoo is sent to Alton Penatenciary.

With that, Smith was excommunicated, but the damage was done: Turley and several other prominent Saints were arrested and charged with bogus-making. That they were later released due to lack of evidence was little help since the long-simmering pot of antipathy in Illinois was once again boiling.

If the exodus of the Nauvoo Mormons did not begin soon, Young knew, an actual war would break out between them and the Illinois residents and, even though the Saints had previously proven their ability as fighters, this was a war the Church could not possibly win. With that in mind, Young determined that the exodus shaping up should take the Saints to an area where no one else in his right mind actually wanted to be—the desolate Great Basin that stretched across desert expanses from the west slope of the Rocky Mountains to the east slope of the Sierra Nevada. But in order for the Saints to be able to sustain themselves, it would have to be in an area with a permanent, dependable water supply and one that was close to a trade or emigration route. The Santa Fe Trail was considered but rejected, not only because water sources were scarce and unreliable, it was almost exclusively a trade route and the traders who plied it were sharpers, largely from Missouri, who could easily take advantage of Mormon vulnerability. The Oregon Trail was much more promising, busy as it was with emigrants migrating westward who would be quite as eager for trade as the Mormons.

The choices for a new Zion were therefore, in Brigham Young's reckoning, down to three general sites: The Cache River Valley, the Bear River Valley or the Great Salt Lake Valley.

[December 2, 1845 · Tuesday]

President James Polk's message to Congress today was strong, straightforward and in many respects terrifying. It was vigorously applauded by war-hawks and appalling to doves because it unequivocally nudged the United States closer to war on two separate fronts.

That the United States and Mexico would ultimately go to war over matters in the Southwest was generally being accepted as a *fait accompli*, but Polk's unexpectedly harsh defiance of the British in regard to matters in the Northwest was unsettling in the extreme. It was anticipated that some sort of comment would be made in regard to Oregon and such was exactly the case. The President had asked Congress to look favorably upon the measure that had previously been submitted, for the formation of a regular mail system to Oregon via ships in Atlantic and Gulf waters from East Coast ports to Panama, across the Isthmus by land, and in Pacific waters between Panama and Oregon—a system that would, he stressed, aid in rapidly increasing American emigration to Oregon, as well as improving communications.[60]

Polk, for the first time since its inception, was not only utilizing the Monroe Doctrine as an actual force in international relationships, he had boldly added to it what reporters instantly termed the Polk Doctrine—specifically involving Texas and California, but applicable to the Oregon Territory too—that expressly prohibited protectorates in America. He strongly advised that American settlers in Oregon, as they had been requesting for the past two years, be afforded American legal jurisdiction and that immediately upon expiration of the one-year advance notice to the British, land grants be made to American citizens there. Such grants would not only benefit those citizens, they would strengthen United States' claims to the disputed territory.

Nothing substantial during the ensuing years, he told them, had resulted from the many sessions between British and United States commissioners in regard to settling the territorial controversy. The British, he added, refused to offer any compromise toward a boundary establishment north of the course of the Columbia River, although such boundary was unreasonable, illegal and impertinent in view of the stronger claim of the United States by reason of Spain's having ceded to the United States the territory north of California long before the British made any claim to it. America's title to the territory remained, he said, "clear and unquestionable."

The President pointed out to Congress that in the Convention of 1827, when Great Britain and the United States were at odds concerning their respective claims to Oregon, while the United States had the better-founded claim, the matter had been put in abeyance by mutual agreement to a joint occupancy treaty on a ten-year basis; a treaty that had been renewed by both countries at the expiration of the first ten years. That very treaty, however, carried with it a provision that permitted it to be ended by either party at any time through a simple one-year-in-advance formal notification.

"Due to the situation that has developed in the Oregon Territory," Polk told them, "and the jeopardy that our citizens already established there are presently facing, I now ask that Congress sanction that one-year notice. We have reached a period," he added, laying the issue on line, "when the national rights in Oregon must either be abandoned or firmly maintained...and they *cannot* be abandoned without a sacrifice of honor and interest! If no resolution has been reached at the end of that year, the cup of forbearance will then have been exhausted. Nothing can remain but to take the redress of the injuries of our citizens and the insults to our Government into our hands."

There was a gasp from the entire body of assembled congressmen, but Polk continued after only a brief pause. He delivered a lengthy discourse restating the provisions of the Monroe Doctrine that had made it a binding force ever since its adoption; provisions, he noted, that had only been reinforced by the pending issues of Texas, California and Oregon.

Turning to the matter of Texas, Polk declared that Mexico was required to pay the several millions of dollars, already adjudicated by a commission, in claims made against her by American citizens by reason of damages incurred, confiscations perpetrated and the loss of many lives during the past quarter-century of Mexican revolutions. Since Mexico was consistently bankrupt, such payment could not be made in cash, only in lands. The Rio Grande, not the Nueces River, must be recognized as the border and the disputed strip between the two rivers regarded as Texas land.

The United States, Polk continued, would not pay a single penny for Texas, but if Mexico would acknowledge that the Rio Grande was the boundary and accept the adjudication of Texas claims, the United States would then take responsibility for those claims and make redress. Additionally, if Mexico accepted the Rio Grande as its northern and eastern boundary throughout its length—and in this manner adding a sizeable portion of the New Mexico region to the area of Texas—the United States would give Mexico, as a definitive act of appreciation, the gift of $5 million.[61]

For the first time, the vast New Mexican region of the Southwest was mentioned in connection with any possible Texas settlement, but it was moot; everyone knew this type of reference was mere political ploy. Since the June 4 proclamation issued by President José Herrera, it seemed apparent that no settlement of *any* kind was on the horizon so far as the Mexicans were concerned.

### [December 13, 1845 • Saturday]

John Bidwell decided that he neither liked nor trusted Captain John Fremont.

Bidwell was again working for Sutter and was in charge of Sutters Fort during his absence. He had overseen the loading of more than 850 bushels of wheat and almost 600 pounds of ship bread for the Russians just a few days before Sutter headed downstream aboard a launch for Yerba Buena. Except for the additional packing and shipping of 1,000 pounds of dried meat to Hock Farm and thirty sides of sole leather to Don Pedro Pedrorena, Bidwell expected the days following, until Sutter's return about mid-December, would be without event. Four days ago, however, on December 9, Captain John Fremont, accompanied by Kit Carson, unexpectedly appeared quite late in the season. The Sierras were well cloaked with snow and it was almost unheard of for an outsider to show up from the mountains at such time. As they dismounted, Bidwell met them at the main gate and directed an Indian youth to hold the reins.

In almost a repeat of what had happened last year when he was here, Fremont had left some of his party in the mountains, this time not because of wagons breaking down or disaster having struck, but because it was part of a plan. Fremont gave Bidwell a barely discernable nod and walked into the fort. It was from Carson, then, that Bidwell learned some of the details of their having returned.

Their portion of the party had just arrived and were setting up a temporary camp on the American River some three miles above the fort. There, Fremont and Carson had remounted and continued here. Their full party, Carson added, was sixty men who had left St. Louis together on this newest expedition. They had followed the Oregon Trail again to South Pass but this time, instead of taking the new Greenwoods Cut-off to Fort Hall, which was by-passing Fort Bridger—much to the irritation of Jim Bridger and Louis Vasquez—they had followed the older route in order to stop and visit the trading partners. At Fort Bridger they talked about the new route to California, described by Lansford Hastings in his most recent book and immodestly called the Hastings Cut-off.

# The Infinite Dream

Carson looked at Bidwell and laughed without humor. "I was the one who tol' him 'bout that cut-off an' described it to him, an' then that sumbitch goes an' writes 'bout it like he *discovered* it an' even names it after hisself. Damnation! That sumbitch Hastings, he ain't never even been acrost it."

He described it briefly: After leaving Bridgers Fort, instead of heading northward along the old Oregon Trail following the Bear River and ultimately to Fort Hall, the new cut-off which Carson had used and later described to Hastings, crossed the Bear River and headed straight west into the Wasatch Mountains. It was a rough passage, but at its western slope it dropped sharply into the Great Salt Lake Valley, went westward paralleling the south shore of the lake, across the brutal desert of blindingly white salt flats and, using Pilot Peak as guidepost, reached the upper St. Marys River and soon rejoined the main trail from Fort Hall to California.

It wasn't a new route, exactly. Major Benjamin Eulalie de Bonneville had led his party across that treacherous passage in 1833 and, since then, several mountain men had made the crossing—most of them only once, since once was quite enough. Carson, however, had crossed it a few times and recognized it as a distinctly good cut-off for packers who didn't have wagons to worry about and who made sure they carried enough water. The fact of the matter remained: Perilous though it was, it *did* cut off between 200 - 300 miles of rugged travel encountered by those who took the safer, more clearly demarked trail east of the Wasatch Range and northward to Fort Hall, then southward again from Fort Hall down the west side of Great Salt Lake to the St. Marys River.

"The Spaniards, they named the river St. Marys," Carson told Bidwell, "but I figgered that warn't a good name for it. Runs right past the Humboldt Range, pretty much straight west toward California, so I give it a new name. It's the Humboldt River now. Purty good stream for a long way, but the damned thing goes into a sink 'bout a hunerd miles east of the Sierras an jus' plain disappears. Desert jus' swallows it up. Makes a rough stretch, that there final hunerd to the mountains." The mountain man shook his head, remembering, then continued, "Anyways, we took that cut-off an' it warn't no picnic, but we got through. When we got near the Sierras, Cap' Fremont, he splits the party an' sends 'bout half of 'em south with Joe Walker guidin'. Now Joe, he says he's found him a good pass, 'bout twenny-thirty mile or so south an' that's where we're 'sposed to hook up with him again."

Kit Carson went on to say how he'd strongly advised Fremont against trying to cross the Sierras this late in the season. The odds were against them and they were apt to get snowed in and be stuck on the heights all winter long. If that happened, survival would be dubious at best. Fremont wouldn't listen, however, and they did it, following the Truckee River up into the heights, surveying and mapping the route as they traveled. Then Fremont again split what was left of his party, sending off this second split under guidance of the mountain man known as Broken Hand–Thomas Fitzpatrick. He expected that second party, which included a couple of blacksmiths, would be catching up and joining them shortly. As soon as they got some new mules from Captain Sutter, they'd be heading south to rejoin Joseph Reddeford Walker's group at the west end of the pass.

Captain Fremont had walked briskly back to them just as Carson finished his narration and the officer planted himself in front of Bidwell, a bit closer than Bidwell thought necessary but he didn't let Fremont see any inkling of the nervousness he was feeling. Carson, however, moved a few steps away.

"Where's Captain Sutter?" Fremont demanded. "I haven't been able to find him."

"Went to Yerba Buena. Ought to be back in a couple of days or so."

Fremont's expression tightened. "I need sixteen mules," he said, "and six pack-saddles. I want flour and some other provisions. When my 'smiths come in, I'll need to use the smithy's shop to shoe the mules and then we'll be heading south to meet the others."

Bidwell shrugged and apologized. "Unfortunately, we have no mules on hand, or pack saddles, but we can let you have horses and we can make the pack-saddles quickly. Your men are quite welcome to use the smithy's shop, but we're entirely out of coal."

Expression ugly, Fremont stepped to Carson and spoke to him briefly in an undertone, then turned and strode toward his horse without another glance or word to Bidwell. After a moment, Carson followed and the two men mounted.

"Obviously," Fremont said to Carson, loudly enough for Bidwell to hear, "this hired hand is unwilling to accommodate me. Let's go."

Bidwell was stung by the remark, wondering what else he could have done to please this obnoxious officer. Here at Sutters Fort they had always welcomed Americans, especially those in authority, and in view of his employer's help to Fremont last year, Bidwell knew Captain Sutter would do anything in his power to help the man. Bidwell felt he'd acted as properly as he could under the circumstances, yet he had offended the American commander. He turned and strode to where Dr. W.B. Gildea was standing and asked him to accompany him. The pair mounted and rode to Fremont's camp. Bidwell was surprised at how well armed the soldiers were. He approached the commander.

"Captain Fremont," he said, "please be aware that I have in no way meant to appear unfriendly or discourteous. It's just that we don't have what you need at this time. However, Captain Sutter will soon—"

"I am an officer of one government," Fremont interrupted, "and Captain Sutter is the officer of another. There are difficulties at present between those two and I therefore assumed that you were unwilling to accommodate me." His voice softened a little, but still retained an imperious tone. "I remind you that on my first arrival here last year, Captain Sutter sent out and in half an hour brought me all the mules I wanted."

"Which I was quite willing to do," Bidwell protested, "*if* we had them. As I said, we have horses, but at this time we simply don't have the mules. I want to help you with anything it is in my power to provide, but I can't provide what we don't have. Captain Sutter was in considerably better circumstances when you were here last year. At that time, Peter Lassen had just arrived with a hundred mules, from which Captain Sutter bought what you needed. I have to tell you that this created a hardship for Captain Sutter. The drafts with which you paid for those mules had to go all the way to Washington D.C. before they were paid. My suggestion is that you remain in camp here until Captain Sutter returns and then perhaps he may in some way be able to help you. In the meanwhile, I will ride out with some of our men and see if we can locate any mules beyond those we must have for work here at the fort."

This seemed to satisfy Fremont and Bidwell, with Dr. Gildea beside him, along with the two newly arrived military blacksmiths, returned to the fort. While the 'smiths set about preparing to make horseshoe nails and repair broken bits and buckles, Bidwell and a dozen of the herders rode out into the hills and through three days of hard searching, managed to round up fourteen mules that might satisfy the Americans. They returned to the fort early today, arriving at close to the same time Sutter returned. Bidwell explained all that had happened, not failing to mention that he thought Fremont's party was much more militaristic, far more heavily armed and much larger in number than seemed necessary for the simple topographic mission Fremont claimed they were on.

Sutter nodded, approving of all Bidwell had said and done and grateful that he had rounded up the mules. He then set off to visit Fremont. He was gone for three hours and when he returned, ordered herders to accompany him with the fourteen mules back to Fremont's camp.

With dusk well advanced, Sutter returned. He and Bidwell sat smoking their pipes in the gathering darkness. Sutter said Fremont had accepted the fourteen mules with poor grace and given him vouchers for their purchase as well as in payment for other items he required, which Sutter would have delivered tomorrow. Sutter shook his head and said, "I agree with you, John. There's something not quite right about this whole business. I don't know what it is, but those men have more in mind than just a mapping expedition. Fremont and some of his men are heading for Yerba Buena tomorrow, but he wouldn't tell me why.[62] Those he left in camp will be riding south to intercept Joe Walker's group and head for Monterey to rejoin Fremont there. I wish I knew just what the hell is going on."

[December 29, 1845 • Monday]

Alone in his office in the White House, President James Polk looked again at the document in his hand and smiled. This piece of paper handed to him only a short while ago represented the culmination of one of his principal goals in this Presidency and he read it once again, savoring the words:

**United States Congress**
*Joint Resolution for the Admission of the State of Texas into the Union*
*[No. 1] WHEREAS the Congress of the United States, by a joint resolution, approved March the first, eighteen hundred and forty-five, did consent that the territory properly included within, and rightly belonging to, the Republic of Texas, might be erected into a new State, to be called The State of Texas, with a republican form of government, to be adopted by the people of said republic, by deputies in convention assembled, with the consent of the existing government, in order that the same might be admitted as one of the*

*States of the Union; which consent of Congress was given upon certain conditions specified in the first and second sections of said joint resolution; and*

*Whereas the people of the said Republic of Texas, by deputies in convention assembled, with the consent of the existing government, did adopt a constitution, and erect a new State with a republican form of government, and, in the name of the people of Texas, and by their authority, did ordain and declare that they assented to and accepted the proposals, conditions, and guarantees contained in the first and second sections of said resolution; and*

*Whereas the said constitution, with the proper evidence of its adoption by the people of the Republic of Texas, has been transmitted to the President of the United States and laid before Congress, in conformity to the provisions of said joint resolution:*

*Therefore—*

*Resolved by the Senate and House of Representatives of the United States in Congress assembled, that the State of Texas shall be one, and is hereby declared to be one, of the United States of America, and admitted into the Union on an equal footing with the original States in all respects whatever.*

*SEC. 2.*

*And it be further resolved, That until the representatives in Congress shall be apportioned according to an actual enumeration of the inhabitants of the United States, the State of Texas shall be entitled to choose two representatives.*

*APPROVED, December 29, 1845.*

President Polk leaned back in his chair, the vestige of a broader smile still tilting his lips. Fourteen years after its separation from Mexico as an independent Republic, Texas had today become the twenty-eighth state of the Union.

*[December 30, 1845 • Tuesday]*

The influx of Mormons from all over the East during this year had doubled the population of Nauvoo and all were making final preparations for when Brigham Young would give the word for the great exodus of those 20,000 Saints.

Elder Henry Bigler and his father were among those living on outlying farms who, this past autumn and early winter, had been forced to abandon them and move into the greater protection afforded by Nauvoo, where 'round-the-clock patrols of soldiers of Young's army patrolled the city's perimeter. Although the Biglers had voluntarily abandoned their farm, they had done so because they couldn't bear the thought of all their hard work going up in flames.

The burning of Mormon farms had become more systematic in recent months. Word that these people were soon to be evacuating spread among the Illinois "gentiles" and organized arson became more common than random mob activities. After nightfall, armed parties would knock on a farm door. Politely, but with menacing firmness, they would tell the Mormon farmer that he and his family had thirty minutes to gather up whatever they wanted to save and carry away undisturbed. Occasionally they would assist the family in removing such items, but at the end of the stipulated time limit, the house and outbuildings would be torched. Sometimes, if owners resisted they were beaten, even killed, to drive home the point that there was no choice in the matter. Lately, however, personal greed had been creeping in and after the owners of some of the better places were driven off, such houses were spared and then claimed by leaders of the groups. For whatever gratification the Biglers gleaned from this, their farm was one that was spared and confiscated.

Very little disapproval was voiced in the Illinois press. Many editors, especially those relatively close by, were themselves afraid of the threatened retribution that would ensue if they took such a position. Newspapers much farther distant lopsidedly reported what was happening and editorially tsk-tsked, as if scolding naughty children for damaging pranks. Governor Ford and other political leaders, apart from suggesting that the Saints save themselves by leaving Illinois for Oregon or California as quickly as possible, generally ignored the matter and no State aid was organized for the beleaguered Mormons whose own safety now lay within the city limits of Nauvoo.

It was a repetition of what had occurred in Missouri, but this time when they evacuated they would be heading into an area where they would be their own masters, under control of no jealous or fearful State bodies, where Mormonism could flourish and expand, safe from any further attack and eviction.

This was what Brigham Young promised was awaiting them in their new Zion.

*[December 31, 1845 · Wednesday]*

In a decrepit abandoned adobe on the outskirts of Mexico City, false moustache in place, skin darkened, and traveling in mufti under an assumed name, United States Marine Lieutenant Archibald Gillespie still did not feel safe. No gringo was safe. Only hours ago, the Herrera government had fallen to a junta led by General Paredes y Arrilaga and an order had been issued to round up all Yankees.

Gillespie felt a twinge of pity for President José Herrera, victim of his own altruism. He had come to believe, since the admission of Texas as a State, that by negotiating the claim of the United States to that strip of desolate territory between the Rio Grande and the Nueces was a part of Texas, bloodshed could be avoided and perhaps a war averted. It was a serious misjudgment. The Mexican people in general were in no frame of mind to cede *any* portion of Texas to the grasping talons of the American eagle. The Mexican military, commanded by General Paredes, were far less tolerant of such a willingness on Herrera's part to negotiate. Paredes, who long ago had deposed Santa Ana and sent him into Cuban exile, had once again moved in swiftly, unexpectedly, and removed Herrera and his administration from power, confident that both France and Great Britain would honor his appeal that they support him against the United States and that the Yankees would be too cowardly to fight. For this coup, Paredes was named President *pro tem* and, intent upon strengthening his position, ordered the immediate arrest of all gringos in the Mexican capital, who were to be held under threat of deportation… or worse. Mobs quickly formed and roamed the streets of Mexico City. They rang bells, fired muskets, ripped down business signs of Yankee merchants and beat anyone who protested.

That Gillespie would, under these circumstances, be able to get out of the area and travel undetected to Mazatlan was chancy and he could no longer afford the slightest risk. Having blanketed the single window of the adobe, he broke the seal on his pouch and inspected the papers. The personal letters to Fremont from his wife, Jessie, and his father-in-law, Senator Benton, were left intact as they contained nothing damaging. But all the confidential special order documents for Consul Larkin and Captain Fremont were carefully committed to memory in the flickering firelight, then burned.

The task took much of the night and, sighing with relief and weariness, Gillespie—alias Antonio Azua—crushed the paper ashes with a stick, then settled down to nap until daybreak when he would continue as rapidly as possible toward Mazatlan.

### [January 1, 1846 · Thursday]

Sitting at his desk in the Sutters Fort office, John Sutter, in the midst of writing a letter to his friend Victor Prudon in Sonoma, paused to pour himself another large whiskey and relight his pipe. As small billows of blue-white smoke lofted, he reflected on the occurrences of the past year. In more important matters, it had clearly been a disaster for him with its devastating crop failures, troubles with the Californio government officials and the suffocating mounting of debts. Yet, he was regarded as a savior of travelers, a far-sighted developer of the largest personal land grant in all California, the most dependable employer in Central and Northern California, a true champion of the people.

The trouble was, Sutter admitted to himself, he was a long way from being a champion in any respect. He probably would not even be in possession of New Helvetia had not the little revolution occurred. At that time, the Russians had already appealed to Governor Micheltorena about Sutter's continuing unpaid debt to them, asking that the Mexican authorities force Sutter's payment by assuming his debt to them and then they acquiring a mortgage on the fort which, when the debt remained unpaid, they could legally confiscate. The plan might have been confirmed except that the revolution broke out and now the Californios were in charge, Californios who had already expressed a desire to *purchase* Sutters Fort. Ever since turning down that offer, Sutter had been assailed with second thoughts: It could be a resolution to many of his problems. He had already cracked open the door that let the government know he might be receptive to a renewed offer.

Sutter lay his pipe aside, took a large swallow of whiskey and resumed writing the letter to Prudon:

> ...*Do you believe the government will buy it? I would like to be sure of that, so that I might take the necessary measures. In case the government decides to make the purchase do you think it would be possible to obtain a part of the price on account, sufficient to pay a part of my debts? I could give possession of the establishment after Harvest. I believe the Government would do well not to neglect this Matter, for next fall there will be many immigrants from the U.S.*

> *Think of it! From 1841 through 1844, only about 50 U.S. residents came to the fort. But last year alone it jumped to 250 U.S. immigrants. So here is this surging flood of immigration, accompanied often by hunger, death and distress. At times my buildings are filled with immigrants. So much so that I can scarcely find a spot to lay my own head to rest. My farm-houses and store-houses are filled with poor, wet, hungry men, women and children seeking a fortune in a new land. They are of my breed and they love the promise of the soil...*

Sutter paused and pushed the letter an arm's length away, tired of writing. He would finish it later. He drank off the whiskey and half-filled the glass again. So, what did the future hold in store?

"I have no idea," John Sutter said aloud, and his words seemed to hang in the room like a ghostly apparition.

*[January 12, 1846 • Monday]*

This had been the day originally set for the embarkation of the ship *Brooklyn* from New York to California, but preparations for the exodus of the Mormons in the East had taken somewhat longer than anticipated and departure was now tentatively scheduled for "around the first of February." Some of the delay was through unforeseen circumstance, but much of it was Sam Brannan's fault, though no one really held him responsible since from the beginning he had moved things along with speed and efficiency. Perpetually in motion, the twenty-six-year-old seemed to be everywhere at once, requiring little rest.

The alterations within the ship cost $16,000 and with carpenters working around the clock, the *Brooklyn* had been rapidly transformed into a combination passenger and cargo vessel. The so-called staterooms were tiny, only minimally large enough for their occupants, poorly ventilated and, as with almost everything else below decks, poorly illuminated since portholes were not installed. That included a large room for religious services primarily led by Brannan, plus a small mess hall served by two hired black men who were cook and steward.

So, while certainly not luxurious, the *Brooklyn* was anticipated to serve the basic needs and provide reasonable comfort for those aboard. At least that was what Brannan informed those 250 Saints who had signed on for the voyage and paid deposits. He told no one but

Captain Richardson, a few crew members and the carpenters making the alterations that part of the delay was occasioned by his own private little scheme.

A fair portion of the area that was to have been converted into more comfortable stateroom space for the travelers had been sealed off into a secret cargo area. Within it, Brannan had been surreptitiously loading a horde of 500 barrels of quality goods he had purchased, mainly on consignment, which he was sure he would be able to sell at substantial profit to merchants at the scheduled stops in Valparaiso and Honolulu. Hidden here, as well, was a large case containing smooth-bore muskets and ammunition.[63]

Brannan had considered well what would be necessary for such a migration and the *Brooklyn's* principal cargo areas were already stocked. The largest single item was Brannan's five-ton printing press with all its accoutrement, including a two-year supply of paper, that had so satisfactorily turned out issues of *The Prophet* and *The Messenger* and which, when they reached California, would be the heart of the newspaper he was already determined to publish; this time not a Church publication but his own profit-making venture. There were adequate provisions for the trip, as well as mechanical and agricultural tools and equipment that would be needed for upwards of 800 men—shovels, saws, wedges, sickles, axes, pitchforks, scythes, hammers, plows, hoes, sledges, harness goods, along with quantities of plant seed, and the provisions to sustain them for the journey. Additionally, there were crates of poultry, forty swine, and two cows to be milked on deck each day. There was equipment for the construction of three small gristmills, turning lathes, schoolbooks and slates, bars and ingots of copper, brass and tin.

There were still many New York Saints who had chosen not to be included in the voyage and Brannan was still trying to convince them to "become part of this glorious venture." They continued to vacillate, some clearly disliking the idea of Brannan as leader. Although Sam Brannan was well-built, six feet tall and normally dashing and personable, ever since having been placed in charge of the exodus he had become somewhat pompous and a tough commander demanding instant obedience to his bellowed orders. Members of this company had been required to sign contracts that specified not only their indebtedness for the trip costs, but absolute obedience to Elder Brannan in all matters during the voyage.

The rumors that Brigham Young intended to lead his great flock only to that vast desert area called the Great Basin, between the Rocky Mountains and the Sierras, had not reached Brannan. He remained firmly convinced that California was to be the new Zion of the Mormons and that he and his charges would be first to reach it. He was already calculating how his new colony should be established and placed in readiness for the arrival of the other Saints Brigham Young would be leading overland.

Brannan had continued making brief trips to Washington D.C., visiting any dignitary who would see him, in an effort to secure help for the Mormons who would be migrating by land. Amos Kendall, on the other hand, visited Brannan in New York and continued attempting to interest him in various intrigues. Brannan remained aloof from most of them, but Kendall did succeed in convincing him that a definite government plot, supported by President Polk and his cabinet, was afoot to prevent the Mormons' westward move. This was allegedly on the basis that it was illegal for any armed group of people from the United States to march into the territory of another government. Alarmed, Brannan wrote to Young:

> ...*I have received positive information that it is the intention of the government to disarm you after you have taken up your line of march in the spring, on the ground of the law of nations, or the existing treaty between the United States and Mexico. Amos Kendall was in the city last week, and positively declared that that was the intention of the government, and I thought it my duty to let you know, that you might be on your guard.*
>
> *Kendall has also learned that we have chartered the ship* Brooklyn *and that Mormons are going out on her. It is thought that she will be searched for arms and, if found, taken from us, and if not, an overland express order will be sent to Commodore Stockton on the Pacific to search our vessel before we land...*

Brannan finished the letter, sealed and posted it without delay, but with communication so slow, he considered it unlikely that he would receive any response from Young before the *Brooklyn* embarked. He shrugged. He had done what he could and now everything—including the upcoming voyage of the *Brooklyn*—was in the hands of the Almighty.

*[January 13, 1846 • Tuesday]*

James K. Polk was keenly aware that he was at this moment on the brink of the most important decision of his Presidency—in fact, of his entire career—and what he was in the process of doing today would forever be the foundation upon which his value or worthlessness to the United States would be judged.

The namby-pamby character, timidity and subtle betrayals of his Secretary of State, James Buchanan, was bothersome, but by no means a determining factor in the direction being taken; nor was the fact of a clearly sobering Congress and a press growing distinctly more frightened of what lay ahead in regard to both international crises—Mexican and British.

The defiance Polk had exhibited in the face of British anger and the remonstrance of America's own press to the President's unwillingness to compromise on the issue of Oregon's north border was underlined by his determination to force England to make the initial advance of compromise or declare war. That stance was a delicate balancing act, but Polk was convinced that England would not go the route of aggression at this critical juncture; the Crown would begrudgingly suggest compromise and once that became reality, the President would conciliate without losing face with Congress. His own administration would not appreciate the tactic, but if and when the British offer of compromise was tendered, Polk would then submit it to the Senate. In view of what Polk was prepared to do in regard to Mexico, the Senate would be in no position to do anything but advise that the British compromise be accepted.

Part of the problem with Buchanan was the result of ambition, not just timidity. Among the more reliable whispers circulating in Washington D.C. was that James Buchanan was angling for an appointment as Associate Justice of the United States Supreme Court as a stepping stone toward eventually becoming the nation's President and that he had used the powers of his present office to sway the Senate in its decision to reject President Polk's nomination of George W. Woodward to that seat. This was clearly in violation of the pledge Polk had caused Buchanan to sign before his appointment as Secretary of State, to abstain from using his office to enhance a move toward the Presidency.

The intelligence Polk had already received confirmed that Buchanan had indeed torpedoed the Woodward nomination and if proof could be obtained, Polk was prepared to fire him without hesitation. At subsequent Cabinet meetings, Buchanan acted like a sullen child, letting loose supercilious objections to almost all proposals and expressing his fears in regard to the Oregon situation. Availing Buchanan nothing, his adherents had been leaking rumors that if President Polk would not consider the views of the Secretary of State in so delicate a matter, Buchanan would have no recourse but to resign.

Polk smiled upon hearing that tidbit. His comment was cold and unwavering: "Mr. Buchanan will find that I cannot be forced to act against my convictions and that if he chooses to resign, I will find no difficulty in administering the Government without his aid."

Sympathetic toward Buchanan, South Carolina Representative Black had visited the White House on January 4 and begged the President to ease off his non-compromising and insulting stand against the British, since they would never *ever* accept the Fifty-four-forty parallel as the U.S. northern border of Oregon. The President did not back down from his unrealistic position. His own party's powerhouse, South Carolina U.S. Senator John Caldwell Calhoun, who had previously championed Polk, last month, led his coalition of Southern Senators to vote against the Oregon termination of rights as Polk had requested.

Polk, who distrusted Calhoun above all other Democrats, shook his head. "The only way to treat John Bull," he said, "is to look him straight in the face. I consider a bold and firm course on our part to be the pacific one. If Congress falters or hesitates in its course, John Bull will immediately become arrogant and more grasping in his demands. Such has been the history of the British nation in all their contests with other powers for the last two hundred years."

The following day, January 5, the President's requested resolution was introduced to the Senate to terminate joint occupancy of Oregon. Buchanan darkly warned Polk that despite the apparent national support for "Fifty-four-forty or fight," the country would not support it. Not unexpectedly, Calhoun, with his junior from South Carolina, Senator McDuffie, immediately initiated a bloc against termination and would be demanding that negations with the British be reopened in a manner favorable to giving them what they wanted.

Powerful though Calhoun's opposition might be, what bothered Polk more was the position taken by confirmed expansionist Senator Thomas Hart Benton of Missouri, upon whom he was counting for strong support. Benton, as usual, was working behind the scenes and informed Polk that while he did indeed favor the termination, he would support it no further than he thought justified. Still, it made little difference to Polk: He had explained himself fully in his message to Congress and if the Democratic senators did not support those ideas, it would result in the ruination of the Party. And even though reports from London indicated increasing preparation for war, the banner of Manifest Destiny still fluttered over the country and the *status quo* remained.

President Polk strongly believed in the Manifest Destiny concept; believed that America, to be fulfilled, must eventually stretch from coast to coast in order to form the solidarity of a nation uninterrupted territorially by any other. The same concept had sprung from a bare flicker to burning intensity in the breast of most Americans who, politics and political boundaries aside, were pioneers in heart and to whom uncharted frontiers were irresistible.

Rhetoric concerning who owned California or Oregon, Texas or New Mexico, the disputed territories of the Southwest and the vast Indian Territory bisecting the continent's mid-belt, had made all the issues cloud in the minds of run-of-the-mill Americans. Bolstered by *"Fifty-four forty or fight"* or *"Remember the Alamo"* or, especially, *"Manifest Destiny"*, expansion had become the by-word, acquisition took precedence over moral right, and ethical consideration had all but vanished. The American West was a great pie from which everyone wanted his slice.

Today, then, with Congress still a beehive of manipulation and maneuverings as debate continued on the resolution to terminate joint occupancy with the British, and negotiations with Mexico were no longer possible, President James K. Polk set the ball into an unstoppable roll. Through Secretary of War William Marcy, he ordered General Zachary Taylor—still sitting with his impatient army on the Texas coast at Corpus Christi since last summer—to march his force through the disputed territory south of the Nueces and take up a defensive posture on the north bank of the mouth of the great river that, Texas first and now the United States, claimed as the nation's southern boundary, the Rio Grande.

*[January 29, 1846 · Thursday]*

Captain John Fremont was frustrated, not knowing exactly what was expected of him at this juncture. His written orders were clear enough, directing him, among other matters, to lead his company of sixty northward in California for the purpose of surveying a good route through the mountains and into the Willamette Valley of Oregon. That, however, was not what he was doing now. There was more here than was spelled out and he felt strongly that he should be doing more. Much more.

A sense of unrest and suspicion prevailed everywhere, even at Sutters Fort, where Fremont's needs for mules and supplies were neither so swiftly nor abundantly met as had occurred during his first visit. He'd finally obtained the mules his party needed, once John Sutter himself had returned to the fort, but even the New Helvetia leader, despite his politeness, had acted as if he were suspicious of Fremont's motives and was clearly skeptical of the avowed purpose of simply exploring, surveying and mapping. At one point Fremont had overheard Sutter talking with his chief aide, John Bidwell, and the two were questioning why this American military party was in California, why it consisted of sixty well-armed soldiers when a party of a dozen topographical engineers with surveying tools could have done what they were supposed to be doing.

While the questions were legitimate, the answers were none of Sutter's business, nor anyone else's for that matter. Fremont and Kit Carson had just finished spending several days on horseback, tracking southwestward of the fort in an effort to pick up some trace of Captain Joe Walker and the detachment he was guiding, but discovered nothing. The pair returned to their own camp, just upstream on the American River from Sutter's on Thursday afternoon, January 15, and that evening Sutter and Bidwell, both clad in fresh uniforms of Mexican officers, visited the camp and invited Fremont to dine with them. The officer accepted, changed into a fresh uniform and, with Carson beside him as usual, all returned to the fort where, as they approached, a cannon was fired.

The discussions over dinner and wine were pleasant enough, but unrevealing.

"I've heard," Sutter remarked, carefully setting down his glass, "that some of the Americans at my fort here, including several employed by me, have visited your camp and volunteered for a year's service under your command."

Fremont smiled and touched napkin to lips. "As a matter of fact, some did, although of course I have explained that our business here is geographical, not political. Yet, should word be received that war has broken out between Mexico and the United States, that would likely alter matters and whatever help was offered would be gratefully accepted. I was," the officer added, "pleased to note that among the first to volunteer his services was your chief carpenter, John Marshall."

Sutter was irritated. He depended upon Marshall and thought his foreman should have at least discussed the matter before taking any action. Nothing in his expression, however, reflected his feelings as the meal was finished and they smoked their pipes.

Fremont requested more supplies. Sutter said he could fill the order and promised to deliver the goods to the American camp in a day or two.

"You mentioned, Captain Fremont," Bidwell put in, "that you wanted to visit Yerba Buena and Monterey. Our launch *Sacramento* is scheduled to head down to Yerba Buena on Monday—that's the nineteenth. Would you and perhaps others of your party be interested in booking passage? Captain Sutter can provide the necessary passports."

Fremont nodded. "Actually, yes. Passage for seven of my men, plus Mr. Carson and me. There are some people in Yerba Buena we should visit and then it's important that we continue to Monterey where I need to confer with Consul Larkin."

The 100-mile downriver journey was uneventful but Fremont was disappointed with what they found. They had heard that Yerba Buena, in the seven years since being established on San Francisco Bay, had become a thriving new port, but it was only a small village with forty or fifty ramshackle houses, a couple of poorly-built trading posts and a total population of about 200. Those he had planned to visit were not on hand and his small party met with the same sense of subtle suspicion that they had encountered at Sutter's.

Fremont sent his men back upstream to his main camp while he alone continued to Monterey. There he was granted an immediate meeting with Thomas Larkin. The American Consul appeared nervous, reserved in his responses as to California's political situation and said he had nothing of any real importance to share in regard to what was happening concerning the United States with Oregon or Mexico.

"I can tell you, however," Larkin added, "that the Californio general, José Castro, has lately been at odds with Governor Pico. They've had some heated words about letting foreigners move about the California countryside practically at will. Californio ranchers are uneasy and Castro agrees, even if Pico's not so concerned." He did not add that he perceived this as the first flick of a revolutionary aspect toward Governor Pico's administration. In accordance with his instructions from Washington D.C., Larkin had been sympathetic with Castro's concerns, quietly fanning the fiery-tempered general's little flame of resentment.

"My advice to you," Larkin went on, more gravely now, "is that if you are planning on roving about the country and joining, as you say, with the remainder of your party somewhere in the San Joaquín Valley, it would behoove you to request a meeting with the top three men here—Governor Pico, General Castro and the Californio prefect, Don Manuel Castro—for official permission."

Fremont had already done exactly that earlier this morning. Governor Pico had been unavailable but, adopting his friendliest demeanor, Fremont had met with the prefect and the general.

"Gentlemen," he had begun, "it is important for you to know that my party is not comprised of soldiers. My men are a simple topographical unit of civilians hired by the United States for an entirely peaceful mission of establishing the most ideal trade route to the Pacific. I must admit that those men who were detached by me several weeks ago are at present in the Sierras or its foothills somewhere to the southeast of here—where, I'm not exactly sure, though probably they'll soon reach the San Joaquín Valley—and it is my intention, with your official permission, to intercept and join them. We would continue to camp and rest there for a while, then continue with the project of mapping the river systems. Following that, I would like permission for this party to head southeastward toward the valley of the Colorado River as spring progresses, most likely via Tejon Pass and the Mojave Desert, then upstream on the Gila toward Tucson before returning to the United States."

Behind his desk, Don Manuel Castro leaned back and smiled, his stubby fingers interlocked across an immaculate buff vest. "I see nothing wrong with your request, Capitan Fremont, and will be pleased to provide you with the permits. And you will no doubt inform your superiors of our swift and peaceful cooperation with these people from the United States."

"You may count on that, sir," Fremont had replied.

Don José Castro, however, was not so easily mollified. A lithe, swarthy individual, heavily mustached, he came to his feet and stared down at Fremont. "You need to be aware," he said, "of the unsettling effect it has created among our people to have a party of armed American foreigners—who you claim are not soldiers—moving through their country. Something warns me that this is not a good thing to do, granting you such permission." He paused a moment, then softly slapped his hand to his thigh. "However, since the San Joaquín Valley is well east of our more settled coastal areas, the army will honor the permits Don Manuel has said he will issue. At the same time," his tone sharpened, "you are instructed to keep your party well away from any settled areas so as not to annoy the people. Is this understood?"

Captain John Fremont came to his feet, smiling, and extended his hand.

"Yes, General, perfectly."

*[February 3, 1846 · Thursday]*

At Corpus Christi, the early enthusiasm of General Zachary Taylor's men had waned and instead of a disciplined army they had transmuted into little more than a mob: The officers had become lazy and careless, as much among themselves as with their men; dysentery and scurvy plagued the encampment and sanitary facilities hardly existed; constant bickering occurred, often punctuated by serious altercations; drinking and gambling were rampant; the largely Mexican citizenry unhappy with the continuously boisterous camp life that interfered with normal routine and unhappy, as well, with the 2,000 camp followers—mainly prostitutes and gamblers—drawn here as if by magnetism. Everyone wanted change. For half a year the commanding officer had been holding this 4,000-man, so-called army of occupation—the Third Infantry—here, frustrated by interminable delays and wanting nothing so much as definitive orders from headquarters to do *something*.

Today, at last, General Taylor had received the January 16 orders from Secretary of War William Marcy: He was to march his army into and through the disputed territory between the Nueces River and the Rio Grande and take up a defensive position, while simultaneously—and paradoxically—taking care not to antagonize the Mexicans, since no war had yet been declared. While Marcy did not make it a habit to talk down to his field commanders, he did so this time: "You should consider establishing sentinel duties as soon as the new position is selected; the Mexicans are known to be a hotheaded people, who might make some sort of move toward retaliation."

General Taylor read the orders eagerly, then felt sickened at the realization that he was in certain respects guilty of dereliction: He had ignored or overlooked fundamental steps that should long ago have been taken; steps that Old Rough and Ready *would* have taken. While some of the infractions had been beyond his control, others were clearly his own fault; his curious neglect in failing to dispatch scouting detachments to reconnoiter both the terrain and the enemy situation between the Nueces and Rio Grande, of which virtually nothing was known; his failure to establish and maintain adequate patrols.

Not a man inclined toward self-recrimination, Taylor moved swiftly to rectify the deplorable situation and bring order out of chaos. Half a dozen reconnoitering cavalry parties were dispatched at once, ordered to watch closely for any trace of enemy activity, carefully study the difficult terrain, spread out southward all the way to the northern bank of the Rio Grande, and move downstream to converge near the river's mouth at Point Isabel. He ordered the purchase or commandeering of wagons and mules wherever encountered and using them, the entire coastal base to be transferred with all possible speed to the same destination, located only a short distance from Matamoros at the southern side of the river's mouth, which he considered a logical site for a Mexican army stronghold.

It was a haphazard start for any kind of military operation but, as General Taylor had long clamored for, it was at last *something!*

[*February 4, 1846 • Wednesday • 8:00 a.m.*]

Samuel Brannan experienced a strong welling of pride and excitement as he stood on the bridge of the *Brooklyn* with Captain Richardson. They watched silently as the procession of 238 Mormons mounted the broad gangplank leading up to the deck, their demeanor a dichotomy of fear and eager anticipation. They included seventy men, sixty-eight women and 100 children and infants, just a few more than Brannan had estimated when he wrote on February 1 what he was sure would be his last letter from New York to Brigham Young. He had written:

> ...*The ship is now loaded, full to the hatchings, about five hundred barrels of which we leave at the Sandwich Islands, and the remainder is ours. There are now in the city, and some on board the vessel, about two hundred and thirty souls that will sail next Wednesday at two o'clock; all happy and cheerful at the prospect of deliverance.*

The Infinite Dream

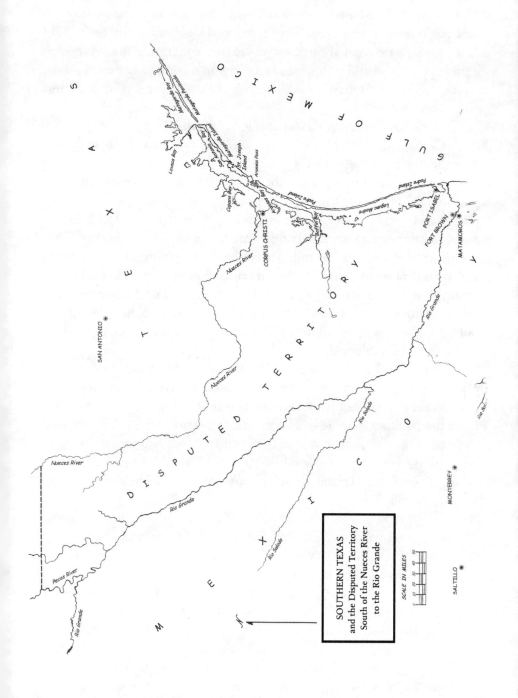

Now that day had come and, with the heavier baggage already stowed, most of these remaining refugees boarding in the early light of a cold sunrise carried bundles or satchels containing the final small items that they would be taking with them on the long journey that now lay before them. Embarkation was still scheduled for two o'clock this afternoon.

"Well," Brannan remarked at last, "it's begun."

Captain Richardson nodded. "Aye, Mr. Brannan, it's begun, and may the good Lord let it end as peacefully."

The culmination of more than two months of intensive effort in refitting the ship, organizing the preparations, loading and stowing cargo, and finally boarding these passengers had exhausted Brannan and he slumped slightly against the rail, thankful that the greater effort was now substantially behind. There would be plenty of time for rest and rejuvenation in the weeks and months ahead en route to California. In addition to the Mormons, the ship's crew, Captain Richardson and Brannan himself, ten non-Mormons had taken passage on the ship, but only after agreeing to abide by the rules of shipboard comportment Brannan had established.

Only one thing had occurred to diminish enthusiasm for what lay ahead: Yesterday, in the final mail he would receive here in New York City, Brannan had received an envelope containing a small notice cut from the January 20 issue of *Times and Seasons* magazine. There was no indication of who had sent it to him, but the item had struck Brannan with all the force of a physical blow and he wished he could dismiss it as fallacious. It was a public announcement placed by the Mormon High Council at Nauvoo:

> *It is herewith officially declared that a policy has been adopted by the Church of Jesus Christ of Latter-day Saints to remove itself and all its followers from headquarters in Nauvoo, State of Illinois, to some good valley in the Rocky Mountains within the Indian territories beyond the Western border of the United States. This permanent evacuation is scheduled to begin as soon as favorable weather permits.*
>
> *In the event of President Polk's recommendations to build block houses and stockade forts on the route to Oregon, becoming a law, we have encouragement of having that work to do, and under*

*our peculiar circumstances, we can do it with less expense to the government than any other people.*

Brannan had been entirely convinced that the new seat of the Church was to be in California, not in some undisclosed valley of the Rocky Mountains and it irked him that he had not been informed earlier of this plan. He could only hope, though with little conviction, that the information was in some way distorted and that the Rocky Mountains location was actually only to be a temporary stopping place, perhaps a wintering camp, for the Mormon exodus while en route to California. If it were true, however, then it would be up to him to establish the new Mormon colony in California as so ideal a community of Saints that he would personally be able to convince Brigham Young and the Mormon High Council to amend its plan and continue to the West Coast. He had fully convinced himself that he would have no problem doing so.

Now, in only a few hours more, the *Brooklyn* would cast off and a great adventure would commence. But Sam Brannan was no longer quite so pleased about it as he had been before Brigham Young's letter had arrived.

*[February 4, 1846 · Wednesday · 3 p.m.]*

The help that Brigham Young had hoped to get from government officials with the migration of the Mormons was apparently bearing little fruit; at every turn their efforts had been balked.

On January 20, Young had the High Council issue a circular avowing Mormon assistance to government if and when a time should come that it was needed. It read:

> *Should hostilities arise between the Government of the United States and any other power, in relation to the right of possessing the Territory of Oregon we are on hand to sustain the United States to that country. It is geographically ours; and of right no foreign power should hold dominion there; and if our services are required to prevent it, those services will be cheerfully rendered according to our ability.*

The offer had thus far fallen on deaf ears and the stronger hope that government would employ the Mormons to build the string of Oregon

Trail posts and forts proposed by President Polk from South Pass to the Pacific had also faded considerably and now seemed out of the question.

A final effort remained yet in the works: Young had commissioned Elder, newly appointed head of the New England Saints, to visit Washington D.C. and endeavor in any way possible to bring the federal government into some sort of position to understand and help the Mormons in their great migration. The need was so great that Young was even willing to back away to some degree from the notion of a Rocky Mountain site for the new Zion to one on the West Coast. A week ago he had written to Little:

> *If our government should offer facilities for emigrating to the western coast, embrace those facilities if possible. As a wise and faithful man, take every honorable advantage of the times as you can. Be thou a savior and a deliverer of the people, and let integrity and truth be your motto—salvation and glory the prize for which you contend.*

It was of little help that at this same time new counterfeiting charges were levied against the dozen leading Mormons at Nauvoo and even named Brigham Young and Orson Pratt in the indictments. On January 24, Young had been forced to concede the existence in Nauvoo of "a set of bogus-makers determined to counterfeit coin here by wagon loads and make it pass upon the community as land office money," but he blamed the outrage on Thomas S. Williams' upstart clique of criminals within the Church who, he claimed, "wish to be avenged upon us for not consenting to the establishment of their bogus mints and dealings in base coin. The Lord will be against him and all those who partook of such corruption."

The only good news that had come to Nauvoo involving the United States Government was derived in a strangely negative manner. Only five days ago, U.S. Senator James Semple of Illinois reported to President Polk that the Mormons were on the verge of migrating out of his state and into the West, beyond the jurisdiction of the United States. He requested that, due to possible consequences, they be prevented from leaving.

Polk shook his head and replied, "I possess no power to prevent or check their emigration. The right of emigration or expatriation is one which any citizen possesses. I cannot interfere with them on the ground of their religious faith, however absurd it might be considered. If I could interfere with the Mormons, I could as well with the Baptists, or any other religious sect. By the Constitution, any citizen has the right to adopt his own religious faith."

Senator Semple had wisely backed down at that point, but it rankled the Saints in general and Young especially that a President of the United States should actually have implied that the religious faith of the Mormons was absurd. So now, with virtually all avenues of government assistance closed to them, they were on their own and the day scheduled for the great Mormon migration to begin had finally arrived.

That the Mormon exodus from Nauvoo was commencing across the Mississippi on this very day of the sailing of the *Brooklyn* from New York City was a coincidence that Brigham Young chose to interpret as an augury from God. However, the prevailing weather was not in accordance. The sky had been heavily overcast this morning and brittle bits of dry snow rattled through the naked tree branches, driven by a bitter, merciless wind. The Illinois bank of the Mississippi at Nauvoo was choked with great mounds of stacked goods and heavily laden wagons ready for transport across the river to the Iowa side aboard the fleet of broad, low ferry boats that had been constructed over the months past. The near one-mile-long pull-and-guide ropes had already been strung and stretched tautly from shore to shore. In addition to all the worldly goods assembled and packed during the long period of preparations, there were the living creatures awaiting their turn to be ferried across: thousands of chickens, ducks, geese, milk cows, horses, swine, and sheep...and a multitude of human beings.

The projected danger of the crossing was magnified by the fact that the river was not solidly frozen, as had been prayed for. Great chunks of ice, separated by patches of muddy water, floated haphazardly downstream in a steady six-mile-an-hour current, deceptively innocent in appearance but capable of grinding and crushing those craft now beginning to be launched.

Preliminary parties of heavily bundled men crossed first. They were laden with tools and accompanied by work horses and mules. Their job was to push onward after the crossing to the previously selected area nine miles west along Sugar Creek, an area only vaguely protected by a stand of timber; there the first campground would be established. Trees were felled, limbs chopped, downed branches interlaced to form windbreaks. Available tents were erected and secured, or makeshift huts were quickly set up, comprised of skeletal branches overhung with pieces of bark, blankets, quilts and canvas, anything to form a shelter. Numerous fires were built and kept stoked by mobs of boys who collected fallen wood. Women with cook-pots and fry-pans prepared food without pause, replenished as needed with whatever was available and constantly feeding those exhausted from their labors and ravenous.

No time was wasted back at the river. Unceasingly the ferries crossed over and returned as swiftly as possible, touching the far shore and dumping all cargo, then moving back to the east side to repeat the process while the newly deposited load on the Iowa side was gathered, lashed to wagons or sleds and moved out of the way for the next to be brought across.

There were tragedies: Lashings snapped, loads shifted, bundles and furnishings skidded on icy decks and slid into the murky waters; bobbing tables, chairs, bedsteads, rockers, dressers drifted swiftly away with no chance of recovery; ice floes struck causing cows and horses to lose their footing and fall into the maelstrom, their terrified bawling and screams cut off sharply as the current sucked them down; ferries were struck by other floes, tilted, canted, overturned and lives were lost. Elder Hosea Stout, crossing with his family, saw one such occurrence and, as the boat capsized, cried, "The Destroyer broods over us! The Revelation saith the Lord has cursed the waters in the Last Days and in my heart it is verily true!"

All through the day of unrelenting bitter wind the staggering, disheveled but unbroken line of refugees and wagons stretched westward from the river well into the gathering darkness and collected themselves at the grove along Sugar Creek and simply strove to survive. Some sang hymns and others prayed. Elders offered gritted words of comfort to the distressed. Men grumbled, women moaned, children cried, babies screamed, people were injured, a number died. And during this first memorable night, of this great exodus, nine babies were born.

Several hundred had successfully made the crossing today, but they were hardly even a vanguard. Hundreds of others had stood on the Illinois side, merely bidding farewell and Godspeed to friends and relations. This was only the first of a multitude of days that must stretch into weeks, possibly months, before all 20,000 gathered at Nauvoo had joined the throng west of the Mississippi and headed into a future even less assured.

# Chapter 3

♦

[*March 1, 1846 • Sunday*]

Some 15,000 Mormons had already crossed the Mississippi, with only about 5,000 more to do so, when Brigham Young announced it was time for them to begin following him westward. None of the Saints as yet had any idea where they were heading but by far the greater majority had implicit faith in Young, whom many had taken to referring to as Israel. What concerned more than just a few of the followers, however, was when Young stood before them and said with conviction, "I *am* Israel!"

The crossing of the Mississippi, begun on February 4, continued to be very hazardous, but at last, after nine successive days of below zero temperatures, the great river froze solidly enough that the ice could support them and the number that could cross in a day quintupled. Two days later, on February 15, Young himself crossed the ice and they clustered about him as he led them on to the greatly expanded camp at Sugar Creek, where conditions were less than ideal. The temperature was twenty degrees below zero and the vast flock of Saints was suffering severely, a situation compounded when the temperature moderated for a day and a heavy snowfall all but buried them. The bark huts and makeshift lean-tos provided little shelter and only by clustering about the numerous fires could any degree of relief be gained. More and better shelters were erected and they helped, but the situation remained grim and several of the very young and very old died. As ever more of the Saints arrived, some found work, exchanged for food, among nearby settlers.

Brigham Young, ever active, established a sense of order, putting most on a schedule of chores, anointing those who were sick and by night encouraging the holding of hymn sessions and prayer meetings and even dances. All the while preparations were being made for resuming their migration on foot and in wagons. Hosea Stout organized the temple guards and marched them in formation until they had tramped fully an acre of the snow into a hard-packed parade ground. Eliza Snow, the secret widow of Joseph Smith, wrote poetry, some of it in praise of Brigham Young, whose proposal of marriage she had just accepted, but more often concerned with the plight of the Mormons:

> *The Camp, the Camp—its numbers swell—*
> *Shout! Shout! O camp of Israel.*
> *The King, the Lord of Hosts is near,*
> *His armies guard our front and rear.*
> *Though we fly from vile aggression,*
> *We'll maintain our pure profession,*
> *Seek a peaceable possession*
> *Far from Gentiles and oppression.*

Today, at last, the actual movement westward was begun in earnest, with Young leading the throng and no one but he having anything but guesses as to their ultimate destination. Some thought Texas, near the mouth of the Rio Grande, others somewhere in the Great Basin and still others to Oregon or Vancouver Island or California. Even those high in the hierarchy of the Church, such as Lorenzo Snow, were baffled and he wrote to a friend that they were moving *"...to we know not where"*.

Young divided the throng into organized groups of tens or twenties or fifties, each commanded by a newly appointed "captain;" and today some 3,000 bedraggled Saints blindly but joyfully followed their leader, accompanied by more than 300 wagons. They traveled relatively slowly, slogging through snow squalls that gradually turned to icy cold rain, their feet clogged with heavy clumps of mud, pausing often to build bridges where necessary, for those thousands following, creating roads through difficult terrain, but almost constantly moving westward. Feet became frostbitten, then turned gangrenous and some of the victims died in agony. Sickness was all but endemic, yet they plodded on toward an unknown destination as they knew they must continue to do for the weeks and months to come, doing so because they believed in their leader, their Prophet, their Israel—Brigham Young.

*[March 14, 1846 • Saturday]*

Of all the men in his command, Captain John Fremont respected none so much as he did his two principal guides, Kit Carson and Joseph Reddeford Walker. Though Carson had become more an actual friend to him than the somewhat more aloof Walker, the natural hot-headedness of Carson was worrisome and that was why Fremont had weeks ago chosen Walker to head the larger detachment he had sent south to seek out a new and better route across the Sierras. And, not unexpectedly, Walker had done just that. His men and horses had, in fact, come through the new pass he had located in much better shape than Fremont's and the two detachments had finally reunited and moved together westward out of the San Joaquín Valley and across the low Santa Cruz Mountains into the more populated coastal area between Yerba Buena and Monterey.[64]

That this move was a violation in strict defiance of Don José Castro's order seemed of little consequence to Fremont and on March 5, as they entered the last little valley before reaching Monterey, while on the Hartnell Rancho near Salinas, they were met by a Mexican lieutenant carrying terse messages sent by both the prefect and General Castro which said, in essence:

> *Capitan Fremont: You have disobeyed our strict order to maintain your force no farther west than the San Joaquín. You have broken faith with Mexican officials, you have lied about both your instructions and your intentions, you have broken our laws, defied our courts and condoned the misbehavior of your men. You must withdraw immediately back to the San Joaquín or face the most severe of consequences.*

To the dismay of most of his men and to Joe Walker in particular, Fremont treated the Mexican officer with gross disrespect, hastily wrote a defiant answering note which he gave to the lieutenant to carry back to his superiors and savagely ordered him away. He then hurried his own men to the top of a nearby eminence called Gavilan Peak.[65] There he ordered a breastwork of logs erected and as this was being done, he nailed the American flag to a pole and planted it in the ground, then hastily wrote and dispatched a note to Consul Larkin in Monterey, in which he declared grandly:

> ...If we are unjustly attacked, we will fight to extremity and refuse quarter, trusting our country to avenge our death.... If we are hemmed in and assaulted here, we will die, every man of us, under the flag of our country.

Upon receiving the note, Larkin was horrified. His own subtle intrigues were being destroyed by what was occurring. Certain that Fremont must have misunderstood, he wrote him an answering note recommending he back off and explaining the Californio *commandante's* action. He also sent a hasty message to Don José Castro begging him to withhold aggression and endeavor to engage Captain Fremont in peaceable talk.

For his own part, Castro quickly called up his militia and on March 13 sent out a strong proclamation saying that Fremont and his men were nothing more than a band of highwaymen and urging the already angered citizens of the area to hold themselves in armed readiness at Sonoma but to take no other action unless so ordered. He then quickly moved his militia to the base of Gavilan Peak and paraded them there in a show of strength, but not intended to presage any form of attack. The tactic succeeded.

Though Fremont ranted irrationally with emotional fervor for three days, he finally ran down and began to more clearly assess the humiliation of his own situation. His position, both in tactics and in law was untenable; he had no authority for his action from his own government which would, if he continued, simply disavow him. When the flagpole he'd poorly planted abruptly fell over of its own accord, he commented lamely, "Well, I guess that shows we've done enough for honor," and at last gave in to the wiser counsel of his officers, including Joe Walker. During the night of March 8 he marched his force off the hill and, without opposition, headed them back toward the San Joaquín River, which they reached at noon today and established an overnight camp more safe than they'd had for about a fortnight.

Now that they had done so, Fremont was approached by Walker, whose expression was set in grim lines. The mountain man stopped before the commander and regarded him scathingly for a moment, then shook his head.

"I quit," he said. "I refuse to serve any longer under so stupid a son-of-a-bitch!"

*[March 20, 1846 • Friday]*

War was in the air.

It hadn't yet been declared, but a giant step in that direction was taken today as General Zachary Taylor's advance moved southward through the disputed territory between the Nueces River and the Rio Grande. As they came to a large salt pond at the Arroyo Colorado, General Francisco Mejía appeared on the other side with a number of skirmishers and called to the Americans in reasonably good English: "Stop, Yankees! If you come any farther, you will start a war!"

They were precisely the words the "Yankees" had been longing to hear ever since they had been sent out as an advance unit from Corpus Christi on March 8. They had been heading for Point Isabel, where a supply depot was to be built. Some twenty-five miles southwest was where, on the opposite side of the Rio Grande lay the town of Matamoros, which was where General Mejía had established his headquarters. Directly across, on the Rio Grande's north bank was where General Taylor intended to construct his principal fortification and he sent an advance force there to reconnoiter.

While Taylor was still at the Point Isabel depot with the bulk of his troops, a force of Mexican soldiers under General Mariano Arista made an unexpected move to engage the American detachment, but the advance fought well and repulsed the endeavor, forcing Arista to take up a defensive position at Palo Alto.

This was not a good time for Taylor. His troops remained largely undisciplined and there was considerable friction between his principal officers in regard to the matter of seniority. There were also swamps to cross at first, then desert country and finally higher chaparral country where the lack of water became a very real problem.

It was only the day before yesterday—March 18—when Mexican General Francisco Mejía posted a biting proclamation inveighing against United States aggression, a copy of which was brought in and delivered to Taylor by one of his rangers. The American general had trouble digesting the vitriol, as well as the inherent truth of the document, but one sentence in particular stood out in its verity:

> *Fellow-countrymen: With an enemy which respects not its own laws, which shamelessly derides the very principles invoked by it previously, in order to excuse its ambitious views, we have no other resource* (recourse) *than arms.*

Now it was March 20 and the advance had just heard the threat by General Mejía on the other side of the big salt pond and it did nothing more than spur all the madly yelling Americans into a wild charge through the cloudy, calf-deep waters in a startling rush. A few shots broke out but no one was struck. Incredibly, before the Americans were even halfway across, the Mexicans broke and fled.

The cries of the Americans turned into victorious cheers and all the Rangers were convinced it wouldn't be the last time.

[March 24, 1846 · Tuesday]

"White flag coming across the river, Sir," reported Ranger Lieutenant Edward Johnson, who had just run across the under-construction earthen and timber fieldwork to the commander's tent. The soldier standing guard nearby remained at attention but could not mask his curiosity.

General Zachary Taylor returned the officer's salute and nodded. "Took a bit longer than I expected," he said. "Thank you, Lieutenant. How many in the boat?"

"Two rowers and an officer in the bow. He's the one holding the flag."

"Escort him here, please, Mister Johnson. Him only. Put a watch on the others."

"Yes Sir!" Johnson saluted again and raced back the way he had come.

Taylor reentered the tent and set aside the report he had been writing on the small folding table beside his bunk. As he pressed fresh tobacco into his pipe, he considered recent events. He had arrived with his full army of 4,000 men at Point Isabel during the forenoon four days ago and had immediately set the men to work on establishing fortifications as a supply depot. With a full company of mounted men he had then moved on at speed to the site directly across the Rio Grande from Matamoros and where the detachment sent out earlier had made considerable progress in clearing the broad area and erecting a timber breastwork facing the river. He was well pleased with the work that had been done and eager to begin construction of the fort itself; the new installation he was already planning to call Fort Texas.[66] Now he lighted his pipe and the blue-white cloud of aromatic smoke wafted above his head just as Lieutenant Johnson returned with the Mexican officer and he bade the pair enter. Obviously nervous, the messenger saluted and then extended a folded and sealed paper to him.

"From General Mejía, Señor, who asks American commandante to make reply I take back." His command of English, though stilted, was reasonably good.

"*Gracias*," Taylor replied, accepting it and, shifting his gaze to his junior officer, added, "Take him outside, Lieutenant, while I read this and make my reply."

As soon as they were gone he sat down on his bunk, breaking the note's seal as he did so, gratified to see writing in English:

*From General Mejía to the American officer in command.*

*Sir—You have trespassed into Mexican territory, which cannot be tolerated. The presence of your army can be regarded in no other manner than as a hostile act against Mexico. You are herewith ordered to gather your forces wherever you have set them and return with them north of the river Nueces. If you do not withdraw completely within three days, my army will attack and your force will suffer bloodshed and death until you comply in full measure. By your actions, you have declared war upon Mexico.*

FRANCISCO MEJÍA<br>*Commanding General*

Taylor sat quietly for a moment and then sucked on the pipe stem, but the coal had gone out and he set the pipe aside. Removing a fresh sheet of paper from a leather pouch, he sat behind his makeshift desk and swiftly penned his reply:

*General Mejía—*

*Pleased be advised that I and my men have been sent here by the Presidentof the United States, and until President Polk directs me to leave, we intend to stay. The territory north of the Rio Grande is American, not Mexican.*

*We have come here peacefully and, in my opinion, have taken no Hostile action whatever. If a war begins, the responsibility for it will lie with whomever fires the first shot, which is something I and my troops will not do. It would indeed be foolhardy for you and your men to do so.*

Z. TAYLOR, *General.*

He folded the paper, placed it into an envelope and sealed it, then wrote General Mejía's name on its face. He strode out of the tent, handed it to the Mexican officer, then beckoned the lieutenant a few steps away and spoke, his voice low: "Take him back to his boat, Lieutenant, but detain him by whatever subterfuge you can, for as long as you can without the use of force. I will be heading for Point Isabel as soon as you're away with him." He tipped his head toward the Mexican officer.

"Sir," Johnson whispered back, "an express came for you several minutes ago. Wanted to see you immediately, but I had him wait over there." He motioned and for the first time the general saw the dismounted runner impatiently standing beneath a tree, holding his horse's reins.

"All right, take this man back to his boat now."

"Yes sir!" The lieutenant saluted, rejoined the Mexican officer and set off with him toward the river. Taylor watched them go until they were out of earshot, then turned and found that the messenger, leading his horse, had approached and was waiting a few yards distant.

The news brought by the rider was that the general's transports and supply ships had made harbor at Point Isabel and the troops were awaiting orders. Taylor immediately ordered the runner to see to his jaded horse, then take some rest himself. As the grateful messenger led his horse away, the commander had one of his own runners provided with a fresh mount, then told him to wait. He returned to his tent and swiftly wrote out orders for the full army at Point Isabel, with the exception of a sizeable guard for the supplies and fortifications, to march at speed for this site. Most of them, he knew, had earlier been primed to leave Point Isabel to come here to aid in constructing the new fort. Now there was a far more pressing reason for them to get here quickly. The messenger left immediately.

Taylor conferred with his second in command, ordering him to keep the men working at their assigned tasks, but warning him as well to keep alert for any movement toward crossing the river of the several hundred Mexican troops. Should that occur, the entire company was to ride out at once and join him somewhere on the trail to Point Isabel.

Within the hour, General Taylor was mounted and riding northeastward at a mile-eating trot, intent on intercepting the main army, at which time he would personally lead them back here. He hoped they'd be in time to thwart, by sheer numbers, any attempt by the Mexicans to cross the Rio Grande.

*[March 28, 1846 · Saturday]*

California Governor Pio Pico was considerably irked with General José Castro.

When the incident occurred recently with the Americans under Fremont "invading" coastal California and actually getting rather close to Salinas and not all that far from Monterey, it had been Pico who had warned the countryside, mustered troops and kept the whole Fremont party bottled up atop Gavilan Peak for several days. Yet it was Castro, who hadn't even been there, who had overstepped his authority and was essentially taking credit for the whole affair. It was Pico who was preparing a proclamation to that effect when Castro stole his thunder by making the announcement in person this morning to a very large crowd gathered in the central square of Monterey. It had been the braying voice of Castro that had drawn him out onto the palace balcony in the first place and he had become livid with what the general was thundering about the Fremont affair.

"Compatriots!" Castro bellowed. "The act of unfurling the American flag on the hills, the insults and threats offered to the authorities, are worthy of execration and hatred from Mexicans; prepare, then, to defend our independence in order that united we may repel with a strong hand the audacity of men who, receiving every mark of true hospitality from our country, reacted with such ingratitude for the favors obtained from our cordiality and benevolence."

On and on he went about how the show of force at the base of Gavilan had kept the *gringos* bottled up for days at the top and, without one shot being fired, had finally frightened those cowards away. The throng cheered mightily and the governor had heard enough. He left the balcony, closing the French doors behind him and sent one of his guards to bring the speaker to him.

Governor Pio Pico was unsure he could ever forgive General Castro.[67]

At this very moment, some 250 crow-flight miles to the north, a greatly subdued John Fremont, leading his entire original force of topographical surveyors and mappers, was arriving at the Neal Rancho on Butte Creek near where it emptied into the Sacramento, some fifty miles upstream from Sutters Fort. He looked as if he had been whipped and, except for necessary commands, he had hardly spoken to anyone except Kit Carson since they had reached the valley of the San Joaquín.

# The Infinite Dream

On March 15, the morning after Joe Walker had quit as his chief guide and Carson had immediately assumed that role, they had traveled steadily and with some speed northward until reaching Sutters Fort six days later. As much as it had galled him, there was nothing to do but refit his party there, including horses and mules, and mostly refusing to even respond to John Sutter's questions other than to say he was carrying out his original mission, which would take him up the Sacramento and eventually into the Oregon country. As usual, everything he received was to be charged to the U.S. Government by Sutter; a billing Fremont officially signed even though Sutter had not yet completed writing out the inventory.

The members of the expedition, as Fremont was referring to it again. camped at their previous site on the American River and were on their way up the Sacramento as soon as the order was completed several days later. They arrived at the mouth of Butte Creek in the forenoon today, moved upstream on the tributary a little distance and now had just reached Tom Neal's Rancho.

Neal had been a blacksmith on Fremont's second expedition, and at his request been given permission to stay and establish a homestead. Neal himself emerged from one of the several cabins as they approached and his face lighted when he recognized both his former commander and guide, as well as a number of men in the topographic unit.

He began talking animatedly to old friends but was disappointed when Fremont rather sourly explained that they could only stay overnight, as they'd be continuing up toward Oregon country in the morning.

Neal shook his head. "That ain't very good news. Hardly never get much of visitors here." A grin split his features again. "By gum!" he chortled. "Kinda' figured I'd never see you fellers again! Got a coupl'a untapped kegs in the shed there that're just plain ripe to be unbunged. Reckon from the looks of things, ever' last one of you could stand a good stiff jolt!"

Neal slapped his own thigh and laughed aloud, not noticing that hardly anyone among the new arrivals even smiled.

*[April 17, 1846 • Friday]*

Marine Lieutenant Archibald Gillespie was finally able to disembark from the U.S. sloop *Cyane* at Monterey and was pleased to feel solid ground under his feet once again. It had taken him just slightly less than six months to get here from Washington D.C. and he was delighted his travels were over for the time being.

Getting directions from a lounger on the wharf, in less than ten minutes Gillespie presented himself at the office of American Consul Thomas Oliver Larkin in the United States Embassy. After the door was closed, the mufti-clad lieutenant repeated the instructions he had memorized before burning the papers in Mexico. Larkin listened closely and then shook his head. Too many changes had occurred here; the orders were nearly half a year old, no longer germane to existing conditions. The troubles here had begun with Fremont at Gavilan Peak and swiftly escalated into a highly volatile situation. It was clear that the Californio provisional government was breaking down: Governor Pio Pico and General Castro were at one another's throat more than ever and neither had any real interest in continuing to even try to maintain civil stability. Larkin was sure the unstable government would collapse of its own neglect in less than a year. The fiasco at Gavilan Peak had been especially traumatic for Larkin, almost destroying the intrigues he had been carefully developing for so long. Now he would need time and the exercise of caution to convince Castro that the United States was interested in his cooperation and well being.

Lieutenant Gillespie admitted he was sorry to hear that, but with such being the case, he still needed to deliver special oral instructions to Fremont, too. Did Larkin know where he could find him?

Consul Larkin shook his head slowly, ruefully. "You'll just have to follow where he's gone," he said, "up the Sacramento."

"How far?"

"Past its headwaters and over the mountains. He's probably in Oregon by now."

Lt. Gillespie groaned. His long journey was not over after all.

[April 25, 1846 • Saturday]

The chilly war occurring near the mouth of the Rio Grande was finally beginning to heat.

For weeks the situation had remained fairly static. There had been an almost constant flow of communications between General Taylor and Washington D.C. and between himself and the Mexican force across the river at Matamoros. Internal tensions continued at Fort Texas and

Point Isabel, senior officers vying for position through tenure. Taylor coped by strengthening defenses at both posts and writing letters, mainly to Secretary of War Marcy, requesting not only that some of those bickering officers be transferred, but more troops be sent to counter a steadily increasing build-up of the Mexican forces occurring across the river. Simultaneously, he exchanged reasonably cordial letters with the succession of commanding officers occurring at Matamoros. First, General Mejía was replaced by General Pedro Ampudia and when Taylor blocked the mouth of the Rio Grande with the revenue cutter *U.S. St. Anna* and the brig *U.S. Lawrence*, Ampudia complained bitterly. Taylor responded calmly, stating that his action was not to be taken as bellicose but "a simple defensive precaution." When Ampudia followed up with no offensive action, he was replaced by General Mariano Arista, who arrived with even more troops, increasing the Mexican force at Matamoros to more than 6,000 *soldados*—more than twice the size of Taylor's force at the improved Fort Texas.

Taylor sent out a ten-man reconnoitering party commanded by Lieutenant Lucius Porter. When Porter promptly got himself killed by some Mexican foragers, Taylor deemed it a "tragic incident" but not an act of war. Then, after Captain Trueman Cross was listed as "missing" for many days, his largely skeletal remains were found not far from Fort Texas; again, Taylor refused to treat this as an act of war but rather "a murder that appeared to have been perpetrated by Mexican civilians." Even as Lieutenant Porter's remains were being given a formal burial, Arista moved a sizeable force of his men across the river in a plan to catch the Americans in a pincer movement, while simultaneously sending Taylor a personal letter replete with courtly expressions. The plan failed due to the alertness of Taylor's guard patrols and Arista withdrew, but with a better understanding of Taylor's defense at Fort Texas.

Then, just yesterday, General Taylor received a letter from General Arista that was clearly not cordial; the Mexican commander promised that before long his army would cross the Rio Grande and this time would attack, in force, Taylor's so-called "Army of Occupation." Taylor's response was terse:

> ...When and if the time comes to respond, we are ready. From your known high character, both as a public officer and private citizen, I was strengthened in my hope that some arrangement could be made

by which friendly relations might be maintained on the frontier, until a final settlement of the question of boundary.... But if such is not to be the case—if hostilities are to ensue—the responsibility must rest with them who actually commence them.

Arista's response was swift: Under cover of pre-dawn darkness today, he sent 1,600 men under command of General Anastasio Torrejon to the Rancho Carricitos, some twenty-five miles northwest of Fort Texas. An hour or so after sunrise, a cavalry squad of fifty-two patrolling U.S. dragoons under command of Captain Seth Thornton encountered a solitary civilian who fearfully told the officer that General Torrejon was nearby with a sizeable force. Thornton did not believe him and continued with his squad until they reached the sprawling, chaparral-walled Rancho Carricitos. There was a barred entry which they opened enough to enter into the enclosure in single file and, without a guard having been placed at the bars, found the rancho seemingly deserted. At last Thornton himself found an old man inside and had begun questioning him when an alarm was abruptly given. Its cause was far more savage than anticipated. Scores of previously hidden Mexican soldiers appeared at the bars and fired. Thornton was wounded and fourteen men of the American patrol were instantly killed and the remainder captured.[68]

Later that day, when word of the encounter reached Fort Texas, Lieutenant Colonel Ethan Hitchcock wrote:

> ...My heart is not in this business. I am against it from the bottom of my soul as a most unholy and unrighteous proceeding. It looks as if government sent a small force on purpose to bring on a war, so as to have a pretext for taking California and as much of this country as possible; for, whatever becomes of this army, there is no doubt now of a war between the United States and Mexico.

General Taylor may or may not have agreed with the whole of the officer's comments, but he was definitely in full accord with the conclusion that Hitchcock had reached. Most especially with the information just received that the most bellicose of the Californio leaders, Pio Pico and Castro, were sworn in on April 18 at Los Angeles as, respectively, governor of California and commandant general. Taylor fired off an express message to President Polk with that intelligence, plus whatever details about the skirmish that he was able to assemble.

While not yet officially declared, this was quite clearly the beginning of the Mexican War.

*[April 28, 1846 • Tuesday • 7:00 a.m.]*

Samuel Brannan's complexion was more than a little green this morning and he steadied himself with a firm grasp on the *Brooklyn's* starboard rail. On the bridge ahead of him, his back to Brannan and apparently unaware of the Mormon leader's presence, Captain Richardson stood motionless in the pose he so often assumed, gaze fixed on the distant horizon, the sea a beautiful blue-green, the waves small and only here and there breaking into a brilliant whitecap; ideal sailing weather.

Considering himself unnoticed for the moment, Brannan breathed deeply, giving himself time for the still lurking nausea to diminish, giving himself time to think. He pushed from his mind the thoughts of their largely spoiled food supply and greatly diminished and tainted water remaining; he had already this morning ordered it rationed in pints. As he sometimes did to settle his mind when upset, he considered matters with an arithmetical concept: For three full months—twelve full weeks this very day, eighty-four days in all—they had been at sea without the feel of solid earth beneath their feet. He remembered the excitement, the ebullience among so many of his Mormon throng as they had filed aboard on February 4, anticipating a long, peaceful, *indolent* cruise. And how quickly they had become disenchanted.

Brannan had immediately taken absolute charge of his flock, inaugurating a militaristic system of work and behavior. Aided by Samuel Ladd, the only Saint aboard who had been a soldier, he established a schedule that involved every male who was sixteen or older except for the *Brooklyn's* crew. First thing every morning after breakfast, the women did the clean-up and the men filed onto the deck for an hour of military close-order drill. They were initially less than happy about it until Brannan dug out bolts of navy blue cloth from the hold and set the women to measuring, cutting and sewing, making uniforms for each male in what he termed his "shipboard battalion." It was a brilliant stroke, imbuing in all a sense of "belonging" and they began following orders better, even adopting a sense of jauntiness as Brannan and Ladd barked commands. Other tasks the leader devised kept every Saint aboard reasonably occupied from dawn until nightfall.

Only a few days after clearing New York Harbor they had encountered their first gale; a blow lasting two days, the seasickness among the flock creating a clean-up problem lasting for days. Brannan prided himself on being one of the few essentially unaffected. But the first real tragedy occurred when Phoebe Robbins lost her toddler son, George Edward Robbins; the little boy had slipped and fallen headlong into the hold, breaking his neck. The mother was deeply bereft when later Brannan led the services over the small, bundle-wrapped corpse which was then, amid voices raised in prayer, gently lowered over the side and into the sea.

Following the celebration when they crossed the equator, extreme boredom finally reared its head. Brannan realized discipline was slipping and at once took a definitive step to control it. He drew up a set of rules to take effect immediately which he planned to continue even after they made landfall and had established their own community in California.

"These regulations," he intoned, holding up the paper before the assembled Saints, "are for the brotherhood and protection of one and all. They represent a pattern of government strong enough to withstand whatever adversities or problems may beset us, whether here aboard ship or later when our commune is established in California."

He then read what he had written: It was a plan generally based on the Prophet's grandly entitled "United Order" but with certain important amendments of Brannan's own creation. Every Saint aboard would have to sign the agreement. Though the list was extensive, it condensed to six salient points:

1. *All Saints aboard will unite to establish a single company.*
2. *All Saints aboard, as this single body, will make every effort to pay the debt of transportation at the journey's end.*
3. *The Saints will, with single accord, prepare for their brethren Saints who are en route overland.*
4. *All signers of the document shall give the entire proceeds of their labors for the next three years into a common fund, from which all will be provided a living.*
5. *Any Saint refusing obedience of the rules here established will be expelled and thereafter be denied any subsistence from the order.*

> 6. *Should any Saint depart from this covenant, the common property is to revert to the Elders; should any Elder fall from grace, the common fund shall pass to the First Elder.*

The "First Elder" in this case was, of course, Samuel Brannan, who announced himself titular head of the commune's body politic and sole custodian of its assets and property. The crowning touch came with what he flagrantly named the Order: "Samuel Brannan & Company."

A certain amount of grumbling resulted, but after missing a few meals—which were withheld from those who had not yet agreed—every Saint aboard, Brannan excepted, finally signed the agreement.

Exactly a month ago, on March 28, the steady hand of Captain Richardson skillfully guided the *Brooklyn* through the treacherous currents and frigid waters of Drake's Passage while seabirds flapped and screamed above as if in warning. Without difficulty, however, the passage was made and Cape Horn lay behind them as they sailed steadily into the vast waters of the Pacific off the multi-islanded coast of southernmost Chile. Great anticipation sizzled in them all as their first landfall since leaving New York lay not so far ahead.

That was when a storm struck with a fury so monstrous that even Captain Richardson blanched.

For three days that seemed like weeks, the *Brooklyn* ran southwestward with the wind, lashed and battered by waves that at times loomed higher than the masts themselves. Whipped by savagely furious winds and almost constantly soaked by spray and leakage, the Saints were buffeted until all were badly bruised and some even suffered broken bones.

At last, close to dawn this very day, the storm blew itself away and in this morning's brilliant sunlight the bright sea lay quiescent before them.

"Well, Mister Brannan, you wish to see me?"

The booming voice shattered Brannan's train of thought. The Captain was still standing where he had been, hand gripping the wheel, gaze still toward the horizon, his back still toward Brannan, who was unaware that the skipper had evidently known of his presence all along.

"I do, Captain," he replied, crossing the deck and climbing the short ladder to the bridge. "We've obviously blown off-course, so how long before we can get back to Valparaiso and replenish?"

"We're not going to Valparaiso."

Brannan's stomach gave a slight lurch, but he replied evenly, "We're not? *Why* not?"

"Much too far. We're 'way off course. Only one reasonable chance for us now."

"Which is?"

"Juan Fernandez Island..." Richardson's chest rumbled deeply with one of his rare chuckles, "...presuming I don't miss it."[69]

*[April 28, 1846 · Tuesday · 2:00 p.m.]*

The Whigs were chortling among themselves, convinced they finally had President Polk in a pincers grip. This situation had its inception with Senator Calhoun's effort to discover some sort of leverage in the proposal made by the President to actually buy a treaty from Mexico. Polk continued to mention it when Calhoun called on him to suggest that a possible escape from the current Oregon problem was to propose a negotiation through the foreign ambassadors. That was clearly placing the President in the position of admitting defeat; the first time Polk had allowed himself to be so seemingly cornered.

The Whigs knew there was no way they could back away from Termination since that ending of the old treaty was precisely what the country wanted. To protect themselves in case their stance should result in complications, they were now determined to make sure President Polk would have to take full responsibility when the measure failed, as they were quite certain it would.

The House resolution told Polk to "cause notice to be given" to the British regarding Termination, but the Senate resolution in its preamble carefully stated President Polk was "authorized, at his discretion" to give the British such notice, which was a considerably weaker platform. The Senate had passed that resolution on April 16, but then the House quickly amended that vital to read "authorized and directed." Polk, believed this imperiled the administration's primary objective because there was such objection on cleavage lines among the senators that if provided with such an opportunity they would, in relief, let the resolution perish. His sharp resentment to this was obvious in the bitter comments he penned in his private journal. Nevertheless, he responded by allowing the Senate to eliminate the word "directed" and, in so doing, lost his final opportunity to present Termination as the nation's united will. Beyond that, Polk refused to budge. However, the Senate's modification was accepted by the House and both congressional bodies, on April 23, passed the resolution to abrogate the 1827 convention. The Termination Notice was already prepared and Polk signed it the following day.

This morning, securing it with the Great Seal of the United States, Polk sent it to Great Britain's sovereign via special packet. Joint Occupation of Oregon was officially ended and now all breaths in political Washington D.C. were being held in anticipation of John Bull's response. In the meanwhile, Polk had at least won, if perhaps only momentarily. His own position on Oregon had carried through Congress and notification of the British to this effect had been made. What their reaction would be, he didn't know, but he remained convinced he had read the signs correctly.

Now the President of the United States could turn his full attention to Mexico.

*[April 30, 1846 • Thursday]*

The California that Mariano Guadalupe Vallejo had known all his life was rapidly disappearing and he was one of few who fully recognized that fact.

Governor Pio Pico in Los Angeles and Commandante General José Castro, hardly caring that their respective titles had been officially approved in Mexico City, remained constantly at one another's throat, their fomenting hatred for each other coming into full bloom, but now, like the last rose of summer, ready to perish at the first frost—that being, in this situation, when one might gain ascendancy over the other. Neither understood, as Vallejo saw only too clearly, that the destruction of one would ultimately sound the bell of destruction for the other.

Vallejo knew that such destruction would engulf him as well, meaning that the wealth, the estate, the holdings and the life style he had spent his entire existence acquiring were imminently jeopardized. He had long wracked his mind over how to avoid such an eventuality and had found only one vague possibility, inherently distasteful though it might be to him. He was aware that Sutters Fort, though originally founded by a Swiss, was now more American than anything else, with all indications being that this trend would not only continue, it would increase.

The Americans had brought with them an energy and possessiveness that was anathema to most of those of Mexican heritage, to whom their more relaxed style had become a way of life that could not exist alongside the vigor and unity of the Yankees. Unless he were reading all the signs incorrectly, which Vallejo did not believe for an instant, California and all of Mexico's other North American land possessions would become American territory within five years and, quite possibly, even Mexico itself. The realm that had been so much an adjunct to his existence was about to tumble and, perhaps for the first time in his life, Vallejo largely put patriotism aside and allowed a degree of selfishness to the forefront.

For now the inhabitants of the Sutters Fort vicinity, Americans dominating, had held themselves aloof from the internal troubles besetting California but most likely this would not last for too much longer. Americans were an enterprising lot, opportunistic to a fault, perhaps, but this often became a benefit rather than a liability. Sooner or later, Vallejo believed, they would temporarily align themselves with either Pio Pico or Castro and aid in the downfall of the other. Having known Castro since his academy days, he believed it was Castro they would support. What would happen after Castro's ascendancy he had no clear idea, except for his own strong personal belief that the Californio military commandant could not possibly hold California together for very long and when it finally broke apart, it would be the Yankees who would pick up the pieces and fit them together again to their own benefit. With but little uncertainty, annexation by the United States would quickly follow.

Vallejo sighed and reached for his pen and paper to write what he had been putting off for too long already. The decision made, his quill pen raced across the paper with faint scratchings. When he neared the end of what he felt was imperative to say, he paused for a moment to consider how best to conclude. Then he dipped his quill, bent forward again and added a final paragraph to the declaration he was writing to the citizens of Alta California:

> ...Why then should we hesitate still to assert our independence? We have indeed taken the first step, by electing our own governor, but another remains to be taken...annexation tothe United States. In contemplating this consummation of our destiny, I feel nothing but pleasure, and I ask you to share it...When we join our fortunes to hers, we shall not become subjects, but fellow-citizens, possessing

*all the rights of the United States and choosing our own federal and local rulers. We shall have a stable government and just laws. California will grow strong and flourishing, and her people will be prosperous, happy, and free."*

[*May 7, 1846 • Thursday*]

As much as General Vallejo was concerned for the future of his Californio compatriots, so too was John Sutter concerned with what was occurring in and around Sutters Fort and what was to be the future of the inhabitants in the area. Most of them, at this point, were Americans and Sutter was becoming ever more convinced that sooner or later this entire California region would come into United States ownership. The question he asked himself was this: should he maintain his standing as a displaced Austrian? Should he continue with his adopted Mexican citizenship, now that the fortunes of Mexico in California seemed to be waning...and what if they should be ousted? Who would do the ousting? The answer was patently apparent: it would be the Americans and those Americans would need homes and supplies. Would not, then, his lot be better if he were to throw in with them than if he maintained his Mexican connection? And the most important consideration on his mind now was his own Sutters Fort and the very strategic role it was being forced into. For the first time, Sutter was beginning to become convinced that in order for him—and for his little empire—to survive, he would have to become an American citizen and convert Sutters Fort into an American installation.

The fact of it all seemed almost overwhelming to him, yet the probable actuality of it and what it portended was all but staggering. While he must definitely keep his leanings and opinions to himself for the time being, it was apparent to him that such survival would be dependent upon filling the immediate needs of the growing American population. Adequate housing was an immediate need and, to this end Sutter now devoted his thinking in his usual methodical way. For homes to be built, those emigres already here and those yet to come would require lumber in considerable quantities and so it became requisite for Sutter to locate the best possible site for adequate timber to be harvested and to establish a mill at such site to convert the timber into planking. While there were some fairly good stands of hardwoods—oaks and maples and the like— the greater prospects by far would come from harvesting the pines, which were in great abundance, but at higher elevations. The mill site, therefore, would have to be situated where the readied lumber could be shipped most expeditiously to Sutters Fort. And not only to the fort, but even down to the settlements at San Francisco Bay, where the demand for lumber was already great and growing with each passing day. All this meant that the eventual site would have to be located either up the Sacramento River itself or its tributaries, or up the American River or the streams from which it was generated.

With that conclusion having been reached, Sutter set about at once putting the wheels into motion. The sawmill, he was fairly certain, would almost certainly have to be built somewhere in the foothills of the Sierra Nevada. Toward this end he sent out one of his most trusted employees—John Bidwell—to ascend the Sacramento in an effort to locate a site that would meet his criteria, suggesting the powerful Feather River as a likely first choice. Bidwell left at once.

At the same time he also decided it would be a wise step for him to establish a grist-mill relatively close to the fort area, where a good current, swift and strong, would provide the power required for turning the great mill-wheels he had already ordered from the east, even though it would undoubtedly be months before they arrived here. Until then, he would continue having the grain ground by hand in rounded-out stumps by Indian laborers wielding heavy oaken pestles.

The most important decision Sutter made at this time, however, was to act at once to align himself and his fort with the Americans.

[*May 9, 1846 • Saturday • 9:00 a.m.*]

The *Brooklyn* had left its mooring in a cove on the south side of the largest of the islands of the San Fernando Archipelago just after dawn, maneuvering under Captain Richardson's skilled hands around its southern and eastern extremities and then taking an exact northwest heading to the Sandwich Islands—only some 6,500 miles dead ahead.

The three-day stopover on Robinson Crusoe Island, which early yesterday had gradually disappeared from the horizon behind them, had not only been their salvation, it had been a boon beyond all expectations.[70] In the ship's hold there was now an abundance of fresh fruits, vegetables, barrels of salted fish and meats and, most important, scores of barrels holding eighteen thousand gallons of fresh water to see them through the tedious voyage ahead. This was the largest they had gathered at a cost much less than they would have had to pay, according to the *Brooklyn's* skipper, had they been able to make the originally planned stop at Valparaiso.

They had all been suffering from hunger and lack of good water when they finally reached the island on May 3. As one of the Saints, Caroline A. Joyce, wrote:

> ...As we approached, being yet a great distance away, the island looked like a mass of immensely high rocks covered with moss; which moss, on nearer scrutiny, turned out to be heavy forests covering lofty peaks...

Their first task, after anchoring and going ashore, was a melancholy one; the burial of Laura Goodwin, mother of seven, who had died of scurvy shortly before their landing. As Caroline continued to write:

> ...Although the occasion was so sorrowful, the presence of the Seven [sic] little children sobbing in their uncontrollable grief and the father in his loneliness trying to comfort them, still, such was our weariness of the voyage that the sight of terra firma once more was such a relief from the ship life, that we gratefully realized and enjoyed it....

The service for the deceased was attended by the majority of Saints and almost the full crew of the *Brooklyn*, as well as some of the island's native population. It was conducted by Sam Brannan and he did an adequate job of it, having already had considerable practice with those who had died on shipboard en route. He spoke of motherhood and its important place in the world, as well as adding somewhat mysteriously, "motherhood's value in the eternal worlds, even before those worlds were created." No one really understood this allusion, but no one seemed to care.

The island, they discovered, owned by Chile, was a penal colony. There had once been a coastal settlement here, they were told, but four years ago an earthquake had caused the entire island to sink about fifty feet and that settlement became submerged. Now there were only the scattered grass huts of natives, a few other more substantial homes built by families who had chosen to live here, along with a large number of more poorly constructed shacks which were those of the convicts, plus a pair of houses inhabited by their keepers.

Two of the civilian families living here invited the *Brooklyn's* crew and passengers to help themselves to the abundance of wild fruits on the island and, for a very nominal fee they could also pluck the vegetables growing in the numerous haphazardly distributed garden plots.

The first task, however, was to fill the water barrels with some of the best water they had ever tasted, cool and fresh from bubbling springs no more than thirty feet from the shoreline. Firewood for cooking was lying about and available simply for the chore of picking it up, tying it into bundles and stowing it on shipboard. Fruit and vegetable gathering was next and they picked and stowed a remarkable supply of peaches and various wild fruits as well as potatoes, squashes, cucumbers and a variety of other vegetables from the gardens. The cost for the "crops" was minimal, easily ten times less, according to Captain Richardson, than the cost would have been for the same at Valparaiso, and paid for gladly with communal funds by Samuel Brannan & Company. Fish, easily caught, were equally abundant and barrels were filled with the de-gilled, gutted and salted-down varieties, as well as a species of crawfish almost as large as lobsters and equally tasty. Also added to the ship's larder were barrels of salted meats from the easily hunted goats, hares and wild pigs that inhabited the island.

To all the Saints the island was truly a paradise and Brannan easily convinced them that the fierce storm they had endured that had forced them away from Valparaiso was God's intervention and that their reward for not faltering in their faith in Him was this island and its abundance.

Finally, with the essential chores completed over a period of two days, the Saints were given leave by Brannan to roam and enjoy themselves during the final day. Some strolled through the forests or climbed the smaller mountains. Others strolled along the beaches or swam in freshwater pools or played games or explored a bit.

The third evening, after preparing for the *Brooklyn's* scheduled departure at dawn, Caroline Joyce wrote:

> ...*The passengers bathed and washed their clothing in fresh water, gathered fruit and potatoes, caught fish, some eels—great spotted creatures that looked so much like snakes that some members of the company could not eat them when cooked. We rambled about the*

island, visited the caves, one of which was pointed out to us as the veritable Robinson Crusoe cave, and it was my good fortune to take a sound nap there one pleasant afternoon.

At the first light of dawn today, after bidding farewell to their island friends, the Saints re-boarded the *Brooklyn* and as the rising sun began brightening the water, the anchor was hauled and the ship began moving, coasting easily eastward along the south shore, then bending northward as the island ended. Soon they were skimming along at six or seven knots under full sail along the island's eastern coast until finally there was naught ahead but the far horizon. As the island disappeared from sight, Caroline Joyce wrote a final comment:

...Many mementoes and souveniers [sic] were gathered, and after strewing our dead sister's grave anew with parting tokens of love, regret, and remembrance, we departed from the island, bearing away a serene, though shaded picture of our brief sojourn. The memory of the place will never fade from our minds.

*[May 9, 1846 • Saturday]*

During the week that ended at noon today, the Mexican Army had been attacking the Americans in two separate wings, one commanded by General Mejía and the other by General Arista, and three distinct engagements had occurred.

On May 1, having previously moved the majority of his troops from the American supply depot at Point Isabel to Fort Texas, which some of the men were calling Fort Taylor, so they could aid in rapidly constructing the defenses there, reliable intelligence reached General Taylor that the Mexicans had made this split, with one wing moving to cross the Rio Grande above Fort Texas and the other doing the same below the fort. It was this lower crossing that most concerned Taylor, igniting the fear that its aim was to attack his army's now vulnerable supply depot at Point Isabel. Immediately he had assembled the majority of his troops and marched them back to that site, arriving there on May 3, but found no trace of a Mexican advance in that direction. Still concerned, however, Taylor held his army here to help strengthen defenses and keep alert for any indication of the enemy's approach.

General Mejía, advised of Taylor's departure with the bulk of his army, took advantage of the situation and while a portion of his force continued to cross the river above the under-construction installation, moved cannon into place on the south bank of the river and, with Taylor's force now out of earshot, commenced his bombardment on Fort Texas. Almost immediately the American officer left in command, Major Jacob Brown, was critically injured and Sergeant Horace Weigart of the Seventh Infantry was killed. Major Brown was carried to a safer location behind the earthworks already in place, but it was obvious his wounds were so severe he would not survive and Captain Edgar Hawkins assumed command.

With what artillery they had, an eighteen-pounder and a six-pounder, Hawkins ordered a return fire. It was not terribly effective except that it held the enemy at bay. It had become a one-sided artillery duel, with the Mexicans lobbing in a dozen or more shots to every one returned by the Americans. When a message from Mejía arrived on May 3 demanding the Americans' surrender, Hawkins refused and continued sporadically lobbing cannon shot back across the river at them; sporadically because their supply of ammunition for the big guns was disturbingly limited. The situation worsened when the Mexican detachment that had crossed over the river above them moved into position and began musketry fire from the rear. Hawkins ordered the six-pounder howitzer turned around and fired back at them, holding *them* at bay as well.

The bombardment of Fort Texas continued practically unabated until May 9—the day Major Brown finally died—but without any significant damage and finally ceased that day. No other Americans had been killed but nine were very slightly wounded and two others more seriously, one with a fractured arm, the other with a fractured leg. Evidently, though far more limited, their own cannon fire had gratifying effect. A Mexican deserter who surrendered to them said that General Mejía had ordered their dead buried where they fell and their wounded carried to safety.

Meanwhile, back at Point Isabel, General Taylor's men had completed improving the supply depot's earthwork defenses and on May 7, leaving part of his army there as added protection, Taylor started to move his remaining 2,228 men and a number of well-loaded supply wagons back toward Fort Texas.

The next day, May 8, as they approached Palo Alto, eight miles north of the Rio Grande, Taylor's army found its way blocked by the

Mexican force under General Arista and fully three times the size of their own. The Mexicans began lobbing artillery shots but all fell far short. Taylor moved his force closer, to within range of his own cast iron twelve- and eighteen-pounders and began firing back with great effect.

Back at Point Isabel, troops at the supply depot heard the distant artillery and brought themselves to high alert. One lieutenant who knew that this signaled the war had begun, and which he considered a conspiracy of slaveholders, jotted in his journal: *...I felt sorry I had enlisted.* His name: Ulysses S. Grant.

Despite the punishing fire being taken, the Mexican army held its ground and continued firing back throughout the day with little significant effect on Taylor's force. A cavalry attack against the right rear of the Americans was easily repulsed. As dusk began gathering, there was a concerted infantry attack against the American left and another cavalry onslaught on the right, but well-placed artillery shots caused both to quickly withdraw. Casualties were fairly light among the Americans, but heavy for the Mexicans and when at last the battle ended as darkness closed in, the two forces settled in for the night. The engagement just concluded—the first battle of the Mexican War—was rather grandly designated the Battle of Palo Alto...and both sides claimed victory.

By first light today, General Arista began moving his force southward to find a more defensible position. Taylor's force followed, though moving slower to keep alert for possible ambush. As the pursuit continued well into the afternoon, General Taylor's concern mounted, and with justification. When they overtook Arista's force, the Mexicans had taken a strong position amid dense chaparral in an old bed of the Rio Grande at a place known as Resaca de la Palma, about three miles from the actual stream. Though to advance into such cover seemed almost certain suicide, Taylor bellowed for the army to advance anyway and the two forces quickly engaged.

What ensued was far bloodier than at Palo Alto. All was confusion amid the heavy undergrowth, and severe casualties were suffered by both sides. Heavy local duels erupted, were savagely fought and died out. A charge by Mexican cavalry against Taylor's artillery came within a hairsbreadth of overwhelming it and Taylor countered, to the consternation of his staff officers, by ordering his dragoons under Captain May to charge a battery set up by the Mexicans...and they captured it. Not long after, the Mexican line faltered, gradually bent under a withering fire, then broke and ran. The terror spread through their entire force and the Mexican Army turned and fled in the direction of Matamoros.

Though casualties were heavy for both sides, it was the far weaker American force that had emerged victorious in the Battle of Resaca de la Palma.

The loss most deeply felt among all the Americans was that of Major Jacob Brown who had always been so highly regarded. Now, with virtually unanimous agreement and with the concurrence of General Taylor, the name of the installation he had died to protect, Fort Texas—sometimes called Fort Taylor—was officially changed to Fort Brown.[71]

*[May 10, 1846 • Sunday]*

Neither Brevet Captain John Fremont nor Lieutenant Archibald Gillespie revealed to anyone else what the imperative secret orders were that the former received from the President, but what became so clear was that Fremont's whole attitude, as well as his course of action, abruptly changed: The deep cloak of depression that had enveloped him since his inglorious retreat from Gavilan Peak instantly disappeared, as did his determination to resume the surveying duties that had allegedly sent him to the West in the first place.[72]

Immediately after his principal guide, Joe Walker, had quit and walked away on March 14, Fremont had filled that position with Kit Carson, who had coveted it since the beginning of the expedition. But the massive depression that had descended upon Fremont with Walker's angry abandonment had made him taciturn and, except for giving orders, he spoke to no one except Carson as they headed north. Even when they'd stopped at Sutters Fort on March 21 to exchange their weary mounts for fresh ones, he refused to satisfy John Sutter's curiosity about where he and his men had been and what they had done and only said they'd be stopping by to see Peter Lassen at his rancho on Deer Creek.

They did reach Lassen's place, 250 miles up the Sacramento, on March 28, to exchange mounts again before continuing with the surveying mission up into the Oregon country.[73] When Lassen presented him with a letter dropped off a week or so earlier by Jim Clyman in case Fremont should come by, he read it quickly. It was an offer of assistance in guiding him wherever he wished to go in California. Fremont at once jotted his reply on the back of the same letter, thanking Clyman for the offer but rejecting it:

> *The California authorities object to my presence here and threaten to overwhelm me.*
>
> *If peace is preserved, I have no right or business here; if war ensues I shall be outnumbered 10 - 1 and be compelled to make good my retreat by a pursuing enemy...*

Leaving the letter with Lassen, Fremont resumed doggedly leading his freshly mounted team up the narrowing Sacramento but for the first time admitting to himself that much of his depression was being evoked by his tormenting notion that while other U.S. officers were probably already making great reputations for themselves battling the Mexicans, he was relegated to facing no greater an enemy than mosquitoes as he pursued the mundane act of surveying. The admission had not improved his mood.

His force pressed on but the weather itself thwarted him. The team managed to reach Mount Shasta but a heavy spring snow in the Cascades forced him back to Lassen's, where they remained until a wave of several days of much warmer weather sent them on their way north again on April 24.

Yesterday, finally in Oregon Territory, they had camped beneath the huge pines on the mid-east rim of Upper Klamath Lake. It was dusk when Bill Sigler, whom he'd sent earlier to carry dispatches back to Lassen's, came galloping in, attracted by the glow of Fremont's fire and calling his own name aloud so he wouldn't be shot. He thundered to a halt at the edge of the ring of firelight.

"Colonel!" He was obviously excited. "Ran into a feller with important dispatches for you. Wouldn't give 'em to me. Says they're secret stuff."

"Who was it?"

"Marine lieutenant. From Washington D.C. Feller named Gillespie, with a coupl'a guides from Lassen's. Ran into him 'bout sunset. Ridin' a pretty wore-out horse. Looks like they're bein' trailed close by some Injins. Modocs, I 'spect."

Fremont shook his head, unfamiliar with the name but his pulse quickening at the thought of secret dispatches and possible Indian trouble. "You fit to ride back and lead 'em in, Bill?"

"Yep."

"Do it then. Lead them in and watch your scalp. We'll meet you on the way along the lake edge."

Sigler grinned, wheeled his mount around and galloped off into the darkness. Fremont immediately doubled the guard, then selected ten good men to accompany him at daybreak, including Kit Carson. In addition, the pair of Delawares who had nominated themselves to be Fremont's guardian angels decided to trail along. The ensuing night was tense and no one got much sleep as they double-checked their carbines in the firelight. At last, however, they did turn in for an hour or so.

This morning, as first light was silhouetting the eastern peaks, they saddled up quickly and moved off southward along the big Upper Klamath's eastern shore. Throughout the day they followed the lake shore and it was close to sunset as they were nearing the southeastern tip of the big lake where the Klamath River flowed out of it when they were hailed by a dual call from Bill Sigler. With him were a pair of guides the commander had met at Lassen's—a Frenchie named Basil Lajeunesse and a half-breed known only as Denny—plus another rider unfamiliar to him whom Fremont took to be the marine messenger named Gillespie.

He was, and Sigler said there'd been no sign of the Modocs for most of the day and he figured they'd given up trailing them. Fremont was glad to hear that and they set up a little camp for the night. Fremont and Gillespie moved some distance away from the others and sat on the trunk of a wind-fallen pine and talked for a long while with no one to overhear. The commander was pleased to get the letters from Jessie and her father, but it was the oral transmission that intrigued him. Now with Gillespie's secret orders from President Polk safely—and orally—delivered, Fremont fairly bubbled with a newborn enthusiasm for what he hoped lay ahead.

After a bit they moved back and rejoined the others at the fire. One of Fremont's men had cooked soup and all shared a small portion before turning in. Weary as they were, sleep came quickly. Except for Fremont. The fire was dying and the commander sat alone by the glowing coals, his gaze inward. He had an important decision to make and he considered several alternatives before fastening on the one that set his heart thumping with excitement: For the glory and honor it would bring him, they would turn around and go back to California to do a great deed; they would raise as large a force as they could among the

Americans at Sutters Fort and, with himself as commander of course, they would engage the Californios, whoever they were presently under, defeat them, then make a gift of the whole of California to the United States, in the process of which his own greatness would shine. He would trust that in the war which followed, as he was convinced it would, his recent brigandage would be forgotten and he would be regaled as America's most current great heroic figure.

His head began to droop and he would undoubtedly have fallen asleep had not the faintest snap of a breaking twig jerked him into alertness. Dismay flooded him in the instant realization he had overlooked posting a guard. And Kit Carson, who *never* made the kind of silly mistakes that could wind up killing a man, had tonight neglected to reload his carbine after cleaning it. Just as Fremont bellowed an alarm, the war party of eighteen to twenty Hot Creek Modocs, who had, unseen, been continuing to follow Gillespie and his guides all day, burst onto the scene with fearsome shrieks. Almost instantly two of the sleeping men—Lajeunesse and the half-breed Denny—had tomahawk blades sunk in their skulls. Kit Carson leaped up and snatched his carbine leaning against a bush and snapped it repeatedly to no effect and he finally plunged away into the darkness. Fremont, who had no gun with him, jerked out his sheath knife and buried it to the hilt in the chest of one Modoc just as that Indian tomahawked the nearest man, who had jumped to his feet, one of the Delawares. The Modoc stabbed by Fremont staggered and fell. Instantly his followers halted, unbelieving. Their chief had fallen! They turned and fled into the darkness.

The whites took cover behind trees or logs and throughout the remainder of the night the two groups fired intermittently at one another. No one else was harmed and before dawn the Modocs disappeared.

*[May 11, 1846 • Monday • 3:00 p.m.]*

At last the cards, that in Washington, D.C. had been so unfavorably stacked against the Mormons for so long, abruptly changed and they were dealt a good hand.

The change in governmental attitude was due to the efforts of Elder Jesse C. Little, leader of the Eastern States Mission of the Mormons. Acting on orders received from Brigham Young to "...*make one more effort to convince Government that the Mormons can be of great value to the present Administration specifically and to the People of America generally,*" Little left

New Hampshire for the nation's capital bearing with him material sent by Young, including letters of introduction to Vice President George M. Dallas, Secretary of the Navy George Bancroft and other notables, along with instructions to officially seek whatever help for the Mormons the Government deigned to grant. There was great need of assistance: The Mormon flock had all but abandoned Nauvoo by now and this throng of nearly 20,000 on foot stretched three-quarters of the way across Iowa, frequently beset with complaints and quarreling. Despite this, even though none of them—except for Brigham Young—had any clear idea of their final destination, they remained motivated by faith alone that God Himself would sooner or later reveal to them The Promised Land.

Elder Little was empowered to offer Government the services of the Mormons in whatever capacity best served the interest of the United States: They could volunteer troops to occupy California; they could do the same to assist in the present difficulties with Mexico; they could massively occupy the disputed Oregon Territory; they could offer to transport army supplies with their teams and wagons; they could erect and garrison a series of forts along the Oregon Trail or elsewhere in Indian country for the aid of migrating U.S. citizens; they could build, wherever needed, good roads and ferries, improvements on the rough trails in the West; they could, in fact, perform quite well any task Government might have in mind.

As he passed through Philadelphia, Little took the time to convene a "special conference" of the Saints remaining. A young man named Thomas Leiper Kane, passing by the hall rented for this purpose, had his curiosity whetted and joined the crowd that was entering. Somewhat neurotic and definitely a romantic, Kane became entranced with the power of Elder Little's speaking and was deeply moved by his message. Kane was the son of John Kenzer Kane, Pennsylvania's attorney general and leader of the bar, who was not only the Democracy's elder statesman but a staunch political ally and friend of President James Knox Polk.[74]

After the address by Little, young Kane, who had been ailing for the past fortnight, sought him out, introduced himself and invited Little to his nearby home, hoping to gain further information and instruction about the Mormon order. Sensing a possible benefit of some magnitude, Little did so with especial eloquence, concentrating on the sufferings of the Saints, and Kane was even more moved. Then Little laid hands on the young man for a moment and prayed fervently. By the time he finished,

Kane had brightened considerably and enthusiastically declared himself cured, which surprised Little not at all, since he had long been noted among the Mormons as a healer and was affirmed to have cured many followers of their ills. Kane announced he was now determined to go west with the Mormons, share in whatever difficulties faced them, and become a devoted disciple of Brigham Young.

Upon reaching Washington D.C. two days ago, on May 9, Little met not only with Bancroft and Dallas, he had a brief introductory visit with President Polk that the Mormon Elder considered less than satisfactory. Upon leaving the White House, Little visited the final name on his list, the former U.S. Postmaster General Amos Kendall and again expressed the plight of the Mormons, the help they needed and what they were prepared to offer as repayment. Kendall, evidencing interest, promised to see the President about it. Despite fading hopes and well-concealed skepticism Little struck gold.

Two days later—this afternoon at three o'clock—he was summoned to Kendall's office and found the man looking pleased with himself. Kendall shook his hand vigorously and invited him to sit as he seated himself behind his massive desk.

"I have good news for you, Mr. Little," he beamed. "I have met with the President and he has agreed to help you Mormon people. The President designs to take possession of California for the United States and has decided that he will make this effort with Mormon help. You will be receiving orders for a force of Mormon men to march to California, occupy and fortify it in the name of the United States."

Little was stunned into silence and, after a slight pause, Kendall continued: "You are instructed to go forthwith to the Mormons and handpick two thousand of the most fit men among them. Of these, a thousand are to march to California and, as before stated, dash in and take possession. This body of men are to have their own selected chain of command, except for the commander, who will be appointed from among our military by the President. The second thousand are to be transported by ship, via Cape Horn, for the same purpose. All will receive pay, according to their rank, commensurate with that of regular United States troops.

"None of this," he added hastily "has yet been ordered by the President, but I have been assured that it will be in a few days; probably a week at the outside. Until that time, do please keep yourself available for instant call."

"I shall do so," Elder Little promised, having recovered his voice.

"The President, incidentally," Kendall concluded, "also asked me to convey to you his most sincere thanks for your forthcoming efforts."

[*May 13, 1846 · Wednesday · 11:00 a.m.*]

The United States Congress today declared war on the Republic of Mexico.

It was, for President James Knox Polk, the gratifying culmination of the planning, labors and maneuverings he had put into motion many weeks ago with his order sending General Taylor's army to occupy Texas all the way south to the Rio Grande, but with the admonition not to instigate any form of aggression against Mexico except in self defense, at which he, Polk, was to be informed by the swiftest possible communication.

The wait had seemed interminable and in the meanwhile, on May 9, at a meeting of his own Cabinet, full agreement had been reached: Should any hostilities be committed against Taylor's army, the President must at once recommend to Congress that war be declared. This was, of course, precisely what Polk had been attempting to instigate, but still no word of Mexican aggression had come.

The President, on the verge of preparing a message to Congress, had no intention of letting the matter drop. He suggested that this message he would prepare immediately after the Cabinet meeting should strongly recommend, on the basis of the number of insults already committed by Mexico against the United States, that Congress declare war. To this end he polled the Cabinet, beginning with the Secretary of War.

"Well," Buchanan replied, shifting uneasily in his chair, "I would be much better satisfied if we had actual hostilities occurring against our troops to go on, but I do feel we have ample cause without that and so I would recommend war."

The remainder of the Cabinet agreed, except for Secretary of the Navy Bancroft, who adamantly held out for an actual act of hostility to be committed by the Mexicans.

The President nodded. "I will then ask Congress today for a declaration of war. Mr. Secretary," he faced Buchanan, "will you please prepare the supporting documents." It was not a question.

Polk adjourned the two-hour meeting, immediately returning to his own desk. His pen flew across the pages as in succession he wrote about

Mexico's unpaid claims to America, the Mexican failure to acknowledge the true Texas boundaries, its refusal to accept Slidell as U.S. ambassador, plus considerable incidents of rhetorical bellicose defiance directed by the Mexicans at America. It was, Polk admitted to himself, a fairly weak basis upon which to ask Congress for a declaration of war, but he was reasonably confident it would have the desired result.

About six in the evening, just as he was finishing, the Adjutant General arrived at the White House in an excited state with news that the Southern mail had just arrived and, with it, an urgent dispatch from General Taylor informing the President that on April 25 a Mexican military force had crossed the Rio Grande and killed or captured the entire complement of two dragoon companies under command of Captain Thornton.

Polk immediately sent a messenger to summon Cabinet members for an emergency meeting at seven-thirty this evening. Later, just as they were seated, Buchanan arrived with his draft requesting Congress to declare war and handed it to the President who looked it over, a tightened expression developing as he read. Buchanan had written:

> ...I want to memorialize foreign courts.... In the making of war, we do not intend to acquire New Mexico, California, or any other portion of Mexican territory.

There were other such remarks and Polk noticed with sardonic amusement the looks of consternation on the faces of the other Cabinet members, one of whom murmured in a barely audible voice, "Not take California? Then why all this labor?"

"Gentlemen," said Polk as he put down Buchanan's paper and picked up another from his desk, "before we go any further, I would like to read you an express dispatch received just this evening from General Taylor." He did so swiftly and then added, as he lowered the letter, "Obviously, we now have causative justification for a declaration of war from Congress. And we will take California and other such lands as may be necessary to indemnify us."

"If this be made known," Buchanan burst out angrily, "then we shall have war with England certainly and very likely with France, too!"

"I don't really think so," the President said, a distinct tightness still in his voice. "But I would rather accept war with England or France or all the powers of Christendom rather than make this pledge that we would not, if we could fairly and honorably acquire California or *any* other part of the Mexican territory which we desired."

Buchanan bristled even more and didn't back down, despite the verbal assault received from other Cabinet members. For upwards of two hours the heated discussion continued until finally Polk put a stop to it. He dipped his pen and struck out from Buchanan's draft those passages with which he took issue and substituted new comments of his own. When finished, he read it aloud—all but Buchanan and Bancroft approving—and handed it to the Secretary of State, who was still red-faced and angry.

"Here," he ordered, "take this and do a final for Congress."

That night Polk finished his diary entry with the comment: *"...much exhausted of incessant application, anxiety and labour."*

In the morning, however, he worked hard writing a series of notes to the Congressional majority leaders and committee chairmen, keenly aware that even with the better ammunition of General Taylor's report, it was not a given that Congress would go along with a declaration of war. Once again the final sentence in his day's diary entry reflected his concern: *"It was a day of great anxiety to me."*

The following morning, May 11, he summoned to the White House Senator Thomas Benton, Chairman of the Committee on Military Affairs. Polk let the Senator read the revised recommendation to Congress. When Benton finished, he handed the document back to the President and shook his head.

"While I can assure you," he said sadly, "that I will vote the required men and dollars, I think I need to remind you that I did not favor sending our army to the Rio Grande, and I am not in favor of an aggressive war such as this." With a brief dip of his head, Benton turned and left the office.

At noon the President personally took the important document to the Hill and addressed a joint session of Congress. The opening comment for authorizing and financing an army asserted that "the Rio Grande is an exposed frontier" and then after relating what had occurred up to April 25, Polk went on to state:

> *...the cup of forbearance had been exhausted even before the recent information from the frontier of the Del Norte* [Rio Grande]. *We*

> *have tried every effort at reconciliation...But now, after reiterated menaces, Mexico has passed the boundary of the United States, has invaded our territory and shed American blood upon the American soil. She has proclaimed that hostilities have commenced, and that the two nations are at war.*
>
> *As war exists, and, notwithstanding all our efforts to avoid it, exists by the act of Mexico herself, we are called upon by every consideration of duty and patriotism to vindicate with decision the honor, the rights, and the interests of our country."*[75]

The senators weren't so sure and were far more enrapt at first with the grinding of their own political axes and, so far as the President was able to determine, were considering outright war with Mexico most pertinently as merely a factional element disruptive to the Democratic Party. The House, however, took the matter far more seriously. For ninety minutes after assimilating the principal document, the joint session listened to supporting documents until they finally terminated hearing any more and in a half-hour approved the President's measure by an overwhelming vote of forty-to-two from the Senate and 173 - 14 from the House—an aggregate vote of 213 - 16.

Afterward, President Polk stood again and the excitedly murmuring senators and representatives quickly quieted. It was the chief executive's crowning moment and his voiced boomed with clarity in the great hall: "I call upon this joint session of the Congress of the United States to now fully authorize a Declaration of War against the Republic of Mexico."

It wasn't quite that easy. Congress wanted more time for serious contemplation, but there was actually little doubt of the outcome. Two days later—today, May 13, 1846—the Senate and House agreed that a state of war existed against México due to that country's own aggressive actions and its own already declared war against the United States and they voted the drafting of 50,000 men and $10-million for the prosecution of that war.

# Chapter 4

◆

*[May 16, 1846 • Saturday]*

Secretary of the Navy George Bancroft, in his office at the War Department in Washington, D.C., this morning dictated a set of secret orders to be transmitted without delay to the U.S. Naval Commander in the Pacific, John D. Sloat. They were orders that would leave no doubt in Sloat's mind as to what he must now do to protect and further the interests of the United States on the continent's West Coast. As always, it would take weeks for the orders to reach their destination, but at least now the die was cast. Among the dictates Bancroft laid out were these:

*You will consider the most important object to be, to take and hold possession of San Francisco; and this you will do without fail.... You will also take possession of Mazatlan and Monterey, one or both, as your force will permit.... If information here is correct, you can establish friendly relations between your squadron and the inhabitants of each of these three places.... A connection between California, and even Sonora, and the present government of Mexico is supposed scarcely to exist. You will, as opportunity offers, conciliate the confidence of the people in California, and also in Sonora, toward the government of the United States; and you will endeavor to render the relations with the United States as intimate and as friendly as possible....*

*[May 28, 1846 • Thursday • 11 a.m.]*

The senior U.S. Senator from Missouri, Thomas Hart Benton, had throughout his tenure, always been considered a powerful voice in that body. He was also considered by many to be a big bag of wind—there were few in Congress who could come anywhere near matching his filibustering skills. Early on he had learned an important lesson and today it worked to perfection: He knew that if he maintained the filibuster long enough, those enemies who might try to block passage of a bill he wanted to propose, would be unable to tolerate his droning voice any longer and would eventually give up and walk out. That was precisely what occurred today: As soon as the odds tipped in his own favor, he broke off the filibuster and set about ramming through the bill he was currently supporting. The maneuver almost always worked.

In fact, it worked today to perfection.

Old Bullion, as Benton was sometimes called, had begun this particular filibuster three days ago. Only a few moments ago, as a few more of the opposition members drifted out of chambers and, with the odds now stabilized in his favor, he introduced his bill, and once again, when the vote was called, his measure passed by a slim margin. Few of the Senators recognized its importance: When the Oregon Territory boundary question was opened again, no territory north of the forty-ninth parallel could be requested.

*[May 28, 1846 · Thursday · 6 p.m.]*

General Zachary Taylor smiled, as much pleased by what met the eye as his cheering army behind him. They had just topped a low rise and saw before them the city of Matamoras. It was the city that had, at least temporarily, become his base of operations.

Though he would not admit it to anyone just now, the commander of the army was undergoing a prolonged ambivalence. It had been riding him ever since he'd ordered the withdrawal, much to the disappointment of many of the men following him at this moment. The situation had its genesis almost immediately following the Battle of Resaca de la Palma. It had taken General Taylor two full days to write out the official reports of the battles to submit to Adjutant General Roger Jones in Washington D.C.. The first day, May 16, had been spent writing out the details of the Battle of Palo Alto, and the entire next day doing the same for the Battle of Resaca de la Palma. Despite his inability to correctly spell most Mexican words and many English ones as well, the reports were quite well done.[76]

The next day—May 18—Taylor temporarily abandoned Fort Brown

and moved his army across the Rio Grande and occupied a foreign city. It was the first time any American force had done so since the War of 1812 and he was proud that he had it to his credit...and highly pleased that war correspondents were feverishly writing copy. On the same day he left a guard squad behind and marched his army in pursuit of General Arista's panic-stricken army. They followed the trail to the vicinity of the town of Linares, about sixty miles southwest, but Taylor finally called off the pursuit and returned with his fatigued troops in mid-afternoon today to await additional transportation and reinforcements.

The correspondents thought this the action of a very wise general.

*[June 3, 1846 • Wednesday • 10:00 a.m.]*

Before noon today, John Fremont had established his corps of topographical engineers in a bivouac at the foot of the rather strange buttes ten kilometers northeast of where Butte Creek emptied into the Sacramento River.[77] This was sixty miles upstream from Sutters Fort, which Fremont was avoiding, although they had camped nearby previously. There was good reason—too many people at Sutters Fort, residents and visitors alike, and not all of them would be favorably inclined to what Fremont had in mind. Not even Sutter himself, who had turned his place into a largely American installation, would Fremont allow to become privy to his plans; Sutter had too much to lose if current plans went awry. That was a lesson he'd learned earlier, when he had supported Micheltorena.

They hadn't left their camp near the foot of Upper Klamath Lake quite so quickly as Lieutenant Gillespie had thought they would after he'd delivered his secret messages to Fremont. The expedition leader had a score to settle and he'd taken three days doing so. He'd sent a message to the other camp and had the remainder of his force join him here. Then the majority of them, Gillespie included, went on what Kit Carson laughingly designated as "Johnny Fremont's Injin Hunt." They tracked the retreated Modocs to their village about ten miles distant, killed a good many of them on the spot, burned their village, then tracked down a number of the retreaters and killed them, too. That a fair portion of the latter were women, children and the aged, who could not flee as rapidly as the males, made no difference, all were slain.

Their savagery sated, they headed down the Sacramento and arrived at Peter Lassen's spread again, who eagerly told them the latest news: The warship *U.S. Portsmouth*, under Captain John B. Montgomery, was presently anchored in San Francisco Bay close to Yerba Buena and was reported well packed with supplies. Although Fremont still had ample goods to see him through for some time yet to come, he immediately dispatched Lieutenant Gillespie there with an official requisition of what were listed as "urgently needed supplies" and at the top of his list were 300 pounds of American rifle lead, a full keg of gunpowder and 8,000 percussion caps. The lead alone was sufficient for the molding of close to 10,000 bullets. This material, Fremont added, was to be sent to him at once, directed to the place where he would establish a substantial camp at the Buttes, to which Gillespie could guide the shipment. Gillespie left down the Sacramento at once in a large open cargo boat rowed by four of Lassen's hired men and Fremont wasted no time continuing with his force to the Buttes.

Word quickly reached Sutters Fort of Fremont's arrival and everyone was questioning why he had returned. A rumor quickly solidified that he'd come back to take control of California for America and launch an attack against Castro or Pio Pico, while that pair were trying to unseat one another. Almost immediately scores of the Americans at Sutters Fort left to join Fremont. They flooded into his camp, eagerly volunteering to serve in whatever move he would make against the Californios.

One of the men from Sutters Fort brought some interesting news: A squad of eight Mexican soldiers, led by Castro's personal secretary Lieutenant d'Arce and another of the same rank named Alviso, had been sent to Sonora with a requisition for nearly 200 horses, which Castro intended using in his attack on Pio Pico.[78]

The squad had herded the animals to a crossing of the Sacramento just above Sutters Fort, picketed the animals there and stayed overnight. They'd told Sutter they would be crossing the American River and moving on with their herd some sixteen miles south to the Cosumnes River where they planned to camp for several days to rest the horses.

Fremont quickly conferred with a group of about twenty-five of his men who immediately, changed into civilian garb and, led by Ezekiel "Zeke" Merritt, mounted and went off at a brisk trot. The commander then met briefly with his remaining men, after which he announced to the civilian assemblage standing about curiously that he and his surveyors were heading for his old campground just up the American River from Sutters Fort, which would be more convenient for them. Within an hour they were on their way, leaving behind two men to escort Gillespie and his supply boat to the American River site when he arrived. Most of the civilians who had flocked to the Buttes to see him, perhaps to join him in whatever he was contemplating, trailed after them at a distance. By noon the next day, May 18, Fremont had reestablished his old camp.

An hour or so later, Fremont arrived at Sutters Fort in bad humor. He was met by John Sutter who was flushed with excitement over the rumor he'd heard about Fremont having returned to lead a force against the Californios and to take the whole of California for the United States. Fremont became irate and lashed out at him: "You are a damned Mexican! If you don't like what I'm doing, I will set you across the San Joaquín River and you can go and join the other Mexicans!"

Captain Sutter was stunned by the rebuff and Fremont immediately realized the mistake he'd made and actually apologized. Sutter, entirely believing Fremont was acting in accord with orders from Washington D.C., accepted the apology and matters warmed between them. Soon Sutter was gossiping that none other than Governor Pio Pico had stopped by briefly in the morning the other day before moving on toward Sonoma, but without divulging anything about his mission. Toward evening that same day, a large herd of horses from Sonora had been brought past here by a squad of men under a Californio lieutenant named Don Francisco d'Arce. Trying to get them across at the Straits of Carquinez would've been much too slow, they'd said, and this was the only reasonable alternative, even if much longer. D'Arce and his squad had stayed at the fort overnight, Sutter told him, and had moved southward early the next morning, May 16.

"Interesting," Fremont remarked in a barely interested manner. "Where were they going?"

"To General Castro, evidently, who I believe is at Santa Clara. Lieutenant d'Arce said they were going to rest for a few days when they reached the Cosumnes. Which means he'll probably be heading out from there early tomorrow."

"Interesting," Fremont repeated, apparently disinterested, his expression not betraying concern as he wondered if his men had reached the herd in time. He was glad, though, that he'd come here and talked with Sutter, since that had effectively established his own alibi if his men succeeded. He was well aware that he was an officer of the U.S. Army and prohibited from participating in such an action without specific orders, which was not what his secret orders included.

# The Infinite Dream

Fremont returned to his camp and waited a bit nervously. Well over 100 civilians—hunters and settlers, good men and reprobates, the majority Americans—had joined his own men at their fires and were chatting amiably, mainly about what might possibly lie ahead, but getting no satisfactory answers from the surveyors. In his tent, Fremont lay atop his blanket, eyes open, senses alert. It was nearly midnight when he heard the thumping of hooves and he instantly leaped up and stepped outside. A broad smile creased his features as his men surged into camp with the horses and herded them into the rope corral that had been prepared.

Ezekiel Merritt, grinning broadly and obviously very pleased, rode up to him, dismounted and saluted. "Got 'em, sir. All of 'em. Easy as pie."

"Tell me what happed, Zeke" Fremont said, still smiling.

Merritt related the events succinctly: They had ridden unopposed into d'Arce's camp, weapons leveled, and demanded the horses. There was no resistance and d'Arce himself and his men were permitted to ride off toward distant Santa Clara without harm, but with verbal abuse from several of the raiders ringing in their ears.

A die, of sorts, had been cast.

Over the days following, many meetings were held with the civilians who still flocked to join them and a sizable number, the best and most anti-Californio—were "unofficially" inducted by Fremont as supernumerary to his own force and given immediate basic drilling for several hours each day so at least they would be able to follow elementary commands and not be merely a rabble.

On May 24 a special messenger arrived from Sonoma with urgent news that the Americans there, under self-proclaimed leader William Ide, had formed themselves into an anti-Californio unit inspired by Fremont's presence at the Buttes and near Sutters Fort. They easily took over the befuddled little Mexican garrison at Sonoma, and when they learned that a fair number of Californios, estimated as anywhere from forty to eighty men, had formed under Joaquín de la Torre, a quickly raised force of thirty of the Americans under Henry L. Ford met the enemy near Vallejo's Petaluma Rancho and a brief fight ensued. Four or five of the Californios were killed or wounded and the rest fled, but were thought still to be in the area and preparing to make another attack. Could Fremont come and help? Fremont could.

Leaving his American River installation under command of "...

one of my better civilians...," Fremont and his regulars rode at once to Sonoma and, for miles around, searched for the supposedly hidden De la Torre's force, of which no trace was found.

General Castro, learning of a largely impromptu army presence on the American River, immediately concluded that it presaged an invasion of Southern California. Consul Larkin, also learning of it, wrote what appeared to be an innocent letter to Fremont, inviting an exchange of news and lightly chiding him for not having written to him. When those previously uninformed Americans of the countryside heard of it, many of them flocked to Fremont's camp to enlist. The same thought seemed to be close to the surface in everyone's mind: Fremont had returned to initiate war against the Californios and occupy California for the United States. Even more men came to help.

A plan was juggled about: If they could raise a small group of Americans. with little to lose, who could egg Castro into attacking them, Fremont could then march his force to their protection. If this caused Castro's army to attack Fremont's, which seemed very likely, then the American force would be justified in retaliation with a counter-attack and the actual hot war for California could begin.

Even Fremont believed the plan just might work.[79]

*[June 3, 1846 · Wednesday · 11:00 a.m.]*

The order to Colonel Kearny was written in Washington D.C. today in the War Department, but stemming from a direct order by President Polk. It would, of course, be some while before the written order reached him, but in the very writing of it, a die had been cast that would affect nations and their important leaders for a very long time to come. On this day, President James K. Polk issued the order to Colonel Stephen Watts Kearny of the First Dragoons to move at once with his force to take official possession of New Mexico and California for the United States.

In essence, these orders—so long anticipated by the residents of those territories—were a commencement of the official connection of the United States with California and a vast portion of the American West; all of it stemming from the initial Exploring Expedition that had been undertaken six years earlier by U.S. Navy Lt. John Wilkes through orders originating from the President.

Hardly even noticed at this moment, the face—and the future—of the United States of America had just become irrevocably altered.

## The Infinite Dream

*[June 7, 1846 • Sunday]*

All matters of interest that occurred at Sutters Fort were carefully noted through faithfully maintained entries penned into the fort's daily logbook entitled *New Helvetia Diary: A Record of Events, Kept by John A. Sutter and His Clerks*. The entries, however, were often exasperatingly brief and today's was no exception:

*Sunday 7 Arrived Capt Sutter and party from Campaign.*

What was not explained was what kind of campaign, against whom, and the results. It said nothing of the unidentified spy who had arrived in the midst of night more than a week ago and conferred for some time with John Sutter, nor of the man's departure, as surreptitiously as his arrival. There was no explanation of his bringing word that General Castro had learned that the Americans at Sutters Fort were preparing to mount a force against him, that he had immediately summoned a party of Mokelumne Indians under Chief Raphero to his headquarters at Mission San José and, with gifts distributed and promises of more, engaged them to launch a surprise attack against the foreigners. They were to kill all the Americans, burn their houses, the fort and wheat fields and take their horses. The gifts were probably superfluous, as Raphero envied and despised all Americans, but he and some of his subchiefs accepted the fine clothing offered them and were pleased when good weapons were distributed to some of the warriors.

Sutter's informant had no idea when the projected attack was to occur, but that it would be led by Raphero was disconcerting. The Mokelumne chief was well noted for his courage and sagacity, his leadership abilities and, most of all, for his innate cold-blooded ferocity, exemplified in the fact that recently, for an infraction of rules, he had blandly slain his own brother-in-law. He was a formidable enemy and though in this essentially lawless frontier, he would probably never have been prosecuted for the crime, Sutter considered him such a threat that, acting under his authority as a Mexican *alcalde*, he sent a squad of his own Indian guards to arrest him. Scornful of such apprehension, Raphero made no resistance and allowed himself to be bound and brought to the fort.

At once an impromptu trial was held and the Mokelumne chief was found guilty of murder. Sutter sentenced him to immediate death. When

James Marshall refused an order to head up a firing squad, Sutter himself selected a squad of his Indian trappers to carry out the execution. The riflemen positioned themselves but then a brief delay ensued to remove a horse standing well behind, but in the line of fire.

"Why don't you shoot me?" Raphero snarled. "Are you afraid?"

Within a minute the firing squad raised their rifles, the command was given, six lead balls slammed into his chest and he fell dead without another sound. So impressed was Marshall with such bravery on the chief's part, he raised his own squad of whites and buried Raphero with full military honors, complete with a volley fired over the new grave.

The following day, marauding Mokelumnes were reported in a distant pasture trying to steal horses. Sutter instantly decided that rather than waiting to be attacked, he would initiate his own assault and selected forty men—twenty-five whites and fifteen Indians—to make up his force. They moved out at once and detected the marauders in a thicket, but a rain swollen stream would have to be crossed. Swiftly building a small raft on which to float their ammunition and weapons, they started across, pushing the raft before them. Abruptly the water was too deep and the men were swept off their feet. Some could not swim and they snatched at the raft and tried to climb aboard, causing it to tilt severely and many of the weapons slid off and went to the bottom.

Despite the disturbing accident, all got safely across and the remaining weapons were distributed to the best shooters. The Mokelumnes had taken advantage of the incident to slip away and, since it was late, Sutter's party camped for the night and dried their saturated clothes at the several fires that were built.

Early in the morning the tracking was resumed as rapidly as possible and they overtook their quarry by mid-morning, who immediately took cover in a patch of very dense cover; so dense, in fact, that Sutter's men had to cut their way through it with their knives. Marshall and one of the Indian hunters were first to reach the inner clearing where the marauders had hidden themselves behind two large fallen tree trunks, between them a gap through which the Mokelumnes could shoot their bows.

Almost at once a whining arrow barely missed Marshall's head and struck his companion just above his ear, lodging itself under his scalp. The pair withdrew a bit and Marshall extracted the arrow. The wounded man, realizing the arrow was poisoned, quickly gathered up some selected plants and chewed them into a wad to make a poultice, which he applied, and Marshall reached into his own mouth and extracted a large, well-masticated wad of tobacco to seal the medicinal herbs in place over the poultice.

Without sufficient weapons, Sutter and his men continued their firing for several hours, but at such a distance they only succeeded in wounding one Mokelumne and another of their own took an arrow in his arm. Both sides eventually withdrew. Later, following the return of Sutter and his men to the fort, the scribe of the *New Helvetia Diary* felt compelled to pen an explanatory note which, for him, was much more elaborative than he was accustomed to writing:

> *Rufino* [sic], *Chief of the Moquelumnes* [sic], *was today tried for murder, found guilty, and executed.*[80]

[June 14, 1846 • Sunday • 9:00 a.m.]

William L. Todd was weary. He had worked all night in his quarters in Sonoma on creating a flag design for California, which he intended to have become the banner of the Americans here. It was meant to be a symbol of those who were opposed to stringent controls over their adopted California lands, whether by the Mexican government or by the Californios, who lately, under the influence of both Governor Pio Pico and Commanding General Castro, had become so insurgent against their parent government. Now that flag was finished and, while hardly what Todd considered a memorable piece of artwork, he was nevertheless proud of his own efforts.

To resounding cheers from American neighbors, Todd's friend, William B. Ide, had immediately raised the new banner to the top of a seventy-foot pole.

The flag's basic background was a rectangle of the unbleached light brown cotton, known as "common domestic", about three feet wide and four and a half feet long, on which Todd, who admittedly was no artist, had very clumsily rendered a single crude star in the upper left corner, exemplifying the lone star symbol of Texas. At top center, in reddish brown paint, was the clumsily-rendered figure of what Todd declared was a grizzly bear—representative of the many bears of this species that roamed the area—but Todd's illustration looked so much more like a shoat than a grizzly that the native Californios were calling it *Coche*, their common name for a pig. Along the flag's bottom edge, just as crudely rendered in relatively small letters, were the words *California Republic*.

Immediately dubbed "the Bear Flag," this was now officially, in the view of Todd and his friends, the flag of the newest possession of the United States of America—California.[81] Fremont, upon viewing it, roared with laughter and declared it was certainly a good enough banner under which to fight what he now dubbed "the Bear Flag Revolt."

*[June 14, 1846 • Sunday • 3:00 p.m.]*

That the Saints were now being given the opportunity to officially serve the United States in the newly declared Mexican War was a matter of great joy for the Mormon leadership specifically and its membership generally. In its own way, it also gave the people of the United States a clearer view of the order that was now not only being sanctioned by the Federal Government through order of President Polk himself, it provided the Saints with a gigantic boost in self-image at a time when the entire sect was teetering perilously on the brink of extinction.

None of this was intended, since it all resulted from a colossal error.

The matter had its genesis several weeks back, when the ragtag Missouri Volunteers were given the order to present themselves to Colonel Stephen Watts Kearny at Fort Leavenworth for service in the Mexican War. Nothing was stated in the official orders that prohibited these men from being mounted so, almost to a man, each arrived on his own horse and Kearny had little real choice but to accept them as mounted troops in the United States Cavalry, a branch already top-heavy in its ranks, but leaving Kearny still more or less bereft of the foot troops that he so sorely needed. Worse yet, though all these recruits were experienced riders, they arrived in tattered homespun, most of them weaponless, none having any real inkling of military organization, chain-of-command protocol, or requisite Cavalry horsemanship.

Kearny immediately had them formed into a regiment; the First Missouri Mounted Volunteers. He also had them equipped with weapons and uniforms and ordered his officers to inaugurate a crash course in military drill, establishment of camps and fundamental military discipline and tactics, all in the hope they would be to some degree effective in the coming campaign.

Whatever his other military skills, Kearny was acknowledged by his peers as "one of the very best" in the business of military organization and in a remarkably short time he had established what he had been ordered to call the Army of the West. The core of this body was his already well established and thoroughly experienced First Dragoons, comprised of six troops of his own regiment. The officer selected to command the First Missouri Volunteers was, in a major irony, none other than the former Missouri attorney from the town of Liberty, who not so terribly long ago had prevented an out-of-control mob of Missourians from executing the Mormon leadership in the town of Far West, Colonel Alexander W. Doniphan.

Himself no slouch at military organization, Doniphan formed his raw volunteers, 856 in number, into eight companies, with the left-overs incorporated into a battalion of infantry, including 145 men in two basic companies, plus 250 men tagged as companies of light artillery. The majority remaining at that point were ear-marked as an elite company of cavalry comprised of 107 men from St. Louis, who named themselves the Laclede Rangers. Finally, there were also those who comprised his staff troops, plus a single detachment of topographical engineers.

Kearny had just finished approving these formations when Colonel Thomas L. Kane arrived at Fort Leavenworth from Washington with orders directly from the President to Colonel Kearny concerning the projected army of Mormons. On his journey toward this frontier post, Kane had been accompanied by Mormon Apostle Jesse C. Little as far as St. Louis; Little then moving on to connect with Brigham Young in Iowa with the good news of the accomplishment of their goal with the President; Kane heading directly to Fort Leavenworth with the President's orders for Kearny in regard to the Mormons.

Still deeply concerned over his lack of infantry, Kearny was highly pleased with the order, which would undoubtedly provide those foot troops so sorely needed. He immediately dispatched Captain James Allen to take the offer at once to Council Bluffs, on the western rim of Iowa Territory and deliver it personally into the hands of Brigham Young. The Fort Leavenworth commander was gearing up to march for California and he wanted those Mormons here, prepared to march, as swiftly as possible. Allen mounted up and left immediately.

That, finally, brought the matter more clearly into focus in regard to the major error that had originated in Washington D.C. Polk's order to Kearny regarding the Mormons for use in the Mexican War was dictated in line with his strong conviction that none of the Saints should be officially enrolled in the United States Army until Kearny's force reached California. However, the order thereafter issued by the War Department was carelessly drafted, in such a way as to make it official that as soon as the Saints reached Fort Leavenworth, a Mormon Battalion was to be formed and its men to be immediately inducted into the Army of the West.[82]

[June 15, 1846 · Monday]

The deed was done; the first of President James Polk's four principal objectives had been accomplished. With the signing of the Oregon Convention in Washington D.C. today, the line permanently separating British territory from American in the far Northwest was agreed upon by both nations to be the forty-ninth parallel.

Polk considered it a distinct victory—successfully grasping a great mass of Pacific coastal territory from the British without becoming engaged in a war the Americans could not have won. Such victory, however, had not come without cost; a steep cost, indeed, and one that could now very easily thwart Polk in his goal to succeed in the remaining three measures so paramount on his agenda.

In the midst of all this, on June 2 while President Polk was engaged in a cabinet meeting to address the problem of how to occupy New Mexico Territory and still move on before winter to invade California, Jesse Little's not-so-subtly threatening letter landed on his desk. If accommodation was not afforded the Mormons, Little wrote—almost wholly without basis for his threat—he would have no recourse but to "...*cross the trackless ocean*" and negotiate with the British, throwing the weight of the entire worldwide Mormon manpower behind the Crown "...*for certain concessions*" to the Saints.[83] For Polk, who had little accurate idea of the strength or manpower of the Mormons, although he had been deliberately misled by Little to believe it was in excess of 40,000 men *domestically*, and only that they were presently migrating westward to some undisclosed destination, the threat had to be taken seriously and he took immediate steps to nullify it. As he wrote in his diary before turning in:

> TUESDAY, 2nd June, 1846—*The Cabinet met today; all members present except the Atty. Gen'l, who was detained at his residence by severe indisposition. The manner of conducting the war with*

Mexico was the chief topic considered. The expedition against California was definitely settled, the Cabinet being unanimous in favor of such an expedition.

In pursuance of a conference on the subject between the Secretary of War and myself on yesterday, the Secretary read the rough draft of an order to Col. Kearney [sic] of the U.S. army, who was designated to command the expedition. Upon several points the order was modified upon my suggestion. It was in substance that as soon as Col. Kearney took possession of Santa Fe, he was to leave a sufficient force to hold it, and proceed without delay with the balance of his command & the mounted men ordered out from Missouri some three weeks ago, towards California, if in his judgment he could reach California before the winter set in. 1,000 additional mounted volunteers were ordered out from Missouri to proceed to Santa Fe, or follow Col. Kearney to California as he might order.... It was agreed that Col. Kearney should be authorized to take into service any emigrants (American citizens) whom he might find in California or who may go out with these munitions of War and Military stores. Col. Kearney was also authorized to receive into service as volunteers, a few hundred of the Mormons who are now on their way to California, with a view to conciliate them, attach them to our country, & prevent them from taking part against us...

The following day, in a private meeting with Little and Amos Kendall, President Polk told Little that the U.S. was at war with Mexico and asked if 500 or more of the Mormons now en route to California would be willing *on their arrival in that country* to volunteer and enter the army in that war, under command of a U.S. officer. Little, masking his elation, replied that he had no doubt they would quite willingly do so, adding that if the U.S. would take them into service, he would immediately overtake them and make such arrangements.

The President nodded and said he would see Little on the morrow; he did not, however, reveal to him anything about the present projected Kearny expedition. The Mormons, if taken into service, would constitute less than a quarter of Kearny's command and Polk's principal reasoning for taking them into service would simply be nothing more than the dual purpose of conciliating them and preventing them from assuming a hostile demeanor toward the U.S. after arriving in California. He instructed Secretary of War Marcy to this end and Marcy, this same day, wrote an extensive letter to Kearny in which, in part, he declared:

> ...It is understood that a considerable number of American citizens are now settled on the Sacramento river near Suter's [sic] establishment, called "Nueva Helvetia," who are well disposed toward the United States. Should you on your arrival to the country, find this to be the true state of things there, you are authorized to organize and receive into the service of the United States such portion of these citizens as you may think useful to aid you to hold possession of the country. You will, in that case, allow them, so far as you shall judge proper, to select their own officers. A large discretionary power is invested in you, in regard to these matters, as well as to all others in relation to the expedition confided to your command.... I am directed by the President to say that the rank of brevet brigadier general will be conferred on you as soon as you commence your movement toward California, and sent round to you by sea, or over the country, or to the care of the commandant of our squadron in the Pacific. In that way, cannon, arms, ammunition, and supplies for the land forces will be sent to you.[84]

Now it was June 15 and at last, whatever the ramifications might be, the Oregon Treaty signed with Great Britain today gave that portion of Oregon south of the Forty-ninth Parallel to the United States, while the portion of territory above that line, to the Alaskan border, was given to Great Britain, including Vancouver Island, thus providing the British access to Pacific coastal waters.

Everyone, it seemed, breathed a sigh of relief that at least one potential war had been averted.

*[June 16, 1846 • Tuesday]*

On this day, when Stephen Watts Kearny commenced the march of his troops westward from Fort Leavenworth, he relinquished forever his military rank of colonel. Beginning this day, by special order of President James Polk and transmitted by Secretary of War William L. Marcy, he was Brevet Brigadier General Kearny.

Although most definitely gratified with his promotion, Kearny was also irked that the anticipated arrival of the Mormon men from Council Bluffs had not occurred. Since Captain Allen, whom he'd sent to fetch them, was one of his most reliable junior officers, his irritation was also spiked with an element of genuine concern.

While the force with which he left Fort Leavenworth amounted to 1,558 men, he'd already dispatched a detachment of 242 men of the First Missouri to convey 100 wagons and 800 head of cattle to Bents Fort on the Arkansas River in the Colorado country. This was to serve as a supply and staging area for Kearny's expedition. The Army of the West that Kearny was personally leading was comprised of a full battalion of Missouri Mounted Volunteers, five squadrons of the First Dragoons, and the First Regiment of Missouri Volunteers, led by Colonel Doniphan. In addition, there were a number of Indian guides, a French interpreter, and a handful of U.S. topographical engineers under command of Lieutenant William Emory.

This, then, comprised the total of 1,800 men that left Fort Leavenworth today on a march that would eventually take the main body of troops to Santa Fe in New Mexico and, providing conditions were favorable, on into California. But where, General Kearny wondered, were the Mormons, who were to become a quarter of his entire force and the majority of his infantry troops? He had left orders at Fort Leavenworth for them, as soon as they showed up, to follow on his trail immediately and overtake him if possible. But the question continued to haunt him.

Where was Captain Allen and his 500 Mormons?

*[June 25, 1846 • Thursday]*

The very little, essentially ineffective, so-called Bear Flag Revolt, in which John C. Fremont played a significant role, for all intents and purposes ended today after less than a fortnight of existence. The brief role of the group, mainly Americans, was of little moment except to a few individuals in particular.[85]

After his loss of the fine herd of horses, Lieutenant Francisco d'Arce had hastened to General Castro at Santa Clara and reported on June 12, quite accurately, that the entire number of horses he was in the process of herding here, had been stolen at gunpoint by a group of *Americanos*. Castro's fury bloomed and assuming, rather accurately, this to be the initial move in an American effort to take California by force, he issued a proclamation to raise a force of Californios to defend their land. In that proclamation, Castro exhorted his fellow citizens:

> ...to rise en masse, irresistible and just.... Duty leads me to death or victory. I am a Mexican soldier and I will be free and independent or die with pleasure for those inestimable blessings.

That, however, took a couple of days and it was not until June 14 that he marched this force of 250 men forward. It was a bit too slow. Fremont had already set up camp on the American River a few miles upstream from the Sacramento and was busy arousing the settlers there when an express reached him the day before yesterday—June 23—from eighty-mile distant Sonoma, revealing that Castro's whole force was crossing San Francisco Bay, with Sonoma as its intended target. Fremont wasted no time leaping to action and at 2 a.m. today, leading ninety American riflemen, he arrived in that valley ahead of Castro. Fremont immediately sent out a scouting party of twenty men, which encountered a squadron of seventy of Castro's dragoons led by Captain Joaquín de la Torre and attacked it without hesitation, defeating it soundly, killing and wounding five men without any casualty whatsoever to themselves. De la Torre barely managed to escape, but only with the loss of his transport boats and having nine brass cannon spiked.

By this time Zeke Merritt's force, now numbering thirty-three men, was already approaching the sleepy little hamlet of Sonoma. The move was not approved by Fremont and he refused to take part, but Merritt went ahead anyway and "captured" the dazed little community. Even though it had held nine readied pieces of brass artillery and 200 stand of rifles, no defensive moves were made. Merritt's force then immediately descended upon La Hacienda where they found the unsuspecting General Mariano Vallejo and his guests sound asleep—those guests including Lieutenant Colonel Victor Prudon, as well as the general's brother, Captain Salvador Vallejo, and the general's brother-in-law, trader Jacob P. Leese. Awakened, the erstwhile general was more than a little confused.

"What is this all about?" he demanded.

"You and these others," Merritt replied, "are prisoners of war."

"What war?" Vallejo asked, still confused.

Merritt grinned. "The war between the United States and Mexico, of which California is a part. Get dressed, all of you. You are being taken to Sutters Fort, where you will be incarcerated as prisoners of war until further notice."[86]

Vallejo provided fine brandy for his "guests" and they sat down to discuss the matter. When it was explained and a formal statement of "terms" written out, which, by its third paragraph, created the Republic of California, all present quite willingly signed it. They also learned that four white men had been captured recently on the nearby Rancho Cabeza de Santa Rosa, owned by Vallejo's mother-in-law, Maria Ignacia López Carrillo. One was unidentified, but he and two others, William Cowie and William Fowler had been captured and brutally tortured to death. The fourth was none other than William Todd, who had created the Bear Flag and who was rescued ten days later, on June 24, during the so-called Battle of Olompali, when eighteen Bear-flaggers under Lieutenant Henry L. Ford held off the entire force led by Joaquín de la Torre.

Another early action, if such it can be termed, of the Bear Flag Revolt occurred when Kit Carson and some other scouts sent out by Fremont, fired from a distance on a small boat just landing that had approached from the direction of Castro's force on the other side of the bay. Three individuals in the boat, an unarmed old man named José de los Reyes Berryessa and his twin nephews, the Berryessa boys—Francisco and Ramón de Haro, also unarmed—were all killed without being afforded any opportunity to surrender or explain their presence.

Before the so-called "bear" emblem could be implemented into a standard banner, however, word was received that the United States and Mexico were now actually at war. Immediately following the President's orders for what to do in such event, Commodore John D. Sloat took possession of Monterey in the name of the United States and the Bear Flaggers were swiftly assimilated into the military as "volunteers". At this, Fremont and his men returned to their camp and, as Fremont stated it, "...well satisfied with our initial efforts."

Immediately upon his return, Fremont seized Sutters Fort from the control of its founder, "...*in the name of the United States*," which perturbed John Sutter very little. Concerning Fremont, he had written in his diary:

> *...He regarded me as an ally. By the simple act of throwing open my gates I renounced my allegiance to the Mexican Government and declared for the United States. When the Sonoma prisoners*

*arrived I placed them in my best rooms and treated them with every consideration. I did not approve of these arrests...They took their meals with me and walked out with me in the glory of the evening. I appreciated them as gallant gentlemen under stress of misfortune...*

Fremont, in his characteristic bad humor, did not agree and chided Sutter for "*...treating prisoners too well...*" and immediately curtailed the freedoms Sutter had afforded them. He also, on June 20, arrested and similarly detained as prisoners, two civilian visitors to the fort, José Noriega and Vicente Peralta.

This same day, while belated in his own oratory, Pio Pico easily outdid the proclamation of Castro, by declaring in flowery terms:

*...Fly, Mexicans, in all haste in pursuit of the treacherous foe; follow him to the farthest wilderness; punish his audacity; and in case we fail, let us form a cemetery where posterity may remember to the glory of Mexican history the heroism of her sons, as is remembered the glory won by the death of that little band of citizens posted at the Pass of Thermopylae under General Leonidas...*

At this point the insipient megalomania of John Fremont erupted unequivocally. He moved his camp to the north side of the American River nearly opposite Sutters Fort and, now determined to openly join the uprising, drew up his own resignation from the army and ordered two of his men to carry it as an express to Washington D.C. Two days later, the same two express messengers unexpectedly returned, to the utmost surprise of everyone...except Fremont.[87] When spies reported to Fremont that General Castro was en route with 250 men to attack the small U.S. garrison left at Sonoma, he at once marched his entire force to relieve the town. They arrived in ample time to rescue the imperiled Americans.

Fremont continued to arrest and incarcerate all visitors who arrived at Sutters Fort, including even Americans who had no idea what was occurring. At the same time, he busied himself writing a plethora of letters, especially to Consul Larkin, Captain Montgomery of the *U.S.S Portsmouth*, and his father-in-law, U.S. Senator Benton; letters rife with deception, explanation and manifesto and in the strongest terms expressing the perilous situation currently existing, his upright

# The Infinite Dream

intentions to combat it, and the steadfastness of his heart and mind in such pursuit. He reported that the Mexicans were prowling the countryside of California in *"angry armies"* and *"murderous masses"* and that their situation was *"nothing less than critical"* and that although he *"was being insulted and hunted down"*, he most assuredly *"would persevere"* and that, in addition to soundly defeating the Californios, *"I intend to force an apology from them!"* He gleefully accepted Admiral Stockton's appointment of him as Commander of the California Battalion, and boasted of himself as being *"liberator of the province"* and *"ruler of a new nation on the Western Coast."*

The signs of combined paranoia and megalomania rising in John C. Fremont were both clearly apparent and increasing.

*[June 28, 1846 • Sunday • Noon]*

Their stay here in the Sandwich Islands was nearly finished and most of Samuel Brannan's followers were eager for commencement of the final run to California. Brannan was not particularly in favor of any members of his flock broadcasting their opinions publicly unless they cleared it with him first. Today was a case in point and he was decidedly irked.

Early this morning several of the Saints had decided, on their own, to attend a native religious service held in a non-Mormon church and heard an American missionary address those in attendance in their native tongue. When the service ended, the little Mormon group was met by a reporter in a hurry to interview them in time for his story to be included in today's newspaper. When he asked them what they thought of the experience, one of the Mormon sisters replied with a frankness that now had irritated Brannan on reading about it in the paper. She was quoted as saying:

> *"...I don't think the missionaries have done much good here; they degrade the natives. Here the white ladies are drawn around in two-wheeled vehicles by the natives. I saw a great many of them drawn to church by them and men too. I think it would have looked better had they gone on foot. Many of the natives wear scarcely any clothing at all!"*

The remark, Brannan thought, apart from not being approved by him for publication, was simply both inappropriate and negative and, in his opinion, cast a bad light on the entire Mormon group in his charge. After some consideration, however, during which he reviewed his own activities and remarks since arriving here eight days ago, on June 20, he began reconsidering reprimanding her.

Actually, they would have arrived much sooner than this, since they'd left Robinson Crusoe Island in the San Fernando Archipelago on May 9 after having spent several excellent days there. They'd had virtually perfect weather almost all the way to these lovely islands, with day after day of coasting smoothly along at about seven knots across the deep blue surface.

During their progress, as if to rectify for the ten lives lost during their passage, a lovely little baby girl had been born to John and Phoebe Robbins and their infant was christened Georgianna Pacific Robbins. Her arrival brought them a great surge of joy, since two of their sons had been among the ten thus far lost. Everyone was cheerful during this month-long passage on a northwest heading when abruptly, on the thirtieth day, the wind died and they were becalmed. One Saint quoted their dilemma as being *"as silent as a painted ship upon a painted ocean."*

For more than a week the *Brooklyn* lay motionless on the glass-flat surface and for those aboard, who had been at sea in extremely cramped quarters for 100 days, the sudden stop of forward progress was an all but unbearable experience. The Saints were nearly driven out of their minds with the monotony that ensued and many of them offered up prayers that their dilemma be relieved. As if in answer a gentle breeze swept in and swelled to a wind that bellied the sails and they were once again moving well and they sang praises to God.

On June 20, just one week later and forty-two days into this leg of their voyage, the *Brooklyn* rounded Diamond Head and all aboard were startled to see a number of cannon-armed American warships at rest. Shortly afterwards their own anchor dropped into the harbor at Honolulu. It was their one hundred thirty-sixth day since leaving New York City. Here they would be taking on necessary supplies, as well as dropping off the half-thousand barrels of freight that Brannan had surreptitiously contracted to deliver.

Brannan learned that the presence of the warships was due to the fact that Mexico and the United States were now at war and, as he interpreted it, California would soon be a United States possession. The frigate *U.S. Congress* was one of these, under command of Commodore Robert F. Stockton and all the ships were taking on provisions in anticipation of assaulting the California coastal cities. The news was unsettling and many of the Saints at once favored moving on to Oregon or Vancouver Island. Some actually suggested turning back. Brannan however, wondered if the persecution they had taken such drastic steps to escape would actually be awaiting them when they arrived. Yet, if dispossession of the Mexicans had not already occurred, suppose his Saints were to land and take Yerba Buena through force of arms; suppose they were first to raise the American flag there? Would not Government then be disposed to treating his Mormons with the greater concern that being beholden so often begets?

"You must," he said loudly, addressing them, "remember your promises made to Brigham Young. You must remember our plans to make that port our place of disembarking and nowhere else. Have you forgotten your solemn promise—and now your obligatio—to ready a place in California for your brothers and sisters from Nauvoo? Our duty is only too clear; we must go on to California, come what may!"

Brannan quickly made it a point to confer with the American naval commanders. At Commodore Stockton's suggestion that the Saints just might help in the war effort, Brannan purchased from him 150 outdated military arms, with their ammunition, for four dollars each or less. It was Stockton himself who suggested that the *Brooklyn* head directly to Yerba Buena and the Saints help to secure that port for the United States. But it was Brannan whose imagination soared as he considered actually conquering California and transforming it into a Mormon territory within the United States.

Fear remained high among the Saints, however, and to alleviate it to some degree, Brannan gave them liberty to leave the ship and explore the island as they wished. At the same time, he reminded, there were fresh fruits and vegetables, meats and casks of water to be brought aboard. And, of course, while they were all gone on this unexpected freedom, Brannan had the arms and ammunition rather stealthily brought aboard and secretly stowed. So he thought, but Captain Richardson was hardly so lax in alertness and he feared a possible mutiny. As soon as Brannan left, the skipper had all the war materials put under lock and key and Brannan had no recourse but to accept his decision.

Even more perturbing to Brannan at the moment was the

growing sense of mutiny arising among his own Saints, who ever more were resenting the fancy living their Elder was enjoying, the unusual favoritism he was receiving, and the rather imperialistic tactics he was employing in regard to them. To combat this, Brannan named the four most vociferous and troublesome of the protestors and held a shipboard trial, with himself as judge, of course, and quite simply and wholly incontrovertibly, found them guilty of wicked and licentious conduct and improper views and excommunicated all of them. Thereafter, loudly voiced complaints of his leadership fell off almost completely.

The act, however, only fanned a growing rebelliousness among his Saints.

*[June 28, 1846 • Sunday • 4:00 p.m.]*

James Marshall was part of the delegation of "settlers" who had presented themselves respectfully yesterday to Captain John B. Montgomery, commander of the *U.S. Portsmouth*, temporarily moored relatively near shore just below The Presidio. It was Marshall who acted as spokesman and he handled his role well.

"Sir," he said, "we have come here representing American settlers on California soil, most of whom are sorely in need of aid. We would like you to help us if that is possible." His words seemed to convey considerably more than he actually said.

"It is part of our purpose here, Mr. Marshall," Montgomery responded, "as an American warship, to aid any Americans it might be possible for us to help, within the scope of our ability to do so. Exactly what," he added, with no change of expression, "would constitute the type of aid you are seeking?"

Marshall steeled himself and then took the plunge. "We are in great need of gunpowder, sir, and lead."

The captain of the *Portsmouth* did not recoil or in any other way exhibit shock at the request, but when he spoke, his words did indeed convey some degree of surprise at the bold request. "Gentlemen, I am astonished at your audacity. Are you not aware that you are rebels? Are you not aware that you are in arms against the Government of this country, and that I am an officer of the United States Navy, a power with which Mexico, here, is at peace? I cannot entertain your proposition for a moment, and even though, if you were to succeed in your endeavors, the case would be altered, it is utterly impossible that I should assist you in any way *at present!* "

At this apparent rebuff, Marshall glanced at the other members of his delegation and saw they were watching him closely, awaiting his response. They appeared to be as melancholy and crestfallen as he. He was on the verge of retorting to the churlish captain with a remark that would surely insult him, but then he thought better of it and turned to leave, beckoning the others to follow. As the commander himself hurried away and left their line of sight, they reached the side and were about to descend when the senior lieutenant, who had been standing mute with other officers while the captain and Marshall spoke, hurriedly stepped forward now and addressed Marshall in a grave undertone:

"You must have known that Captain Montgomery could not give you any ammunition. It would be as much as his commission was worth." He paused and then, a slight smile curling his lips, added: "Besides, a good bit of our ammunition has been slightly damaged by moisture and we are planning to land a quantity of it tomorrow for the purpose of drying it."

Marshall's own lips curled slightly as he caught the drift. "And exactly where," he asked, "might such a process take place?"

"Well," the lieutenant replied, eyes twinkling now, "I was looking around this morning for a favorable place to dry the powder and I have chosen that spot." He pointed to an area of sandy shoreline between jumbled rocks at the water's edge. The delegation of junior officers behind him were now smiling themselves. Marshall's whole little group broke into grins as well and Marshall turned back to the lieutenant.

"We fully understand," he said levelly, "and regret that the rules of the service are so inexorable, but please assure Captain Montgomery that we bear him no ill-will and that we understand he has only been doing his duty." He turned then and led his men down to the boat that would return them to shore.

Early this morning a large lifeboat put off from the *Portsmouth* and was rowed ashore by six seamen under command of a lieutenant. They landed, drew up the boat firmly and then unloaded a number of kegs, which they deposited on the sandy area. As the last was put ashore, a dozen armed and masked men appeared, seized their arms and then rapidly carried off the kegs. The leader of the bandits, who, as much as could be determined, bore a striking resemblance to James Marshall, emptied the confiscated weapons and returned them to the sailors and then escorted them back to their boat. Unharmed, they were sent back to the man-of-war.

There was every reason to believe, of course, that Captain Montgomery would be irate at this outrage, and so it appeared he was. The big guns at four of the cannon ports were uncovered, aimed somewhat high and shot in succession, the quadruple booms echoing in the still morning air across San Francisco Bay. The balls they fired landed on the slopes well above to left and right and the "bandits" decided it would be wise to leave, lest one of the balls roll down the slope and possibly injure someone.

It was expected by "bandits" and sailors alike that the commander of the *Portsmouth* undoubtedly filed a report of "ammunition expended."

As indeed it was.

*[June 30, 1846 • Tuesday]*

The forty-year-old Ohioan, Captain James Allen, though an eighteen-year-veteran of the U.S. Army, had long felt he had become mired in an extended period of stagnation in his rank. Any officer in the army, he knew quite well, encountered precious little opportunity for advancement in peacetime. It was why he had secretly exulted in the fact that his country was now involved in a declared war with Mexico. With that having begun, it then became the responsibility of the ambitious officer, eager for promotion, to place himself in advantageous position for same.

In this respect, Captain Allen had become, over the past few years, Kearny's most dependable subaltern. And the great opportunity he had so long envisioned had at last presented itself when Kearny's Special Order of June 19 had appointed him to go to the Mormons in Iowa Territory and gather the 500 there who would augment Kearny's Army of the West.

The initial portion of that Special Order dealt with how he was to go about gathering those men, enlisting them as the First, Second, Third, Fourth and Fifth companies, equipping them and marching them to join Kearny at Fort Leavenworth or, if the troops had already marched from there, overtaking him somewhere on the Santa Fe Trail. It was, however, a brief passage in that order that had caused Allen's heart to suddenly pound so furiously in his chest he feared it might burst; the passage that read:

*...You will, upon mustering into service the 4th Company, be*

considered as having the Rank, Pay, Emoluments of a Lieut. Col. of Infy and are authorized to appoint an Adjt. Sergt. Major and QMr Sergt. for the Battalion.[88]

Allen, himself mounted and with four mounted privates and a fifth driving a baggage wagon, arrived among the Mormons who were still assembling in the westernmost quarter of Iowa Territory. Very quickly, however he discovered that every Mormon he addressed became suspicious or afraid as soon he saw their uniforms. All his efforts to point out the benefits of enlistment seemed not to be understood and though he adopted a conciliatory attitude toward the religious movement, doing his best to solicit the favor and confidence of the Mormon leaders, it didn't seem to help. He was having such little success that when he reached the Mormon emigration encampment at Mount Pisgah on June 26, he had an announcement printed up and posted:

### CIRCULAR TO THE MORMONS

*I have come among you, instructed by Colonel S.W. Kearny, of the U.S. Army, now commanding the Army of the West, to visit the Mormon camps, and to accept the service for twelve months, of four or five companies of Mormons who may be willing to serve their country for that period in our present war with Mexico; this force to unite with the Army of the West at Santa Fe, and be marched thence to California, where they will be discharged. They will receive pay and rations, and other allowances, such as volunteers or regular soldiers receive, from the day they shall be mustered into the service, and will be entitled to all comforts and benefits of regular soldiers of the army, and when discharged, as contemplated, at California, they will be given, gratis, their arms and accoutrements, with which they will be fully equipped at Fort Leavenworth. This is offered to the Mormon people now. This gives an opportunity of sending a portion of their young and intelligent men to the ultimate destination of their whole people, and entirely at the expense of the United States, and this advanced party can thus pave the way and look out the land for their brethren to come after them. Those of the Mormons who are desirous of serving their country, on the conditions here enumerated, are requested to meet me without delay at their principal camp at Council Bluffs, wither I am now going*

> to consult with their principal men, and to receive and organize the force contemplated to be raised. I will receive all healthy, able-bodied men of from eighteen to forty-five years of age.
>
> J. Allen, Captain, 1st Dragoons
> Camp of the Mormons at Mt. Pisgah
> One hundred and thirty-eight miles east of Council Bluffs
> June 26, 1846
>
> NOTE:—I hope to complete the organization of this battalion in six days after my reaching Council Bluffs, or within nine days from this time.

At a meeting called of the High Council of Mount Pisgah, Allen's announcement was read, but the Council did nothing more than provide him with a letter of introduction to President Brigham Young and other high Mormon officials who would be at Council Bluffs. Present at the time was Elder Wilford Woodruff of the Quorum of Twelve Apostles, and he immediately dispatched an express messenger to inform Brigham Young of Captain Allen's arrival and the object of his mission.

Unaware of this, Captain Allen repaired at once toward Council Bluffs and soon many Mormon men were heading that way, too, to enlist. However much an augury that seemed, the way was not yet at all clear. Suspicion abounded on all sides and urgent messages were dispatched to Council Bluffs for all cannon and other arms to be hidden immediately. Hosea Stout was loud in his declaration that he viewed this as a test by the U.S. Government of Mormon loyalty and suspects "they want five hundred of our men in their power, to be destroyed as they had done to our leaders at Carthage."

This morning, finally, Captain Allen and his few men with the baggage wagon rolled into the outskirts of Council Bluffs. Two men walking the road ahead of them stopped as they approached and Allen's party pulled up.

"I am Captain James Allen, U.S. Army, out of Fort Leavenworth. I am seeking Brigham Young. Can you tell me if there is a man in this camp by that name?"

The two men happened to be Henry Bigler and his cousin, Jesse Bigler Martin, returning from hunting lost stock. It was Henry who replied, suspicion evident in his voice that these were men come to arrest their leader and take him away, so his answer was accordingly hedged: "There is a man in this camp by that name, but *where* he is I couldn't say."

It didn't matter; the news of Captain Allen's mission had already reached Brigham Young and he instantly viewed it as an answer to his prayers and sent several of the Elders to escort Allen to his presence: here was the permission the Mormons needed to settle for a while west of the Missouri River on Indian lands; the opportunity to give the Mormons greatly needed time to prepare for the much more difficult move west; an opportunity to move 500 Mormons to California entirely at Government expense; most importantly at this precise time, the pay that would be received by the soldiers would help the dispossessed Church of Jesus Christ of Latter-day Saints to survive. Would Brigham Young agree to provide Colonel Kearny with the requisite men? He most certainly would.

On a far more personal level, where Captain Allen was concerned, it would allow him to advance two full grades in rank and become lieutenant colonel of a semi-independent command. And now, thinking of his presently renowned classmates of long ago at West Point, Joseph E. Johnston and Robert E. Lee, the soon-to-be-former Captain James Allen was suddenly very deeply pleased.

*[July 1, 1846 • Wednesday]*

The fact that The Presidio, overlooking the entrance to San Francisco Bay on its southern point, had not been garrisoned for many years and that its ten cannon were so old and rusted and most probably were entirely incapable of being fired was of little consequence to Lieutenant Colonel John C. Fremont. He meant to make sure the installation and its guns were never again even remotely a threat to United States ships.

With a handful of mounted men, including Lieutenant Archibald Gillespie, beside him, Fremont left Sonoma and reached the northern shore of the strait by mid-afternoon yesterday. He had learned from one of his spies that the old ship *Moscow* was anchored there close to shore and this gave him the idea for perhaps accomplishing a feat that would probably be easy enough to undertake, while at the same time, with careful phrasing, could be reported as a highly significant event in the earliest stages of an American takeover of California.

The small party of Americans was delighted to find the *Moscow* still riding at anchor where it had been reported to be. This was the ship whose captain had offered Fremont and his men refuge during the Gavilan Peak fiasco still so fresh in their minds and though the offer of refuge had been refused at that time, it seemed the captain, whose sympathies were clearly with the Americans, would still be willing to offer assistance.

So he had been. The skipper, now Captain John Phelps, would not allow the ship itself to participate in Fremont's plan, but he did offer a longboat, as well as a select small crew of four husky seamen to man the oars and carry them across the strait to its southern shore. At first the going was easy enough, as the tide was all but quiescent, but as they moved into the main mouth of the strait, the newly-turned, powerful incoming tide thrust them eastward until the land on both sides was clearly visible and rather spectacularly rimmed with the golden light of the setting sun. They all stared at the scene, mesmerized by its beauty, but it was John Fremont who found the words to describe it.

"It's like a gateway to the Pacific," he said. "And to California as well. It's *Chrysoplylae*—a beautiful golden gate."

The crewmen from the *Moscow* and his own men all agreed most heartily and Fremont had unwittingly given this strait its new name—the Golden Gate.[89]

Despite the strong efforts of the quartet of crewmen from the *Moscow*, the powerful thrust of the incoming tide swept the longboat far eastward, defeating all they did to combat it. Dusk came quickly as the golden orb of the setting sun slipped below the western horizon, and full darkness enveloped them shortly afterward. Throughout the darkness, only ten days past the shortest night of the year, the oarsmen labored at their task, but it was a difficult job with the weight of so many men in the boat. By the time they crossed the strait and reached the somewhat calmer waters close to the southeastern point of land and followed the shoreline back to a point directly below The Presidio's location, the first streaks of dawn had begun streaking the eastern skyline.

They all worked together to pull the longboat well up onto shore in the growing daylight. When they had it firmly above the high-tide watermark, Fremont left two of his own armed men with the four *Moscow* crewmen to guard the boat and, after a short conference of whispered instructions from their commander and their weapons at ready, the remainder spread out and began scaling the steep slope.

With a certain amount of justification, Fremont fully expected the old installation, which the Spanish had initially called *El Castillo de San Joaquín*, to be entirely abandoned. He was not disappointed. Hardly anyone had been there since it was an active fortification a third of a century before. Ten ancient Spanish cannon were still in their emplacements, none of them in any condition to be fired. Nevertheless, Fremont ordered each of them spiked with the wooden pegs; the plugs driven deeply inside the fuse hole with a mallet they had brought along, then snapped off level with the rusted metal, making the big guns even more incapable of firing than they were previously.

As soon as this was accomplished, Fremont and his men returned to the longboat, one of the men painfully turning an ankle on the way down, and launched it for their return to the north shore. Already, in his mind, their leader was composing the report he would write; a report of how a small party of gallant Americans, led by a wholly intrepid commander, braved fierce tidewaters in the dark of night, climbed almost unscalable cliffs, invested a commanding fortress and spiked every one of the installation's numerous cannon, then escaped without a single man being lost and only one man injured. It would be an inspired account of great heroism and Fremont was sure the exploit, as he described it, would quickly be blown all out of proportion and not only fire the public's imagination, but equally propel Lieutenant John C. Fremont's name, even more than previously, into the imagination and onto the lips of virtually everyone in the East. He would become noted as the fearless leader in one of the boldest and grandest achievements thus far in the war with Mexico.[90]

The projected conquest of California by the United States had irrevocably begun.

*[July 2, 1846 • Thursday]*

As a well-trusted and time-proven Elder among the Mormons, Henry Bigler had an opportunity yesterday and today to have a close look at the upper echelon of the Church of Jesus Christ of Latter Day Saints as it deliberated on matters of great importance to all the Mormons. The boon had been granted to him as a sort of reward for his excellent work and devotion to the Mormon cause. He'd promised to remain absolutely silent...but that certainly didn't curtail his thoughts and he wasn't, at this point, entirely sure that he approved of what was occurring.

Ever since early yesterday he'd been wrestling in his own mind with the proposals laid before all the assembled Saints and the Quorum of Twelve Apostles by the American officer, James Allen, in the temporary quarters here in Council Bluffs. Among the members of the Quorum present were Willard Richards, Orson Pratt, Levi Richards, Orson Hyde and George A. Smith. The session had been opened by Brigham Young and it was not possible, at first, to know whether he approved or disapproved of the officer's appearance here. In his own mind, Bigler didn't trust the man at all; this man who was here representing a government that had for so long mistreated or ignored the Mormons and their cause. Brigham Young, however, had been very noncommittal in his introduction of their visitor. He'd started out the meeting with a sense of urgency, yet evidently not relating to the American officer's visit. Young had declared that it was time for the Mormon governing body to:

> "…issue their own call for recruits to go over the mountains to set up the Kingdom of God or its Standard yet this year. Despite the church's [sic] poverty or disarray, we hope to bring between two and five hundred able and effective men to accompany us to the Bear River Valley, or Great Basin, or Great Salt Lake."

There had been murmurs of approval from members of the Quorum of Twelve, but then an Apostle had respectfully hurried in and whispered something close to The Prophet's ear and Young had immediately excused himself, saying he'd be back in a moment. And so he was, trailed by the uniformed officer who had addressed Bigler on the road several days ago to ask how he could find Brigham Young or whoever might temporarily be filling his place. Without dalliance, Young said he had sent out runners to summon all Saints to assemble immediately near the tent of Elder John Taylor. Then he introduced Captain Allen to the Twelve and it became clear that in his brief moments with Allen, he'd heard enough to be unquestionably approving.[91] He said Allen was scheduled momentarily to address the crowd, including the Quorum of Twelve if they would adjourn here and reassemble outside. It was exactly 11:45 a.m. Within moments all of them, including Bigler, were outside, where Young and Allen mounted a wagon bed amid a great throng of assembled Saints. Young raised his arms and immediately the murmuring crowd silenced, at which the Mormon leader introduced the U.S. officer beside him, adding that this officer had some important information to impart. Allen thanked him and immediately raised his voice and began his address:

"I have been sent here by Colonel Stephen Kearny, through the benevolence of the President of the United States, James Polk, to enlist the aid of five hundred Mormon men between the ages of eighteen and forty-five, for a period of one year, to take part in the newly declared war between Mexico and the United States." Those who volunteer will have ten days to prepare before we march to join Colonel Kearny."

A strong murmur rippled through the assemblage at this and, as he waited for silence to resume, he removed two documents from his pouch. Then, he continued:

"While we have hundreds of thousands of volunteers ready in the United States to aid us in this endeavor, I will read to you now the orders I have received from Colonel Kearny, as well as a circular I personally posted the other day at Mount Pisgah."

He unfolded the papers and read to the crowd both of the documents and once again a strong murmuring arose, during which he refolded the documents and replaced them in his pouch. A near pandemonium broke out among the Saints as everyone seemed to speaking simultaneously. The tone of the sound was not at all pleasant, as it was rife with a considerable resentment. Henry Bigler was only one of many of the Saints who instantly experienced a strong sense of pique that a proposal be given them to fight and risk their lives for a government that had given them virtually no protection against mobs, whose own representatives had openly threatened them with extermination, and now they would be required to go off and fight while leaving their families in Indian Territory without food or shelter. It was altogether galling to most of them, Henry Bigler included.[92]

The resentful murmuring continued, but Allen simply nodded to Brigham Young and stepped back slightly as the President of the Mormons stepped forward and once again raised his arms for silence. He addressed Captain Allen first:

"You shall have your battalion," he said, "even if it has to be made up of our elders. I wish the Saints here assembled," he said, turning back to them, "to consider carefully what President Polk and Captain Allen have proposed to you. I ask that all of the brethren assembled here, in your own minds, make a clear distinction between this action of the general government, and your former oppressions in Missouri and Illinois.

"You would be justified in asking," he continued, "is it prudent for us to enlist to defend our country? If we answer in the affirmative, all are ready to go. Suppose we were admitted to the Union as a State and the government did *not* call on us? We could feel ourselves neglected. We *want* the requisition made upon us, and we will do nothing else till we have accomplished this thing. If we want the privilege of going where we can worship God according to the dictates of our consciences, we *must* raise the battalion. Let the Mormons be the first Americans to set their feet on the soil of California. Captain James Allen has assumed the responsibility of saying that we may locate at Grand Island until we can prosecute our journey. This is the first offer we have ever received from the Government to benefit us. I *proposed* that the five hundred volunteers be mustered, and I would do my best to see all their families brought forward, so far as my influence can be extended and feed them when I had anything to eat myself."

Young stepped back and once again Captain Allen addressed them: "I will write to President Polk to give us leave to stay on the route wherever it becomes necessary; the soldier's daily ration would be eighteen ounces of bread and twenty ounces of beef, or twelve ounces of bacon, and they will be paid every two months."

It was Elder Heber C. Kimball who climbed aboard the wagon bed then and, when silence had once again settled, called out loudly: "I move that five hundred men be raised in conformity with the requisition from the government."

Immediately the motion was seconded by Willard Richard. Kimball called for a vocal vote and the measure was carried unanimously in a tremendous din. There were no "nays" uttered when this second vote was called for. President Young then called for volunteers to approach and, with his clerk, Richards, took down the names of the first few volunteers. Then the Quorum of Twelve and President Young led Captain Allen into John Taylor's nearby tent. Inside, Young tuned to face Allen and addressed him:

"Does not an officer enlisting men on Indian lands have the right to say to their families: 'You can stay until your husband's return'?"

There was no hesitation in Captain Allen's response: "I am the official representative here of President Polk. I can act until I notify President Polk, who might ratify my engagements, or who might indemnify for damage. The President may simply give permission for the Mormons to travel through Indian country, and stop whenever circumstances require."

On request that he do so, Captain Allen left the tent and the Quorum of Twelve continued for a time to converse about the favorable prospects now before the Saints. They voted, without dissention, that President Young and Elder Kimball should themselves go to Mount Pisgah to raise volunteers there.

Young nodded. "I will start soon, and I desire that the companies here be organized so that it may be correctly ascertained who can go and establish camp at Grand Island and who must remain after raising the troops. You Quorum of Twelve are directed to go westward with your families.

Although probably a large majority of the male Saints would have elected not to serve the U.S. Government in a military role, the matter had quite efficiently been taken out of their hands by Brigham Young. Mormonism was a totalitarian organization and they knew they *had* to obey. The power of President Young left no room for dissention and his decision went unchallenged; there was no choice but to obey orders.

Young had already made out a list of the Elders he wanted to be named as captains and non-commissioned officers over the volunteers and sent each one the same message: They were to come hither and receive special instructions from him, arriving before 6:00 p.m. on the evening of July 18. He gave them specific instructions of where this important private meeting would be held, in a distinctive cottonwood grove flanking the Missouri River.[93]

Despite his own personal misgivings, one of the very first hale and hearty Mormons to volunteer as a private was Henry Bigler.

# Chapter 5

♦

*[July 4, 1846 • Saturday • 10:30 a.m.]*

The information received by Colonel Stephen W. Kearny in his Bents Fort temporary headquarters yesterday, from what he supposed was good authority, stated that California had been taken by the Americans there and no realistic danger remained. This altered his plans considerably and he busied himself by preparing to discharge, or distribute elsewhere, immediately after taking Santa Fe, his entire brigade, save for a hand-picked escort of 100 men...although he fully expected the 5,000-man Mormon Battalion to overtake him before that destination was reached.

This morning, when Kearny set off from Bents Fort for Santa Fe, he had already determined on paper who would accompany him for the remainder of his march to California: He would take this relatively small body of men as his escort, most of the officers selected from among the West Point graduates: Captain H.S. Turner of the First Dragoons, Lieutenant William H. Emory of the topographical engineers, and Captain A.R. Johnston, ADC of the First Dragoons. The 100 picked men of the First Dragoons would be commanded by Captain Ben Moore and his junior officer, Lieutenant T.C. Hammond, mounted on mules. Lieutenant J.W. Davidson of the First Dragoons would be placed in charge of the two mountain howitzers being brought along on wheeled carriages. All the baggage required would be packed on mules.

That everything had gone so relatively smoothly since their departure from Fort Leavenworth was gratifying, but it was also a source of worry to Kearny; wars, he was well aware, were simply not fought with such ease and he had to consciously put down the prickly feeling that there were bad things to come.

# The Infinite Dream

The march from Fort Leavenworth to Bents Fort in the Colorado Territory had been something of a surprise. The general had fully anticipated that news of the war with Mexico would have caused a significant diminishing of traffic on the Santa Fe Trail. Quite the contrary; the war had, in fact, stimulated rather than deterred traffic and the route was filled with a variety of wagons; so much so that goods being shipped farther west were arriving upwards of six months later than expected in Chihuahua and the villages beyond.

The immense wagons of the traders on this route, fully twice the size of those utilized by settlers heading westward on the Oregon Trail, strung out for great distances, their heavier than usual loads slowing the oxen pulling them, and slowed as well by the greater number in evidence. Such traveling merchants were under military guard and army supply trains, with wagons considerably smaller than the commercial conveyances, only complicated the road congestion. Added to that of the regular trade, there was Kearny's force, including his train and supports, plus the quickly developing services of scouts, supply, couriers and expresses, surveyors, ambulance wagons and a large walking assemblage of soldiers that had been discharged or were invalided and being transferred to new posts.

Despite the inherent unruliness and obstinate mentality of the Missouri Volunteers, the privates were slowly—often *very* slowly—being whipped into a semblance of a command by the West Pointers, who knew they would never quite overcome their distaste for such rabble. The standard pace of fifteen miles march daily was distained by Kearny, who demanded a minimum of twenty and, under good conditions, often pushed them to as much as thirty-two. No one lagged; there simply wasn't time for it. Companies A and B of Colonel Doniphan's regiment excelled in the marches, often outdistancing the mounted troops, whose horses or mules were so often sick from the lack of good graze.

When Kearny received word on June 22 that two of the more important Mexican leaders, Armijo and Speyer, were still fleeing ahead of them, he sent out two troops of the First Missouri and two of the Dragoons to sprint ahead and attempt to apprehend them. Although they pursued very rapidly, all the way to the Cimarron Crossing, the fleeing pair simply had too much of a head start and the Americans could not overtake them.

They gave up the pursuit at that point and today returned to

Pawnee Fork, where they camped in the forenoon and waited for the army to catch up.

*[July 4, 1846 • Saturday • Noon]*

Zachary Taylor was more than just a little irked, though he prided himself on the belief that no one around him was aware of it. Nevertheless, he was plain damned mad and he knew exactly where to place the blame.

Throughout the late spring and now into early summer, he had been besieged with volunteers arriving in numbers he had never believed possible. At first it had been gratifying, as it would have been to any field commander requiring support in facing an enemy, but now it had become a major problem in and of itself. So many volunteers had arrived that his once small army, which had initially been in danger of being overrun by the Mexican Army, now had swelled to some twelve *thousand* men and he simply did not have the means to support such a force, insofar as maneuvering and supplying them was concerned.

Part of it, he knew, he could blame on the multitude of war stories that had appeared about him in the nation's press; stories that had portrayed him as the fearless and brilliant strategist whose little army had won serious battles and forced the far-more-numerous Mexican troops to scatter in panic. With such successes, he had enjoyed the influx of volunteers whose imaginations had been stirred by the victories, such as they were, and wished to become part of the winning team.

Two things occurred then, almost simultaneously; a surplus of troops became a sudden serious problem and news stories about the "great American general" abruptly vanished from the newspapers. The first problem was the knottiest: The new troops, who had volunteered for periods as short as three months or for as long as a year, became considerably more a burden than an asset. Some he was able to send home at once, but far too many more stayed on, with nothing to do and particularly susceptible to southwestern maladies never before encountered and against which they had acquired no previous immunity, as had the regulars. Quite literally hundreds died at base camp.

In addition to illnesses, for which there were inadequate medical supplies, the newer troops were beset with an overwhelming and seemingly contagious plummeting of morale. Behavior disintegrated, fierce fighting broke out among themselves, sometimes with fatal results.

# The Infinite Dream

Insubordination was rampant and desertions to Mexico increased alarmingly, into scores of men. Instead of being supplied with mules, the War Department sent several thousand wagons, which were essentially useless in the Mexican terrain west of Matamoros. Some mules were finally sent, but only about half the number necessary for carrying out the campaign envisioned by General Taylor.

That was hardly the end of the problems besetting this army; there was no shortage of food, but most of the food sent had, to some extent, gone bad and, in eating it, most of the troops became candidates for hospitalization rather than the front lines. Quite probably the only individual who truly grasped the magnitude of all these combined problems was a virtually unknown lieutenant named George Gordon Meade, who was sorely depressed by all he saw. By no means had he ever favored this war against Mexico, but once the nation was committed, he felt it should be engaged in with every degree of efficiency possible, which was not occurring at all. While he considered General Taylor a good general in combat, he had grave issues with the preliminaries to battle and was convinced that the only thing that had thus far prevented annihilation of the American force was an equal or surpassing incompetence among the Mexican troops.

The next logical step for Taylor, after putting the Mexicans on the run, Meade reasoned, was to move forward to take and occupy the major city of Monterrey, but in view of existing shortages, ineptitudes, and inexperience among the American troops, he had grave doubts it could be accomplished. As with other West Pointers on hand, he strongly resented having to take care of the volunteers "as you would so many children", fully a third of whom were sick and all of whom, including their self-elected officers, had any real conception about how to fight a war.

Lieutenant Meade was appalled at the behavior of the troops from both Texas and Missouri, considering them suitably brave but imbued with a totally unconscionable bull-headedness, aggravated by an overriding vindictiveness that clearly clouded judgment. On the basis of each force having roughly equal numbers, he had grave doubts the Mexican troops could ever hold up in formal battle against the Americans, but if they resorted to any form of guerilla warfare, the American forces would surely be doomed.

It was on the personal level, however, where General Taylor was both angered and frustrated. There were still numerous newspaper accounts of heroism and fierceness and dedication occurring among the Americans, but these were now centered most closely on such acts among the troops and their superior officers, but almost studiously avoiding any mention of the commanding general. This peculiar turnaround transpired as soon as Taylor, in offhand remarks, had more or less announced his own forthcoming aspiration to become a candidate for the Presidency of the United States. Ever since then he had been practically wholly ignored by the press and he was certain he knew exactly who was responsible for this selective muzzling of the nation's news reporters and editors.

That individual was President James Knox Polk.

*[July 4, 1846 · Saturday · 2:30 p.m.]*

Samuel Brannan was to some degree irked with the decision made by the skipper of the *Brooklyn* shortly after they had re-embarked from Honolulu, but which he had not discovered until today. In his usual philosophical manner when he had no choice in the matter, he simply accepted it and readjusted his own mind-set.

He had not noticed Captain Richardson paying any kind of real attention to him or the cargo he'd had loaded aboard the ship just prior to their departure from Honolulu on July 1, but admitted to himself now that he should have known better. The skipper was constantly aware of everything that occurred aboard the *Brooklyn* and the newly discovered step he had taken came as no real surprise to Brannan; it had, in fact, only made him respect the ship's captain even more.

Under cover of darkness in the per-dawn hours just prior to their departure from Honolulu for California, Brannan had directed a crew of workers in the loading aboard the *Brooklyn*, the 150 rifles and fifty Allen revolvers, as well as ammunition for both, procured surreptitiously from U.S, naval officials. They had been hidden fairly well in the hold, he thought, and he hadn't gone near them since. He'd thought Independence Day a most satisfactory day to bring out the weapons and commence drilling the Saints with them in preparation for what resistance he envisioned they might encounter on their arrival at the Port of Yerba Buena; an encounter, he thought, that just might earn for him in the pages of American history the aura of a great American patriot. He was, therefore, more than shocked when early on this morning of July 4 he descended into the *Brooklyn's* hold and found all the weapons and ammunition gone. In addition, a safe-room in the hold was now heavily padlocked and an armed seaman stood on guard at the door. It was clearly obvious that Brannan's secret stash had been confiscated and locked away.

He had, of course, confronted Captain Richardson about this immediately upon emerging from the hold. The skipper made no attempt to deny the fact that he'd locked all the armament away. Since he could not believe that Brannan and the seventy male Saints at the Elder's disposal could possibly have conceived of storming the Mexican garrison at Yerba Buena, he had deduced the possibility that Brannan meant to use the weapons in a mutinous attempt to take over his ship. The two had conversed about this for some time and Brannan managed to convince the skipper that the weapons and ammunition were to be utilized, when they reached their destination, for an assault against the Mexicans garrisoned there. Brannan and Captain Richardson had a good laugh together about this, but the skipper remained adamant that the weapons would remain locked away until the *Brooklyn* arrived at the port in San Francisco Bay, and that even any further drilling of the Saints by Brannan on deck before then was now forbidden. Captain Richardson was not a man prone to taking unnecessary chances where his ship was concerned.

So now, on this beautiful afternoon of July 4, 1846, Brannan stood on deck and stared eastward toward the not-yet-visible California coastline. Captain Richardson's decision was hampering, but certainly understandable. The Saints all knew well enough how to load and shoot and they really needed no further drill. He was quite sure they would function well as a unit under his command when they reached Yerba Buena and assaulted and captured it in the name of the United States of America.

*[July 7, 1846 · Tuesday · 2:00 p.m.]*

Commodore John Drake Sloat was not a well man. Although he was entirely convinced that he would soon die, he had informed no one else of such conviction. Despite his own dire premonition, he was pleased with himself; pleased with what he had done during these past few days that would secure his place in history as one of his country's great patriots. It was he, after all, who raised the stars and stripes over Monterey and he who had claimed California for the United States.

It had been touch and go, for a while, he admitted to himself, and a matter of timing. Three short days could have made a world of difference. That was when, in his flagship, the frigate *U.S. Savannah*, he had coasted into the harbor at Monterey and anchored, as his two smaller escorts, the *U.S. Cyane* and *U.S. Levant* had followed and anchored in line with him, all three having done so on his command but without written orders.

It had been a ticklish—and quite possibly career-ending gambit—for him to have done so. His small squadron, just as the more powerful fleet of the British had done, was positioned at Mazatlan when news arrived that a state of war may have begun between Mexico and the United States. Ambiguous and unverified as the report was, Sloat did not hesitate for an instant. That he, with his escorts, had been able to slip away before the nearby British battleship, *HMS Collingwood*, could do so, had turned out to be more a matter of pure happenstance than anything else.

Commodore Sloat had arrived here at Monterey three days ago, landed 250 armed men, raised the American flag over the Customs House in the principle city square and issued a proclamation that California was now a possession of the United States. In that proclamation, which was also posted in the always bustling city square, information and instructions were given to the citizenry: California was proclaimed free from Mexican rule and was now a possession of the United States; no tyrannous rule would be imposed, but until the United States established democratic government here, California citizens would be governed by, and be under protection of, American military law; the rights of citizens to conscience, property and suffrage would not be abridged; the clergy should maintain possession of their churches; American manufactures would hereafter be admitted free of duty and only a quarter of the previous duty rates would be charged of foreign imports. In the event any former officials of Mexican authority wished to retain their positions as prefects of districts or *alcaldes* of municipalities, under the jurisdiction of the United States, they were encouraged to remain in their positions and function as previously; further, any provisions furnished to U.S. officers and soldiers were to be fairly purchased and resident property owners would be provided with reconfirmation of their titles. All these provisions were met with somewhat befuddled equanimity by the Monterey citizens and no outbreaks of violence or even discord occurred. It was as benign a takeover of governmental control as could have been imagined.[94]

It was not until all this transpired that the full impact of what he was doing struck home with Commodore John Drake Sloat and caused him to experience nerve-shattering second thoughts. What if the unofficial "report" he had received regarding the alleged war declaration was untrue? That he had met with no resistance from anyone when he raised the American colors over this capital city of a Mexican possession was hardly an affirmation of the rightness of his move; nor was the flight from the city of the top Californio officials, without any attempt at defense, an affirmation that he had acted correctly. There was also the unnerving fact that American Consul Thomas Larkin had quickly paid a brief visit to him aboard the *Savannah* and, having received no official notification of a declared war between Mexico and the United States, gravely advised him to "move cautiously." He was also haunted by the memory of a disturbingly similar situation that had occurred four years previously when Commodore Ap Catesby Jones, anchored at Callao, had heard rumors of war and rushed off to Monterey and ran up the American colors, only to have the Secretary of the Navy disavow the act and relieve Jones of his command. Sloat's own reputation, his lifetime of unblemished service in the United States Navy, could well be destroyed by the same sort of precipitate action he had taken and he was more than nervous over what the end result would be.

Now, three days after Commodore John Drake Sloat had made his rash move, the stately British battleship, *Collingwood* sailed into Monterey Bay and took up anchorage at 2 p.m. within cannon range of his own much smaller flagship, *Savannah*. Although Sloat's own gun ports remained closed, all hands were at their posts, prepared to battle if such became necessary, despite the knowledge that they could not survive against so formidable a warship. But British Admiral Seymour took no aggressive action against the American ships and this, more than anything else, was affirmation to Sloat that he had, in fact, made the right choice and a great flood of relief coursed through him.

Monterey was firmly in American hands and the whole of California itself was now, at least for the time being, an American possession.[95]

[*July 9, 1846 • Thursday*]

With the skill of his many years of experience in naval command, Captain John Berrien Montgomery directed the approach of the warship *U.S. Portsmouth* relatively near the shore at Yerba Buena before ordering full stop and release of opposing anchors fore and aft. Already on shore, not terribly far away from where a Mexican flag barely fluttered atop a sturdy pole amid the fifty or so structures, some 200 of the inhabitants—Mexican, Indian, English and American—silently observed the arrival of the American warship, but more with curiosity than fear.

A few moments later a lowered whaleboat bearing five high-ranking officers and ten carbine-armed seamen, plus four rowers, left the ship and headed for shore. In the bow stood the captain and, beside him, Lieutenant Washington Allen Bartlett, the only officer of the *Portsmouth* who spoke fluent Spanish. Behind them one of the seated officers bore on his lap a triangularly folded bundle of cloth, unquestionably a large American flag.

Almost as if by common consent, the assembled crowd took several steps backward as the whaleboat approached a landing site on shore. As the craft thumped lightly ashore no one made any immediate attempt to disembark. Instead, the captain stepped aside slightly and nodded at the lieutenant who, in turn, nodded to the crowd and then spoke loudly:

> *Damas y caballeros, yo tengo el honor para informarle esta en los Estados Unidos de America.*

The crowd erupted in a great babble of voices and then, as the sound died, one of the listeners stepped forward and led the assemblage in three cheers. As the final *Viva!* died away, Captain Montgomery, broadly smiling, nodded at Bartlett. "Evidently they understood, Lieutenant."

Bartlett grinned in return. "I might be a little bit rusty, sir, but I think I told 'em just what you said. 'Ladies and gentlemen, I have the honor to inform you that you are in the United States of America.' Haven't told 'em yet, though, that I'm their new *alcalde*."

"That can wait for a moment," Captain Montgomery said, turning to the waiting junior officers. "All right, gentlemen, first things first. Let's get the honor guard ashore, take that Mexican flag down and raise our colors."[96]

*[July 11, 1846 • Saturday]*

The twenty-six-year-old lieutenant, graduate six years ago of the U.S. Military Academy at West Point, stood at the bow of the *U.S. Lexington*, filling his lungs with great draughts of salt air, a broad, irrepressible grin cracking his features. He was on his way to his first truly major assignment and anticipation of it set his heart beating faster and caused a flush of his cheeks not entirely attributable to the freshening breeze off the Atlantic.

He was being assigned as principal aide to the new military governor of California, although neither he nor headquarters seemed able to pinpoint exactly who that was at the moment...or even if a tentative hold on California as a new possession of the United States had truly been effected. If not, then perhaps the 4,000 military muskets in the ship's hold would help in achieving that status. But if the United States actually held that fabled territory, thought of by practically everyone in the East as truly a paradise, then this assignment, which he considered decidedly a plum, would surely be a significant stepping-stone for him in his military career. He chuckled aloud at the thought of it, then glanced about guiltily to see if he had been overheard, but no one else was nearby.

He grinned again and spoke slowly aloud, clearly savoring his own barely audible words. "California, here I come. You *are* going to do well by me, or I'm not Lieutenant William Tecumseh Sherman!"

*[July 14, 1846 • Tuesday]*

In the shabby room that he had usurped as a temporary headquarters, General Zachary Taylor, though proud of his accomplishments and the victories his army had won to this point, was abruptly saddled with a force of men so sick they could barely stand. For the moment, at least, further pursuit of the fleeing enemy was out of the question and this was what had abruptly placed him, personally, in a very untenable position.

The dilemma in which the American general found himself at the moment had actually had its inception only a few days short of a month ago. With such an enviable plethora of men available to him, he was limited only by what supplies were available to maintain the army. He and his principal officers selected those privates judged the least offensive of the multitude of miscreants and fugitives who had taken refuge from apprehension by enlisting for a year and were shipped to the front. At the same time, a multitude of discharges were occurring of those who had previously enlisted for periods of three or six months. With such an enviable source of manpower available to him, the commander had been limited only by what trustworthy men he could gather from the horde on hand and by what supplies were available to maintain his army; those supplies, in this case, dictating a maximum of six thousand effectives. At best it was an extremely confused atmosphere.

At last, on July 6, commencing from his occupational headquarters at Matamoros, General Taylor began to move this largest force possible up the Rio Grande via a flotilla of steamboats, intent on taking and occupying every town encountered en route. Once on its way the army had behaved quite well and in succession during the remainder of the month of July captured, on their way upstream, every tiny community or village of Mexicans encountered. Even the largest town of all and their immediate destination, Camargo, was taken handily earlier today by the army's advance guard.

That ambushes could have been perpetrated against them with ease at numerous places along the 250-mile journey was a fact not lost on Taylor. The army's commanding general was nagged by an ever-growing and very disturbing conviction that the administration in Washington D.C., aware of his Presidential aspirations, was actively seeking to destroy his national image by deliberately setting him up for defeat in the field.

General Zachary Taylor, however, was determined to win every battle he would fight, including whatever opposition he encountered in the nation's capital.

*[July 24, 1846 • Friday]*

Over these past many weeks, Lt. Col. John Fremont had been a very busy individual, turning up in various places all over California and constantly finding, among the Californios, men willing to drop everything else and assemble under his leadership as a new American force. For the Americans at Sutters Fort, of course, there was no question that the vast majority would support—with their lives, if necessary—the possibility of California becoming a United States territory and even, at some future time, another state of the union.

Although still refusing to comment in regard to whether or not he was acting under orders from Washington D.C. in any of this, Fremont had announced on July 3 that he would make an important address the following day. Conferring in private with Pierson B. Reading, William B. Ide, and John Bidwell, he told them it would be necessary to have some sort of plan of organization ready and asked them to act as a committee to report such plan.

The men were eager to do just that, especially now that fear had become an element in the motivation: In past years frequent rumors had circulated that were regarded as threats to the Americans and other foreigners at Sutters Fort, often causing them to hasten during the night from all places within a hundred miles or more from the fort, sometimes remaining as much as a fortnight, during which time they had drilled and prepared to resist attack. Such alarms had occurred at intervals from 1841 through 1845, yet in every case they had proven groundless and gradually the Americans and other foreigners at Sutters ceased being so apprehensive. With the population at Sutters Fort so increased by immigration of late, the sense of security had grown, even though Fremont himself was presently absent with his exploratory force of sixty men.

Then, actual hostilities had commenced and the danger was suddenly again quite real and everyone realized it was a matter of self-preservation to organize themselves to some degree. A widespread rumor had begun—some said originating from Fremont himself—that the war was begun in defense of American settlers and American interest but there was greater truth in the fact that this was a pretense to justify a war that would henceforth be carried on in the name of the United States.

Expectations for a salient comment and plan of action to be delivered by Fremont at Sonoma on July 4 fell somewhat short. The committee he had formed, consisting of Ide, Reading and Bidwell also left much to be desired, since they were unable to come to any sort of strong agreement in regard to what needed to be done. Ide's contribution, almost laughable in its simple-mindedness, suggested they paste together his long proclamations that had been affixed to the flagstaff and make them their report for Fremont. Reading's contribution was a document much shorter but, in Bidwell's view, "*...altogether too long, ponderous and unclear.*"

It was Bidwell's submission that was pithiest and most pertinent to what needed to be done at the moment. He had written:

*The undersigned hereby agree to organize for the purpose of gaining and maintaining the independence of California.*

The committee of three submitted, anonymously, what they had written to Lieutenant Gillespie and asked him to select. Without hesitation he selected Bidwell's and the meeting was called, but though Fremont made his appearance and spoke briefly to the assemblage, his remarks were generalized and provided no new light on their present situation. He did, however, announce that in addition to himself in command of the California Battalion, Fremont, acting on Commodore Stockton's request that he nominate his own officers for his California Battalion, submitted the name of Pierson Reading as paymaster, Henry King as commissary, John Bidwell as second lieutenant and Ezekiel Merritt as quartermaster.[97] As before, however, Fremont neither confirmed nor denied that he had been acting under orders from Washington, D.C. and extraneous events abruptly impinged and got him off-track; some of the men who had assembled had admitted to an incident of substantial misconduct in an Indian village not far distant and he reprimanded them soundly.

"I refuse to have anything to do with this movement," he said, "unless the men who will make up our force can and will conduct themselves properly." Everyone seemed in agreement on this accord and all listened next to a few non-conclusive remarks by Gillespie, who finished up by reading Bidwell's brief statement. The words struck home with them and every man present signed his name to the document.

Organization of a sort then took place, the men assembled into three separate companies under Captains Granville P. Swift, Henry L. Ford and Samuel J. Hensley, following which they marched into the Sacramento Valley and to Fremont's camp on the American River some five miles upstream from Sutters Fort. There, more of the men who had not been at Sonoma signed the document and more would sign, they were sure, at the Mokelumne River while the force was en route to Monterey.[98]

With his new "army" trailing behind, Fremont now returned to Sonoma and late today he organized officially what he called the California Battalion of the United States Army, with himself as its commanding officer and Marine Lt. Archibald H. Gillespie appointed as adjutant. Their avowed purpose was to carry on the revolution and they hadn't long to wait.

The following day, July 6, word was received that Castro, with a body of 400 men and two pieces of artillery, was entrenched on the south side of San Francisco Bay at Santa Clara. It meant that a circuit of more than 100 miles had to be traversed in order to reach him, but Fremont did not hesitate. He set out immediately, leading 160 mounted riflemen. However, when they reached his American River camp once again, late that same day, reliable word was received that Castro had abandoned Santa Clara and was en route to Los Angeles. Fremont instantly determined to pursue him there but, as they prepared to move on, another messenger arrived, this time from Monterey and with what Fremont considered most gratifying news: The declared war between the United States and Mexico had commenced, Monterey had been taken without resistance by the naval forces two days before. That eased the necessity for speed and Fremont delayed at his camp for another fortnight, strengthening and instructing his little army before moving on to Monterey.

Most important to Fremont was the further word received just this morning, as they reached the major port city, that the U.S. fleet would be pleased to cooperate with his little army against the Castro forces and John Bidwell wrote about the war in his journal this evening just after their arrival:

> ...There is now no longer any uncertainty and all are glad. It was a glorious sight to see the Stars and Stripes as we marched into Monterey!

### [August 1, 1846 • Saturday]

Captain James Allen finally arrived back at Fort Leavenworth with what he at first described as his "ragtag collection of five hundred Mormon recruits" averaging about twenty-seven-years old, but ranging in age from fourteen to sixty-eight, that he had led here from western Iowa. As part of the "deal" Allen agreed to, in the effort to raise the battalion, he had given in to the demand by Brigham Young that he and "my people" be given permission to over-winter in Potawatomie Indian Territory on the west bank of the Missouri River, where they would be safe from any marauding Missourians bent on harming them.[99]

The entire force of 500 Mormons volunteering for U.S. Army service under command of Lt. Col. Allen had finally assembled by July 14 and on that day the commanding officers of the five companies comprising the Mormon Battalion were hand-picked by Brigham Young and his choices were unanimously approved by the membership. Jefferson Hunt, forty-three, a bearded Kentuckian with an appearance both rugged and decidedly patriarchal, was chosen senior captain and commander of Company A.[100] The remaining four selected by Young as company commanders and approved of by Allen included Jesse D. Hunter, forty-one, for Company B; James Brown, forty-four, for Company C; Nelson Higgins, thirty-nine, for Company D; and Daniel C. Davis, forty-two, for Company E. Their subordinate officers were to be chosen and approved of by the recruits themselves.

The process of bringing them together initially at Council Bluffs had been a monumental one and except for the efforts of none other than Brigham Young himself, it would never have happened. Once convinced of Captain Allen's sincerity and need, which coincided well with the needs of the Mormons themselves, Young devised the only plan that could possibly have worked within the allotted time frame of having a full regiment of recruits assembled at Council Bluffs. The Mormons en route west at this time stretched in a virtually continuous line from the Mississippi River at Nauvoo some 300 miles to Council Bluffs on the Missouri, directly across the river where it had been determined to establish winter quarters.[101]

Using the swiftest riders he could assemble as express messengers, Brigham Young sent them eastward to recruit wagon drivers to come at once and at utmost speed to the encampment at Council Bluffs, which they must reach no later than July 6. In his urgent instructions, dictated hastily to his clerk, Willard Richards, he implored such drivers to enlist:

> *...for the purpose of raising five hundred "Mormon" volunteers to enter into the service of the United States, under the command of Captain J. Allen of the U. States army, who will be Lieut. Col. of the Regiment. Each company will elect their own officers under Col. Allen, to be marched forthwith to Fort Leavenworth, there receive their arms, ammunition, camp and hospital stores, and immediately follow Col. Kearney's trail to Santa Fe. This is no hoax.... We must take these five hundred men from among the teamsters, and send them without delay. If there is any one among you over eighteen and under forty-five that wants to and can go, let him be at Council Bluffs forthwith...*

Brigham Young went on to assure all who showed an interest that their families would be cared for and that they would fare as well as his own family did and that he, personally, would see that they were helped along. In addition to his instructions, Young then made some unusual predictions, stating that:

*...not one Saint who enlists will fall by the hands of the nation's foe; your only fighting will be with wild beasts and there will not be as many bullets whistling about your heads as occurred at Carthage jail.*[102]

However much the urgency to gather and induct these men into service, it was unrealistic to assume it could be done in only a matter of a few days and so Allen had delayed their departure from Council Bluffs until more than a sufficient number had arrived, at which time they were all sworn into service with a very pleased Brigham Young looking on. And though the men were given the right to select their own officers, except for the principal commander, it was Young himself who usurped that right and personally named the men who were to be the officers of the five companies of the Mormon Battalion.

It was not until July 16, however, that the assembled Saints who were to be the privates of the Mormon Battalion were sworn in and assigned to specific companies.[103] The swearing-in ceremony was conducted by Allen beneath a US flag hastily erected at Council Bluffs, by Brigham Young's order, on a tall slender sapling stripped of its lower branches. At the same time, James Allen adopted his own new rank of lieutenant colonel. Almost immediately he issued his first three orders to the new troops:

*Head Quarters, Mormon Battalion,*
*Council Bluffs, Iowa, July 16, 1846:*
*(Order No. 1—In virtue of authority given me by the Col. Commanding the army of the west, I hereby assume the command of the Mormon Battalion, raised at this place for the service of the United States. Therefore, companies now organized will be held in readiness to march at the shortest notice, and as soon as the fifth company be filled all will be ready for movement.*

*(Order No. 2)—The following appointments are made in the Battalion: First lieutenant, George P. Dykes, to be Adjutant; Private James H. Glines, to be Sergeant Major; Private Sebert C. Shelton, of Company A, to be Quartermaster Sergeant. They will be respected and obeyed accordingly.*

*(Order No. 3)—William L. McIntyre, of the Mormon people, is hereby appointed assistant surgeon to the Mormon Battalion*

*of volunteers of the United States, and under my command. He will be obeyed and respected accordingly, and will be entitled to the pay and emoluments as an assistant surgeon in the United States Army.*[104]

*J. Allen, Lt. Col, U.S.A., Commanding*

That evening, Henry Bigler dutifully wrote in his diary:

*...The Battalion was made up of five companies—A, B, C, D, and E—one hundred men in each company. We had the privilege of making our own officers from among our own men. I attached myself to Company B, Jesse D. Hunter, Captain. The battalion was mustered into service July 16, and Capt Allen took command as Colonel; the same day he marched us some six or eight miles to a trading post on the Missouri River kept by some Frenchmen. I think the proprietor's name was Sarpea.*[105] *Here Colonel Allen issued to his men blankets, provisions, camp kettles, knives, forks, plates, spoons, etc.*

They returned to the Council Bluffs camp and remained there until Company E was brought to its designated strength and then, at noon on Tuesday, July 21, lustily singing the traditional marching song, *The Girl I left Behind Me*, commenced the 180-mile march down the trail following the east bank of the Missouri River to a point opposite Fort Leavenworth.

The initial singing did not last long, as it had been by no means an easy march, especially since some of those that had joined the battalion at Council Bluffs were so ill they were unable to walk and had to ride in the several wagons accompanying them. One of these, Samuel Boley of Company B, had actually died during the short journey, just before 1:00 a.m. on July 23 and was buried, wrapped in his blanket and contained in a hastily constructed box as a coffin, shortly after daybreak that very day.

Clouds of mosquitoes plagued them periodically and several rainstorms en route made the trail a quagmire of mud, but they plodded doggedly on, averaging at least ten miles per day. Colonel Allen was among a number of the men who contracted malaria while en route, but he was less able than his men to overcome the effects of the malady. For a while he tried, but this only aggravated his condition, making him less able to the task of trying to transform these men in a very short time into an effective body of fighting men, a task that at first seemed patently absurd. It was perhaps his own suffering from malaria that prompted him to appoint Dr. George B. Sanderson as battalion surgeon today, not fully realizing how much that doctor was detested by the Saints, who had quickly dubbed him Dr Death. One of the Saints, Elijah Allen, complained bitterly that this surgeon "...*would rather kill the damned Mormons than cure them*" and another private, William Johnson, added that the doctor's medicine "...*would kill a dog on short notice.*"

Allen's whole force of the Mormon Battalion finally reached a point along the Missouri River opposite Fort Leavenworth and here an entire day was spent in ferrying the men across the river, where they were immediately issued tents, muskets and ammunition. The fundamentally humorous good nature of their commander surfaced again and endeared him even more to his men when they gathered in a sizeable crowd outside the arsenal before it was opened. Colonel Allen accompanied the officer who was to issue the arms and as he reached the front of the crowd before the entry, he paused and held up his arms until they silenced. With a twinkling expression he lowered his arms and, in a voice strong enough to carry to all, said: "Stand back, boys! Don't be in a hurry to get your muskets; you'll want to throw the damned things away before you get to California!"[106]

By nightfall a whole new tent city of the five hundred Mormon recruits had blossomed outside the walls of the fort and despite how progressively worse Allen was feeling, he was amazed at how quickly these Mormons, so "raw" in military movements, learned the orders of arms and march. They seemed to work together with such universal purpose of mind that the training of one appeared to transfer itself through a peculiar form of osmosis to others. In a remarkably short time they were becoming reasonably well coordinated and were, in fact, doing better than many of the other troops that had been training for weeks or sometimes even months.

Further, the commander of the Mormon Battalion was especially cheered by one element of news that was imparted to him almost immediately upon his reaching the fort: General Kearny had already successfully taken Bents Fort in the Colorado country and was presently approaching Santa Fe in the Spanish New Mexico Territory, which might take him a while to conquer, and immediately after which he would be poised to set out for California. Allen continued to be disheartened, however, by the fact that more than 30 of the men had brought their families along; some of them, such as their senior captain, Jefferson Hunt, actually bringing two wives. In addition, there were forty-four children, plus a scattering of other family members and camp followers who brought the extraneous total to about 100. These latter "civilians" Allen was quite determined to leave behind once his force reached Santa Fe.

With the time quickly at hand for these Mormons to march out on the trail to Santa Fe, Lieutenant Colonel James Allen was very pleased, not only with himself and his own highly important and well-earned promotion, but also with the rapid accomplishments of his Mormon Battalion and, perhaps most of all, with the trust they evinced in him. So far as he could see, there was but one "fly in the ointment" at this time: the Mormon Battalion *had* to be marched out at once if there was to be any chance at all of overtaking General Kearny in his own march to California. However, Allen, who yearned for the duty he had been selected to perform, was now finding it necessary to absent himself, at least temporarily, and relegate that role to someone else. He had delayed too long already, barely able now to move under his own power and wracked by fevers and chills such as he had never before in his life experienced.

Only two decidedly linked matters remained pertinent to him during his moments of clearer thought: He *had* to be hospitalized and submit to truly professional treatment to combat the malaria presently assailing him; at the same time, he had no choice now but to send them off the Mormon Battalion under Jefferson Hunt as their temporary commander until he could regain his health and subsequently overtake them.

*[August 2, 1846 · Saturday · 4:30 p.m.]*

The uniformed third lieutenant, accompanied by a squad of six musket-armed privates, marched in reasonably precise formation from their tent city just outside the fort, through the main gateway and headed directly for the main quarters in which former Californio General Mario Guadalupe Vallejo was still being held under house arrest. The lieutenant wore a grim expression, evidently unhappy with his present assignment, but orders were orders and he had no choice but to obey.

At the portal to the main quarters, the soldiers came to a halt at attention and transferred their weapons from shouldered arms to ready arms and stood waiting. The lieutenant mounted the single step of the wooden porch and crossed to the door where he knocked authoritatively—three sharp raps. After a few moments the door was opened and John Sutter, a faintly steaming cup of coffee in hand, stepped to the threshold and stopped, frowning.

"Yes, Lieutenant, what is it?"

"By order of the commander of Fort Sacramento, we have come for General Vallejo. Summon him, sir."

"Fremont?" Sutter questioned. "What the hell does Colonel Fremont want with General Vallejo?" His voice sharpened "And this is Sutters Fort, not Fort Sacramento, Lieutenant."

"No sir, it is no longer Sutters Fort. By order of our new commander, First Lieutenant Edward M. Kern, this installation, now under Federal authority, has been renamed Fort Sacramento. You are ordered, sir, to summon General Vallejo."

"I'm well aware of the fort's name change, Lieutenant."

As he was; that sailor, what was his name again?... Scott! That was it, William Scott. He'd shown up and told Sutter about the U.S. takeovers at Sonoma, Monterey and Yerba Buena and that his own fort would hereafter be Fort Sacramento. Scott said all of California was in American hands now, but Sutter hadn't believed that. He still didn't, but these days he was becoming less sure of himself. Scott told him that Lieutenant Revere at Yerba Buena had sent him with the American flag he was carrying, that Sutter was to haul down the tattered Swiss flag and replace it with the stars and stripes. Which, of course, he had done, on the next day—July 11. That was when Sutter had summoned all the inhabitants at the fort and addressed them.

"Gentlemen," he'd said, "we are now under the protection of a new flag, a very great flag, the American flag. Today Sutters Fort passes out of existence. It has now become Fort Sacramento.[107] The fort, you and I, and everyone living in California, are from this time on, under a new master. From this moment, we will take orders only from Washington. Let us salute the flag. Let us love, honor and obey it, and defend it with our lives."

They had then fired all the cannon repeatedly in salute and the heavy reverberations had broken a number of the fort's windows. Then the New York Volunteers had arrived from Sonoma under Lieutenant

Anderson. If that weren't enough, word had come at the end of July that the Hudson's Bay Company had sold its holdings at Yerba Buena and pulled out, but instead of cutting down the number of settlers there, they were flocking in and new houses were being built by the dozens, with more than ninety expected to be raised by the end of this year and the population to probably be close to four hundred by then. Finally, the influx of new settlers from the East had been tremendous. From May to the end of July, half a thousand new settlers had crossed the Sierras by the Truckee River route alone. All these changes were so great and so frequent, Sutter was having a hard time keeping up with things. Even *he* had been changed somewhat, as a stipend of fifty dollars monthly was regularly paid him.

Now, he'd just been told Lieutenant Kern was the new commander here and he shook his head as if he were some kind of wounded animal. "Ed Kern's commander here now?" he asked. "My God, the man's an artist, not a soldier! Where the hell is Fremont? Where's Bartlett?"

The lieutenant was obviously becoming agitated, but he managed to respond politely enough. "Sir, Lieutenant Colonel Fremont is no longer commander here. He is now in full command of our California forces. At present he's with a body of 250 men—the California Battalion—en route under orders to Monterey. He anticipates he will be leading them against the Méxi—excuse me, against the Californio—forces under Generals Pico and Castro. We remain under martial law. Lieutenant Bartlett, as ordered—as soon as he'd organized the garrison here—has turned over control of the fort to First Lieutenant Kern, who is now this installation's commander. I ask again, sir, that you summon General Vallejo immediately."

Sutter shook his head. "General Vallejo's resting. I'll rouse him. Wait here, please." He shut the door quickly, before the young officer could object, and strode toward the back room where Vallejo was resting, pausing briefly at the table to set down his cup of coffee. *Now what the hell's going on here?* he wondered. He didn't at all like what was occurring. *Fort Sacramento? What the hell was wrong with Sutters Fort?*

As a matter of fact, Sutter hadn't really liked much of anything that had occurred here since Vallejo and the others had been brought in and incarcerated as prisoners of war. The whole countryside was in such flux, no one seemed to be sure what was occurring: That Mormon group under Samuel Brannan had come in and settled themselves and were starting to farm somewhere southeast of the Bay, except for the limited number of them he'd hired to help him build the grist mill, upstream a few miles at Natomo; Bob Semple and Walt Colton were preparing to establish within a fortnight their own new weekly newspaper, *The Californian*, at Monterey, evidently to compete with Brannan's *California Star* at Yerba Buena; the whole countryside south of Monterey was in a state of active revolt and God only knew who was going to come out ahead on that one, though Sutter was betting on the Americans.

Sutter paused outside the door to the store-room where Vallejo was resting. Then he knocked softly and was surprised when the door opened almost immediately and Vallejo stood there, fully dressed but not yet with his boots on, smiling quizzically. "Well, John! How can I help you?"

Sutter made his decision without even realizing that he'd been weighing the options. "There's a squad of soldiers out front, with a lieutenant in charged. Armed. They've come to take you away. Better get out while you can, through the back. I'll keep 'em busy and…"

"Hold it, John!" Vallejo was shaking his head. "I'm not running from anything or anyone. Just let me get my boots on and we'll go out together."

A few moments later they stepped out onto the porch. The lieutenant took a backward step and then snapped the order, "'Ten-shun!" The squad, standing at ease, came swiftly erect with their weapons at present arms. The officer turned back to Vallejo.

"General, sir," he said. "I've been ordered here by Lieutenant Kern. I'm to inform you, sir that you are no longer to consider yourself under arrest. You may stay here, if you wish, or you may leave the fort anytime you wish. Lieutenant Kern has a pass for you if you wish to return to Sonoma."

"Thank you, lieutenant," Vallejo replied. His gaze shifted momentarily to Sutter and the corners of his eyes crinkled a bit with restrained laughter. He returned his gaze to the officer. "Thank you for delivering the message, Lieutenant. You can inform Lieutenant Kern that I will drop in on him directly. Then, I believe I'll go home."

*[August 4, 1846 • Tuesday]*

James Knox Polk, President of the United States, was on the verge of committing an act that was not only criminal but would likely, if the facts ever became publicly known, not only result in his being impeached, but also accused of, and tried for, high treason. It was unnerving but, he felt, necessary, if he were to accomplish the principle goal he had set for himself and, in effect, for the American people: A unified order of States of the Union that stretched across this land from Atlantic to Pacific coasts.

The first matter he had tacitly approved, which had set the Whigs on fire with resentment, was his condoning, as far back as Independence Day, the action undertaken by General Taylor down in Mexico; his ordering the actual shooting of deserters detected in the process of defecting to Mexico. So far a dozen or more such defectors had been shot and killed as they attempted to cross the Rio Grande to join the enemy.

The instant word of this reached Washington D.C., the *National Intelligencer* led the Whig press in a roar of protest so prolonged that its echoes still reverberated today. President Polk was accused of tyranny, of advocating the murder of American soldiers without courts-martial. In the House chambers, John Quincy Adams loudly proclaimed the need that existed to court-martial *every* American officer who should order such killing, as well as every soldier who carried out such orders. Further, Adams declared, an inquiry should be made into the *causes* of such desertion in the first place. Even though his proposed measure was cut down, the uproar continued and the *Calm Observer* added its own attack against both Polk and Taylor by writing that discipline would become impossible among the American troops if such brutality were to continue. Fortunately, these attacks against the Administration were nullified to some degree when the not-yet-one-year-old *National Police Gazette* began publishing its own voluminous lists of deserters from the Army, which the War Department quickly reprinted in volume to distribute among the American troops.

Another Whig publication, the *Baltimore American*, fired off a punishing salvo against the Administration, listing all the Mexican provinces it claimed the Administration intended to take over, which was near half of that country. Polk countered by writing in his diary—and telling a select few of his callers—that he had always wanted the California and New Mexico territories, to unify the nation, adding that "perhaps something more was not unlikely, but that was strictly a contingency based on the cost of the war to America."

The war was producing a shortage of arms and so President Polk, after consulting with Texas Ranger Samuel Walker, placed an order on July 10 with Samuel Colt for his new, now well-proved six-shooter revolver. Colt, in turn, engaged E.K. Root to assist in mass production of the revolvers, with interchangeable parts, in Root's new factory at Hartford, Connecticut.

Polk's ill-advised venture into territory forbidden to a President of the United States commenced with his secret contact of General Santa Ana, still in exile in Cuba. All along, Santa Ana had been directing his Mexican co-conspirators to do what they could to undermine the Paredes government, which he feared. Paredes was one of the few Mexican leaders who was champion of his country and his people, but he *did* have two grievous faults: his elemental stupidity and his alcoholic dependency. Last January Paredes himself had written:

> *...Order is precarious, peace insecure, and the nation, in the midst of the anarchy which consumes it and the chaos which surrounds it, moves toward dissolution and the fear of death.*

Now, with the U.S. President himself "forgiving" Santa Ana for the affair at the Alamo in Texas and offering him substantial payment to unseat Paredes and resume control of Mexican forces, the deposed general was ready for his return and readily agreed to be a "benevolent" protector of the Mexican people and a "considerate friend" of the United States. He agreed to return as a "liberator" of his people and with the help of the United States would deliver his country "from the tyranny of monarchists," of which, he declared, Paredes was worst. He agreed that as soon as he returned to power, he would cede to the U.S. the land Polk wanted, to indemnify the U.S. for its war expenses...although, of course, the U.S. would have to pay for the ceded territory. He promised to assist in determining a permanent boundary between the U.S. and Mexico and absolutely guaranteed that San Francisco Bay would be to the north of that boundary. He added, cautiously, at the end of his oral agreement, a solicitous reminder: "Let the President see to it that the personal publicity of Santa Ana in the American press is conducted in the most favorable terms."

On the surface it all seemed a good idea, but in reality it was idiotic to think Santa Ana could ever have been anything but a dangerous despot. Unfortunately, this was a factor the American President failed to consider. Nevertheless, the deed was done. Santa Ana was paid by Polk a secret "first payment" of $2 million, roughly one-sixth of the war cost Polk could commit himself to underwrite, and this, he was assured, was how that initial payment would be utilized: Even though Mexico owed U.S. citizens a considerable sum, already duly adjudicated, the fact of the matter was that Mexico had no money and the only way it could pay would be by ceding territory and this, as Polk understood it, was what Santa Ana would do. It was, however, a badly tangled web with "strands" attached that had to be considered; no Mexican government could possibly make such a cession of land unless it had support of the army and, to maintain that support, Santa Ana would have to be able to pay his army. The $2 million advance on the ultimate payment in full would, Santa Ana assured Polk, pay the Mexican Army and conciliate his country into ceding New Mexico and California to the U.S., upon which Polk would be able to end his war and bring peace to both Mexico and the U.S. The remainder would be paid, Polk promised, when he could get Congress to approve it in the secret war fund, of which he had no doubt they would do. His subsequent proposal went to Congress and was approved as "an appropriation for foreign negotiations" at the behest of President Polk alone. Immediately, though not quite so confidently as previously, Polk believed he had actually arranged permanent peace between the two warring nations and at once he sent an order to Commodore Conner to allow Santa Ana to pass unmolested through the U.S. naval blockade.

Passage of the bill set the Whigs into paroxysms of muffled laughter: When the measure failed, as surely it *must*, Congress would be held entirely blameless and the whole weight of "fiscal responsibility" would have to be borne by one person alone: the President of the United States, James Knox Polk.

[*August 15, 1846 • Saturday*]

Although it was Commodore Robert F. Stockton, from his headquarters at Monterey, who first suggested that a weekly newspaper be inaugurated here, to be called *The Monterey Californian*, it was frontiersman Robert F. Semple and U.S. Navy Chaplain Walter Colton—presently Monterey's first American *alcalde*—who turned the notion into a reality.

The idea had been generated as a need to compete with Sam Brannan's *California Star*, which Stockton feared to be merely a mouthpiece for Brannan's band of Mormons now inhabiting a tent city of their own creation along the San Joaquín River southeast of San Francisco Bay. Though not really in concert with Stockton's conclusion in regard to Brannan, Semple and Colton nevertheless thought the idea of a weekly newspaper for Monterey to be a good one and leaped to the challenge.

The pair had at once gone to the city's abandoned quarters of Augustin V. Zamorano and there located the old Zamorano printing press in a store room and set to work in preparing it for the jobs ahead. It hadn't been used in a considerable while, though its history had been to some degree illustrious: This was the press on which Zamorano had, in 1834, published California's first book and had, as well, been the source of all the governmental proclamations published and posted in the years that followed under a variety of Mexican governors. Nevertheless, it had been in storage for many months now and required prodigious cleaning to rid it of the caked inks that had not been cleaned away after its last use.

Quite equal to the proposed task, Bob Semple and Walt Colton rejuvenated the old press, prepared the new inks and type-faces and today—Saturday, August 15, 1846—they published the four-page weekly newspaper they had decided to name in a slightly altered version of what Commodore Stockton had suggested. They printed this initial issue half in Spanish and half in English.

With justifiable pride, they had named it *The Californian*.

[*August 17, 1846 • Monday*]

Commodore Robert Field Stockton, the new American commander in California, sat at his desk today and, in his fine handwriting that he had practiced so diligently, wrote in bold letters across the top center of the blank page before him, the first line of the proclamation that would forever after enshrine his own name as the officer who had made California a possession of the United States:

*"To the People of California"*

He paused before dipping his pen and writing more, pleased at the quirk of fate that had brought him, a newcomer to this country, to the place where he would forever after be hailed as California's "liberator"—a title which, by rights, belonged to Commodore John Drake Sloat. A soft chuckle escaped him. Perhaps it ran in the family; his own grandfather had been one of the signers of the Declaration of Independence. That it had fallen to himself to be author of *this* document was simply fate. Wasn't it?

"The fortunes—or misfortunes—of life in the Navy," he muttered, but it made him pause as he thought of what had occurred since his arrival here. It had been on July 23 when Commodore Sloat, because of his own illness, had turned command over to him. He smiled at his own vow to himself when he had arrived that day: "I swear," he had told himself, in regard to the matter of California independence, "that I will expend half my private fortune..." which was quite substantial "... rather than fail of success."

Stockton quickly embarked the Navy Battalion of Mounted Rifles aboard the *U.S. Cyane* to occupy San Diego and claim it in the name of the United States, just as Commodore Sloat had already claimed Monterey, Yerba Buena and Sonora before his arrival. But such "claiming," Stockton had been pleased to note, had been done by simply raising the Stars and Stripes and vocally making the claim without proper documentation. Stockton was swiftly rectifying that little error with the documentation of his own that he was now in the process of preparing.

When Fremont had first met Sloat and the then duly constituted commander of the U.S. forces in California had asked him by what authority he was acting, Fremont had been forced to admit he had acted on his own. This had greatly shocked Sloat and made him determined to get out from under at once. Old and sick as he was, Sloat was still resolute enough to withhold permission for Fremont to march against Santa Barbara and Los Angeles, which were meant by Fremont to complete his conquests, and he also refused to muster Fremont's battalion into United States service. More than anything else at the time, Sloat wanted to let someone else take responsibility. That "someone" had, of course, been Stockton...and the self-assured Stockton had no doubt he could control the ambitious Fremont.

To properly place Fremont in his own niche, subservient, of course, to himself, Commodore Stockton quickly rescinded Sloat's orders and commissioned Fremont—though definitely by dubious authority to do so—as a major in the Army, made Archibald Gillespie a captain, then mustered in Fremont's irregulars as the Navy Battalion of Mounted Riflemen—in other words, the Horse Marines. Then he prepared to "conquer" the rest of California, for which he'd clearly need the document he was presently preparing.

Fremont had not been at all happy to be cast in a subservient role, even though one of the highest ranked. He had envisioned himself in the role of supreme commander in California and it irked him considerably that the wand had passed him by. Even more, he deplored the declaration Stockton had made against Castro, Pico and the Californios in general in his initial proclamation on July 26.

In that document, Stockton blandly accused Castro of

> ...*lawless violence; a man who intends, with the aid of hostile Indians, to keep this beautiful country in a constant state of revolution and blood. Castro is...a usurper, has been guilty of great offenses, has drained the country of almost its last dollar, and has deserted his post now, when most needed. Therefore, moved by reports from the interior of scenes of rapine, blood and murder, and, as the only means to save from destruction the lives and property of the foreign residents and citizens of the country who have invoked his protection, it is my duty as military commander here to drive the criminals and usurpers out of California and restore peace and prosperity.*

So far as Stockton was aware—and he had quickly made himself aware of just about everything—there had been no rapine, pillage or murder, no one had invited either his participation or protection, and those he was vilifying as usurpers and criminals were, in fact, the constituted authorities. Stockton was not only flat-out lying about the entire situation, he was ignoring the stated purposes of his own government. What Fremont had failed to take into consideration was there just might be another officer of the line quite as hungry for glory as was he—and it happened to be an officer who outranked him.

Pursuant to his orders, Fremont raised the American flag at San Diego on July 29, impressed horses for his own and his men's needs and started north to rejoin Stockton on August 8. For his own part, Stockton called up a landing force of 360 marines and sailors and left Monterey with them aboard the *U.S. Congress* on August 1, intent on reaching Los Angeles and pausing only briefly at Santa Barbara to raise the United States colors and leave behind a small force to maintain the occupancy.

On August 13, Stockton, entered and took possession of Los Angeles and raised the American flag.

Fremont's command joined Stockton's the following day—August 14—and the peculiar "land army" of sailors occupied Los Angeles. With that, the so-called conquest of California—with John Fremont second in command—was completed...but only for a while. On this same day, Stockton caused to be arrested on suspicion of disloyalty, former American citizen Jonathan Trumbull Warner, owner of the 49,000-acre Warner's Ranch.[108]

Now, fully satisfied with his own actions thus far in the takeover of California from Mexican control, Commander Stockton returned his attention to the document he had begun and wrote swiftly, in his elegant handwriting, directly below the title of:

### To the people of California

*On my approach to this place with the forces under my command, José Castro, the commandant general of California, buried his artillery and abandoned his fortified "camp of the Mesa" and fled, it is believed, towards Mexico. With the sailors, the marines, and the California battalion of mounted riflemen, we entered the 'City of Angels', the capital of California, on the 13th of August, and hoisted the North American flag.*

*The flag of the United States is now flying from every Commanding position in the Territory, and California is entirely free of Mexican domination.*

*The Territory of California now belongs to the United States, and will be governed, as soon as circumstances permit, by officers and laws similar to those by which other Territories of the United States are regulated and protected. But, until the governor, the secretary, and the council are appointed, and the various departments of the government are arranged, military law will prevail, and the commander-in-chief will be the governor and protector of the Territory.*

*In the mean time the people will be permitted, and are now requested, to meet in their several towns and departments, at such time and place as they may see fit, to elect civil officers to fill the places of those who decline to continue in office, and to administer the laws according to the former usages of the Territory. In all cases* where the people fail to elect, the commander-in-chief will make the appointments himself.

All persons, of whatever religion or nation, who faithfully adhere to the new government, will be considered as citizens of the Territory, and will be zealously and thoroughly protected in their liberty of conscience, their persons, and property.

No persons will be permitted to remain in the Territory who do not agree to support the existing government, and all military men who desire to remain are required to take an oath that they will not take up arms against it, or do or say anything to disturb the peace. Nor will any person, come from where they may, be permitted to settle in the Territory who do not pledge themselves to be, in all respects, obedient to the laws which may be from time to time enacted by the proper authorities of the Territory.

All persons who, without special permission, are found with arms outside of their own houses, will be considered as enemies and will be shipped out of the country.

All thieves will be put to hard labor on the public works, and there kept until compensation is made for the property stolen.

The California battalion of mounted riflemen will be kept in the service of the Territory, and constantly on duty, to prevent and punish any aggressions by the Indians, or any other persons, upon the property of individuals, or the peace of the Territory; and California shall hereafter be so governed and defended as to give security to the inhabitants, and to defy the power of Mexico.

All persons are required, as long as the Territory is under martial law, to be within their houses from 10 o'clock at night until sunrise in the morning.

R.F. Stockton, Commander of the Territory of California
Ciudad de Los Angeles, August 17, 1846[109]

[August 18, 1846 • Tuesday]

On this day, Brigadier General Stephen Watts Kearny entered the oldest city in the West—Santa Fe, in the Spanish New Mexican Territory—with his force of 1,800 men and claimed it for the United States, without a single shot having been fired. After the slight resistance overcome at Bents Fort, both with the residents there and the Indian tribes in the vicinity, he had fully expected that the Mexican leader fleeing ahead of him—General Manuel Armijo—would make his stand at Santa Fe, especially after the proclamation he had issued before abandoning Bents Fort. The Armijo proclamation had been issued on August 8 and rattled on extensively, but said, in essence, that General Armijo was

> ...*willing to sacrifice my life and all my interests in the defense of my country.*

The Kearny Army of the West plodded on, intent on reaching Santa Fe and engaging the enemy there, but the very next day, August 9, Captain Weightman of the artillery, arrived from Bents Fort, where he'd remained to convalesce, with another American officer in tow—Major Thomas Swords, the quartermaster. They had traveled all night in order to overtake Colonel Kearny and had reached him just at reveille as they prepared to march into the little town of Las Vegas. Swords, inordinately pleased with himself, delivered into Kearny's hand the special orders he'd brought from Fort Leavenworth: Stephen Watts Kearny was now officially promoted to the rank of brigadier general.

Brigadier General Stephen Kearny, fiercely proud on his new rank, wasted no time. Las Vegas was devoid of protectors in any form and Kearny, from a roof-top overlooking the public square, immediately issued a proclamation of his own, informing the residents that they were now Americans. He reminded them of the oppression under which they had been living and promised them security in both their religion and their property, assuring them that the United States would hereafter protect them from the roving bands of Indians as they had never before been protected in over two centuries of occupation. The gentle residents smiled and cheered, provided the soldiers with wines and fruits and gravely swore the allegiance demanded of them to the United States of America, not overlooking Kearny's terminal warning to them: "... *But, listen! He who promises to be quiet and is found in arms against me, I will hang!"*

Without delay, Kearny's force moved on with less jollity in the ranks now, fully expecting to be ambushed, as they approached Santa Fe, by the army of 4,000 men under Governor-General Armijo's command. But when the Army of the West moved fearfully through the mountain pass where they had expected such ambush to occur, the Mexican Army had disbanded and was nowhere to be found and its commander, so they were told, was fleeing ahead of them... and he no longer had an army.

Governor-General Manuel Armijo was no longer a threat of any consequence to the Army of the West under Brigadier General Stephen Watts Kearny.[110]

# Chapter 6

♦

[*August 20, 1846 • Thursday*]

President Polk was frustrated at the inter-party disruptions that were causing both of the major national political parties—Whigs and Democrats—to endure as many internal problems as they regularly caused one another. Had one or the other maintained a stability within itself it could have emerged as a forceful entity and easily taken over American politics, but both were in utter chaos and needful of complete reorganization and a greater sense of unity. So, what frustrated Polk was also the factor that helped preserve him in his office.

It was Congressman David Wilmot who set both House and Senate back on their heels on August 8 this year when, almost certainly for motives of his own, he delivered a brazen and fervent ten-minute speech—which became known as the Wilmot Proviso—that made both parties recognize their own failings and the desperate need to reorganize. He told Congress that for the past twenty-six years both parties had ignored the very paradox at its own core, the unresolved conflict at the foundation of its economy and politics; a conflict that now as an undeniable repression distinctly threatened destruction and death to both parties. Repression instills neuroses and both parties were now on the very lip of collapse due to such repression. Whatever motivation Democrat David Wilmot and his supporters may have had is of little consequence; what does matter is that *someone* had to bring into full light the profound disruption in both parties and cause the repression to end, and it was Wilmot who did it here and now.

All this had been occasioned by the highly secretive deal being negotiated between Polk and the deposed Mexican General Santa Ana, in which Santa Ana promised that for the sum of $10 million to pay the troops of the Mexican Army—and the guarantee of his being permitted to reenter Mexico—he would reorganize the Army and take it from the grasp of the Mexican President he accused of being a despot, Paredes y Arrilaga. The initial payment of $2 million that had been pending in the House was, as Polk had delineated it, for "extraordinary expenses" that had originated in, and was paramount to, the intercourse between the United States and foreign nations. Several speakers had risen to defend or sneer at the President's request and the bill was on the verge of being voted today—successfully, Polk believed—when David Wilmot, the junior Democratic Representative of Pennsylvania took the floor.

"I did not think of this present war with Mexico as a war of conquest when I voted for it," he said, "nor do I think it one now. I will support the President, but there are questions I must needs ask: Just why does the President want this money? Since we will not pay for land we claim to be ours," meaning that to the Rio Grande, "there must be an intention to acquire more land. I approve of our acquiring territory on the Pacific, including the Bay of San Francisco, by purchase or negotiation. But I am most definitely opposed to the peculiar institution of slavery. It exists in Texas, so I accept it there. But if, now, free territory comes in—and Mexico is free soil—then God forbid that we shall plant this peculiar institution in it. I therefore suggest this amendment to the Bill: *Provided:* That as an express and fundamental condition to the acquisition of any territory from the Republic of Mexico by the United States, by virtue of any treaty which may be negotiated between them and to the use by the Executive of the moneys herein appropriated, neither slavery nor involuntary servitude shall ever exist in any part of the said territory, except for crime, whereof the party shall first be duly convicted."

Thus was the Wilmot Proviso, which fastened the question of slavery to the President's request for $2 million advance for the purchase of territory. It was already 8:20 p.m. on that August 8 Saturday evening and the measure fell quietly now in the House chambers that were clearly disorganized, decidedly weary, obviously inattentive and to some degree drunk. The Southern coalition was lax, its nerves frayed, and only a weak opposition could be mounted. News of the projected amendment flashed through the city and the gallery filled with the likes of such cabinet members as the Secretary of State and the Secretary of the Navy and the Postmaster General to witness what maneuvering would occur. There were few and, after a few customary and inconsequential substitutions, the Wilmot Proviso was amended to apply particularly to a treaty of peace. Without any further substantial opposition the House quickly passed the bill and then adjourned itself into the sickeningly hot August evening.

President Polk had his desired $2 million bribe as a down-payment to Santa Ana, one of America's most loathed enemies, while the Paredes government, which sought only peace, could not help but fall and the despotic Santa Ana, back in power once again, *might* live up to his promises. But with the $2 million snugly in his grasp and not recallable, the Mexican general just might not honor *any* promise.

Now, President Polk was furious over what had occurred and wrote in his private journal:

> *I consider that Proviso a mischievous & foolish amendment.... What connection slavery has with making peace with Mexico is difficult to conceive.*

It was much too late now for second thoughts in that context. With his ten short minutes of House oratory, David Wilmot and his *Proviso* had its unprecedented effect; it had forced Polk to acknowledge the bribe he had made with the nation's worst enemy. The $2 million advance of the $10 million payment in full to Santa Ana, he argued, would enable that general to pay the Mexican Army, oust its tyrannical president, conciliate its countrymen and ultimately deliver the cession of the vast New Mexico and California Territories to the United States and thus end the war. This, President Polk believed, in the deepest recesses of his own heart, was the simplest and most straightforward road to peace, as well as finally permitting the United States that ultimate goal that this country should eventually stretch from Atlantic to Pacific.

All this was, Polk believed, a most worthy and selfless plan to benefit the people of the United States. Unfortunately, no one could have been more blinded than he to the consequences he had set in motion. His "secret deal" with Santa Ana, when it became known, had quite rightfully been construed by the public as an act little short of traitorous and for which he would be fortunate to escape censure and impeachment; even if he did, it effectively ended any possibility of Polk ever running for a second term in the Presidency; and, most important of all, the issue of slavery in the United States was now, at last, out of the closet and there it would stay and already, over the past twelve days since the bill's passage, it was well on its way to driving an implacable, ever-widening wedge between the Northern and Southern States.

[*August 23, 1846 • Sunday • 12:00 noon*]

It was at exactly noon today that Lieutenant James Pace mounted his horse and set off from Fort Leavenworth to take the sad news to Brigham Young at his Council Bluffs headquarters. Of the three sealed letters he bore with him, addressed to Young, the one finished by Lieutenant Samuel Gully shortly before Pace's departure, was in his pack, along with the letters for the Mormon leader written earlier this morning by Dr. George B. Sanderson, aspiring to become surgeon to the Mormon Battalion, and the West Pointer, First Lieutenant Andrew Jackson Smith of the First Dragoons. All three dealt with the same subject but were of somewhat different elemental theme; those of Sanderson and Smith being clearly motivated more by an aura of self-aggrandizement as by sympathy for what had occurred. That of Lt. Gully, however, bore a strong sense of genuine bereavement over the loss.

Almost exactly six hours earlier, at 6 a.m. precisely, Lieutenant Colonel James Allen, commander of the Mormon Battalion, died of his acute malaria, exacerbated by consumption.[111]

As soon as the announcement was made of the commander's death, both Lt. Smith and Dr. Sanderson immediately wanted to push Lt. Gully out to join the Battalion. Gully was furious at the suggestion and after venting his rage for a few moments, added, "I am not under your command, nor will I remove until it suits me!"

The argument may easily have become much more heated except that both Pace and Gully were approached by a headquarters orderly who told them they were to report at once to the quarters of the post commander, Lieutenant Colonel Clifton Wharton.[112] The pair shrugged and followed the orderly and were, in turn, soon followed by Smith and Sanderson.

"I'd like to know," Wharton said to Gully, as soon as the pair entered, "the present whereabouts of the Mormon Battalion and if every necessary requisition has been filled and completed. Lieutenant?"

"Yes sir," replied Gully. "All necessaries filled and completed." Before he was able to add more, however, Smith and Sanderson immediately stated their complaints concerning Gully and their arrogant assumptions in regard to their own intentions respecting the Mormon Battalion. Wharton heard them out with a bit of an exasperated air and then turned again to Gully.

Lieutenant," he said, "as I understand matters, the Mormons now have the perfect right to elect their own company commanders, but no one else." He shot a meaningful glance at Smith and Sanderson, "I repeat, *no one*, has any *right* to assume the command. Is that correct?"

The lieutenant and the doctor remained silent and it was Gully who replied. "Yes sir, that's correct. I have written a letter to that effect to Captain Hunt, who was given nominal command of the Battalion by Lieutenant Colonel Allen before he took sick, and I will send an express forthwith to General Kearny and inform him of our situation. We Mormons are, of course, a separate corps from all other soldiers in the service. If I may suggest it, sir, either Lieutenant Pace or I—or even both of us—as duly appointed Mormon officers, should return at once to Council Bluffs to inform our President of the situation and return with his instructions to this command as soon as possible."

Wharton shook his head, his eyes fixed on the younger of the three officers. "Lieutenant Gully cannot go, as he is quartermaster in charge your entire outfit. That leaves you to carry the news, Lieutenant Pace. I direct you to do so as soon as you can make yourself ready, by noon, if possible."

Pace nodded and replied, "Yes sir, I'll leave by noon at the latest."

Lt. Col. Wharton nodded and dismissed them and almost at once Sanderson and Smith converged on Pace, their entire demeanor changed. Both now, in very glib language and with considerable sophistry asked the lieutenant if he would do them the favor of taking a letter from each of them to Brigham Young. Pace agreed to do so and these were two of the three letters currently in his pouch. He had not read those two, as they were sealed, but Gully had let him read his before sealing it:

*Fort Leavenworth Sunday Morning Augt 23rd 1846*
Prsdt B Young,
My dear Sir

*It becomes my painfull* [sic] *duty to announce to you the death of Lt. Col. Allen; he died at 6 oclock this morning, with congestive fever, as the doctors say. He was sick eight days. This Sir is to us a very great loss in our present situation, as he was a good friend to us, as well as to our people.*

*The companies are now ten days in advance of us. Lt. Pace is with me & 8 others who were detailed to take the staff waggons [sic] along.*

*It is impossible for me to express to you my feelings on this occasion. We are here, alone, and no one to counsel with. Whose hands we are to fall in, is yet to us unknown.*

*Our men having left this post, makes it our right to make our own officers, but as to its policy for us to do so, is to me doubtful [sic]l, until we get to Genl. Kearney [sic]. Coln. Allen never spoke to any person on the Subject; he requested me yesterday Morning to call on him in the after noon alone, that he had some private business with me, but wished to take a little sleep first, as he had had a restless night of it; in the evening I called but he was so much worse he could not make his business known. I sat up with him last night and in the night he requested me to lift him & called me by name, and that was the last word he ever spoke.*

*The Coln. has many warm friends here and many more in the Army.*

*It was my wish for Lt Pace or myself to return to the Bluffs this morning, but Lt Smith, a Gentm [gentleman] in the regular service, and Doctr Sanderson, the Surgeon in the Battalion, objects to it and Mr. Smith seems to be inclined to assume some authority over us; if he should it will only be temporary, as we shall act decidedly, and as we hope wisely, considering our situation for the future and accomplishing the thing we set out to do. We hope to act wisely and be governed by the dictates of the Spirit of the Lord.*

*We shall doubtless go through to California without having any difficulty to contend with from the Mexicans, & hope to see you all Safe there with us early in the next season. I hope if you should send us any person to return with the funds we might be disposed to send to our friends [and] that you will write some one in the Battalion, and give us all Necessary Council for our future welfare. We re[ceive]d news from the Command yesterday Morning & it is favourable there [being] but few sick none dangerously sick & most recovering. In haste your Servant*

*Samuel Gully*[113]

The letter written to Brigham Young by Dr. George B. Sanderson, though unread by Pace, was not only misdated, it clearly bore a sense of self-serving misinformation:

> Fort Leavenworth August 22d 1846
>
> Mr. Brigham Young & others
> Council Bluffs
> Gentlemen
>
> I have the painful task to perform informing you of the death of our friend Lt. Col Allen of the Mormon Battallion. He died this morning about 6 oclock after a confinement of about 10 days to his bed. He died of Congestive Fever, was indisposed for many days previous to taking to his bed. Your people have lost a devoted friend and good officer. I am in hopes in fact I have no fears nor you need not entertain any your people will be taken care of. The most perfect harmony has been preserved among themselves since their arrival at this post and every one speaks to their praise. Lt. Smith of U.S.A. will go out with them until they overtake Genl Kearny who will take them on in his official care. I am going out myself as Surgeon to the Battalion—I was appointed by Col Allen on the 1st Inst. and every thing that I have in my power shall be extended to them for their Comfort. Please to give kindest regards to Col Kane and had it been in my power I should have visited him during his illness. I have just learned he is much better.
>
> I am the honor to be your obt. Servt.
> Geo. B. Sanderson Surgeon M.B.[114]

In the meanwhile, preparations having been completed, it was time for the Mormon Battalion to move out in an effort to overtake General Kearny, who was now six weeks ahead of them. This they did on August 13 and, as Henry Bigler wrote of it in his diary:

> "We remained in garrison till the thirteenth, when orders were given to be on the march for Santa Fe. The Colonel remained behind intending to overtake his command in a few days. The weather was still hot and the roads half-leg deep with dust and sand, water scarce, for the brooks and creeks were dry, and it seemed that some of our sick would die for want of water.

Traveling separately, the Battalion's various companies maintained a distance between them of as much as five or six miles, and two of them—Companies C and D—finally caught up with the others six days later. The days passed relatively uneventfully until, on August 19, Bigler recorded a near disaster:

> "On the nineteenth, just as we made camp, a storm of wind, hail, and rain from the west was upon us, capsized our tents, upset wagons, and blew some of them several rods into the brush. Hats flew in all directions, and as the hail began to fall ever[y] horse and mule put for the timber, leaving their masters to face the storms themselves on an open prairie. This was severe on our sick. On the twentieth, Captain Hunt baptized the sick people, and in the late afternoon a religious-patriotic meeting was held, with addresses by several officers, which raised the spirits of the Battalion.

The following day, August 21, saw the arrival of Adjutant Dykes from the garrison, who brought word that Colonel Allen was still very sick and, as Bigler wrote of it in his diary:

> ...the whole Battalion prayed for the Colonel's recovery because they "Believed him to be a gentleman" and were afraid a "more tyrannical man" might take command.... Nothing on next day's travel but on the twenty third day of August we passed an old stone wall. Some five feet thick. Ruins of an ancient citty [sic] were also plainly visible, showing us that this prairie country must have been inhabited sometime long ages past by a civilised people...

This same day the second unopened letter to Brigham Young was placed in the hand of Lieutenant Pace only moments before he left his quarters to mount up and ride out. It was the letter written by First Lieutenant A. J. Smith, in which he wrote:

> Fort Leavenworth, August, 23, 1846
> President Brigham Young:
> SIR:—It is with the deepest regret that I have to inform you of the death of Lieutenant Colonel James Allen, late commander of the Mormon Battalion. The command left this post last week,

*and is now encamped about forty miles from here. The particulars of the lamented and universal favorite, Colonel Allen, will be communicated to you by Lieutenant James Pace, the bearer of this note. If it is the wish of your people that I should take charge of the Battalion, and conduct it to General Kearney [sic], I will do it with pleasure and feel proud of the command.*

*I have in my possession most, if not all, the papers that relate to the movements of this Battalion, which is presently under command of Captain, temporary Lieut. Col., Jefferson Hunt, and will use my best Endeavors to see all orders and promises heretofore given, carried into execution.*

*I am, sir, very respectfully, Your obt. Servant,*
*A.J. Smith, 1st Lt. 1st Dragoons*

Despite the seeming courtesy of their letters to Brigham Young, both Dr. Sanderson and First Lieutenant Smith had no intention of awaiting permission or approval for the roles each keenly desired to fill for the advancement of his own career—Sanderson, as Surgeon Major to the Battalion, and Smith, as Lieutenant Colonel Commanding.

Both men peremptorily took over the entire Mormon Battalion by vowing they had the required seniority, despite strong protests from the Mormon officers previously designated by Brigham Young to fill those roles. It was a situation that bred some significant internal troubles now, when it occurred, and which held the promise of growing only worse as time passed.

*[August 27, 1846 · Thursday]*

In the new temporary headquarters of the Mormons on the west bank of the Missouri River a bit over a dozen miles upstream from Council Bluffs on the opposite side, Brigham Young officially named the site Camp of Israel, Cutler Park, Omaha Nation, but everyone else was quickly referring to it simply as Winter Quarters.[115] Here, as constantly more of the Mormon flock daily straggled in on their continuing exodus from Nauvoo, all would assemble and remain until next spring when more clement weather would permit the continuation of their overland journey to the new Mormon permanent home...wherever that would be.

Now in his headquarters tent at that site, Young looked with distaste

# The Infinite Dream

at the two letters he had just signed in response to those delivered to him by Lieutenant Pace; letters from First Lieutenant Smith and Dr. Sanderson at Fort Leavenworth. He had found it expedient to more or less have his clerk gloss over their comments about the future command positions of the Mormon Battalion and to make no commitment concerning their requests. It was the next two letters he had yet to draft that would require more thought and more care in preparation: a response to the Mormon Battalion Quartermaster, Sam Gully, and an official letter to the Commander of the Army of the West, General Kearny. The letters to Smith and Sanderson were just short of being brusque:

> *Camp of Israel, Cutler Park, Omaha Nation*
> *August 27, 1846*
>
> Sir:
>
> *Your letter of the 23rd inst. to President Young, announcing the death of Lt. Col. Allen, was received this day, and we feel to sympathize with you and our friends in the Battalion in this deep affliction.*
>
> *You kindly offered to take the charge of the Battalion and conduct it safely to Gen. Kearney [sic]. We have not the pleasure of a personal acquaintance, and consequently can have no personal objections to you; but, sir, on the subject of command we can only say, Col. Allen settled that matter at the organization of the Battalion; therefore we must leave that point to the proper authorities, be the result what it may. Any assistance you may render the Battalion while moving will be duly acknowledged by a grateful people.*
>
> *Most respectfully, Sir, Yours in behalf of the Council.*
> *Brigham Young, President.*
> *Willard Richards, Clerk*
> *A.J. Smith, 1st Lt., 1st Dragoons, U.S. Army of the West.*

The letter to Dr. Sanderson was no less non-committal:

> *Camp of Israel, Omaha Nation.*
> *Aug, 27, 1846.*
>
> Sir,
>
> *Your letter of the 22nd inst, to Mr. Young and others has just arrived, and while we mourn the loss of a gentleman, and noble*

*officer with our friends in the Battalion, and his brother officers of the army, we are consoled with the assurance you have made that our brethren have won the praise of their country, by their harmony and good order, and we doubt not your services to the Battalion will be duly appreciated.*

*Your regards have been presented to Col. Kane, who is convalescent, and thinks he shall be able to ride out in a few days.*

*Most respectfully, In behalf of the Council,*
*Brigham Young, President.*
*Willard Richards, Clerk.*
*To. Geo. B. Sanderson, Surgeon, Mormon Battalion.*

Young's clerk, Willard Richards, in response to Sam Gully's letter, addressed the whole battalion as well as the quartermaster in particular and Young read the missive carefully, noting in particular the reference to his appointment of a new battalion commander, before appending his own signature above that of the clerk:

*Camp of Israel, Cutler Park, Omaha Nation,*
*August 27, 1846.*
*Samuel Gully, Quartermaster, and the Mormon Battalion.*

*Beloved Brother,—Your letters of the 21st and 23rd inst., per Lieutenant Pace, we received, and feel to mourn the loss we have sustained in the death of Lieutenant Colonel Allen, who, we believe, as a gentleman and officer, had the affection of all his acquaintances.*

*To such dispensations of Providence, we must submit, and pray our Heavenly Father to guide your steps, and move in all your councils.*

*You will all doubtless recollect that Colonel Allen repeatedly Stated to us and the Battalion that there would be no officer in the Battalion, except himself, only from among our own people; that if he fell in battle, or was sick, or disabled by any means, the command would devolve on the ranking officer, which would be the Captain of Company A, and B, and so on, according to letter. Consequently the command must devolve on Captain Jefferson Hunt, whose duty we suppose to be to take the Battalion to Bent's Fort or wherever he has received marching orders for, and there wait further orders from*

*General Kearney* [sic]*, notifying him by express of Colonel Allen's decease at the earliest date.*

*From the great confidence we had in Colonel Allen's assurance of the order of making officers in command, and the confidence we have in General Kearney* [sic] *and the officers of the United States, that they will faithfully perform, according to the pledge made by Colonel Allen as an officer on the part of the Government, we consider there is no reasonable chance for a question on the future command of the Battalion, and as to expediency, we know of none worthy of consideration. But should General Kearney* [sic] *propose any other course, we presume the Battalion would not feel disposed to act upon it until they had notified the General of the pledges they had received from the Government through Colonel Allen, and received his answer, and we know of no law that could require the brethren to act contrary to those pledged, or under any circumstances contrary to their wish.*

*We trust there is not a man in the Battalion who would let pass the first opportunity of procuring the rules and regulations of tactics of the United States Army and making himself master of the same before the close of the year.*

*For the Council,*
*Brigham Young, President*
*W. Richards, Clerk.*

The sadness of Lt. Col. Allen's death aside, other matters needed attention and there was no doubt that Brigham Young expected a true windfall of cash when Parley Pratt returned today from collecting the wages and allowances that were paid to the men of the Mormon Battalion before they left Fort Leavenworth. The total of their pay was estimated to amount to approximately $22,000. Allowing that some of the men would undoubtedly keep a few dollars for their own expenses, Young nevertheless expected Pratt would bring back somewhat close to $20,000, which was seemingly fairly commensurate to the amount actually taken by the Mormon "collectors" from the soldiers of the Mormon Battalion. His consternation was great, therefore, when Pratt showed up with a total amount he said he collected of only $5,835...of which he finally turned over to Bishop Newell K. Whitney only $4,375.19—a peculiar disappearance of nineteen cents less than $1,460. The more "prominent" of the Mormon families somehow never seemed to be in want for food or supplies, but the "poorer or less recognized" families of Mormons who were part of the emigration, remained constantly in want and hungry. When the abundance of these latter families complained bitterly of their poverty and need, Brigham Young lost no time in blaming the shortages on soldiers themselves: "You ought not grumble and complain to The Twelve for not having enough to live on," he told them in a general meeting of the unfortunate dependants. "Your dear husbands sent you only about five thousand dollars out of the twenty-two thousand they received at Fort Leavenworth, evidently reserving to themselves some seventeen thousand dollars for the grog shop, the ballroom and the card tables. This shows the great love they have for their families, but their greater love for the pleasures around them."

But then, of course, there actually were no "pleasures around them" for the Mormon Battalion soldiers to spend money upon, assuming they had any to spend. Unfortunately, the "missing" money—approximately $15,000—remained missing. There was little doubt in anyone's mind that the forthcoming winter would become one of the most grim in the Church's history, at least for the impoverished dependants of the soldiers of the Mormon Battalion.[116]

[September 5, 1846 • Saturday]

Thomas Kane, who was today in the quarters of Major Thomas H. Harvey, the Commissioner of Indian Affairs in St. Louis, read the express letter just received by Harvey from Undersecretary William Medill in the War Department in Washington, D.C. and immediately broke into a smile.

"You can forward that letter—a copy I had my clerk make up—to the Mormon president, if you wish," Harvey told Kane, "since the Winter Quarters do meet with my approval."

Kane's smile broadened. He knew Brigham Young would be very pleased when he received it, since it clearly negated one of his most prevalent fears for the Saints of his flock. The letter read:

*War Department*
*Office of Indian Affairs*

Sir: –
 *Since my letter to you of the 27th July and the 22nd ult. in*

*relation to the Mormons and the desire expressed by them to remain for a time on the lands recently purchased by the United States from the Pottawattomie [sic] Indians, and which lie within the limits of Iowa, the subject has been brought to the immediate notice of the president and secretary of war.*

*The object and intention of the Mormons in desiring to locate upon the lands in question, are not very satisfactorily set forth, either in the application to the President or in the letter transmitted to this office, which contained the assent of the Indian chiefs. If their continuance is really to be temporary and for such length of time only as will enable them to supply their wants and procure the necessary means, for proceeding on their journey, the government will interpose no objections.*

*The want of provisions and the near approach of winter, which will have set in before they can reach their proposed destination, would necessarily expose them to much suffering, if not to starvation and death; while on the other hand, a location and continuance for any very considerable length of time near Council Bluffs, would interfere with the removal of the Indians, an object of much interest to the people of that region of country, delay the survey and sales of the lands in question, and thus in all probability bring about a difficulty between Iowa and the general government. Both these extremes, in the opinion of the President, should be avoided. The rights and interests of Iowa, now that the Indian title has been extinguished, may not be jeopardized, while the laws of humanity and rights of hospitality should not be disregarded.*

*You will ascertain, if possible, the real intention of these people in desiring to remain, and if you are satisfied that they will leave and resume their journey in the spring, or at such period as the season for traveling will justify, and that no positive injury is likely to arise to the Indians from their stay among them, you will instruct the subagent and give notice to any other officers of the general government in that quarter, to interpose no objection to the Mormon people remaining on the lands referred to, during the suspension of their journey, or to their making such improvements and raising such crops as their convenience and wants may require; taking care, however, at the same time, to impress upon them the necessity of leaving at the earliest moment their necessities and convenience will justify, and of observing all laws and regulations in force upon the territory for the time being.*

*Very respectfully, your obedient servant,*
*W. Medill*
*Major Thomas H. Harvey, Supt., etc., St. Louis, Mo.*

*[September 6, 1846 • Sunday]*

It hadn't really dawned on Lt. Col. John Fremont yet that the disappearance of the foe—personified by the two Californio leaders, Pio Pico and José Castro, who themselves were still at odds with one another—hardly betokened the end of Californio resistance to an American takeover of the territory. It had all been just a bit too easy, a bit too snug, but Fremont was inexperienced enough to almost completely convince himself that the transition of California into an American Territory marked the end of all hostilities.

There were other things that gnawed a bit more permanently at Fremont's consciousness these days, chief among which was having allowed Commodore Stockton to become aware of his chief subordinate's own yearning for greater power, well beyond his rank as lieutenant colonel. It was a conclusion that he knew would continue to gnaw at him indefinitely hereafter.

In the meanwhile, Stockton was busy feathering his own nest. On August 28 he had sat at his desk and wrote out a detailed report for Secretary of the Navy George Bancroft, who was already ensconced in his new position as Minister to England, in which he told his chief:

> *...In less than a month, I have chased the Mexican Army more than three hundred miles along the coast, pursued them thirty miles into the interior of their own country, routed and dispersed them and secured the Territory to the United States, ended the war, restored peace and harmony among the people, and put a civil government into successful operation!...*

It would not have required a terribly astute observer to have questioned, what war? What Mexican Army? Harmony to what people? What kind of civil government was put into successful operation? But the Secretary of the Navy was close to 3,000 miles distant in Washington, D.C., and he had no one to check with, even if he had doubted the authenticity of the report...which he did not. Nor did he seriously question any of Stockton's remarks, particularly the last one. Stockton, *de facto* governor of the California Territory did, in fact *begin* to prepare a constitution to organize California into a United States territory, but his skills toward that end were sorely lacking and he soon gave up, not only because he fathomed the Californios still might have something to say in that regard, but also because that particular job had been relegated by the President to General Kearny. Instead, Stockton thought it would be a very good idea for him to consider more attacks by sea, especially down the west coast of Mexico and most particularly against the major ports of Mazatlan and Acapulco. In the meanwhile, before launching such an enterprise, there were a few matters to take care of here in California. He appointed Fremont civil governor of California and ordered him to launch a recruitment effort that would bring the unorganized Navy Battalion of Mounted Riflemen—the Horse Marines—to a strength of 300. That same day he ordered Kit Carson, accompanied by Ned Beale, to go "...*as swiftly as possible*..." overland with dispatches for Washington D.C., announcing the entire conquest of California by the United States, and he also reaffirmed martial law as the "code" of what he considered to be his territory. Finally, he set about reorganizing the military and, on September 2, toward this end, he divided California into three distinct military districts commanded by subordinate officers. One of these was the District of Los Angeles which he placed under command of Lieutenant Archibald Gillespie. Even worse, today he appointed Fremont as military commandant of all of California. Fremont immediately set out for the north, leaving part of his force with Gillespie at Los Angeles, part with Lieutenant Talbot at Santa Barbara, plus a few others at other points.

While Stockton and Fremont were taking care of all these "odds and ends," Pico, who had been in hiding for a month near San Juan Capistrano, quietly, undetectably, followed the swallows to Baja on his escape into the arid wilds of Lower California.

[September 9, 1846 · Wednesday]

Despite his former resolve to no longer be a part of the Californio military and his interest in throwing his energies to the influx of Americans, Lt. Col. Vallejo, perhaps in residual resentment for those Yankees who had incarcerated him, today once again threw his weight behind the Mexican military.

There was one aspect of it that, however much his loyalties were still rooted in his heritage, was undoubtedly a deciding fact in his decision. With his acceptance of the role of commandante-general of all California, he also accepted with gratitude and pride, his new rank, effective today, as full colonel of cavalry in the Mexican Army.

Despite the turmoil and uncertainty that raged all about him in his beloved California, thirty-eight-year-old Colonel Mariano Guadalupe Vallejo was very pleased with himself.

*[September 11, 1846 • Friday]*

At noon today, the Mormon Battalion arrived at the bank of the Arkansas River. Great cries of delight erupted from the Saints who, for long days of strenuous marching over essentially desert terrain, had been unable to even wash their face and hands, much less bathe. What they found at the river, however, did not at first encourage any serious degree of bathing. The river was mostly a bed of sand and debris, as much as a quarter mile across, with only here and there a small rivulet appearing, bubbling up in the sand and coursing downstream in a miniscule current for perhaps fifty or one hundred feet before abruptly disappearing again beneath the sand.

Because the small amount of actual stream was visible only fairly close to the opposite bank, some of the soldiers dug holes close to the near bank, delving as deeply as three feet or more before finally encountering water. When they did, the holes filled quickly, providing them with water to drink and to ladle out to use for bathing. Much of the day was spent here in such clean-up pursuits and it wasn't until later that some of the more daring, despite the possibility of encountering quicksand, moved closer to the actual stream. Here they found pot-holes of water in the stream itself or isolated from it by many feet, in which fish—mainly carp, suckers and bass, some of them upwards of five pounds apiece—had been isolated and were easily impaled on sword-points or, in some cases, speared with javelins. These efforts quickly provided a delicious repast for the entire Battalion.

The fresh food and the ability to wash and relax were working wonders for the men. Henry Bigler was one of those who reveled in the opportunity to lie back, push his hat over his eyes and give the appearance he was asleep. He wasn't. His mind clicked back over the past two-and-a-half-weeks, ever since that night of August 26, when they'd camped on Beaver Creek.[117]

That was the day when both Lieutenants Sam Gully and James Pace arrived from Fort Leavenworth and caused universal grief among the Saints with their news that their commander, Lt. Col. James Allen, had died. Immediately, rising to the crisis, a vote was taken among the Mormons as to who the new commander among themselves should be, and Captain Jefferson Hunt of Company A was by far the most popular choice. Before he had an opportunity to do anything substantive, however, two more men, accompanied by their own personal Negro slaves, arrived from Fort Leavenworth with news that quickly changed grief to consternation.

The new arrivals were the first lieutenant of the Second Dragoon—but now acting Lieutenant Colonel and commander of the Mormon Battalion—Andrew Jackson Smith and Dr. George B. Sanderson, with the title of Acting Battalion Surgeon. Both men were now authorized by Leavenworth's Colonel Wharton to assume their temporary roles and continue in them until the Battalion could overtake and fall under the command of General Kearny.[118]

There was a great outcry from all the Mormons but none louder than that issued by Jefferson Hunt. All protests were unavailing, however. Smith declared in no uncertain terms that even while Captain Hunt might be the popular choice of the Battalion, it made no difference; he was not a regularly commissioned officer of the United States and until his commission was approved by the War Department he was officially powerless. Adjutant George B. Dykes concurred.

"Get this through your heads, men," Smith announced bluntly to the assembled Battalion. "Only a regularly commissioned officer has the authority to command an American fighting force. Mr. Hunt does not hold such authority. I am your new commander, under specific orders from Colonel Wharton, and will remain so until ordered differently by General Kearny."

With apparently no other choice, Hunt resentfully resumed his duties as Company A commander and the force of Mormons accepted grudgingly the West Pointer's appointment. The succession might not have occurred with so little protest had they been aware of the letter Smith had written only yesterday to the Adjutant General of the United States:

*Camp Near Ft Leavenworth*
*Augt 25th 1846*

Sir:
*I was requested by Lt Col Allen of the Mormon Battalion, a few*

days before his death to take charge of & select such papers as were directed to the Adj. Genl. U.S.A. & forward them to Washington. The enclosed are all I can find. The Batallion [sic] left the Fort several days before the death of Lt. Col. Allen & are now encamped at Council Grove, about 150 [miles] on the road toward Santa Fe. I am now on my way to report to Genl. Kearney [sic] and having his instructions to Capt. J. Allen 1st Drags.

In relation to the Mormons in my possession, I deem it my duty as an officer of the Government to have these instructions carried out. I will therefore with the consent of the Mormons, take charge of the Battalion at Council Grove & conduct it to Genl. Kearny, or until I receive further orders from him in relation to them. As no officer has been assigned to the command of the Batallion [sic] I am in hope that my course will be approved of by the department.

*I am Sir, Very respectfully, Your Obt. Servt.*
*To Genl. R. Jones.*
*A.J. Smith, 1st Lt. 1st Drags.*
*Adj. Genl. U.S.A., Washington, D.C.*

That night Henry Bigler, as disgruntled as the rest, wrote in his diary the substance of a disquieting rumor that was swiftly moving through the camp:

*...I have since understood that there was strong suspicion that Colonel Allen had been poisoned, fearing perhaps he would be too friendly to the Mormon Battalion...*

As with so many rumors that circulate in the military, there was no truth whatsoever in regard to this allegation and the rumor quickly died away. The distrust of Surgeon George B. Sanderson, however, escalated. This was as much due to his stern treatments as anything else. Many of the men were suffering from illnesses ranging from simple colds to deep bronchial infections and to one and all the doctor's remedy was the same. Instead of believing in the efficacy of faith and herbs as the Mormons so customarily did, Sanderson—backed up by the equally unrelenting Lt. Smith—now brevet lieutenant colonel—poured down their throats a mixture of calomel and arsenic that was so vile that few of the men ever returned for a second dosage and from that moment on, Sanderson and his big iron spoon became the Battalion's collective symbol of intolerance, evil and cruelty. Sanderson became quickly known more by the nickname they dubbed him—Captain Death—than by his true name.

The persistently drier march was aggravated by the fact the commissary wagons often did not keep pace with the march and when the day's tramping was done, instead of meals ready to eat, the Mormons often waited hours for their food. Occasionally the wagons did not show up at all and the men went hungry and tempers grew short. The Mormons detected—or fancied they did—punishments and aggravations in every order Smith issued and their hatred of him intensified to such degree it became truly a passion. For every Mormon who became sick, with whatever ailment, it was the "gentile commander" who was held to blame and they neglected even more their own health and hygiene until the few wagons were filled with the ailing.

Even Henry Bigler, who normally managed to stay reasonably aloof from the "general mentality" exhibited by the majority of the men in his battalion, felt his own anger rise almost as a gorge in his throat at the treatment the men were undergoing. Though he did not discuss his feelings with others, he clearly unleashed them in his diary. On September 3 he wrote:

> …Sptb 3…Colonel Smith begins to show his simpithy [sic] for the sick by ordering them out of the waggons [sic] and he swears if they do not walk he will tie them to the waggons and dragg [sic] them. Now the surgeon, who is a Missori man, dont [sic] belong to our people and was herrd [sic] to say he did not care a damm wether [sic] he killed or cured. Because of this our sick men refused to go at sick call and take his Medesin [sic]. But Col. Smith was told strate [sic] up and down, there & then, befor [sic] we would take Doctr Sandersins [sic] medesin we leave our bones to bleech [sic] on the prarie first…

As much as anything else, the resentment—virtual hatred—for Lt. Col. Smith and Dr. Sanderson was turning out to be a blessing in disguise. The resentment fueled fires in the men they did not know they possessed and provided them with the dogged determination to persevere, sick, bewildered, unhappy, no matter what, just to show the two men up.

Bigler, on September 6, ate his first meat of a large bison calf and was amazed at how much better it was than that of the adults. As he wrote in his diary that night:

*We not only saw plenty of buffs but one of our boys kilt [sic] one. We thought it was good eating. The meat very good. But, like most of the males that stay alone, it was tough. Now we have learned to get for our eating the younger animals, which are more tender,'stead [sic] of shooting the oldest, which are loners away from the herd. We saw hundreds and several were shot and the whole Battalion had good suppers.*

On September 8, when they stopped for the night at Pawnee Fork, a messenger arrived on horseback, bearing instructions from General Kearny and the good news that Santa Fe had surrendered without opposition. Colonel Smith was instructed to lead all his troops by way of "the Semirone [sic] route" to Santa Fe, so instead of taking the route that would have led to Bents Fort, the Battalion was turned onto the Cimarron Route, which was drier and more difficult, but shorter. Crossing Pawnee Fork the next morning was very difficult. The water was as muddy as the Missouri and the banks were high and steep. Each wagon had to be eased down with ropes and, on the opposite steep bank, upwards of thirty men with ropes assisted the teams in getting the wagons back up to level ground. Just as they were finishing, one of the Saints—no one seemed to know who—caused a general guffaw to erupt when he called out:

*"Anyone care if I go home?!"*

[September 15, 1846 · Tuesday]

John B. Montgomery, commanding the District of San Francisco, was not at all pleased with the reports he'd been receiving of whites in the area mistreating the Indians of the various California tribes. This was most definitely *not* the way to open the California interior, neither for settlement nor the means by which to establish friendly relationships with the tribes. Whichever of those two considerations was dominant at the moment was unclear—perhaps they were of equal importance—but Montgomery sighed and leaned forward to complete the writing he had begun a few moments before—a new proclamation to all inhabitants here:

*15 Septb 46—Yerba Buena*
**PROCLAMATION**

*It having come to the knowledge of the Commander in Chief of the district that certain persons have been and still are imprisoning and holding to services Indians against their will and without any legal contract, and without a due regard to their rights as freemen when not under any legal contract for service—It is hereby ordered that all persons holding or detaining Indians shall release them, and permit them to return to their own homes, unless they can make a contract with them which shall be acknowledged before the nearest Justice, which contract, shall be binding upon both parties.*

*The Indian population must not be regarded in the light of slaves, but it is deemed necessary that the Indians within the Settlement shall have employment, with the right of choosing their own master and employers, and after having made such choice, they must abide by it, unless they can obtain permission in writing to leave, or the Justice on their complaint shall consider they have just cause to annul the contract, and permit them to obtain another employer.*

*All Indians must be required to obtain service, and shall not be permitted to wander about the country in idle and dissolute manner; if found doing so they will be liable to arrest and punishment by labor on the Public Works at the direction of the Magistrate.*

*All Officers, civil or military, under my command are required to execute the terms of the order, and take notice of every violation thereof.*

*Given at head quarters in Yerba Buena.*
*September 15, 1846*
*JOHN B. MONTGOMERY,*
*Commanding, District of San Francisco*
*Published for the government of all concerned.*
*Washington A. Bartlett, Chief Magistrate*

On this same day, at the Yerba Buena Customs House—known as The Old Adobe—ninety-six ballots were cast. Lieutenant Bartlett, by heavy majority, was elected as the new *alcalde*.

*[September 19, 1846 • Saturday]*

For the Saints who were not of the 500 comprising the Mormon Battalion—those left behind to continue, or just begin the journey westward to an unspecified destination—now came the most difficult time of all and everyone among them paid a stiff price; some the gravest price of all.

The situation had reached its crux just two days ago, on September 17. At that point there were still approximately a thousand Saints left at Nauvoo on the Illinois side of the Mississippi—the very poorest of the entire throng. They had hoped for leniency, a respite of sorts from the angry mobs converging on them from all direction. But the savage gentiles besetting them had no such mercies to bestow; they had waited far too long for this day to have their retribution sullied by any degree of compassion. They lusted for blood, destruction and personal gain.

Fearing what was coming, the remaining Nauvoo Saints sold off what they could of what they owned at a paltry five cents on the dollar and the wealthiest among them—those still with three or four wagons apiece and perhaps a small herd of cattle—dispossessed themselves of what they could, loaded what they considered dear or essential and left behind all else to be ravaged. The majority, much poorer, carried all their possessions in wheelbarrows or on their own backs.

The Illinois attackers besieged them as they made their way to the boats to cross the great river, pausing only long enough to destroy first the things left behind and then the structures themselves. The great temple was hideously besmirched with urine and feces. When this degradation was not enough, it was set afire. Any Saints who lagged behind—those weakest or most ailing—were mowed down by sporadic gunfire.

The very disorganization of the mob, blinded and fueled by its hatred, was its own greatest detriment, stalling itself for superficialities, preventing a determined following. The fleers reached the boats and crossed the river, over and over again and only a remaining few still on the east shore suffered the wrath of the attackers who had finally better directed their fury and followed.

The large skiffs that had ferried the residue Mormons across were set adrift and whirled away in the Mississippi's muddy current. Their former human cargoes, gathered now on the Iowa side, began their pitiable shuffling march westward as if they were lemmings, driven onward irrepressibly but without known destination. Exhausted at nightfall they camped and because there was no food, no warmth, no encouragement, they collapsed and simply aestivated until the morning when they could begin again their journey. And during the night, some wept softly and some cried aloud and some became even more ravaged by sickness…

…and some died.

*[September 24, 2005 · Thursday · 4:00 p.m.]*

Of all the men who made up the five companies of troops in the Mormon Battalion, probably none took more enjoyment out of this parched, cross-country march than Elder Henry Bigler. To their recollection, none had ever heard him complain about anything. It was not that Bigler was an automaton who accepted cheerfully whatever outrages of man or nature their rigorous march plagued them with, since his own diary entries were replete with serious and well-advised commentary on such occasions; it was just that he, unlike any of the others, openly complained about nothing; an attitude that led others to utilize him as a sounding board for their own complaints and which, through his own diary, helped Bigler create one of the more unbiased documents relating to the Mormon Battalion and its officers.

It was the relationship of Brigham Young's adopted son, John D. Lee, to everyone else that most perplexed Bigler. The bullish Howard Egan was clearly Brigham Young's chief "enforcer and avenger" in maintaining the Saints themselves as adherents to the strict rules and regulations of The Church of Jesus Christ of Latter-day Saints.[119] Yet, Egan clearly feared and respected Lee and kowtowed to his apparent authority. Though nominally no more than a private, Lee, who had arrived with Egan and Lieutenant James Pace on September 11, exhibited neither fear nor reticence in confronting Lt. Col. Smith and Surgeon Sanderson as soon as he learned how these two had been callously mistreating virtually everyone. With an element of menace in his demeanor, Lee confronted the pair and unequivocally "ordered" them to "cease oppressing my Brethren"—the Mormon Battalion's officers and men. When the bullying and other mistreatment of the Saints hardly even slackened, Lee met with many of the Mormons and actually advocated mutiny against the authority of the U.S. Army if such persecution continued. Immediately following this, he met privately with both Smith and Sanderson and very calmly but very coldly threatened to slit the throats of both if immediate improvement was not noted.

Immediate improvement was noted.

As well as the privates, the higher officers among the Mormons were equally aware of Lee's awesome powers and few had the courage to attempt to override or thwart him. One of those who did, however, was Captain Jefferson Hunt, who was so scandalized at Lee's behavior—and the possible repercussions it could evoke from highly-placed U.S. officials—that he confronted Lee himself.

"If, Mister Lee," he advised coldly, "you do not at once cease counseling mutiny within this Battalion, I will have no recourse but to place you under guard."

Lee smiled, faintly, coldly, and when Hunt did not continue, gave the superior officer a lackadaisical salute, turned on his heel and departed. It took a while for Captain Hunt to recognize the magnitude of his own error. Lee subsequently reported Hunt's imperiousness to Brigham Young in person and Hunt's career, both militarily and in the Church, was, from that point on, severely damaged.

Bigler noted all this carefully in his diary and he also noted a vague but certain change in Colonel Smith's demeanor in regard to the Saints a little later, on the ides of September, when Sterling Price once again interfered in Mormon affairs. As Bigler penned this in his diary:

> On the fifteenth we overtook Colonel Price encampt [sic] in the bank of the Arkansas River with five hundred horsemen on his way to Santa Fe, where I believe he was to take command of that post.
>
> Now it had been Colonel Allen's intention, before leading the Battalion away from Ft, Leavenworth to go via Bents Fort in order to reach Santa Fe.[120] Stored there were a lot of supplies Col. Allen had ordered for his command., but Col. had decided he would not go via Bent's Fort, it being too far around. He determined to take a much shorter route, although wood and water were less plentiful. The Battalion, being short of grub, and would be more short as they had now abandoned the idea of going by way of Bent's Fort, the Colonel sent his quartermaster over to Col. Price's Company, about one-fourth of a mile to get a little provision. Word was sent back that they did not haul grub for the Mormons. This raised Colonel Smith's Irish a little, and he sent back word and swore if they did not

> let him have some he would let loose the Mormons and come down on them with his artillery. This had, on Smith's part, the desired effect. Colonel Price was in command of a company of mob militia at Far West and sanctioned the shooting of Joseph the Prophet and others on the public square in '38. We remaind [sic] here 2 days. Alva Phelps of our Battalion, E company, a martyr to his country and religion, died and was buried at this place. It was believed that Doctor Sanderson's Medecine kilt [sic] him. He gives calomel and the sick are almost physicked [sic] to death. It is understood that he begged Doctor Sanderson not to give him any strong medicine [sic], as he needed only a little rest and then he would return to duty—but the Doctor prepared his dose and ordered him to take it, which he declined doing, whereupon the Doctor with some horrid oaths forced it down him with the old rusty spoon. A few hours later he died, and the general feeling was that the Doctor had killed him. Many boldly expressed the opinion it was a case of premeditated murder. When we consider the many murderous threats previously made, this conclusion is by no means far-[fetched]. Brother Phelps was buried on the south side of the Arkansas River, in a grave only about four feet deep, its shallowness being due to the fact that the water was very near the surface of the soil. On the evening of Brother Phelps death what appeared to be a star was noticied [sic] in the east as dancing in the air. It continued to move both North and South, up and down; it was directly in the course we had traveled. It attrackted [sic] considerabl [sic] attention while it remained in sight and finally disappeared below the Eastern horizon. We believe in healing a person by "laying hands" on him or by use of Botanic medecine [sic].[121]

The already present animosity toward the commander of the Mormon Battalion abruptly became a burning fury when, as the force was halted at an inter-connecting trail, Lt. Col. Andrew J. Smith waited until the trailing wagons, containing perhaps fifteen families of the soldiers caught up and stopped. Close at hand was the last crossing of the Arkansas River.

"The wagons containing dependents and some of the sick," he announced loudly, without preamble, "will leave us here under command of Captain Nelson Higgins." Instantly there rose the murmur of protest, but Smith was having none of it and went on virtually without pause. "It is no longer feasible or practical for dependants to travel with us. They will follow this trail," he waved a hand at the trail leading northwestward "which leads toward Pueblo. Once there, there will be food and medical supplies and comfort available to one and all. The main body of the Mormon Battalion will be able now to travel with increased speed and, hopefully overtake the main body of troops at or near Santa Fe, just as Brigham Young himself planned."[122]

The main body plodded on but it quickly became very clear that the Mormon Battalion was rapidly approaching its limit. The more than liberal doses of calomel administered by Dr. Sanderson, along with their having to undergo the heavy, bitter, alkaline dust of the desert, combined with horrible food and the near total lack of water—all these had their effect upon the men and, in conjunction with a smothering blanket of despair in regard to leadership issues, those of the Battalion that were sick became steadily worse and those who were physically well gradually sank into a state of exhaustion all but unendurable.

Matters came to a head the following day—August 17—when, while the Battalion was at rest, John D. Lee confronted Lt. Col. A. J. Smith and demanded changes be made. Before the meeting could take place, however, it was made clear to Lee by Captain Hunt that despite the hardships the Battalion was undergoing, the men had accepted Smith's leadership and the march would continue as it was. Lee, slightly deflated but not to be deterred, had his meeting with Smith and it was not a pleasant one.

Lee presented Smith with a letter from Brigham Young and then loudly expressed his own view that the entire Battalion was being mistreated. "These men," he intoned, "deserve greater consideration from you, Sir. I formally request that since these men have been under a forced march for three weeks and have been traveling twenty to thirty miles each day, when by law they are required to travel no more than thirteen miles daily, that the Battalion be stopped and the men be given two full days of rest before proceeding further."

Lt. Col. Smith heard Lee out but then shook his head. "Sir," he said, "I cannot and will not draw this march to such a halt, which would help defeat the purpose of overtaking and joining the Army of the West under General Kearny, several days ahead of us. The men may rest for an hour, but then we move on."

With Captain Hunt present as a witness, Lee let his oratory flow and castigated Smith sternly. "The men of this Battalion are my brethren, sir," he said, "and they have suffered together, for the sake of our Holy Religion, sufficient by the hand of ungodly men, without having everything now that tyrants and oppressors can inflict upon them to make them miserable! When I came up with the Battalion and saw the suffering and oppression of these soldiers, my blood boiled in my veins to such an extent that I could scarce refrain from taking my sword in hand and ridding them of such tyrants."

"I have not," Smith said, drawing himself up warningly, "designedly oppressed any man of this Battalion."

Lee sloughed off the commander's words with a slicing motion of his hand and continued without pause: "You, Sir, are the man who made one of the soldiers get down off his horse and damned him, threatening to tie him to the wagon, there to drag him like an ox—when he was scarce able to stand alone—burning with fever, unless he would report himself to the doctor and take whatever he should prescribe. And when that man begged the liberty of being nourished with food and mild herbs by one of his Brethren—who was very skillful in baffling diseases—your reply, Sir, was that if you ever knew of our doctors administering medicines to any man in this Battalion, you would cut his throat; the surgeon was the man to prescribe and administer medicine. Yet, you were knowing at the same time that he gave double portions of calomel through spite, saying he did not "care a damn whether it killed or cured and that the more it killed, the better, that the damned rascals ought to be sent to hell as fast as possible." Lee's eyes glinted madly, but he continued unchecked: "Such conduct is incredible and more than what I can bear and should I see him or your honor impose upon and abuse one of my Brethren as you have done in times past, I don't know but I would cut your infernal throats."

The harangue went on but gradually tapered off as Lee finally ran down, his point made and Smith remarkably tolerant of the tirade.[123] He might have replied, but just then they heard, from outside, shouts of "Water! Water!" and they rushed out to join the others at their life-giving discovery—a small swampy area where percolating muddy water had filled the tracks of livestock and was greedily being sucked up, mud, insects, debris and all, by the thirst-crazed Battalion members. It was the first semblance of water they had encountered for the past fifty miles and most of the canteens had been bone dry for at least the last twenty-five.

Nothing further of consequence occurred within the Mormon Battalion until today, August 24, when the marchers encountered the bones of a hundred mules that had died in a storm here about a year ago. A human skull was found among the remains, which Dr. Sanderson concluded was that of an Indian herder. An emigrant returning East paused and chatted with them for a while, stating that he had been a member of that train and he considered it a miracle that anyone other than himself had escaped the fury of the storm, which was said to have been the worst since records were begun. No one doubted that at all.

*[September 25, 1846 • Friday • 8:00 a.m.]*

Impatient at the delay, which he arbitrarily blamed on the Mormons, General Kearny had no intention of remaining in the Santa Fe area any longer. With the expected opposition to his advance having failed to materialize and the way perfectly clear for him to move on, so far as the general was concerned, the Mormons, who still weren't expected here until about ten days into October, could simply follow at double time and overtake him on the march. Or not. Kearny didn't much care either way. Not having encountered any substantial opposition here at the Spanish headquarters in Santa Fe, he was convinced there was little likelihood he'd encounter it elsewhere in this New Mexico Territory; a little Indian trouble here and there, perhaps, but hardly anything to constitute an armed force strong enough to pose any real threat to his own army.

Having reached that conclusion last night, General Kearny lost no time informing his officers to prepare for the march to be resumed this morning and for his second-in-command, Colonel Alexander W. Doniphan to report for orders at 8 a.m. It was precisely that time when Doniphan appeared at the general's tent flap and remained at attention until Kearny bade him enter. The general launched into his instructions without preamble.

"I don't like the idea of leaving you behind, Colonel, but there's no help for it. Several reasons. Don't know for sure when that damned Mormon Battalion will get here, but as soon as it does, you're to send it on my trail with instructions to overtake me as quickly as possible. Clear?"

"Clear, sir." Doniphan's head bobbed once and he waited, knowing the commander had more to say. Kearny had no inclination to delay. "I'm taking only a select force—300 of the Dragoons and we'll be moving rapidly. I don't think the Mexicans themselves are going to be much of a problem. They're docile enough and disinclined to opposition if not egged into it. I don't want that to happen and we've come too close already."

Doniphan nodded, quite as aware as General Kearny of the disturbing situation that had built up under the command of Brigadier General John Ellis Wool. That outfit, moving as an advance unit and heading for Chihuahua, was made up almost in half by Kentucky volunteers who had started out as unruly and then quickly degenerated into little more than a mob, disdainful of the discipline observed by Wool's regular troops. This resulted not only in a cleavage between the regulars and volunteers but in actual feuding between them that was little short of intolerable. General Wool was willing to let their increasing infractions go, for the most part, in a sort of "boys will be boys" frame of mind, but it was one of Wool's subaltern officers, unable any longer to tolerate such abuses, who reported the situation by runner to General Kearney and opened a whole keg of worms that Wool had been more than inclined to keep capped. That officer was Lieutenant George Gordon Meade who, despairing of the lack of discipline among the men and lackadaisical control exhibited by the colonel, as well as by a majority of his inferior officers, risked his own career by going over Wool's head to report the situation to the commanding general of the Army of the West. His written report minced no words:

> *General S. W. Kearney* [sic], *Commanding*
> *American Army of the West*
> *Temporary Headquarters at Santa Fe*
>
> *Sir—A distinct and decidedly disruptive rivalry currently exists between the two troop factions currently serving under General Wool in this theatre of operations en route to Chihuahua. I fear that it might very well cause problems for us of a highly significant nature.*
>
> *Without a modification of the manner in which they are officered, the Kentucky volunteers with us are almost useless in an offensive war. They are sufficiently well drilled for practical purposes, and are, I believe, brave and will fight as gallantly as any man, but they*

*are a set of Goths and Vandals, without discipline, laying waste to the country wherever we go, making us a terror to innocent people, and if there is any spirit or energy in the Mexicans, will finally raise the people against us who are now perfectly neutral...they cannot take care of themselves; the hospitals are crowded with them, they die like sheep; they waste their provisions, requiring twice as much to supply them as regulars do. They plunder the poor inhabitants of everything they can lay their hands on, and shoot them when they remonstrate, and if one of their number happens to get into a drunken brawl and is killed, they run over the country, killing all the poor innocent people they can find in their way, to avenge, as they say, the murder of their brother.*

General Kearny was furious at the report and lost no time in reacting. While the advance was temporarily bivouacked at Saltillo, Kearney ordered the Kentucky Regiment to the rear in disgrace for the rapes and indiscriminate murders they had been committing.

In the meanwhile the Mormons, who had yet to fire a shot in this war, marched across the entire width of what the Mexicans considered as their territory and they even built a substantial wagon road as they marched. In doing so, they were turning into actuality the vision of President Polk of the United States becoming a fully continental nation. The secret to the military success had little to do with planning or strategy concocted in some hidden-away war room. It had to do with the simple basics of who had the more powerful military force and could take as desired. What any nation could claim was considered good and entirely acceptable, so long as that nation had the strength to defend its claim. The claim of these advancing Americans provided the Mexican colonists not only with a promise of political freedom, but equally a distinct hope of protection from Indians hostile to any invaders. The Indians, however, were holding their hostilities in check in view of the forces of Americans advancing unopposed across their lands.[124]

"Your orders," Kearny continued, "are to pacify all the tribes in this area and southward to the Mexican border; even beyond if it appears necessary. Avoid conflict if possible, but be alert for possible surprise attack and, should that occur, you are to retaliate in kind without delay. As soon as acceptable quiescence has been accomplished, you are to continue your march south and place yourself and your force at the disposal of Colonel Wool who, I assume, will by that time be in occupation of Chihuahua. In the meanwhile, before leaving this station, your force will complete the work already begun on the fortification overlooking Santa Fe. When complete, it is to be named Fort Marcy in honor of our Secretary of War."

"Yes sir," Doniphan replied without hesitation. "All will be done according to your orders. Am I to have any instructions in regard to providing for the civil government of this territory?"

Kearny grunted. "Glad you mentioned it. That's been taken care of. I've named Charles Bent as governor of New Mexico and his young friend, Frank Blair—a good man, by the way—as attorney general. I'll be setting off at once with the Dragoons for California and Tom Fitzpatrick, our guide, has recommended our taking the lower trail, which we will do.

"I think that about wraps it up, Colonel," Kearny concluded. "Colonel Sterling Price with his Second Missouri Mounted Volunteers should arrive here in another two or three days. When you set off with your force to the southwest, you're to hand over command here to him. Are we clear?"

"Clear, General. It will all be seen to exactly as you've ordered. Allow me, sir, to wish you well on your mission."

"Noted, and I thank you. However, I don't expect much from it. I'm afraid California's not where the action is and I'd far rather be heading down south to help Taylor bring the Mexicans to their knees."

# Chapter 7

♦

*[September 25, 1846 • Friday • 9:45 a.m.]*

Major General Zachary Taylor, seated before the lantern-illuminated desk in his dim, windowless quarters at Monterrey, Mexico, looked with distaste at the small stack of blank sheets of paper awaiting him and scowled. Of all the tasks he had to perform as commanding general of United States forces there was none he detested more than the writing of post-battle reports to Washington, D.C. He fully intended to make this one, concerning the latter stages of the Battle of Monterrey, just fought, as brief as possible, yet still he knew it would be an hours-eating task and he sighed at the thought. The fact that the authorities in Washington, from the President on down, would revel in what he had to say was little compensation to him for the effort it entailed to put everything into proper perspective.

As usual he leaned back in his chair and with unseeing eyes closed to mere slits, reviewed in his mind the war situation as it was now and the events that had occurred to bring them to this time and place. His last full report had been written some seven weeks ago, on August 8, when his army had halted to rest at the town of Mier before resuming its sixty-mile march to Cerralvo on the road to Monterrey.

The Army was in better shape now in regard to general health than it had been in the early part of the campaign when they were in the coastal lowlands, where the heat was decidedly oppressive, the water very bad everywhere and the roads in deplorable condition. As their march had carried them westward, however, and the swampy lowlands were left behind, the air cooled and cleared as elevation of the land increased and with it, so too the health of the troops improved and, significantly, their morale.

After ten solid days of uninterrupted rest at Mier, during which welcome reinforcements and transportation wagons and supplies were received, they resumed their march toward Cerralvo and first established an advance base at Camargo. Here General Taylor built some new companies of Rangers from his force and shoved them back toward the border of Texas at the Rio Grande, while at the same time maintaining the elite force—Hays's Texas Rangers—to ride ahead of the Army. While some of his force would definitely be left behind to occupy Camargo, Taylor quickly prepared as large a force as he could muster—6,641 men—to move out as swiftly as possible on the march to Monterrey, where he expected he would have to lay siege to that city and fight the more than 7,300 Mexican soldiers defending it.

First, however, they had reached Cerralvo, which turned out to be an exceptionally beautiful town in the foothills, the enjoyment of which was further enhanced by the unexpectedly warm welcome they received from the populace. In addition, here the water was sparkling clear and cold, the food abundant and well-prepared, the surrounding countryside a joy to behold. Little wonder, then, that morale among Taylor's troops rose accordingly. The feeling elevated even more when copies of newspapers—the New Orleans *Delta*, in particular—depicted the Mexican troops as being,

> ...*the lowest classes of cross breeds, who have been taken in chains to the capital and there, in their half-naked state, they are furnished with a musket and taught roughly and toughly how to load, aim, and fire...*

That the Mexican press described Taylor's army in virtually the same terms was of little consequence and mostly taken as bravado. Nevertheless, Lt. Meade made it very clear that if either Army thought its opponent would not fight, they were clearly deluding themselves.

The general himself had not experienced so sharp a rise in his own emotions as his troops were experiencing. Thus far there had been a virtual absence of hostilities, but everything in his experience cautioned him not to put alertness aside. Spies continued to bring in messages, often contradictory to one another, yet all foretokening a serious encounter ahead. What intelligence could be gathered that was not suspect indicated the forces that had scattered ahead of them were once again drawing together under General Arista's successor, General Pedro de Ampudia, and more were arriving in Monterrey every day. It seemed clear that with these reinforcements, it was in Monterrey that some very serious fighting would occur. Even the most momentarily emotionally elevated of the American troops blanched to some degree when confirmed reports arrived that the fifty-one-year-old former dictator of Mexico, Santa Ana, had returned from exile and was now once again installed as top commander of the Mexican Army. No one in the American Army had forgotten the stinging defeat General Santa Ana had handed them at the Alamo.

He did, indeed, have to put Monterrey under siege and it was not an easy job they faced. As the American troops, with the peaks of the Sierra Madre behind them, descended into the valley of the San Juan on September 19, they found themselves within cannon range from the city, just as Taylor's engineers, who had reconnoitered the situation, predicted would occur. Taylor at once prepared to order his force into his favorite maneuver—a bayonet charge—but was forced to put that in abeyance when the enemy's cannon opened up on them. Having not too wisely left the greater bulk of his own artillery behind at Cerralvo, the American general had to do some rapid rethinking of what tactics to use and he relied heavily on the intelligence acquired by the Corps of Engineers. They reported that southwest of town the road to Saltillo was clearly both the line of Mexican reinforcement and, if necessary, retreat. That road was commanded by lighter gun emplacements, but the terrain they overlooked was formidable. The engineers contended that despite the obstacles, Monterrey could be turned and the Saltillo Road effectively cut and that was the plan Taylor wisely elected to use. He immediately threw the First Division under General Garland to take the city's eastern forts with bayonet. That was easier said than done. Garland led his troops past some of the redoubts and then into the city streets where they were promptly blown to pieces by the Mexican artillery in the forts. Garland immediately withdrew to re-form, at which point Taylor sent in the division under Major General William O. Butler with this same type of approach against the northern and eastern faces of the city simultaneously. It was a bad mistake. Lieutenant Ulysses S. Grant and the Fourth Infantry ran into severe opposition and had a terrible time of it, finally withdrawing with something less than half the entire unit left alive.

Late on Sunday afternoon, September 20, a fresh brigade was sent in under command of President Polk's appointee, General John Anthony Quitman, but farther to the south. That body, too, was met by fierce rifle fire and the troops began melting away. It was discouraging to the Americans, but was also playing havoc with Mexican morale since they could not understand why the Americans insisted on coming back after taking such dreadful fire from cannon and rifles.

A rush of fear filled General Ampudia's breast and he withdrew some of his men, which others took as a sign of retreat and themselves fled at a very crucial moment. At this wavering, Colonel Jefferson Davis of the First Mississippi Rifles waved his sword and led his men in a charge of one of the redoubts, which they took.[125] Then another, which they took as well, while all the while withstanding a flurry of concentrated rifle fire from the other forts.

Encouraged, Taylor then sent in another wave of bayonet-wielding soldiers who met such devastating fire they were three times driven back to their starting point with casualties numbering into the scores. By late in the day Taylor had no choice left but to pull his entire army, except for Davis' volunteers in a captured redoubt, out of range of the Mexican big guns. It was not a good day for General Taylor, who had lost a great many of his men and, in the process, taught his subordinate commanders certain lessons about strategy he could not seem to master himself. His army was so fatigued by this point they could do no more fighting throughout the entire next day, even though the Mexicans had withdrawn during the night to the city's center.

Before day's end, however, Taylor finally sent Brigadier General William J. Worth with his Second Division of seasoned regulars, supported by Hays's Texas Rangers, to take the Saltillo Road but they were delayed by a heavy rainstorm which forced them to bivouac and the mission was not completed until the following day. When Worth did engage in combat, he coordinated his attacks well and gave them sequence, as the light and actually insufficient American artillery disrupted a strong charge of Mexican lancers, making it possible for the Rangers to turn them back with their own losses negligible. The Saltillo Road thus being taken, the Mexican force, now within the heart of the city, could neither retreat to the interior nor receive supplies or reinforcements from outside. Wasting no time, Worth formed an assaulting force under command of Captain C.F. Smith, which had to cross a river and work its way up a thousand-foot hill while under fire from artillery and rifle. These men had both guts and good leadership from competent officers and, upon reaching the crest, they charged the first bastion with bayonet. Resistance was well organized and the fighting fierce, at first from a distance but gradually narrowing the gap until at last it became vicious hand-to-hand combat. By mid-afternoon the whole ridge had been taken at light cost, at which point the Americans turned the captured Mexican artillery against their owners with devastating effect. They then turned these cannon on another stronghold that was across the river and nearer the city.

Worth endeavored to mount an attack here, but his own skirmishers had advanced no farther than the base of the hill when nightfall, accompanied by yet another fierce rainstorm, set in and curtailed the operation. Although Worth's men had not eaten since Sunday morning and they had no blankets, they nevertheless had won a very important battle against a strong opponent.

On Wednesday, September 23, Taylor's troops began a block-by-block movement through the city, fighting every step of the way as they strove to reach Monterrey's grand plaza in the city's center. The force was shot up very badly, yet the men kept advancing. Finally, in mid-afternoon, they ran out of ammunition. Lieutenant Grant, who was quartermaster, swiftly rode back in an effort to organize a new supply to be brought forward, but Taylor, unwilling to sacrifice more lives, ordered his men back and withdrew well out of town, even as the Mexicans continued shooting at them.

Worth, meanwhile, with no specific orders from Taylor, sent two of his columns right down the city's main streets, fighting their way house to house and, though they had a very bad time of it and suffered numerous casualties, they persevered in the advance. Lieutenant Meade and other engineers taught them to pierce the soft adobe walls and lob grenades through the gaps to clean out pockets of the enemy. Block by interminable block they continued this deadly mopping-up of the enemy and they were within a single block of the plaza at nightfall and Worth did not call them back, knowing that they had just won Taylor's third major victory for him.

For six days—September 19 - 24—this fiercely contested Battle of Monterrey was fought vigorously by both sides and with heavy losses.[126] However well the city was fortified and protected by its military installations—the Citadel, Fort Tenería, and Fort Diablo—the Mexican supply line from Saltillo was poorly guarded and, in his well-executed turning movement around the west end of the city, Brigadier General Worth had cut the Saltillo Road and attacked the Mexican defenses from south and east, which was, for the most part, unexpected by the defenders.

General Taylor, who feared the fight might continue for days longer, was very gratified when, early on Thursday, September 24, a Mexican messenger appeared before General Taylor bearing General Ampudia's proposal to surrender on terms quite favorable to himself and including a two-month armistice to follow. Ampudia's force would surely have been destroyed with just one more day of fighting but General Taylor, though without actual authority to grant any kind of armistice, and in order to avoid any further bloodshed to his own troops, which had already suffered twenty per cent losses among the effectives, generously accepted Ampudia's terms and the Battle of Monterrey was over.

Now, with the Mexicans withdrawn and heading southward, General Taylor bent to the distasteful task of relating all the details to the Army's Adjutant General Roger Jones in Washington, D.C., writing with a steadily flowing hand and few pauses:

> *Head-Quarters, Army of Occupation,*
> *Camp before Monterey, September 25, 1846*
>
> *Sir—At noon on the 23rd inst., while our troops were closely engaged in the lowerpart of the city, as reported in my last dispatch, I received a flag of communication from thegovernor of the state of New Leon, which is herewith enclosed (No. 1) To this communication, I deemed it my duty to return an answer declining to allow the inhabitants to leave the city. By eleven o'clock, P.M. the 2d division, which had entered the town from the direction of the Bishop's Palace, had advanced within one square of the principal plaza, and occupied the city up to that point. The mortar had, in the mean time, been placed in battery in the cemetery, within good range of the heart of the town, and was served throughout the night with good effect.*
>
> *Early in the morning on the 24th I received a flag from the town, bearing a communication from General Ampudia, which I enclose (No. 2) and to which I return the answer (No. 3.) I also arranged with the bearer of the flag a cessation of fire until 12 o'clock, which hour I appointed to receive the final answer of Gen, Ampudia at Gen. Worth's headquarters. Before the appointed time, however, Gen. Ampudia had signified to Gen Worth his desire*

*for a personal interview with me, for the purpose of making some definite arrangement. An interview was accordingly appointed for one o'clock, and resulted in the naming of a commission to draw up articles of agreement regulating the withdrawal of the Mexican forces and a temporary cessation of hostilities. The commissioners named by the Mexican general-in-chief were Generals Ortega and Requena, and Don Manuel M. Llano, Governor of New Leon. Those named on the American side were Gen, Worth, Gen. Henderson, governor of Texas, and Colonel Davis, of the Mississippi volunteers. The commission finally settled upon the articles, of which I enclose a copy, (No. 4) the duplicates of which (in Spanish and English) have been duly signed. Agreeably to the provisions of the 4th article, our troops have this morning occupied the citadel.*

*It will be seen that the terms granted the Mexican garrison are less rigorous than those first imposed. The gallant defence [sic] of the town, and the fact of a recent change of government in Mexico, believed to be favorable to the interests of peace, induced me to concur with the commission in these terms, which will, I trust, receive the approval of the government. The latter consideration also prompted the convention for a temporary cessation of hostilities. Though scarcely warranted by my instructions, yet the change of affairs since those instructions were issued seemed to warrant this course. I beg to be advised, as early as practicable, whether I have met the views of the government in these particulars. I regret to report that Capt. Williams, Topographical Engineer, and Lieut. Terrett, 1st infantry, have died of the wounds received in the engagement of the 21st.— Capt. Gatlin, 7th infantry, was wounded (not badly) on the 23d.*

*I am, sir, very respectfully, your obedient servant,*
*Z. TAYLOR, Major-general, U.S.A. Commanding*

[September 25, 1846 • Friday • 2:30 p.m.]

The recognition and appreciation of what Colonel Mariano Guadalupe Vallejo had done for the American cause in so many different ways was clearly reflected in the letter being penned this afternoon by Captain John Berrien Montgomery, in command of the war ship, *U.S. Portsmouth*, who wrote to say he was sending his:

*...hearty thanks for the service you have rendered as well as for the*

> *prompt and sincere manner in which you were pleased to tender your assistance to the Government of the United States in the recent emergency, and to your associates, whose ready obedience to your call has done much toward allaying natural prejudices and unfriendly suspicions among the various classes comprising the society of California, and for hastening arrangements for the establishment of peace, order and good government in the country.*

Almost simultaneously, in his home at Petaluma, Vallejo, who had been in a bad mood before he even began writing his own letter to Consul Thomas Larkin at his headquarters office in Monterey, now having finished it, read it through and felt his anger increasing even more. Despite all he had done to aid the Americans in becoming established in California and subsequently championing their cause to make this land an official territory belonging to the United States, all of which Captain Montgomery was at this moment acknowledging, other United States officials could hardly have treated him in a manner more shabby and disrespectful.

A highly self-controlled individual, Vallejo rarely exhibited his emotions outwardly, but he did so today as he wrote to Larkin, concerning the unbelievably bitter aftermath of his unjustified imprisonment at Sutters Fort:

> *...I left the Sacramento half dead and arrived here* [Sonoma] *almost without life, but am now much better.... The political change has cost a great deal to my person and mind and likewise to my property. I have lost more than one thousand live horned cattle, six hundred tame horses, and many other things of value which were taken from my house here in Petaluma. My wheat crops are entirely lost for the cattle ate them up in the field and I assure you that two hundred fanegas* [near 25,000 bushels] *of sowing, in good condition as mine was, is a considerable loss. All is lost and the only hope for making it up is to work again.*

That the Americans could actually have treated him so abominably after he had discarded his own significant standing in the Californio military in order to openly protect and aid those Yankee newcomers in their cause for the United States was both perplexing and vexing to him.

For the help and aid he had provided them and for his support in using his own considerable prestige and influence to support them, they had imprisoned him and, while he was still incarcerated—long after United States authorities had taken possession and the American flag fluttered over his prison—looted his home and lands until now virtually nothing remained.

The once enormously wealthy Mariano G. Vallejo was presently sliding headlong into the process of losing virtually all he owned; his own personal wealth in funds, millions of acres of land, many tens of thousands of cattle, sheep and hogs, thousands of saddle horses and mules and practically all of his family's personal possessions. Vallejo, who was quite probably at one time the wealthiest individual in all of California, found himself now teetering on the very brink of poverty.[127]

*[October 2, 1846 · Friday · 10:00 a.m.]*

California was turning out to be more of a "dream come true" for Samuel Brannan than he might have envisioned, even in his most optimistic fancies. His new colony for the Mormons under his control was still only a seed newly planted, but his vision had it becoming, one day, a grand metropolis and his own vision in this respect tended to transfer itself to the Saints in his charge.

Everything had gone extremely well for Brannan since their arrival at Yerba Buena. Only a short time thereafter, the assembling of his Saints aboard the deck of the *U.S. Portsmouth* on the morning of August 2 had been a tribute to his early accomplishments here in Yerba Buena and Brannan was more than satisfied with his accomplishments. He had not been so assured of success when they had first arrived and their arrival that morning at the tiny port on San Francisco Bay had been both a joy and a disappointment. A loudly raised comment from one of the women aboard the *Brooklyn* caused a stir of "Well saids," rising from the passengers as they filed ashore.

"Of all the memories of my life," she proclaimed fervently, "not one is so bitter as that dreary six months voyage on an emigrant ship around the Horn!"

The joy had been there simply because the interminable voyage from New York City to San Francisco Bay had indeed finally come to an end and it was glorious to feel the solidness of Mother Earth underfoot again. The disappointment, though short-lived, was occasioned by the fact that the American colors fluttered from the top of the mast protruding above Yerba Buena's principal trading post and, in a way, Brannan's sense of adventure had risen high over the prospect of meeting and driving out whatever Mexicans occupied the place. Instead, they were being cheered by Mexicans, Americans and a horde of Indians on the shore. In addition, a longboat that put off from the nearby warship, U.S. *Portsmouth*, contained half a dozen of the principal brass from the ship, which included her skipper, Captain John B. Montgomery. When that craft tied up to the *Brooklyn's* pad and the five subalterns climbed the swaying steps after their captain, introductions were quickly exchanged and then Brannan spoke.

"We expected to find some resistance awaiting us, Captain Montgomery. Evidently you took care of that before our arrival. How long have you been here, sir?"

Montgomery blinked as he thought for a moment. "Nine days," he said. "Well, nine days *today*. There was no resistance, just as there was none at Monterey. We simply walked in, took down the Mexican flag and put up old glory—to numerous cheers, I might add. Seems no one's very happy with what had been going on under the old regime, such as it was. They took the oath to the U.S. and everyone seems happy enough."

"We're eager to get our Mormon agricultural community started here," Brannan said carefully, adding, "presuming there's no problem with that, of course."

"None so far as I know," Montgomery said. "You will have to stay on board, however, for the first couple of days while cargo and personnel are checked out. Then you just go where you want to without restrictions."

There were a few raised eyebrows among the sailors when the store of firearms was encountered, but everyone laughed when Brannan explained they had expected to have to fight off the Mexicans to gain a toehold here and were glad that hadn't been necessary. He said nothing, however, about the somewhat graver problems that had occurred aboard the *Brooklyn* when some of the Saints began taking exception to the preferential treatment Brannan had been receiving from the captain. It had begun as whisperings about the "fancy living" he was having and the more pronounced "high handed tactics" he was employing with his flock.

Brannan had decided to nip the problem quickly and did so by ruthlessly making examples of several of the most vociferous. Setting himself up as prosecutor, jury and judge, he held a farcical trial aboard ship during early July and, concentrating on the four "worst" offenders—

which included even his own counselor, E. Ward Pell—he wound up excommunicating the quartet. Instead of silencing the other Mormons, however, his action served only to make the prevailing resentment of him fester more and complaints became louder. When he was finally able to found his Mormon community on July 31, he also immediately set up his presses in Yerba Buena and established the *California Star*, whose editorial opinion reflected that of its owner.

Paying for their passage to this place was the first matter on the agenda. Few had any cash resources but the captain of the *Brooklyn* had an idea that suited them all very well: They could pay Captain Richardson by filling the hold of his ship with freshly cut lumber, which they did quite speedily by cutting timber on the Marin Peninsula. As soon as the hold of the *Brooklyn* was filled to capacity, farewells were said and the sturdy old ship sailed out of San Francisco Bay and out of the lives of the Mormons who had just become the first new settlers of American California.

Locating the "perfect" place to sink the new Mormon roots had been neither easy nor swiftly accomplished. Brannan inspected dozens of possible sites for the new town's establishment and discarded each for one reason or another. Finally, though, after long discussions with the trappers and mountain men who were most familiar with California's interior, he was guided to a spot some thirty miles up the Sacramento River from northeastern San Francisco Bay, to where the mouth of the San Joaquín River was located, its substantial stream entering the larger river from the southeast. Up the San Joaquín some twenty miles more they at last encountered Brannan's dream world. Even before the first stake was driven he absolutely *knew* this site of breath-taking beauty was the place where one day the new Zion of the Mormons would become a reality. With hardly a moment's hesitation he named the location New Hope.

Here, just a mile or so upstream from where the tributary Calaveras River emptied into the San Joaquín was a beautiful broad valley and here, Brannan knew, was where he and the Saints in his charge must plant a city; a place to become a haven of welcome rest for the overland travel-weary Saints who were sure to arrive during the next year or so. This was the place where the climate rivaled that of southern Italy, where broad acreages of great natural beauty surrounding the proposed city-site must be planted in life-giving crops, where substantial houses could be built and everything made ready for the Zion to be established.

The rich, loamy topsoil here was not just a few inches deep but several feet or more. Wild game was present in amazing abundance—antelope, deer, bear, geese by the tens of thousands, ducks in flocks so great that they blackened the waters; chirring grouse were here as well and great coveys of quail. There were also fine furbearers—beaver and muskrat, mink and weasel and hordes of river otter; the rivers themselves amazingly abundant with fish simply there for the taking. The trails made by the bigger bears, the grizzlies, were as numerous through the riverside swamps as the multitude of trails on cattle ranches and bear hunting would surely provide the entire colony with enough meat for a week, to say nothing of the rich bear-oil to be rendered that would serve admirably as lard. As for the crops they would raise, for the time being these would be comprised primarily of unground wheat, unrefined sugar, and coffee beans. There would also undoubtedly be the goods the Saints would themselves create with their skills. For all this, they would construct a fleet of boats that would carry them and their agricultural products and manufactures swiftly down the beautiful, deep waterway of the San Joaquín, which quickly and easily emptied into the even broader and deeper majesty of the Sacramento that itself flowed at last into San Francisco Bay and the seaports of the vast Pacific Ocean would become their market.[128]

Brannan could imagine no place else in the world more suitable for the establishment of the home of the Mormons—the new Zion that Brigham Young was always seeking but had never found—and now it was one of his youngest apostles who had discovered its location. The very thought of it and the fame it would bring him made Brannan positively giddy.

Infected with their leader's enthusiasm, the Saints in Brannan's charge fell to work with unlimited vigor. They built a sawmill, powered by the current of the San Joaquín and to it they brought the trees that were sawn into lumber for the construction of the homes and other buildings they would require. By next spring everyone would be well housed and many acres would be plowed and sewn with wheat and barley and other crops.

Unfortunately, what seemed a promising beginning had flaws that were directly attributable to none other than Brannan; he was spending far more time in Yerba Buena than with his flock and becoming, in the process, the leading entrepaneur of the rapidly expanding town. There were, he found, opportunities for considerable profit in virtually every direction and he let none of them slip past. While he still allowed himself time with his Saints, it was decidedly a minimum effort and resentments were beginning to rise among some members of his flock. His austere and exacting demands of strict obedience to him in respect to all the orders and instructions he levied out to them were still being followed, but only grudgingly now. Each Sunday while New Hope was being established, he held religious services for his flock in the Yerba Buena portmaster's *Casa Grande*, and demanded unwavering attendance from all, calling the Saints to worship with the tolling of a small bell hung in the central plaza. He hammered at them verbally to remain faithful and to shun the many temptations they were being confronted with in this land of gentiles. Brannan was, in fact, the only bona fide preacher in Yerba Buena—a situation that showed little likelihood of changing in the near future.

Still, discontent seethed among the Mormons, primarily over management of the affairs of Samuel Brannan & Company, over which only he had a vote. The agreements the Saints had signed aboard ship still bound them and all business transactions involving these Mormons were transacted through the firm's name and under the sole direction of the "First Elder"—Brannan himself, who was so uncompromising a leader. Sensing the growing rift between himself and his flock, Brannan tried to solve the problem by excommunicating three more of the Saints who were among the most complaining, but this only stirred an already agitated hornet's nest. Several of the Saints appealed to Captain Montgomery for redress and Montgomery immediately instituted a court of inquiry.

The suit, brought by the most discontent of the Saints, William Harris, claimed the entire party of Saints was weary of Samuel Brannan & Company, appealed for a withdrawal from the chafing obligations it imposed, complained bitterly of generally bad treatment from Brannan and demanded, in accordance with the stipulations of the agreement, their shares of the common stock of the joint company. Since at this time there was not yet any duly authorized court in Yerba Buena, absolute power for such judgment rested in the hands of that pompous naval officer who had become the town's *alcalde* under military administration Lieutenant Washington A. Bartlett. It was he, therefore, before whom the case was heard.

One of the Saints, who was a lawyer by profession, Stanley Hyde, presented the case for the plaintiffs in rather eloquent manner and it was Col. C.W. Russell who acted as counsel for Brannan. The trial, however, was a lock-down from the onset. Harris had no truly supportive grounds for his lawsuit and Brannan, in his usual obstreperous manner, presented most of his own defense personally. He was brilliant in stating his own case and with such stirring oratory that he quickly captivated the members of the first jury trial in California and swayed them to his cause. They swiftly brought a verdict of *"not guilty,"* declaring, *"...the contract the Saints have signed for a period of three years is legitimate and cannot legally be abrogated."*

On hearing the verdict, the defendant rose from his seat, made a slight bow to both Bartlett and the jury and then remarked loudly, "The truth is mighty and has prevailed!"

Moving swiftly to take advantage of his victory, Brannan quickly took on other printing jobs for the Yerba Buena community—business advertising, civil notices, naval proclamations and municipal deeds. It was profitable and Brannan pocketed virtually all of the proceeds.[129] Much of this was used by Brannan in furnishing the house he quickly had built for himself—the very finest house in town—with most of the labor done by his Mormons at no cost to him; the structure quickly becoming a very popular rendezvous for any important visitor, of which there was a constantly increasing number. None of the Saints, with the exception of Brannan himself, was ever invited to such social or business functions. As complaints against him continued, Brannan sporadically excommunicated the leaders and, for some while, managed to keep the lid on the foment brewing against him.

At one point the Saints were invited by Captain Montgomery to attend the Sabbath services being held for the military men on the main deck of the *Portsmouth*. Brannan accepted on behalf of his flock and they gathered at his behest, the women and children being provided with seating beneath a large spread canvas. The common sailors, who were eager for their first glimpse of Mormon women seemed disappointed; one, in fact, was overheard by Brannan, remarking to another, "I'll be demned! They look like any other woman!"

Thwarted in their attempt at legal redress, many of the disgruntled Saints settled in to work and wait patiently for the remainder of the Saints to arrive here at New Hope under Brigham Young. Refusing to believe the prevalent rumors that those Saints would never come here and would settle at the west foot of the Rocky Mountains, they lived with the hope of being able to complain in person to the Mormon Order's chief figure exactly how they felt about Samuel Brannan.

Brannan, as usual, was supremely confident he could handle any problems that arose. Most observers agreed, but there were those who darkly predicted that "Mr. Brannan will one day find his come-uppance!"

[October 4, 1846 · Sunday]

Commodore Robert Field Stockton had returned to California only hours ago and was immediately being feted as guest of honor at a large reception held at the rapidly growing town fronting on San Francisco Bay.

Not surprisingly, William H. "Owl" Russell, proclaiming himself to be "one of the first true-blue Yankees" to take up permanent California residency, was in his cups and gave a long, flowery speech that delighted all in attendance, but which was entirely unmemorable, except that he introduced Commodore Stockton as the principal speaker for the evening. Then Stockton, wholly unaware of what had been occurring lately in regard to the California conflict, began his own enthusiastic oratory.

"I have returned," he announced to the audience of self-proclaimed American "victors" plus many conciliated Californios, "for important business; that of enlisting a thousand Americans here in California, transporting them by sea to Mazatlan and thence marching them eastward into the heart of Mexico. There we will join and assist General Zachary Taylor, whom I suspect will be awaiting our arrival close to Mexico City. The reason Colonel Fremont is not in attendance here with us today, I'm pleased to say, is because he is presently out drumming up new recruits for this operation. He will..."

The sentence was left hanging as one of the guests urgently tugged at Stockton's sleeve and, when the colonel stopped in momentary confusion, informed him *sotto voce* that Gillespie's force, which he thought was still occupying Los Angeles and would, with that force, assist him in the Mexican operation, had actually been driven out of Los Angeles and fled to safety aboard the *U.S. Vandalia*. Los Angeles was now firmly back in the hands of the Californios, and the same held true for both San Diego and Santa Barbara. After a bit of blustering and a few swallows from his water glass, Stockton regained better control and, realizing now that he would have to begin all over to re-conquer those places, delivered an absolutely hell-fire, gore-thirsty speech that of itself was almost enough to send the enemy to perdition.

One thing, however, was now very clear to all: despite American claims to the contrary and their related promises of prosperity and freedom for the native people, California was not yet a United States territory and whether or not it would ever actually became one remained to be seen. Achieving that goal seemed altogether likely now to take just a wee bit longer than the Americans had initially anticipated.

### [October 6, 1846 • Tuesday]

The news General Kearny received today in regard to the situation in California was far more encouraging than he had dared hope; yet, there remained within him a pang that the likelihood for martial glory was yet again being denied him. So it had been since the beginning of this entire campaign and so it seemed to be continuing.

He had harbored high hopes that the mission he'd assigned to Doniphan to engage in with General Wool would have prompted at least some kind of conflict, but even that had hardly borne the fruit expected. It was two weeks ago, on September 26, that Wool had set his army marching from San Antonio en route to clashing with the enemy in the vicinity of Chihuahua, but it hadn't quite worked out that way.

Doniphan's orders from Kearny read that he was to turn over command of Santa Fe to Colonel Sterling Price as soon as the Second Missouri should arrive, but that first he was to clean up the unfinished business in regard to the tribes in the Santa Fe region; defeating them, if it came to that, but preferably rounding up the Indians and exhorting them toward peaceful co-existence with the whites and making treaties with them toward that end. Once that was done and Santa Fe was snug under Price's control, then Doniphan was to head out with his small force to locate and join with Wool in the Chihuahua area for the purpose of occupying that city.

Kearny, continuing to head for California from Santa Fe, almost immediately ran into outcropping problems with the Indians that slowed him down somewhat. The supposedly peacefully-inclined Navajos were suddenly making their presence known in a series of aggravations toward the scattered settlers in southern New Mexico Territory; incidents that might well escalate into a full-fledged war. One wealthy Mexican rancher alone had already lost some 6,000 sheep to them. Kearny immediately sent new orders to Doniphan to put teeth into his pacification efforts. He was to invade the Navajo's territory, release their captives, reclaim properties they had stolen and awe them into submission. If the latter was not possible, he was to beat such submission into them without delay. Kearny thereupon continued his march toward California.

Just four days ago—on October 2—General Kearny, while at La Jolla, about 130 miles south of Santa Fe, finally learned by express of Col. James Allen's death and immediately ordered the commander of the First Dragoons, Captain Philip St. George Cooke, to return eastward and take command of the Mormon Battalion, at the same time promoting him to lieutenant colonel.[130] The very next day, learning that the Navajo had raided a village only a dozen miles from his army, he sent reiterated orders to Doniphan to speed up his Indian campaign and then move at once to join General Wool's force in the vicinity of Chihuahua.

Finally, today, with his dragoons along the Rio Grande, Kearny met Kit Carson en route back East from California with dispatches from Commodore Stockton and Colonel Fremont, both of whom were reporting that they had already conquered the Californios. So now, assured by dispatches from the two commanders that he would experience no difficulty from the California inhabitants, Kearny reduced his mounted force by three fifths, retaining only two dragoon companies of about fifty men each. He sent the remaining three companies back to Santa Fe under Major Sumner and Captain Burgwin and hurried on with his 100 packmule mounted dragoons as a guard, to take charge of events in California as ordered by President Polk.

Westward progress of Kearny's remaining force over the Santa Fe Trail was reasonably rapid and they encountered no more than the usual difficulties such travel normally experienced; lack of good water for man and beast, shortages of food and shortages of animals to hunt for food, except for the rare occasions when they came across buffalo herds and there was suddenly such a plethora of meat that it could not all be consumed at once and time had to be taken to jerk and smoke and dry portions of the flesh as reserves for times when nothing else was available. Kearny was a stickler about no more animals being killed for this purpose than was absolutely necessary for their needs and that no meat of any such buffalo slain was wasted, the hides and heads of those killed salted down and carried along to be given in gifts and trade to whatever Indians were encountered.

So it was that today Kearny's force intercepted the smaller eastbound party led by Kit Carson—the mountain man himself now a U.S. Army lieutenant by Stockton appointment. Carson was accompanied by sixteen men and half a dozen trail-skilled Delaware Indians as his escort, moving rapidly and steadily with saddlebags well filled with dispatches, mail, papers and detailed reports about the situation in California to be delivered personally to the President, Secretary of War, Senator Benton and other highly-placed governmental officials. That Stockton's and Fremont's dispatches related the easy takeover of the western territory from the Californios, that the American flag now flew there and that the country was forever free from Mexican control was both welcome news and a bitter pill for Kearny to swallow. Once again Kearny found himself in the position of having missed whatever opportunity there may have been to participate in the glory of claiming and assuming control for his country over a vast and highly important Western territory.

Lt. Carson had left the western headquarters at Los Angeles with the dispatches just a month and a day ago—on September 5—and he conferred with General Kearny at length, describing for him the prevailing conditions when he left there, with the native generals in flight to Mexico, all principal ports and towns occupied by Americans, the native people themselves pacified and reconciled to the momentous changeover of government, Commodore Stockton having taken over as top military commander and Fremont now "probably" established as both civil and military governor of the territory. All that remained for Kearny to do, it seemed, was to continue his march westward and, as required by his Presidential orders, officially take possession and command of the whole of California in the name of the United States, just as he had already done with New Mexico.

One of the chores that had been left to Kearny and his army was to establish, as quickly as possible, a wagon road from Santa Fe to San Diego and Los Angeles, the old trail itself at this time sparse and difficult and all but impassable for wagon traffic. Kearny now directed his chief guide, Tom Fitzpatrick, to assist in carrying Carson's dispatches to Washington D.C. Carson, who had not laid eyes on his own family since joining Fremont in the spring of '45 was at that moment seriously considering going AWOL, if necessary, to effect that reunion, but eventually he accepted and obeyed the orders and returned with Kearny, whose orders sent his wagons back to Santa Fe and directed Colonel Cooke to follow with the Mormon Battalion and establish, in the process, a decent wagon road. The Dragoons themselves packed horses and mules and even a few oxen, but the going was tough and very hard on the livestock. As Kearny wrote in his official report today to the President:

*...we met Mr. Kit Carson, with a party of sixteen men, on his*

way to Washington city, with a mail and papers, an express from Commodore Stockton and Lieutenant-colonel Fremont, reporting that the Californios were already in possession of the Americans under their command; that the American flag was flying from every important position in the territory, and that the country was for ever [sic] free from Mexican control, the war ended, and peace and harmony established among the people. In consequence of this information, I directed that 200 dragoons under Major Sumner should remain in New Mexico, and that the other 100, with two mounted howitzers, under Captain Moore, should accompany me as a guard to Upper California...*

[October 9, 1846 • Friday]

The westward march of the Mormon Battalion, as it attempted to overtake General Kearny's advance had become hardly less than a nightmare of monotony and thirst and seemingly endless marching. The greater the effort made to overtake the commander and his dragoons, the more Kearny seemed to be leaving them behind. In the evenings, when camp was made, the Saints were so weary of marching they were too tired to do much more than pitch their tents and tumble into exhausted sleep, often even neglecting to eat their meager rations; the erecting of tents, at first so precisely accomplished in neat rows and spacings, had gradually become haphazard, with little semblance of uniformity and often scattered over an area of five acres or more. Despite such exhaustion, however, there were some of the men who faithfully recorded the events of each day, even if only tersely, though often with surprising detail. One of these was John D. Lee, adopted son of Brigham Young, who, while his command of grammar and spelling left much to be desired, was nevertheless keen in his penned observations. In his diary entry for September 25, he wrote:

*New Mexico, Simeroan [Cimarron] R., Commancha [Commanche] Nation Friday, Sept. 25th, '46 Morning cool & cloudy, wind North, fuel scarce. The country So barren that buffallos [sic] scarce could subsist or were hunted out, for the Spaniards & French came even 50 ms [miles] East of this to hunt Buffallo [sic]; about 8 the Bat. received marching orders about 11 we left the Simerone [sic] River & on ascending the ridge Several Peaks & Spurs of the Mountain hove in sight, I in co. with several of the Bat. Ascended several of those Spurs—on the top of one was a cave the mouth of which was about 3 by 4 feet the stone around the cave were perfectly smoothe [sic], of a sand cast, about the door of the Stone, were a great no. of singular characters—representing the Egyptian Hyroglifics [sic]. I would have penned some of them down—but the Teams were on the move—between two of those Spurs formed a smawl [sic] valley in which was a few Trees; the most beautiful for cottonwood & Hackberry that I ever saw, their green foliage appeared so fresh & tender, that it brought quite forcible to my mind the saying of the scriptures—shall flourish like a tree by the side of the fountain that is well watered,*[131] *the country around us is parched up, at this place we haulted [sic] to water our teams—Several antelopes were killed & brought into camp, Some few Deer also—traveled 5 ms more & came to the Cold Springs—where we encamped for the Night—feed scarce, Buffallo [sic] dung also. Dis 19 ms, Total 519 ms.*[132]

By late afternoon two days later—September 27—the slipping morale of the entire Mormon Battalion due to the rigors of the forced march became clearer than ever to John D. Lee and he chronicled them in his journal entries while, at the same time, demanding that the officers under acting Lt. Col. A.J. Smith give the men greater consideration than was occurring. His displeasure sharpened when Smith ordered fifty men and the best teams from each company to engage in an even more stringent forced march in an effort for them to reach Santa Fe, as Gen. Kearny had ordered, by October 10 and who had warned if they did not make it, they would forfeit the opportunity of continuing the march to California. With that selection of the most able men and animals to meet the deadline, Smith assigned Lt. George Oman to follow with the rear guard through the ruins of ancient pueblos and past the first present Mexican settlements.

The going remained very rough during the day and the Saints marched fully a dozen miles over very difficult desert that was both broken and almost universally sandy. It was at 3 p.m., as the men were near the point of exhaustion, when Smith, to their immense relief, called for a halt and camp to be made in a broad open area of the desert to the left of the trail they were following. They were informed that this was the site, almost 200 miles from Santa Fe, where a major conflict had occurred along a creek bed in 1828, with Comanche raiders pitted against—and defeating—a caravan of white traders.[133] As Sgt. Daniel Tyler wrote about the day's march in his journal:

> On the 27th we marched over rough sand hills and encamped by a pond of stagnant water. There were a few buffalo chips which were soon gathered, when some, who had none of this kind of fuel, traveled two miles to timber and brought wood on their shoulders. A few antelope added to our short rations were quite a treat. The monotony of the barren plains in our rear was considerably relieved by the view of the numerous mountain peaks in front, the first many of us ever saw, including the Rabbit's Ears.[134]

The next day's travel was even worse, especially for the animals. Early in the day they passed Rock Creek, but then the terrain became even drier and virtually bereft of any grazing material, forcing them to travel farther and longer than usual and with no stop made for the night's camp until about 9 p.m., by which time men and beasts alike were practically falling in their tracks. The following day the route they traversed was, for a considerable distance, over hills and high ridges. A number of antelope were killed and some bears and wild turkeys were seen, but no buffalo were visible, as the men were now out of the country over which the animals ranged. The high temperatures, combined with the fundamental lack of water and the forced pace at which they were marching now began having a singular effect upon the men, who began failing as badly as were their teams, and the majority placed the blame squarely on the shoulders of Lt. Col. Andrew Jackson Smith, condemning him for what they termed "his lack of judgment."

On the final day of September, the Mormon Battalion covered a solid two dozen miles, besides killing a number of antelope as food. Then, on the first day of October they encountered an inexplicable construction—two apparently ancient parallel walls of rock and cement, some four feet apart and running north and south for approximately 190 feet. There was much speculation among the men as to who had built the walls and why. As Daniel Tyler wrote in his journal:

> Whether these had been partition walls of a castle or some large building, or part of a fortification, it would be difficult to determine. It was evident that the whole face of the country has undergone

a change. There were numerous canals or channels where large streams had once run, probably for irrigating, but which were quite dry and, to all appearances, had not been used for generations.

John D. Lee was less impressed with the construction and more with the condition of their animals. He wrote:

> New Mexico, Commancha Nation, Barron Encampment
> —Thur, Oct. 1st, 1846 Clear.
> Wind southwest. About 5 the battalion was on the move & at the distance of three ms we came [to] Stillbetter Creek, called a Hault [sic], grass good. Orders was given to graze 3 hours during which time our victuals was to be prepared. Marching order was given, traveled 12 ms, encamped in a valley—that was completely encompassed on three sides with a chain of Rocks—that was called the Point of Rocks.[135] Water & willow wood, but grazing short. Dis 16 ms. T 620 ms.

On the first day of October the Mormon Battalion reached what they called the Red River.[136] This was where, the following day, the sick were left with a few officers to take charge and bring them up, while all the strong and able proceeded on their forced march for Santa Fe in an effort to try to get there by the tenth, which was Gen. Kearny's limitation date for how long he would await them before moving on.

The morning was clear and the healthier men of the Battalion moved on at daybreak at a brisk pace and in twenty-one miles reached what was called Wagon Mound—a natural formation shaped much like an overloaded wagon—and here they found good water and grass in abundance. They camped amid a number of mounds and were joined by the ill detachment bringing up the rear at one o'clock in the morning. The mounds were a great curiosity to the Mormons and the majority of the Saints flocked close for a first-hand view.

The Battalion divided on October 3 and the hale and hearty, including most of the commissioned officers—with Lt. Col. Smith and Dr. Sanderson among them—moved on at top speed toward Santa Fe. The sick, feeble and worn out were left to follow as best they could. The fact that Dr. Sanderson moved out with the healthy instead of staying behind to attend to the sick was, to most of the Mormons, a clear indication of how little he was concerned for the Battalion's health or in attending to those who were ailing. For once, however, the Mormons did not complain; they were very glad to see him go and, with him, his pronounced cursing and the dispensing of medications they didn't feel they needed, with calomel, which they most definitely despised. Perhaps not too surprisingly, many of those who had been seriously ill now suddenly took a swing for the better and the ailing, following in the rear, did not fall as far back as most had thought they would.

As the main body of Mormons marched along briskly, the Saints saw, for the first time, Spanish sheep and goats. They were amused by the milking of the goats and chuckled at how, as a nanny was being milked, very frequently her droppings fell into the pail being filled with milk and were subsequently skimmed out by the milker, usually with his fingers.

Sergeant Daniel Tyler created a roar of amusement when he opined that possibly this dropping of the "nanny-berries," as he termed them, into the milk might contribute to some degree to the extreme richness of goat's milk cheese.

[October 12, 1846 · Monday · 10:00 a.m.]

The President of the United States was extremely displeased.

Not only had General Taylor blandly ignored Polk's explicit orders to avoid, if possible, a confrontation with the enemy in Mexico, he had evidently placed his Army in a position where battle became unavoidable and then, at its conclusion in a questionable "victory," had the temerity to offer the Mexican forces an armistice. And General Antonio López de Santa Ana, the new Mexican president, had wasted not one moment in beginning to reorganize that force of his that had fallen back to San Luis Potosi.

President Polk had learned about the Battle of Monterrey just last evening and had been as utterly dismayed as he was furious. With approximately 900 Americans killed or disabled in the three-day action, American newspapers had plenty to write about for a change and they didn't hesitate at the opportunity. They pounced on wonderfully dramatic stories of heroism under fire and the snatching of victory from what had quite apparently been the jaws of defeat and the unavoidable conclusion that a flag-waving nation was now widely lauding Major General Zachary Taylor as perhaps the greatest military genius in history and most definitely in the uppermost echelon of consideration as the next

# The Infinite Dream

Whig candidate for the American presidency. It also quite neatly placed President Polk in the unenviable position of today having to disavow the unauthorized armistice and order its termination. This, in essence, was an official declaration that nine hundred American soldiers had pointlessly become casualties in a battle that never should have been fought in the first place; a battle that had accomplished precisely nothing.

This was exactly the sort of ammunition against President Polk that the opposition press had been striving to find.

Brigadier General William Worth did his part, as soon as the battle ended, in trying to undermine Taylor's effectiveness through a succession of letters to political allies in Washington D.C., but such a ball, once rolling in Taylor's behalf, was difficult to stop or divert and Worth was unable to do either. Though various newspapers were already pointing out Taylor's lack of sensible generalship and detailing a list of serious errors he had made, the fact of the matter could not be shaken: even though it had been only the courage of the private soldier that had won the Battle of Monterrey for him, it was clearly Taylor who was both the victor and the deserving recipient of glory. That glory was already being utilized by the Whigs to bring the War with Mexico into disrepute and to undermine President Polk himself. It was a simple matter now to lay all blame for the nine hundred American casualties at the President's doorstep, while simultaneously promoting Taylor's generalship as the factor that had saved the nation's face; his first stepping stone to the principal seat in the White House.

Justifiably.

And, of course, as a Whig.

*[October 12, 1846 • Monday • 3:00 p.m.]*

This afternoon, three days after advance companies of the Mormons reached Santa Fe, the remaining "sick or impaired" division of the battalion showed up and, desperately weary and many of the men limping or barely able to struggle along, marched up the same street to the cheers and jubilation of their fellows. The joy all of them were experiencing at this reunion was much enhanced by two elements of news that awaited them.

There had been those among them who had almost lost faith that they would ever become joined again as a unit and the relief they felt that such had now occurred was almost palpable; there had been little of encouragement for them over the past ten or twelve days. John D. Lee, after several exhausting days of marching with the advance unit, had written in his journal on October 4:

> *New Mexico, Waggon* [sic] *Mounds, Wooharapahoo [Arapaho] Nation, Sund, Oct 4th, '46 Morning clear, cold. W.S.W. At 7 Guard Mounting was beat at which signal the Bat. was put on the march—through the day several groves of Pine & Spruce were seen. Traveled the dis*[tance] *of 20 ms & encamped on the East branch of the river Morough* [Mora River].[137] *Excellent feed & water. At this is—a singular chain of Rocks & is said to be Mill Stone grit of the best quality, over the face thereof is covered with Santafe Chinchapin Shurbs* [shrubs] *& Cedars—between sun down & dark, 5 or 6 Spaniards came into camp with pies & cakes—to sell—told us that it was 4 ms to the 1st Settlements on the Moree* [sic] *river. W.S.W. clear. Dis 22ms, T 667.*

The Battalion moved along the next morning and in about five miles came to where the East Branch of the Mora emptied into the parent stream, although the Mora itself was not much larger than its tributary. It was a beautiful flush-running stream, very clear and quite obviously fed by springs in the nearby mountains. Along the Mora they encountered large herds of cattle, sheep and goats who sustained themselves by grazing on the slopes, though Lee had a difficult time believing there was graze enough for them.

Nothing of outstanding note occurred the next day and, on the day following that—October 6—they traveled over broken, mountainous country until, about noon when, after marching twelve miles, they reached the town that Lee referred to as Taucaulute, but which was actually Telecote—a village about the same size as Bagoes. They then traveled another six miles before camping in a valley at another small settlement. In the evening about 9 p.m., as Lee wrote in his journal in Adjutant Dykes' marquis, they were joined by a drover named Symington, who brought fifty head of oxen from Santa Fe, sent by General Kearny for their assistance. He also bore a dispatch for Lt. Smith revealing that Kearny had heard rumors of Lt. Col. Allen's death but had not learned positively of it before the express reached him. Kearny wrote that he had decided to wait no longer for the Mormon Battalion and had resumed his march for California on September 20. He added that he had left orders with Col. Doniphan, whom he had placed in command at Santa Fe, to have all the troops—meaning specifically the Mormons—who arrived before October 10 to follow on his trail, that he would undoubtedly be detained somewhat in opening a path through the mountains at a pass that he planned to open, which would make the trek to California "...*much nigher than the usual travel.*"

In the following days the Battalion encountered a few aspects of interest, which Lee wrote about in his journal, though nothing of an imperative nature. On the seventh of October they traveled between mountains most of the way, encountering large beds of permanent snow. Lee continued to better cement his relationship with Lt. Col. Smith, Adjutant Dykes and others as they progressed, hopefully to gain their approval for an idea he'd had to prevent the Battalion from being divided. In the process, at the southernmost part of the trail that skirts the mountains to enter Santa Fe from the south, they passed through the little town of San Miguel del Vado—Ford of St. Michael—on the Pecos River, which had been established there just over half a century earlier. On entering the village Lee traded some colorful calico for corn and here he observed five Spaniards engaged in hauling wood in what he considered to be "remarkably heavy loads." Then, on the following day, October 8, dating his remarks as having been written at *Spanish Settlements, River, NM*, Lee continued writing his observations with delightful astuteness and a distinct flair for the unusual:

> ... *at the distance of 13 ms came to first rate Spring of water that gushed out of N bank of Paco Creek (which is the name of the creek that runs between the mountains—on our route.) Around this Spring are Silver ore in abundance—near the same Stands the walls & many of the rooms of a large ancient Mexican or Nephite building—Built entirely of clay, sand & rosin cemented together. Some of the walls were about 50 feet in heighth* [sic], *I should think there were about 40 rooms & apartments. The most of the* [wood] *work were carved & exhibit far more art & ingenuity than the present race who now inhabit those regions can produce. I was told by the Pilott (who had been in the Spanish trade for 25 years) that this Building was discovered about 250 years ago—which was about the time Santefe* [sic] *was settled—the whole structure at a glance*

*exhibits great antiquity.*[138] *We traveled 2 more ms stopped & fed, & while my mules were eating [I] improved the time in writing. Along in this valley are additional growths of timber the Palm trees & the Balm of Gillead or rather Santefe* [sic] *in this valley— while I was sitting here an Express passed from Gen. Kearney* [sic] *instructing the Mormon Bat., that as soon as he heard of the death of Col. Allen—& that Lt Smith was at their head, he appointed Capt Cook* [Philip St. George Cooke] *to the office of Lieut. Col. to take command of the Bat & to lead them on to California as soon as they would reach Santefe* [sic]*—This information struck Lieut Smith and Adj Dykes as well as many others of the officers almost speechless as they had been anticipating some thing* [sic] *very different, yet it was just what I predicted to Capt Hunt & the officers of the Bat when they refused to send Pres's Young's letter immediately to Gen. Kearney* [sic] *apprising him of the Death of Allen & of his pledge to the Bat.*

*What favorable impression might have been made in time!— but instead of doeing* [sic] *this—I was overruled & the letter was delayed until Smith's Express reached him & in fact it is doubtful whether Kearney* [sic] *has yet received the letter referred to. Kearney* [sic] *is now about 150 ms from Santefe* [sic] *& I look for nothing else than to see the officers* [agree] *to the present arraignments* [sic] *without ever ascertaining whether Gen Kearney* [sic] *was apprised of the pledges made by Col. Allen.*

It had been a rapid and difficult forced march for the Mormon Battalion to reach Santa Fe by October 10, as Gen. Kearny had proscribed, but they actually made it a day early and entered the dusty streets of Santa Fe on October 9, extremely weary and discouraged. Or so they were until abruptly cannon fire in salute of the Battalion began coming from the rooftops and continued until fully one hundred of the blasts had been fired in their honor by order of Colonel Doniphan, acting under the command of Gen. Kearny. The effect on the marching Mormons was miraculous; the weariness seemed to vanish and the deep-seated aches and pains of the grueling march were suddenly forgotten as their own cheers in response melded with those of the troops who heralded their arrival. The joy they felt was even more greatly intensified when it was learned that Col. Sterling Price, who had arrived several days before them with his contingent of Missouri cavalry, had been received without any form of public demonstration; when he learned of the salute that had been fired to honor the Mormons, he was greatly chagrined and enraged.

On the arrival of Lt. Col. Philip St, George Cooke at Santa Fe in the early evening of Sunday, October 11, with an express from Gen. Kearny, Captains Hunt, Brown and Hunter, along with Lieuts. Clark, Egan and Lee, visited him at the new headquarters, where he received them courteously and conversed freely with them. He told them that Gen. Kearny had been at La Jolla, New Mexico, about 130 miles south of Santa Fe when he received the report of James Allen's death, at which he at once ordered First Dragoons' Captain Cooke to return to Santa Fe and take command of the Mormon Battalion, which was also to arrive at Santa Fe and await orders. In his orders, Kearny said to Cooke that he was:

> ...reposing Special trust & confidence in your courage, good conduct & ability, I therefore appoint you Lieut. Col. in place of Col. Allen to take command of the Bat. when they arrive at Santa Fe.... Fit them out with 60 days provisions—not to encumber your selves with baggage, as a part of the route will be difficult for the passage of wagons—and follow on my trail. Mr. Fitz Patrick, the pilot that I sent will conduct you to the Pacific, where you will wait further orders & if necessary I will have a vessel meet you to convey the Bat. to Monterae [Monterey]—as their probable destination will be the Sacramento Valley, which is probably 1,000 ms from this place.—I have sent Mr. Fitzpatrick (the bearer of this) who will conduct you through.[139] *He was with Capt Fremont as a pilot through his exploring expedition. The American flag has been hoisted and the American coulours [sic] waving over California for the last 3 months. Capt. Fremont by assistance [of a] Man of War subdued the whole country & Fremont claims to be governor of that province...*

Lee, on the other hand, finished off his more than ordinarily busy day by commenting in his own journal:

> ...Early in the day I went with a French Bro. Markse Mcwell & procured about 3 bushels of corn—for our journey.[140] Corn is worth from 6 to $10.00 per bushel. Bro Alburn Allen[141] browned and ground our coffee while I brought my Journal [up to date].

> *Bro Egan was walking about to the groceres [sic] with some of the officers—apparently unconcerned about the things that I thought should immediately concern us both, but I submitted the whole arraingement [sic] to him that rules the destinys [sic] of men. At 1/2 past 2 p.m. the rear of the Bat. that was left back—arrived with much rejoicing – part of our divisions met them at the edge of the city & escorted them in—We were escorted by a Horse Co. of Mo'ians [Missourians] when entered—I must say that I seldom saw the same No. of men greet each other with the same warmth of feelings as did this Bat. Every Spirit was elated with the hopes that the dark cloud of gloom that had hovered over the Bat & threatened them with despairaition [sic] was about to be blown over & that the Smiles of Freedom would again gladden the hearts of the oppresd [sic] Sons of Liberty, but alas in this we were Sadly disappointed—the Serpent (that little Wolfish Lieut Smith) which the officers, contrary to the wish of the Bat., took into their bosom as a counselor to lead them to Santefe [sic]—Some of the officers were not satisfied with the sting of his enmity allready [sic] endured by the Lord's anointed or many of them but worked the Wires secretly—in behalf of this Serpent until they prevailed in removing the Most active & true friend to suffering Humanity, that the Bat. could afford—a man who had in his station the good will & confidence of 9 tenths—of the Bat. & loss of his service is sorely lamented (as well as being sevierly [sic] felt.[142] Two of the most bitter enemies to our people now are appointed & the Bat. must take them in exchange for a man whose real work & worth but few ever realized.[143]*

It was when the "sick" division finally showed up and straggled limping down the same Santa Fe street that the reunited Mormon Battalion was finally made happier with a dual promise from their general—first that they'd have a full week of comforting and much-needed rest from the rigors of their march, but, far more pertinent to their morale,—they were promised a new commander.

Lee continued in his journal:

> *...Until my arrival Gen, Donethan [sic] & Col. Cooke proffered to Send all the sick the Women & children of those belonging to the Bat. to Touse [Taos] (where there is a branch of the church[144]), there to*

> *winter as an escort of our Brethren & in the spring intersect the main body of the church & go such at the expense of the government. This I considered to be a fair & liberal proposal for I was well persuaded that neither the Sick, Women & children could stand the fatigue & exposures of the Journey to go around with the Bat.*

Lee, for once, was in complete accord with Capt. Philip St. George Cooke, whom he knew had observed, several years earlier, that Santa Fe was

> *...probably the most abandoned and dissolute community in North America...*

To acquaint them with their new surroundings, the newly arrived Mormon Battalion soldiers were informed that Santa Fe was the oldest continuously occupied seat of government in all of North America, that it had been founded in 1610 by Don Pedro Peralta along Santa Fe Creek, which, after flowing twenty miles, empties itself into the Rio Grande.[145] Since the Mexicans had gained their independence from Spain, it had been a bustling frontier fur-trading center with a population that varied wildly from year to year. At present the settlement stretched out for close to four miles in a lovely valley, through which ran that fine stream of water. John Steele had offered the ebullient opinion, during his stay here, that *"all went merry as a marriage bell."*

Lee, however, abruptly became extremely outraged upon being told that some of the Mormon soldiers were spending all their money on drinking, gambling, and fadangoes, rather than give their pay to him, to be transferred to their needy families back in the grueling march of the Mormon dependants. At once—and without checking the story's reliability—Lee reported this negativism to Brigham Young.

The Mormon soldiers were truly incensed when they learned of this from their wives; incensed that they should be belittled to their own families in such a hateful and untrue manner when, in actuality, they had sent "home" virtually every penny of their earnings since, obviously enough, even were they so inclined, there was nothing to buy for their own comfort, ease or pleasure. They were angry with John D. Lee and vowed they would "not soon forget that it was he who carried news from Santa Fe that was so unjustifiably disrespectful of those of the Mormon Battalion.[146]

# Chapter 8

♦

*[October 13, 1846 • Tuesday]*

To Henry Bigler, the appointment of Lt. Col. Philip St. George Cooke as the new commanding officer of the Mormon Battalion was the best possible thing that could have happened. Here was a man in whom they could invest great confidence to lead them safely and well from Santa Fe to California. While from hearsay he knew of Cooke's reputation of being a stickler for strict discipline and almost addicted to the proper filling out and filing of military forms, Bigler felt, as did the majority of the Battalion, that Satan himself would have been more welcome as the Battalion's new leader than anything further from Lt. Col. Andrew Jackson Smith or his medical cohort, Dr. George B. Sanderson. Adjutant George P. Dykes, so flagrantly the toady of his superior officers was, unfortunately, still on hand but without the dictatorial hand of Smith guiding him or the antipathy of Dr. Sanderson for the members of the Battalion to taint his judgment, he was no longer quite the aggravation he had been when those two had been in charge. Besides, Dykes was himself a Mormon and the Mormons had a knack for seeing to whatever problems might develop among themselves, irrespective of rank.

Today, however, on his first inspection of the Battalion and transference of command to himself, Cooke was more than just a little dismayed by its condition. The march thus far had been quite detrimental to the Battalion, what with its forced marches, lack of sufficient food and water, plus prevalent sicknesses. Yet, despite Cooke's awareness of all this, he was deeply appalled by what he saw drawn up in ranks before him this morning. The fact that by far the greater majority of the Saints had sent their own clothing allowances to their families left them in abominably ragtag condition. As Cooke himself viewed their condition:

> ...Everything conspired to discourage the extraordinary undertaking of marching this Battalion eleven hundred miles, for the much greater part through an unknown wilderness, without road or trail, and with a wagon train.
> It was enlisted too much by families; some were old, some feeble, and some too young; it was embarrassed by many women; it was very undisciplined; it was much worn by traveling on foot, and marching from Nauvoo, Illinois; their clothing was very scant; there was no money to pay them, or clothing to issue; their mules were utterly broken down; the quartermaster department was without funds, and its credit bad; and animals were scarce. Those procured were very inferior, and were deteriorating every hour for lack of forage or grazing. So every preparation must be pushed—hurried.

One of the wisest assignments Cooke made was to appoint as Assistant of Substance the young but highly talented recent West Point graduate, Lt. George Stoneman.[147] At the same time, the commander saw to diminishing the detrimental influence of so many of the ill in the Battalion, as well as those of limited benefit to the Battalion, such as the many laundresses. As Cooke penned in his journal:

> A small party with families (Captain Higgins' company) had been sent from Arkansas Crossing up the river, to winter at a small settlement close to the mountains, called Pueblo. The Battalion was now inspected, and eighty-six men found inefficient, were ordered, under two officers (Captain James Brown in command), with nearly all the women, to go to the same point. Five wives of officers were reluctantly allowed to accompany the march, but furnished their own transportation.
> By special arrangement and consent, the Battalion was paid in checks—not very available [negotiable] at Santa Fe.
> With every effort, the quartermaster could only undertake to furnish rations for sixty days; and, in fact, full rations of only flour, sugar, coffee, and salt; salt pork for only thirty days, and soap for

twenty. To venture without pack-saddles would be grossly imprudent and so that burden was added.

In his own inimitable manner, Sgt. Tyler responded:

*...Colonel Cooke's assertion that the Battalion "...was much worn by traveling on foot and marching from Nauvoo, Illinois...", while strictly correct, it* [the Battalion] *was much worse "worn" by the foolish and utterly unnecessary forced marches of Lieutenants Smith and Dykes, which utterly broke down both men and beasts, and was the prime cause of the greater part of the sickness and probably of many deaths. I am satisfied that any other set of men but Latter-day Saints would have mutinied rather than submit to the oppressions and abuse thus heaped upon them...*

As for Henry Bigler, he continued to have no doubt whatever that, come what may, the Mormon Battalion would never fail to be an exemplary unit in the make-up of the Army of the United States.

[*October 19, 1846 • Monday*]

For the Mormon Battalion, it seemed that time-consuming delays had at last become a thing of the past and the selected Saints were finally on the move to actually perform the duties which had been ordained by Brigham Young who, as he made no bones about pointing out, was simply uttering "the Will of God" to His children.

Although the Battalion had undergone much too long a siege of what virtually all the Saints proclaimed to be a punishment from on high, now at last the fomenters of such dissention—"Doctor Death" Sanderson and "Dictator" A.J. Smith—were reverted to their previous roles and no longer such bones of contention to the Mormon Battalion. Now, at last, in their new commander they had a leader whom they could respect, admire and obey without question. There were still, however, ill feelings rampant among many of the Saints, including some of those of considerable influence, such as John D. Lee, who wrote in his diary:

*Morning clear, pleasant & calm. We are yet detained and how much longer we will have to wait the slow operation of the officers I no* [know] *not—Last evening 9 of the officers received their pay—*

*at Night the Capt's & Lieut all but G. [George] W. Rosecrance [Rosecrantz] of Co C, Lieut [Sylvester] Hulett of Co. D & Lieuts. Pace, Lytle & Gully of Co. E & Adj Dykes went to a ball that was got up by some Spaniards & Mo volunteers. About 3/4ths of the Bat. also attended. The bill was $2.00 per Head—I had several invertations [sic] to attend & have my bill Paid—but I refused—on the grounds that our covenants to the House of the Lord prohibited me at least from associating with unbelievers, much more to take the Daughters of Zion in among prostitutes—& to mingle in recreation with men whose hands & garments are stained with the blood of those martyred Saints in Mo.*[148] *I consider it a disgrace to the Priesthood for the Saints of light to mingle with the children of darkness, saying nothing about $1,000 spent foolishly—which had better been sent to the poor in Israel.*

*Some of the Brethren considered the council good & proposed to Send the amount $2.00 that others spent extra to the Poor in Israel & risk the consequences—Capt Hunter & Hunt & many other officers said there was no harm in the Soldiers going into any thing that their Capt encouraged—as they had power to control the Spirits. Lieuts Barnes and Omen [sic] were as drunk as sots. Oman, acknowledged to be at the gambling table, said that he won $5.00, gave me 50 c[ents], said it was his tithing—sat down to eat—but was so far gone that he could not discern between his waiter's finger (a little boy), & a piece of meat and plunged his fork through 1 of the boy's little fingers into the table. After dark Br. David P. Rainey & Wm Hyde and myself walked down thinking to look on privately but could not get within 10 feet of the entrance for the throng of ruffians that stood around using the most vulgar language—we were soon Satisfied so returned with disgust from the scene—about 50 of Co H Mo volunteers some of our old Friends [mobbers] composed a part of the party – The Capt of Co H said that it was with much difficulty that he could keep his men from kicking up a row. Said that the Mormons had the same op- pressive spirit that they had in Mo. No more than what would be expected when Lambs fondle or play with Wolves—the commanders said they took this course to gain friends, but I am certain that the Bat. lost ten lbs of influence to where they gained one ounce of credit or pleasure.*

Nevertheless, the greater topic of conversation among all the Saints was their new commanding officer, who had been chosen by General Kearny himself to lead the Battalion from Santa Fe to California. Lt. Col. Cooke, already noted for being a stickler for military forms and discipline among the men, was appalled when the five Mormon Battalion companies lined themselves up for his initial inspection as he assumed command; the forced marches they had undergone with meager food rations had taken their toll among them in sickness and simple overall fatigue. The men were clad in rags and tatters, since by far the greater majority had sent to their families almost all of their cash advances that had been designated for the use of the Saints to clothe themselves. In such a sorry spectacle it was rather amazing to Cooke that they still exhibited such remarkable discipline among themselves and such a sense of *esprit de corps*.

In three sets of Special Orders dictated by the commander, Cooke directed Captain James Brown to take command of the men already reported as incapable of undertaking the march to California, due to sickness and debility, and establish winter quarters for them near the source of the Arkansas River at Pueblo. With them would go almost all the laundresses, for whom the march to California would prove to be too much and they would become an encumbrance to the expedition.[149] He did, however, promise them that the government would pay the expenses of their journey to Zion the following year, which mollified them considerably.

As if in a final slash of pique at the Saints in general, before the orders were given Dr. Sanderson played an unexpected card; he called up twenty-five men from the Mormon Battalion and, contrary to their wishes, ordered them to be discharged instantly, with neither the privilege of conveyance back to the States or pay for their enrollment. It was an act of retaliation that galled the Saints as much as anything that had occurred thus far and Lee went to Adjutant Dykes immediately and complained bitterly:

"I would consider it more honorable," he stormed, "to command those men to be shot and put an end to their suffering than to discharge and leave them here to rot among prostitutes, without a friend to assist them! The man who raised his voice or assented to this move..." meaning, of course, Dr. Sanderson, "...will have to atone for the sufferings and lives of those men."

When Dykes merely shrugged helplessly, Lee whirled away

contemptuously and went at once to the company captain and restated his anger for what was occurring, though now in more cool and collected terms, but still with no less force. So impassioned was his delivery that he was escorted to newly promoted Brigadier General Alexander Doniphan, to whom he repeated yet again his complaint. This time, however, there were more definite results.

Brooking no delay, General Doniphan confronted Lt. Col. Cooke with the outrage and Cooke, previously unaware of what was occurring, immediately took control of the situation. He summoned Dr. Sanderson and, with devastating harshness, chided him for such presumptive action and countermanded the order.

"You must know, Doctor," Cooke told him coldly, "that General Kearny would *never* discharge a man under like circumstances, to perish in desert conditions such as this."

"Sir," Sanderson protested, his anger clearly apparent, "I was but following the orders of my own commander in the medical division."

"You're telling me this action was a move ordered by Dr. Samuel DeCamp? I find that hard to believe, Doctor, but even if true it is an improper and unjustified course and is hereby revoked. You will, without any further discussion, send those men at once to join the other sick and disabled preparing to leave for Pueblo. Is that understood?"

"Yes sir, understood."

The order was relayed to Captain Brown at once and when the company under his command marched for Pueblo in the dawn light on October 18, it numbered 130 individuals, including not only ninety-one privates, but seventeen additional wives, two other women and ten more children.[150] At Brown's request, Sgt. Major James H. Glines of the Battalion staff was reduced in rank to Private and sent to Pueblo with the detachment for the purpose of making out morning reports, provision returns and other such company matters, and his place in the principal command taken by Cooke's selection of eighteen-year-old James Ferguson.[151] Also, just in the nick of time to ease the Battalion's dangerous lack of supplies for the march ahead of them, a shipment arrived of salt pork, plus a seeming sufficiency of beef cattle as part of the fulfillment of a previous contract for the Battalion, as well a quantity of pack saddles to replace those badly worn. At least the unhealthy and unfit had finally been separated from the main body of the Battalion and were en route to Pueblo.[152]

Now, at last fairly well unencumbered for the first time, the relatively

*The* Infinite Dream

fit members of the Mormon Battalion were poised and ready to move out in the morrow's dawn with California their objective. Cooke's guides were three of the most experienced mountain men available—Pauline Weaver, Antoine Leroux and Baptiste Charbonneau. This trio of highly experienced mountain men met with the commander and, strongly advised, he lay in a full four-month's worth of supplies for his troops on the march before setting out, but Cooke demurred.

"I cannot," he told them during their private meeting, "acquire teams enough to haul that amount. Besides which, it's almost certain we're going to hit terrain eventually where supply wagons simply can't be brought through and we'll have to rely on the mules. And," he added ruefully, "the mules we have available leave a great deal to be desired." He was silent for a moment, then shook his head decisively. "No, we'll take along a sixty-day supply of provisions and ration provisions accordingly—three-quarter rations immediately and half-rations later, if that becomes necessary."

"As it undoubtedly will," Weaver muttered glumly.

"As it undoubtedly will," Cooke replied, his own tone grim, "but there's no help for it, gentlemen; it's going to be a hard march and a hungry one. But, by God, we *will* do it!"

By late forenoon today—the tenth day after their arrival in Santa Fe—the entire force was in place in two companies and ready to move out temporarily along the Old Spanish Road connecting Santa Fe with Mexico City.[153] John D. Lee and Howard Egan would not be accompanying the march; instead, they, along with the ex-quartermaster, Lt. Samuel L. Gully, and Roswell Stevens as their guard, they set off with the majority of the Saint's pay checks for their families at Council Bluffs.

Cooke's force now consisted of 397 men in all, including both officers and enlisted troops, with a total of fifteen wagons, including six large, well-filled mule-wagons, three to each company, plus four other wagons for the field staff, quartermaster, hospital, and paymaster, as well five private wagons for the officer's wives still being included. However, even Cooke's pessimistic estimate of half the recommended amount of rations to be included had necessarily been scaled down further. Twenty-eight head of beef cattle would be driven along with them as their principal meat staple and there would be enough flour, sugar and coffee for sixty days, but salt pork enough for only thirty and soap enough for only twenty.

# The Infinite Dream

"Gonna be a hungry and grimy bunch of sol'jers by the time we get to Californy," Charbonneau muttered.

"Assuming," Leroux added sourly, "we ever reach California. One thing sure: it ain't gonna be no easy march."

In that final assessment, they were all in accord.

*[October 28, 1846 · Wednesday]*

For John Sutter the impending conflict with the Californios remained more a vague threat than an actuality. From what he could gather out of the numerous reports he received from guides and emigrants and itinerant travelers, the Californios were vacillating in where their allegiance lay, where their own interests could best be served. Sutter had his own small army in readiness—comprised of a corps of the emigrants and about a hundred of his own Indian employees—to march to wherever the action was occurring, when the time came; the problem was, at this point, more one of ennui than anything else. While the Californios, with few exceptions, seemed quite content to let matters hang unresolved, the American emigrants were growing more impatient for action with each passing day.

As best he could under such tentative circumstances, Sutter kept his own workers busy with numerous improvements in and about the fort, augmented by the far-reaching plans he envisioned for the future. Even with creditors now almost continually barking at his heels—most especially the Russians at Bodega Bay, who were more than a little concerned about recovering the indebtedness of some $27,000 Sutter still owed them and had lodged a legal attachment against all his real estate—he continued to further his own grandiose plans for what might occur under the flag of the United States. It was a decided gamble on his part; if the militant Californios under Castro and Pico were successful in regaining governmental control, Sutter was in distinct peril of losing everything, including his own life. It was a possibility he chose to largely ignore as he continued to sink ever deeper into debt while at the same time expanding his interests. Sutters Fort was no longer merely a toehold in the wilderness; under Captain Sutter's direction it had evolved into a constantly growing core of enterprise with numerous avenues of endeavor which he had the vision to project. As he optimistically wrote in his log:

*Things go on prosperously with me and my empire seems assured under the new flag. I plan night and day to advance it and render it a permanent place in the California sun. I find an excellent market in the newcomers and also in the San Francisco Bay region. People from below come to buy leather, shoes, saddles, hats, spurs, bridle bits and other articles and my manufacturies [sic] have increased. Good mechanics are plentiful and I own large fields of ripening grain and great herds of cattle, horses, and sheep. Beside farmers and rancheros, I have a large number of Indians employed as hunters and trappers and at present have 800 beaver traps employed with excellent results.*

Among Sutter's prime interests was the grist mill he was presently in the process of building some five miles up the American River from its confluence with the Sacramento, which was coming along quite well, with the millstones presently on order and assumed to be en route to him from the East. Not content to merely sit back and wait, now he was also sending out parties under John Bidwell and others to locate an ideal place to harvest, assemble and mill the lumber requisite not only for his own expansive pursuits, but equally for the imperative needs of others. Thus far the parties that had gone out in such searches had not located one that was ideal for such purpose, but he was confident that somewhere upriver—along the Sacramento or the American Rivers or their tributaries—it would be.

Eventually.

### [October 30, 1846 · Friday]

For the fully active portion of the Mormon Battalion presently on the march to overtake and become assimilated into the force ahead of them being led by General Kearny, this latest portion of their forced march since leaving Santa Fe was quite as arduous as the earlier portion had been; they marched twenty-four miles on this day.[154] Though the assistant quartermaster attempted to obtain fresh mules and oxen from the Mexicans, their prejudice against the United States was such that they refused to sell them anything beyond a small amount of feed and perishable vegetables. The following day they passed four tiny but nicely styled and maintained villages, these inhabited by Indians. There were also some large farms with extensive peach and apple orchards and vineyards, the latter producing very large, sweet grapes.

Now, however, each day's marching became even more difficult due to the half-rations they were being subjected to by order of Lt. Col. Cooke.[155] The effort of attempting to establish a wagon road to the southwestern tip of California drained them of their energies far beyond what any similar force could have been expected to endure, yet the Saints had borne up almost miraculously well under the rigors imposed upon them by their commander as they overcame the monumentally treacherous terrain of deserts and mountains inhabited by hostile Apache Indians.

The Saints, accustomed to the maliciousness of medical officer George Sanderson, plus the prejudices of their former temporary commander, Lt. Col. A.J. Smith, who gave officers highly preferential treatment over the enlisted men, they expected little different from their new commander, but Lt. Col. Cooke surprised them all. It was actually an officer—Capt. Jesse D. Hunter, commander of Company B—who first drew his wrath and, as Pvt. Henry Bigler voiced the sentiment of the majority of the Battalion, "He came down on him like a duck on a June bug!"

Lt. Col. Cooke placed Capt. Hunter under arrest the morning of October 21 for having remained overnight in Santa Fe with neither the knowledge nor consent of the commanding officer. For such offense, admittedly relatively minor, Hunter was ordered to march at the rear of his company during the day which, to him, was a paramount humiliation and embarrassment. The punishment, however, swiftly levied, showed the troops conclusively that their new commander was not only strict in his discipline, he was unswervingly impartial and that his officers would be held every bit as accountable for their infractions as the enlisted men themselves would be. To the men, this act established the fact in their own minds that now they had a commander whom they could respect and admire.

The physical hardships were difficult in the extreme to bear, made even more so when they labored under the gaze of their commander, as Cooke perched himself hawk-like on one of the hills and sent down unrelenting orders. Yet somehow the Saints not only bore them but had the fortitude to carry on and even laugh a little at their own dilemma, as was exemplified by the marching song entitled *The Desert Route*. The piece was composed by Pvt. Levi W. Hancock of Company E, as the Battalion broke itself into units of twenty men each, with long ropes by which the Saints could help the exhausted oxen pull the wagons over the sand hills:

> *While here, beneath a sultry sky,*
> *Our famished mules and cattle die;*
> *Scarce aught but skin and bones remain*
> *To feed poor soldiers on the plain.*

A brief two line chorus followed each quatrain, to which, eventually, virtually everyone in this march raised his voice:

> *How hard, to starve and wear us out*
> *Upon this sandy desert route.*

Verse after verse followed, chanted by the composer or one of the lustier, farther-carrying voices:

> *We sometimes now, for lack of bread,*
> *Are less than quarter-rations fed,*
> *And soon expect, for all of meat,*
> *Naught less than broke-down mules to eat.*
>
> *Now, half-starved oxen, over-drilled,*
> *Too weak to draw, for beef are killed;*
> *And gnawing hunger prompting men*
> *To eat small entrails and the skin.*
>
> *Sometimes we quarter for the day,*
> *While men are sent ten miles away*
> *On our back track, to place in store*
> *An ox given out the day before.*
>
> *And when an ox is like to die,*
> *The whole camp halts, and we lay by:*
> *The greedy wolves and buzzards stay,*
> *Expecting rations for the day.*
>
> *Our hardships reach their rough extremes,*
> *When valiant men are roped with teams,*
> *Hour after hour, and day by day,*
> *To wear our strength and lives away.*
>
> *The teams can hardly drag their loads*
> *Along the hilly, sandy roads,*
> *While trav'ling near the Rio Grande,*
> *O'er hills and dales of heated sand.*

> *We see some twenty men or more,*
> *With empty stomachs, and foot-sore,*
> *Bound to one wagon, plodding on*
> *Thro' sand, beneath a burning sun.*
>
> *A Doctor which the Government*
> *Has furnished, proves a punishment!*
> *At his rude call of "Jim along Joe,"*
> *The sick and halt to him must go.*
>
> *Both night and morn, this call is heard;*
> *Our indignation then is stirr'd,*
> *And we sincerely wish in hell,*
> *His arsenic and calomel.*
>
> *To take it, if we're not inclined,*
> *We're threatened, "You'll be left behind:"*
> *When bored with threats profanely rough,*
> *We swallow down the poisonous stuff.*
>
> *Some stand the journey well, and some*
> *Are by the hardships overcome;*
> *And thus the "Mormons" are worn out*
> *Upon this long and weary route.*

As always in military involvements, rumors went rampant among the troops. Rumor had it that James Magoffin had been robbed by Apaches and had barely escaped with his life. Untrue, as it turned out. Another circulated that Commodore Stockton had taken all of California, though no one seemed able to account for such a coup on the part of a naval officer. Today, for the first time in the past three days, the pessimism that had gripped the Battalion's soldiers finally began fading away, resulting from the rumor somehow begun that General Wool, in fighting a fierce battle at Chihuahua had lost a thousand men, but captured the city. No one could say who initiated the rumor, nor could anyone elucidate why, once begun, it simply died away.

On October 23, Cooke managed to convince the Mexicans in one of the small towns they passed to exchange thirty of the Army's now almost worthless mules for fifteen fresh animals, though these from the Mexicans were smaller animals than those the Army had. Better yet, on encountering the two companies of First Dragoons commanded by Capt. John Henry K. Burgwin that General Kearney had ordered to remain in New Mexico, they were able to exchange another thirty of their worn-out mules for fifteen better ones, plus another ten purchased at forty dollars, and also obtained ten yoke of relatively fresh oxen. At the same time they were able to exchange two of their heavier—and poorest—wagons for a pair that were lighter and better.

On October 24 they encountered another large village with a population roughly half-Mexican, half-Indian—a rather pleasant place just west of the Sandia Mountains called Albuquerque.[156] Although some fruits and vegetables were purchased from the villagers here, the Battalion did not pause long, but crossed the Rio Grande and continued down its west bank along the long-established Chihuahua Trail.

A heavy snowstorm that blanketed the mountains had the effect of impacting for a few days the deep sand through which they had been wading, but it remained sand nonetheless and the difficult walking prevailed again only too soon. Ditches dug for irrigation were discovered all along the banks of the Rio Grande, several of them actually carrying water to isolated ranchos. Unaccustomed to irrigation practices, the Saints were fascinated with how the water was made to flow over the ground surface until the sandy soil was sufficiently saturated, then shut off until more was needed for the same purpose.

Four days ago—on October 26—they reached the village of Valencia, one of the oldest Spanish settlements along the Rio Grande, arriving only shortly after the Navajo Indians in an audacious foray had attacked here, killing two Mexican shepherds and driving off more than 10,000 sheep. All the able-bodied men in the village were gone in pursuit of them when the Battalion arrived and the women in town begged Lt. Col. Cooke to stay and protect them until their men returned. Though he sympathized with them, Cooke's orders from General Kearny prohibited him from doing so and he moved the Army along without significant pause.

It was not until today, however, that they finally reached another fairly substantial village—the first of any real consequence since their departure from Albuquerque. It was fairly large and shaded here and there by scattered groves of cottonwood trees. This was the Mexican town called La Jolla, a farming village frequently used as a stopover by caravans traveling along the Rio Grande.[157] And it was here that the Saints, for the first time since leaving Santa Fe were, by order of Lt. Col. Cooke, given a full day free of marching; a rest unquestionably well deserved.

Nevertheless, as all among the Saints were now keenly aware, they were still a very long way from California.

*[October 31, 1846 • Saturday • 6:00 p.m.]*

With matters for the Mexicans not going at all well—their battles with the Americans thus far lost and the American forces under Taylor, Kearny, Sloat, Stockton and Doniphan making serious inroads into their territory—President Polk today directed his emissaries to offer Mexican leadership an opportunity to treat for peace. He felt certain they would hardly dare to refuse such an opportunity to, as Polk put it, "...end the war with honor, dignity and relatively little loss."

The President was quite well aware that if the Mexican governing body accepted this opportunity, it would be noted as a distinct feather in his own cap—an achievement that would almost certainly go a long way toward helping to remove some of the stigma he had been shouldering due to his abortive support of General Santa Ana. It might, in fact, so vindicate his efforts that a second term in the White House could once again become a possibility. Unfortunately for Polk, it simply was not meant to be. There was still some sting remaining in the Mexican scorpion's tail and the offer for peace talks to be opened was flatly refused.

The war with Mexico would continue.

The greater number of men that the United States military forces were able to bring against the Californios seemed to matter little; they were outfoxed at every turn. Even though Commander Stockton had some time ago summoned Fremont to help and loosed his own force of some 400 sailors and marines from the *U.S. Savannah* under Captain Mervine against them, the latter turned out to be simply no match for the guerilla tactics used against them by the Californios, who probably had fewer than one hundred men plus a small cannon and some homemade gunpowder. When Stockton himself landed at San Pedro and saw what was occurring, he disgustedly ordered the Americans back to the ship and sailed down to San Diego. His intelligence agents quickly told him the city was filled with Californio soldiers ready to do battle, so Stockton anchored in the bay and simply sat there for the better part of three weeks before realizing the intelligence he'd received was in error and that there was no enemy waiting in the city at all. So the force was landed and in tune with his orders, prepared themselves to move by land against Los Angeles.

It was actually a pretty good plan except for one small factor: The revolutionaries had swept the countryside clean of horses and there was no transportation left available to take them there.

[*November 6, 1846 · Friday*]

The continuing march westward of the Mormon Battalion had become no easier for the Saints than it had been in previous weeks and whether they would ever actually overtake and join Gen. Kearny's force was becoming ever more a matter of conjecture. Whenever they seemed to be moving ahead at better speed, something always seemed to intervene to slow them down again and increase the difficulties they were facing. Today was just such an occasion.

Twenty-seven-year-old Private Samuel Holister Rogers of Company B was among the limited number of Saints who maintained a daily journal throughout the entire march of the Battalion.[158] What he wrote, while often intriguing, just as often created questions. This evening's entry was no exception, as he wrote:

> *Fri. 6. Continued our journey over a very hilly road. I was detailed to push wagons up the hills. Camped near the river in a hollow formed by a creek coming down from the bluff. Here Kearney* [sic] *left his wagons and went on with pack mules.*

What Private Rogers failed to note was that Gen. Kearny's decision to go on with pack mules only, four weeks earlier, was made because the way being forged through hilly, rocky, desert country had simply become too difficult to continue with wagons. He had solved the problem to his own satisfaction by simply taking the very best animals and outfits and leaving the cumbersome vehicles behind, along with orders for Cooke and his Mormon Battalion, when they reached this point, "*...the task of opening a wagon road.*"

As one of the Saints summed it up with weary humor, "I guess ol' General Kearny figured we were comin' along too fast and just decided to slow us down a bit."

When the Battalion finally reached Socorro in the New Mexico Territory just eight days ago, Pvt. Rogers was one of the few to comment in his Journal about the fact that, indigent though he accused the Mexicans of being, they somehow managed to produce substantial crops in their fields. As Rogers wrote at that time:

> *Fri. 30. Hilly and very sandy. Camped near the town of Socorro.*[159] *Saw a cotton patch, the first cotton I ever saw growing.*

While the Saints had at first been delighted to encounter the Rio Grande and then follow that major river downstream, their initial enjoyment was dulled by the sandy valley the river had created, where each footfall sank deeply in the hot, dry sand and then became a drudgery in pulling free. What surprised them all the most was the numerous Mexican and Indian towns they encountered close to the river and the numerous orchards and vineyards being maintained in this desert area through irrigation. As twenty-two-year-old Pvt. Henry G. Doyle described it in his diary:

> *...We marched 105 miles down this Stream over an almost continual bed of Sand. The fatigues of the Journey have been great Since we came on this Stream. Following this river we have traveled a little west of South. & evry [sic] day the Snow has been visible on the Sieras [sic] to our right. We have passed through towns or villages nearly every day. There are considerable many Spaniards or rather I may say Mexicans living on this River. Thier [sic] mode of living & farming is singular enough to me but they Seem to get along. & seem to be happy enough. Thier [sic] land for cultivation is enclosed by ditches, hedges & adoba Walls. On account of the dry Seasons in this country, they have to irrigate all this farming land, all thier [sic] vineyards & orchards which is done by leading the water from the River through ditches through all their grain & every thing else that is raised or produced.*[160]

On November 1, after the usual guard mounting and general parade, Order No. 13 was read aloud, returning 1st Lt. George Dykes to Company D, to command in the absence of Capt. Nelson Higgins, who had failed to return in time to join the march from Santa Fe after escorting the sick or incapacitated to Pueblo. Dykes resigned as battalion adjutant and was replaced in that post by 2nd Lt. Philemon C. Merrill, which lifted the morale of the Saints considerably, but was not at all appreciated by the men of Co. D. Nor was it very helpful to Lt. Col. Cooke, who wrote in his journal today:

> ...*A dumb spirit has possessed all for the last twenty-four hours, and not one of my orders has been understood and obeyed. All the vexations and troubles of any other three days of my life have not equalled* [sic] *those of the said twenty-four hours.*

The following day another death occurred in the Mormon Battalion when Pvt. James Hampton, forty-three, of Company A, who had been sick for three days and had been seen by Dr. Sanderson with his usual harsh treatment and then returned to duty, abruptly fell violently ill again at 2 p.m. and quickly died. The march of the Battalion was halted for twenty minutes as Hampton was failing and then resumed again after his death, when his body was placed in a wagon and carried to the evening's camp, where he was buried the next morning after being rolled into a blanket and given a brief service. As Cooke wrote in his Journal, Hampton's death was "...*very sudden*..." but he did not blame Sanderson for it. Sgt. Daniel Tyler and others of the Saints, however, bitterly attributed his demise to Dr. Death. The animosity filling Tyler, however, was not limited to his hatred of Dr. Sanderson. As he wrote in his Journal that evening:

> *While traveling this day, two weary soldiers were tied behind an ox wagon and obliged to march in that position through wind and dust, for neglecting to get up and salute Lieutenant Dykes while* [he] *was on his grand rounds of the camp last night, to visit the guards stationed at different points. They had just been relieved from standing guard for two hours and lain down to take their rest, of which...they stood in much need, when the officer of the guard, seeing Dykes approaching, gave the usual order, "*Turn out the guard! Officer of the day!*" As the two men failed to "turn out," Dykes considered it a great indignity and reported it accordingly to Colonel Cooke, who was obliged, under regulations, to order the humiliating and disagreeable punishment...*

William Hyde, 2nd Orderly Sgt. of Co. B., was only one of the many Saints who sided with the punished men and said, "It was plainly manifest that Lieutenant Dykes sought to gain favor of and please the wicked rather than favor his Brethren." From that day forward, Dykes, because of his officious and captious manner, was termed throughout the Battalion as *Accuser of the Brethren*.

Not unexpectedly, rumors continued to rise, spread, and dissipate among the companies. The latest of these was the rumor, following the arrival of a runner, that a movement was afoot among the Mexicans in the region through which they were traveling, to revolt against American rule. Further, so the story went, the same thing was occurring among the Mexicans at Santa Fe. It caused considerable concern among the companies for a while since, were it true, their situation would have been extremely perilous, as they were less than four hundrd strong and surrounded by hostile Indians as well as Mexicans who, of course, had the advantage of a knowledge of the countryside, while the men of the Battalion were strangers there, with little to depend on but their muskets. The Battalion's guides became quite downcast with the "news" that Cooke, when he learned of it, took the matter very coolly and maintained an air of indifference. It was just what was needed and the rumor quickly died away and was gone.

Yesterday Pvt. Rogers wrote in his diary:

*...I remained in camp and washed and patched my clothes. Soap being scarce, I substituted a root called* arinola *by the Mexicans, which makes good suds.*

Even Rogers' generally sunny disposition had taken a nosedive this morning, however, with the news that the Battalion would now be responsible for pushing along the wagons Gen. Kearny had abandoned. As he now wrote in his diary:

*...The prospect before us from this point is anything but encouraging. Besides what we have previously endured from hunger and having to help our worn-out animals pull the overloaded wagons, we now have before us this additional task of having to construct a wagon road over a wild, desert and unexplored country, where wagons have never been.*

But, as Lt. Col. Cooke was becoming more assured of with every passing day with this remarkable Mormon Battalion, the Saints somehow always seemed to rise to the challenge and overcome whatever difficulties arose before them. He was quite sure this instance was no different.

It wasn't.

*[November 19, 1846 • Thursday]*

The decision being made by Lt. Col. Cooke this evening was not an easy one. If he chose incorrectly, he could very well be placing the Mormon Battalion into such jeopardy it might be damaged beyond recovery. They were camped this evening at Oho de Vaca—more familiar to the Americans as Cow Springs—and ahead lay the final leg of this grueling journey across the Southwest.

If they turned here and moved southward, Cooke knew, they could follow the easy-to-travel—even though gradually ascending—Spanish road running from the old Santa Rita Copper Mine to Janos, deep in Mexico and, from there, the existing road past Fronteras to the historic San Bernardino Spring, which would be the jumping-off place for the penetration of California.[161] Or they could continue due west from where they were and move across an unknown desert wasteland to the same destination, which would cut off at least 120 miles of marching. The problem with the first choice was tackling it with an army already jaded from its cross-continent march, which might well be marching directly into confrontation with the Mexican Army, possibly quartered now at Fronteras; the problem with the alternative was marching at least sixty miles through a wholly unknown desert wasteland where, from what their guides could gather from natives, there was no water available for man or beast. Either choice had to be accomplished with animals so unfit they might well drop in their tracks at any time.

It was, to Cooke's reckoning, a career-making—or career-*breaking*—decision to make. How much harder could he dare push these men, these *Saints*, who had already endured such hardships in the march westward from Fort Leavenworth—or, for that matter, all the way back to Nauvoo, Illinois? How much more could they take? The past dozen days alone had pointed out only too clearly that a long, recuperative rest was quickly becoming requisite, yet their orders from General Kearny precluded any such latitude.

On November 7 a few of the men had a wondrously rich treat when one of the privates brought down a black-tailed deer with a shot that would have been a tribute to the most skilled of mountain men, but a herd of such animals would have been needed to satisfy the hunger of all. The troops were ordered to be on the alert for more possibilities of fresh meat when, the following day, they encountered a Mexican trapper who told them there were bears in the nearby mountains and fat beavers in the river, yet since they encountered none of them and the Army's rations were cut even more, the entire force was constantly hungry.

The following late afternoon, when the Mormon Battalion paused in its march, Private Rogers noted in his diary:

> Mon. 9. Continued on over hills and hollows as usual. Pioneers have been sent forward to look out the road. White frost seen for several nights past. We have got into a land of dew again. Camped on a bench or table land where Kearney [sic] left the river.[162]

That evening four of the pilots Cooke had sent forward several days previously to explore a route returned and dejectedly reported that the terrain ahead was of such hostile nature that they deemed it impossible for wagons to pass through. Cooke refused to accept that verdict and remained adamant that the march continue forward, wagons and all; he had been given the responsibility of establishing a wagon road across the great American desert and a few difficulties were not going to deter him.

Sgt. Tyler was impressed with Cooke's resolution and commented favorably about it in his journal, as well as remarking about the vegetation, noting:

> "During the same day we encountered the first mesquit [mesquite] brush that we have seen. It is a thorny shrub, bearing a slight resemblance to the honey locust."

On this same evening as well, Colonel Cooke estimated that over the previous six days the army had traveled merely forty miles, yet with an enormous amount of exertion caused by the broken country which was so sandy underfoot. It was very difficult for the loaded mules to walk and as he wrote in a report to Gen. Kearny:

> ...The guides say that most of the mules could not be driven loose [i.e., free of loads] to California. I have examined them, and found

*that whole teams seemed ready to break down. Twenty-two men are on sick report. Quite a number have been transported in wagons. I have ordered fifty-seven of the sick and "least efficient" men and one woman, Sophia Gribble, to go to Pueblo under Co. A Lt. William W. Willis.[163] I shall thus get rid of 1,800 pounds' weight of rations, and by means of what they leave, particularly the livestock, increase my rations for the remainder, seventeen days of meat and thirteen of flour. Even after these two weedings of the old, the feeble and sickly, lads and old gray-headed men still remained.*

From this point on it became customary for the soldiers of the Mormon Battalion to kill any of the work animals that showed signs of giving out and then butcher the carcasses and issue the meat as rations to the troops. No portion of the carcass was ever thrown away for which there was any possible use as food. Even the hides, tripe and entrails were all eagerly devoured, often without benefit of having water with which to initially wash such organs. Marrow bones were a considerable luxury and were issued in turns to the various messes, where they were eagerly accepted, especially for soup stock.

Much as he disliked doing so, on November 10, Cooke issued an order requiring the acting assistant quartermaster to leave behind the two remaining ox wagons, but retained the teams for them as being absolutely necessary for the further march of the Battalion. To further lessen the loads being transported by wagon, the commander ordered the company commanders to make sure that hereafter each tent would sleep nine men instead of six, which would allow the discarding of extra camp kettles, which were so heavy, and many of the cumbersome upright tent poles thrown away, with muskets to be used in their stead as tent supports.[164]

A considerable amount of repacking of gear was required as a result, since now much of it would be carried by both oxen and mules. Loading the oxen, however, which were nowhere near so patient as the mules, was the cause of a considerable amount of merriment that helped to dispel the monotony of the march. The antics of the frightened oxen tickled the men and, as Sgt. Tyler wrote of it:

*The loading taken out of the two abandoned wagons was packed on mules and oxen, the latter scarcely knowing which end they stood upon, nor we either, for that matter. As some of the boys put it, "They* kicked up before and reared up behind!" And they bellowed and snorted, pawed and plowed the ground with their horns, whirling and jumping in every direction. Even our sedate commander had his nature overcome sufficiently to wryly write in his report: "Thirty-six mules were lightly packed, besides oxen; some of which performed antics that were irresistibly ludicrous, such as jumping high from the ground in quick-step time, turning 'round the while—a perfect jig."

While all this was occurring, one of the Battalion's better hunters, Pvt. Ephraim Hanks came into camp with a large black-tailed deer over his shoulders that he had shot, at which the men cheered loudly.[165] Unfortunately, the meat from one deer served to fill far too few bellies and the need for water increased dramatically as the creek being followed became first a series of small water-filled potholes, then more scattered scummy ponds and finally only damp spots in the creek bed as the life-giving moisture percolated through the sandy soil and simply disappeared.

Cooke sent the guide, Charbonneau, well ahead to seek water as a camp site but he was hardly gone when the sharp-eyed commander spied a line of stunted willows and a patch of cane, into which he spurred his mount at once. As he suspected, after following the bottom for about a mile, he found water and good grass in plenty and the army camped at the bluff nearby.

When the march resumed they soon encountered the Gila River—a beautifully clear and swift stream running almost due west and they followed it without hesitation, soon encountering some well established villages of Pima and Maricopa Indians. They were cheerful, engaging people who made the passing army welcome and, unlike other tribes thus far encountered, exhibited no vestige of threatening manner. The morale of the Battalion elevated accordingly as they marched now through nicely irrigated farmlands where numerous units of hived bees were established and honey plentiful, where watermelon, cantaloupe, corn and wheat grew abundantly and where Cooke was even able to purchase a few bullocks to drive along with them as a living meat supply for when the present supply of meat gave out. It was, to the Saints, like a touch of Heaven after having marched so long through a desert Hell. When they were asked the price of their fragrant, tasty cornmeal cakes, a spokesman looked at them quizzically for a moment and then laughed aloud.

"Bread is to eat, not to sell," he said simply. Gesturing toward a substantial stack of loaves, he added, "Take what you want."

So different in temperament and generosity were these people that Captain Johnston succinctly summarized what all the Saints were feeling. "They are greatly superior," he said, "to the Apaches, who have bayed at us like their kindred wolves." Lieutenant Emory was quite as laudatory, declaring, "They surpass many of the Christian nations in agriculture, are but little behind them in the useful arts and," he added with a short, barking laugh, "immeasurably before them in honesty and virtue."

Pvt. Henry Bigler's journal entries continued to be brief in the extreme, nonetheless intriguing as when, on November 14, he wrote:

*...During our next day's travel, we found the ruins of an ancient building, aboutthirty-six feet square, and containing five rooms.*

There was no indication who built the structure, though it was apparent these ruins had been on this spot for a very long time, "...perhaps," as Bigler judged, "a century or more."

By this time, with November half gone, Lt. Col. Cooke was coming to realize that he was commanding a Battalion of quite extraordinary soldiers; men who followed orders almost without question, who accomplished their duties practically without complaint, who marched longer and better and harder than any he'd ever before commanded... or even encountered. Their physical endurance and exploits were, Cooke decided, virtually beyond explanation except by their quiet determination to trust in God.

The supply of dried beef from the long-horns, which had seemed so much in the beginning, all too quickly disappeared and soon they were subsisting again only on those wasted oxen and mules no longer physically capable of pulling the wagons. These were butchered as needed and nothing of them wasted as food. Rationing was again strictly enforced in respect to the rapidly dwindling salt, flour and coffee. Sgt. Daniel Tyler continued to maintain his journal entries almost daily and today he wrote:

*...We find our road extremely sandy in many places, and our men, while carrying blankets, knapsacks, cartridge boxes (each holding three dozen rounds of ammunition), and muskets on their backs and*

> living on short rations, continue having to pull at long ropes to aid the teams. The deep sand alone, without any load, is enough to wear out both man and beast.... The men are ready to eat almost anything that will afford them nourishment, the rations issued to them being insufficient to satisfy the cravings of hunger.... An old white ox which had seen at least a dozen summers, and which we had driven all the way from Fort Leavenworth, having given out...a few miles back, was brought into camp, butchered and issued as rations. He was a mere skeleton, and his small amount of remaining flesh was more like a sickly jelly than real meat. In consequence of this incident we named the valley in which we were encamped "White Ox Valley," and the little rivulet "White Ox Creek."
>
> The day was stormy, snow and rain falling alternately. Some of the hunters went about five miles from the camp, up a ravine, and found an old deserted vineyard, with some good grapes still hanging on the vines, upon which they feasted.... We found a marshy water hole, which was given the name of Cooke's Spring, where we found much broken earthen ware scattered all over the ground. By whom it had been made or why it was scattered so extensively, could only be conjectured...

On November 17 the Battalion passed through a gap in the mountains and encountered a place where gold mining had evidently been carried on some time in the distant past. They found no less than thirty holes, from six to ten inches deep and about fourteen inches in diameter which had evidently been cut for the purpose of catching rainwater when showers occurred. Here they also found, for the first time, California quail, which some of the Saints called partridges. Swift birds that often ran rather than flying, they were of a bluish color and sported beautiful top-knots.

Yesterday, November 18, the Saints celebrated Thanksgiving Day, though with little food to commemorate it. As their march continued, they found a variety of oak tree new to them and a beautiful variety of Spanish bayonet, which the natives called *oose*, the leaves of which were three feet long, with serrated, saw-toothed edges and thick bloom stalks rising from the center to a height of near twenty feet. They marched twenty miles on this day and camped in the evening near a grove of cottonwoods on a stream the natives called *Mimbres*.[166]

The Mormon Battalion was now at the site in their march where

Lt. Col. Cooke had to make the important decision of either continuing straight westward through what could well be entirely waterless desert terrain, where the possibility of their perishing from thirst was very real, or following the existing road southward to the Mexican village of Janos, then westward via Fronteras, where it was possible the Mexican Army was lying in wait to ambush them, the latter route smoother traveling but at least 120 miles farther. Even if the Mexican Army was not there, such a distance meant adding another six days to their journey and they were again on strict rations and all but destitute of food.

There was little doubt that the lives of the remaining members of the Mormon Battalion were hanging in the balance and wholly dependant upon the decision that must now be reached by Lt. Col, Philip St. John Cooke.

*[November 22, 1846 • Sunday • 2:00 p.m.]*

Although every bit as strict with the Mormon Battalion he was shepherding as his predecessor, Andrew Jackson Smith, had been, with Lt. Col. Philip St. George Cooke there was a difference: the Saints had never ceased despising Smith but, amazingly, Cooke had begun winning their trust and admiration because of his adamant fairness in both rewards and punishments. He was, in essence, a splendid officer.

As for Cooke himself, he was a dichotomy in many respects: as much he was a gourmet who doted on elegant cooking and fine wines, so too he ate without complaint the same dismal diet his own men endured and shared the same limiting of rations; as much as he was a romantic, so too was he a strict West Point precisionist, with no one in his command below genuine praise or above deserved criticism. Favoritism was not in his make-up; no man – privates, non-coms and officers alike – was coddled over any other; he kept them to the job needing to be done and if punishments were in order for the rare cases of carelessness or malingering, they were meted out as required.

In his own private journal, Cooke often exploded with frustration over what he termed *"the stolidity, ignorance, negligence, and obstinacy"* of the Saints and the maddening influence of their apostles and priests over them, yet at the same time he was developing a boundless enthusiasm and admiration for their generally good humor, their spirit and solidity, their immediate obedience of orders and their plain old-fashioned guts in the face of adversity. For their own part, the Saints came to respect, even admire, Philip St. George Cooke's leadership and they honored his unmitigated fairness in all matters. His counsel to them was invariably and unquestionably inspired and certainly on a par with, if not surpassing, that of the priesthood.

For one of the very few times in their history, the Saints had actually begun to like a *gentile*.

*[November 22, 1846 · Sunday · 4:00 p.m.]*

Lieutenant William H. Emory, the West Point topographical engineer who always took such great pride in both his appearance and decorum, was haggard and disheveled, his uniform sweat-stained and dust-dirty as he presented himself to General Kearny, who had halted his army late yesterday along the bank of the Colorado River.

Kearny, for his own part, was well aware of the lieutenant's return—it being difficult to hide the approach of a herd of about a thousand horses—and silently approved of the fact that Emory had wasted no time trying to become more presentable before reporting.Cleanliness was a behavioral trait of which the commanding officer highly approved, under normal circumstances; the general was of the same character. There were times, however, when attention to physical appearance could prove to be a serious detriment and this was just such a time.

Standing beneath the posted door-flap of his headquarters tent, Kearny himself straightened to attention as Emory reined in his horse, slid from the saddle and handed off the reins to the commander's aide, then strode toward him. Kearny gravely returned the junior officer's salute.

"Sir, Lieutenant Emory reporting from reconnaissance."

The tiniest of smiles tugged at the general's mouth corners. "So I see, Lieutenant." He tilted his head toward the horses now crowding to the river's edge to drink and being kept from swimming across by some of the men of Emory's squad, who were quite as sweaty and bedraggled as he. "Glad you have your priorities aligned. You could hardly have brought anything else that would've pleased me more."

"Thank you, sir." The smile touched Emory's lips as well. "Afraid I didn't have much choice—wouldn't have been able to keep them from the water, no matter what, once they caught scent of it. They're all pretty dry...as are we. Sir."

Kearny nodded and, at the general's bidding, Lt. Emory reported on his squad's mission that had begun at sunrise; a mission that had issued from what the army had found when it reached the Colorado at the first light of dawn today. They were all in exhausted condition at that point, having marched through much of the night to reach the big river's valley, with most of the Dragoons then afoot and having to lead their horses and mules; so worn were the mounts that many of them could no longer carry their riders and a fair number, in fact, had given out entirely and dropped dead in their tracks. The cavalry had at that point become foot soldiers and veterinarians, caring for the ragged animals that remained. Men and beasts alike were a sorry lot.

Arriving at the Colorado River at dawn, however, it immediately became clear that a huge number of horses had been there not long prior to the army's arrival. Kearny had at once sent his chief guide, Kit Carson, on a scout to follow their trail a while. Sunrise was just at hand when Carson returned, reporting the huge herd evidently was being driven at a rather slow pace toward Chihuahua and probably were no more than ten miles ahead.

That was when Kearny had quickly sent the twenty men under Lt. Emory on their trail, mounted on the best cavalry horses still available to them. Emory's detachment had followed the trail until near mid-day before overtaking it. The horses were being driven by Mexican vaqueros who were evidently very afraid of the unexpected appearance of a detachment of U.S. Cavalry and without the capability to resist when ordered to halt. The story their leader had told Lt. Emory—that they were horse traders who had captured these animals from the massive wild herds roaming California in the remote, lushly meadowed foothills of what they called the Sequoia River Valley—was reasonable enough and the officer was inclined to believe it.[167]

"Even so, Sir," Emory continued, "I didn't want to leave anything to chance, so I had the baggage and pockets of every man searched and found nothing at all of a suspicious nature. Fully aware of our desperate need for horses, though, I required that they and their herd return with me here, assuming you would want to engage in purchasing some to replace those we've already lost and those still on their way out"

Kearny nodded. "Good thinking," he murmured. "We'd not make it much farther without fresh mounts."

General Kearny removed a shiny brass telescope from his saddlebag hanging from the tent-flap pole and studied the milling horses through it. As he did so, Lt. Emory signaled toward his detachment and three men immediately came toward them; two were Emory's men and the third a Mexican whom they were evidently guarding. As they neared, Emory spoke again to his commander: "General Kearny, this is the man, who seems to be in charge. Says his name is Gómez. Salazar Gómez. As I've said, we've searched him and he appears to be legitimate; a horse-trader heading for Mexico City with their latest annual round-up results of wild horses."

As the trio came to a halt, the commander lowered and collapsed his spyglass and returned it to his saddle pouch. He eyed the Mexican, who was smiling in amiable manner. The general did not smile in return, nor was there any warmth in his voice.

"Señor Gómez," he said, "I am told that you are a horse trader and that these animals," he tilted his head toward the herd, "are wild horses you have rounded up in the Sequoia River Valley."

"Sí, General." The man's smile faded somewhat.

"You, sir," Kearny snapped, "are lying and I cannot tolerate liars. Remove your boots."

"Señor General," Gómez protested indignantly, "you have no right to—"

"One more word, sir," Kearny interrupted, "and I'll have you thrown to the ground and forcibly disrobed. Entirely. Remove those boots, *now!*"

Clearly dismayed, Gómez sat himself down on the ground as the two guards stepped toward him, then began tugging at his left boot, muttering to himself in Spanish.

"The other boot, Señor!" Kearny ordered.

Gómez shot him a hate-filled glance and tugged off the right boot without difficulty. A packet of papers wrapped in oilskin and molded around his right ankle fell out. At once Emory snatched up the parcel and handed it to his commander, which General Kearney opened and quickly scanned, one paper after another.

"Dispatches, Lieutenant," he murmured, "to General Castro and others in Sonora who are apparently gathering forces to retake California." Frowning, he refolded the papers and returned them to the oilskin, then tucked the packet into his pouch. The little he had seen was enough; evidently there had been fighting in California since Carson left there: The Americans no longer held Los Angeles and they were obviously in trouble.

"Rouse the men. Each to have a fresh horse. The rest to be brought along with ours and the mules in the rear." He indicated Gómez. "Turn him and his men loose, after we leave. Afoot. We can't afford to be bothered with them. Inform the officers; we move out at noon."

Lt. Emory saluted and turned to obey, but then hesitated and turned back.

"Sir," he said, "if I may?" He glanced at the Mexican being led off by the guards. "How could you possibly know he had hidden messages?"

"Intuition, in large measure, Lieutenant," Kearny replied, then smiled slightly. "Plus the fact that wild horses don't sport saddle sores and bridle burns."

*[November 24, 1846 • Tuesday]*

For the Mormon families, left behind when their menfolk became part of the Mormon Battalion, the forthcoming winter was already promising to be a great tribulation and the death toll would undoubtedly be high.

Those families who were among the earliest Saints that had started the westward migration from Nauvoo were now getting themselves established in their temporary settlement called Winter Quarters on the west bank of the Missouri River within the Indian country of Nebraska Territory. None had an easy time of it and camps of destitute Mormons dotted the Iowa Territory landscape all the way from the west side of the Mississippi opposite Nauvoo to the Missouri.

Apostle Hosea Stout, a captain of Israel's Guard was among those Mormons fortunate enough to have become settled in at Winter Quarters, but there was nothing elegant nor even very comfortable in respect to accommodations available for the many who had made it this far. Stout's journal clearly reflected the horrors of what they had already been through and what was certainly yet in store before spring reawakened the land. Concerning his new "home," Stout wrote, it ha *...neither door nor window not even but a few of the craks* [sic] *was yet stoped* [sic] *up and a hard North wind blowing.* Still, his quarters provided about as good a shelter as any of the Saints had who had made it this far and was quite probably better than most. He continued:

> *...It will be hard to burn us out so many of us are living in caves in the bluffs dugouts or log shacks covered with dirt. My family has had no roof over there* [sic] *heads sine we left Nauvoo 10 weks* [sic] *less than a year ago during which time we have under went*

*almost every change of fortune that could be imagined. One half of my family so dear to me has been consigned to the silent grave & we who yet remain have been brought to the verge of death often in storms & rains have I stood to hold my tent from uncovering my sick family expecting every moment to see them exposed to the wind & rain which would have been certain death...How often in sorrow & anguish have I said in my heart when shall my trials and tribulations end. But amid all these adverse changes, these heart wrenching trials not once yet have I ever regretted that I set out to follow the council of the people of God & to obey the voice of the spirit to flee from the land of the Gentiles.*[168]

The Missouri Bottoms, at which the migrating Saint families finally rooted themselves for the winter suffered conditions so bad that the location soon became more familiar to them all as "Misery Bottoms." All of them now began paying in full measure for the year of terrorism they had just survived, as well as the summer and autumn of forced migration during which they had been so constantly harassed by the Missouri gentiles, whom they termed "mobbers".

Deaths among the Saint families that had finally reached Winter Quarters were appallingly frequent and even though it was the healthiest and wealthiest of the various Saint parties, the burial parties were always at work. Equally, the trail through Iowa, east to west, was even worse and was dotted with individual burial sites as well as clusters of graves. Afflictions took their grim toll throughout the entire line, especially where groups of them had gathered to withstand together the rigors of an especially severe winter. None of those temporary Saint colonies escaped death, but none had it worse than the six hundred Saints who had congregated at the over-winter colony they called Garden Grove. Veritable plagues of pneumonia, scurvy and ague settled upon them and they died by scores. When the United States government ignored their pleas for help, they memorialized the British government for similar aid, but with a reaction no different.

Except to their tormentors, who harassed them wherever encountered, the fleeing Saints had become a wholly ignored people.

*[November 30, 1846 • Monday]*
The farther the Mormon Battalion followed the old copper mine road

southward, the more it angled to the eastward and the more frustrated Lt. Col. Cooke became.

To the west was a rocky, rugged land through which even the pack mules would have to pick their way with delicate care; getting any wagons through seemed an insurmountable problem. At last Cooke had enough of the old copper mine road detour, such as it was and, riding at the head of the companies with his scouts, he abruptly raised his right hand high, halting the column. Ignoring the worried exclamations of his guides, who declared it was an impassable area, even though none of them had previously been across that terrain before, Cooke rode to the highest point and studied the fiercely jagged landscape spread out before and below him by about a thousand feet. In that morass he thought he detected a trail and he was determined they must reach it if they were to get through. He returned to his staff and ordered the command be turned directly west.

"By God," he declared aloud, "I don't want to go home again; I don't want to go there and be under General Wool's command. My orders were to California." He turned and motioned to the musicians behind and ordered, "Blow that trumpet!" Then, more to himself than to his staff, he raged: "I will be goddamned if I am going all around the world to get to California!"

Despite the additional hardship this decision of Cooke's was creating for them, the Saints generally applauded the move and, as the good Father Pvt. David Pettegrew wrote in his journal, expressing the command's universal sentiment: *God bless the Colonel!*

The commander had previously sent out a newly hired Mexican guide under Leroux to reconnoiter the route to San Bernardino, at which they had failed, but yesterday returned with an ancient Apache chief named Manuelito. Cooke hoped to convince him to become the Battalion's pilot, since he knew the country well and none of Cooke's own guides had been there before. He also hoped to get some additional fresh mules through his influence, since the Apaches reportedly had many. Manuelito, however, was both suspicious and timid, his people having so often been tricked by the Mexicans previously that he was wary of trusting strangers. Cooke's patience with him quickly flagged and he made his own decision without hesitation. As Private Henry Bigler wrote of it:

> ...*Accordingly, one hundred fifty pack mules were sent over the*

> mountain with some details [work squads] to pioneer and work the road. Lieutenant Dykes of Company D was sent with a company of men to guard the baggage from Indians. The distance across was some eight or ten miles and believed to be in the province of Sonora. We were two days transporting our baggage across. Empty waggons [sic] had to be let down over ledges by means of ropes, let down by hand. I think no other man but Cooke would ever have attempted to cross such a place, but he seemed to have all the spirit and energy of a Bonypart.[169] The remainder of the men, I being one, returned to camp. The route is very rough and rocky, never saw one more so. A large number of pioneers out preparing the road. It rained some last evening. I sold my butcher knife to Azariah Smith...We divided our mess, I sleeping with Lawson in the wagon.[170]

That Cooke mistrusted the evaluations of his own guides was to his credit; that he forged ahead with the work needing to be done to move men and wagons ahead across seemingly impossible terrain was an entirely remarkable achievement. As he wrote this evening in his report to General Kearny:

> ...having reluctantly assented, I took the Yanos Road. A mile or two convinced me (and them) that its general direction was very different from their representations; and east of south. I then took the full responsibility of turning short to the right, and ordered them to guide me to the water hole. I had some confused information of water to be found in the direction of San Bernardino. Mr. Leroux had been very decided that it would be necessary to go by this southern point, even if I ventured that far on the unknown prairie. I then marched 40 miles without water, except for a drink for part of the men, where I had hoped to find enough for encamping. The battalion were not prepared for it, and suffered much. These were anxious circumstances, and the responsibility I had taken weighed heavily upon me; their safety and my success seemed both doubtful...

That the Saints were capable of following Lt. Col. Cooke's orders at all under such adverse conditions was little short of miraculous and their doing so impressed the commander greatly. As Sgt. Tyler wrote in his journal about it:

> *Here it was decided and ordered that the men walk in double file in front of the wagons, just far enough apart to make trails for the wheels, and that at the end of an hour's march the leading companies and teams halt and allow the others to precede them and take their turn at breaking the road. This gave us all an equal share of the burden in traveling over all the heavy, sandy road...It was much like trampling snow—very hard on the men, especially those who took the lead, as we had no road or trail to follow. Here, also, Charboneaux [sic], one of the guides, came into camp, packing his saddle and pistols on his back. He said he got off to let his mule graze, when the animal kicked him, ran off and would not be caught; hence he shot him down to save his saddle and pistols, as he claimed, from falling into the hands of the Apache Indians."*

Charboneau continued to exhibit extraordinary coolness and courage in the execution in his duties. On November 25, when he was ascending a mountain several hours ahead of the command, he was abruptly confronted by a large female grizzly and her two well-grown sub-adult cubs. She immediately charged him, but Charboneau calmly held his ground and fired at her. His first shot, at almost 100 yards struck her full in the chest and tumbled her, but she rose and resumed her charging, more frantically furious than previously. Charboneau had quickly reloaded and his second shot, at less than fifty yards caught her in the lower abdomen and whirled her around, causing her to fall again. For a second time, as the enormous grizzly regained her feet and resumed the snarling charge, the mountain man reloaded and fired, this time with the female only yards away, the ball catching her in the neck, severing her spine and killing her instantly.

The sub-adult cubs, about half the size of their mother, had followed some distance behind her charge, but just as fearsomely. Charboneau quickly scaled a large emergent rock to its peak and then held off the two yearling animals by jabbing at them with the muzzle of his musket until they finally gave up and withdrew, still snarling ferociously. After a time, making sure the two were gone, Charboneau descended from his perch and butchered the big female grizzly which, he estimated, weighed almost half a ton. By then the leading supply wagons of the Mormons were upon him and the fresh bear meat was placed in them and served for supper that evening.

Cooke continued his written report to General Kearny, making rather light of the extraordinary hardships his Mormon Battalion had overcome in blazing an entirely new trail.

> ...*Fortunately a large spring was reached the second night, after a continuous march of thirteen hours, and when men and mules were at the point of exhaustion, for the weather was quite warm.*[171]...*we found a trail leading toward San Bernardino; and the fourth day, early, just after Charbonneaux* [Charbonneau], *the only guide then present, had very unwarrantably gone off hunting, we fell into what was believed to be the trail or road from Yanos to Fronteras; and it immediately led us to a precipitous and rocky descent, of perhaps a thousand feet, amongst broken, wild and confused mountain peaks, which extended as far as could be seen from our great height. I soon found the trail could not be made passable for wagons; and I hunted myself for a more promising descent, and, in fact, saw a part of the proper one; but very inaccessible from the mountain height on which I then was. My next care was to seek the nearest ground suitable for a camp; fortunately I found water about a mile off. All guides pronounced the country lying before us impassable for wagons; I nevertheless immediately organized a large working party, under Lieutenant Stoneman, and sent him to make a passage. That night Leroux arrived, bringing an Apache chief, whom he had got hold of with difficulty, and probably great address; so shy were they found. Next morning, it was owing to Leroux's decided assertions and his arguments that there could be and was no other known pass but the horse trail, that I did not* insist *on his thorough examination. He even asserted, but was mistaken, that he* had *examined the opening I had seen and described, and believed might be a wagon road. Meanwhile, the party continued the second day hard at work with crowbar, pick &c.; whilst I sent one company and about half the baggage, packed on mules, to the first water on the trail, in a deep ravine below. It was about six miles, and the mules were brought back in the evening. Next morning they took the rest of the loading, and I succeeded that day, with much labor and difficulty, breaking one. In getting the wagons to the new camp. Dr. Foster accidentally found the outlet of an old wagon road, (into mine,) and, following back, it led him to the verge of the plain about a mile from our point*

> *of descent. He says this is called the pass of the Guadalupe; and that it is the only one, for many hundreds of miles to the south, by which the broken descent from the great tableland of Mexico can be made by wagons, and rarely by pack mules. I hold it to be a question whether the same difficult formation does not extend north, at least to the Gila. If it is so, my road is probably the nearest and best route. But if the prairie, to the north, is open to the San Pedro, and water can be found, that improvement will make my road not only a good but a direct one from the Rio Grande to the Pacific.*[172]

In this instance, Sgt. Tyler—observing his thirtieth birthday this day—and others who were sent forward to act as pioneers in establishing a wagon road over the backbone of the mountains—found the task feasible, but extremely difficult. The advance had started early and, after about a dozen miles of travel they came to a crevice in the rock where water had collected enough to perhaps provide each man with half a pint. As the commander and his staff rode up to it, Tyler overheard Cooke remark, *"The men can do without water better than the animals."* Cooke then spied Tyler standing nearby and was displeased at his being near enough to overhear. Nevertheless, his mule and his staff and their mules drained the spring and moved on. Tyler waited a few moments for a little to seep in and managed to get perhaps an eighth of a pint of muddy water into his canteen. Others of the command, coming up from behind, cast wistful looks into the crevice and passed on, though a few stopped. Of this, Cooke wrote in his journal:

> *...the water was soon gone and the poor fellows were waiting for it to leak from the rocks, and dipping it with spoons! There was nothing to do but toil on over the ridge.*

The downgrade immediately before them that they had now to contend with presented far more difficulty than had the ascent, since it was at an angle of approximately forty-five degrees for more than half a mile. With their usual aplomb at facing the seemingly insurmountable, however, the Mormon Battalion, essentially waterless for the past thirty hours or more, struggled through. They even continued to note and comment in their journals or diaries about aspects of their journey, as when Pvt. Rogers noted:

> *Wed. 25. Continued on, two antelopes were killed and one of the pilots killed a grizzly bear. We traveled southwest for 20 miles and camped near a stream of water. This day observed specimens of the maguey plant in great perfection. The stalks of some of them were near 25 feet high and from 4 to 6 inches through at the butt, all of the growth of one year.*

This plant referred to as the maguey was, of course, the fleshy-leafed century plant, from which it was known the Apaches brewed a drink called mescal, a mild intoxicant used in a variety of tribal ceremonials. That the Saints abstained from attempting to emulate the brew was a testimonial to their tenet of alcoholic abstinence. Rogers continued in his journal the following day:

> *Thu. 26. Traveled 15 miles and camped near a creek. There is a mountain with timber on it. The most of the mountains lately passed are destitute of timbers. This country seems very barren of timber. The Creeks also soon sink in the sand in their descent from their fountains. There are high rocky mountains with gravelly and loamy plains.*

When at last they reached the trail, they encountered almost immediately a small party of Spaniards who had been out trading amongst the Indians. Tyler noted:

> *…Our Colonel purchased twenty mules and some of the soldiers bought some dried beef. I thought it was the best meat I ever ate.*

Though he maintained his essentially austere demeanor with officers and men alike, Lt. Col. Philip St. John Cooke was immensely proud of his command.

# Chapter 9

♦

*[December 6, 1846 • Sunday]*

For Brigadier General Stephen Watts Kearny, the war from which he initially thought he was being excluded suddenly came to life today. This evening, with his three wounds—in left upper arm, left shoulder and upper right hip—treated but still sending stabbings of pain through him, he sat alone in his tent, staring at the blank sheets before him as he reviewed in his mind the events that had led him and his forces into so severe a battle against the native California Mexicans—the Californios.

Weary though he was—more so than at any other time during this long march from Fort Leavenworth to California—he knew he could not rest until his report was written. The officers and men of his command were already referring to it as the Battle of San Pascual and so, too, he decided, would he in this official report to Washington D.C. which he was poised to write this night. It had been a fierce fight and even now, though his own forces grimly held the field of battle, he was not entirely sure who were the actual victors.

"If this was our victory," he muttered aloud, shaking his head sadly, "then God forbid that I ever live to see a defeat."

There was good reason for his vacillation; never before in his career had he led so fatigued an army—men and beasts alike—against a force so much stronger and fresher than his own. That they had withstood the withering assault by General Andreas Pico's expert horsemen and still held the ground at its conclusion was an accolade for the American force, but to any but the most optimistic could it possibly be regarded as a victory. His casualties far surpassed those of the enemy's.

Had he been able to ascertain with any degree of accuracy how many casualties had been suffered by the force under General Pio Pico's brother, Kearny might have felt better and perhaps more inclined to write this pending report, but he had no way of knowing what the number might be, since they had carried off most of their dead and dying before leaving the field. However many it might have been, however, he knew it had to be far fewer than his own force had suffered.

Twenty-two of his own men, including some of his very best officers, were being interred in a mass grave by the burial squads this evening and there was simply no way he could look upon such a result as a victory, yet that was how he knew he had to portray it in this report that he would write before morning's light. Still, he hesitated and instead reflected on the events leading to this momentous day.

His army, such as it was – now only about one hundred twenty-five men, pared down by three-fifths its initial size, primarily because of the reports received from Commodore Stockton that he was occupying Los Angeles and that all of California was firmly in American hands—had crossed the Colorado River ten miles south of the mouth of the Gila and entered California on November 25. They immediately found it to present severe desert terrain as bereft of food and water as any ground thus far encountered.

While irked to some degree that the Mormon Battalion had not yet overtaken him as anticipated, to a degree General Kearny was glad they had not, simply because of the hazards his select dragoons had been forced to face. The sprawling desert of southeastern California had quickly become their deadliest foe. When Kearny sent the majority of the wagons back, the meager quartermaster supplies had gone with them. Cactus had ripped uniforms to tatters and the sharp rimrock had done the same to boots. Hunger had quickly become a foremost enemy and the cavalrymen had been forced to butcher the oldest, lamest and most fatigued of their horses as food, just in order to survive. As Lt. Emory noted, *"Meat of horses may be very palatable, but ours are poor and tough."* Even the reasonably fresh horses on hand—intercepted and confiscated but virtually unbroken—including those that were accustomed to being used as saddle mounts, were unaccustomed to the rigors of desert travel and they faltered badly.

The Spanish, Kearny learned from traders, called this severe landscape of sprawling desert *Journada del Muerte*—the Route of Death—and the poorly delineated trail the army was following was justifiably referred to by them as the Devil's Highway. Fearful of what lay ahead once they left the valley of the Colorado, Kearny had wisely ordered the Dragoons to gather and tie behind each saddle bunches of grass for the subsistence of their mounts. Had they not done so, the death toll among their horses would have been much more pronounced, since the only vegetation encountered was spiny cactus and bitter yucca.

For thirty hours after striking westward across the desert here, the army encountered only one trace of water and even then barely managed to fill their bone-dry canteens by digging out and deepening an old dry well they encountered. They had, at this point covered a fifty-four-mile traverse of deeply sand-covered terrain in just two days. It was a remarkable achievement considering how badly broken-down their animals had become. Many of the mounts simply collapsed and died beneath their riders; others were saved only through the manual efforts of the Dragoons themselves—one man afoot tugging at the halter, another bracing his shoulder against the rear of the horse and pushing with all his strength—on that final stretch before the well was reached.

On December 2 they had finally reached Warner's Ranch, also called Agua Caliente—the southern route's equivalent of Sutters Fort. Here they met the current foreman, who was essentially uncommunicative, but a neighboring English rancher named Stokes, who was a bit reserved toward them at first, finally opened up to Kearny a bit, saying "Mr. Warner, I've been informed, is being held prisoner by the Californio revolutionaries. I must advise you, I absolutely want no part of a revolution and wish only to remain neutral."

As he and Kearny continued, however, Stokes—owner of the ranchos San Isabella and Santa Maria, the latter only forty miles from San Diego—informed him that it was as Kearny feared: while Commodore Stockton still had possession of San Diego and its important port, the enemy Californios were occupying the country from there northward to Santa Barbara.

"I am, in fact," Stokes said, "leaving tomorrow for San Diego and, as a neutral, I can pass through the lines without concern."

Kearny was immediately interested and interjected: "If it will not cause you difficulty, I would greatly appreciate your carrying along a letter to the Commodore."

"I can do that," Stokes agreed, "and I will keep it well hidden from possible prying eyes. Fortunately," he added, a conspiratorial twinkle in his eyes, "I will not have to pass through the area, about fifteen miles from here on the road to Los Angeles, where General Flores is holding his force. There is also a large *remuda* of horses and mules being held in reserve there."

Kearny's pulse quickened at this intelligence, though he masked it from Stokes, whom he doubted he could trust completely. As soon as he returned to his own headquarters tent, however, he summoned Kit Carson and Lt. Davidson.

"Take a squad of fifteen men," he ordered Davidson, explaining the situation. He then added, "With Mr. Carson's help, locate that *remuda* and see what you can do about obtaining some fresh mounts for us."

"Yes sir," Davidson replied. "We'll leave as soon as possible. It'll be full dark by the time we get there." He was grinning. "We'll see what we can do about liberating as many as possible and hopefully be back here by daybreak."

As soon as they were gone, Kearny dashed off a letter to Commodore Stockton, alerting him of his small army's presence here and his determination to attack the Californios, but also his imperative need for necessary supplies and reinforcements from Stockton to support and sustain his move. He sealed the letter and gave it over to Stokes, who planned to set off early the following morning.

By noon of December 3—Lt. Davidson and his squad returned, herding a fair number of horses and mules before them—animals "liberated" from the Californio's *remuda* without interference—but the animals were found to be unbroken and not of much service. Kearny nevertheless alerted his force that they could enjoy one more day of rest but would march along the route toward San Diego first thing the following morning, December 5, at which time they would have to be especially alert as they would almost surely encounter either the Flores force or another somewhere along the way.

The additional day of rest helped considerably to rejuvenate the men, though Kearny was only too well aware the animals would require much more rest and nourishment to regain their strength. They did not have this luxury of time, however, and set off with most of their mounts still in a weakened state. It was a rainy, foggy morning and Kearny's hope of quickly encountering the additional force of men requested of Commodore Stockton was soon realized, though with hardly the strength the general had hoped to acquire. What had been sent was a detachment of thirty-five sailors under command of Lt. Gillespie, Lt.

Edward Fitzgerald Beale and Midshipman John Duncan, armed with nothing larger than a tiny brass field piece which Kearny immediately added to his own meager howitzer unit. He conferred with the three at once, but gained from them little of real intelligence regarding the enemy beyond unfounded theories. Kearny then wrote another letter, this to Washington D.C., addressed to Brigadier General Roger Jones, the U.S. Adjutant General, in which he reported, in part:

> ...on the 5th, were met by a small party of volunteers under Captain Gillespie, sent out from San Diego, by Commodore Stockton, to give us what information they possessed of the enemy, 600 or 700 of whom are now said to be in arms and in the field throughout the territory, determined upon opposing the Americans and resisting their authority in the country...The journals and maps, kept and prepared by Capt. Johnston, (my aid-de-camp,) and those by Lt. Emory, our topographical engineer, which will accompany or follow this report, will render anything further from me on this subject unnecessary...

At nightfall he sent out a reconnoitering party under Lt. Hammond, which quickly returned with their findings.

"There's a body of Californios holding the road to San Diego only a few miles ahead of us, sir," Hammond reported. "They're at a small town called San Pascual, roughly nine miles from here, and appear to be pretty well mounted, but without any detectable sign of artillery."

The general nodded. "No choice," he muttered, "but to clear them out."

Lt. Gillespie and Kit Carson chimed in almost simultaneously that, in their opinion, the force of Californios appeared weak and they very much doubted they'd stand and fight against any sort of concerted assault; they were poorly armed and hardly a force to be feared very much, armed as they were, as Gillespie put it, "...with not much more than a bunch of spears."

Kearny was not so sure, but he nodded. "Even with the reinforcement, such as it is, we're still too small to do anything much except attack. Perhaps we can surprise them." He paused, as if prepared to say more, but after a moment merely shook his head. "Well, we'll see, won't we, gentlemen?"

As soon as the pair left his headquarters tent, Kearny summoned his much trusted aide de camp, Captain Johnston, and sent him out with a small party to investigate the same route Lt. Gillespie and Kit Carson had just reported upon. At two o'clock this morning, Johnston returned from his mission and reported immediately to Kearny: "We found the enemy, sir, camped pretty much where the lieutenant and guide found them and they're armed with muskets and lances, though I don't believe the force is in quite the numbers they reported. I estimate they're less than two hundred in number. We also learned from a sentry we captured that their force is being led by General Andreas Pico. He's the brother of Pio Pico—"

"The late commanding general and governor of the Californios," Kearny murmured, aware that Pio Pico had died of natural causes only a month or two previous.

"Yes sir, that's right. But evidently his appointment then was more than mere nepotism. Andreas is reputed to be every bit as skilled a general as Pio had been. At any rate, I'm sorry to say we were seen and had to flee, but we were not pursued by them. I'm somewhat at a loss to explain why not."

"Thank you, Captain Johnston," Kearny said. "Go get some sleep now while you still can. You won't have long. I suspect we're going to have a busy day ahead."

Johnston saluted, wheeled about and was gone. Kearny sat in thought for a considerable while and finally decided, just before 3 a.m., that the time would quite probably never be any better than the present: Even though his own force was evidently weaker numerically than the enemy, if they could hit the Andreas Pico camp at daybreak, taking them by surprise, they just might gain an important advantage. And his men's carbines were better, more accurate weapons by far than the enemy's muskets. Decision made, Kearny ordered the army roused and prepared to march within the hour.

The troops assembled without delay and Kearny instructed his officers. It was still two hours or more before daybreak when he put his force into motion and they headed for San Pasqual, southward on the San Diego Road. They had not gone far when they were overtaken by a sizeable company of American volunteers on foot, jovial and joking amongst themselves and nearly all of them armed with carbines. These were a ragtag, un-uniformed and disorganized bunch and Kearny was disappointed in what he considered to be their potential in actual fighting; so much so, in fact, that with hardly a second thought, he ordered them to the rear to guard the baggage. This irked the volunteers considerably and, though they gave voice to considerable grumbling, they formed as ordered, as a guard for the trailing wagons.

Kearny's force arrived within sight of San Pascual just at dawn, but any hope he nurtured that they could attack the enemy by surprise was quickly demolished. His Dragoons jogged along with their sabers jingling and clashing so loudly that, even though a light rain continued falling, the noise of their approach had preceded them by several miles in the still morning air and the enemy was alert and waiting. As General Kearny wrote later this day:

> *My aid-de-camp, Capt. Johnston, dragoons, was assigned to the command of the advanced guard of twelve dragoons, mounted on the best horses we had; then followed about fifty dragoons under Capt. Moore, mounted, with but few exceptions, on the tired mules they had ridden from Santa Fe, (New Mexico, 1050 miles,) then about twenty volunteers of Capt. Gibson's company under his command, and that of Capt. Gillespie; then followed our two mounted howitzers, with dragoons to manage them, and under the charge of Lieut. Davidson, of 1st regiment. The remainder of the dragoons, volunteers, and citizens, employed by the officers of the staff, &c., were placed under the command of Major Swords, (quartermaster,) with orders to follow on our trail with the baggage, and to see to its safety.*

In the dim morning light the Californios and Americans clashed in the Battle of San Pascual.[173]

It was a remarkably short battle, not lasting much more than a quarter-hour and, for the American force, it was a devastating debacle. The small advance guard Kearny sent forward under his aide de camp Capt. Johnston was mounted on the best animals the Americans had remaining, but they were still sorry steeds. The shambling charge of the Dragoons on animals that were largely jaded and only half-broken at best was far too slow to outmaneuver the fresh horses the Californios quickly mounted and the enemy were themselves some of the most skilled horsemen in the world. The overnight rain had made the firearms of the Americans all but useless and in that first attack Capt. Abraham R. Johnston and quite a few of his men of the First Dragoons were killed outright. Johnston was among the first to fall, shot dead.

The main body of the Americans, following not far behind and led by Kearny himself, managed to turn the Californios and drive them away and a ragged pursuit was attempted. Very soon, however, the American force became strung out and the Californios, seeing this, reversed direction and came charging back at a powerful gallop, their deadly lances leveled. Those who could, among the Americans, used their rifles as clubs and the officers wielded sabers, but such weapons were woefully inadequate against lances and the clash was very one-sided. A fair portion of the ninety Americans were on foot and many were immediately impaled. Kearny himself quickly received three lance wounds which very nearly unseated him—one through the shoulder, another through his upper arm, a third high in the hip—and his horse was badly wounded.

The two howitzers, pulled all the way from Santa Fe for just such an engagement, turned the Californios momentarily, but the team pulling one panicked and stampeded and the Californios easily overtook the shambling mules, captured the field piece and pulled it away. The other was aimed but could not be fired.

Lt. Thomas Hammond was lanced twice and unseated, but managed to regain the saddle, then was lanced again and killed. His brother-in-law, Capt, Benjamin D. Moore, was overtaken and took a lance thrust through the center of his back, which killed him instantly. Kearny, reeling from his three lance wounds but still maintaining his saddle, was clearly in bad shape, while beside him Lt. Warner was lanced twice and had four rents through his blouse that barely scored his flesh.

General Kearny's mount finally fell dead from its wounds and the commander, afoot, was weaponless and staggering. American reserves ran up behind Captain Turner, who now took command from the unseated and disabled Kearny and led a charge that clashed with, then turned, the Californio horsemen. Several of the enemy had been killed but the Californio losses were slight compared to eighteen Americans who lay dead on the ground and the many others who were wounded, four so severely they were dying.[174]

It was at this point that the American volunteers—those that Kearny had disparaged and sent to the rear to guard the baggage—came to the front and, with their long rifles and deadly accuracy, swiftly changed the tide of the battle and sent the enemy into full flight. They saved the day for the American force and General Kearny, remorseful now over how he had treated them on their arrival, vowed to himself he would never again refer to them as "riff-raff," no matter how poorly they marched nor how slovenly they were clad.

Captain Turner, who continued in command for the remainder of the day, called a halt to the pursuit of the enemy and set up a temporary camp and the surgeons began treating the many American wounded, including General Kearny, whose lance punctures were very painful but not life-threatening. As Lt. Emory wrote, with shaking hand:

> ...Our provisions were exhausted, our horses dead, our mules on their last legs, and our men, now reduced to [he meant "by"] one-third of their number were ragged, worn down by fatigue and emaciated.

In the evening Captain Turner had the American dead gathered up and buried in a common grave on the cactus-grown hillside and he sent mountain man Alexis Godey and two others, who had just arrived, to Commodore Stockton at San Diego, asking for reinforcements.[175]

General Kearny, in addition to the wounds he received, was clearly devastated by what had occurred and wrote in his journal:

> ...What a loss to my regiment! Ah! Who but loved Johnston—the noble, sterling, valued Johnston! And who had warmer friends than poor Moore? Peace to their ashes! Rest to their souls! May their country honor the memories of its heroic champions, who, serving her, have found their graves in distant and desolate regions!

General Kearny's official report to Washington D.C. concerning what had occurred was very brief, almost sketchy. He did not, however, as many field commanders were inclined to do, falsify. He wrote:

> ...As the day, December 6th, dawned, we approached the enemy at San Pascual, who were already in the saddle; Captain Johnston made a furious charge upon them with his advanced guard, and was, in a short time after, supported by the dragoons, soon after

> which the enemy gave way, having kept up, from the beginning, a continual fire upon us. Upon the retreat of the enemy, Captain Moore led off rapidly in pursuit, accompanied by the dragoons, mounted on horses, and followed, though slowly, by those on their tired mules.
>
> The enemy, well mounted and among the best horsemen in the world, after retreating about half a mile, and seeing an interval between Captain Moore, with his advance, and the dragoons coming to his support, rallied their whole force, charged with their lances, and, on account of their greatly superior numbers, but few of us in front remained untouched;
>
> Their number was thirty-eight, all of whom, save two, were killed or wounded. For five minutes they held the ground from us, when, our men coming up, we again drove them, and they fled from the field not to return to it, which we occupied and encamped upon. A most melancholy duty now remains for me: it is to report the death of my aid-de-camp, Captain Johnston, who was shot dead at the commencement of the action; of Captain Moore, who was lanced just previous to the final retreat of the enemy; and of Lieutenant Hammond, also lanced, who survived but a few hours. We also had killed, two sergeants, two corporals and ten privates of the First Dragoons; one private of the volunteers, and one engaged in the topographical department. Among the wounded are myself (in three places), Lieutenant Warner, topographical engineer (in three places), Captain Gillespie and Captain Gibson, of the volunteers (the former in three places). one sergeant, bugler and nine privates of the dragoons; many of them receiving from two to ten lance wounds, most of them when unhorsed and incapable of resistance. The enemy proved to be a party of about one hundred and sixty Californians, under Andreas Pico, the brother of the late governor.[176]
>
> Our provisions were exhausted, our horses dead, and mules on their last legs; and our men now reduced to [actually, "by"] one-third their number, were ragged, worn down by fatigue, and emaciated.

It had been a very bad day, indeed, for the American Army in California.[177]

*[December 7, 1846 • Monday]*

Commodore Robert F. Stockton was becoming very tired of the continuing aggravation of having to contend with the hard core of Californios who still formed a stumbling block for the American cause. It was clear that the greater majority of these Mexican-Americans supported the cause of the United States and wished to be a part of the Republic, but their fear of the revolutionary leaders—Castro in particular—was such that they preferred to maintain a wait-and-see attitude. Everything seemed to depend on what would happen, especially now that the army of General Kearny had been so soundly trounced by the lancers under General Andreas Pico.

Almost all the American forces were now concentrated in the San Diego region. Stockton's men-of-war and other ships rode at anchor in the San Diego Harbor, constantly on alert and poised for action...but waiting. The single exception was Colonel John Fremont's new force of rag-tag volunteers, primarily American, which was still roaming the countryside to the northeast of Los Angeles, but gradually moving closer, a force presently augmented by the body of men under Capt. Merritt and Lieutenant Gillespie.

Commodore Stockton, now temporary governor of the California Territory, had a force of some eight hundred men gathered in the port city, but they remained a rather disorganized collection of sailors, marines and volunteers who had been at dalliance for much too long and who now, despite his defeat at San Pascual, were anticipating that General Kearny would take control and provide the strength and disciplined military leadership they needed.

At the same time they wondered who would emerge victorious in the power struggle that seemed certain to develop between the well-entrenched Commodore Stockton and the newly arrived commander of the Army of the West, Brigadier General Stephen Watts Kearny.

*[December 11, 1846 • Friday]*

Almost with a sense of infusing fatalism, the Mormon Battalion was now marching along the bone-dry course of San Pedro Creek in the southern New Mexico Territory as if it were a treadmill into the depths of some sort of Hell. Few thought of Kearny's dragoon force treading this same ground a month ahead of them or, for that matter, contemplated anything much more complex than the process of constantly placing one foot before another in the march that seemed as if it would never end.

This present terrain, since December began, was the driest they had yet encountered, the landscape having become a sort of phantasmagoria more appropriate to nightmares than to reality. Only a fortnight ago they had crossed the continental divide for a final time in the relatively low Animas Range, but felt little lifting of their spirits in the knowledge that all streams now passed drained, eventually, into the Pacific Ocean.

"Nothing to drain from this creek into the Pacific," muttered one of the Saints of Company B, "except a whole lot of dry sand!"

The remark elicited a few chuckles from Saints nearby, but groans as well. All the marchers were incredibly fed up with this land they'd entered in which water rarely ran fresh and clear, where leaves were not lush and green and thornless, where the punishing rays of the sun hammered one with the intensity of physical blows. A sense of Midwestern homesickness was affecting them all and, with it, a pervasive moroseness all but equivalent to physical illness.

The march for the Mormon Battalion had been little more than a plodding monotony, enlivened only occasionally by incidents disproportionately amusing, saddening or exasperating. Once in a while, however, things occurred that tended to lighten the burden each man was bearing. A case in point occurred on the first day of December when one of their own, the detested Lt. George P. Dykes, came rather close to getting himself killed. They'd been traveling down a bone-dry canyon when it came time to cease the day's march and establish the night's camp. Despite the near abject weariness of the men, Dykes, who was on duty as officer of the day, decided he'd play the role of spy, evidently with the hope of finding some new cause for complaint in regard to security.

The lieutenant slipped about in the darkness until he was inside the sentry lines and was stealthily making his way toward where the guns were stacked when he was suddenly spotted and challenged by one of the sentinels on duty, Pvt. Henry G. Boyle. Supposing the shadowy form of Dykes to be an infiltrating enemy, Boyle rasped *"Halt!"* He simultaneously raised and cocked his rifle in one fluid movement, the muzzle pointed steadily at the center of Dyke's chest. The lieutenant was momentarily struck speechless by the challenge and Boyle was in the process of squeezing his trigger when he recognized the Officer of the Day and relaxed. Another second or two of non-recognition on Boyle's part or continued muteness on the lieutenant's and a half-ounce lead ball and a dozen pea-sized buckshot would have crashed into his chest and surely killed him.

While their journey afoot was extremely arduous, nevertheless there were some among the Saints who reveled in the experience. One of these was Sgt. Daniel Tyler, who wrote in his diary on December 1:

> ...*Being on the west of the dividing ridge, we found that all of the streams run westward instead of eastward, as previously. The scenery is most beautiful, with mountain preciipices and rocks in all shapes and sizes heaped upon each other. The mescol* [mescal], *a wild vegetable, sometimes roasted by the Indians for food, is found here, as well as the Spanish bayonet, evergreen oaks, cottonwoods and sycamores, the leaves of which are nicely tinted by frost. Everything here, even to the rocks, bears a brilliant shade or tint of some kind...*

Pvt. Rogers, on the other hand, was more interested in the human aspect of the territory as, on the following day, he wrote in his journal:

> *Wed. 2. Left the valley and entered a plain traveled 10 miles and camped at a deserted village in another valley. The place had been occupied by Mexicans who had been driven out by the Apache Indians. The place was called San Bernardino Ranch and was built like other Mexican houses we have seen*[178] *This was the 31st day since we saw a house. A number of Indians in camp for the purpose of trading.*

This was the area in the southern New Mexico Territory where long ago the Spanish settlers had established cattle ranches of great size upon which they were breeding a new variety of long-horned cattle. Apache depredations, however, had driven the Spanish settlers out and their cattle had reverted to a wild state, learned to survive well in the hostile terrain and eventually grew into large migratory herds. Unlike the buffalo, however, alongside which they shared the desolate land, their viciousness was unparalleled. With little or no provocation, the long-horns were almost eager to tackle any enemy *en masse*.

There were remains of two adobe walls at the site but little else.

When the Battalion arrived, they found one of their scouts already there, who had killed one of the wild long-horned bulls and was drying the meat. Lt. Col. Cooke immediately sent out a few hunters to down some of the wild cattle for meat, and several other small parties, once camp was made, went off to hunt on their own. Tyler was with one of these and after following several of the animals in succession, which ran off at sight of him, he finally encountered one as yet unaware of his presence. He was at that time about four miles from their camp.

The big animal, with horns spanning six feet or more, was beneath a solitary tree about half a mile distant. Tyler immediately crouched to make himself small as possible and slipped from one clump of mesquite to another until he'd covered about half that distance with the animal still unaware of his approach. With little cover left between himself and the big bull, Tyler steadied his gun and was squeezing the trigger when there was the crack of another rifle being fired and the bull bellowed as a lead ball struck and broke his thigh bone. A second shot put the big bull down.

Unsure of who else was hunting nearby, Tyler walked toward the fallen animal and was still about fifty feet distant when a voice halted him and he spun about. It was one of his messmates, Walter Barney.

"Stand still, Tyler, until I can fire again. He may still be alive."

"Hold your fire and save your ammunition. He's dead. I'll cut his throat to bleed him out."

"Don't just walk up on him," Barney warned. "He might just be playing 'possum until you get close and then he'll jump up and gore you."

Tyler considered this and shrugged, not believing the animal could possibly have survived, but nevertheless more cautious. He picked up a rock about the size of his fist and threw it the final ten feet. The rock bounced off one horn and instantly the bull roared and struggled to its feet and then charged at Tyler on three legs. The sergeant held his ground and fired. The bull fell once more but in moments struggled to his feet and continued the charge yet again, with wild, shrill bellow and even greater fury. Another shot from Barney struck the beast but seemed to have little effect.

Tyler was below the bull on a hillside and, as the fearsome animal neared, he whirled out of its way, the point of one great horn just barely missing him. The sergeant reloaded yet again and, as he did so, Barney fired and for a fourth time the bull slammed to the ground. Without hesitation now, Tyler brought up his weapon and shot again, this time the ball striking the skull just below the base of the horn and killing the animal. With due caution, the two men inspected the carcass and found six bullet holes.

"Harder to bring down than a buffalo," Barney commented. He was grinning but obviously shaken.

"Glad you were close by," Tyler panted. "He'd've nailed me for certain. Look at those horns—six feet easily, maybe even more, tip to tip."

They cut away a large patch of skin and then cut out two sizeable chunks of meat from the haunch and set off back to camp with it. By this time the sun had already set and Tyler, who had been sick ever since they'd reached the Arkansas River, soon was unable to walk farther. Barney suggested Tyler remain in place and build a fire while he went back to camp, promising to return with comrades and pack mules, using his fire as a beacon, to bring him in along with the best part of the meat. Tyler agreed it was a good plan. He later wrote in his journal:

> I had but little fear of other wild beasts or Indians, although the country abounded with both. I made my supper from the roasted melt or spleen of the animal. My comrade, with others, returned with mules about 10 p.m. We took what meat the mules could pack, I mounted the one with the lightest load, and reached camp about 12 o'clock, some time having been occupied in dressing the beef.
>
> This same evening, John Allen, assigned to Company B, the desperado and hunter who was supposed to have deserted, came into camp, having been absent five days. He was minus his gun, coat, vest, shoes and butcher knife, which he said were taken from him by Apache Indians. They made signs to him to take off his shirt, also; but the weather was cold, and he felt if they did not kill him he must soon perish, hence he bared his breast and signified that he would prefer them to shoot him. They then let him go.
>
> He finally struck our trail, and finding Captain Jesse D. Hunter's dead horse, gnawed through the posterior like a wolf and got his first meal since leaving the command. He had killed a turkey, but the sound of his gun betrayed him to the Indians, who took it from him. The poor fellow had even picked up the hoofs of dead animals and gnawed off the most tender portions and eaten them.

*He was, for once, humbled, and much of his disagreeable, wicked, profane and quarrelsome nature seemed for a time to have left him. Cooke sets him down as "the only member of the Battalion not a Mormon."*

Quite soon the Battalion encountered more of the wild long-horned cattle and as Henry Bigler wrote about it in his diary:

*On the fifth we marched about twelve miles. This day there were supposed to have been seen about 4,000 wild cattle. Four were killed for beef, I believe all bulls.*

The following day another of the Mormon Battalion's men died. This was Elisha Smith, who was not an enlisted soldier but, rather, a man hired early on by Capt. Davis as both teamster and servant and whose wife had separated with one of the detachments to winter at Pueblo. The night was made hideous with the howls of wolves and many of the Saints believed they were attracted by corpse of Smith. They buried him without benefit of coffin or slab and a mound of brush and wood piled on his grave was set afire in an effort to disguise the grave and prevent either Indians or wolves from digging him up.

After several days of march without finding water, on December 9 they encountered a good stream, running fast and cold. Henry Bigler identified it in his diary as the Rio San Pedro and wrote:

*It affords plenty good running water and runs north, emptying I suppose into the Gila, and seems to abound with plenty of fish. Our course now was down this river and quite a lot of salmon trout was taken. Bands of wild horses were seen, as also an antelope and wild cattle.*

Once more Providence stepped in with a mixed blessing, both disconcerting and yet inestimably valuable, occurring as the Battalion plodded wearily along the San Pedro in southern Arizona Territory. Almost without warning the thunder of hooves brought them to alertness as a massive herd of hundreds of longhorns, many with powerful horns spanning as much as eight or nine feet from tip to tip, bore down upon them in a cloud of dust, erupting with guttural rumblings of rage erupting. There was little time for the foot soldiers marching in columns to do anything except try to shelter themselves from the murderous throng. Men and mules alike were gored by those terrible horns, wagons were overturned and for a time the world had become total chaos for the marching Saints. As Bigler chronicled the event:

> ...A number of wild cattle, I believe mostly bulls, came running from the west and ran through our ranks, plunging their horns into two team mules, goring them to death almost instantly and running over men.... One of those mad brutes made a charge at a soldier. The soldier to escape fell flat to the earth. The bull ran lengthwise over him, looking down at the same time, and caught the soldiers cap on his horn, and carried it off, I suppose, in triumph. There was no timber or trees to climb out of their way, except a few scattering ones. They were soon mounted by those who were most handy. Some guns were empty, for orders had been given not to carry a loaded gun in ranks. There was one man by the name of Lafayette Frost, whose gun was loaded. When one of these enraged animals made a charge at him, the Colonel seeing it hollered, "Run! Run, God damn you, run!" Frost, raising his gun, fired. Down dropped the bull, dead in his tracks.
>
> The Colonel turned around and swore, "That man is a God damned soldier! One of the bravest men I ever saw!"
>
> Some of those rascals actually made a lunge and seemingly tried to upset some of the wagons. I saw a bull make a charge, and it appeared to me that he threw the near mule slick and clean over his off-mate. Then he plunged his horns, letting the guts out of the off-mule, while the near one received no injury. There was so much dust made that everything was out of sight for a few seconds. Ten bulls were killed...several of our men wounded, but not fatal.

Sgt. Tyler, while quite aware of the danger the herd presented, still could not help but admire the maddened animals. He wrote:

> ...In the open ground, where the cattle could see us from a distance, they would run away, but when near us, whether wounded or not, they were the assaulting party. Their terribly beautiful forms and majestic appearance were quite impressive. Contrary to the orders

of the Colonel, as previously noticed, many of the men had their muskets loaded, and a battle followed. Hence, the roar of musketry was heard from one end of the line to the other.... The end-gates of one or two wagons were stove in, and the sick, who were riding in them, were frightened. Some of the men climbed upon the wheels of the wagons and poured a deadly fire into the enemy's ranks. Some threw them selves down and allowed the beasts to run over them; others fired and dodged behind mezquit [mesquite] brush to reload their guns, while the beasts kept them dodging to keep out of the way. Others, still, climbed up into small trees, there being, now and then, one available.

Brother Amos Cox was thrown about ten feet into the air, while a gore from three to four inches in length and about two or three in depth was cut in the middle of his thigh near its junction with the body. Albert Smith, quartermaster sergeant of Company B, was run over by a wounded bull, and, I understand, had three of his ribs partially severed from the backbone.

Major Clowd [Cloud], our paymaster, had one of his pack mules killed. Dr. William Spencer, assistant surgeon's steward, shot six balls into one bull, and was pursued by him, rising and falling at intervals, until the last and fatal shot...was fired.

Henry Standage and Sanford Porter, who fell behind on account of trying to catch some salmon trout...on entering our trail saw nine bulls lying dead in one place. After stopping and roasting what choice cuts they wanted, they followed on and overtook the command. The number of bulls killed is not known, but it is probably not less than 20.

Probably twice as many or more were fatally wounded; thus making the number about 60 [sic; 40?]. This is considered a very low estimate; one soldier says 81 were killed outright.

Finally, with Lt. Col. Cooke roaring commands, volleys of musket shots turned the charging beasts and they raced off, disappearing over a low rise as swiftly as they had appeared. It was a tremendous relief they were gone. For the commander, however, it was not enough. After caring for the wounded and ordering a good night's rest for all, early in the morning Cooke ordered a hunt. Now, with muskets charged and ready, it was the Saints who bore down on the longhorn herd as it rested and the guns dispatched scores of the big animals before the remainder finally fled in a diminishing thunder of hooves and bellowings.

Drying frames were quickly built and the downed longhorns butchered, their stripped meat hung to dry and quickly becoming a life-sustaining larder for the Saints. For the first time since their long journey began, all bellies throughout the Battalion were well filled and supply baskets were overflowing, and once again the Saints looked upon it as an unusual but entirely Providential blessing. The larder filling only momentarily delayed the march and soon the Saints were plodding ahead once again, although now much more rejuvenated.

"Forever after," Henry Bigler predicted, "the Saints will remember this occasion as The Great Bullfight."

*[December 13, 1846 • Sunday]*

General Stephen Watts Kearny, presently ensconced and recuperating from his wounds at San Diego, was walking a very precarious path in regard to the chain-of-command in California.

His orders, directly descended from President Polk through the War Department in Washington D.C., stated in unmistakable terms that upon reaching California, he was to take command of whatever land forces had been raised there to occupy the territory—which meant, in essence, Fremont's California Battalion—and to then organize and establish a civil government. There was, however, a distinct glitch apparent: Commodore Stockton clearly regarded himself as the conqueror of California and he had—though on paper only—already organized a civil government. While his authority for doing so was through the force of circumstance, that command position of Stockton's would be terminated the moment Kearny showed his orders. Stockton felt himself so secure in his self-exalted position that, prematurely, he had already named Lt. Col. John Fremont as civil governor of California—which suited perfectly Fremont's own self-aggrandizing instincts for treachery—and Col. William Henry Russell as Secretary of State. Russell, a Kentuckian, was a bosom friend of Henry Clay, who was himself one of the most powerful Senators in the United States government.

The dilemma, exacerbated by the wounds Kearny had received in the Battle of San Pascual, became more pronounced when Stockton not only refused to at once acknowledge Kearny's authority and withdraw his U.S. Navy and Marine detachments from Kearny's command, but also attempted to suspend Kearny from command of the Dragoon companies that had accompanied him to California. In the latter instance the Commodore was unsuccessful but, even so, this left General Kearny with only a handful of Dragoons, plus a field commander, Fremont, who, in a hastily contrived message, baldly informed Kearny, his commanding officer, that he would not obey his orders, only those originating from Stockton.[179]

Kearny, at this point, was clearly being upstaged by his very ambitious and well-connected countrymen and he had little recourse but to remain in San Diego and await the arrival of less mutinous troops, meaning, of course, the Mormon Battalion under command of Lt. Col. Phillip St. George Cooke. Wisely biding his time in this manner would, Kearny reasoned, provide him not only with the opportunity to recover to some degree from the lance-wounds he had suffered but would also prevent giving Mexican leaders any indication of dissention among the American forces.

On the morning of December 7, weak from blood-loss, Kearny had set his Dragoons on the march toward San Diego, trailing his wounded men with them on travois constructed by his mountain men guides. After about ten miles of travel, they reached San Bernardo, the ranch of another Englishman, where they paused to feed the wounded. Just beyond them were the Californios, who had been hanging on their flanks and riding across the front just out of gun range. When one of the scouts brought word that the Californios had suddenly spurred ahead to occupy a small hill, it seemed likely they would try to provoke a fight here. Kearny, however, quickly sent out a small party under Lt. Emory which drove them out, killing and wounding five of the enemy in the process, with no loss to the American detachment. It seemed obvious to Kearny, however, that if his march continued, the free cavalry of the Californios would eventually capture his horses, his remaining howitzer and perhaps even his wounded. He decided to remain encamped with his force on the hilltop here, but maintained the position only at the price of losing his remaining beef cattle which, now well behind, fell into enemy hands.

The following day, learning that his messengers had been captured, Kearny decided to stay forted where he was for at least another day. That night Lt. Edward Fitzgerald Beale and his Indian servant, led by Kit Carson, crept out of camp at midnight in an effort to carry another summons to Stockton. Their crawl, mostly on their bellies through darkness and the lines of a vigilantly patrolling enemy expecting them to do just that, was successfully completed, adding even more fuel to the reputation of Carson being a master mountain man whose career was already packed with desperate exploits.

By dawn on December 9, the trio had finally left their besiegers behind, but they had also lost their shoes, which they had tied around their necks, and had to travel barefoot through areas of cactus toward San Diego. They thought it wise, then, to separate and enhance the chances of at least one of them getting through. Actually, all three made it, arriving at San Diego the following evening within an hour of one another, although Beale collapsed just as he made it and actually had to be carried to Stockton's headquarters to make his report. Even Kit Carson suffered severely for several days from effects of their ordeal.[180]

Trying a new tactic, the Californios, in a pre-dawn maneuver on December 10, tried to drive a herd of horses over Kearny's position to rout his force, but the hill was too well protected by nature on three sides and the effort failed, at the cost to the enemy of having some of their better horses killed by Kearny's men, who eagerly devoured them for breakfast as a welcome change from the stringy mule meat upon which they had been living for the past several days. As yesterday's daybreak came upon them, one hundred sailors and eighty marines sent by Commodore Stockton under command of Naval Lieutenant Gray arrived on horseback with food and clothing for Kearny's besieged unit, simultaneously causing the enemy force to flee. By 10 a.m. Kearny's entire force was again on the move over the remaining miles to San Diego, this time unopposed.

For Kearny, the principal drawback to all this was that such delay also gave Stockton an opportunity to entrench himself even more deeply into California Territory politics and it provided the insubordinate Fremont with ample opportunity to begin a series of appeals to his father-in-law, Senator Thomas Hart Benton, who also had considerable influence in American government. This could well, Kearny knew, result in the defacement of his own reputation and character in Washington D.C. and, as a result, in American history. The general, however, possessed the one essential element clearly lacking in both Stockton and Fremont; the self-discipline to step back for the time being, accept a subordinate's assumed leadership and allow both men to entrap themselves through their own grandiose ambitions. With Fremont presently moving in on Los Angeles from the north, Stockton and Kearny were ready now to start to the same place from the south. Since Stockton's sailors and marines comprised the majority of the force Kearny would have and since the general was still favoring his wounds, Stockton had placed himself to command the expedition.

To add impetus to his report, Kearny wrote now to Brig. Gen. Roger Jones, U.S. Adjutant General in Washington, D.C.:

> ...*On the 12th (yesterday) we reached this place; and I have now to offer my thanks to Commodore Stockton, and all of his gallant command, for the very many kind attentions we have received, and continue to receive from them.*
> 
> *Very respectfully, your obedient servant,*
> *STEPHEN W. KEARNY, Brig. Gen., U.S.A.*

It was a decidedly ticklish tight-rope to walk, but a very necessary one for both military and political survival...and, clearly, Brigadier General Stephen Watts Kearny was, above all else, a survivor.

### [December 16, 1846 · Wednesday]

The *U.S. Lexington*, out of New York Harbor, had now been en route to California for just a few days over five months and all aboard—crew members excepted—were overfilled with the deadly monotony of this extensive sea voyage. Yet, still they sailed in sight of Chile's capital city, Valparaiso, and a long way from their goal.

One of the very few who avoided voicing complaints about ennui was the young military officer presently standing at the bow rail, watching the shoreline diminish as their journey resumed. The pulse of twenty-six-year old Lt. William Tecumseh Sherman quickened at the thought that the layover here was finally finished and they were once again on their way; this time, please God, with no more delays before they finally headed into the dockage at Monterey Bay on California's West Coast.

This had been only their second stop since leaving New York Harbor, the first a fortnight's layover for the three Rs—rest, relaxation and replenishment—in Buenos Aires. Though the pause there had been interesting and everyone had enjoyed the many activities that the cosmopolitan port city afforded, Sherman had chafed at the delay and was pleased when they had finally set sail again.

Now they were just finishing a stay of similar duration here in the Chilean anchorage, where they had paused to replenish supplies of fresh water, fruits, vegetables and heavily salted mutton in brine. While the respite was highly important and certainly interesting, for Sherman the zenith of their two-week layover here had been the opportunity to visit yesterday the captain and crew of the *U.S. Independence*, freshly arrived from Sherman's own destination. Commodore William Branford Shubrick seemed to enjoy the visit of officers and guests of the *Lexington* to the *Independence* and himself led them on a fairly thorough tour of his warship. Sherman had stayed as close as possible to him and plied him, at every opportunity, with questions. What quickly irked the esteemed Commodore, however, was that the lieutenant's questions were not so much about his ship as they were about where his ship had been—in California's coastal waters.

In his tiny cubicle last night, Sherman had penned in his journal:

*All the necessary supplies being renewed in Valparaiso, our voyage is resumed. Having settled down to sailor habits, time passes without notice by some. We have brought with us all the books we could find in New York about California, and have read them over and over again: Wilkes's* Exploring Expedition, *Dana's* Two Years Before the Mast, *and Forbes's* Account of the Missions. *It is generally understood we are Bound for Monterey, capital of Upper California. We know, of course, that General Kearny was en route to the same country overland, that Fremont was there with his exploring party, that the navy had already taken possession, and that a regiment of volunteers, Stevenson's, was to follow us from New York; but we are nevertheless impatient to reach our destination.*

[December 17, 1846 · Thursday · 5:00 p.m.]

In the rapidly settling twilight, Lt. Col. Philip St. George Cooke looked out over the assembled Mormon Battalion with no expression on his face to betray the exasperation he harbored for what lay ahead, for what he now felt it was necessary to tell the Saints, who had assembled and stood at ease in their company ranks before him.

They had marched some eight miles out of Tucson today and an aspect of general weariness cloaked them, yet there were few murmured grousings; only an apparent curiosity over why their commander had, in this unusual manner, assembled them for an evening announcement, even before they'd had an opportunity to establish their night's campground and ignite their campfires.

Before the Battalion could be called to attention, rumors quickly circulated among the Saints as to the reasoning behind this impromptu assembly, especially since the enemy force was earlier this afternoon ascertained to have evacuated from Tucson. Had some aspect of their previous marching suddenly become a threat to the Battalion? A review of the past five days' march seemed to indicate such was not the case but, except for the commander himself, who could know for certain?

On December 12 their march had carried them generally north by northwest and time and again they had been forced by the terrain to cross and re-cross the San Pedro River. It was during the morning hours that they passed the ruins of some old Spanish buildings and a fortification. Though they remained keenly alert because an element of possible peril seemed to be hovering, no enemy had been found there.[181]

Leroux and others of the Battalion's guides returned from an exploration of the tableland to the west and brought with them the welcome news that twenty miles distant, on a trail leading toward Tucson, they had found water. Other news they brought was not so encouraging: They had found a party of Apache Indians and Mexicans distilling mescal into whiskey and, with circumspect questioning, learned of the presence of a force of at least 200 Mexicans stationed at Tucson and that they had two cannon. Leroux, however, was certain they could be frightened off and convinced Cooke to send ahead to Tucson their interpreter, assistant surgeon and scout, Dr. Stephen C. Foster, on a dangerous mission with a concocted tale.

"I want you to tell the Mexican commander at Tucson," Cooke directed Foster, "that a large army of Americans has been detected en route to California, that its front guard is comprised of about three hundred sixty men and that if this advance stops to drill, it is simply to provide enough time for the main army to overtake them; that the Mexican commander could judge the strength of that army by the size of its advance guard. If you don't return by the end of the time framework I've outlined to you, it will be understood you are being held prisoner at Tucson."

Dr. Foster had left at once, but ominously had not returned with the guides and there was no choice remaining then but to assume he had been taken prisoner. In that regard, Cooke quickly had a Special Order drawn up and posted for the Battalion:

> *Camp on the San Pedro—December 13th, 1846*
> *Thus far on our course we have followed the guides furnished us by the General. These guides now point to Tucson, a garrisoned town, as our road, and assert that any other course is a hundred miles out of the way and over a trackless wilderness of mountains, rivers and hills. We will march, then, to Tucson. We came not to make war on Sonora, and less still to destroy an important outpost of defense against the Indians; but we will take the straight road before us and overcome all resistance. But shall I remind you that the American soldier ever shows justice and kindness to the unarmed and unresisting? The property of individuals you will hold sacred. The people of Sonora are not our enemies.*
> By order of LIEUT COL. COOKE,<br>[signed] P.C. Merrill, Adjutant

In view of this order issued nearly at noon, the Mormon Battalion, which had assembled with some confusion, accepted without grumbling the prospect that they might actually have to fight in Tucson. The men were issued up to twenty cartridges apiece for their rifles and the weapons were promptly cleaned, the men themselves mustered and drilled once again, this time by the commander himself, in loading and firing. A sense of excitement abruptly swept through the Battalion, which caused Pvt. Azariah Smith of Company B to scribble hastily in his diary that the afternoon muster

> *...was somewhat awkward which made the Colonel swear very much.*[182]

The following day the Battalion, as ordered by Cooke, left the Rio San Pedro and struck out on a course at first near due west and before long were traveling through terrain that was bare of timber and the ground itself of a decidedly yellow cast.[183] They soon struck a trail leading toward Tucson, at which point Cooke selected a detachment of fifty men, whom he personally led forward past his own front guard and soon encountered good water, where they also found five Mexican soldiers cutting grass. Their horses were staked nearby, saddled and armed, but Cooke ignored them, easing the concerns of the Mexicans. Casual conversation with the Mexican sergeant in charge revealed that Cooke's plan was evidently working well: Rumor of a large approaching force of American soldiers had reached Tucson and the town was in something of an uproar. As Sgt. Tyler wrote in his journal:

> *Of course, the Colonel, who was possessed of generalship as well as discipline, took no pains to disabuse their minds, and thus expose our little army to unnecessary peril. Indians who had seen us in the distance had largely overestimated our numbers, and this served to impress the people of Sonora with the truth of the statement made by guides.*
>
> *The Colonel also learned from the Mexican sergeant that the commander of the garrison had orders from the governor not to allow an armed force to pass through the town without resistance. A message was, therefore, sent to the commander by this same Sergeant that the people need not be alarmed, as we were their friends, we would do them no harm but would simply purchase some supplies and pass on.*

Concerned for the safety of Dr. Foster and to guarantee his release, Cooke had four Mexican dragoons taken prisoner, then sent one of them to the presidio with an offer to release the other three in exchange for Foster being set free by midnight. The ploy worked very well; the doctor was brought to Cooke at close to midnight by two officers, one of whom said he was authorized to make a special armistice. Cooke readily released the hostages and prepared to head into Tucson on the morrow.

The Battalion was led by Cooke into Tucson yesterday, December 16, arriving there just after noon and finding the place to be nothing more than an outpost for control of the Indians. The Saints were half-expecting to be attacked, but the Mexican garrison had cleared out during the night and most of the inhabitants had fled as well, leaving much property behind. At the town's edge the companies were formed into line and Cooke addressed them briefly, sternly repeating his order about meddling with private property and threatening to punish any who failed to observe his edict. The entire Battalion then moved into the town and, as Pvt. Bigler remarked in his diary:

> ...Only a few old people and the infirm were left, and they were scared almost to death. The place looked delightful to see: the green wheat, the fruit trees, swine running about, and fowls. It was music to hear the crowing of the cocks. I suppose the reason was, we had been so long without seeing such things. There were two mills for grinding grain by mule or jackass power. The top stone revolving just as fast as the mule was of a mind to travel.

Without pause, the Battalion then marched completely through the town, which they found to be quite clearly an island of Spanish colonization much in need of repair and isolated in a region controlled by hostile Apaches. The Americans confiscated whatever public property could be found as they passed, mainly some tobacco and about 2,000 bushels of wheat, but did not touch private property. Possession of the fort—from which its garrison of 130 men with two brass cannon had fled to the nearby Mission San Xavier del Bac—was taken without any opposition and the town itself was found to have a population of about five hundred, composed mostly of soldiers and their families.

Now, after marching some eight miles out of Tucson today and having stopped at a fine water source, the Battalion awaited with a certain uneasiness to learn why their commander had assembled them for an announcement even before camp was established. They were not kept uninformed for very long. With his usual directness, Lt. Col, Cooke addressed his entire command in words clear to every man.

"This place," he said, "is not our stopping place for the night. It is, in fact, more our beginning place for a difficult passage. This water source you see here is, according to our guides, the last water that will be available for at least the next forty miles. As soon as dismissal is ordered, all troops are to drink from the source to their own full capacity. Each man, without exception, will then fill his canteen, being certain to cap it tightly. Once this is accomplished, what few livestock we have—*every animal without exception*—is to be watered until it can drink no more. With those matters seen to, we will be marching out immediately and continue throughout the remainder of the night."

He paused and let his gaze sweep across the entire Battalion for a long moment, then continued with words that hammered home in the ears of every listener: "The possibility exists that there may not be a sufficiency of water available to replenish us even then. Therefore, the water in your canteens is to be considered your salvation, to be conserved to the utmost, to be drunk in the greatest moderation and to be made to last for as long as possible. To conserve bodily fluids, we will march by night and lay by under canvas cover during the day.

"What lies ahead of us," he concluded, "is not pleasant, but neither is it impossible. I intend for us—*every single man and beast of us*—to get through this all with nothing worse to be undergone than possibly some thirsty discomfort."

He stared at them sternly for a long moment and then seemed to relax from the tenseness that had been gripping him. The faintest trace of a smile touched his lips and he dipped his head slightly. Though he spoke more softly now, his concluding words carried clearly to every ear.

"Good luck, men. We will all need it."

[December 25, 1846 • Friday • Daybreak]

Throughout the night, once the Christmas Eve festivities in the White House were completed and the multitude of guests at last all gone, President James Knox Polk had labored uninterrupted at his desk. Most of such labors had been cerebral rather than physical, but no less exhausting for that. Now, as dawn began streaking the sky over Washington, D.C., he bent again to the task of writing the proposal he planned to present to Congress when it reconvened following the Holidays.

Things had not been going well in halls of the Democracy over the past few weeks: Plans Polk had instigated and nurtured had soured, undermining both his own disposition and that of Congress toward him; the war with Mexico had become tedious and was no longer a fuse igniting fires of patriotic enthusiasm among the citizenry and Congress alike; criticism of his administration was becoming far more vocal, far more demanding; nothing he initiated seemed to coalesce as he had initially assumed and the frustrations had made him irascible at best.

It had all begun going downhill for Polk when it became public knowledge that he had used a major portion of the war funds appropriated to him to bring America's arch enemy, General Santa Ana, out of exile in Cuba and foster his resumption of power in Mexico, all in the misguided supposition the Latin-American general would live up to his secret agreements with Polk and the war could be quickly ended. That, of course, had not occurred and rumors of the President's complicity in Santa Ana's restoration to power—rumors unproven but severely damaging, nonetheless—continued to cause an erosion of public faith in Government generally and in Polk specifically.

The news, early in December, that Santa Ana had learned of General Zachary Taylor's ambitions toward the U.S. presidency and was steadily amassing a succession of minor victories against the Mexicans that promoted those aims, had caused Santa Ana to raise a new army of 20,000 troops in Mexico City. The additional fact that General Winfield Scott had similar ambitions and was presently honing a plan to capture and occupy Vera Cruz and open a massive assault from there into the very heart of Mexico, caused Santa Ana to hasten north out of Mexico City with his troops to confront and repel Taylor before Scott could make his move, and then move swiftly to bolster the Vera Cruz defenses and defeat Scott as well.

The public approbation General Taylor had won for his victories was, to Polk, ominous news. Taylor was, after all, a Whig, not a Democrat and his ascendancy could well mark the beginning of the end of governmental control being in the hands of the Democrats. That was when Polk had begun undermining Taylor's Mexican accomplishments and sending him orders that took him out of the limelight. The only logical choice for Taylor's replacement seemed to be General Scott and this was what Polk had been banking on, until Scott, who had maintained political neutrality, abruptly made clear his own ambitions toward the Presidency...and he, too, as a Whig.

For Polk, the dilemma now was all but overwhelming. With Taylor already aiming for the Presidency as a Whig, with Scott poised to do precisely the same, also as a Whig, with Congress in growing opposition to support of the War with Mexico, and with the American public confused about everything, but weary of the war and beginning to lean away from the Democrats, the immediate future prospects for Polk and his party clearly were dimming daily.

The only saving grace for the Party lately, it seemed, was the fact that since the end of the past summer, the country's finances had improved both rapidly and considerably. The United States, through no doing of its own, had benefited enormously from Ireland's famine, which swiftly brought farm prices not only back to their pre-1837 levels, but actually exceeded them, and the substantially increased export of cereal grains had created a shipping boom. Whether the American public approved of the war or not, wartime manufacturing had sent the American economy soaring.

The fact that Congress had adjourned in little short of chaos simply reflected the country's prevailing emotions; the public was deciding they really did not want a war and, in particular, they didn't want a continuing and expensive war with neighboring Mexico. The Second Session of the Twenty-Ninth Congress had been convened in political chaos and it accurately reflected the confusion reigning in the public mind, when election time came, for the vote clearly undermined the certainty of political interpreters of the Twenty-ninth Congress and, as a result, they not only did *not* increase the power of the Democrats, they voted the Whigs into a House majority for the Thirtieth Congress. Thus far that had done little good and only served to emphasize the greater insufficiencies of the Polk administration.[184]

John C. Calhoun, as leader of political revolution in the United States, was convinced there was only one way to save the country, desperate though the device might be: The U.S. simply had to be reborn as, in his estimation, the whole direction of the country had been wrong since June of 1788. As he thundered to Congress: "We must go back to the preceding September, reconvene the Constitutional Convention that then adjourned *sine die*, and start all over. If we do not, the consequences are grave. As the esteemed Ralph Waldo Emerson has said: 'The United States will conquer Mexico, but it will be as the man swallows the arsenic which brings him down in turn. Mexico will poison us.'"

For the moment, in Polk's view, while he found the notion of success by any Whig general distasteful, Scott was presently the lesser of two evils. The President realized only too clearly that since he had been unable to bribe or buy a victory through his cloaked dealings with Santa Ana, he had to reassess what remained. In view of the fact that peripheral campaigns had thus far virtually given him all of the West, as well as all the principal Mexican seaports with the exception of Vera Cruz, plus a strip of territory in northern Mexico, he was at a loss to understand why the Mexican government adamantly refused to submit. With such conquests as already provided by General Taylor, Polk had been convinced nothing further need be done except sit back and await Mexico's capitulation. That hadn't occurred and by the beginning of this month it had become clear to him such a "wait and take" policy was not working, that it was shaping, instead, into a much longer war and a longer war was something the nation simply wouldn't tolerate.

What this meant was that Polk found himself now with no recourse but to step up the national war effort and strongly support a decisive campaign for Mexico's reduction. Reluctantly then, Polk finally approved Scott's rather grandiose plan to reduce San Juan de Ulua and progress into Mexico's heartland from Vera Cruz, with the capture of Mexico City and total Mexican capitulation the ultimate goal.

Polk had already all but exhausted any hope of getting the military into safely Democratic control. While it was clear to the President that a campaign of such scope was well beyond the talents of General Zachary Taylor, it simultaneously fed the rapidly blooming political ambitions of General Winfield Scott, who was a highly trained soldier. With little choice remaining to him, President Polk's intention now was to throttle Scott's insipient insubordination and keep him in line with a set of instructions that minced no words in their conclusion: "If you win, it will be a victory for the administration; if you lose, the responsibility will be yours alone and no one will share it with you."

Pleased with his own solution, Polk believed he was severely undermining Taylor in his bid for the Presidency and, at the same time, with ample grounds for the conclusion, convinced himself that he could prevent Scott's candidacy from blossoming any further. This would require some very careful maneuvering, but it could be accomplished because of Scott's recent laboring at his job. The fact that the current war effort had not broken down altogether was because of Scott's success through the man who worked closely with him, Secretary of War William Marcy. Marcy had been appointed to his Cabinet post for past services rendered, but the situation with Mexico had surprisingly transformed him into a top-notch Secretary of War, who could now be cultivated as a distinct asset to Scott's escalating ambition.

President Polk's ace-in-the-hole, however, at least to his own way of thinking, relied upon his own personal cultivation of a never-before-experienced accord that had developed this past fall between himself and his former adversary, the U.S. Senator from Missouri, Democrat Thomas Hart Benton. The proposal Polk was carefully drafting this Christmas night was that Congress revive the rank of lieutenant general, which—if Congress did so—Polk could then bestow that title upon Benton, effectively advancing him in rank over either Taylor or Scott. This would neatly result in an appointment not only of economical value to the country, which the public would appreciate, but it would simultaneously prevent the Whigs from grasping a military command victory and also effectively undermine the Democratic Party's Van Buren faction, which would undoubtedly please just about everyone.

At least that was the current belief of President James Polk.

*[December 25, 1846 • Friday • 9:00 a.m.]*

Lt. Col. John Charles Fremont, slowly but surely leading his California Battalion down the length of coastal California, had as yet encountered no real difficulties but, as always, he was taking no chances. The messages he had received just outside Sutters Fort had informed him that the Los Angeles area—and perhaps certain areas north of that, too, had been overtaken by the Mexicans under General Flores—or was it General Andreas Pico, or maybe José Castro?—and the situation was not good.

The urgency of the message received from General Kearny that his force had suffered badly in the battle at San Pascual and ordering Fremont to bring his irregular force swiftly was largely ignored except for Fremont's reassertion which said, in essence, he was under command of Commodore Stockton, who was now the self-appointed commander of California Territory and who was, insofar as Fremont was concerned, the American commander-in-chief.

Now, this Christmas morning, Fremont uncharacteristically benevolent to his troops, allowed them this day free of marching or seeking trouble. They had passed San Luis Obispo yesterday and were struck by a severe rainstorm just as they stopped to make camp last evening. It was only with great difficulty that tents were erected, as the violent winds were extremely difficult to combat and it was well into the night before shelters were ready. Even then, the men were very wet and uncomfortable and only a few campfires were successfully ignited. Some, such as Edwin Bryant, stripped themselves of every vestige of clothing and attempted to dry their garb overnight, though without much success.

Fremont's men sat gloomily in soggy tents and contemplated past Christmases that had been much better. Under such conditions, it was not at all surprising that there were few among them who offered or received the traditional American greeting of "Merry Christmas."

*[December 25, 1846 • Christmas Day • 5:00 p.m.]*

This had not begun as a very pleasant Christmas Day for the Missouri troops under command of General Alexander Doniphan. They had thought they might have an opportunity to celebrate Christmas to some degree as most of them had always previously celebrated it, with better than usual food, with rest and relaxation, overlain with a prevailing sense of serenity and Divinity. Such had not quite been the case. Instead, this evening they found themselves embroiled in an overblown skirmish with Mexican troops that some were already, somewhat grandiosely, calling the Battle of El Brazito.

While preparing to merge with General Wool near Chihuahua, the Doniphan force had made a detour, just over a month ago, to the Zuni Pueblo where, on November 23, they'd made a treaty with them and expected no further trouble from that quarter. They were disappointed to learn as well, however, that at the same time the Navajo, who had agreed to follow them back to the Rio Grande, had turned back when met by a group of unidentified "cousins," who convinced them Doniphan's agreement was a ruse and that he planned to massacre them.

A disturbing number of Doniphan's men had died while they were in the Indian country and others had sickened, though not through his fault; orders had directed him on his march but without providing him the proper preparation time and so they had experienced considerable difficulty, with supplies inadequate to their needs, their food both poor and sparse and with precious little shelter from the elements.

Back among his various detachments holding their positions between Socorro and Santa Fe, Doniphan learned that Wool's force, while on its march to Chihuahua, had been diverted to join General Taylor's command at Parras, once again leaving Doniphan's force in a sort of limbo. There was, however, one bright spot: Doniphan was finally able, on December 12, to provide his men with the $42 clothing allowance he had expected to have for them in May. It was the first pay they'd received for their service thus far and eased considerably the tension that had been rising among them.

The on-again, off-again march of Doniphan's force was abruptly on-again when he received orders on that same day to once again head his force of 856 effectives toward a union with General Wool, just as before, at Chihuahua. He had set off with his force at once, at the same time directing Col. Price in Santa Fe to forward to him his artillery, which was still on hold there but which Price, abruptly assailed with rumors of revolt, was loathe to let go.

Doniphan immediately began preparing for the campaign with Wool. Under such conditions and with the Chihuahua invasion again imminent, Doniphan abandoned the regulation forbidding him to requisition food and supplies from the inhabitants. If his army were to be judged on appearance alone, the general reasoned, it would not fare well: most of the original uniforms the men had worn were now in absolute shreds; some of the troops had bought pieces of clothing from natives or traders and others acquired buckskins from the Navajos. The foraging parties Doniphan now sent out did, in fact, sign receipts for all they took, but they also confiscated whatever they wanted, bringing in several hundred head of beef cattle and a few thousand sheep. If nothing else, they reasoned, from now on they'd eat regularly and well. A small amount of gunpowder was brought in, too, as well as a paltry few medical supplies. It was not, however, under any conceivable measurement, a fairly well supplied army.

Doniphan reasoned that if his force was to encounter opposition anywhere along the way, it would most likely originate from where the Rio Grande would break through the mountains to the high plains, close to the ancient bastion of El Camino Real near the town of El Paso del Norte. It was on December 12 that Doniphan set his advance guard of three hundred, under Major Gilpin, on its move and followed up with the rest of his command in two sections over the next six days, but irked that the traders and camp followers at Valverde quickly packed up their goods and followed close behind.

The first news of enemy activity occurred on December 19, when a trembling Mexican non-combat civilian—believed to be reliable—came rushing past and paused only long enough to impart to General Doniphan the news that had allegedly sent him into flight: Major Gilpin's entire advance unit had been captured and sent as prisoners to Chihuahua and now a force of seven hundred determined Mexican dragoons was marching to intercept the remainder of Doniphan's army. As the Mexican hurried on his way, Doniphan shook his head and muttered, as much to himself as to his aide: "I do not, by God, believe one word of it. Nevertheless, alert the company commanders to be prepared, just in case."

As Doniphan suspected, the story proved false when Gilpin's force united with Doniphan's again at Doña Ana, having encountered no Mexican military whatever. That Doniphan's unit was being spied upon by individuals at a distance became obvious last night, but the Americans soon became scornful of any possibility of their betokening a larger force. It was Christmas Eve and, though Doniphan ordered the army's weapons be inspected and further gunpowder issued, the night patrols encountered no trace of an enemy in force. Alertness was by this time so dulled that this morning—Christmas morning—no sense of impending danger remained and the scouts were directed to precede the marchers no farther ahead than was normal.

The army was in fine fettle and greeted this Christmas Day with exuberance, firing their guns skyward and taking up the march, accompanied by band music, in high spirits. The increasing lackadaisical air that had become noticeable among them yesterday, was even more pronounced this morning. Much of the stock had scattered by daybreak and so when the day's march was begun, Doniphan's train and a third of his regiment was strung out for miles behind. The marchers sang songs and traded ribaldry with one another and finally General Doniphan called an early halt after only eighteen miles and camp was established at a place called El Brazito, about thirty miles distant from El Paso.[185]

The troops, overjoyed at the easy day's march and early stop, whooped with joy and then set off to water their mounts and collect firewood. All were impressed with the beautiful white stallion the scouts had brought in during the day and now General Doniphan and several of his officers spread a blanket on the ground and gambled in a game of Loo for possession of the animal. Doniphan was winning when he glanced up and saw a force of Mexicans establishing a battle line half a mile distant and instantly he ordered a general alarm. Evidently not at all inclined to participate, the white stallion pulled free and sped off to parts unknown.

The Mexican force, rather resplendent in dashing new uniforms and led by a temporary general named Ponce de León—larger than Doniphan's army and, of course, much fresher—had ridden out from El Paso del Norte.[186] Their banner, borne by an officer who came forward to invite Doniphan to surrender, displayed two skulls and the words *Libertad o murte!*—Liberty or Death! Not surprisingly, the American general refused the invitation with very special and uncomplimentary words inspired by the occasion and sent the crestfallen Mexican officer back to his commander.

The delay while all this was occurring had allowed time for at least a portion of Doniphan's men to come shouting back to the scene and they assembled quite enthusiastically into a rather ragged defensive line comprised of about four hundred men, rifles at ready. The Mexican force, evidently dismayed that the Americans had not immediately submitted, advanced no closer but began lobbing two-pound howitzer shots at them, their cannonballs loaded with copper slugs. This they followed up with rifle fire at the Americans from their whole line, enthusiastically but disconnectedly and, because of the distance, with phenomenally poor effect.

A squad of men from Doniphan's Company G of the First Missouri, annoyed by the howitzer firing at their flank, raced out with wild cries, captured the gun and brought it back amid the whooping and hollering and cheering of their fellows. The Missourians were finally getting their first long-anticipated taste of action against a bona fide enemy and they were positively reveling in it.

At length the Mexican infantry and lancers alike broke into a trot and charged toward the American line, firing as they came and filling the air with their own version of battle cries. Doniphan steadily ordered his men to lie down and prepare, but hold their fire. When the Mexican charge finally reached a point about a hundred yards distant, Doniphan gave the order to fire and two separate volleys stopped the charging Mexicans as cold as if they'd run into a wall. The enemy infantry at once spun around and began running off, except for one formation of a couple hundred lancers who veered to the American flank and tried to attack some of the wagons, where return fire was much less prevalent.

Captain Reid coolly got some twenty of his company mounted and led them in a charge that almost immediately broke the spirit of the lancers and sent them hightailing after their fleeing infantry. When it became obvious the Missourians' own weary mounts made pursuit pointless, Reid recalled his men and they returned in high spirits. Fortunately for all concerned, casualties were relatively light.

The entire battle, so called, had taken less than thirty minutes.

For their part, the Mexicans under General Ponce de León returned to El Paso and reported gloomily that the war was lost, that the Americans had won. It was an exaggeration, of course, and the war was far from over, but the American troops were highly elated with today's result and General Doniphan himself quickly sent off his report, listing forty-three

Mexicans known to be dead, 150 others wounded, the enemy force in shambles.

None of the Missourians had been killed and only seven slightly wounded, their injuries proudly flaunted before their less fortunate companions as trophies of battle. For the remainder of the day they argued companionable among themselves about who had accomplished the most as they swooped down on the abandoned Mexican supply wagons and confiscated their considerable stores of bread, boxes of quality cigars and a very large number of kegs of surprisingly excellent wine.

With those liberated benefits of the Battle of El Brazito, only a little belatedly, the First Missouri happily settled down to enjoy the remains of a Christmas Day that had started rather poorly but had turned out to be quite satisfying.

[December 25, 1846 • Christmas Day • Friday • 5:15 p.m.]

The Mormon Battalion encampment ordered by Lt. Col. Philip St. George Cooke this evening was not a festive one, even though it was the evening of Christmas Day. Few of the Saints even acknowledged it was Christmas and far fewer accorded it any sort of celebration, even though the fact they still survived had to be considered as some sort of minor miracle.

The final week prior to Christmas had been, for the entire Mormon Battalion, an effort that tried their very souls, a desperate battle with the insidious demon called thirst as they had trudged through ankle-deep sand across a trackless desert. When at last they reached the Gila River again on December 22, they were so weakened that any kind of enemy force could have quickly had its way with them; instead, fortuitously they had encountered a village of close to four thousand friendly Pima Indians. As Pvt. Sam Rogers of Company B noted in his diary:

> *Tues. 22. Last night a mule was drowned in the river. Off at the usual time the river here running west 10 miles, camped at noon in an Indian village. Saw a squaw suckling a papoose in a most singular manner, it was in a round basket with a hole in the side of the basket through which the child sucked as she held the basket under her arm. The squaws were naked except a breech clout. As soon as we camped the Indians, Squaws and Children all came into*

*camp with corn, beans, meal, dried and green pumpkin and bread to trade for Clothes or other articles. They have also water melons; the land appears very dry and barren. They have good horses and poneys* [sic]. *It is said that this tribe of Indians have never shed the blood of white men neither do they war with other Indian tribes but obtain their living by agriculture, having large farms.*

All the Saints seemed favorably impressed by the gentle humanness of the Pimas, a fact that became apparent in their writings. Pvt. Thomas Morris, also of Company B, wrote today in his journal:

*...Here, for the first time in my life, I was introduced to a tribe of Indians unadulterated by the immoralities of the civilized white population where there were drunkards. Here no degrading vulgarity, no pinching poverty, no tippling loafers, no prodigal aristocrats imposing taxes and titles on the communities.*

Sgt. Tyler wrote along the same lines in his journal:

*...On the 22nd, we marched ten miles and arrived at the Pima village, supposed to contain about 4,000 inhabitants. They were quite a large-sized, fine-looking race of people and very industrious and peaceable. They engaged in agriculture, and manufactured blankets and other fabrics by hand. The poison of the civilized asp is unknown among them, and our American and European cities would do well to take lessons in virtue and morality from these native tribes.*

*Long before we reached the village, we were met by the Indian women and children, many of whom were quite pretty and graceful, and walked generally by twos, with arms lovingly entwined around one another, presenting a picture of contentness and happiness that was very pleasing to look upon. Even our stern and matter-of-fact Colonel was not proof against their bewitching charms. In writing of them he says:* "One little girl particularly, by a fancied resemblance, interested me much; she was so joyous that she seemed very pretty and innocent; I could not resist tying on her head, as a turban, a bright new silk handkerchief, which I happened to wear to-day; the effect was beautiful to see—a picture of happiness!" *Kindness to the natives, by military officers, as manifested in several instances by Colonel Cooke, is so rare in this age, that this circumstance may be mentioned, as one of the note-worthy events of our journey.*

The observations of Pvt. Henry Bigler were equally penetrating in their portrayal of the Pimas:

*...their settlements extend down the river for twenty-five miles. The Chief turned over to the Colonel some mules and store goods that had been left in his charge by General Kearny for Cooke. The Chief said that some of the Mexicans had been to him representing them selves as being part of Cooke's command and wanted the goods, saying that the Colonel had sent for them, etc., but he said he did not believe it. He was glad we had come, for he believed we were the right men. These were fine-looking Indians. They said they did not fight and steal to get their living. They seemed to have plenty of corn, beans, pumpkins, some poultry. I saw a few cattle and a good many fine ponies, some mules, and jackasses. Our Colonel bought a beef from them. They brought into camp large quantities of corn and corn meal, wheat, and flour, also beans and squashes to trade for old shorts, old shoes, pants, vests, beads and buttons. They would not have [take from us] money. They said it was of no use to them. I saw their women grinding wheat by hand, the largest stone about fifteen inches by twenty, a little scooped. The grain was put into this and rubbed with another stone, about the same length and six inches wide. They raised cotton and manufactured it into blankets and breech-clouts.*

Lt. Col. Cooke was very taken by the simple and benevolent lifestyle of the Pimas and presented as a gift to their chief three pregnant ewes, which he hoped would encourage their culture of sheep both as a source of food and of wool. Before the Battalion moved on, Cooke paid a final brief visit to their chief in his house.

"I want to congratulate you," he said, "on having the most prosperous and happy tribe I have ever encountered. A bit of advice, however, as we leave: while you and your people are peaceful and never trouble your neighbors, be prepared for any emergency that might arise.

# The Infinite Dream

Be sure, as well, to resist any outside pressure that others may try to use against you."

The chief smiled at that and shook his head slightly. "Throughout our history," he replied, "we have resisted pressures brought against us by others who think to use us in some way as tools for their own needs. We have always resisted them in the past, just as now we resist them with you. We are, and always will be, our own people. We will not be changed in our ways." He paused a moment and then added with a wry smile, "Not even by such as you, as are considered friends."

The journey downstream along the Gila, was a very trying one for the men. Their mules, now only best described as "bags of bones", were becoming ever more useless in pulling the heavy wagons that Cooke was determined to transport into California, despite the strain it created for the men, who very often became virtually beasts of burden themselves as they strained to drag the wagons forward. It was here that Cooke came up with a plan that, at first, seemed ingenious. He ordered a number of the wagon-boxes lashed together to form a crude raft and, well loaded with their remaining food stores, had the men launch it on the Gila. His plan was to float it downriver by day and moor it for the night. However, as the army moved on ahead to the Colorado River, the barge became tightly lodged on a sand bar. Some of it was salvaged and back-packed but the majority was lost and it suddenly became a worry if they would ever again taste staple food.

During the night of December 23 and again last night, the Mormon Battalion camped at a village established by the Maricopa Indians, although calling it merely a village tended to grossly underestimate its size. Cooke estimated the population as being in excess of ten thousand and he assumed a deferential attitude in his dealings with their chief, Don José.

The Maricopas, who showed no indication of fearing the Americans, lived largely in dome-shaped structures ranging from twenty to fifty feet in diameter, thatched with corn stalks and straw. Their animals included horses, oxen, mules, dogs and Spanish fowls and they were well stocked with hoes, shovels, rakes, axes and harrows. They were also scrupulously honest.

Having learned from his guides that the river ahead made a gigantic loop, the general today ordered the Battalion away from the river, to travel in a straight-line southwest course around some mountains and over a heavily sandy area where marching was extremely difficult but by which they would have to march only forty miles that would have required over a hundred if the river were followed closely. Marching forty miles through a blistering desert, however, was a difficult matter indeed and they only finished half of it by nightfall.

A similar march of twenty miles of desert lay before them for the morrow and a fair number of the Saints believed they simply would not be able to make it. Small wonder, then, as the Battalion established its camp for this night of December 25, there was little of Christmas cheer evident in any of them.

*[December 31, 1846 • Thursday]*

The year 1846 came to its conclusion at midnight as essentially cheerless for any of the migrating Mormons as its previous days and weeks and months had already been.

For Brigham Young and many of his homeless, drifting Mormon families, a temporary surcease from their long march was a relief, though it hardly betokened an end to the tribulations that had plagued them throughout the year. All had finally departed from Nauvoo, crossed the Mississippi and left behind them permanently the terrorizations inflicted upon them by the Illinoisans, who had driven them out.

The majority of the Saints were now clustered on the west bank of the Missouri, already undergoing a frightful winter that had yet only begun, but there were still a great many who had not yet reached that point and their miserable camps stretched nearly the length of Iowa. Such camps lacked the fundamental necessities for survival, each plagued by sickness and suffering, each struggling against whatever elements of weather and misfortune could possibly befall them, problems both pervasive and persistent.

The Iowa prairies were abundant with rattlesnakes that terrified the walkers and occasionally struck at the steadily weakening legs of the oxen that thudded past, sickening many, killing as many more. They were still hundreds of miles east of where great wild herds of bison could supply them with meat. The smaller animals—the varieties of fowl as well as rabbits and woodchucks and ground squirrels, prairie dogs, opossums and raccoons, either went into estivation or migrated or were quickly depleted. Each camp of the Saints became its own hospital where far too many of the weak, the sick and the aged barely clung to a life that had become a living torment. All of these Latter-day Saints were struggling to ward off illness, starvation and death; far too many were failing in their efforts.

That large numbers of these pilgrims, despite such odds, despite being drained of the prime of their menfolk, continued to persevere—continued to believe in their chosen God and, even more, in their own self-proclaimed chosen prophets who, Moses-like, were leading them to a new and more permanent Zion—was a tribute to the incredible depth and strength of their faith.

Many of the Mormon groups had separated into bands that, while adhering to their beliefs, sought various ways of maintaining themselves during the self-imposed migration. The band being led by Captain John Pitt was only one such, but exemplary of the majority, stopping to work where work was available, earning a living where such earning was possible, and, if all else failed, begging from the gentiles the means of survival. That band, even after a rigorous day's march of eight miles, established a campsite and, while the women prepared the evening meal, the remaining old men and boys split one hundred thirty rails before dark, traded these to a farmer for corn and then actually gave a concert during the evening.

They played their instruments every evening, wherever the gentiles might be or would gather; played their fiddles and jew's-harps and mandolins and mouth organs and drums; sang their ballads or folksongs or hymns and, though they didn't actually dance themselves, they strummed out their dance tunes and quadrilles, their minuets or their hoedowns, all for whatever fee could be gleaned from such audience. This might be a half-dozen or more bushels of corn, or a gallon or two of milk or honey, or five or six or seven dollars in cash in areas where the gentile parsons opposed them, or perhaps twenty-five dollars and meals for everyone at another place and even, from villages of awed and admiring Indians, meals or skins or vessels.

They studied en route as well, their Apostles calling them together in large or small groups: Studying together the mysteries of life and of death; learning of their religion's founder, Joseph Smith and his teachings; damning to eternity those who slew him and his brother; children and adults alike learning their alphabet and arithmetic, their logic and oratory and religion.

They learned to do all that was required of them to survive, and then even more; learning new skills from others and passing on their own skills to those of their brethren who would learn. And, depending on circumstance and where they happened to be, they labored incessantly for their Lord God. And when they settled down in any one place for a while, they established semi-permanent farms and smitherys, dug wells and privies, fashioned nails, tanned hides, turned bad wood into good charcoal, learned to shape oxbows in temporary wagon shops and made harnesses and reins and plaited ropes and bullwhips, always working together and depending upon one another.

They hired themselves out for any job at any time for any wage and thanked their God for the opportunity to do so, if and when such opportunity transpired. They learned to deal placidly with gentiles who were friendly, or cautiously with those who were cool or suspicious, or even with those who were openly hostile; learned to make examples of themselves with their skills and their honesty and their ethic of working hard and long and steadily for whatever was earned.

The leading portion of the migrating Mormons had reached the Missouri River on June 14, and those who were among the last to arrive there—even though many others had set up temporary camps—finally reached Winter Quarters on November 27. They brought with them frailty and sickness and most especially respiratory diseases—influenza, pneumonia and whooping cough—that killed many of the children and aged. They fought, often unsuccessfully, that form, of scurvy they called "black canker" and they underwent waves of diphtheria and typhus and plain old septic sore throat; malnutrition was as common as the common cold.

By far, however, the most pervasive, persistent and persevering aspect of this massive migration of the Mormons throughout 1846 was *faith*: An absolute faith in their God, Jehovah, in their prophet, Brigham Young, and in themselves. The Promised Land was out there somewhere and no matter what else might occur, their faith would lead them to it.[187]

Where the Mormon Battalion itself was concerned, at least now it seemed to the majority that the end of their long cross-country march was nearing, as was the term of their enlistment. What would occur at that point was a significant uncertainty and only one matter remained paramount in the minds of most: Almost to a man, they wished to return to their dependants at the earliest opportunity and by the simplest and most direct route. In the meanwhile, there were still some very knotty problems facing them. By runners, Lt. Col. Cooke maintained as close a contact as possible with General Kearny, but that was all too often easier said than done. As Cooke wrote in his letter of December 17 to Kearny:

> ...I remained in camp the next day, December 16. There was very little grass, and I fed my mules, cattle and sheep, on the wheat (and brought off enough for two more days in the adjoining desert.) That day, to cover some small parties of mule hunters, I made a reconnaissance, with about sixty men, marching halfway to an Indian village, ten miles off, where the enemy were stationed. (I intended attacking him under favorable circumstances, but the path led me through a dense mesquit [sic] forest, very favorable to an ambush. I learned, however, that this demonstration caused him to continue his retreat.)
>
> The garrison attempted to force all the inhabitants to leave the town with them. Some of them returned whilst I lay there, and I took pains that all should be treated with kindness. The day I arrived there, a detachment of twenty-five men, who had been posted at the Pimos [Pima village], to observe or harrass my march, having been sent for by express, passed unobserved, round a mountain, near town, and joined the main body. (I afterward learned that they had made a threatening demand for the mules and goods left for me with the Indian chief. He refused, and expressed his determination to resist, by force, any attempt to take them.) On leaving, I sent to its late commander, Capt. Comaduran, by a citizen messenger, a letter for the governor of Sonora, (and I afterward received an answer that it would be transmitted.) It is appended. All things considered, I thought it a proper course to take toward a reputed popular governor of a State, believed to be disgusted and disaffected, to the imbecile central government. It was intimated to me, whilst in Tueson [sic], that if I would march toward the capital of the department, I would be joined by sufficient numbers to effect a revolution...

Having found the Mexican military command absent from Tucson upon his arrival, and before marching from the town, Cooke left a message in Spanish to the commander of the presidio and a letter to be delivered to the governor of Sonora, which he penned later that same day. In his letter to Commander Comaduran at Tucson, he wrote:

# The Infinite Dream

*Battalion Headquarters*          *Camp at Tueson [sic], Sonora,*
*December 18, 1846*

Sir: Having received no orders, or entertained an intention to make war upon Sonora, I regret that circumstances have compelled me to break up your quarters at this post. Making forced marches for the want of watering places, and finding no grass or other forage here, I have found it necessary to use about thirty fanegas of wheat from the public granary. None has been wasted or destroyed, and no other public property has been seized. Herewith you will receive a letter for his excellency, the governor of Sonora, on the subject of my involuntary invasion of the state. I respectfully request that you send it to him with your own dispatches.

           With high respect, your obedient servant,
           P. St. Geo. Cooke, Lieutenant-colonel
           Commanding battalion U.S. volunteers

To Don Antonio Comaduran,
Commandante, Presidio of Tueson [sic]

Immediately upon completing that letter, Cooke wrote in a more conciliatory manner to the governor of Sonora:

           *Camp at Tucson, Sonora, December 18, 1846*
Your Excellency: The undersigned, marching in command of a battalion of United States infantry from New Mexico to California, has found it convenient for the passage of his wagon train to cross the frontier of Sonora. Having passed within fifteen miles of Fronteras, I have found it necessary to take this presidio in my route to the Gila.

Be assured that I did not come as an enemy of the people whom you govern: they have received only kindness at my hands.

Sonora refused to contribute to the support of the present war against my country: alleging the excellent reasons that all her resources were necessary to her defence [sic] from the incessant attack of savages; that the Central government gave her no protection, and was therefore entitled to no support. To this might have been added that Mexico supports a war upon Sonora.

For I have seen New Mexicans within her boundary trading for the spoil of her people, taken by murderous cowardly indians who *attack only to lay waste, rob, and fly to the mountains; and I have certain information that this is the practice of many years; thus, one part of Mexico allies itself against another.*[188] *The unity of Sonora with the States of the north—now her neighbours,—is necessary effectually to subdue the Parthian Apaches.*

*Meanwhile I make a wagon road from the streams of the Atlantic to the Pacific Ocean, through the valuable plains & mountains rich with minerals, of Sonora: this, I trust, will prove useful to the Citizens of either republic, who if not more closely* [be observed], *may unite in the pursuits of a highly beneficial commerce.*

*With Sentiments of Esteem & respect, I am your Excy's most obt.*
*Servt.*

| | |
|---|---|
| *To His Excy.* | [signed] *P. St. Geo. Cooke* |
| *Sn. Dn. Manuel Gandara* | *Lt. Colonel* |
| *Governor of Sonora, Ures Sa.* | *Comdg. U.S. Forces.* |

Continuing his previous report to General Kearny, Lt. Col. Cooke wrote:

*On the 17th, I marched late, as I did not expect to find water. At 8 o'clock, P.M., I encamped 24 miles from Tueson* [sic], *with no water or grass. Ten or fifteen miles further there is a little water, in a mountain, close to the road, but it could not be found.*

*On the 18th the command resumed its journey. At the end of seven miles, the mules were watered. This was the last water for a considerable distance, as the stream sank at that place. We traveled about three miles down the dry bed, and found the sand very heavy. Our progress, after leaving the bed of the stream, although over level clay ground, was frequently obstructed by mezquit* [sic] *thickets. We made camp without water at 9 p.m., having traveled twenty-four miles. The mules were tied up and fed grain.*

*Struggling, worn-out, famishing men came into camp at all hours of the night and the rear guard did not reach camp until near daylight, and I marched, the second day, thirty miles, and, at 9 P.M., again encamped, without water; but the men, about sundown, had a drink from a small puddle, too shallow for the water to be dipped with a cup.*

It was not until close to noon on December 20 that the advance unit found several rainwater pools and camped. At that point several groups of men took somewhat refreshed mules and full canteens and made their way back to relieve their companions, many of whom had faltered and lain down and would undoubtedly have died had such relief not returned for them. All were saved, but stragglers continued coming in to camp for the remainder of the day and well into the night. As Pvt. Bigler wrote of it:

> *The next morning, being the twentieth, we found some of the mules were dead, and it was most impossible to get some of the teams along, and no wonder, for they had neither grass or water for two days. The country seemed to be as dry as an oven, not a piece of grass to be seen anywhere....we marched but a short distance, when we were met by one of the guides with the welcome news that about two miles and a half ahead were seven holes or ponds of water, sufficient for the whole army. As we made up to those ponds, another guide came up and reported that about one and a half miles farther on our course, he had found plenty of water and grass. We rolled up to this last spot and encamped, making this day about eight or nine miles.*

It was on the following day—the twenty-first—that the Battalion's march took them to the Gila River again and here, where once more they encountered the trace of General Kearny's passage some five weeks earlier, they halted.[189] Almost immediately they began being visited by hordes of Pima Indians, some two thousand of them, who were very curious about the Battalion, but very polite. While the Battalion's property was exposed and could easily have been stolen, not a piece was touched and mountain man Pauline Weaver, who had been this way and encountered these people years before, said "Honestest bunch I ever met up with. These fellers are so honest they once followed us up for half a day, just to restore some lost property to its owner. They're good people!"

In continuing his report to General Kearny, Lt. Col. Cooke wrote:

> *...The next day [December 21], I found it ten miles to the Gila, at a small grass bottom, above the Pimo [sic] villages. The mules were forty-eight hours without water; the men marched twenty-six*

*of thirty-six consecutive hours, and sixty-two miles in rather more than two days, (in one of which no meat ration was issued).*

*Thus the 90 miles of the guides turned out to be 128 to the village, 57 miles nearer than the reputed distance by the San Pedro. Excepting four or five miles, the road was excellent; but over a true desert. There is, however, a better watered road from Tueson [sic], which strikes the Gila higher up. I believe this route can be well taken for six months in the year; and, like that much of the road on this side, it is impassable in summer, unless for travelers. It is a great gold district, rich mines have been discovered in many of the mountains in view; but it is so barren and destitute of water that even a mining popu-lation can scarcely occupy it.*

*About eight o'clock we took up our line of march, and in the afternoon encamped on the banks of the Gila River, where the Pimas came out by the hundreds to see us. They said the Spanish had been there and wanted them to unite with them and give us battle, and promised the Indians, if they would, they should have all the spoil. But the Pima Chief said he told them his men should not fight, that they never had shed the blood of any white man, and for this reason he was not affrighted at the coming army and had no objections to us passing through their towns. Our Colonel bought one hundred bushels of corn for his teams. At this place we intersected General Kearny's trail, where he had come down the Gila with packs.*

Lt. Col. Cooke then discussed in considerable detail the visit of the Mormon Battalion with the Pima Indians. When that portion was finally concluded, he moved on to his receiving General Kearny's instructions, written to him from Warner's Ranch in California and brought to him by the messenger named Francisco. Cooke continued:

*...he brought with him seven mules found on the Gila; and, altogether, I obtained at the villages, twenty, which had belonged to the dragoons. They were not sufficiently recruited to be of much service. I traded the Indian goods, and every spare article, for corn. After feeding it [them] several days, I brought away twelve quarts for each public animal, which was fed in very small quantities. With the aid of a compass, and closely estimating the distances, I have made a rude sketch of my route from the point on the Rio Grande,*

> *where our roads diverged, to their junction, near the villages. It is herewith submitted.*[190] *I have good reason to believe that, even with pack mules, better time can be made on my route than yours; and the mules kept in good order, for mine improved on the greater part of it. I halted one day near the villages of this friendly, guileless and singularly innocent and cheerful people, the Pimos* [sic].

After discussing in considerable detail their stay and dealings with the Pima Indians and his unbounded admiration for them, the skirmish with Mexican lancers at El Brazito, and the arrival of the Messenger Francisco with further instructions from their commander, Lt. Col. Cooke moved on with his report to General Kearny;

> *On the 27th December, (after making the forced march, without water, across the head of the Gila,) in consequence of the information in your letter, I determined to send my useless guides express, to give you information of my approach, &c: hoping thus, as I said, to meet orders at Warner's ranche on the 21st of January, and to be of service to your active operations. I also sent for some assistance in mules, understanding that you had placed a number of them in the vicinity.*

Private Rogers, on the other hand, in his journal entry for this same day, was somewhat more explicit and detailed in regard to the skirmish they had with the Mexicans at the Battle of El Brazito on Christmas Day and the intelligence received from General Kearny that a quarrel had erupted

> *...between two of the leading Mexican generals and that the people of Califfornia* [sic] *are fleeing from there. This morning an expresss was started to General Kearney* [sic] *and we resumed our journey.*[191] *Traveled 18 miles.*

Private Bigler commented about the rather remarkable ancient hieroglyphics the Battalion encountered on December 29, describing them as "*...a mass of rocks on our right, carved all over with birds, beasts, serpents, and men...*" but Rogers did not mention them at all.[192]

It was the day before yesterday when the Battalion encountered what was supposed by Cooke to be a steep down-slope barrier that would probably require anywhere up to ten days for them to descend. Most of the animals were packed with goods from the wagons and sent ahead some six miles into the valley, where they were unloaded and left under guard. The animals and majority of the men then returned and undertook the strenuous job of lowering, one by one, all the empty wagons through the use of long ropes. All but one were safely done in this manner—the single exception being one wagon that accidentally broke free and plummeted down the slope with such destructive force that it was smashed beyond use and had to be abandoned. A few others were slightly damaged, but repaired quickly at the bottom. The Saints were extraordinarily proud of the job they had done, accomplishing the gargantuan feat in a mere two days. As Sgt. Tyler commented in his journal:

> *During the three days that we were encamped on the ridge the weather was extremely cold and disagreeable, but when we arrived in the valley, which was perhaps three-quarters of a mile in altitude, it was warm and pleasant...*

As for General Kearny himself, his own card had been well-filled since the debacle at San Pascual. The wounds he received there, though painful and for some time debilitating, were not life-threatening and he quickly resumed his command for what he envisioned lay ahead. That included not only clashing with the disjointed Mexican leadership for possession of California but equally—and as importantly to Kearny himself—wresting the self-proclaimed leadership of the American forces in the West out of the hands of Commodore Stockton, and his ambitious puppet, Col. Fremont, into his own hands, as directed by U.S. Secretary of War Marcy.

Not surprisingly, Commodore Stockton simply could not be convinced that the administration could have contemplated any commander for California other than himself. Kearny, on the other hand, trying to organize a Kearny-Stockton jointly-commanded expedition to retake Los Angeles, simply had no time at the moment to concern himself with such army chain-of-command politics. He marched out of San Diego for Los Angeles on December 29, leading some five hundred men. This force amounted to sixty dismounted dragoons under command of Capt. Henry Smith Turner, fifty California volunteers, and the remainder of Stockton's marines and sailors, plus a battery of artillery. Lieutenant William H. Emory of the topographical engineers was acting as assistant adjutant-general for this campaign.

Meanwhile, General Doniphan was having to cope with his own set of troubles, not the least of which was that General Wool, into whose force his own had been scheduled to be assimilated, had been recalled to Taylor's command and Doniphan's force was more or less left hanging. His quartermaster service was near collapse and his army had been more or less living off the country ever since the events back in San Miguel in August and even had to provide its own munitions. Doniphan met that latter challenge in remarkable form: His patrols had "liberated" ten tons of gunpowder at El Paso, as well as five hundred stands of small arms, four tiny cannon with a fair supply of balls for them, plus a roomful of ancient weaponry, such as culverins and swivels. He took whatever he needed and then sank the remainder in the Rio Grande.

Now, however, Doniphan found himself more or less out on a limb. With General Wool having been recalled by Taylor and no orders from the President or the War Department, it was hard to know what was expected of him. Rumors floated everywhere, none of them encouraging; it was "reported" that General Taylor had been defeated and he was himself a prisoner of the Mexicans; that southern Chihuahua, along with its neighbors, had risen en masse to destroy the American invaders; everything suggested strongly that Doniphan turn his army back, but he shook off the idea, deciding he would simply get his supplies and troops in shape and go on and do by himself the job he had expected to be doing under Gen. Wool's command.

As for General Taylor, he chafed under the realization that the President was subtly but steadily eroding his military power and standing. Polk had sent in General Scott to take over full command from Taylor, but Scott had found it impossible to do what was expected of him without sufficient manpower to back him up. He did take over about half of Zachary Taylor's army and ordered Taylor to stay in place and concern himself only with defensive measures, which was pretty much what Taylor had been doing anyway. Since late September's Battle of Monterrey, Taylor had been in a sort of limbo at Saltillo, watching discontentedly as a number of his quasi-expeditions petered out to virtually nothing. His greater concerns these days centered on consolidating preparations and promoting himself for Presidential candidacy.

All the jockeying for political position was also having its effect in California. Commodore Stockton, who had been busying himself with attempting to put down the revolt of the Californios, abruptly decided his fortunes lay elsewhere and he began preparations to leave California and head for Mexico to continue the war efforts there. Stockton, with little other choice, selected Lt. Col. John Fremont as his gubernatorial successor, wholly disregarding the official orders from both the President and the War Department, which placed General Kearny in top command in California. Fremont blandly ignored orders from Kearny and considered himself subordinate only to Stockton, which was a very serious mistake that could not help but come back to haunt him.

In the San Francisco Bay area, General Mariano Guadalupe Vallejo, was still very active and, at this point, intent upon not only having California become an official state in the union of the United States, but upon establishing the capital city of that state. To that end Vallejo deeded to the seven-foot-tall Dr. Robert Semple an undivided half of a tract of five square miles of his Soscol Rancho on the Straits of Carquines, that site to be the basis of a great new commercial city and seaport on San Francisco Bay which he wanted to be named Francisca in honor of his wife—Doña Francisca Benicia Carrillo—and which Vallejo envisioned as becoming the capital city of California.

U.S. Consul Thomas Larkin, still at Monterey, became so interested in Vallejo's proposal that he actually took over the greater part of Vallejo's ownership of the property and Larkin's attempt to establish the city of Francisca into commercial supremacy in the bay area fell through, simply because the rapidly growing city of Yerba Buena provided a better and more accessible port for the entire bay area. Even changing the proposed name of Francisca to the Señora Vallejo's second name—Benicia—proved of no benefit. While that site was admittedly attractive, and even though General Persifer F. Smith established the army's headquarters there, the trade still did not leave Yerba Buena as Dr. Semple hoped would occur. Further, despite his attempt to have the new city of Benicia named capital of California—and made very generous offers of land and money to the legislature to effect this—it was all to no avail.

Dr. Semple was not the only Californian who wished to have the capital city of California moved elsewhere. The entrepreneurial Capt. John Sutter believed that the rapidly growing city he had founded as Sutters Fort was ideally located to become California's governmental center. He realized, as well, that in order for this to become reality, the adobe structures of the Californios would never do; what was needed was timber, both in the form of logs and in planking. If a good supply of timber could be wrested from California's natural forests, it would likely change a whole way of life where California was concerned.

The problem was, as Sutter saw it, the forests where harvestable timber was located were too far away and it would be much too costly to try to raft logs downstream for construction use. But, Sutter reasoned, why couldn't he do with timber what he was already in the process of doing where grain was concerned? His grist mill, already being constructed five miles up the American River from the fort, held great promise for the production of flour from the wheat that grew so well in the lowlands of the Sacramento River's drainage. Quite some time ago he had begun thinking, why couldn't he locate a site for the development of a lumber mill in the midst of the timber country, where logs could be harvested, brought easily to a sawmill and cut into the planking so sorely needed for building by the influx of new residents? With such a mill, he could virtually establish a monopoly in the lumber business.

With Sutter, the entrepreneurial possibility had excited him and, as always, was the first step in his embarking on a new enterprise. This was no exception. He had last year ordered huge timber saw-blades and gears and related paraphernalia from the East Coast, which should be arriving soon. Then had come the crucial task of finding the ideal site for establishment of such a mill and already he had sent out several of his employees at the head of exploratory teams for that purpose. Unfortunately, thus far such expeditions had been costly and essentially fruitless; the sites they had located up the Sacramento and such of its tributaries as the Feather, Bear and Yuba Rivers had always turned out to be unsuitable for one reason or another.

It had struck Sutter then: what if he sent out a team or two led by a man who had a vested interest—who was, in fact, an equal partner in the enterprise; one who could not only locate a proper site, but who would be willing to stay on and oversee the construction of the sawmill and get it into production? Such an incentive might bring rewards. There were several of his employees that he could think of off-hand who might put special effort behind such an endeavor. One of these was the skilled New Jersey carpenter he had hired immediately upon that man's arrival from the East; the man who had turned out to be not only a dependable worker but an individual who could think and had leadership qualities of his own.

That man was James W. Marshall.

# Chapter 10

◆

*[January 1, 1847 • Friday]*

For James Knox Polk, New Year's Day of 1847 was perhaps the most glum beginning of a new year he had ever experienced and, for the first time since becoming President of the United States, he began to doubt the wisdom with which he had led his nation. Was he wrong, he wondered, in his belief that this country of his should stretch unbroken from the Atlantic Coast to the Pacific? Was he wrong in striking a bargain with the British that the 49th Parallel should be the northern boundary of the United States? Was he wrong in launching a war against Mexico in order to seize California and a great swath of the West for the United States?

Both houses of Congress had all but turned their backs to him and decried the methods he had used to make what gains had thus far been accomplished and all the Senators and Congressmen, it seemed, had settled back now, either in outright opposition to him in what he had accomplished in spite of them, or had assumed an air of standoffishness, as if fully expecting him to fail entirely and not wanting to be closely associated with what they whispered among themselves was the worst President the country had ever had,

The early fervor of war that had initially swept through the nation had shriveled to either apathy or outright anger toward what the public now generally deemed a dead-end for whatever goals their leader had aspired to for his country; they no longer cherished those aspirations of his that had sapped the nation's manpower and finances to near the breaking point, and with no ending yet in sight.

There had been a slight bending of the masses in the President's favor when, within mere days of the close of the previous year, the territory of Iowa had been granted the honor of becoming the twenty-ninth State of the Union, with its capital at Des Moines, and became, at the same time, the second state of the United States created west of the Mississippi. Such bending, however, had been minor and Polk was painfully aware it was insufficient to sustain a national turn-around in his favor. Iowa was a very long way from the West Coast and the problems of drawing all the westward regions into a national unification of statehood along the lines envisioned by Polk seemed, to the masses, an insurmountable barrier, especially since so much of the West remained essentially Spanish/Mexican territory. It was true that some barriers had been pushed back through United States military endeavor and occupation in Texas and the New Mexican and Arizona regions but none of that appeared at all permanent and, as the war dragged on, the likelihood of those regions eventually becoming divided into states, as Polk foresaw, seemed farther away than ever.

It had been President Polk's plan to supplant the ambitious southwestern field commander, General Zachary Taylor, with Senator Thomas H. Benton, but Benton himself admitted that *"my inexperience in matters military make such a selection a poor choice indeed..."* and so, in the interim, a new commander was named who had the experience needed to pick up the military leadership reins from Taylor. This was Major General Winfield Scott, commanding general of the entire United States Army. He was unquestionably an excellent and experienced officer, very popular with the American public, but one, as well, who was not only a heavy drinker, but a man who aspired quite as much to the United States Presidency as did Taylor himself.

Despite his own wavering self-confidence in regard to resolving the Mexican question, President Polk remained unshakable in his belief that:

> *...in order to survive and increase in stature among the more powerful nations on earth, the United States must stretch from coast to coast.*

The Chief Executive had every intention of seeing this occur during his own Presidency and what he considered to be a vital step in that direction had to be the undermining of General Zachary Taylor's reputation in the public eye. But the public was simply not all that easily swayed and not even supplanting him with Winfield Scott as commander was significantly diminishing him in the public eye, as Polk had hoped would occur.

Then Scott had abruptly become just as much a political rival for the Presidency as Taylor had been and Polk wasted no time, once Taylor was removed from command of the Army of the West, in setting the wheels in motion to wrap up the Mexican fracas quickly and completely. Scott had swiftly assembled a force of 13,000 men—including a large portion of Taylor's force—for his planned assault against Mexico. Though much of the material he had requisitioned had not come through—such as more wagons, lighters and siege cannon—he was now working in concert with the United States Navy to take Mexico's most important port city on the Gulf coast—Vera Cruz. He was also viewed at present by Polk as quite as much a threat to himself politically as was Taylor.

President James Knox Polk fully intended to thwart Scott's rampant ambition just as much as he believed he had already thwarted Taylor's.

*[January 9, 1847 • Saturday]*

Samuel Brannan was finally beginning to focus his energies on what clearly most excited and motivated him and was finding, both to his dismay and delight, that it was distinctly out of line with the precepts of The Church of Jesus Christ of Latter-day Saints.

His latest and most exacting—as well as exciting—enterprise was his establishment of California's first regularly published newspaper, which he named *The California Star* and which he planned on publishing each Saturday hereafter with the press he had brought west with him aboard the *Brooklyn*.[193] It was the same press upon which he had first published *The Messenger* in New York City and which was housed now in a second-story loft on the north side of Yerba Buena's Clay Street, above one of the two grist mills he had already built there and which were now thriving businesses.

In addition to turning out the Saturday four-page newspaper on fifteen by twelve-inch stock, which was the most abundant paper he had on hand, and which was purchased by virtually each of the 459 souls declaring Yerba Buena residency, plus many others in outlying districts, Brannan's press ran almost constantly, preparing public notices, printing naval proclamations, and publishing a variety of municipal deeds, notices

# The Infinite Dream

and commentaries. Not only were such jobs immensely satisfying to him, they were profitable far beyond his expectations, though he declared none of such profit as assets to the common fund of the Mormon Church.

Utilizing the labor of the Saints still under his dominion at New Hope, Brannan built what all agreed was the finest residence in Yerba Buena; a home which was quickly becoming the town's most popular rendezvous for such illustrious individuals as Commodore Robert Stockton, as well as California's new territorial governor, Lt. Col. Richard Mason and Missouri's former governor, Lillburn Boggs, who was now serving as *alcalde* of Sonoma. None of the Saints, however, were ever invited by Brannan to any functions occurring in his sumptuous residence. With such "dismissal" of his flock, Brannan was becoming the target of complaints lodged by them of his mismanagement and gross neglect of them and their interests.

Instead of becoming chagrined or humiliated at such charges being levied against him and making some attempt to alleviate the deplorable situation by reestablishing himself in their estimation as being "one of the least," in accordance to Mormon doctrine, Brannan swiftly took up the offensive and arrogantly excommunicated several of the more vociferous of the complainers. He was obviously hoping—and succeeding—in this manner to stifle what he termed "the open rebellion" against his authority. Simultaneously, he kept the other Saints busy constantly, preparing for what he believed would be the arrival of the vast number of Saints presently migrating westward toward a new "Zion" under Brigham Young's leadership.

"Our weary brethren," he contended, "must have a city to come to next summer that will be their own—a haven of rest where they will be safe and secure and capable at last of exercising their communal religion in absolute safety.

"The site for our new Zion," he intoned to them, "must be carefully chosen; it must have a multitude of houses built in preparation of their arrival and its acreage must be planted and become fruitful for them from this time forward; a home for them and their children and their children's children throughout the future. As our Prophet Brigham Young has declared, this new Zion that we are now initiating will become the bedrock home of our faithful Saints for all time hereafter."

That Brigham Young had never said any such thing to him, most particularly in regard to the California site, seemed of little consequence to Brannan, so sure was he that such would actually become the case. In the meanwhile, continuing to tithe those of his flock who received payment through working for others, but not declaring such income to Young, Brannan concentrated almost exclusively of late in establishing *The California Star* in Yerba Buena as the prime—and only—declared reliable source of information for the public on the West Coast. Among its first articles was a piece declaring that Yerba Buena's exports for the past year were valued at $49,597 and its imports at $53,589.

Cleverly, Sam Brannan did not, either in editorial policy or in other activities, publicly stress the strong Mormon influence in his newspaper or in his own private affairs. He was, in fact, becoming far better known to the California populace as quite likely the most enterprising young man in the entire territory. It became all but axiomatic that the more the public read what was written by him—whether newsworthy or editorializing or of commercial content—the more it became entranced by his words and the more his own private coffers filled with income beyond any expectation he may have previously harbored.

As the income of Samuel Brannan increased almost incrementally, so too did his renown...and, equally, his incipient, well disguised greed for personal gain.

*[January 12, 1847 · Tuesday · 10:30 a.m.]*

Brigadier General Stephen W. Kearny, again faced with writing a battle report to General Roger Jones, the U.S. Secretary of War in Washington, D.C., sighed heavily and stared glumly at the blank sheets before him that it was his duty to fill. Though alone this morning in his temporary headquarters in Los Angeles, Kearny spoke aloud, his voice low and rumbling, clearly reflecting his hatred of the detestable chore ahead, for the completion of which he alone was responsible:

"Damned official reports! I'd rather stand off the whole Mexican Army with sword in hand than write just one of them!"

There was, of course, no answer and he sighed yet again, reviewing in his mind the events that led to what was now being referred to jubilantly by his troops as the Battle of St. Gabriel. Though General Kearny, since it had not immediately involved him or his force, had no intention of including the matter in his report, it had all actually begun with the skirmish that had taken place just south of San Francisco Bay near Santa Clara on January 2. It had been at that point that the Californios had showed fight, at least to the extent of hovering about the American force there, but just beyond rifle range.

At that time the enemy, trusting to its expert horsemanship, had moved in relatively closely in an effort to provoke the Yankees to an attack. It was a ploy that might have worked a year before, considering the American conception of contempt at that time for all "Greasers" as fighting men. The subsequent battles at Natividad and San Pascual, however, had taught them the bloody lesson that the Californios were most dangerous when they seemed to be retreating and were instead luring their enemy into ambush from their deadly lancers.

Having learned the fatal lesson well, the Americans refused on this occasion to allow themselves to be drawn into mortal hand-to-hand combat with a much better-mounted enemy armed with lances. Instead, they had marched along stolidly and, unlimbering their six-pounder artillery, had held the Californios at a distance with well-placed grape-shot. Only two Americans became casualties in that set-to and the Californio lancers abruptly wheeled about and galloped off into the shelter of the surrounding hills, which for all intents and purposes ended the so-called Battle of Santa Clara. That same evening a Californio embassy had come in under a white flag and requested terms for a truce, which was immediately granted when it became clear these northern Californios were fighting not so much for territory or glory or some sacred cause of freedom as they were simply trying to protect their sprawling ranches from indiscriminate American plundering in the name of military requisitions.

The truce enacted then and there was clearly an augury that no more trouble from the mid-country Californios seemed likely at any time in the immediate future. That was when Lt. Col. John Fremont, in tardy response to Gen. Kearny's summons, had headed his substantial, rather motley force southward to aid in whatever action was occurring at or near Los Angeles. Even then, it was not so much Kearny's order that set Fremont into movement as it was that the only officer Fremont considered his superior in California, Commodore Stockton, had attached himself to Kearny's force.

Kearny sighed yet again and shook his head sadly. As always, he was wearied quite as much by military politics as by military reports. But, as he thought now of the subsequent Battle of San Gabriel, his exasperation vanished and he gave silent thanks for the six hundred men of his command who had come through so well, so decisively in that action.

General Castro having absented himself, General José Maria Flores was now in command of the 450-man Californio forces and the arena of action in that conflict, where the Americans under Kearny and the Mexican Californios under Flores crossed swords, was at Seal Beach, some eight miles south of Los Angeles proper. At that point the road crossed just up from the river's mouth at a right angle and continued up a steep bank and over a minor plateau on which the Californios had positioned their four big guns. Between the river and the plateau lay a stretch of bottomland some 600 yards wide, to the left of which was a respectable copse of trees. There General Flores had hidden his cavalry force—the Lancers—with which he intended to capture the American artillery during its river bottom crossing.

The American force had been divided, their six cannon in front and a considerable body of men bringing up the rear. The elevated position of the Californio artillery was such that it would have been extremely difficult and dangerous for the American force to cross the wide-open bottom, yet that was precisely what Commodore Stockton advocated in an effort to storm the Californio battery on the crest of the hill. It was clearly a suicidal, all but maniacal plan and, fortunately, Stockton was persuaded by Kearny to leave the opening of the battle to the artillery.

Very quickly the Americans' Number Two gun—on which James Marshall was serving—incapacitated with well-directed shots, two of the enemy's cannon. At that moment the Mexican cavalry charged out of their woodland concealment, the lancers galloping forward in an attempt to overpower the big American gun. The six-pounder was quickly aligned and about ready to fire when Marshall bellowed an order: "Give them a stand of grape!"

The change was made swiftly, professionally, as the lancers thundered toward them. The cannoneers held fire until they could clearly see the eyes of the charging lancers; only then did they apply the match. The big cannon roared and flamed and bucked and when the smoke cleared away, the lancers were scattered and torn and in hopeless confusion. Riderless steeds galloped frantically over the plain, which was strewn with bodies of the dead and dying. As the Mexican officers strove to rally their men, the American rear guard opened up a murderous crossfire which totally demoralized them, driving them into headlong flight from the action. Several of the men at Marshall's gun fell in the attack, one killed so nearby that Marshall's face was bespattered with the artillerist's blood and brains.

This single action was the key to the entire battle and it effectively ended the fight. The Californios were unable to rally and the American rear charged up the slope and carried the plateau. They camped there and, as dawn broke on January 9, were set into motion to cross the Mesa. Before the maneuver could be completed, they once again encountered General Flores' force. A desperate fight occurred then, the Americans most often massed in square formation. Two full hours of hard fighting ensued—already dubbed the Battle of La Mesa—during which many of the Californios slipped away—and ending only when hostilities were halted by the appearance of a delegation from Los Angeles, offering to surrender the city. The offer was accepted and Kearny's Army, along with Commodore Stockton's force, unopposed, retook the city on January 10.

General Andreas Pico, accepting what remained of the Californio/Mexican force from General Flores, retreated northward. General José Maria Flores, himself, retreated to Mexico...and into oblivion.

Now Kearny snapped back from his unbidden reverie, dipped his pen and bent without further procrastination to composing his report to the War Department:

> *Head-quarters, Army of the West*
> *CIUDAD DE LOS ANGELES, UPPER CALIFORNIA    Jan 12, 1847*
> *SIR:—I have the honor to report that at the request of Com. Robert F. Stockton, United States navy, (who, in September last, assumed the title of Governor of California,) I consented to take command of an expedition to this place, (the capital of the country,) and that, on the 29th of December, I left San Diego with about 500 men, consisting of sixty dismounted dragoons under Capt. Turner, fifty California volunteers, and the remainder of marines and sailors, with a battery of artillery—Lieut. Emory (topographical engineer) acting as assistant adjutant general. Commodore Stockton accompanied us.*
>
> *We proceeded on our route without seeing the enemy, till on the 8th instant, when they showed themselves in full force of 600 mounted men, with four pieces of artillery, under their governor, (Flores,) occupying the heights in front of us, which commanded*

*the crossing of the river San Gabriel, and they ready to oppose our further progress. The necessary disposition of our troops was immediately made, by covering our front with a strong party of skirmishers, placing our wagons and baggage train in the rear of them, and protecting the flanks and rear with the remainder of the command. We then proceeded, forded the river, carried the heights, and drove the enemy from them after an action of about an hour and a half, during which they made a charge upon our left flank, which was repulsed; soon after which they retreated and left us in possession of the field, on which we encamped that night.*

*The next day (the 9th instant) we proceeded on our march at the usual hour, the enemy in our front and on our flanks; and when we reached the plains of the Mesa, their artillery again opened upon us, when their fire was returned by our guns as we advanced; and after hovering around and near us for about two hours, they occasionally skirmishing with us during that time, they concentrated their force and made another charge on our left flank, which was quickly repulsed; shortly after which they retired, we continuing our march, and we (in the afternoon) encamped on the banks of the Mesa, three miles below this city, which we entered the following morning (the 10th instant) without further molestation.*

*Our loss in the actions of the 8th and 9th was small, being but one private killed, and two officers (Lieut. Rowan of the navy, and Capt. Gillespie of the volunteers) and eleven privates wounded. The enemy, mounted on fine horses, and being the best riders in the world, carried off their killed and wounded, and we know not the number of them, though it must have been considerable.*

*Very respectfully, your obedient servant,*
*STEPHEN W. KEARNY, Brig. Gen. U.S.A.*
*Brig. Gen. Roger Jones, Adjt. Gen., U.S.A.*

### [January 13, 1847 • Wednesday]

Though Lt. Col. John C. Fremont's exterior demeanor remained flatly calm, it masked an interior jubilation that all but bellowed for release. Rarely, he felt, had such a boon dropped unbidden into his lap and he was quite determined to milk it for whatever gain he might acquire. What had occurred might well turn into his stepping-stone to full Army generalship, perhaps chief of staff of the entire United States Army.

Perhaps even the Presidency of this great nation.

A peculiar power play was occurring right here in California that could not help but deeply affect all who were in some manner connected with it, of which Fremont was keenly aware he was a prime factor. General Kearny had arrived with his small army from the East, allegedly with orders from Washington D.C. to take command of the California Territory, yet Commodore Stockton had already declared himself commander-in-chief and governor of the entire territory and none had risen to dispute his claim, not even Kearny himself.

The Commodore, busy with war tactics against the Mexicans, had relinquished the California governorship to Fremont; still there had been no cries of outrage from Kearny, which was a clear indication to Fremont that Kearny fully accepted Stockton's superiority, both politically and militarily. That Kearny had, in fact, kowtowed to Stockton in all respects was evident even more in the fact that while so far Kearny had led his military force successfully against the Californios, it had apparently been done with Stockton unobtrusively directing the strategy behind the scenes.

Now, wholly unexpectedly had come the windfall yesterday of such unexpected proportions that Fremont was entirely convinced it would catapult his own entire career to higher echelons than even he had allowed himself to truly believe. In fleeing the Los Angeles area with his troops, General Andreas Pico had inadvertently encountered Fremont's force and Don Andreas, who had of course heard of Fremont and knew of his aspirations for glory, assessed the situation and took instant advantage of the opportunity to enter into negotiation with the American commander toward a capitulative permanent peace between the Californios and the Americans, but with very generous terms for the Californios, who were hardly in a position to make demands. It was, Pico knew, a capitulation far more beneficial to the Californios than he could ever have expected from either Commodore Stockton or General Kearny.

Fremont was only too willing to oblige and immediately set up a board consisting of some of his highest ranking officers to negotiate with a similar board established by General Pico. Within mere hours the terms had been agreed to between them and the documents had been drawn up and properly signed by both parties. It was undoubtedly one of the briefest international capitulations ever officially engaged in by a military representative of the United States:

*Articles of Capitulation Made and Entered Into at the Rancho Couenga* [Cahuenga],
*this 13th Day of January, 1847, between*
*P.B. Reading, Major Louis McLane* [McClane, actually]. *Jr., commanding Third Artillery;*
*William H. Russell, ordnance officer, Commissioners,*
*Appointed by J.C. Fremont, United States Army, and Military Commandant of California, and*
*José Antonio Carrillo, commandant squadron,*
*Augustin Olivera, deputado,*
*Commissioners appointed by Don Andreas Pico,*
*Commander-in-chief of the California forces Under the Mexican flag.*

ARTICLE I — *The commissioners on the part of the Californians, agree that their entire force shall, on presentation of themselves to Lieutenant Colonel Fremont, deliver up their artillery and public arms, and that they shall return peaceably to their homes, conforming to the law and regulations of the United States, and not again take up arms during the war between the United States and Mexico, but will assist and aid in placing the country in a state of peace and tranquility.*

ARTICLE II — *The commissioners on the part of Lieutenant Colonel Fremont agree, and bind themselves on the fulfillment of the first Article by the Californians, that they shall be guaranteed protection of life and property, whether on parole or otherwise.*

ARTICLE III — *That until a treaty of peace be made and signed between the United States of North America and the republic of Mexico, no Californian, or any other Mexican citizen, shall be bound to take the oath of allegiance.*

ARTICLE IV — *That any Californian or any citizen of Mexico desiring, is permitted by this capitulation to leave the country without let or hindrance.*

ARTICLE V — *That by virtue of the aforesaid Articles, equal rights and privileges are vouchsafed to every citizen of California as are enjoyed by the citizens of North America.*

ARTICLE VI — *All officers, citizens, foreigners and others shall receive the protection guaranteed by the second Article.*

ARTICLE VII — *This capitulation is intended to be no bar in effecting such arraignment as may in future be in justice required by both parties.*

*CUIDAD DE LOS ANGELES*
*January 16, 1847*[194]

> ADDITIONAL ARTICLE—*That the paroles of all officers, citizens, and others of the United States and of naturalized citizens of Mexico, are by this foregoing capitulation, canceled, and every condition of said paroles, from and after this date, are of no further force and effect, and all prisoners of both parties are hereby released.*
> P.B. READING, *Major, California Battalion.*
> LOUIS McCLANE, *Commander Artillery.*
> WM. H. RUSSELL, *Ordnance Officer.*
> JOSÉ ANTONIO CARILLO, *Command't of Squadron*
> AUGUSTIO OLLIVERA, *Deputado*

Both Commodore Stockton and General Kearny were stunned when they learned of the capitulation later today and the American intermural military command problems it intensified. Their anger that Lt. Col. Fremont could have the temerity to enter into such a negotiation with a foreign power without any effort to seek authorization or sanction was, to them both, unmitigated brashness bordering on actual criminal behavior conducive to insurrection. Many of the enemy were noted to be in sympathy with Fremont and it was no secret that previous to the capitulation the lieutenant colonel had been Stockton's senior military advisor and field officer. Many of Fremont's officers simply refused to surrender public property to General Kearny's command without a direct order from Fremont himself.

Most galling to both Stockton and Kearny was that the capitulation, though deemed excessively lenient by both, was remarkably close to what either of them would have organized with the enemy had they been given the opportunity. The fact that they had *not* been given such opportunity and that they were deprived of the honor for such a coup was what rankled most and both considered this to be indicative of gross insubordination.

Fearful for the light in which this placed him and the potential jeopardy to his own ambitions and eventual retirement, Commodore Stockton immediately issued an official report to the Secretary of the Navy in Washington D.C.—a statement meant to absolve himself of any complicity or guilt in the matter, but equally to make it clear that while disapproving of the *manner* in which it was executed, it was, in essence, a document worthy of approval. He wrote:

> *José Ma* [sic] *Flores, the commander of the insurgent forces, two*

*or three days previous to the 8th, sent two commissioners with a flag of truce to my camp to make a "treaty of peace." I informed the commissioners that I could not recognize José Ma Flores, who had broken his parole as an honorable man, or one having any rightful authority worthy to be treated with; that he was a rebel in arms, and if I caught him, I would have him shot. It seems that, not being able to negotiate with me, and having lost the battles of the 8th and 9th, they met Colonel Fremont on the 12th instant, on his way here, who, not knowing what had occurred, entered into capitulation with them, which now I send you; and although I refused to do it myself, still I have thought it best to approve it.*

General Kearny, on the other hand, was not quite so amenable as Stockton, nor so forgiving. Fremont had flatly rejected Kearny's authority and had boldly usurped authority not his to grasp and, for such malfeasance, Kearny was now resolute in his determination that Fremont must pay.

In time.

*[January 14, 1847 • Monday • 10:30 a.m.]*

No hint of the agitation General Kearny had bottled up inside him for Lt. Col. John Fremont appeared in the letter just completed to Adjutant General Roger Jones in Washington, D.C., and Kearny complimented himself on his own control. Careful man that he was, however, he now swiftly read through the missive again, just to be certain no trace of vindictiveness was apparent:

*Headquarters, Army of the West*
*CUIDAD DE LOS ANGELES, Jan. 14, 1847*
*SIR:—This morning, Lieutenant-colonel Fremont, of the regiment of mounted riflemen, reached here with 400 volunteers from the Sacramento. The enemy capitulated with him yesterday, near San Fernando, agreeing to lay down their arms; and we have now the Prospect of having peace and quietness in the country, which I hope may not be interrupted again.*

*I have not yet received any information of the troops which were to come from New York, nor of those to follow me from New Mexico, but presume they will be here before long. On their arrival, I shall, agreeably to the instructions of the President of the United States, have the management of affairs in this country, and will endeavor to carry out his views in relation to it.*

*Very respectfully, your obedient servant.*
*STEPHEN W. KEARNY, Brig. Gen., U.S.A.*
Brig. Gen. Roger Jones, Adj. Gen., U.S.A.

Finished with the reading, General Kearny folded the letter and slid it into an envelope he had already addressed, a small smile curling his mouth corners. He had come to this country with specific instructions from the Secretary of War to march from Ft. Leavenworth to California, and to "...*take possession of all the sea-coast and other towns, and establish civil government.*" When he'd arrived, possession had already been taken by Commodore Stockton and a certain form of loose government, half civil and half military, was in place. Without actually having the authority to do so, Stockton had arbitrarily determined that Fremont should be California's military commander and governor and reportable only to Stockton himself as commander-in-chief.

Had the opportunity been given him, as his Presidential orders called for, matters for Kearny would quite probably have been different and had Fremont aligned himself with the general against Stockton instead of vice versa, Kearny would almost certainly have appointed Fremont governor. Those things had not occurred.

A saying Kearney's father had frequently uttered to him when he was a lad flitted momentarily across his mind: *What goes around, comes around.*

General Kearny's smile broadened.

*[January 15, 1847 • Friday]*

For the Saints in the Mormon Battalion, the fabled paradise that California had been purported to be had thus far proven itself to be an absolute hell.

During the mile-wide fording of the Colorado River, their makeshift boat was used all night long to ferry their baggage across, but it wasn't until about noon on January 11 that the crossing was completed. One wagon mired deeply on an island and had to be left. At the same time, where the water in places was up to their necks and very cold, some of the mules got so chilled they simply gave up and drowned. Despite such deterrents, some of the Saints actually waded across the broad river.

In regard to the Colorado River, Lt. Col. Cooke was heartily disappointed in it. As he wrote in his journal:

> The Rio Colorado here resembles the Missouri in size and color of the water. It has immense bottoms difficult to pass; they are of rich soil. I believe it to be the most useless of rivers to man; so barren, so desolate and difficult, that it has never been explored; running through volcanic mountains and sand deserts, at places through chasms of vertical rock perhaps five thousand feet deep.

While the Battalion was engaged in the process of crossing the Colorado River, an express arrived from General Kearny bearing startling news and an order for Lt. Col. Cooke to spur the Mormon Battalion onward for its junction with Kearny's force at the greatest speed possible. Kearny told of an uprising of the native Mexicans in California—the Californios, as they were labeled—against the American Army. Cooke, of course, put the Mormon Battalion into whatever greater speed could be eked out of them toward the conflict, at the same time damning the fact that his men were on foot and only so much could be asked of them, especially over such tortuous terrain. Despite the need for haste, nothing could induce Cooke to abandon the wagons or ignore the primary objective Kearny himself had set for them: the General had ordered the opening of a road into California and Cooke was determined that his general would have that road. Cooke's proof that such a road had been opened would lie in the wagons he brought through. So the rickety wagons were rolled onward and the Saints opened the way for them, carving their roadway through hillsides and passes, rocks and chasms, with such hand tools as crowbars and axes, shovels and spades; a task that was never less than gargantuan. Food supplies were again exhausted and his men subsisted largely on the seeds of mesquite pods. As Private Robert Bliss of Co. B scrawled in his diary:

> We have endured one of the greatest journeys ever made by man & it is only by the faith and prayers of the Saints that we have done it!

Cooke sent a detail of his guides ahead to reach San Diego as soon

# The Infinite Dream

as possible and return with water and edible food. It was clearly apparent that only the unbending determination and harsh direction of Lt. Col. Cooke and the Battalion's own seemingly indefatigable perseverance was keeping them alive and there was no telling how much longer that might last. Petty annoyances at such a time became almost monumental problems. Sgt. Daniel Tyler was particularly irked by the actions of their guide, Weaver, whose carelessness on occasion seemed calculated to jeopardize them all. A case in point occurred when Weaver set a fire which, it seemed to him, was the wisest solution for clearing a path for the road they were building, but in doing so he clearly endangered some of the wagons and the hooves of the mules were jeopardized by live coals from the burning brush.

The trace they made was very sandy and some of their teams simply gave out. Two of the wagons broke down irreparably under the conditions and had to be abandoned, while the baggage they carried was packed upon those mules with the lightest burdens.

The great scarcity of graze available for the oxen and mules at their night's campsite could have become a problem of consequence, but the wisdom of Lt. Col. Cooke won the approval of the Saints when he ordered a quantity of mesquite fruit to be gathered for the animals, which sufficed very well for their needs and actually provided more moisture for them than grass alone could have done.

The well they had been informed about early this morning as being fifteen miles ahead was not encountered until late afternoon and it was initially a great disappointment. Not only was it dry, they found the desiccated remains of a wolf at its bottom, but the manner in which their commander handled this clearly won the approval of Sgt. Daniel Tyler, who wrote in his diary this evening:

> The following will show that the Colonel was not insensitive of our true situation. He wrote: "I was met by a man who told me there was not a drop of water" (in the well.) "The worst prospect for sixty miles ahead instantly arose to frighten me for the 360 nearly worn-out footmen, who confide all to me." When he arrived at the camping place about 6 p.m. today, he found a portion of the men cleaning out and sinking the old well, while another party were digging a new one. Some mud and a little water were struck in the old well, but the quicksand ran in and not only

*obscured the water, but endangered the lives of the men, who were now ten feet or more below the surface. Some one suggested that the wife of one of the Captains*—Susan Davis, wife of Capt. Daniel C. Davis, commander of Co. E—*had a wash tub, which, by boring holes in the bottom, might answer as a curbing. The Captain's team soon came up and the vessel was called for, but the good lady, who perhaps had brought it all the way from Nauvoo or even farther, could not consent, on any account, to part with it. It was, however, pressed into service, and bored, and sunk in the sand. This proved a failure. Then the bottom was ordered to be knocked out, when it worked better; some water came in, but, alas, for human hopes!, the fluid soon disappeared and all seemed lost. In this emergency, Weaver, one of the guides and an old mountaineer trapper, was sent for, to ascertain the practibility* [sic] *of traveling sixty miles more or less down the river. He thought, with our weak teams and worn-out men, it would be next to impossible. According to Cooke's account, which is doubtless correct, he now cast one more anxious look down the old well, and, as a last faint hope of success, ordered a fresh detail to further sink the new well, which was already more than two feet below the old one, with no better prospect. A half hour later all hearts were made glad with the tidings of water deep enough to fill our camp kettles.*

*Colonel Cooke says, of the news of water:* "It was like a great Light bursting on darkness and gloom." *Further on, the anxious commander adds:* "Eighteen hours of unceasing labor has been my lot to-day, with anxiety enough to turn one gray." *With all this anxiety, the ever hopeful officer says:* "My faith had not failed." *Nor, with such example, has our own.*

The southeastern California desert continued to be a fearsome obstacle; so much so that the next day, January 12, their paymaster, Major Jeremiah H. Cloud, whose mules were beginning to falter, was forced to cache a trunk filled with tools, along with some other articles.[195] It was believed that all the cached goods and abandoned wagons would eventually be retrieved by squads sent out for that purpose from San Diego.

The following day—January 13—the Battalion marched sixteen miles in a northwest direction before finally camping. Details sent ahead by Cooke during the day managed to obtain, with great effort, supplies of water in three different wells ranging from twelve to sixteen feet in depth. None of the three wells was very good, but the better of these was one the Mexicans called Alamo Mocha Well.[196] Sgt. Albert Smith of Co. B noted in his diary about this:

> Some went A head with [pick] & Shovel in hand & dug wells in low places So that we did not quite parish [sic].

Private Henry Bigler was a bit more specific in his diary entry, noting that:

> On the thirteenth we made about fifteen miles. Here was another well dug by General Kearny, but like the other was dry and had four dead wolves in it. It was soon cleaned out and dug deeper by a detail under command of Lt. Oman. Also another well at the same time was being dug, and plenty of water was had for the whole command...

The next morning, dispatched by Cooke, Lt. George Stoneman, leading a detach-ment of twenty five men and with Weaver to guide them, headed out early for a well to the north-northwest that Weaver said was called the Pozo Hondo and to prepare it for the arrival of the command.[197] By the time the full Battalion was ready to march, however, it was close to noon and the rear guard did not get into motion until near the middle of the afternoon. Troubles continued to plague them and three of their wagons—one of them the blanket wagon—had to be left behind because the famishing animals could pull them no farther.

For a portion of the way they had to plough through deep sand, which was extremely difficult, and in which they found traces where large herds of cattle and horses had been driven across to reach Sonora, evidently to prevent the livestock from falling into American hands. In other places they encountered solid clay, so hard that neither the animals nor the wagons left much of a trail. While crossing the hardpan of clay they noted many deposits of seashells and pockets of pure salt, leading Sgt. Tyler to deduce that at some time in antiquity the Gulf of California extended over these parts.

Though the march continued until 10:30 p.m. and covered some twenty-two miles, the command was unable to reach the Pozo Hondo Well before nightfall and so they camped for the night on the barren desert ground without water. Before turning in for the night, their commander added another passage to his continuing report to General Kearny, noting that:

> When of no real use to me, some wagons, which were broken on the march, were left, in order to save the mules. At this first well I left three, because the mules were unequal to drawing them. I had then remaining one for each company, and two others. I sent forward a strong party to the next well to prepare it and dig another...

It had been a considerable while since anything had been heard from or about General Kearny, but that changed today. The Battalion reached the Pozo Hondo Well fairly early into their day's march. It was a great disappointment, however, insofar as providing them with a good water supply was concerned. The amount of water it contained was so slight that there was not enough for all the men.

What they did encounter at the Pozo Hondo, however, was the return of their guide, Antoine Leroux, with some of the men in the detail Cooke had sent weeks before from the Gila River as an express to General Kearny. They had brought back with them half a dozen Indians, as well as thirty-five relatively fresh mules and ten beeves. They had something else with them, as well, that was nowhere near so appreciated: They bore dispatches and news of the defeat of General Kearny's force at San Pascual on December 6 and of the General himself having been three times wounded in the affair where a score of Americans had been killed by the Mexican Lancers.

The Saints marched away from the Pozo Hondo Well late in the afternoon and continued their march until well into the night, but there was little of the usual jocularity among the men. When they finally established camp close to midnight, Sgt. Tyler, though fearfully tired, still managed to write in his journal of the day's events:

> ...the 15th...we marched seven miles to the Pozo Hondo wells. A rainbow was visible in the morning, a sight rarely seen on these arid deserts. On arriving at the well, one of our guides, who had been sent ahead to purchase fresh mules and beef cattle, met us

*with 35 mules, all in good condition. He had started with 57, but unfortunately the other 22 were lost by the way. Ten fat beeves were also brought and one was killed, which was a great treat to the men, after having little else than worn-out oxen since leaving Santa Fe. The most of the mules were wild and some got away. One broke loose from three men and made good his escape, harness and all.*

*The well afforded us but a little very poor water; it served, however, to save life until better could be reached. We left Pozo Hondo at about 4 p.m., and continued our march un til 11 p.m., making about ten miles.*

# Chapter 11

♦

*[January 19, 1847 • Tuesday • 9:00 a.m.]*

In a simple quasi-military-civil ceremony held in the Los Angeles temporary headquarters office of the self-proclaimed Commander-in-Chief of California, Commodore Robert Stockton, U.S.N., personally inducted Lt. Col. John Charles Fremont into the office of Governor of the Territory of California.

The commissioning ceremony was neither lavish nor extensive, but it was formal and the relatively few witnesses included mainly other individuals who were similarly being inducted into higher echelon governmental positions. Foremost among them, apart from Stockton and Fremont themselves, was William H. Russell, who was being sworn in as Secretary of State.

A seven-man legislative council was also appointed and sworn in by Stockton, consisting of the former military commandant of California's Northern Frontier District, Mariano Guadalupe Vallejo and the American counsel Thomas O. Larkin, as well as David Spence, Juan Bandini, Eliab Grimes, Juan B. Alvarado and Santiago Arguello. The Legislative Council was instructed to convene for their first session on March 1.[198]

The simple ceremony was completed quickly, handshakes and congratulations were exchanged and the appointees then dispersed to their previously assigned offices. Fremont strode with a decided swagger down the tiled hall to its end, where there was an imposing, oversized double door, to the right of which was positioned a one-word placard: GOVERNOR.

A sense almost of giddiness swept through Fremont. That door, he reminded himself, was not just a portal to the office of the chief executive of the territory. No, it was far more than that: It was the gateway to a future quite as grand and illustrious as he had ever imagined.

At least so it seemed.

*[January 21, 1847 • Thursday]*

The incredible journey of the Mormon Battalion was, for all intents and purposes, finally over. It had ended at 2 p.m. yesterday when the weary Saints had finally reached Warner's Ranch, some sixty-five miles northeast of San Diego.[199] Though badly worn from the long overland march that had begun last summer on the west bank of the Missouri River at Fort Leavenworth, few of the Saints had any inkling that they had just completed the longest foot-march in mankind's recorded history of military maneuvers; a march which had grown progressively more difficult the farther west it progressed.

This final leg of the long journey had begun on January 16 when the Battalion had been aroused at 1 a.m. and the forced march resumed until 3 p.m., without water and with no halts until they had covered about forty miles and reached the first running water they had encountered since leaving the Colorado River. The intermittent stream where they finally camped was called Carrizo Creek—Carrizo being the Mexican term for common reed grass. On arriving here, the mules were so completely worn down that a number of them died from drinking too much too soon.[200] In recording his version of the ordeal, Sgt. Daniel Tyler wrote:

> ...we halted until 2 a.m., of the 16th. As usual, the night was very cold, and the half-naked men suffered for want of more and better clothing. The contrast between an almost tropical sun in the day times and a December cold atmosphere at night was very hurtful and weakening to both man and beast. The Indians call this region "the hot land"—a name which strikes the writer as being appropriate, as it is by far the hottest region he ever saw.... The march of the last five days was the most trying of any we have made, on both men and animals. We here found the heaviest sand, hottest days and coldest nights, with no water and but little food. Language fails to provide adjectives strong enough to describe our situation...there are many occasions during our travels through these deserts, when twenty well-armed men might have nearly used up the command, in our scattered condition.... At this time the men

are nearly bare-footed; some use, instead of shoes, rawhide wrapped around their feet, while others improvise a novel style of boots by stripping the skin from the leg of an ox. To do this, a ring was cut around the hide above and below the gambrel joint, and then the skin taken off without cutting it lengthwise. After this, the lower end is sewed up with sinews, when it is ready for the wearer, the natural crook of the hide adapting it somewhat to the shape of the foot. Others wrap cast-off clothing around their feet to shield them from the burning sand during the day and the cold at night.

Before we arrived at the Cariza [sic], many of the men were so nearly used up from thirst, hunger and fatigue, that they were unable to speak until they reached the water or had it brought to them. Those who are strongest report when they arrive, that they had passed many lying exhausted by the way-side.... About sixteen or more mules gave out entirely during the two last days' travel and were abandoned. During this part of our journey, made in the morning, it is piercing cold. The guides got lost and we traveled a mile or more out of our way, through heavy sand. Our fresh animals are nearly exhausted.

17th—We have traveled fifteen miles over very heavy sand and are encamped between two mountains. The fresh animals, after getting rested, do good work. Some of the men, unable to keep up with the wagons, travel and sleep at intervals, during the night, and do not reach camp until daylight the following morning. The sheep arrived about noon today. They number from 70 to 80, but are so poor that when one is slaughtered and skinned, the bones have but a very thin covering, and the scant flesh that remains contains very little nourishment...

All of our government wagons had been abandoned at this time, but five. During the day, the Indian magistrate (alcalde) of the town of San Philipi, and a companion, brought a letter to the Colonel from the Governor of San Diego, announcing the arrival of our men, who had been sent for supplies, and promising assistance. He welcomed our approach. The Governor's messengers are near naked, and not unlike the Apaches in appearance.

18th—Have not advanced any today, but spent the day in cleaning up our arms, and in the evening the men were paraded and inspected. The Colonel expressed great surprise at seeing the half starved, worn-out men who, only the night previous, had staggered into camp, like so many inebriates, from sheer exhaustion and hunger, now playing the fiddle and singing merry songs. The messengers having heard of several other battles in California, the Colonel entered into precautionary measures, as it was thought we might meet a large force of the enemy retreating towards Sonora. The command reached Vallecito Creek after marching over what the Colonel says was "the worst fifteen miles of road since we left the Rio Grande: and that it was accomplished under all the circumstances, by mules or men is extraordinary." At this camp the Colonel received word from John B. Montgomery, commander of the U.S. sloop-of-war *Portsmouth*, that the California insurrectionists are expected to march for Sonora over the same trail the Battalion is on.

The trail taken by the Mormon Battalion between the Oriflamme and Vallecito Mountains was especially narrow and very rugged. In the event the retreating enemy might pass close enough to overhear them and stage an attack, Lt. Col. Cooke issued a silence order, to be observed as much as possible until further notice and all bugle signals were temporarily cancelled. The narrow defile the Battalion passed through was very difficult, the men preceding the teams and helping them up a mountain, then through another deep valley before passing through the narrow defile. The day's march required intensive hard labor from all hands—including even the commander—as a passage had to be hacked for the wagons in some areas through solid rock and, in others, axes and a pry bar were utilized to widen the trail. Even then, they still had to dismantle and carry some wagons and turn others sideways to get through Box Canyon.[201] As Henry Bigler described it that evening in his diary:

> 19th—Today we crossed over a mountain. Ropes were fastened to the wagons, and every man that could get ahold [sic] pulled and pushed until all got over, falling into a small valley, where for the first time on our tramp, I noticed the wild sage. We soon left this by turning to our right up a little creek but dry, at the head of which we wished to cross the mountain. But the mountain soon closed upon us on each side, that our pass became more narrow than our wagons, and we were obliged to take some of the wagons apart. But

> while we were unloading and making preparations, a lot of men went to work and cut through the rocks so as to admit the passage of our wagons without taking them to pieces. We are encamped to night [sic] on the top of the mountain without wood and water. The night is cold and we have only a little brush for fuel.

The Battalion was on the move again before sunrise on January 20 and started with having a steep sand ridge over which they had to draw the wagons with long ropes pulled by upwards of twenty men to each wagon. The route then turned into an exceedingly rough, rocky descent to a little valley where the going was much easier and they found an Indian road leading to their village, called San Philipi. The village was deserted, but this had evidently just occurred as the inhabitants heard the Battalion's approach and fled.

The mule teams were here turned loose to graze for a while and two beeves were butchered—their only food. After resting briefly they marched again, another seven miles farther, taking them over a low mountain pass where they camped for the night and where they were overjoyed to find plenty of fresh water.

It was here that they met their guide, Baptiste Charbonneau, on his return from San Diego. He told them that the governor there had detained both Hall and Leroux to prevent their falling into the hands of hostile Californios who were apparently holding a specific grudge against the pair, though he did not know why.

For the first time in what seemed to the Saints to be months, the vegetation was now beginning to change. Live oak trees of large size were being encountered at intervals, the trees bearing acorns up to two inches long and a half inch in diameter, plus other vegetation of much greener variety.

Today, then—January 21—the Mormon Battalion finally reached Warner Ranch, the first white habitation encountered since leaving the Colorado River on southern California's eastern border. Their arrival was not at an auspicious time, since it was a cold and drearily overcast day with the scent of approaching snow in the air.

The trail they were following at this point took them over some low mountains—large hills, actually—which were not difficult to overcome. The trail, barely recognizable as a previous passage, led them through a grove of very fine old live oaks and the grass beneath their feet was lushly green. The universal feeling among the Saints was that, despite the gloom of the weather, they were descending from winter into spring.

They crossed a ridge which divided the southerly flowing waters of the Colorado basin and Lower California—the Baja—from those which emptied at last into the Pacific itslf. Fine forests cloaked the snow-topped peaks and high ridges and there was an overwhelming sense of their having entered a new climate, a new land.

Their arrival on the great, sprawling Warner Ranch coincided, remarkably enough, with the arrival there of the guides their commander had sent forward on December 28 to procure supplies for the travel-ravaged Battalion; a quest in which they had been only partially successful. On reaching the extensive Warner Ranch headquarters they were greeted by Jonathan Warner himself, who welcomed them and quickly conferred with Lt. Col. Cooke in a decidedly concerned manner.

"The Californios," he told the commander gravely, "have more or less collapsed in their resistance to American occupation and they are being hard pressed by General Kearny's force in the Los Angeles area. That, in itself, is good, but you need to be aware that there is a strong likelihood you will, in the days ahead, meet a large force of them retreating toward Sonora."

In view of this, Lt. Col. Cooke decided he would give his troops a full day of rest tomorrow before starting that final short trek. He purchased three very large, fat beeves from Warner for $3.50 and raised the rations for the troops to four pounds of beef per man, but there was little else at Warner's that could be provided them, including even salt to season the meat.

The Saints reveled in the warmer temperatures now being experienced which, they agreed, was more like the atmosphere they were accustomed to in Indiana and Illinois in late April or early May. From a jumble of rocks on the ranch there issued a hot spring of considerable volume which raised a cloud of steam visible for a mile or more from its source and near the center of the valley there stood a magnificent live oak whose boughs reached down to within five feet of the ground and its massive foliage that spread in a circumference, according to Cooke's estimate, of two hundred seventy feet.

Pvt. Henry Bigler noted in his diary:

*Went to see the hot Springs near here. The water comes out of the rocks, and is too warm to hold in one's hand with comfort. A very warm stream ran around one side of this tree, issuing from that hot Spring, and a cold branch flowed around the other side. Laid in camp. Washed my clothes. The men are trading their clothes to the Indians for provisions, some even traded off their last shirts from their backs. These are Indians which stay around Warner's ranch. Warner has some fine vineyards. The Quartermaster bought some cattle of him.*

"The Indians here," Warner remarked, "who wear almost nothing where clothing is concerned, will often sleep with their bodies in the warm water and their heads on the sod bank, which keeps them very comfortable even on the coldest nights. They've been very faithful to us here on the ranch. But they've faced some hard times. Not long ago they captured and brought here ten or eleven Californios, whom they executed, but they paid for it when just last week they were ambushed in the Temecula Valley not far from here by some of the Californios who have their own Indian allies and thirty-eight of their own number were killed. It's been a very disturbing time here recently."

The friendly Indians on the ranch converged on Cooke and their chief, named Antonio, begged him to let them accompany the Battalion so that they could collect and bury their dead on the way, to which the commander agreed and employed him and ten of his best men to act not only as scouts but to take charge of and drive the Battalion's remaining beef cattle.

Shortly after the Battalion's arrival here in the afternoon, Lt. Col. Cooke hastily wrote a dispatch to General Kearny, saying:

*On the 21st day of January, I arrived and encamped at the Warner's ranche [sic]: the very day, as it happened, I had promised in my letter of December 27. This was seven miles off the road to San Diego; but I had resolved, the night before, to march for the Pueblo de los Angeles, where the enemy had concentrated, unless I met orders or fresh information. That which I had placed your forces approaching it on the south, and Lieutenant Colonel Fremont's from the north. Thus, I should advance from the east, and from the only pass leading to Sonora.*

Since then, however, further orders from General Kearny had come in with news of the American victories over the Californios in the Los Angeles area and the subsequent retreat of those forces. In view of these circumstances, Kearny directed that the Mormon Battalion be marched directly to San Diego instead of Los Angeles. Lt. Col. Philip St. George Cooke was very pleased with his Battalion and, as he reported in his dispatch to General Kearny:

> *I am forced to admit that I cannot conceive of any other large group of men enduring so extensive and horrendous an on-foot march as this Battalion has undergone, with all its severe privations, who yet have quite universally maintained their good humor and discipline. My very considered estimation of the Mormons now, as soldiers, is far greater than for any other body of men I have ever had the honor to lead. I admire and respect them for their obedience, courage and steadfastness under the most trying circumstances.*

The pride and pleasure he felt in his men was characteristically reflected in the fact that now, after a thorough drilling to sharpen his command, Cooke, without further delay, ordered the final march to San Diego.

*[January 30, 1847 • Tuesday • 3:00 p.m.]*

Today was a very significant date for the California bayside village of Yerba Buena. This community that had initially spawned the growing development of the interior of the territory had become a rather bustling village by now. With its well protected harbor, which was also the mouth of the territory's largest and most extensive river, the Sacramento, draining virtually half the territory, there was hardly any doubt that Yerba Buena held the potential for becoming perhaps a very important metropolis on the continent's West Coast. The town itself, with its population growing steadily, its well protected harbor and its mercantile possibilities was showing definite signs of expanding considerably more. The town, at this point in time, had 300 permanent residents and fifty adobe homes, plus a scattering of business establishments. There were those already—seamen in particular—who believed the waterfront community could conceivably become a premiere world metropolitan seaport.

Among those who were supporters of such a notion, none was more staunch in his belief of it than the city's *alcalde* under military administration, U.S. Naval Lieutenant Washington Allen Bartlett, officer of the warship *Portsmouth*. There was, however, so far as Bartlett was concerned, one particular fly in the ointment of his young city's future development: He saw little hope of the community actually becoming internationally important if it bore such a name as *El Parage de Yerba Buena*—The Place of Good Grass—and he had one much better in mind; one that was much less...well...*localized*.

Since his civil office, however temporary, endowed him with the power to do so, he issued a proclamation today, changing forever the name of the city and some of its important aspects. The central plaza, for example, which until today had always been referred to as simply "the Plaza," he now proclaimed should ever after be known as Portsmouth Square, in honor of the name of his vessel. The principal avenue fronting the harbor, which most of the citizens referred to simply as "the waterfront," he now bestowed with the name Montgomery Street, in honor of his vessel's commander.

The most significant change made by Bartlett in his proclamation today, however, was the name of the city itself. It would no longer be known by the name of Yerba Buena. From this day forward, the city would be known by the name of the great protected bay upon which it fronted.[202]

San Francisco.

*[January 30, 1847 • 5:00 p.m.]*

As was occurring at San Diego with others of the soldiers in the Mormon Battalion, Pvt. Henry Bigler was currently wondering what lay in store for them next. They all still had months of their enlistment left to serve and now that the uprising of the Californios seemed to have been quashed permanently, all were wondering how they would spend the remainder of their enlistment period.

By far the greater majority of the Saints were very eager to return to their families and to become again a part of the communal gathering that, in large measure, formed the foundation of the Church of Jesus Christ of Latter Day Saints. Their commander, however, quickly put that hope to rest by informing them that none need harbor any expectation of discharge before their enlistment term expired, adding, in fact, that he hoped some might wish to stay on in the service and reenlist for another term. There was a notable lack of enthusiasm expressed for that idea.

# The Infinite Dream

Pvt. Henry Bigler was one of those who had formulated no concrete idea as to what he wanted to do when his enlistment expired. He presumed he would probably head to whatever place was finally established as Zion, the new headquarters of the Mormon Church, but there was not really any imperative need for him to do so. He assumed he would probably resume living with his father at that time, but there was no great urgency within him to do so. Word had spread through the Battalion that the town called Yerba Buena on San Francisco Bay was growing rapidly and would no doubt eventually become an important seaport, perhaps even a major commerce center for international trade. Some of the Saints had already voiced the possibility that they might be transported by ship, at government expense, from San Diego to that place. As Bigler noted in his diary:

*The boys feel like they would like a ride of that sort after having footed it so far.*

While the thought of that possibility stirred some of the Saints, it brought little reaction from Bigler. He was, he knew, just a small town person by birth and he expected he would always harbor a fondness for small town living no matter where he happened to end up. But the thought of seeing more of California and staying west for a while intrigued him.

The Battalion had stayed at the Warner Ranch for another day, during which time Lt. Col. Cooke had a very serious talk with Baupista, a prominent chief of the Cohuillo tribe, comprised of some 2,000 warriors, who more or less stood aloofly independent from all the other tribes. Cooke told him very firmly that it would be folly for his tribe to interfere in any way with the Americans, who would soon and forever govern California. Baupista professed friendship and non-interference and they parted on good terms.

The Saints finally were on the march again early on January 23, moving west through rain over hills and valleys for twenty-five miles before camping for the night. The detachment Cooke had sent back to try to recover supplies that were stranded on the Gila River finally caught up with the Battalion again this day, bringing with them some three hundred pounds of flour they had recovered, along with a sackful of bacon. This provided each man in the Battalion only a pound and a quarter of flour as his share and Bigler was convinced that they were not telling the truth when they returned since, as he commented about it in his diary:

> ...There were twelve hundred pounds of flour put aboard the boat. I would not wonder at all, if the truth was told, that they "played off" on the Colonel as well as on the whole command, and were in no hurry about overtaking the army, for if they did, they would soon come on short 'lowance, and while they had plenty they were in no haste.

The storm that first drenched them and then plagued them with high winds lasted for three days and nights and was very discomfiting for man and beast alike. Four of their mules died due to the weather and several others wandered off and had to be recaptured. The storm, however, was far less important than the difficulty they had when they entered the Temecula Valley and encountered a body of Temecula Indians who had assembled to bury some thirty-eight of their dead, who had been killed by the Californios in a recent battle. The Indians mistook the American Army for Californios and the Americans thought the Indians were enemies, so the two sides were close to fighting—the Indians forming quite splendidly and formidably in full battle array—before the error was discovered and the matter resolved through talks. Once convinced the Army was friendly, the Indians were pleased to see the Americans and shook hands heartily with Cooke and some of his officers.

They parted in peace and the Army, following a road that branched off toward San Diego, they passed through the San Luis Valley, where they were pleased to find good grass as high as ten inches and plenty of wild mustard which they found made excellent mustard greens to complement their diet of beef.

More than anything else, the Battalion was pleased with the sudden abundance of animals they observed—thousands of head of cattle and horses, plus a large herd of donkeys and also virtually millions of wild geese, brants, ducks, pelicans and gulls.

Traveling downriver, the Battalion reached the deserted Catholic mission of San Luis Rey at noon on January 27.[203] Just a mile below it they ascended a bluff which, when they reached the top, revealed to them, only about three miles distant, a broad view of the Pacific Ocean—a gigantic cobalt blue expanse stretching to the western horizon. A prolonged, excited cheering broke out in the ranks at the sight of this long-anticipated goal and Cooke, smiling broadly, allowed it to run its course unchecked. The commander himself, rarely given to express praising superlatives, wrote unabashedly in his journal:

> ...The road wound through the smooth green valleys, and over very lofty hills, equally smooth and green. From the top of one of these hills, was caught the first and a magnificent view of the great ocean; and by rare chance, perhaps, it was so calm that it shone as a mirror. The charming and startling effect, under our circumstances, could not be expressed.

Private Henry G. Boyle of Co. C., who never before had been overly effusive in his diary descriptions about anything on their journey, waxed enthusiastically at the sight, writing:

> ...I never Shall be able to express my feelings at this enraptured moment. When our column were halted evry [sic] eye was turned toward its placid Surface evry [sic] heart beat with muttered pleasure evry [sic] Soul was full of thankfulness, evry [sic] tounge [sic] was Silent, we all felt too ful [sic] to give Shape to our feelings by any expression. It has been many a weary day, and we have traveled many a long mile Since our eyes have been permitted to gaze upon as lovely a Scene. The Surrounding hills are covered with wild oats & grass nearly a foot high, green & luxuriant as midsummer and how Sweet and refreshing is the breeze that is winging its way from the ocean up to this fertile Valley which here Stretches itself from the Shore back to the "Sierras." What an expansive view! How bright and beautiful evry [sic] thing looks![204]

As Sgt. Daniel Tyler penned it in his diary with subdued excitement:

> ...The joy, the cheer that filled our souls, none but worn-out pilgrims nearing a haven of rest can imagine. Prior to leaving Nauvoo, we had talked about and sung of "the great Pacific sea," and we were now upon its very borders, and its beauty far exceeded

*our most sanguine expectations. Our joy, however, was not unmixed with sorrow. The next thought was, where, oh where were our fathers, mothers, brothers, sisters, wives and children whom we had left in the howling wilderness among savages, or at Nauvoo, subject to the cruelty of the mobs? Had the government we were serving ordered them off the reservation? If so, had it ordered them back, when they came, to perish by the ruthless mobs it had failed even to rebuke, while the blood of innocence, even of children, cried to heaven for vengeance? Or, if allowed to move on, had they found a resting place where they could dwell in peace until they could raise a crop, or go, unknown, among their enemies and labor to replenish their much exhausted stores of provisions? We trusted in God that they were in the land of the living somewhere, and hoped we might find them on our return in or near the valley of the Great Salt Lake, within the limits of California, now a Mexican state, but this was only hope. We comforted ourselves with the fact that it was the "Lord's business to provide for His Saints," and that He was "not slack concerning His promises." Amid it all we went our way rejoicing.*

*An express from General Kearny directed that we take Quarters in a Catholic mission, five miles from San Diego.*

Oddly enough, Henry Bigler, who had often waxed enthusiastically in his diary about more mundane sights, was curiously subdued it his own diary entry on this occasion, as he wrote:

*January 27. While on the march today, we were overtaken with an express from General Kearny for us to march to a certain mission for quarters. We also learned from the expressman (I think his name was Walker) that we had taken a wrong road and had traveled some 10 or 12 miles out of our way. Our course was now southwest. The whole country appeared to be alive with large bands of horses, mules, and jackasses, and the valleys and hills covered with herds of cattle, and along the larger streams any amount of geese, crane, and brants. We passed San Luis Rey and turned a little to our left over a hill, from the top of which for the first time we got sight of the Pacific Ocean about four or five miles in the distance, and at night camped near the seashore.*

## The Infinite Dream

Sgt. Tyler was still marveling when he continued his voluble diary entry on January 28:

*As nearly all our beeves were lost on the night of the 27th, the Colonel gave orders to gather up more on the march; but as he did not direct how many were to be gathered, our Indian scouts brought to our camp, this morning, several hundred, probably ten times as many as we had lost; this caused a good deal of merriment at their expense.*

*Traveling in sight of the ocean, the clear bright sunshine, with the mildness of the atmosphere, combined to increase the enjoyment of the scene before us. We no longer suffered from the monotonous hardships of the deserts and cold atmosphere of the snowcapped mountains. January here, seems as pleasant as May in the northern States, and the wild oats, grass, mustard and other vegetable growths are as forward as we had been used to seeing them in June. The birds sing sweetly and all nature seems to smile and join in praise to the Giver of all good; but the crowning satisfaction of all to us was that we have succeeded in making the great national highway across the American desert, nearly filled our mission, and hoped soon to join our families and the Saints, for whom, as well as our country, we were living martyrs. Much of the soil over which we passed was very rich, and the vegetable growth exceedingly luxuriant. The water was clear and good, being mainly cold mountain streams, somewhat warmed by the brilliant rays of the sun in the middle of the day.*

Though still not quite so ebullient over their surroundings as some of the others, Pvt. Bigler was at least a little more expansive in his diary description on this same day than previously. He wrote:

*...January 28. Marched about 15 miles over broken country but alive with stock. I heard one of the guides say he knew one man who owned 12,000 head of cattle. In many places there were scores and perhaps 100s of acres of wild oats growing, looking as green as a wheat field at home in the month of May. I noticed another thing. Since coming near the ocean we have some dew, which was not the case in New Mexico, and, indeed, if I remember right, we had none*

*soon after leaving Ft. Leavenworth. Carcasses do not seem to rot in these countries as soon as they do in the United States, but literally dry up like a mummy, and I do not know but the people live longer for I have seen some Mexicans and Indians who looked to me as if they were as old as the everlasting hills. We made about 20 miles when we arrived at the San Diego Mission, where we expected to go into quarters.*[205]

The following day, January 29, assembly was beaten at 8:30 a.m. and the entire Battalion responded, at which time one of the regular officers, Col. Stevenson, addressed them most earnestly, remarking that Commodore Sloat with the American naval squadron had taken Monterey while, almost simultaneously, Capt. Montgomery occupied Yerba Buena, which had just become San Francisco and, as they already knew, Stockton and Kearny had ousted the Californios from Los Angeles: "The Spaniards are whipped, but not conquered," he told them. "Your term of service will soon close. It is of the utmost importance that troops be kept here until others can be transported." He paused as several groans erupted from the gathered men, waited until they had silenced and then continued: "I have the authority to press you into the service for six months longer, if deemed necessary, and have no doubt but I would be sustained in so doing, but believing, as I do, that enough, if not all, will re-enlist without, I have decided not to press you to serve longer. I am required to make a strong effort to raise at least one company, and the entire Battalion if possible. If the whole Battalion, or even four companies, enlist, you shall have the privilege of electing you own lieutenant colonel, major, and all subordinate officers. Your commander will be the third in rank in California. Should either of his superior officers die or be killed or removed, he would be second in command, and should both be removed, he would be first – military governor and commander-in-chief of California.

"I sympathize with you in the condition of your families. I am a father—I have been a husband. Should you re-enlist, you shall be discharged in February with twelve months' pay, and in the meantime a small detachment shall be sent, if necessary, to pilot your families to any point where they may wish to locate. Your patriotism and obedience to your officers have done much towards removing the prejudice of the government and the community at large, and I am satisfied that another year's service would place you on a level with other communities."

# The Infinite Dream

There was no general response from the assembled Saints, although a few irritated rumblings were audible, since what the colonel was saying was clearly looked upon as an insult added to the injuries they had for so long received without due cause. The consensus was generally the same among all the Saints here assembled: They felt—and certainly with justification—that they could compare favorably with any other group in the world where patriotism and other virtues were concerned and they had now reached the saturation point where no longer were they so willing to engage in self-sacrifice to please others who cared little or nothing for them.

Still having made no sort of generalized commitment to the remarks just delivered to them, the gathered Saints were now dismissed by Col. Stevenson into the hands of their own officers, from whom they knew, with a sense of gloom, they were apt to be subjected to similar entreaties.

So it occurred…and without much delay.

They assembled only a short time later perhaps a quarter mile away in a sort of declivity that was almost a natural amphitheater and listened, one by one, to what their more prominent ranking officers had to say at this point. First to speak was Captain Jesse D. Hunter of Company D, who was looked upon by the brethren as a recruiting officer and he made it clear without preamble that he believed it to be the duty of the Battalion to re-enter the service and serve another term, in support of which he listed a variety of reasons.

Next to speak was Captain Jefferson Hunt of Company A, who endorsed the remarks just delivered by Captain Hunter but added that it was essential for the Saints to maintain the ground they had gained; that an opportunity was before them now to gain still more. He recommended that the Saints elect an officer from their number who would be third in command but who would become first should Colonel Mason and Colonel Stevenson be called away. His comments were little more than a reiteration of what Col. Stevenson had already said.

Captain Daniel Davis, commanding Company E, spoke only briefly and, in essence, backed up completely what the previous officers had said.

Third Lt. Cyrus C. Canfield of Co, D. was a bit more thought-provoking in his remarks. "I think," he told them, "that we had all better reenlist, in order that we might have some means of taking care of our families since, at present, it would take all of each man's pay to outfit himself for the journey home and by the time we find the Church itself, we will have nothing left. I know there are some of us here who think we can live on faith alone, but I believe if we don't have something to live on besides faith, we will perish."

George P. Dykes, 1st Lt. of Co. D, probably the most detested Mormon officer, played his usual mealy-mouthed role by subscribing to all that had thus far been uttered by the others and adding: "All that the Saints have done will be lost unless we serve another term."

The Battalion's principal preacher, Father David Pettegrew of Co. E, opposed that notion. He thought it to be clearly the duty of the Saints to return eastward as swiftly as possible and locate and look after their outcast families. "Others can do as they think best," he intoned, "but I believe we have done all we set out to do and more. Our offering was accepted and I have no doubt our swift return will be sanctioned by our Church leaders."

At that point Captains Davis and Hunter, along with Father Pettegrew, were chosen as a committee to draft conditions of re-enlistment. As soon as the articles were drafted, a few more speeches were made. Second Orderly Sergeant William Hyde of Co. B addressed the group in a mild tone but in a peculiarly forcible manner, saying, "We have made one offering which I feel assured has been fully accepted and I think that it is now time we return to our families and be ready for any sacrifice that might become necessary for us to make in the future. Let's face it: All, so far as we have any knowledge of it, have been satisfied with our past service. I, for one, believe God is satisfied as well."

Sgt. Daniel Tyler of Company C was perhaps the most definitive in his remarks and the only one of the speakers to elicit applause from those gathered. "I think," he said, "we need to refer back to the pledges made us by Colonel Allen, who repeatedly assured us that in case of his death or removal, the command would fall upon the senior officer of this corps. Well, sadly, that noble officer did die and all *that* showed us was while a senior officer might be removed by death or otherwise, *our* commander might also be removed, leaving us without any rank in the command of California, where the chances are two to one against us. So where is the realization of those pledges? So far as our own officers taking command was concerned, instead of that, were not our noses put upon the grindstone...*and aren't they still there?* Those who wish can certainly remain, but I feel it my duty to the Church and to my own family to return."

A few more remarks were made by others but without adding anything of real substance to what had already been said and upon their conclusion the meeting was adjourned with no other such meeting scheduled for the future. A request for volunteers was made and sixteen individuals chosen.

The terms of what the Saints had concluded were carefully written up and approved and then taken by the body of volunteers and presented to the day's initial speaker, Colonel Stephenson, a veteran officer of the regular army, who looked at the pages briefly and in a cursory manner, then summarily rejected them.

The Mormon Battalion consisting of some four hundred Saints, having left Santa Fe, New Mexico Territory exactly one hundred two days ago under command of Lt. Col. Philip St. George Cooke, having traveled on foot through deserts, mountains and hostile Indian territory, having dug wells all along the way and having firmly established the Santa Fe Trail, truly expected to receive virtually nothing in return. They found that despite their more than exemplary service given to the United States Government, in many respects, as in their off-hand rejection by Col. Stevenson, the cards of unreasoning discrimination were still solidly stacked against them.

Despite that gloomy conclusion, however, there were signs that finally their worth was becoming recognized and acknowledged. Their arrival had added substantial weight to General Kearny's claim of his legal authority to command all U.S. forces currently in California and to establish a civil government that treated the citizens benevolently and with exacting fairness, as had not thus far been entirely the case with Commodore Stockton or Col. Fremont.

Kearny, after conferring with Cooke, realized and acknowledged that the continued good behavior and industry of the Saints would undoubtedly help him accomplish far more than a show of musketry in conciliating the citizens and establishing trust and stability in the new government being inaugurated. Kearny's unswerving determination now was to defend the rights and interests of all citizens and not in any way to treat them as subjugated enemies, which was precisely as the U.S. Secretary of War had directed. He swiftly established protection for those Californios who had supported the American takeover and who, though to a lesser degree now, were still viewed as traitors by some of their die-hard countrymen. Kearny at once set up programs to defend ranches against raids by hostile natives who had once been pacified under the Spanish mission system, but who had become increasingly belligerent since the secularization of the missions that had begun fourteen years earlier. And now the restlessness of the Saints, which had quickly become apparent to Kearny in the brief time since their arrival, was effectively quelled, as much by how he addressed them in assembly now as by how he turned their seething energies toward having them sink new wells and establish brickyards and start construction of new buildings to improve community life in both Los Angeles and San Diego. His first Special Order to them was quickly posted for all to see:

*Headquarters Mormon Battalion*
*Mission of San Diego, January 30, 1847*
*(Order No. 1.)*

*The Lieutenant-Colonel commanding, congratulates the Battalion on their safe arrival on the shore of the Pacific Ocean, and the conclusion of their march of over two thousand miles.*

*History may be searched in vain for an equal march of infantry. Nine-tenths of it has been through a wilderness, where nothing but savages and wild beasts are found, or deserts where, for want of water, there is no living creature. There with almost hopeless labor, we have dug wells, which the future traveler will enjoy. Without a guide who had traversed them we have ventured into trackless prairies and tablelands where water was not found for several marches. With crowbar and pick, and axe in hand, we worked our way over mountains, which seemed to defy aught save the wild goat, and hewed a passage through a chasm of living rock more narrow than our wagons. To bring these first wagons to the Pacific, we have preserved the strength of our mules by herding them over large tracts, which you have laboriously guarded without loss. The garrison of four presidios of Sonora concentrated within the walls of Tucson, gave us no pause. We drove them out, with their artillery, but our intercourse with the citizens was unmarked by a single act of injustice. Thus marching half naked and half fed, and living upon wild animals, we have discovered and made a road of great value to our country.*

*Arrived at the first settlement of California after a single day's rest, you cheerfully turned off from the route to this point of promised repose, to enter upon a campaign and meet, as we believed, the approach of the enemy, and this, too, without salt to season your sole subsistence of fresh meat.*

*Lieutenant A.J. Smith and George Stoneman, of the 1st dragoons, have shared and given valuable aid in all these labors. Thus, volunteers, you have exhibited some high and essential qualities of veterans. But much remains undone. Soon, you will turn your strict attention to the drill, to system and order, to forms, also, which are all necessary to the soldier.*

*(Signed)* Lieut.-Colonel P. St. George Cooke,
*(Signed)* P.C. Merrill, *Adjutant*

Instantly, upon conclusion of the reading. The Saints cheered heartily and threw their hats into the air. Pvt. Henry Boyle said aloud of their commander, to no one in particular: "He is a man, too, that was strongly prejudiced against us in the start."

[*February 2, 1847 • Tuesday*]

The prevailing question in California Territory at this juncture was clear enough to all, but the correct answer was not: Who was in control insofar as government was concerned?

Each of the several claimants for the territorial seat of power seemingly had both credentials and authority to back him up, so who among these aspirants were the common people—the Californios and the Indian tribes and the land owners and the settlers from elsewhere— to accept as their leader... and who were the civil servants and military personnel to obey?

This was a very serious matter involving far more than just a mere matter of choice by the inhabitants of California. Because the question remained unequivocally unanswered for now, both government and military officials were substantially hamstrung and a strong sense of disorder and impending peril loomed. The possibility was very strong, very real, that the residents of this territory, already outraged by the arrogance of the Americans, would rise in revolt once again and this time be supported more fully by Mexico as the conflict continued. Without a firmly established and controlling government in place, the entire structure could quite easily collapse in a morass of confusion. That was the situation now and it was already more than merely a strong possibility.

With the self-proclaimed Californio leaders clearly no longer vying for governmental control, the role seemed destined to go to one of several American military officials presently on the scene, but the big question remained: To which individual and under what conditions?

Lt. Col. John Fremont, was already loudly proclaiming himself to be Governor, not only by virtue of a letter received from his father-in-law, Senator Thomas Hart Benton—who was himself a man of great influence with President James Polk and his administration—but also through right of appointment by Admiral Sloat, who had taken territorial possession of California for the United States, and then bolstered by confirmation of that appointment by Sloat's successor, Commodore Robert Field Stockton, who fully considered *him*self Commander-in Chief of the Territory and by right its foremost leader; or by General Stephen Kearny, more recently on the scene but who bore with him U.S. Governmental authority to assume top command in California. Then, too, there was Lt. Col. Richard Mason, who had newly arrived with orders to take governmental control from Kearny so that Kearny could return to Washington, D.C., Mason himself with the rank of Brevet Brigadier General in the offing as soon as he took over command from Kearny; there was, of course, also Col. Jonathan D. Stevenson, presently en route to California with a regiment of New York Volunteers, who was already assuming from his orders that he would be in command upon his arrival; and then, equally, there was Commodore Shubrick, whose own unequivocal orders from the Navy Department were to replace Stockton as commander of the Pacific Squadron and himself control all matters currently afloat militarily in the California Territory. Each of those mentioned was utterly convinced in his own mind that he possessed the utmost right and authority for the position.

Little wonder, then, that the very same burning question, as yet quite unanswered, seemed to be on the lips of *everyone* today—especially the younger military officers—throughout the length and breadth of the Territory of California:

*Who the devil is the Governor of California?*

[February 4, 1847 • Thursday]

The struggle for American dominance in the New Mexico Territory was now, for all intents and purposes, drawn to a close. The Army forces

## The Infinite Dream

there, being led by the irascible Col. Sterling Price of Missouri, clamped down mercilessly on whatever pockets of resistance remained.

The first of the two New Mexican battles on January 24, which included the Battle of La Canada—more a rather bloody skirmish than a truly significant battle—was led personally by Col. Price and a portion of his regiment, joined by more of the Second Missouri and a full company of Kearny's dragoons from Albuquerque under command of Capt. John Henry K. Burgwin.

The second battle on that same day—the Battle of Mora—the latter a conflict under command of Capt. Israel Hendley—was decisively won against the handful of Mexican and Indian insurrectionists still functioning there. The same encouragement was experienced with the Battle of Embudo Pass on January 29 and, more importantly, today's fierce fight in the Battle of Taos, which marked the bloody end of a rather excessively bloody campaign.

In the latter struggle, occurring today, the rebels made the fatal error of crowding themselves into the old Spanish mission church at Taos, a large building constructed mainly of thick adobe bricks, which they evidently believed would protect them. It did not, however, once the Americans unleashed their artillery to blast huge holes in the walls.[206] Most of the leaders of the insurgency were killed in the bombardment and those who were not were swiftly rounded up by Price and his subcommanders and, following a brief trial on charges of treason, considered by most of the combatants on both sides to be a mockery, hanged on greased ropes.

The struggle for New Mexico Territory was finally over and the Americans had won it handily. It was one more leg up on President Polk's long-ranging plan to oust Mexican control and consolidate the holdings of the United States from coast to coast.

*[February 5, 1847 • Friday • 4:00 p.m.]*

Lt. William Tecumseh Sherman finished writing the notation in his journal, blotted it carefully, then read what he had just written. It was an interim comment, not terribly long, but he considered it one of the more important entries he had written and he grinned as he read his own words yet again:

*5 Febr '47. Today has been one of the more significant days of my Army career thus far. I have met, even briefly conversed with, a man of great importance; to me, surely, and, I believe, to his country, tho' he exhibits no semblance of recognizing this in himself. He is a Brigadier General—first general I have ever met personally—and I think he will play an important role in my own future career in the Army, just as he has already played, and continues to play, a very important role in U.S. military history. He is the Commanding Officer of the Army of the West—General Stephen Watts Kearny.*

That he would meet so important a person in this land called California was, to Sherman, a most unlikely as well as fortunate happenstance and hardly one he could have predicted on his arrival here at this port city of Monterey just ten days earlier.

That arrival on January 26 aboard the *U.S. Lexington* had been, for Sherman, simultaneously the most exasperating as well as the most exciting event of the entire voyage that had lasted for one hundred ninety-eight days. The ship's master and regular navigator, Lt. Macomb, had made all his observations quite correctly but during the night his relief, Midshipman Nicholson, made an incorrect observation on the north star that, to his reckoning, indicated they were twenty miles father south than should have been the case.

Nicholson's reckoning was relayed to Captain Bailey, who instantly issued orders to alter the course of the ship more to the north and follow up the coastline, keeping good lookout for Point Pinos, which marks the normal entry of Monterey Bay. About noon, the prevailing north wind slackened, which allowed Lt. Macomb to get a good observation, at which time it was discovered that the *Lexington* was already north of Ano Nuevo, the northern headland of Monterey Bay.

The ship was put about immediately, but gradually a southeast storm arose and, as Sherman commented about the situation in his journal:

*...we buffeted about for several days, cursing that unfortunate observation on the north star, for, on first sighting the coast, had we turned for Monterey, instead of away to the north, we would have been snugly anchored before the storm. But the southeaster abated, and the usual northwest wind came out again, and we*

# The Infinite Dream

*sailed steadily down the roadstead of Monterey Bay. This is shaped something like a fish-hook, the barb being the harbor, the point being Point Pinos, the southern headland. Slowly the land came out of the water, the high mountains about Santa Cruz, the low beach of the Salinas, and the strongly-marked ridge terminating in the sea in a point of dark pine-trees. Then the line of whitewashed houses of adobe, backed by the groves of dark oaks, resembling old apple trees, and then we saw two vessels anchored close to the town. One was a small merchant brig and another a large ship apparently dismasted.*

*At last we saw a boat coming out to meet us, and when it came alongside, we were surprised to find Lt. Henry Wise, master of the* Independence *frigate, that we had left at Valparaiso. Wise had come off to pilot us to our anchorage.*

Sherman and a number of the other military men aboard gathered about Lt. Wise while he gave orders to the helmsman. Almost simultaneously he added, in his peculiarly fluent style of speech to those who had gathered, the news that he had assimilated: that the *Independence* had sailed from Valparaiso a week after the *Lexington* departed and had been in Monterey Bay for a week; that the Californios had broken out in an insurrection; that the naval fleet under Commodore Stockton was all down the coast about San Diego; that General Kearny and his force had reached California but had engaged in a severe battle at San Pascual and had been worsted, losing a score of officers and men, himself and others wounded; that war was going on at Los Angeles; that the whole country was full of guerillas…and on and on, imparting to them while piloting the ship in, as Sherman wrote:

*…more news than we could have learned on shore in a week, and, being unfamiliar with the great distances, we imagined that we should have to debark and begin fighting at once. Swords were brought out, guns oiled and made ready, and everything was in a bustle…*

Later that same evening, Lt. Sherman penned more in his journal and in greater detail, as was his custom before retiring. From his position at the rail of the *Lexington*, he wrote:

> ...everything on shore looked bright and beautiful, the hills covered with grass and flowers, the live oaks so serene and homelike, and the low adobe houses, with red-tiled roofs and whitened walls, contrasted well with the dark pinetrees [sic] behind, making a decidedly good impression upon us who had come so far to spy out the land. Nothing could be more peaceful in its looks than Monterey in January, 1847. We had already made the acquaintance of Commodore Shubrick and the officers of the Independence in Valparaiso, so that we again met as old friends. Immediate preparations were made for landing, and, as I was the unit's quartermaster and commissary, I had plenty to do. There was a small wharf and an adobe custom house in possession of the navy; also a barrack of two stories, occupied by some marines, commanded by Lieutenant Maddox; and on a hill to the west of the town had been built a two-story blockhouse of hewed logs occupied by a guard of sailors under command of Lieutenant Baldwin, United States Navy. Not a single modern wagon or cart was to be had in Monterey, nothing but the old Mexican cart with wooden wheels, drawn by two or three pairs of oxen, yoked by the horns. A man named Tom Cole had two or more of these, and he came into immediate requisition.
>
> The United States consul, and most prominent man there at the time, was Thomas O. Larkin, who had a store and a pretty good two-story house occupied by his family. It was soon determined that our company was to land and encamp on the hill at the block-house, and we also to have possession of the warehouse, or custom-house, for storage.

Lt. Sherman's company was landed on the Monterey wharf and the entire unit, in full dress with knapsacks and arms, was marched to the hill where it relieved the guard under Lt. Baldwin. The tents and camp equipage were unloaded from the ship and hauled up to their position and the new camp swiftly established. Sherman, himself—along with his friend, Lt. Edward Otho Cresap Ord—who was rumored to be a cousin of Queen Victoria—remained at the custom-house, where Sherman superintended the landing of the stores and their proper distribution. He then wrote:

> I had brought out from New York City twenty thousand dollars

# The Infinite Dream

commissary funds, and eight thousand dollars quartermaster funds, and as the ship contained about six months' supply of provisions, also a saw-mill, grist-mill, and almost everything needed, we were soon established comfortably.

We found the people of Monterey a mixed set of Americans, native Mexicans, and Indians, about one thousand all told. They are kind and pleasant, and seem to have nothing to do, except such as own ranches in the country for the rearing of horses and cattle. Horses can be bought at any price from four dollars up to sixteen, but no horse is ever valued above a doubloon or Mexican ounce (sixteen dollars). Cattle cost eight dollars fifty cents for the best, and this makes beef net about two cents a pound, but nobody buys beef by the pound, but by the carcass. Game of all kinds — elk, deer, wild geese, and ducks — are abundant, but coffee, sugar, and small stores, are rare and costly. There are some half-dozen shops or stores, but their shelves are empty. The people are very fond of riding, dancing, and of shows of any kind. The young fellows take great delight in showing off their horsemanship, and will dash along, picking up a half dollar from the ground, stop their horses in full career and turn about on the space of a bullock's hide, and their skill with the lasso is certainly wonderful. At full speed they cast their lasso about the horns of a bull, or so throw it as to catch any particular foot. These fellows will work all day on horseback in driving cattle or catching wild-horses for a mere nothing, but all the money offered will not hire one of them to walk a mile.

The girls are very fond of dancing, and they do dance gracefully and well. Every Sunday, regularly, we will have a baile, or dance, and sometimes interspersed through the week.

We were all invited to witness a play called "Adam and Eve." Eve was personated by a pretty young girl known as Dolores Gómez, who, however, was dressed very unlike Eve, for she was covered with a petticoat and spangles. Adam was personated by her brother...God Almighty was personated, and heaven's occupants seemed very human. Yet the play was pretty, interesting, and elicited universal applause.

It was today, however, February 5, that the event occurred which was so significant to Lt. Sherman. He was aboard Commodore Shubrick's flagship, the *Independence*, dining with the ward-room officers, when a look-out's call was clearly heard: "War vessel approaching! War vessel in the offing!"

In a short while everyone relaxed when the ship was identified as the sloop *U.S. Cyane*, which was known to be under command of Captain Samuel F. DuPont. The officers of the *Independence* finished their meal and then the majority of them trooped out onto the deck and positioned themselves at the starboard bow rail to watch the approach of the new arrival—all the while the two ships exchanging signals. The excitement increased substantially when the signals resolved themselves into the message that General Kearny was aboard the *Cyane*.

As the sloop came closer a deck-boat was launched from the *Independence* with Shubrick's flag-officer Lt. Lewis aboard to meet the *Cyane*, bearing the usual messages needing to be relayed, but also with a special invitation to the general to come aboard the *Independence* as Commodore Shubrick's guest. At the rail and agog with curiosity were many of the larger ship's officers, including Sherman and his fellow lieutenants, Henry Wise, Montgomery Lewis and William Chapman, none of whom yet realized the identity of the officer being sent an escort.

Before too long the deck-boat returned with a stranger in Army-blue seated in the stern-sheets. As it drew closer, Sherman became convinced the individual was General Kearny, even though the man was clad in an old dragoon officer's blue coat and was wearing an Army cap to which had been added a broad visor cut from a full dress hat. Though relatively certain his recognition of the officer was correct, Sherman said nothing. It was Chapman who suddenly spoke aloud rather excitedly: "Fellows, the problem is solved. There is the grand *vizier* himself, by God! That's the governor of California! It's General Kearny!"

The shrill pipings of several whistles blew and suddenly the deck of the *Independence* was alive with sailors quickly forming themselves into proper echelons and rankings, the officers drawn up closest to the boarding gate, Commodor Shubrick himself at the portal. In a few moments more General Kearny appeared, saluted the colors and was effusively invited aboard by the Commodore. As he stepped aboard, the two principal commanders shook hands with genuine pleasure and all hands on deck greeted Kearny with a rousing, synchronized cheer, which the General accepted with a pleased smile and nodded warmly at the officers and men. A moment later the two officers disappeared into the Commodore's cabin. It was a telling interval and, as Lt. Sherman recorded somewhat later in his journal:

> *Between Commodore Shubrick and General Kearny existed from that time forward the greatest harmony and good feeling, and no further trouble existed as to the controlling power on the Pacific coast and all friction between Army and Navy disappeared. General Kearny had dispatched from San Diego his quartermaster, Col. F. Swords, to the Sandwich Islands, to purchase clothing and stores for his men, and had come up to Monterey, bringing with him Turner and Warner, leaving Emory and the company of Dragoons below. He was delighted to find a full strong company of artillery, subject to his orders, well supplied with clothing and money in all respects, and, much to the disgust of our Captain Tompkins, he took half of his company clothing and part of the money held by me for the relief of his worn-out and almost naked dragoons left behind at Los Angeles.*

As he prepared to leave the *Independence,* General Kearny passed the gathered officers with a slight smile still curling his lips and crinkling the corners of his eyes. Along the way, he paused before Sherman and asked his name and rank. Sherman, taken aback, quickly recovered and drew himself up into stiff attention and then provided the General with the answers to his questions.

General Kearny reached out and shook Sherman's hand and his smile broadened. "I want to thank you personally, Lieutenant Sherman, for your warm welcome and ask that you relay to your fellow officers my sincere thanks for theirs as well; and to the men, also. You are all to be commended for the important roles you have played in the successful transfer of the Territory of California into the domain of the United States of America."

"On behalf of the officers and men of the *Independence,* Sir," Sherman replied, his voice quavering only slightly with nervousness, "as well as the men of my own Regiment, I wish the General well and Godspeed. You have our very sincere thanks and appreciation in return. It is a distinct honor and pleasure for us all to serve under your command."

*[February 6, 1847 • Saturday • 6:00 p.m.]*

For the Saints, the rigorous journey on foot of over 2,000 miles was finished, but their harassment at the hands of non-Mormons, instigated through rumor, was far from over. The Missourians in Kearny's command, especially those quartered at the Mission San Gabriel, having arrived earlier, brought their own prejudices with them and, even before the Mormon Battalion arrived, had spread their litany of hatred for the Saints before them.

The unjustified distrust and fear induced by those Missourians in the local populations at San Diego and Los Angeles and the territory between through the wild, unreasonable and unrelenting half-truths and outright lies broadcast about the Saints had created an atmosphere of prejudice against them quite as pervasive here as that which they hoped to have permanently left behind. All they could do at this point was, through their own comportment, prove their true worth; a task far easier said than done, since the California populace had been so primed to hatred that they hid behind closed doors and shuttered windows when the Saints arrived.

With the problems of imminent insurgency essentially set aside, at least for the time being, what remained for those of the Mormon Battalion was simply being broken up into their individual companies and shunted about to perform mundane tasks until the time, still distant, when their enlistment period should expire. Very quickly fully a quarter of the Battalion were garrisoned in the missions at San Diego and San Luis Rey.[207] Company C in its entirety was marched off eastward to guard against guerilla bands of Mexicans and Indians who might attempt penetration through Cajon Pass to harass American occupational forces. To the remainder of the Battalion was given the chores of baking breads, restoring damaged village structures and building a new hilltop fortress to be called Fort Moore, large enough to quarter two hundred troops and sturdy enough to fend off assault until aid could come from San Diego or Monterey or even San Francisco.

Among the higher priority tasks assigned to the Saints was rejuvenation of the old Spanish missions, now mostly abandoned and having become looted, sun-bleached and earthquake-cracked structures, the walled gardens severely deteriorated and overgrown with weeds, the sequestered burial places choked with fiercely thorned briars, the interiors of the great sprawling buildings filthied from a generation or more of misuse or disuse. These were systematically cleaned and repaired and whitewashed by the brethren and, rather astoundingly, made quite attractive and comfortable for further use by citizens as well as the military.

The non-Mormon soldiers had certainly proven themselves as fighters to be reckoned with when pitted against organized enemies but, with the insurgency crisis essentially overcome, those soldiers were thrown into the ennui of peaceful occupation, which was far more difficult for them to tolerate than activities of warfare. Disturbingly increased desertions resulted among them, along with gambling, drinking and rapine pursuits, greatly frustrating American military authorities trying to cope with situations not only disgraceful to the Army but of growing concern to the inhabitants. Little wonder, then, that they barred their doors and hid from the Saints who had been portrayed to them as being even more malignant.

Now, however, the Saints had come and what they had been so maliciously described as being was swiftly revealed as lies; instead, they worked diligently with few complaints, abstained entirely from drink, refused to involve themselves in the depravities and follies engaged in with so much gusto by the non-Mormon troops. They met frequently in humble brotherhood and spirit, together breaking bread, passing the cup, acknowledging their own shortcomings to each other, singing hymns in praise of God instead of profane and suggestive brothel songs, abstaining profanity and instead offering prayers of supplication and contrition.

Astounded at such revelations, the Californios and Indians quickly recognized the very intrinsic goodness of the Mormon soldiers and honored them for their faith and stalwartness as compared to the traits of the American soldiers who had preceded them... and who had so maligned them. As testimony to this conclusion, with the Mormons' terms of enlistment rapidly running out, the townspeople were abruptly imploring military authorities to retain the Saints as garrison troops, rather than before long replacing them with almost certainly less reliable and less wholesome troops. At San Diego in particular, where Company B was quartered, a petition was written, signed by every native resident, imploring that the Mormon soldiers be retained permanently. It was a highly gratifying occurrence for the Mormons, but it did not, as the townspeople hoped, result in their widespread reenlistment.

As trying as the situation was for the commander of the Mormon Battalion, who had for so long yearned to be launched into battle, Lt. Col. Philip St. George Cooke somehow still managed to retain his intrinsic sense of humor and took amusement from the fact that with all the varied American forces now present in California, his was the only one that could truly be portrayed as legal, his own standing exactly as earned and not any sort of pretension toward the highest authority in the territory. His rank was equal to that of Lt. Col. John Fremont, yet Fremont was loudly alleging himself to be Governor. As Cooke wrote with unmasked irony:

> *General Kearny is supreme—somewhere up the coast; Colonel Fremont supreme at Pueblo de Los Angeles; Commodore Stockton is Commander-in-chief at San Diego, and we are all supremely poor; the government having no money and no credit; and we hold the Territory because Mexico is poorest of all.*[208]

A sense of awe filled the Saints on February 2 as they passed beneath the hill where, just after the Battle of San Pascual, where he had lost a third of his command, General Kearny and his remaining force, awaiting reinforcement from San Diego, had been pinned by surrounding enemy troops. The hill, eight miles from the San Pascual battle site, had been unnamed then, but now it was being called Mule Hill because during those three days before the reinforcement arrived on December 11, their provisions having failed, Kearny's men had killed and eaten sixteen of the best of their trail-worn mules.

The marching residue of the Mormon Battalion arrived at San Luis Rey the following day, February 3, and were still there now, though far from inactive. As Pvt. Henry Bigler noted in his chronicle:

> *...arrived on the third about noon at that place, some 40 miles. This is a handsome situation and good buildings sufficient to accommodate a thousand soldiers, first-rate barracks. Here also are two vineyards, a number of olive trees, pepper trees, and peach trees. The latter are in bloom. The Battalion [will require] some three days cleaning out and cleaning up the barracks. Here, too, were plenty of fleas.... we are called out every day on duty to drill a few hours.*

Pvt. David Pettegrew of Co. E waxed a bit more eloquently about the situation at the San Luis Rey fortification in his own journal, writing:

> ...Here we have taken up our quarters. The Mission is pleasantly situated on a [sic] elevated piece of land about four miles from the coast. There is a church in the southeast corner built square and on the front or south side is a row of pillars that supports an arch on which is a walk that goes around the top of the building. In the middle is a square and in the center of this is a sun-dial, an orange tree and two black pepper trees. In this square we must drill and parade every day for two hours and sometimes more...

The clean-up the Saints were ordered to accomplish was no easy chore, yet the men fell to at the chore on Lt. Col. Cooke's order and, as Sgt. Daniel Tyler commented in his journal:

> On the 4th, about eighty men are detailed as police to clean up the square and quarters and make necessary repairs, which is being done in good order, making everything look as cheerful and respectable as our dirt floors will permit. Many of the men are almost naked, without a change of underclothing to keep off dust or the worst of the vermin, with which the country abounds, and which even many of the elite of the native Californians are said to be never free from.
>
> What little clothing is in the country is in the hands of army sutlers, and held at extravagant prices. The public square of the mission, with a large adobe Catholic Church and a row of minor buildings forming the outside wall, contain about four acres of ground, with orange and other tropical trees in the center. The olive, pepper, orange, fig and many other varieties of semi-tropical fruit and ornamental trees grow in the garden. Two large vineyards are also connected with this garden.
>
> On the 5th, yesterday, an order was read relating to the duties of the Soldiers when in garrison, such as times of parade, cleaning arms and clothes, shaving, cutting hair, saluting officers, etc., all of which were very good in their way.[209] The only ground for complaint this order afforded, so far as I heard, was that some who had not shaved since leaving home preferred not to do so until they returned. They were probably desirous that their wives, who had

*never looked upon their beautiful visages ornamented with a foot, more or less, of what they doubtless supposed to be very comely hair, should have a chance to see the luxuriant growth before it was sacrificed. Perhaps, in some instances the rich growth proved a shield or covering to features not as inviting as might be desired, hence the dread of submitting to the tonsorial operation. But this, like all other military orders, was quite imperative. It prescribed that no beard be allowed to grow below the tip of the ear; hence the moustache only could be saved. The hair also must be clipped even with the tip of the ear and everything made as neat and tidy as circumstances would permit....*

*After arriving at San Luis Rey, the very able and worthy quartermaster sergeant of Company A, Redick N. Allred, was appointed quartermaster sergeant in Colonel Cooke's non-commissioned staff...*

[February 8, 1847 • Monday]

Together, General Kearny and Commodore Shubrick today solidified Kearny's rightful position in the California Territory as its governor and supreme military commander with the issuance of a joint circular in which the general assumed complete executive powers without opposition in any form. Immediately, General Kearny's first official move, enacted today, was to reestablish the California capital city where it had previously been under the Californios, at Monterey, but now as the Tenth Military District, which encompassed all of California from the Mexican border northward to the southern border of the Oregon Territory.

"This country," Kearny declared publicly, "is to be held for now simply as a conquest in the name of the United States of America and, as nearly as possible, under the previously existing laws until such time as the United States shall provide a duly authorized territorial government."

The general, as yet, made no mention of another matter of a more personal nature that he planned to expedite just as soon as other priority matters were taken care of—the arrest and formal charging, under the rules of court-martial, of Lt. Col. John Charles Fremont.

[February 23, 1847 • Tuesday]

The city of San Francisco was growing very rapidly.

Just a day short of two weeks ago, San Francisco *alcalde* Washington

Bartlett had directed one of San Francisco's more prominent draftsmen, Jasper O'Farrell, who had been living in the community for the past four years, to improve on the *alcade's* current map of the town and produce a new one. O'Farrell fell to the task with gusto and the map he created considerably increased the size of the town.

One of the things he did was to digress from the grid pattern of Vioget to incorporate the existing trail to the Mission, which was on a diagonal to the grid. In doing so, he extended the grid southward in conformance to the grid, thereby considerably enlarging the town's limits. As a result, Market Street was drawn running at a crazy diagonal to all the streets laid out to the north, but in perfect right angle conformity to those running to the south. That this would ever afterward make Market Street a boundary of sorts between the two sections concerned O'Farrell not at all.

His map was also the first of San Francisco's municipal maps to name the streets instead of merely numbering them. To do so, he relied on the use of the names of prominent San Francisco citizens—such as Brannan, Bryant, Harrison, Howard, Hyde and Leavenworth—as well as especially prominent Californians, such as Sutter and Vallejo, and then capped it off with the names of men renowned in the War with Mexico, such as Kearny, Stockton, Fremont, Taylor, Montgomery, Jones and DuPont.

On January 12, Colonel Richard B. Mason of the First Dragoons arrived at San Francisco on the store-ship *Erie,* with his new orders from Washington D.C., authorizing his takeover of the seat of government from General Kearny as soon as the latter felt it was "safe and reasonable" to relax his military hold on the Territory. When that ocurred, Kearny was to repair to the nation's capital as swiftly as might be accomplished, preferably by land rather than by sea.

As one of his last official acts as San Francisco's *alcalde*, Lieutenant Bartlett certified the accuracy of O'Farrell's new town plan before the county recorder, immediately following which Edwin Bryant was elected and sworn in as *alcalde* to replace Bartlett, an appointment that lasted only a portion of one day, before Bryant himself lost his seat to the new *alcalde*, William Hyde.

What it all seemed to betoken was that San Francisco was growing up very rapidly and, as already many of its townsmen fully believed, was destined to play a major role in what every resident was already certain would occur before too many years went by—the Territory of California becoming one of the states of the United States of America.

# Chapter 12

♦

[*February 24, 1847 · Wednesday*]

Matters did not bode well for General Zachary Taylor.

All but fewer than 5,000 of his troops had been reluctantly transferred in January to General Winfield Scott to support the new Army commander in his bold plan to advance, immediately after the taking of Vera Cruz, upon Mexico City. General Taylor had been ordered ignominiously to simply hover with his remaining force around Saltillo and defend his occupation of the north as far as Monterrey. This was an order Taylor found galling in the extreme and he instantly made up his mind that no one was going to deprive Old Rough and Ready of the glory he felt was his, via the White House.

Instead of obeying Scott's order without question, Taylor completely disregarded the Army's Commander and defiantly ordered his remaining force of just under five thousand men forward to Agua Nueva. Though the movement was made with the joyful approval of his own men and the sustained approbation of the various war correspondents, who hailed the act as one of great courage, as he was well aware they would, it was, in fact, a considered ploy in the advancement of his own political advancement, and achieved with much loss of life that needn't have occurred at all.

At almost the same time as Taylor's force began its march, Scott's follow-up message to Taylor, disclosing the latter's weakness and revealing in broad terms Scott's plans for his own force at Vera Cruz, was intercepted by General Santa Ana, who immediately advanced northward with his army of 20,000 men against Taylor from San Luis Potosi. Taylor's reaction was to instantly withdraw his force, of which only 500 men were regulars, a little beyond Buena Vista where, on February 5, he took up a defensive position in the mountains, decidedly outnumbered.

That General Antonio López de Santa Ana had an army at all was little short of amazing, since he had succeeded in raising, arming and equipping his force from a nation already half in revolt against him. It was a good army, though, and deserved better leadership. Santa Ana, using 14,000 of his men, came very close indeed to winning the two-day conflict and undoubtedly would have, had not Santa Ana's own courage failed him. The resultant bloody Battle of Buena Vista was won by the Americans far more by default of the enemy command than by courageous generalship.

While over the two days of the battle—February 22 and 23—the Americans had thwarted every assault General Santa Ana threw against them, in doing so, they had unequivocally come to the end of their rope. They'd been pushed back repeatedly and, by the close of the second day, had become so disorganized that they had allowed the Mexicans to filter around their flanks to within striking distance of the rear. It was indisputably a death-knell for the American force, since one more Mexican assault would easily have turned the tide. Instead, the gallant American defense had finally broken Santa Ana's nerve and, with victory all but within his grasp, the Mexican commander ordered retreat to San Luis Potosi. The order created panic among the troops and this portion of the Mexican army disintegrated.[210]

To the whoop and dazzle of the fired-up accolades of the American war correspondents, Taylor returned with his bedraggled victors to Monterrey and, except for scattered guerrilla actions, the northern portion of the Mexican War was ended.

*[March 30, 1847 • Monday]*

The tableau of internal friction that had begun playing itself out among the top commanding officers of the American forces in the West throughout much of February continued to seethe and bubble during most of March. Now, at last, with only today and tomorrow remaining before April bloomed, a resolution seemed to be on hand and energies previously distracted could better be directed toward bringing the War with Mexico to a satisfactory conclusion.

Reaching this milestone had by no means been a smooth road.

Being named top military commander in the struggle against Mexican forces had, from the very beginning, been no plum for General Winfield Scott: He commanded a force with hardly half the troops that had been promised him and fully a quarter of those were enlistees or draftees with no experience whatsoever in actual battle. Were that not enough to cause him monumental problems, his force was immediately weakened late in January by the loss of whole regiments whose enlistment period had expired. For actual weeks at a time no supplies of any kind arrived, forcing him to abandon the faulty lines of communication and continue fighting only by the expedient of capturing whatever ammunition his men needed, while at the same time living off whatever foodstuffs the country could provide.

That wasn't the worst of it, since instead of being given a free hand to strike the enemy where and when it would result in the greatest damage, his war plan was severely overridden by having to bow to the wishes of a political commissioner sent to treat for peace. In his own estimation, his worst foe was his own predecessor, General Zachary Taylor, whose greed for political notoriety and aspirations toward the Presidency closed off his mind to the elemental needs of his own troops and sharply endangered the entire campaign against Mexico.

That General Scott was able to curb the disorder generated by Taylor in his grasp for power, while at same time, through training and tough discipline, molding this formless mass of a badly disorganized army into a fighting force to be contended with was little short of miraculous, but that was precisely what he did. The United States Navy was superb in providing him with port blockades and seizures, as well as providing immeasurably important strategic mobility and solutions to his seemingly insurmountable problems of supply. Backed as he was by such brilliant subordinate engineering field generals as Persifer Smith, John Anthony Quitman and James Shields, as well as George G. Meade, Pierre Gustave Beauregard, the highly intelligent Ethan Allen Hitchcock and, unquestionably, his superbly outstanding chief of staff, Robert E. Lee, General Winfield Scott conceived a campaign before which the Mexican Army, with its greatest horsemen and lancers in the world, in every quarter would crumble as if built of dried sand.

Almost as difficult was General Scott's chore of keeping the growing rebelliousness of his own Army in check while at the same time governing fairly and well that portion of northern Mexico already conquered. In so doing, he earned the bitterly jealous enmity of Brigadier Generals William J. Worth and Gideon Pillow whose own stars had diminished ever since Scott's arrival on the scene.

The prevailing fear in President Polk that Scott would do precisely as he was doing and, in the process, establish himself as a primary contender for the Presidency on the Whig ticket, caused the Chief Executive to act hastily to nip Scott's ambitions in the bud. He did so by accepting without question the February 18 collaborative perfidy of Pillow and Worth as they smeared the abilities and successes of the commanding general and he quickly turned their lies into a public repudiation of Winfield Scott. Scott's stout denial of the charges soon had the two subordinate generals placed under investigation by a court of inquiry, but the damage was done and Polk sent orders relieving Scott of his command and summoning him back to Washington D.C. in disgrace. It still, however, took a long time for communiqués and orders to reach their destinations and Scott was already well embarked on his campaign for taking the extremely important northeastern Mexico port city of Vera Cruz. If Scott were successful in that venture, then the project to shame him in the eyes of his country would tend to fall flat and Polk would be no better off than previously.

Much as Polk wanted to believe that couldn't possibly occur, it did.

With crucial assistance from the U.S. Navy, Scott and his ten thousand fresh American troops made their unopposed landing just south of Vera Cruz on March 9. Within mere hours the city was placed under investment. At that point an immediate head-on assault could most likely have taken the city, but that would only have been accomplished with heavy casualties to the American force, which General Scott would not tolerate. It would also, the American general knew, be easy enough to establish both land and sea blockades that would eventually starve the city into capitulation. That, Scott knew, was a dangerous course to contemplate; speed of conquest here was essential in order to avoid the oncoming yellow fever season, which could easily wipe out whole armies of men. There seemed but one recourse for the relatively quick taking of the coastal city and Scott wasted no time in implementing it—a sustained bombardment, not only with his own limited supply of cannon, but with every big gun the U.S. Navy could loan him for the duration of the siege.

"With such bombardment," Scott solemnly promised, "it will not take overly long to bring Vera Cruz to its knees."

Nor did it. The siege and sustained bombardment was begun on March 9 and twenty days later the Vera Cruz garrison capitulated. Northeastern Mexico was now firmly in American hands. Despite the fact that this isolated conflict was satisfactorily resolved, and despite whatever head of steam had been building for Scott's nomination for the Presidency, Polk remained entirely convinced that all remaining threat from the Whigs would quickly be dispelled with Scott's demotion.

There was still, however, a war being fought and until there was an unqualified surrender by the Mexican government there were segments of the Mexican Army farther to the south that had to be crushed, which would be no easy task. This was especially true with the withdrawal of Mexican troops from the north now indisputably strengthening the south. The taking of Mexico City itself was clearly the key to ending this war, but before that could occur, enemy strongholds along the way had to be taken.

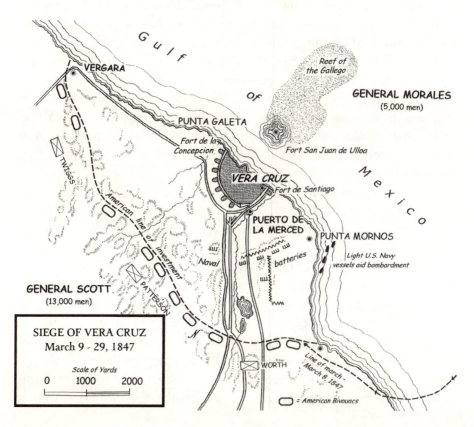

# The Infinite Dream

Under General Doniphan's firm guidance the Army, including the wild, ragtag First Missouri, pressed southward in north-central Mexico, first through Carrizal and then to Ojo Caliente, the latter a large abandoned hacienda named after an enormous hot spring. There, for the first time in too many weeks, this entire wing of the American Army, its commander included, luxuriated on February 21 in a hot, very relaxing bath.

The pause was brief and they moved on some fifty-five miles to where one of Lt. Gilpin's campfires went out of control, became a raging prairie fire that swept up into the mountains and paced their line of march for an entire day. When a sudden gale created a wind shift that drove the flames down toward their camp, forcing the cursing men to shift their horses and wagons wildly about to keep them from being destroyed, Lt. Gibson, grimly remembered the old song, *Fire in the Mountains! Run, Boys, Run*, and led the troops throughout the night of February 25 in setting backfires that finally brought the raging conflagration under control.

The blaze had been an exciting distraction but Doniphan maintained strict discipline and military formation as the Army moved on. The three main reconnaissance parties he sent ahead, led by Captains William Reid, Jonathan Forsythe and Paul Kirker, reported evidence of strong enemy resistance preparations ahead along the banks of Sacramento Creek, some fifteen miles north of the provincial capital city of Chihuahua. Some 4,000 of the enemy—two thirds of them well armed and well-organized, plus about a thousand peons pressed into service and armed mainly with machettes—were poised for battle under their commander, General García Conde.

The men of the First Missouri had been itching for a fight and now they were going to have it—the Battle of Sacramento, Mexico.

Mexican scouts had, of course, observed and reported the approach of Doniphan's force and, despite the previously consistent Mexican losses, a sense of fierce exhilaration had gripped the entire city of Chihuahua. Great victory was promised and expected, proclaimed in placards and broadsides, newspaper articles and priestly sermons. So certain was the anticipation of an overwhelming Mexican victory over the detested "Yankee dogs" that a thousand civilian spectators streamed out of Chihuahua on February 28 to the expected battlefield and there actually erected bleacher seats for the big show. The Mexican Army glowed with confidence and was prepared with a thousand coils of rope to form a coffle with which to lead their anticipated Americans captives into Mexico City.

General Conde had carefully selected and fortified as his attack point a position near the Sacramento Creek crossing, where the hills pressed in and sharply narrowed the approach. Good engineering general though he was, it seemed not to have occurred to him that the American force might bypass such a trap. After a brief reconnaissance, Doniphan and his staff officers wisely committed their men to a detour.

The six cannon being trundled along to the tune of *Yankee Doodle* by the American force under artillery Captains Weightman and Clark were small, yet large enough to well out-range the artillery possessed here by the Mexicans. Doniphan then sagaciously placed his force in an entirely new formation—four parallel columns of infantry, cavalry, artillery and wagons. This was the defensive posture he had noted the trader caravans using so successfully on the Santa Fe Trail against potential Indian attack, whereby if attacked, the wagons could circle to form a corral within which a small force could handily turn the attack of an enemy force many times larger. As he approached the enemy fortifications, Doniphan attacked the enemy's flank instead of approaching head-on as expected, causing the Mexicans to scramble in their efforts to swing their firmly emplaced guns into a half-turn.

It was a wild fight for a while: the disorganized enemy redoubts opened fire at a range much too long and the panoplied lancers formed for their fearsome charge too soon. Doniphan's troops spread out into battle line and Capt. Clark's artillery literally shattered the lancers before their charge could begin. For an hour the opposing artillerists boomed away at one another, the American explosive cannonballs wreaking havoc, the Mexican solid cannonballs lobbing in, bounding and ricocheting so visibly that the Yankees could easily dart from their paths.

A Mexican charge at the rear wagons was easily turned by the American riflemen and Doniphan moved his lines in closer to the half-turned redoubts. Muskets blazed in cacophony from both sides, but that from the Missourians was well-aimed, while that from the Mexicans was at best haphazard and loosed by their inexperienced infantry more at the horizon than at the opposing U.S. troops.

Perched on his horse near the front, Doniphan cursed with enviable eloquence and when his infantry got within four hundred yards of the redoubts, he launched Captain Weightman's artillery and three companies of cavalry under Capt. DeCourcy against the Mexican guns. For a time it was touch and go as the American line halted and then stalled under withering fire from the redoubts but, swiftly assessing the problem, Weightman galloped two of his howitzers halfway to the redoubts and opened fire on them, again with staggering results.

The trader named Owens, with a pair of pals, foolishly put on a show of bravado by galloping their horses down the front of the redoubts and Owens, who had clad himself in white clothing before the battle, made an exemplary target and promptly got himself killed. Captain Reid, ignoring the order to halt, led his company up to and over the parapets. Immediately the two halted companies joined him and the redoubts swarmed for several minutes with men in a wild melee, the Missourians fighting furiously with unleashed sabers, clubbed muskets and even scattered rocks and bare fists as weapons.

Totally unprepared for such an assault so close to nightfall, the Mexicans broke and ran. Some of them tried to rally on a nearby hill but Lt. Gilpin's men swarmed over the fortifications there and abruptly everyone was running. The nearby impromptu bleachers stood empty, their spectators having wisely fled earlier.

The Missourians pursued, chasing and killing and the Mexican troops, most with their sabers still sheathed, ran directly into a cluster of Apaches who had been watching and who now took their own toll of the vanquished, terrified men. With their lives truly on the line, the fleeing Mexicans, heading for Chihuahua under the full moon, handily outdistanced the Missourians, who straggled back to the battlefield and found the surgeons of both armies tending the wounded. Doniphan's subordinate commanders had their hands full in striving to reform their own scattered troops.

Incredibly, considering such close-quarter fighting occurring, the Americans suffered just the two deaths and seven men wounded while at the same time killing more than three hundred of the Mexicans, wounding just as many more and having already taken forty prisoners.

Mexican resistance in the State of Chihuahua was wholly crushed.[211]

On orders from their commander, the Missourians spread out to collect the spoils of their efforts and the rewards were considerable, including ten cannon, hundreds of muskets, tons of rifle and cannon powder, seven fine carriages that had belonged to the Mexican officers and their elite onlookers, literally hundreds of horses, mules, beeves, sheep, wagons and carts that had been hastily abandoned and even General Conde's field headquarters desk, as well as the ropes with which the Americans were to have been tied and herded, plus a huge black death's-head banner that they had first seen at the Battle of El Brazito. As an added bonus, they also recovered the Mexican paymaster's chest containing some $3,000 in copper coins, which they reported to their officers, and probably upwards of $50,000 in silver coins, which they did not and, instead, loaded their pockets and pouches and belts and haversacks with the loot they felt they had earned. The booty they gathered was finally topped off with a large quantity of the best of Chihuahua wines in bottles, kegs and skins which they downed with gusto, toasting time and time again the defeat and dispersal of the enemy.

The next day, March 1, 1847 Gen. Doniphan sent Capt. Mitchell with an advance guard to enter and occupy the city of Chihuahua itself and he followed with the remainder of his victorious army the following morning. The Mexican residents were terrified, expecting pillage and rape, perhaps even death, and what few resident Americans were there expected drastic repercussions at the hands of the victors, but no such outrages occurred. As those possibilities dwindled, the resident Americans came out to warmly welcome their deliverers and the remaining Mexicans hurriedly dressed their beautiful *señoritas* in finest garb and sent them out to mingle with the troops, bearing with them melons and tortillas and yet more wine. And subtle promises.

The First Missouri, led by its blaring band playing *Yankee Doodle*, swaggered into this foremost of northern Mexico cities, singing and shouting, gradually strutting past the mint, the huge cathedral, rounded the Plaza and halted for the ceremony of capitulation.

Later in the evening Private John Robinson succinctly summed up the events in his diary entry for the day:

> *3/2/47 We rode through the principal streets and public square and, on a rocky hill on the south side of the city, fired a national salute in honor of the conquest, stole wood enough to get supper, and went to bed as usual among the rocks.*

For the Mormon Battalion however, far to the northwest in California, the joy of having the strenuous cross-country march finally behind them did not last very long and the new idleness of their existence—despite rigorous daily drilling under the formidable taskmastering of Lt. Col. Cooke and performing a variety of menial tasks—was quickly becoming boring in the extreme. By far the greater majority of the Saints wanted nothing so much as to simply have their term of enlistment expire as swiftly as possible, be discharged and be allowed to make their way to the new Zion. Rumor said it would be found somewhere in the Great Basin; a place where they believed they would finally be free of the prejudice that had plagued all Mormons throughout their existence and where they would at last be reunited with families left behind so long ago.

Pvt. Henry Bigler of Company B, who remained stationed with others of his unit at San Luis Rey, thought it most deserving when Philip St. George Cooke received orders on February 20 promoting him from his regular army rank of lieutenant to the permanent rank of major, though while he continued as commanding officer of the Mormon Battalion he would still maintain the rank of brevet lieutenant colonel. Staunch disciplinarian though Cooke was, the Battalion members had developed a fierce loyalty to him and honored his fairness to all in his command, irrespective of rank.

On this same day that his promotion became official, Lt. Col. Cooke also received word that the long anticipated vessel laden with provisions from the Sandwich Islands had finally reached dockage at the Port of San Diego. He immediately dispatched a few teams and wagons to, as Bigler put it in his chronicle, "fetch the grub" that the Saints so badly needed. Six days later, on Friday, February 26, the detachment returned and, to the gratification of all the Saints, their wagons were laden with barrels of pork and flour as well as a multitude of large bulging sacks, half of them filled with sugar, the remainder bulging with coffee beans.

Two days later, on Sunday, Second Lt. Samuel Thompson was dispatched with a ten-man detachment and a dozen fresh mules to return to the first well west of the Colorado Valley to bring in the three Battalion supply wagons that had been temporarily abandoned there due to their weight and the weakened condition of the animals at that time.

The schedule for the rest of the Battalion continued as a daily ritual: Wake-up roll call at 6:00 a.m., followed by breakfast at 8:40 a.m., then two hour-long drilling sessions, at 10 a.m. and 3 p.m.. tattoo at 8:30 p.m. and, finally, drum taps at 9 p.m., when all lights had to be extinguished—except in cases of sickness—and silence thereafter observed until the next morning's wake-up call. It was, as Pvt. Miles Miller of Co. E put it: *"...a schedule so boring it is downright deadly."*

On March 1 the Saints looked on wistfully as the enlistment period of the regular Army volunteers expired. John Sutter's bookkeeper, John Bidwell, was one of those discharged. As he wrote in his diary:

> *Most of us made our way up the coast by land to our homes. I had eleven horses which I swam, one at a time, across the Straits of Carquinez at Benecia.*

While boredom had become the bane of existence for the Saints in the Mormon Battalion, such was most certainly not the situation in mid-February for General Kearny, who met with Lt. Col. Richard B. Mason in Monterey. Mason had brought with him to California unequivocal orders directly from President Polk in Washington, D.C. by which Kearny was instructed to turn over his First Dragoon command to Mason and himself assume at once the duties of military commander and civil governor of the Territory of California. He was to maintain this position until, in his own considered judgment, the territory could be declared pacified. Just as soon as that was accomplished, Mason was to succeed him in the gubernatorial role and Kearny was immediately to return to Washington, D.C.

Further, if not already attended to, the California Battalion was to be mustered into regular army service and then either utilized at once or discharged as soon as possible. Lt. Colonel John Fremont, the orders went on, was to be sent east to rejoin his regiment there as soon as he could be spared. Shortly after this, another echelon of U.S. Navy personnel arrived, as well as a regiment of enlisted New York volunteers, whose purpose was to be the preliminary colonizing of interior California.

Gen. Kearny instantly set to work, his foremost priorities being the total pacification of California and establishment of the preliminaries of California as a United States territory. He also sent Captain Henry S. Turner to Los Angeles with orders for Fremont to surrender, in person and without delay, all state papers in his possession at the newly reestablished capital of the territory, Monterey.[212]

By this time the tension existing between Kearny and Fremont was all but palpable. Fremont, now Kearny's adjutant, had already sent Stockton's secretary of state, Owl Russell, eastward along the southern trail on a mission having an extremely important objective: he was to turn the father of expansionism, Fremont's own powerful father-in-law, Senator Thomas Hart Benton, loose on anyone and everyone who had in any way hampered the ambitions of one John Charles Fremont.

Upon receiving Gen. Kearny's order, however, Fremont's defiance became brashly open and he responded harshly that while he had advised the irregulars of his California Battalion that they could either be mustered into the regular service or be discharged, they had balked at either choice and preferred to remain as the California Battalion with Colonel Fremont as their commanding officer. There was considerable doubt in Kearny's mind, however, that Fremont had ever presented the choice to his men "to decide, knowingly, upon being mustered into the service." Instead, Fremont made it clear he was continuing to act through Secretary of State Owl Russell in Stockton's bogus cabinet and refused to acknowledge Stockton's self-proclaimed government had completely lost any standing that it might ever have had.

Fremont had already erected a distinct screen of enmity between himself and Lt. Col. Cooke by not only defying his authority but by flatly instructing his adjutant not to obey Cooke and not to turn over to Cooke any military property, including even a howitzer that belonged to the Dragoons. Instead, Fremont continued to foment resentment by deliberately concocting rumors, entirely without foundation, of the Californios reestablishing their revolutionary stance, which he represented as being directed against himself. Such problem, he stated, he would take care of by himself without appealing for outside aid from Cooke or anyone else and added that he would not turn over to headquarters, as Cooke had ordered, his weaponry and supplies. He said that his grounds for such a decision were that "...my battalion will be amply sufficient for the safety of the artillery and ordnance stores..." which, it was inferred, he would continue to hold. Further, Fremont warned that overt conflict was on the point of breaking out between the various branches of the U.S. military in California and was being prevented only by exercise of his own strong control, but that a major clash was quite likely to occur between the Missourians in his battalion and the Mormons in Kearny's.

That Fremont was actually attempting to incite such hostilities between service branches of the United States Army became patently clear; just as it was clear that, in the process of so doing, he was committing treason. When whispers reached his ears of such a charge possibly being drawn up against him at headquarters, Fremont stormed his way to Monterey and confronted General Kearny with blustering and insulting orations about the incompetence of the military leadership in California—specifically Kearny, Cooke and Mason—and galled Kearny virtually to his limit. At last Kearny silenced the bombast with a raised hand and spoke sternly: "Do you, Sir, or do you not, intend to obey orders? I advise you to carefully appraise the gravity of your decision. You have an hour—or a full day, if you wish—to make such an appraisal."

Though furious almost to the point of mayhem, Fremont abruptly got a grip on himself. Requiring neither an hour nor even a day, he replied to the question at once in a voice thready with strain, "Yes, General, I do."

"Then go back to Los Angeles immediately and obey the orders you have already received!"

W. Branford Shubrick, Commander-in-Chief of the U.S. Navy forces, clearly perceiving the inter-agency peril Fremont was fomenting and fearful for his own forthcoming retirement, took immediate steps to absolve himself of any complicity by issuing a brief proclamation of his own this day, in which he stated:

1 march 1847.
To All Whom it May Concern.
Be it known that the President of the United States has invested the undersigned with separate and distinct powers, civil and military.
　　　W. Branford Shubrick Commander-in Chief, U.S. Naval Forces
　　　　　　　　　　　　　　　　　　　Monterey, Territory of California

As for Lt. Col. Cooke, it was only with concerted self-control that he curbed his fury, remained publicly silent and maintained Kearny's wise policy of avoiding overt clashes. As Cooke himself privately wrote:

I sacrifice all feeling of pride to duty, which I think plainly forbids any attempt to crush this resistance of misguided men. It would be a signal of revolt.

Nevertheless, in his written report to Kearny, he allowed his own feelings much broader manifestation:

My God! To think of a howitzer brought over the deserts with so *much faithful labor by the dragoons; the howitzer with which they have four times fought the enemy, and brought here to the rescue of Lieutenant Colonel Fremont and his followers, to be refused to them by this Lieutenant Colonel Fremont and in defiance of the orders of his general! I denounce this treason, or this mutiny, which jeopardizes the safety of the country and defies me in my legal command and duties, by men who report, and say, that they believe the enemy approaches from without, and are about to rise in arms around us.*

It was not until General Kearny and Commodore Shubrick, after meeting in private in Monterey, issued their joint announcement on this same March 1 that the turbulent power struggle between the Americans in California began drawing to its well-overdue ending:

*TO ALL WHOM IT MAY CONCERN*

*Be it Known*

*That the President of the United States, desirous to give & secure to the People of California a share of the good government & happy civil organization enjoyed by the People of the U.S., & to protect the People at the same time from the attacks of foreign foes & from internal commotions, has invested the undersigned with separate & distinct powers, civil & military; a cordial cooperation in the exercise of which it is hoped & believed will have the happy result desired.*

*To the Commander of the Naval forces, the Presdt. has assigned the regulation of the import trade, the conditions on which Vessels of all Nations, our own as well as foreign, may be admitted into the Ports of the Teritory [sic] & the establishment of all Port Regulations.*

*To the Commanding Military Officer, the President has assigned the direction of the operations on land, & has invested him with administrative functions of government over the People & Teritory [sic] occupied by the forces of the United States.*

*Done at Monterey Capital of California this first day of March AD 1847*

*S.W. Kearny*  
*Brig. Genl. & Governor of California*

*W. Branford Shubrick*  
*Com in chief of the Naval Forces*

It was on this same day, March 1, that Gen. Kearny, now alone in his headquarters office in Monterey, wrote out explicit instructions to his most trusted and dependable subordinate, Lt. Col. Cooke:

> Sir—By Dept Orders No. 2 of this date you will see that you are entrusted with the command of the Southern Military District, & required to its protection & defence, for which purpose the California Volunteers (now at the Cuidad de Los Angeles) the Mormon Battalion, & Co. C 1st Dragoons are placed under your orders.
>
> The Southern Dist. is the most important one in the Dept, & the one in which (for many reasons) difficulties are most to be apprehended. The route between California & Sonora leads from the frontier of that District, & that is the only one by which Mexican troops can be brought into this country.
>
> With the knowledge of this fact, I advise you to have the pass near Warner's Rancho (Agua Calliente) well guarded, & the Road from it in the direction of San Felippe & the Desert reconnoitered & examined as frequently as circumstances may render necessary. Troops sent for these purposes should be kept much in motion. The friendship & good will of the Indians on that frontier can easily be secured & it should be done.
>
> It is highly important that a very discreet officer should be in command of the troops you may station at "the city of the Angels," which has been for so long a time the Capital of the Territory & the Head Qtrs. of the Mexicans & Californians when in arms against us. Great discontent, & animosity on the part of the People there towards the Americans have existed & in consequence of complaints ~~on their part~~ [sic] made by them of the Volunteers engaged in our cause.[213] It is not necessary to enquire if these complaints are well founded or not. The fact that the people have been unfriendly & opposed to us is sufficient to make it our duty to reconcile & make friends of them, & this most desirable object may be effected by a mild, courteous & just treatment of them in the future. I urge this subject upon your attention & trust that you will impress it upon those officers & troops you may station there.
>
> In my letter to you of the 11th Ult. (a copy of which is enclosed herewith) I directed you under certain circumstances to send a

*Comp'y. of the Mormon Battalion to San Diego. I have now only to add that should the circumstances alluded to, occur, you will send a Comp'y or more, as you may deem necessary.*

*The selection of a Place for your Head Qtrs. is a matter of some consideration & importance. I suggest that it be the "Cuidad de los Angeles," but leave that subject for your decision, and am unwilling to embarrass you or place any impediments in your way that might prevent you from performing the high duty expected of you.*

*Very Respectfully, Your Obt. Servant,*

*Lieut. Col. P.S.G. Cooke*          *S.W. Kearny., Brig. Genl.*
*Comg. Southern Mil. Dist.*
*San Luis Rey*

The following day, March 2, Lt. Col. Cooke swung into action and dispatched a detachment of thirty-one men—dismounted officers and privates of the First Dragoons under command of Lt. George Stoneman and working in conjunction with the U.S. Quartermaster, Major T. Swords—to San Diego, there to take over the post newly vacated by the American sailors and marines and to protect the town and its citizens as well as its depot of provisions and other public property.

With no longer the immediate peril of attack by Mexican or Californio forces overhanging the Mormon Battalion, Cooke concentrated on turning the men of his command into a more disciplined and precise unit. He enforced strict drill schedules and harangued the troops sharply, profanely, virtually to the point of abusiveness, wherever he felt they did not measure up. So harsh, in fact, was his treatment of them that 1st Lt. James Pace of Company E wrote in his diary:

*Saturday 6th....He drove us through* [as though] *in greait* [sic] *fury. I felt myself highly insulted & could sciercely* [scarcely] *contain my feelings tho* [sic] *I did until morning. I then sent him a few lines of which the following is a true coppy* [sic] *of the original: "Sir With all due respect to your official capacity, I take this method of requesting you if you have any instructions to give in regard to drill dicipline* [sic] *&c that I am ready and Willing at all times to obey your commands but would like to be treated with a little more respect than I was on some occasions yesterday. While on drill, I am aware sir of our awkwardness and that it is enough to Worry your* *patience but all men have to learn that. That they do not know your judgment and experience [they] will doub[t]less admit."*

It was to Cooke's credit that he accepted in good grace such criticism from one of his very junior officers and it was highly gratifying to Pace that the commander had the common sense and courage to openly admit when he was wrong. As Pace later this same day added to his diary notation:

*At ten. Ock [sic] the dril[l] was cald [called]. The Colo presented him self before Company E again to instruct as he had done the evening before but to the supprise [sic] of the company he was a different Man. He treated officers and men with respect which he had not done for a week previous. It was evident to [us] he had changed & for good. How long he may continue is doubtfull.*

Lt. Pace's pessimism proved groundless. Lt. Col. Cooke thereafter curbed any unnecessary abusiveness in his discourse with the troops and the Saints revered him all the more for it. That was not to say he had become any more lax in discipline, as was evidenced the following morning when Sgt. Ephraim Green of Company B was demoted for *"...having failed to learn his duty and drill as a Sergeant, and thus shown his incompetency for his station."* He was replaced by Cpl. David P. Rainey, who was promoted to sergeant of the company.[214] The day after that four more non-commissioned officers were reduced to the ranks for not being expert in learning the drill, their places immediately filled from the ranks.

As was so often the case when the troops had time on their hands, rumors abounded, some amusing but some creating strong momentary concerns, as reflected by Pvt. Henry Bigler's diary entry at San Luis Rey:

*March 8. This evening an express arrived from San Diego. The particulars I did not learn, but there was talk in camp that [a] French vessel had arrived at San Diego and that Colonel Cooke got a paper stating that General Santa Anna had borrowed twenty-five million dollars of the Roman Catholics and had entrenched himself awaiting the arrival of General Taylor.*

It was, of course, a tale made of whole cloth which quickly faded away after running its momentarily scary course through the Mormon companies.

It was two days later—March 16—when an express arrived from General Kearny in which he noted that he did not expect to return to San Diego at all, but that he would quite shortly be returning to the states directly from Monterey. In the same communiqué received at San Luis Rey, he ordered Lt. Col. Cooke to send the First Dragoons and part of the Mormon Battalion to Pueblo de los Angeles to aid in military construction. One company of Mormons, however, was to be sent to San Diego as its new garrison, with the responsibility of protecting the town and its residents from any insipient revolutionary tendencies either from within or without. The latter was clearly an assignment for the best of the Battalion and Cooke immediately selected for this considerable honor the Saints of Company B, under Capt. Jesse Hunter, which included some of the more dedicated of journal-keepers among the Mormons—Lt. James Pace, Cpl. Thomas James Dunn and Pvts. Henry W. Bigler, Azariah Smith and Samuel Rogers.[215] As Bigler commented about it in his diary for this date:

> ...*On the day following* [March 18], *our Captain received a letter from the Colonel giving information that he was on the march with Company C, D, and E to Los Angeles to take possession of that place, and Company A was left to keep San Luis Rey. This morning the marines all went aboard and we took possession of the fort, which was situated on a bluff about one fourth of a mile from the village, with seven pieces of artillery to defend it. The Congress, commanded by Commodore Stockton, was lying in San Diego harbor.*

It was also on March 17 when the Mormon Battalion's senior officer, Captain Jefferson Hunt sent a letter, carried by Captain Turner, to General Kearny, in which Hunt told the General that a goodly number of his men planned to settle in the San Francisco area when their term of enlistment expired and he was, with this missive, formally applying for permission to create a new Mormon force as a United States service branch with himself in command with the rank of lieutenant colonel. His message carried with it a petition for a leave of absence for himself, that he might return to Council Bluffs, Iowa, undoubtedly to obtain the formal blessing of Brigham Young for such establishment. General Kearny rejected the request but in such a sympathetic manner that it encouraged Hunt, who planned to resubmit his petition at least once more before the present enlistment period of the Mormons expired.[216]

Some degree of excitement occurred the following Saturday, March 20, when the largest sailing ship most of the Saints had ever seen slipped quietly into San Diego Bay and dropped anchor. This was the flagship of the U.S. Navy's Pacific Squadron, the massive frigate *U.S. Savannah*, which displaced 1,726 tons, bore forty-four cannon and had a crew numbering 480 men. She was quite a sight to see and, as Azariah Smith commented to Henry Bigler, "When she fires her guns, it makes the air ring!"

There was, among the permanent residents of Southern California generally and at San Diego specifically, an almost ready-made aversion to the American military which focused initially and most particularly on the Mormons. Yet, within a remarkably short time this prejudice began draining away. The director of the little hospital at San Diego, thirty-one-year-old Dr. John Griffin, who was an Army surgeon and who had come to California with General Kearny, expressed this in his diary entry for March 20, writing:

> *The prejudice against the Mormons here seems to be wearing off—it is yet among the Californians a great term of reproach to be called Mormon—yet, as they are a quiet, industrious, sober, inoffensive people—they seem to be gradually working their way up. They are extremely industrious; they have been engaged while here in digging wells, plastering houses, and seem anxious and ready to work. The Californians have no great idea of their soldier like [sic] qualities and in action would not dread them much—this arising in great measure from their dress, carriage, &c, which is as unlike any soldier as anything could possibly be. Yet, I think if brought into action they would prove themselves good men, as I am told they are generally fine shots and they drill reasonably well.*[217]

The detachment under Lt. Samuel Thompson, sent out on February 28 by Lt. Col. Cooke to retrieve the wagons and their supplies marooned on the wagon-rafts in the Colorado River, finally returned on March 16 but, disappointingly with only one wagon recovered, the others having been looted, apparently by Indians, and then burned. Lt. George P. Dykes, in his usual obnoxious persona, at once suggested—unsuccessfully—that Lt. Thompson be held accountable for the loss. Resentment among the Saints for the "sniveling" tactics of Lt. Dykes continued to fester and it helped Dykes' reputation not at all when two of the non-commissioned officers of the Battalion—Sgt. Nathaniel V. Jones and 4th Cpl. Lewis Lane—complained aloud in his presence about the "stingy" policies in the Battalion in respect to the prevailing rations of beef, especially now that supplies had become both plentiful and cheap. Dykes, who had despised Jones from the time of the Battalion's formation at Fort Leavenworth, immediately reported the pair to the commander, leaving Lt. Col. Cooke no recourse but to chastise both, which he did on March 18:

> Orders No. 25
> HEAD QUARTERS MORMON BATTALION
> San Luis Rey, March 18th, 1847
> - *Sergeant N.V. Jones and Corporal Lewis Lane, of Company D, having been guilty of insubordination and conduct disgraceful to them as non-commissioned officers, they are hereby reduced to the ranks.*
> - *On the recommendation of their Captain commanding, private Abraham Hunsaker is hereby appointed a Sergeant, and Privates Sanford Jacobs and William Barger are appointed Corporals, all in Company D. They will be obeyed and respected accordingly.*
> - *Persuant to S.M.D., orders No. 4, of this date, first Lieutenant [George W.] Oman and [2nd] Sergeant [Ebenezer] Brown and nine privates of Company A, Sergeant Hunsaker and five privates of Company D, and eight privates of Company E, will comprise the detachment which will remain to garrison this post. 1st Lieutenant Oman, in command, will receive such public property as will be left and pay special attention to the safety of public mules. Returns will be made immediately for three additional day's rations, including no salt meat. By order,*
> LIEUT. COL. COOKE, Commanding.

Following the posting of the order, Jones, speaking for both himself and Lane, growled angrily, "He [Lt. Dykes] carried false reports to the

Colonel, and through his false reports broke me of my office, which he had proposed to do from the beginning, and had boasted of it." Jones was unable to prove his allegations, however, and the meted punishment stood. The general feeling among the Saints, however, was fairly evident: somehow, some way, some day—and probably in the not too distant future—Lt. George Dykes would finally get his come-uppance.

For Lt. William Tecumseh Sherman, the entire California experience had thus far been exhilarating. He enjoyed moving about the countryside on horseback and visiting with some of the top officials, all of whom, he thought, were very set in their ways, some to their own detriment. Among the latter was Lt. Col. John C. Fremont, whom he had been advised was a very volatile character. So much so, in fact, that only recently he had a set-to with Lt. Col. Richard Mason, who had gone down to Los Angeles by sea with a pay-master and with muster rolls and orders from General Kearny to muster Fremont's irregular California Battalion members into the regular service of the United States, pay them and then muster them out. Fremont, however, had become furious at what he termed was "interference and intercession" and refused to consent to it. Their argument had become so enflamed that Fremont finally challenged Mason to a duel. Mason, never one to back away from any problem, accepted at once and named as weapons "double-barrelled [sic] shotguns and buckshot cartridges." The duel would undoubtedly have transpired had not General Kearny stepped in and absolutely prohibited it.

Sherman learned of Fremont's journey to confront General Kearny in Monterey and his being ordered in the strongest terms to return immediately to Los Angeles, disband his irregulars and to cease exercising authority of any kind in California, an order which, thus far, he had only partially obeyed. Curious as to what kind of a man this Fremont was, since he'd read the man's exploratory accounts and knew of his fame all over the East, Lt. Sherman rode out to his camp to pay him a visit. He found Fremont in a conical tent, conferring with a trapper-mountain man companion whom he referred to as Captain Owens, a member of his battalion originally from Zanesville, Ohio. As Sherman wrote about the meeting in his diary:

> ...I spent an hour or so with Fremont in his tent, took some tea with him, and left, without being much impressed with him.

# The Infinite Dream

It was not too long after that when General Kearny summoned Lt. Sherman to his headquarters in Monterey, remarked that he was soon going to Los Angeles on the *U.S. Lexington* and wanted to know if Sherman would like to go along as his aide. This was exactly the type of assignment Sherman craved and he agreed with alacrity. For the first time, Sherman was able to be in close daily contact with General Kearney and the more he saw of him, the more he admired and respected him. Unlike himself, the general was not a West Point graduate; Kearny had enlisted in the army during the War of 1812 and had steadily worked his way up through the ranks without benefit of a sponsor having political influence. There was no doubt that he held superior performance to be the norm and he was never given to effusiveness in praising either his superiors or those who served in his own commands. He was, however, impressed with Lt. Col. Cooke and the exemplary job he had done in marching the Mormon Battalion across the western half of the continent. As busy as he had become with the requirements of his office here in California, aggravated by his problems with a mutinous John Charles Fremont and complicated by Californians resentful of the American Army's presence, he had been forced to set aside for several weeks any close study of Cooke's report, along with its supporting documents which included his day-by-day journal throughout the expedition. When Kearny was finally able to concentrate on it more, however, his evaluation of Cooke as a fine officer escalated even more and he directed his personal secretary, Capt. H.S. Turner to respond, which he did:

> *Sir:*
>
> *I am directed by the General to acknowledge the receipt of the Journal, Maps & Report of your late expedition from New Mexico to California. The General was highly gratified at this perusal of these interesting papers & instructs me to express his approbation of the successful and officer like manner in which the expedition was conducted by you. Your discovery of the best & most practicable route for the march of the troops from New Mexico to California, will be productive of great advantages to the public interest and the entire success with which your dismounted command was marched through a wilderness unexplored and 1200 miles in extent, justly entitles you to the thanks of the Government. Great credit is also due to the officers & men under your command for*

*the zeal & perseverance displayed by them in the performance of an arduous Service.*

| | |
|---|---|
| *Lt. Col. P. St. G. Cooke.* | *I am Sir Very Respectfully* |
| *Comdg Southern Mil. Dist.* | *Your Obt Serv.* |
| *Pueblo de los Angeles* | *(signed) H.S. Turner* |
| *California* | *Capt., & A.A.A. General*[218] |

Lt. Col. Cooke, in an effort to follow through with the desires of General Kearny in respect to removing Lt. Col. Fremont from his post, took the opportunity on March 24 to mount his horse and ride to the Mission San Gabriel, some eight miles from Los Angeles, where Fremont's battalion was stationed. Unfortunately, Fremont was absent and he found Captain Owens in command and not at all cooperative.

"We don't have any instructions," Owens told him in a tight-lipped manner, "to do anything or go anywhere but wait for word from the gov'nor."

"The governor?" Cooke questioned.

"Colonel Fremont, yes. He's Governor of California and highest in command and he's the *only* one we take orders from. And he's responsible to nobody but Commodore Shubrick." The implication was clear, attested to by nods from others of Fremont's officers on hand, that there was no intention of looking to Cooke as their commander.

"Surely," Cooke persisted, "you have seen Commodore Shubrick's circular regarding the California chain of command?"

"Nope. Nothin' like that's come to us. Far as we're concerned, Colonel Fremont's the highest authority in the land an' he left orders when he left here we wasn't to take orders from anybody else."

"You'll find, sir," Cooke spoke sharply, "that's an error. This battalion of irregulars is to be disbanded immediately."

"No sir, it ain't. Not 'til Gov'nor Fremont tells us so hisself. Ain't likely he's gonna do that."

One of the officers chuckled at that but immediately silenced when Cooke shot a stern glance in his direction.

"All right, since Lt. Col. Fremont's not here, I'll have to deal through you at the moment. We need, immediately, for you to return to us at headquarters in Los Angeles, all the government ordnance—cannon, in particular—presently in Mr. Fremont's possession."

"Uh uh," Owens was shaking his head. "Gov'ner Fremont left

orders we don't turn over no ordnance, 'specially the big guns, to *nobody* 'cept on his say-so."

Obviously they were at an impasse and Cooke, harnessing his own anger, left the camp immediately after leaving instructions for Fremont to present himself at headquarters at once upon his return. Shortly after his own return there, Lt. Col. Cooke received a report that the Mexicans in Sonora were landing arms somewhere on the coast and making other preparations for war and that an army of their men were already assembling on the Colorado River preparatory to invading California. The same story having reached San Francisco, the frigate *Congress* had already set sail southward in an effort to ward off the threat. The whole matter quickly faded away, however, when it all turned out to be nothing but a groundless rumor.

It was today, March 30, that Lt. Col. Fremont returned to the Los Angeles area and an immediate meeting of officers of his battalion was held. This time things did not go at all well for Fremont. The California Battalion officers, evidently having now received Commodore Shubrick's bulletin regarding the military chain of command in California, were suddenly less than convinced about Fremont's authority. Bridling his temper, Fremont replied, "It is my right, and of course you know my willingness, to retain command of this Battalion. I will, however, bow to a decision of a council of the officers here as to whom they wish as their commander."

The officers agreed and an immediate council was held among them. To Fremont's complete surprise and anger, the officers voted him out of command and voted in, as their new commander, Captain C.E. Smith. It was very apparent to all that the house of cards John C. Fremont had constructed for himself had finally begun to crumple.

*[April 19, 1847 • Monday]*

It was just after dawn today that Major General Winfield Scott, in his headquarters tent at the Rio del Plan, Mexico, forced himself to do the task that he, like so many other commanders, most disliked; submitting a detailed account of a battle just fought to the U.S. Secretary of War in Washington, D.C.—in this case concerning the Battle of Cerro Gordo. To Scott, the requisite writing of such reports was every bit as disruptive and painful as the battle itself, but he had vowed to not again, as he had done following the affair at Vera Cruz, let so much time lapse before writing and submitting his report.

In that instance he had written and submitted a partial report of the Vera Cruz Siege on March 25, before the battle was completed. However, it had not been until four days later, on March 29, that Scott was able to complete for Secretary of War William Marcy the concluding details of that affair, which he entitled

### Official Report (2) of the Siege of Vera Cruz
Head-Quarters of the Army, Vera Cruz, March 29, 1847

Sir: — *The flag of the United States of America floats triumphantly over the walls of this city and the Castle of San Juan d'Ulloa.*

*Our troops have garrisoned both since ten o'clock; it is now noon. Brigadier General Worth is in command of the two places.*

*Articles of capitulation were signed and exchanged at a late hour night before last. I enclose a copy of the document.*

*I have heretofore reported the incidents of the siege up to the 25th instant. Nothing of striking interest occurred till early in the morning of the next day, when I received overtures from General Landero, on whom General Morales had devolved the principal command.*

*A terrible storm of wind and sand made it difficult to communicate with the city, and impossible to refer to Commodore Perry. I was obliged to entertain the proposition alone, or continue the fire upon a place that had shown a disposition to surrender; for the loss of a day, perhaps several, could not be permitted. The accompanying papers will show the proceedings and results.*

*Yesterday, after the northern had abated, and the commissioners appointed by me early the morning before had again met those appointed by General Landero, Commodore Perry sent ashore his second in command, Captain Aulick, as a commissioner on the part of the navy. Although not included in my specific arrangement made with the Mexican commander, I did not hesitate, with proper courtesy, to desire that Captain Aulick might be duly introduced and allowed to participate in the discussions and acts of the commissioners who had been reciprocally accredited. Hence the preamble to his signature.*

*The original American commissioners were Brevet Brigadier-General Worth, Brigadier-General Pillow, and Colonel Totten. Four more able or judicious officers could not have been desired.*

*I have to add but little more. The remaining details of the siege — the able cooperation of the United States squadron, successively under the command of Commodores Conner and Perry — the admirable conduct of the whole army, regulars and volunteers — I should be happy to dwell upon as they deserve, but the steamer* Princeton, *with Commodore Conner on board, is under way, and I have commenced organizing an advance into the interior. This may be delayed a few days, waiting the arrival of additional means of transportation. In the meantime, a joint operation, by land and water, will be made upon Alvarado. No lateral expedition, however, shall interfere with the grand movement towards the capital.*

*In consideration of the great services of Colonel Totten, in the siege that has just terminated most successfully, and the importance of his presence at Washington, as the head of the engineer bureau, I entrust this despatch [sic] to his personal care, and beg to commend him to the very favourable consideration of the department.*

*I have the honor to remain sir, with high respect,*
*Your most obedient servant,*
*WINFIELD SCOTT*

Meanwhile, however, General Santa Ana had moved swiftly to oppose Scott's advance inland and began hastily constructing defenses at Cerro Gordo, which included erecting defenses overlooking the Rio del Plan and the twelve-mile-distant road to Jalapa. The rapid fall of Vera Cruz allowed insufficient time for their completion before Scott's force arrived. Swift reconnaissance by American engineers quickly showed that the position could be turned on its left by moving along a rough trail.

General Scott's quickly conceived battle plan was for Twiggs to move along that trail and, by doing so, effectively cut off the obvious Mexican line of retreat. Both Shields and Worth were to follow. As soon as they became engaged with the enemy, Brigadier-General Gideon Pillow was to make a secondary attack against the exposed Mexican right flank. At this time, as well, the cavalry was held in place on the highway, poised for pursuit.

As it turned out, the plan was brilliantly conceived, but its execution was poorly employed; instead of Twiggs going to the Mexican rear as Scott had ordered, he cut in to attack at La Atalaya and El Telegrafo and it

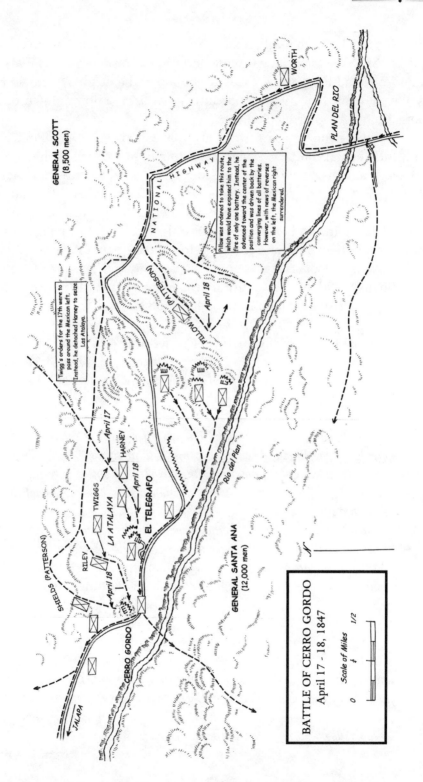

was only Shields who reached the road in the rear, and too late to cut off the retreat of the Mexican left wing and center. Despite the fact that the Americans had to fight their way to the top of the heights commanded by the Mexican army, with a horribly lethal firing raining down upon them, Scott's troops prevailed.

Pillow—who was a former law partner of President Polk and with little actual military experience—totally mismanaged the attack. He was, however, saved by the threat of Shield's advance. That, coupled with the drive of Twigg's attack so demoralized the morale of the Mexican Army that it broke and fled in such precipitous haste that it left behind to be captured not only weapons and baggage but numerous personal items belonging to General Santa Ana, including even his spare wooden leg.

So now, with his usual disdain for composing battle reports, Scott bent to the task of penning his own report of yesterday's victory:

### Official Report of the Battle of Cerro Gordo—18 April 1847
*Headquarters of the Army*
*Plan del Rio, 50 miles from Vera Cruz*
*April 19, 1847*

Sir:—

*The plan of attack, sketched in General Orders No. 111, forwarded herewith, was finely executed by this gallant army, before two o'clock P.M. yesterday. We are quite embarrassed with the results of victory—prisoners of war, heavy ordnance, field batteries, small arms, and accoutrements.*

*About 3,000 men laid down their arms, with the usual proportion of field and company officers, besides five generals, several of great distinction—Pinson, Jarrero, La Vega, Noriega, and Obando. A sixth general, Vasquez, was killed in defending the battery (tower) in the rear of the whole Mexican army, the capture of which gave us those glorious results.*

*Our loss, though comparatively small in number, has been serious. Brigadier-general Shields, a commander of activity, zeal, and talent, is, I fear, if not dead, mortally wounded. He is some five miles from me at the moment. The field of operations covered many miles, broken by mountains and deep chasms, and I have not a report, as yet, from any division or brigade.*

*Twiggs' Division, followed by Shields' (now Colonel Baker's) brigade, are now at or near Xalapa* [Jalapa], *and Worth's division is in route thither, all pursuing, with good results, as I learn, that part of the Mexican army—perhaps six or seven thousand men—who had fled before our right had carried the tower, and gained the Xalapa road. Pillow's brigade alone, is near me at this depot of wounded, sick, and prisoners; I have time only to give from him the names of 1st Lieut F.B. Nelson, and 2nd C.G. Hill, both of the 2d Tennessee foot (Haskell's regiment,) among the killed, and in the brigade 106, of all ranks, killed or wounded.*

*Among the latter, the gallant Brigadier-general himself has a smart wound in the arm, but not disabled; and Major R. Farqueson, 2nd Tennessee, Capt. H.F. Murray, 2d Lieut. G.T. Sutherland, 1st Lieut. W.P. Hale, Adjutant, all of the same regiment, severely, and 1st Lieut. W. Yearwood, mortally wounded. And I know, from personal observation on the ground, that 1st Lieut. Ewell, of the rifles, if not now dead, was mortally wounded in entering, sword in hand, the intrenchments* [sic] *around the captured tower.*

*2d Lieut. Derby, topographical engineers, I also saw, at the same place, severely wounded, and Capt. Patton, 2d United States Infantry, lost his right hand. Major Summer, 2d United States dragoons, was slightly wounded the day before, and Capt. Johnston, topographical engineers (now Lieut. Colonel of infantry,) was very severely wounded some days earlier while reconnoitering. I must not omit to add that Capt. Mason, and 2d Lieut. Davis, both of the rifles, were among the very severely wounded in storming the same tower.*

*I estimate our total loss, in killed and wounded, may be about 250, and that of the enemy at 350. In the pursuit toward Xalapa (25 miles hence) I learn we have added much to the enemy's loss in prisoners, killed, and wounded. In fact, I suppose his retreating army to be nearly disorganized, and hence my haste to follow, in an hour or two, to profit by events.*

*In this hurried and imperfect report I must not omit to say that Brigadier-general Twiggs, in passing the mountain-range beyond Cerro Gordo, crowned with the tower, detached from his division, as I suggested the day before, a strong force to carry that height, which commanded the Xalapa road at the foot, and could not fail, if* carried, to cut off the whole, or any part, of the enemy's forces from a retreat in any direction.

A portion of the 1st artillery, under the often distinguished Brevet Colonel Childs, the 3d infantry, under Captain Alexander, the 7th infantry, under Lieut.-colonel Plympton, and the rifles, under Major Loring, all under the temporary command of Colonel Harney, 2d dragoons, during the confinement to his bed of Brevet Brig.-general P.F. Smith, composed that detachment. The style of execution, which I had the pleasure to witness, was most brilliant and decisive.

The brigade ascended the long and difficult slope of Cerro Gordo, without shelter, and under the tremendous fire of artillery and musketry with the utmost steadiness, reached the breastworks, drove the enemy from them, planted the colors of the 1st artillery, 3d and 7th infantry—the enemy's flag still flying—and, after some minutes' sharp firing, finished the conquest with the bayonet.

It is a most pleasing duty to say that the highest praise is due to Harney, Childs, Plymton, Loring, Alexander, their gallant officers and men, for this brilliant service, independent of the great results which soon followed.

Worth's division of regulars coming up at this time, he detached Brevet Lieut.-Col. C.F. Smith, with his light battalion, to support the assault, but not in time. The general, reaching the tower a few minutes before me, and observing a white flag displayed from the nearest portion of the enemy towards the batteries below, sent out Colonels Harney and Childs to hold a parley. The surrender followed in an hour or two.

Major-general Patterson left a sick-bed to share in the dangers and fatigues of the day; and after the surrender went forward to command the advanced forces toward Xalapa.

Brig.-general Pillow and his brigade twice assaulted with great daring the enemy's line of batteries on our left; and though without success, they contributed much to distract and dismay their immediate opponents.

President Santa Anna, with Generals Canalizo and Almonte, and some six or eight thousand men, escaped toward Xalapa just before Cerro Gordo was carried, and before Twiggs' Division reached the National road above.

> *I have determined to parole the prisoners—officers and men—as I have not the means of feeding them here, beyond to-day, and cannot afford to detach a body of horse and foot, with wagons, to accompany them to Vera Cruz. Our baggage train, though increasing, is not half large enough to give an assured progress to this army.*
>
> *Besides, a great number of prisoners would, probably, escape from the escort in the long and deep sandy road, without subsistence—ten to one—than we shall find again, out of the same body of men, in the ranks opposed to us. Not one of the Vera Cruz prisoners is believed to have been in the lines of Cerro Gordo. Some six of the officers, highest in rank, refuse to give their paroles, except to go to Vera Cruz, and thence, perhaps, to the United States.*
>
> *The small-arms and accoutrements, being of no value to our army here or at home, I have ordered them to be destroyed; for we have not the means of transporting them. I am, also, somewhat embarrassed with the—pieces of artillery, all bronze, which we have captured. It would take a brigade, and half the mules of our army, to transport them fifty miles.*
>
> *A field battery I shall take for service with the army, but the heavy metal must be collected, and left here for the present. We have our own siege-train and the proper carriages with us.*
>
> *Being much occupied with the prisoners, and all the details of a forward movement, besides looking to the supplies which are to follow from Vera Cruz, I have time to add no more—intending to be at Xalapa early to-morrow. We shall not, probably, again meet with serious opposition this side of Perote—certainly not, unless delayed by the want of means of transportation.*
>
> *I have the honor to remain, sir, with high respect,*
> *Your most obedient servant,*
> *WINFIELD SCOTT*

*[April 26, 1847 • Monday]*

Entrepreneur that he was, John Sutter was forging ahead with a couple of grand schemes of his that had long been important to his way of thinking. Both of these were business ventures in which he had no real previous experience, but that did not stop him now any more than such a vexation had ever stopped him in the past regarding other projects. Both involved the establishment of mills which would be of the utmost importance to the settlers beginning to flood into the Sacramento Valley—the first, a very large and productive grist mill somewhere in the vicinity of Sutters Fort; the second, a lumber mill large enough to provide the planking that all these settlers were going to need in order to erect their own buildings that would be far more efficient as homes, barns, stables and work sheds than the clumsy log cabins currently the norm.

Sutter had already built six flour mills at various locations but all were small and inefficient and so it had become important to locate a proper site for a much larger and more effective grist mill of this type. That turned out to be no problem whatever; a good stretch of level ground adjacent to the left bank of the American River about five miles above its confluence with the Sacramento River was ideal and here Sutter had his first really large grist mill built well over a year ago and sent immediately for a pair of huge millstones which had only recently been delivered by ship. With the wheat and barley crops just now ripening, the mill would soon be very busy turning out the flour the settlers already here and those arriving or yet to come would need.

Locating a site similarly for the lumber mill was, however, a much different proposition. The site had to be adjacent to a good stream upon which logs could be floated down to it from wherever the trees were cut and, equally, the sawn planks transported by wagon or raft to Sutters Fort, or wherever needed, with a minimum of difficulty and expense involved. He'd sent for the huge blades at the same time he'd ordered the millstones and they'd arrived here in the same shipment, but they still sat in their crates awaiting the building of the lumber mill and that was where the problem lay.

Three times already over the past year Sutter had sent expeditions upstream on the Sacramento to locate an ideal site to erect such a mill, but thus far they'd been singularly unsuccessful. They simply had not yet been able to locate a site where a steady, dependable supply of lumber trees was reasonably available, nor one that lent itself well to the easy and economical transport of sawn lumber to the fort, either by raft or wagon.

John Sutter was in much better financial condition now than he'd been at any time since establishing the fort and things looked good for a continuation of his good fortune. His debts had not yet been fully paid off by any means, but at least now he was able to make periodic payments that kept his creditors satisfied for the most part. He had been appointed subagent to all the Indians within the enormous land grant he held and presently had half a thousand "tame" Indians working for him on a regular basis and upwards of 20,000 others he could call upon, when necessary, to do specific jobs.

Already many of his Indians had been trained to do exacting jobs, such as weaving blankets or various cotton or linen fabrics, for which he had purchased simple looms. Others he had trained in smithery and in the manufacture of guns—rifles and pistols in particular. He also, by this time, had expansive tracts of acreage currently under cultivation and was already producing 40,000 bushels of wheat annually. Above and beyond those pursuits, he had so many thousands of head of cattle and sheep, plus hundreds of horses, mules and hogs, that he had clearly lost track of their number. His butcher shop within the fort provided meat for settlers for miles around and the tanneries, where their hides were turned into good leather, were constantly at work. In addition to that, he had a number of small stores he'd had built at the fort that provided a variety of goods and services, plus others he rented out to other settlers with entreprenurial bent and his customers included not only the three hundred settlers living at or near the fort, but many others along the Sacramento and American Rivers. He also owned upwards of sixty houses in the area, some of which he rented to more or less permanent settlers and others to transients who were arriving practically every day. Finally, he also had built barracks large enough to be rented out to two companies of United States troops stationed here under Major Kingsbury.

The word about John Sutter over a wide area in central California was that he was well on his way to becoming one of the richest individuals in the territory.

The one enterprise he did not have, however, and which he was completely determined to establish was a good lumber mill. He was not at all satisfied with the results of the teams he'd already dispatched to find exactly the right site. To that end he summoned today the man who had just returned from southern California where he'd been serving for so long in the California Battalion under Lt. Col. John Fremont but who had recently, along with others of the Battalion, been mustered out: James Marshall.

"Do you," he asked Marshall, after explaining to him what was needed, "think you can find the ideal site for the type of sawmill I want to establish?"

"Yes," Marshall replied, without hesitation.

"And can you build it, set it into operation?"

"I can, under certain conditions."

Sutter's gaze narrowed. "Conditions such as...?" He left the question hanging.

"That you continue to pay me as your chief carpenter during the time that I seek and find the proper location, however long that takes, and then build the mill you need, to the exact specifications you want, and build quarters for those needed to harvest the timber, bring it to the mill, operate the mill and transport the cut lumber to wherever you need it..."

He paused and Sutter was certain he was not finished. "And...?" he prompted.

"And at the point that I feel assured the mill is ready to operate as a commercial business," Marshall finished, "you cease paying me as an employee and thereafter accept me as a full partner in that lumber business, with the two of us sharing equally in all proceeds and all costs."

Sutter was silent for a long moment before shaking his head and replying, with a bit of a chuckle, "You continue to live up to my expectations of you from the very first. I agree to your terms."

"As I was sure you would," Marshall said, and the pair laughed heartily together as they shook hands and sealed their bargain.

*[May 4, 1847 • Tuesday]*

President James Knox Polk, for the first time since he took office, was able to relax a bit in his drive for territorial acquisition for the United States. Though the War with Mexico was not yet won and undoubtedly wouldn't be until Mexico City itself was attacked and that nation forcibly brought to its knees there, the foremost goal of the President had clearly been won: America now conclusively stretched as one nation from north to south and from the Atlantic to the Pacific.

Ending the war as quickly and as bloodlessly as possible and establishing firm lines of separation between Mexico and the United States seemed to be the principal desire of everyone except the top Mexican leadership itself which continued to cling with dogged determination to what remained of the nation. Much as Polk disliked the idea, he would have to temporarily rescind his order for Scott to return to Washington D.C. until whatever remained of Mexican opposition could be shattered and the Latin American nation forced to capitulate.

Today, however, May 4, 1847, Polk listened attentively at his Cabinet meeting as Secretary Marcy read aloud General Doniphan's report on the Battle of Sacramento, Mexico. Doniphan had clearly fulfilled Polk's own intent deep within enemy territory. With virtually no backing from the War Department itself, he had captured Chihuahua, the strategically important northern province of Mexico, and its capital city of the same name. All that remained to be done now, it seemed, to force Mexico to final capitulation, was to march into—and take—that nation's capital, Mexico City itself.

In his own diary this evening, the President commented briefly about today's Cabinet meeting and commended Doniphan for having performed "...*one of the most decisive and brilliant achievements of the War.*" It was exactly the type of action needed to rebuild in flagging American hearts the impetus to fight what would have to be the final major battle of the war—the battle for Mexico City itself which, if won by the Yankees, would unequivocally place all of Mexico under American control.

*[May 13, 1847 • Thursday]*

For General Kearny, the closure of his service in the Army of the West was now clearly in sight and a wave of relief washed through him. No assignment he'd ever before fulfilled in his service career had been so disrupted by internal tension and disagreement as had this march to California and the problems faced in carrying out his orders once having arrived here. Bit by bit those problems had been ironed out until now they were virtually all settled and California was firmly in the hands of the United States as its own territorial possession. Only one major problem remained now—that of the unbridled ambitions of Lt. Col. John Fremont—and that was a problem that could not be entirely resolved until those most closely involved were back in Washington, D.C.

From the very beginning, Kearney's orders had been to establish a stable government within California and, as soon as such stabilization had been achieved, to repair to Washington at once for further orders. All that had pretty much occurred thus far and, with the arrival by ship of Colonel Jonathan D. Stevenson and his regiment of New York Volunteers, the final preparations had clicked neatly into place. Kearney ordered Stevenson to accept command of the southern district of California from Lt. Col. Cooke and Cooke himself was ordered to accompany the Kearny detachment back to Washington D.C.

# The Infinite Dream

As was Lt. Col. John Fremont.

General Kearny, in a quick trip to Los Angeles, had directed Cooke, in Special Order No. 16 to *"...select thirteen efficient men of the Mormon Battalion—"* a dozen privates and their officer, Lt. George Stoneman, *"to form part of the escort"* for the journey back to the United States, *"these men to turn in their muskets to the Ordnance Sergeant, & receive from him Rifles in their stead."*

Today, with three of those Mormon men chosen as escort, he prepared to return on the morrow to Monterey by ship, leaving the other nine, under Stoneman, to proceed by land and meet him at his more northern headquarters. The latter party traveled twenty miles this same day and camped for the night next to a pair of bubbling springs only six feet apart, one of which was icy cold and the other boiling hot.

What Kearney had accomplished in stabilizing the California government over these past ninety days had been little short of remarkable, considering the mess that leadership was undergoing when he arrived, in particular the shambles created by Commodore Stockton and Lt. Col. Fremont. With a refreshing lack of bravado, Kearny this afternoon dashed off a note to Lt. Col. Cooke in which he noted that the two of them had:

> *...brought much order to a vast territory so lately given over to chaos. I believe that the Mormons, if left alone, will simply slide back into an ordinary condition, since only persecution has kept them together. I have determined, upon finding the people of California quiet, to close my public business as soon as possible and proceed to St. Louis via the South Pass. I have ordered Lt. Col Fremont to accompany our detachment eastward and am determined to arrest this insubordinate officer when we arrive at Fort Leavenworth or before.*

General Kearny immediately followed up this letter with a preliminary report to General William L. Marcy in Washington:

> *Head Qtrs. 10 mily Dept., Cuidad de los Angeles, California*
> *13 May 1847*
> *No. 11*
>
> Sir,
> My letter No. 10 of May 3 informed you of my intention of

coming to this place with Col. Stevenson and 2 Compys of his Regt of N.Y. Vols. We reached here on the 9th and I find the people of this part of California quiet, notwithstanding some rumors to the contrary circulated & I fear originated by some of our own officers to further their own wicket [sic] purposes.[219]

I leave here tomorrow for Monterey, & will close my public business there as soon as possible, and then proceed to Saint Louis (via the South Pass) where I hope to be by the 20 of August, and where if this reaches you in time (it will go by Santa fe) I shall expect to receive orders for my further movements. I shall be prepared to go at once, wherever it is deemed my services may be needed.[220]

I this morning started Lt. Col. Fremont to Monterey to close his public business there before he leaves for Washington. His conduct in California has been such, that I shall be compelled, on arriving in Missouri, to arrest him & send him under charges to report to you.

I shall be accompanied from Monterey by Lt. Colonel Fremont, Major [Thomas] Swords [Qtrmr.] *who goes to settle accounts and bring his family here*—Capts. Cooke and Turner 1st Drags, who go to join their Companies, & Assistant Surgeon G. B. Sanderson who has resigned. My escort will be the men of the Top[ographical] Parties who came to this country with Lt. Col. Fremont and Lt. Emory & 13 men of the Mormon Battalion.

|  | Very Respectfully |
| --- | --- |
| The Ad't Genl | Your Ob. Servt. |
| U.S.Army | S.W. Kearny. Brig. Genl. |
| Washington | |

[*May 18, 1847 • Tuesday*]

For the Mormon Battalion, still in its disparate companies in southern California Territory, the weeks and months since their arrival seemed to drag interminably. The entire Battalion existed in a sort of stasis while they waited for their term of enlistment to expire and their discharges to become official so they could head back eastward and find their families.

Constant pressure was maintained upon them to re-enlist and some of the offers, if they were to do so, were enticing, including bonuses paid at the time of the re-enlistment and a slightly higher wage scale for their services. A few whose family ties were weak were inclined to do so, but they were very few, indeed, and by far the greater majority wanted nothing so much as to be mustered out of service to the United States Army and be able to head home...wherever "home" might happen to be.

Pvt. Henry Bigler was one of the larger number who simply bided his time and longed for the day to come when his obligation to the U.S. Army was completed and he could make his way back eastward to wherever the Church of Jesus Christ of Latter-day Saints had sunk new roots.

The five companies of the Mormon Battalion remained relatively scattered during this period, some of the men on patrol duties in El Cahon hill country to the east to guard against marauding bands of Indians and scattered bodies of rebellious Californios, some in garrison duty at San Luis Rey or at San Diego, and the majority at Los Angeles. Bigler's Company B remained stationed at San Diego where the duty was relatively easy but altogether too boring—a procession of seemingly endless and purposeless days of eating, sleeping and drilling. Toward the end of March all the companies had been consolidated at Los Angeles except for Company B, still at San Diego, and a guard detachment of only thirty men at San Luis Rey.

Commodore Stockton's warship, the forty-four-gun *U.S. Congress* remained, for the most part, anchored in San Diego harbor, a small city unto itself. Designed specifically as the last of the great sailing frigates for the U.S. Navy and the top of the line in its class, it displaced 1,867 tons and carried a full complement of about 500 men.

Captain Jefferson Hunt was one of the few Mormon soldiers who strongly wished to see the Battalion continue its service to the United States, though more motivated by his own desire to become the unit's commanding officer with the permanent rank of Lieutenant Colonel than for any altruistic reasons. His request to be promoted to this role and to be allowed, temporarily, to return to Council Bluffs, Iowa was, however, not greeted enthusiastically by General Kearny:

> *Head Qtrs., 10th Mil. Dept., Monterey (California).*
> *March 27th, 1847*
>
> *Sir:*
> *I am instructed by the General Commanding to acknowledge the receipt of your letter of the 17th inst., and to say in reply that he does not doubt but that the services of the Mormon Battalion will be needed longer than the period of their present enlistment, and that*

> they will be continued in the service of the U.S. should they desire it. The General does not approve of your going to Council Bluff at this time as suggested by you.

| | |
|---|---|
| | *I am Sir right respectfully,* |
| *Capt. J. Hunt* | *Your Obt. Servt.* |
| *Mormon Battalion* | *H.S. Turner* |
| *San Luis Rey (California)* | *Capt. A.A.A. Genl.* |

The following day, March 28, Lieutenant Stoneman returned to Los Angeles with his detachment of Dragoons, having followed a party of marauding Indians for half a day before overtaking them and killing four of their number. The Indians had been raiding on the Californians and had killed one or two of them. It was believed that Stoneman's reprisal would go far to deter any further incursions by the tribe.

The most inspiring news to reach the Mormon Battalion in a considerable while regarding the war came on Friday, April 2, filtering its way to the troops via Lt. Col. Cooke's headquarters, which put it in a class well removed from the ordinary rumors that circulated so frequently and with so little basis in reality. In this case, however, there seemed little likelihood that the reports reaching them were rumor-based and the entire Mormon Battalion became jubilant with the news of General Taylor having achieved an almost incredible victory at a place called Buena Vista on February 28. As Pvt. Henry Bigler commented about it in his diary:

> ...our Captain...received a letter from the Colonel stating that General Taylor had fought one of the greatest battles ever fought in America. He had scaled the walls of the enemy with four thousand against ten thousand and gained the victory. The Mexicans lost 1400 and Taylor five hundred, and Santa Anna [sic] was still making preparations to fight...

However exhilarating such news was, Cpl. Thomas Dunn of Company B, seemed to better express the general feeling prevailing throughout the entire Mormon Battalion when he wrote in his diary entry two days later, on April 4:

> *The hours seem to pass slowly the nearer the time of our discharge*

*appears. My mind is almost constantly reflecting on my wife and little ones who are anxiously looking for my return to their embrace.*

It was on April 6 that Lt. Col. Cooke, acting on instructions received from General Kearny at Monterey, ended the Battalion's occupation of the small post at San Luis Rey:

> (Order No. 5)
> Head Quarters, Southern Military District
> Cuidad de Los Angeles. April 6th, 1847
> *The post of San Luis Rey will be discontinued until further orders. 1st Lieutenant, Oman, Mormon Battalion, will march his detachment, composing its garrison, to this city [Los Angeles] without delay. He will drive here all the public mules and bring with him other public property in his charge.*
> P. St. George Cooke
> Lieut. Col. Commanding

The matter of the Mormon Battalion troops possibly being awarded an early discharge from the Army remained a matter of considerable discussion in the Battalion. As Sgt. Tyler wrote about it:

> *On the 6th, a petition for the discharge of the Battalion was gotten up and signed by most of the soldiers, on the ground that peace was declared in California and their services could be dispensed with, allowing them to return and aid their outcast families.*
>
> *A council of officers was called, at which the petition was read and thrown under the table, and not presented to Colonel Cooke and General Kearny, as requested. Captain Daniel C. Davis, and Lieutenants James Pace, Charles Lytle and Samuel Thompson, favored the petition, while the majority of the commissioned officers favored a universal reenlistment with Captain Jefferson Hunt as Lieutenant Colonel.*
>
> *General Kearny having sent word to his superiors in office in the East that he was anxious to be released of his charge in California as soon as peace was established, Colonel R.B. Mason was sent to succeed him in command; and he, being superior in rank to Fremont, was, shortly after his arrival, sent by Kearny to*

Los Angeles to enforce the discharge of Fremont's Battalion and obedience to other orders.

After some difficulty, he finally succeeded in discharging Fremont's men and taking ten pieces of cannon held by them, which were immediately brought to Los Angeles and turned over to Colonel Cooke.

For some reason unknown to us, and certainly without just cause, the men who composed Fremont's command manifested a great deal of animosity towards the Mormon Battalion. It was currently reported, and probably true, that Fremont himself did all he could to arouse ill-feeling, not only among his own men but also among the native population. We were assured by some of the Mexicans that he had told them the "Mormons" were cannibals, and especially fond of eating children. It seemed, too, that the story gained some credence among the natives, for their shyness about approaching our camp for sometime [sic] was attributed by them to this cause.

After Colonel Cooke made the demand upon Fremont's men for ordnance stores, which Captain Owens refused to comply with, and especially after their subsequent discharge, their bitterness towards us seemed to increase. We frequently heard of their threatening to make a raid upon our camp and wipe us out of existence. However, they never attempted to put any such threat into execution, and it was probably as well for them that they did not, as they would have been met with a warm reception. A few of the most belligerent of them sought quarrels with some of our men on meeting them in Los Angeles, but beyond this we were not molested by them.

Lieutenant Rosecrantz's Company C was ordered by Lt. Col. Cooke on April 11 to return the following day to Cajon Pass in the mountains forty-five miles east of San Diego to take post in the narrowest portion of the canyon pass and establish a camp there to prevent the passage of Indians and, if necessary, to send out armed parties to protect the ranchos in the vicinity from attack or livestock raids by any wandering parties of "wild Indians" and that the post would be provided with provisions until further notice.

On April 12, the thirty-seven men—many who were sick—from the four battalion companies who were left at San Luis Ray under Lt. George

Oman to guard the public property there, rejoined the command at Los Angeles and the Battalion was once again consolidating. Four days later, on April 16, regular mail service was established between San Diego and San Francisco, with the round trip requiring fourteen days.

On April 22, a detachment of twenty-seven non-commissioned officers and men was dispatched under command of 1st Lt. James Pace of Company E with thirty days' rations to Cajon Pass to relieve the detachment on guard there under Lieutenant Rosecrans and with orders to occupy the same position with the same guard duties but, additionally, Lt. Pace was to detach, on his arrival there, a non-commissioned officer and six horsemen to the nearby Williams Rancho, where they were to "discourage" a party of hostile Indians that had recently been detected moving about in the area.

The men of the Mormon Battalion were not pleased at being stationed at Los Angeles and Pvt. Henry Standage of Company E neatly put his fingers on the causes in his diary entry for May 2, as he wrote:

*May 2. For the last two days I have been more or less through the city of Angels or as it is in Spanish* Cuidad de Los Angeles, *and must say they are the most degraded set of beings I was ever among, professing to be civilized and taught in the Roman Catholic religion. There are almost as many grog shops and gambling houses in this city as there are private houses. Only 5 or 6 stores and no mechanics shops. A tolerable sized Catholic church, built of unburnt brick and houses of the same material. Roofs made of reeds and pitched on the outside (tar springs close by or I may say pitch). Roofs flat. There are some 3 or 4 houses built American fashion. The Spaniards in general own large farms in the country and keep from one to 20,000 head of cattle. Horses in abundance, mules, sheep, goats, &c. Also the Indians do all the labor and Mexicans are generally on horseback from morning till night. They are perhaps the greatest horsemen in the known world, and very expert with lance and lasso. They are in general a very idle, profligate, drunken, swearing set of wretches, with but very few exceptions. The Spaniards' conduct in grog shops with the squaws is really filthy and disgusting even in day time. Gambling is carried to the highest pitch, men often losing 500 dollars in cash in one night, or a 1,000 head of cattle...*

That same evening, Major Jeremiah H. Cloud of the Second Missouri Volunteers, who was serving as an additional paymaster for the U.S. Army in California, arrived from the Pueblo de los Angeles with the six months installment of the Saints' pay.[221] Most of this pay was expended by the Saints individually in purchasing animals, clothing and other gear for the forthcoming journey to wherever their new Zion was being established. Fortunately for the Saints, horses and mules were very cheap; wild mares could be purchased for $3 to $4 each and those broken to ride sold for anywhere from $6 to $20 apiece. Good, sturdy mules were worth just about double the price of common horses.

As the time until their discharge began growing short, the efforts to induce the Saints of the Mormon Battalion to re-enlist continued relentlessly. On May 4 Lt. Col. Cooke assembled the men and read to them an order just received from General Kearny giving the Battalion the privilege of being discharged immediately, but only on condition of immediate re-enlistment for three years in the regular Army as U.S. Dragoons. So intent was Kearny on securing such reenlistment, he journeyed south from Monterey once again to address the Saints and encourage them to re-enlist before their current enlistment should expire in mid-July. As Sgt. Tyler put it in his diary:

> ...*He sympathized with us in the unsettled condition of our people, but thought, as their final destination was not yet settled, we had better re-enlist for another year, by which time the war would doubtless be ended and our families settled in some permanent location. In conclusion, he said, "I will take pleasure in representing your patriotism to the President, and in the halls of Congress, and give you the justice your praiseworthy conduct has merited." As before, however, to General Kearny's dismay, the Saints spurned the offer almost unanimously.*

Hours of considerable jubilation occurred among the Saints on May 6 when news was received that the American forces under Major General Scott and Commodore Perry, after a siege of eleven days duration, had taken the principal Mexican seaport city of Vera Cruz and now Scott was en route with his army to strike Mexico City itself in an effort to bring the Mexican government in its entirety to its knees.

The first real excitement to sweep through the Battalion for many weeks occurred on May 9 when, with Col. Stevenson and other officers of note, General Kearny arrived in Los Angeles—to the thunder of a twenty-one gun salute—for the purpose of selecting a dozen of the Saints as part of the escort the General wished for his forthcoming trip eastward.[222]

# Chapter 13

◆

*[May 20, 1847 • Thursday]*

As greedy and power-hungry as Lieutenant Colonel John C. Fremont had proven himself to be to General Kearny, he was also a very shrewd dealer when it came to securing his own future. His U.S. Army career now clearly on the line with the court-martial charges Kearny was planning to launch against him, Fremont was already taking steps to secure a very special niche for himself here in California in the event he were to be found guilty.

His own roaming for so long a period through the beautiful hill country of the central portion of the California Territory had given him a keen grasp on the availability of what he reasoned was land that could support him and Jessie quite well, even if all else was stripped from him. What he decided to purchase was the sprawling ranch called Las Mariposas—a 44,386-acre land-grant tract presently owned by none other than the former California governor, Juan Bautista Alvarado.

With the considerable amount of funds he had amassed during his tenure here in California, Fremont had no doubt he could afford to buy Alvarado's holdings at a fairly reasonable rate, since Alvarado had fallen upon hard times and had lost much of his fortune through drinking and gambling. The trick, so far as Fremont could imagine it, was to secure the sprawling property quickly, before he could be forced away from California.

This was when Fremont tapped the skills of his old friend, Thomas O. Larkin, the American consul in Monterey, who was more than pleased to aid him in purchasing the Alvarado land grant. This was especially true since Larkin was well aware of Alvarado's eagerness to sell—an eagerness inspired by the fact that while governor of California, he had treated the resident Miwok Indians so badly it would be tantamount to suicide for him to try to use the land himself. Alvarado believed—quite as Fremont was sure would occur—that it would be to his benefit to get whatever he possibly could for the land and get away, leaving someone else to face whatever mischief the Miwoks might mount.

The extensive property encompassing roughly seventy square miles of territory along Mariposa Creek was considered a "floating" grant. This was because Alvarado had not been able to properly survey it due to his problems with the Miwoks, but he reasoned that the property would prove just as profitable for timber harvest as it would for the excellent pasturage it could provide for horses and cattle.

So smoothly and so swiftly did Larkin's negotiations go with Alvarado that well before John Fremont could be forced to leave the territory, the deal was consummated, the papers signed and recorded and, come what may, the Mariposa Ranch was his.

*[May 25, 1847 • Tuesday]*

The friction that had developed between General Kearny and Lt. Colonel Fremont had become, by this time, a palpable menace that generated such a strong sense of impending military upheaval resounding in the minds of all the American officers in the California Territory, that everyone seemed poised in the balance. Among these was 1st Lt. William Tecumseh Sherman, who viewed what was occurring with a combination of alarm, confusion and amusement. As with most of the other officers, he knew better than to express any sort of opinion in regard to what would occur but, unlike those other officers, he became deeply involved despite his desire to remain aloof.

Early this month, on the verge of their embarking for San Pedro, General Kearny—with Sherman as his aide—put plans momentarily on hold as into the harbor at Monterey sailed the huge line-of-battle ship, *U.S. Columbus*, fresh from China with Commodore James Biddle aboard, whose rank clearly gave him supreme command of the U.S. Navy on the California coast. Among his first acts was an order rescinding many of the orders already stemmed from Commodore Stockton and calling in—"lassoing," as he put it—all the various naval officers who, under Stockton's command, had been engaged in a variety of on-shore military and civil services.

Having been informed that Lt. Sherman was on the verge of going down the coast with General Kearny, Commodore Biddle summoned Sherman and handed him, for delivery at Los Angeles, two unsealed parcels, one addressed to U.S. Naval Lt. Wilson, the other to U.S. Marines Major Archibald H. Gillespie. Both were orders and both identical save for the addressee:

> *On receipt of this order you will repair at once on board the United States ship* Lexington *at San Pedro, and on reaching Monterey, you will report to the undersigned.*
> 
> —JAMES BIDDLE
> *Commodore, U.S. Navy*

Immediately upon his arrival at San Pedro with the general, the *Lexington* anchoring inside the broad kelp beds, Lt. Sherman dispatched messages to Los Angeles, twenty miles distant, and the two officers in question were duly "lassooed" and the orders from Commodore Biddle delivered. Good horses were requested for the general and his aide and the pair disembarked preparatory to heading for Los Angeles themselves.

Fremont, who had been asked to attend General Kearny at the San Pedro wharf and accompany them back to Monterey aboard the *Lexington,* had refused and the general, not surprisingly, interpreted this as a distinct rebuff. As the senior and junior officers climbed the steep path up the bluff and Kearny clung to Sherman's arm, Kearney spoke aloud, though more to himself than to Sherman: "I find it strange, indeed, that Colonel Fremont has replied negatively to my invitation that he accompany us back to Monterey aboard the *Lexington*. He gave, as his reason, his propensity for sea-sickness and his preference to travel the five hundred miles to that place on horseback. What do you make of that, Lieutenant?"

Sherman responded a bit hesitantly at first but then with a degree of blooming confidence. "I have to admit, sir," he replied, "that I personally would have construed your invitation as a direct order and would have attended you at once." He paused briefly but then, as General Kearny nodded in apparent agreement, added: "Sir, if I may speak frankly...?"

"By all means, Lieutenant. I'd be pleased to learn your assessment."

Sherman nodded, took a deep breath and continued. "The

# The Infinite Dream

younger officers—myself included among them—have been discussing amongst ourselves what the General will do with Colonel Fremont, whom we all cannot help but regard as countenancing a state of mutiny. Some of us thought he would be summarily tried and shot. Others of us—again, myself included—believe he should be carried back East with us in irons and tried by general court-martial. We all seemed to agree that if anyone else other than Colonel Fremont had put on such airs with his commander and acted as he has, the General would have shown him no mercy, since you, sir, are regarded as the strictest sort of disciplinarian."

Kearny barked a short, humorless laugh. "One must take care," he replied, "despite personal feelings, that rashness never become part of the equation when dealing with so serious a matter as general courts-martial involving a field officer. It is altogether possible I may have been too cautious in that respect, although I think not."

The two officers, riding at the van of their company of following foot-soldiers, clearly enjoyed following the seaside road that took them toward the City of Angels, but though they conversed about many matters during the three hours while en route, Colonel Fremont was not again mentioned. They found Lt. Col. Philip St. George Cooke in Los Angeles living at the house of a resident named Alan Pryor, while in a large adobe house nearby the company of dragoons were quartered, along with their officers, Captain A.J. Smith and Lieutenants Stoneman and Davidson, along with Dr. John Griffin. Fremont, they were told, was close by and had taken as his lodging and headquarters the only two-story frame house in the area.

General Kearny, with Sherman attending him, spent some time at Pryor's house, at which point the general leaned close to Sherman and spoke softly: "I have no doubt Colonel Fremont already knows we're here," he said, "but I want you to go now to where he is, notify him formally of our arrival here and inform him personally that I wish to see him."

Sherman murmured, "Yes sir," and immediately slipped away. He walked to the nearby house that had been pointed out to him as Fremont's and found a man stationed at the front door. Without hesitation he strode up to him and asked bluntly, "Is Colonel Fremont in?"

"Yes, he is. Follow me, please."

The man led him to a large room on the second floor, told him to wait and exited through a different door than the one they had entered. In less than a minute the door opened again and Colonel Fremont himself strode out and looked at Sherman inquiringly.

Sherman, without wasting words, delivered the message he had been given. When Fremont said nothing, after a moment Sherman turned to leave.

"Where are you going?" Fremont asked.

"Back to Mr. Pryor's house, where the General is waiting."

"Well, if you'll wait a moment, I'll go along with you."

Sherman waited as Fremont left the room and returned a moment later clad as the Californios were, wearing the peculiar, broad-brimmed hat that so many of them wore, trimmed with a fancy cord. They walked together to Pryor's, where Sherman announced the colonel's appearance to General Kearny and then turned and left the room.

The aspect of Los Angeles was, to Sherman, most pleasant. Although he had been informed that this was the chief pueblo of southern California and noted for its fruits, wines and grapes, he was unprepared for the scope of such improvements: Vineyards alone were cultivated in a swath perhaps a mile wide and five miles in length and seemed to embrace the entire town. Additionally, every house, it seemed had its own vineyard enclosure, resembling a miniature orchard with rows of vines trimmed closely and arranged so that an irrigation ditch flanking the rows could be regularly filled with water diverted from the San Gabriel and Los Angeles rivers which, themselves were fed by melting snow on the distant peaks. Lt. Sherman was impressed to find that with a climate so moderate, there was an abundance of such fruit in almost constant production as figs, oranges, pomegranates and, of course, a wide variety of grapes.

It was, however, the upcoming journey of General Kearny that was the most pressing matter, along with the disposition of the Saints in the Mormon Battalion. As Sherman wrote:

> *At the time of our visit, General Kearny was making preparations to return overland to the United States, and he arranged to secure a volunteer escort out of the battalion of Mormons under Colonel Cooke and Major Hunt. This battalion was only enlisted for one year, and the time for their discharge was approaching, and it*

*was generally understood that the majority of the men wanted to be discharged so as to join the Mormons who had halted at Salt Lake, but a lieutenant and about forty men volunteered to return to Missouri as the escort of General Kearny. These were mounted on mules and horses, and I was appointed to conduct them to Monterey by land.*

*Leaving the party at Los Angeles to follow by sea in the* Lexington, *I started with the Mormon detachment and traveled by land. We averaged about thirty miles a day, stopped one day at Santa Barbara, where I saw Colonel Burton, and so on by the usually traveled road to Monterey, reaching it in about fifteen days, arriving some days in advance of the* Lexington.

The Saints—at least *some* of them—were finally headed for home.[223]

### [June 6, 1847 · Tuesday · 10:00 a.m.]

San Francisco—formerly Yerba Buena—was now a decidedly more permanent village, with laid-out streets and well-planted frame houses and businesses, but there were some who gloomily predicted it would not—*could not*—last.

By the first of April it had begun to have the burgeoning look of both permanence and prosperity, boasting not only an excellent, protected dockage for ships but a reasonably well-designed city schematic for future growth. Already there were seventy-nine structures, including twenty-two shanties, thirty-one frame houses and twenty-nine substantial adobe dwellings and businesses. The prospects for continued growth in the future were very positive.

On Saturday, April 10, a pair of Methodist ministers arrived en route to Oregon and in short order had established a Sunday school as the forerunner to a more permanent church structure. Here, on the following day, they preached a dual sermon that was surprisingly well attended, but by nightfall on that Sunday they had moved on, leaving no minister behind to carry on with what they had begun, nor even their own names or a name for the church; nothing except a shell of a structure with a cross projecting from its roof and with at least one enthusiastic dichotomous resident who proclaimed, "By God, we got us one dam' fine l'il church!"

The twice-monthly shipboard mail run between San Francisco

and San Diego had been augmented now by a supposedly regular land-based mail service between those two communities—"...and any place in-between"—by a pair of volunteer horsemen. The two men traveled a fortnight apart from one another between the two destinations...although the yet-to-be-uttered postal maxim of "...neither rain nor storm nor dark of night..." seemed not to apply to these "worthy couriers" who rarely passed a grog shop without pause of indeterminate length.

On Saturday, April 24, pioneer resident J.D. Marston opened, in a windowless shed of sorts attached to his home, a private school—the first school of any sort in San Francisco, It had bench-space for half a dozen students which, while not much and not yet filled to capacity, was, according to Marston, "...a noteworthy start on the road to education in San Francisco."

Not to be long outdone by the Methodists, the Reverend Thaddeus M. Leavenworth, a Connecticut Episcopalian who had recently vacated the post of chaplain to Col. Stevenson's Volunteers, inaugurated outdoor Protestant Episcopal services on Sunday, May 2. No immediate plans were proposed for construction of a church.

Considered by the residents as "truly a significant benchmark in San Francisco's growth" was the permanent move of the weekly newspaper, *The Monterey Californian*, from its namesake city to San Francisco on June 1 with the four-page weekly's new masthead banner proclaiming it now to be simply *The Californian*. It its very first issue it chronicled the resignation of Edwin Bryant as the city's *alcalde*, who was to be replaced on the morrow by George Hyde, who had come to San Francisco aboard the *Congress*, upon which he has served as clerk to Commodore Stockton.

Finally, early today, June 6, saw the arrival of Mormon Elder Addison Pratt, who had come to confer with Sam Brannan at New Hope, only to find him gone and apparently well on his way to visit Brigham Young at the Great Salt Lake. What he heard about Brannan's high-handedness with his flock of Saints and the growing instability of the Mormon establishment at New Hope, augmented by Brannan's frequent absences directly attributable to his many entrepreneurial ventures, especially in San Francisco, made Pratt decide he just might stick around a little longer than originally intended, in order to confront Brannan with "the error of his ways."

*[June 6, 1847 • Sunday • Noon]*

Brigham Young, who had spent the winter with much of his flock of Saints along the western bank of the Missouri River, was now once again well on the move westward in his search for the perfect Zion. Early in April, with a relatively small party of hand-selected pioneers from those at the winter camp, including eight top-echelon Apostles, eighteen high priests and eighty members of the exclusive group called the Seventies, Young had struck out westward, keeping his promise to the Government not to delay in the eastern fringe of the Indian Territory for any longer than absolutely necessary. This vanguard party he was leading now consisted of one hundred forty-three men, three women and two children, traveling in seventy-three wagons and herding with them a significant total of livestock—ninety-three horses, fifty-two mules, nineteen cows, seventeen dogs and a large number of crated chickens.[224]

On this Sabbath day, however, Young took the opportunity of relative peace and no walking to at last write to Sam Brannan not only an accounting to some degree of what had occurred with those left behind after Brannan's departure, but equally to ask questions of him that made it clear the string of letters he had written to Young had evidently never reached their destination. Young wrote:

> *Black Hills, Bitter Creek, 30 miles west of Ft. John, or Laramie, on the Oregone [sic] and Calif. route from the Platte, in camp of Israel's Pioneers*
> *—June 6, 1847*
>
> Mr. Samuel Brannan: My dear Sir:
> *By my date you will discover my location, and as there is an emigrating company from the States camped about one-fourth of a mile back from [us] this eve, some of whom, as I understand are destined for San Francisco, I improve a few moments to write you.*
>
> *About the time you left New York, the first company of friends left Nauvoo for the west, and in June arrived at Council Bluffs, where they were invited by Pres. Polk, through Capt. James Allen to enlist in the services of the United States and march to and be discharged in California...About 500 enlisted. Capt. Allen died at Ft. Leavenworth, and was succeeded by others in command, and the Battalion was marched to Santa Fe, from whence 150*

*were returned to Pueblo, on the Arkansas, invalids, etc., and the remainder continued their route to Mexico or towards Calif. by the South route.*

*After the Battalion left Council Bluffs, the remainder of our camp settled on the west bank of the Missouri about 20 miles north of the Platte River, and threw up log cabins, etc., so as to make themselves as comfortable as possible. And thus passed the winter.... This camp, which left Winter Quarters between the 6th and 14th of April, consists of something less than 200 men—two men to a wagon, accompanied by two thirds of the Council and men in pursuit of a location for themselves and friends, which they expect will be west of the Rocky Mountains.*

*We left upwards of 4,000 inhabitants at Winter Quarters and expect a large company which have since started, and are now en route, among whom will be as many of the families of the Battalion as can be fitted out. If any of the Battalion are with you or at your place, and want to find their families, they will do well to take the road to the States, via the south bank of the Salt Lake, Ft. Bridger, South Pass, etc. and watch the path or any turn of the road till they find this camp.... The camp will not go to the west coast or to your place at present; we have not the means.*

*The papers report your arrival and that you have the only printing office in Upper Calif., but I do not know the name of your paper.... I should have mentioned that from information received at Ft. Laramie, it is expected that the command, belonging to the Battalion at Pueblo is on their route toward Calif. by the South Pass and will be at this point in a few days.*

BRIGHAM YOUNG

*[June 18, 1847 • Friday]*

It was only four days ago—on Monday, June 12—that the Mormon Battalion learned officially of the details of the Battle of Buena Vista near Saltillo, Mexico. A wave of relief and joy swept through the companies and the troops were formed up and gave a rousing cheer for what the American force under General Taylor, had accomplished against a Mexican army almost twice as large, led by General Santa Ana.

The Americans, the Saints were informed, numbered 7,000 troops against 18,000 of the Mexicans, but the training of the American troops against the badly directed enemy had resulted in the Mexicans being ousted and thrown into a greatly disorganized retreat.[225] Santa Ana, it was reported, had returned to Mexico City and was marshalling forces there for a great stand against the Americans.

The Mormons in California, having nothing better to do than to await their time of discharge, had been given permission by Lt. Col. Cooke to accept employment at various tasks in the community if so they desired. A considerable number of them immediately hired themselves out to a rancher named Williams, who had about a thousand acres of wheat to cut. He also raised crops of barley, beans and peas, as well as having large vineyards and a herd of some 1,500 cattle.

The cattle at this time were selling for about $1 to $5 apiece and good healthy work oxen, well broken, sold at $30 to $50 per yoke. Many thousands of head of beef cattle were butchered for their hides and tallow alone, the meat being left to rot on the ground and creating a terrible stench lasting for weeks. Much of the tallow was used in the manufacture of soap, while that which was not was shipped, along with the raw hides, to eastern and southern markets.

Williams had established a soap factory of sorts which worked quite well: a boiler some ten feet deep and ten feet in diameter was placed over a furnace and filled with tallow and the fattest pieces of meat. A little water was poured in and this rendered down, after which the meat was discarded and the thick grease floating atop the water was dipped into a box a dozen feet square. Mineral earth was then leached like ashes and the lye obtained from it was mixed with the grease and boiled into a soap as white as snow and of very good quality, which was then cut into bars for sale or shipping, much of the product sent to the Orient.

The routine was broken somewhat today, however, when the Saints were assembled to hear an order read from Lt. Col. Cooke; a call for volunteers to reenlist for a period of six months. Not a man among them did and in the resultant embarrassment it was feared that the entire Battalion would be pressed into service, which could have been done if deemed necessary, even against their will, to give the government time to assemble other troops. All breathed sighs of relief, however, that such had not occurred and for the first time if seemed likely the discharges would occur just as soon as the current span of enlistment was completed. All were most eager for that to take place.

*[June 22, 1847 • Tuesday]*

For General Stephen Watts Kearny the scene that met his eyes at the deserted cabins of the Donner Party was horrible in the extreme and deeply depressing, both to himself and his escort. He very quickly made up his mind to eliminate, as much as possible, what remained of it and move along eastward as swiftly as possible, though knowing the scenes they had found could never be entirely obliterated from their memory.

Skulls and other bones as well as fragments of bodies, human and animal alike, lay strewn about the cabins and bore mute but gruesome testimony to what had occurred here. Assembling his escort and all others who had been traveling with them, he delivered his orders in a level but strained voice:

"I want all these remains—*all of them,*" he reiterated, "every scrap of bone, flesh, clothing, bedding, tools, whatever, collected and brought into the cabins, whereupon the cabins themselves will be burned. No one else," he added darkly, "should be subjected to viewing such a scene of human destruction and depravity."

As the men set about in the unpleasant task assigned to them, the General moved off a short distance and set up a very brief camp for himself in a small grove of pines near the shore of the lake and rummaged in his pack for writing materials to record the events of this ugly occurrence.

As he browsed through the notes already written in his journal and prepared to elaborate in some detail about today's discoveries, he knew he would have no difficulty refreshing his memory to all that had occurred over the past month. When the time became appropriate, he would prepare his report for the Adjutant General in Washington, D.C. and report on the activities of the past few weeks, which had been an extraordinarily busy period as he prepared to turn command of his troops in California over to his successor.

On the evening of May 27 the sloop *Lexington* had deposited him and Lt. Col. Cooke at Monterey, joining the frigate *Congress* and the battleship *Columbus* already at anchor in the harbor. Even though the 214 foot length of the warship *U.S. Congress*—forty-five feet from topsail mast to the stern hold and bearing an impressive forty-four guns—made her decidedly an impressive vessel, she was all but dwarfed by the mighty *U.S. Columbus,* riding at anchor nearby and herself boasting three decks and mounting ninety-eight cannon as well as a crew of seven hundred sailors and mariners. Though seldom impressed very much by anything, General Kearny admitted to being impressed by the battleship and his thoughts were more or less mirrored by Pvt. Nathaniel V. Jones of Co. D. who briefly but glowingly described the ship in his diary:

> ...In every way it is a splendid, well-finished craft.[226]

The Kearny escort, having several days earlier arrived under command of Lt. Sherman, had already drawn seventy-five days rations for the journey ahead, as well as some additional mules. The following couple of days had been occupied in fitting out in preparation for the long journey eastward. General Kearny, for his part, did not stint in his approval of San Francisco as the finest port landing on the continent's west coast, writing:

> ...The site of the town of San Francisco is known to all navigators and mercantile men acquainted with the subject to be the most commanding commercial position on the entire eastern coast of the Pacific Ocean, and the town itself is, no doubt, destined to become the commercial emporium of the western side of the American continent.

It was most definitely not false praise. San Francisco not only had a much safer and far more commodious harbor than Monterey, the waters of San Francisco Bay afforded an easy means of communication and transportation between the town and the hundred bayside valleys. Further, it had a ready means of communication by water with such large, rich valleys as the San Joaquín, the Sacramento and the American. Anyone who knew anything about shipping, anchorage and accessibility rated it as one of the best harbors anywhere.

On the final day of May, Colonel Richard B. Mason succeeded General Kearny as military governor of California Territory, freeing the latter for whatever preparations remained to be made for the long journey eastward. Before that day ended, General Kearny had set his small company into its march, John C. Fremont included, plus a few discharged dragoons who, along with Lt. Col. Cooke, were eager to join the main theater of war in Mexico.[227] Also with the party was U.S. Congressman-elect William Preble Hall, who had marched to California with the Battalion and would return to take his seat in the Thirtieth Congress. Included in the party was General Kearny's brother-in-law, U.S. Naval Lieutenant William Radford, Donner Party survivor William Graves, and two guides—one identified only as a man named Murphy, the other William O. Fallon, acting as guide to the party and, finally, "Dr. Death" himself, Dr. George B. Sanderson.

The party stopped briefly at Sutters Fort as they passed and John Sutter, very pleased to see them, fired a salute from his battery of eleven cannon and the fort's garrison of two dozen soldiers was paraded in the general's honor. Here they acquired an additional horse each for the journey over the Sierra Nevada and some hours were spent in drying some extra supplies of beef, pork and flour. Sgt. Tyler recorded that the Sacramento Valley

> ...had a very inviting appearance and the soil appeared as good as any in the world. Mechanical and other labor is very high-priced and scarce. Good land can be obtained for twenty-five cents per acre under Mexican title and a great proportion of the land is open to squatters. Wheat sells for a dollar a bushel..."

They crossed the American River and camped for the night of June 13 on the ranch of *alcalde* John Sinclair. By June 17 they had reached and camped at Johnson's Ranch on Bear Creek, where they were informed they were forty miles from Sutters Fort and that this was the last inhabited house they would encounter until they reached Fort Hall north of Great Salt Lake.[228] Two days later they camped at Mule Springs, now clear of snow and so attractive with its timber that Nathaniel Jones wrote in his diary:

> *June 19. Started early; came through the mountains all day. Came Fifteen miles, plenty of pine timber, very rough. Plenty of water. Camped in a small valley near the top of the mountain. I must say that this mountain is as good a part of California as I have seen with but few exceptions. The timber is the best I have ever seen.*

The following day, as they began again to encounter patches of snow at the higher elevations, they discovered what remained of Charles Stanton's body where he had seated himself to smoke his final pipeful.

His body had been mostly devoured by wild animals but some of the men with Kearny identified the remains of clothing and the pistols as Stanton's.

Yesterday, on reaching the summit at Emigrant Pass, they found the snow in places to still be as much as fifteen to twenty feet in depth, but rapidly melting. General Kearny, without realizing it, may have been responsible for renaming the pass, as he said, while they mounted it, "Instead of Emigrant Pass, this place should be called Donner Pass in memory of the Donner Party, who came here at so desperate a time."[229]

Today, however, whatever degree of levity might have been present in the Kearny Party disappeared as they finally came to the abandoned cabins near the lake and the gruesome remains scatted within and about them. The ground was reasonably clear of snow except in occasional sheltered patches and the grisly, mutilated remains of humans and beasts alike seemed to be scattered everywhere. Some of the corpses had become desiccated; shrunken by exposure until now they appeared all but mummified. Others had been partially eaten, some by humans, some by beasts.

Major Henry Smith Turner, General Kearny's adjutant general, wrote of the grisly scene that greeted them:

> *Reached the 'Cabins,' where 25 or 30 of a party of emigrants, in attempting to pass the last winter, had perished from starvation. Their bodies & bones were strewed about, presenting a revolting & distressing spectacle. The Gen'l directed Maj. Swords to collect these remains & inter them.*

It was Sgt. Dan Tyler who preserved the ghastly scene for posterity in the words he hastily wrote in his diary:

> *22d. A more revolting and appalling spectacle I never witnessed. The remains were, by order of Gen. Kearny, collected and [some] buried under the supervision of Major Swords. They were interred in a pit which had been dug in the center of one of the cabins for a cache. These melancholy duties to the dead being performed, the cabins, by order of Major Swords, were fired, and, with everything surrounding them connected with this horrid and melancholy tragedy, were consumed. The body of George Donner was found at*

his camp, about eight or ten miles distant, wrapped in a sheet. He was buried by a party of men detailed for that purpose.[230]

Another of the party wrote that the body of Donner Party member Lavinia Murphy:

*...was found lying near one of the huts, with her thigh cut away for food and the saw used to dismember her body lying along side of her...we Gathered up there [sic] remains and Covered them up and past [sic] on...*

For his own part, Major Swords assigned a detail of five men to gather up remains and inter them in one of the cabins with the remains already discovered there In his own journal he wrote:

*...five miles from the lower end of [Truckee Lake] we came to the remains of the cabins built by a party of emigrants. Stumps twelve or fifteen feet high afforded evidence of the immense quantity of snow by which they were surrounded.... We collected and buried the remains of those that had perished from hunger; some of the skeletons were entire; parts of others were found, the flesh having been consumed by the last survivors.*

Pvt. Nathaniel Jones of Co. D penned in his own private diary one of the more stark accounts that said, in part:

*The General called a halt and detailed five men to bury the deserted bodies of the others. One man [Louis Keseberg] lived about four months on human flesh and brains. He sawed their heads open, ate their brains and mangled up their bodies in a horrible manner. This place now goes by the name of Cannibal Camp. While we were stopped here the men came up with our pack mules. Colonel Fremont passed us here, the first time we have seen him since we left Fort Sutter. After we had buried the bones of the dead, which were sawed and broken to pieces for the marrow, we set fire to the cabin, which having been done we continued our march 10 miles further; and encamped on Greenwood's Creek. I started about two in the afternoon, came seven miles and camped. One mile above here there was another cabin and more dead bodies but the General did not order them buried.*

In all, the episode was deeply depressing to everyone and now General Kearny bent to his report, quickly closed it off and then shut away the words but not the ghastly pictures that would remain etched in his mind till the end of his days.

*[June 26, 1847 • Saturday • 2:00 p.m.]*

At last, after what had seemed to him had been interminable searching, James Marshall had finally located the ideal site to build the lumber mill and camp in which he and John Sutter would be partners. It had been no easy task to locate the spot, but now that it had been accomplished, the work of construction could move on apace and Marshall was well pleased that he'd had the foresight, two months ago—on April 26—to cut himself in as a partner to Sutter, rather than simply as an employee.[231]

The events since they had struck that bargain had become of extreme importance to both men for their own personal reasons. Immediately upon his return from the bellicose events occurring in Southern California, Marshall had discovered, to his dismay, that his personal holdings had all but disappeared; the majority of his livestock had either strayed or been stolen during his absence and this loss was accentuated by the fact that after spending upwards of a year in the service of his country, he was not to be paid for the time, risk and effort he had provided.

Not given to lamenting his losses, Marshall had immediately returned to work for Sutter as a wheelwright and carpenter but also with a view toward enhancing his own future and the notion of creating a lumber mill struck him as the ideal course to follow. Sutter was certainly in accord with the idea but, with his grist-mill still in the preliminary stages and skilled labor very hard to come by, delays resulted. It was not until Marshall—accompanied by an Indian guide and two itinerant white men from Sutter's named Graves and Treador—began his third exploratory search for a lumber mill-site on May 16 that definite results began shaping themselves.

Marshall, who had been engaged in stocking the plows at Sutter's, put that work aside for the time being and decided his next search for an adequate timber-site should be concentrated, upstream on the South Fork of the American River some forty miles distant above the grist-mill site. When he arrived, he found a site he considered ideal, with a heavily timbered hillside reaching the water on the right bank and, directly opposite on the left bank, a fine level stretch where a mill-race could be dug and the proposed mill itself positioned. This was only a few miles upstream from a small Digger Indian village called Culuma which, because of its pronunciation, Marshall spelled Coloma.[232]

Having found the location he felt was perfect for the lumbering operation, Marshall quickly laid out the course of the millrace he would have his laborers dig in the left bank in order to channel the current for the lumber mill's operation, then returned to complete the work he had promised Sutter he would oversee for the four-mile race at the grist-mill on the American River some five miles upstream from its merging into the Sacramento. He arrived there on May 31 and immediately set his crew to work on the grist-mill's race with plows and scrapers.

Today, however, early in the afternoon, Marshall closeted himself in private with John Sutter and explained in detail to him the setting he had found on the South Fork of the American River and its evident great potential as a lumbering mill site.

"The South Fork at that point," Marshall explained, "flows through the center of a very narrow valley. On the north side the heavily forested hills come right down to the river in a steep pitch. On the south side it's reasonably level for a fair distance and this is where the mill should be set up and a race dug which probably won't have to be more than a half mile long to get the current power-flow needed for the big saw. The wood there," he admitted, "won't last forever, but it'll last a damned long while and even when its finally gone, there's plenty more on the upstream hills on both sides, just as easily harvested. A sawmill built where I propose it there will produce beautifully for years!"

Sutter nodded slowly, wanting to believe but hardly daring to; the search for such a site had gone on for so long at this point that it was hard for him to accept it had finally come to an end. He had sent Marshall's expedition out almost entirely convinced at that point that an ideal lumber site was no more than an unattainable dream. Now Marshall had evidently proven that image wrong.

"Not only is it a productive site," Marshall went on, beaming enthusiastically, "transporting the sawn lumber to the fort can be done handily either by raft on the river itself, right to the fort here, or a good wagon road can be built without difficulty for direct and dry land-hauling. We can begin preparing the mill-site and the road just as soon as you're ready. I don't think we should waste any time in getting started."

Sutter nodded slowly and then abruptly smiled. "Nor do I," he said. "We'll get it started as soon as the grist-mill's up and running—within the month, probably."

Marshall gripped Sutter's hand and shook it. "Very soon as full partners," he said, his grin broadening even more.

"As agreed," Sutter replied, his own grin matching Marshall's.

*[June 26, 1847 • 4:00 p.m.]*

The War with Mexico was finally over...at least it was for the First Missouri Mounted Volunteers.

There was still a major chore ahead for the Army in the task of taking the Mexican capital city and bringing the Mexican Republic to its knees, assuming such a feat could be accomplished at all, but for the rough-and-tumble First Missouri, the war was definitely over.

General Santa Ana had most emphatically been put on the run by the American forces and was now ensconced in Mexico City, putting together what he hoped would be the strongest and most determined force the Yankees had yet faced; his goal not to merely stop the Americans in their inexorable push into the capital city, but to wholly annihilate them. It would be a battle which, if it came about, would either culminate in the great American victory President Polk had yearned for...or a defeat unlike any the Americans had ever before suffered and the loss of all they had striven for in the war thus far. However it turned out, one thing was clear: the First Missouri would no longer be a part of it.

Ever since Santa Ana had evacuated Puebla and retreated to Mexico City, General Scott had remained at Puebla, awaiting reinforcements that were excruciatingly slow in coming. When they did arrive, they came not in force but in dribs-and-drabs over the weeks since then, traveling in small, vulnerable columns and all too frequently under fierce guerilla attacks which left them reeling and genuinely hurt. And, though Scott managed to establish good relations with local civil and clerical authorities and acquire from local sources the food and clothing his replacement army would need, Santa Ana's control over the central Mexican government was not only reestablished but grew remarkably and the thousands who flocked to volunteer under his command exhibited more determination than any force he had previously led. Quite possibly much of this was attributable to the Americans themselves.

The campaigns thus far carried out in northern Mexico had much too frequently been excessively brutal and included all too often the murder of prisoners, by both American and Mexican forces alike, but because so many Mexican civilians had been brutalized as well, it seemed the whole Mexican populace had risen in its anger and its need to retaliate. *Tejanos* and *Mexicanos* alike were fueled by a feverish pitch for vengeance and no longer was there any realistic sense that either side would cut and run as had always been the case before.

General Taylor had been wholly unable to curb the brutalities perpetrated by his own forces while awaiting discharge and he reported to Washington D.C. that the Americans on every front, unable yet to clash with the principal Mexican military, were "…committing extensive depredations and outrages upon the peaceful inhabitants. Were it possible," he reported, "to rouse the Mexican people to resistance, no more effectual plan could be devised than the very one pursued by some of our volunteers about to be discharged." The phrase "some of our volunteers" clearly indicted the incorrigible First Missouri.

Generals Scott and Taylor had marched these men to Reynosa, where they had at last reached navigable waters after having traveled, mostly on horse- and mule-back, including detours and diversions, almost exactly 3,500 miles from Fort Leavenworth. Here, having committed their extensive murders and rapes and robberies across the whole of northern Mexico, they had gathered at last in swampy terrain, pelted by torrential rains, matted with dirt and filth and crawling with lice and other vermin, awaiting final transportation home and congratulating themselves on their own wondrous deeds and great victories. And when there were no civilians left to endure their cruelties, they groaned and cursed their own leadership and government; a government that refused to transport their horses home by boat but instead would make an effort to drive them overland back to their starting points; a government that would not transport their outfits and so they burned their blankets and saddles; a government that crammed them aboard bad transport vessels and fed them weevil-infested hardtack, that ignored their seasickness and its resultant stench and mess, that provided no means for bathing while in transport, that provided them with so little fresh drinking water it was as if they had embarked on yet another *journada*, but this time with no tangible enemy to fasten their rage upon and so they harbored and fostered it deep in their own hearts where, in some, it would burn until they died.

Still, however severe the deprivations they faced, however gross the atrocities they committed against the innocents, however much they deplored their own lot and cursed their own leaders, they had at last, in the late afternoon of this June 26th, marched themselves down the long gangplanks into the center of New Orleans—some wearing only greatcoats, some clad only in bedraggled underwear, all of them dirty and rumpled, heavily bearded and tanned almost to blackness by the Mexican sun.

For its own part, New Orleans recognized these returning warriors with great festivity, loudly proclaiming their heroism, ignoring their crudeness, their filth and bad manners, gurgling happily over such "wonderful achievements" as they had performed, turning them loose on whole steers roasted for their pleasure and watching in wonder as they carved them with sheath knives and ripped the flesh into chunks to stuff into their mouths with both hands.

The First Missourians had come home at last and they read in the New Orleans newspapers of their own adventures, their own grandiose heroism and some of them even believed it. And they were today finally discharged and paid, after a year without pay, and though it was less than expected or promised, it was pay nonetheless, and it bought them, temporarily, at least, those things of which they had been so long deprived—the good food, the excellent wines, the gut-wrenching liquors and the wild, wild, wonderful women of their own fancies.

And some of them actually thought it had all been worthwhile.

*[June 27, 1847 · Sunday]*

There was, among the family-grouped Mormons traveling westward now from Winter Quarters through unknown territory to an equally unknown destination, a sense of what might well have been called a divine fatalism. None among them, with the possible exception of Brigham Young, had any idea where they were going, where they would settle, where the new Zion would finally be established.

Their belief in the Church of Jesus Christ of Latter-day Saints generally and in Brigham Young specifically was so strong, so rock solid, that they followed their leader and obeyed his instructions virtually without question. Their belief was unshakable that if it had not already been revealed to Young where Zion would be found, at least the route to get there had been made known to him and that when he, himself, finally came to know where their new Zion was to be located, he would clarify this to all the Saints.

They had by this point, since leaving Winter Quarters on the west bank of the Missouri River, traveled westward unhindered through Indian Territory and encountered the broad, shallow Platte River. At Brigham Young's direction, they had crossed the Platte at a fording place and resumed the westward march along the north bank of the river rather than the customary Oregon Trail along the south bank; a move, Young assured them, that would lessen the likelihood of their encountering other émigrés and stirring whatever dormant hatreds they bore for the Saints. What few travelers they met, however, not only expressed no enmity toward them, they seemed oblivious of any such proclivity to do so and treated the Nauvoo expatriots with simple trailside friendship and courtesy. It was, Brigham young intoned, clear evidence that the Saints were being cupped in the benevolent hand of God and would continue to be so blessed for so long as their faith in God and their mortal leader remained unshaken.

From the few travelers they encountered returning eastward, they heard tales of the great rivers ahead—the Snake and the Columbia, if they were en route to Oregon, and the Humboldt if they were California bound, the latter substantial stream ultimately swallowed up totally in the fearsome dry gullet of the Great Basin. They heard tales from passers-by of Astoria, the fur-trading post near the mouth of the Columbia and they learned of the broad, fertile valley of the Willamette and the treacherous sheer-walled passage of The Dalles; tales of boiling springs and burning sands in the Black Rock Desert and a vast lake so dense with salt that a man could not sink beneath its surface; of mountain ranges so great they could be seen for a hundred miles or more before they were reached, with peaks so high they were topped with the glistening purity of perpetual snow, like bare white wolf fangs grasping at the sky.

The vanguard of the Mormon procession, led by Brigham Young had, by June 1, camped opposite Fort Laramie and it was here that they

## The Infinite Dream

encountered the families of two Saints—Robert Crow and his son-in-law, George Therlkill—who had wintered at Pueblo with the detached sick of the Mormon Battalion. The two families, numbering nine men, five women and three children were traveling in a richly outfitted party of six wagons, some forty oxen and driving a herd of several hundred cattle and what they were seeking they had now found in this encounter with the Brigham Young Party, since they, too, were seeking the new Zion. They reported that over the winter four deaths had occurred among the Saints there at Pueblo, as well as two births, and that the rest of their own party as well as the Mormon Battalion's sick were impatient to move on to Zion, but had no idea where to go.

Brigham Young immediately dispatched Apostle Andrew Lyman at the head of a party of four to gather up all the saints still at Pueblo and guide them in, to merge with the main party en route to Zion. As they camped and discussed what still lay ahead, they were joined by more parties of travelers, some Mormon, some not, some from the north and west, having crossed South Pass, some from the West, some from the Southwest and the Santa Fe Trail and even more from the east, the year's emigration having caught up with them. Most amazing to all, the Mormons and Gentiles mingled companionably with no trace of hostility and Brigham Young intoned yet again that it was God's way of showing them that they were His children, His chosen people and en route, in their faithfulness, to their ultimate Zion which would before long become revealed to them.

At the Crossing of the Platte, the Saints occupied both fording places and established ferries for the dozens and scores and hundreds of wagons—Gentile and Mormon alike—that needed to be ferried across and paid in cash or, even better, in foodstuffs at prices commensurate with this at Independence. In addition to the ferrying systems, they set up blacksmithing operations and did so well that many of the Mormon entrepreneurs, with Young's blessing, dug in and resolved to stay and operate the ferries for so long as the season's traffic made it worthwhile… and to help their own people across. It was Brigham Young himself who gave the ferrying operations proper sacerdotal organization, invoked the Lord's blessing upon them, set the Lord's schedule of fees for services rendered and then started the remainder of his pioneer advance westward again.

They passed the monolithic Independence Rock and Devils Gate and followed the trace of the wagon trains that had carved the road westward before them over the past year. Yesterday at last, June 26, they had crossed the Continental Divide at South Pass and they camped beside the bubbling water they called Pacific Spring. When the light of their own campfires became beacons stabbing through the night, a party fresh from the Oregon country who were camped nearby paid a visit. They were led by a man who identified himself only as Black Harris, who was en route to meet the year's westward emigration and offer his services as guide. He bore with him some Oregon newspapers and, of all things, a copy of *The California Star* which, they were pleased to learn had been founded by Brother Samuel Brannan at a town called San Francisco, and which they accepted as further proof that the blessing of the Lord was upon them all.

Harris stayed with them through the night and much of today as the trailing portion of the Mormon pioneers came up, and all the while Brigham Young listened intently to what he said about the Great Basin and beyond, but most keenly about the eastern edge of the Great Salt Lake, and he questioned Harris exhaustively about what lay ahead. A specific destination was not yet known, not even to Young himself, though he kept this to himself. What he was able to glean from what Harris told him was that the Great Salt Valley was not terribly good because there was too little timber available, and the Bear River Valley was not much better. Thus far the Cache River Valley seemed possibly to be the best site, but they would have to see for themselves to ascertain which was most suitable. As Mormon William Clayton wrote:

> *We feel that we shall know best by going ourselves for the reports of travelers are so contradictory it is impossible to know which is the truth without going to see.*

Now it became Brigham Young himself who was as eager as any of his followers to see what lay within reach ahead...and to determine what site among these, if any, was to become the new Zion.

### [July 3, 1847 • Saturday]

For Samuel Brannan the ride over Emigrant Pass—now Donner Pass—and down the eastern slope of the Sierras along the Truckee River to the western floor of the Great Basin had been rigorous, but without serious snows or other bad weather encountered, he and Charlie Smith and Tim Tully had made excellent time without the loss of any of their horses and mules. Their passage across the forty mile desert west of the Humboldt Sink had been strength sapping, but with strong, fresh horses and mules, they had done it in record time. The long haul up the Humboldt River to its headwaters had been accomplished without incident and on June 9 they had reached Fort Hall and the main Oregon Trail, which was already swelling with wagon trains on their way west.

They paused only briefly at this point to visit with the station commander. Richard Grant, who had long been chief trader for the Hudson's Bay Company, and who was no little amazed at their arrival from California—the earliest west-to-east crossing of the Sierras in his experience—and deeply disturbed over news of the Donner Party tragedy.

It was finally on Wednesday, June 30, that Brannan finally encountered the west-bound advance party of Mormons under the leadership of Brigham Young himself on the shore of the Green River near the mouth of the Big Sandy. He accompanied the Mormon prophet and his trailing flock to the site Young was considering for the establishment of the order's new headquarters at the southeastern rim of the Great Salt Lake. Almost with a sense of desperation, Brannan at once engaged in long and serious discussions with Young, using all of his persuasive powers to induce Young to leave this place behind and lead his throng directly to the New Hope settlement in the San Joaquín Valley of California, which Brannan extolled as the true new Zion.

"The Saints have been well-received in California," Brannan reported, brimming with enthusiasm and self-satisfaction, confident in the conclusiveness of his argument, "in all the principally populated area—San Diego, Los Angeles, Monterey and, especially, in San Francisco, where we have established a substantial part of the population. I am already considered a civic leader of importance and, of course, we own and operate the only printing press and newspaper there." He proudly handed Young the sixteen copies of *The California Star* he had brought along as proof.

His enthusiasm dampened considerably, however, when Young told him their scouts had already selected this site at the southeastern rim of the Great Salt Lake as a perfectly ideal location for the order's new Zion and Young was very inclined to agree. Almost instantly Brannan's focus became one of convincing the Mormon leader of the error of such a decision. With all the persuasive and logistical skills he could muster, Brannan tried to convince the Mormon president what a great error it would be to establish the new Zion in such an unlikely place.

"How, Sir, he asked earnestly, "can human life expect to subsist in this Great Salt Valley when every plainsman and trapper knows full well it is an alkali desert fit only as a home for wolves and jackrabbits and coyotes? Besides which, I have been informed by those who know, that it freezes here nearly every day of the year and the growing season is far too short for the adequate maturing of any kind of crops. California, on the other hand, is a crop-grower's heaven—the place where every kind of fruit and vegetable imaginable grows to huge size and in abundance throughout the entire year, where literally millions of acres of the finest pasturage I have ever seen grows waist-deep the year 'round. And the fact that we have already established New Hope in the midst of the most fertile and temperate zone imaginable provides us with a site of unparalleled benefit. Everything is ready to receive whatever thousands of the Saints as will come and we can establish the permanent seat of our Church, *our Zion!*"

Brigham Young only smiled, his mind already closed off against any argument Brannan or anyone else might forward. He shook his head and squeezed Brannan's shoulder in a manner he may have felt was fatherly, but which Brannan interpreted as condescending.

"What we find here," he told Brannan, "is not what we can make of it in a very short time. A touch of the Lord's hand, along with the strength and determination of the Saints themselves, can make an Eden of any place selected. And *this* is that place."

The discussion, often heated on Brannan's part, continued for days, but the obstinacy of Brigham Young was a barrier he could not even begin to penetrate and the minor concessions Young offered were little compensation: "When the Saints in the Army have finally fulfilled their obligation and are soon discharged," the Mormon president said, "they are free to have their own choice; they can come here to their families at once; or, if they prefer, they can remain there in California, at New Hope or wherever else they wish, through another winter and find what employment they may and then join us the following spring. In the meanwhile, I wish you to ride to the site where those of our brethren of the Mormon Battalion were detached to spend the winter and lead

# The Infinite Dream

them back here. This, Mr. Brannan, *this* is the The Promised Land for our church. I know now, having come here, that this is the place of our Divine destiny. *This is our new Zion!"*

[*July 9, 1847 • Friday*]

The year's enlistment period for the Mormon Battalion was finally coming to an end. It had been an extremely difficult year for the 500 men who had endured a brutal march on foot across more than half a continent of parched deserts and rugged, arid mountainous terrain, yet, oddly enough, it had become, for the majority, the single greatest event of a lifetime. It would live in their memories forever as an achievement beyond compare.

These final weeks of waiting had been, for all of them, quite as difficult in their own way as the cross-country march had been. Now the order had been given for the final discharge to occur on July 16 at Los Angeles and that was where the five companies were headed, Company B in San Diego having the farthest to travel. It was, in fact, to Company B that the new commander of the Southern District, Colonel Jonathan D. Stevenson, had journeyed nearly three weeks previously in his last-ditch effort to encourage re-enlistment. For those of the Battalion already assembled at Los Angeles, virtually all attended the Sunday meeting on June 20 and, as Third Sgt. Daniel Tyler of Company C recorded in his journal:

> *Excellent remarks were made by Father Pettegrew, Levi W. Hancock, Lieutenant Holman and others. One of the principal topics was our return to hunt up and relieve, as far as possible, our outcast, disenfranchised families, and the Saints generally. While Colonel Stevenson was absent at San Diego, visiting Company B, considerable anxiety was felt by the Battalion for his safety, as threats of personal violence had been made against him by some of the New York volunteers of his command.*

Colonel Stevenson arrived at San Diego on June 22, accompanied by Lt. George Stoneman and an immediate assembly of Company B was called, at which the Colonel spoke in the highest terms to them of the uncommon and highly commendable industry and morals of the Battalion and the excellent record and reputation they had established among the Californio residents, urging them most earnestly—especially the younger Saints, to re-enlist. Some of the local citizens were on hand and addressed the company as well, saying very seriously that if the Mormons would not stay, they too would leave the town, having no confidence at all in whatever other troops might be appointed to guard the place. The men were then dismissed to talk it over among themselves and provide him with their answer the next morning.

When the men assembled again the next morning, the company's commanding officer, Captain Jesse Hunter was first to speak, briefly and quite to the point: "Speaking for myself alone, and hoping the company will follow my lead, I will re-enlist for not a year, but for six months if certain conditions are met. First, permit us to send for the written approval of our leader, Brigham Young and, secondly, that on the expiration of that six-month term, the Colonel will grant the company pay and rations to either San Francisco or Bear River Valley. Finally, a guarantee that a small detachment of our men will be sent to meet our families, wherever they will be found, and act as pioneers for them, guiding them safely here to California."

The requests did not daunt Colonel Stevenson in the least. "I not only agree to those conditions for you *and your men*, I will also guarantee those of Company B who will remain here that they shall be given the privilege of continuing to work and earn whatever money they can during their off-duty hours."

About twenty of the Saints sided with Captain Hunter and agreed to extend their enlistment, but the majority hesitated and allowed Privates Albert and Azariah Smith to speak for them, who agreed that: "We first want to hear the counsel of the priesthood we have here with us in California, the principal part of whom are presently in Los Angeles."

Col. Stevenson agreed to this as well and so, to seek the proper priestly direction, Sgt. William Hyde and Cpl. Horace M. Alexander were selected to return to Los Angeles for that purpose with the Colonel and Capt. Hunter. At the same time, succeeding Henry Delano Fitch, one of Southern California's earliest settlers, Lt. Robert Clift of Company C was appointed *alcalde* of San Diego until further notice. Four days later, on June 27, Lieutenants Charles Lytle and James Pace were elected, by acclamation, to lead back to the main Mormon party, wherever it should happen to be, in companies of 100 men each, those among the Saints who had no intention of reenlisting and wished only to be reunited with their families. As Sgt. Tyler expressed it in his own journal on June 29:

> As the time for mustering-out drew nearer, many attractive offers were dangled before Mormon eyes to induce them to remain in service. When praise and cajolery failed, there were threats of impressment. Honest justice to these faithful men forestalled so drastic a move, and in the end the call of loved-ones and the stronger cry of duty were the deciding issues. Mail from the east revealed that Brigham Young and the vanguard had left Winter Quarters, and already were nearing the Rockies. The war was ending, hostilities in California had ceased, their obligation to the nation valorously paid. Zion-to-be-built had need of their sturdy hearts and brawn.... Here in San Diego they had dug from fifteen to twenty good wells, the only ones in town, several of which were walled with brick, besides building brick houses, including a courthouse, to be used for courts, schools, etc. They had paved some of the sidewalks with brick, while some, being house carpenters, had done the finishing work on the inside. It is proper to state here that the company [Company B], having greatly improved the town, as well as being peaceful, honest, industrious and virtuous, the citizens pled with them in the strongest terms not to leave.

It was five days later on July 4 that grand festivities occurred in San Diego and Pvt. Henry W. Bigler wrote about the occasion enthusiastically in his diary:

> July 4. At daylight five pieces of cannon were fired off to salute the day of American Independence. The "Star-Spangled Banner" was played by the New York volunteer band, while the colors were being raised. Nine cheers were given for the stars and stripes, and "Hail Columbia" was played by the band, after which thirteen guns were fired by the First Dragoons. The companies were then marched back to their Quarters. After that the boys shouldered their muskets by order of Mr. James Sly, whom they had selected for their Captain for the present occasion, marched in order, and gave the officers of Company B and the citizens of San Diego a hearty salute. In Los Angeles at 11 a.m., the command was called

*out, under arms, and the Dragoons and the Battalion paraded inside the fort. Many Californians and Indians were present to witness the ceremonies. The Declaration of Independence was read by our worthy quartermaster, Lieutenant Stoneman, of the First Dragoons, "Hail Columbia" was again played by the band and Colonel Stevenson made a brief and appropriate speech, giving the fortification the name of Fort Moore, in honor of the brave Captain who fell at the Battle of San Pasqual. The band then played "Yankee Doodle," and a patriotic song by Musician Levi W. Hancock, of the Battalion and a march tune by the band, after which Colonel Stevenson proposed to have the Declaration of Independence read, if the Californians desired it, in the Spanish language, but the offer was respectfully declined. In San Diego the inhabitants of the town were so well pleased with festivities that they brought out their bottles of wine and* aguardiente *and called upon the boys to help themselves to all they could drink, and the day passed off nicely.*

*In the evening Captain Hunter and Sergeant Hyde, who had gone with Colonel J.D. Stevenson up to Los Angeles to lend their influence in raising volunteers, returned, but only thirteen men, out of three hundred had reenlisted. The boys shouldered their pieces and marched to their quarters and gave them a hearty cheer. Thus ended all ceremonies of the day. And throughout the evening all Battalion hands were kept busy making preparations to leave for their homes, wherever that was; whether on Bear River, California, or Vancouver Island up in the British possession. For the truth is, we do not know where President Young and the Church is.*

Now five days more had passed uneventfully and then today, at last, was the day for the Mormon Battalion to leave San Diego forever. As Pvt. Bigler put it in his diary this evening:

*On the 9th we took up the line of march for the Pueblo, for Los Angeles.*

[*July 15, 1847 • Thursday • 2:00 p.m.*]

The sojourn with Brigham Young and his advance group of the Mormons had left Samuel Brannan both angry and frustrated and yet, oddly enough, the occurrences of this past week had become very gratifying for him since it had solidified a resolve within him that he had held in check only with the greatest of effort.

It had become quite clear to Brannan, as the obstinacy of Young had clearly revealed itself to be immovable, that the Mormon President had made up his mind; the new Zion was going to be in this barely habitable valley between the west slope of the Rockies in the incredibly rugged Wasatch Range region and the barren, desolate and deadly salt flats bordering the southern rim of the Great Salt Lake.

So inhospitable was the region and so apt to be viewed as such by the thousands of Saints yet to arrive, Brannan was convinced that the lure of California could not help but cause a schism in Young's following, regardless of how devoted they may have been to him up to this point. It was, Brannan judged, one thing to have to *travel* through country that sapped one's energies and ate at one's mind and soul; it would be quite another when they were told that just such a spot was where Young had now decided they must *settle*—the new Zion!

The masked rebelliousness of Brannan, held in abeyance in view of Brigham Young's incomprehensible decision that this would be their new Zion, still seethed within him, but suddenly with a more clear direction. How hard would it be to convince those coming behind that Brigham Young had misinterpreted the Almighty's intent for the Saints? How easy would it be, in view of his wholly incomprehensible selection of this sort of territory as Zion, to lay before them the glory and richness of California as the alternative Zion that God Himself had intended for them?

All this had begun to gel for Brannan while they were still in the Green River area when, on the fourth of July, a dozen dust begrimed American soldiers had ridden into the camp and announced they were the advance guard for Captain James Brown, who was in charge of the Mormons General Kearny had left behind to winter at Pueblo. The twelve, in search of horses stolen from their party, had encountered Young's camp at the Green River quite by accident. Since they had heard rumors from passersby that the horses and their thieves were currently at Fort Bridger, that was where they were headed. Their main body, however, under command of Capt. Brown, had decided to march to California via the Fort Hall route in order to receive their discharge and back pay.

Brigham Young and his Council quickly changed their minds,

encouraging the platoon to return southward in an effort to intercept Captain Brown's main command and have them join him and the Mormon advance at the southeastern fringe of the Great Salt Lake. As Young wrote of it in his journal:

> *The council decided that Sergeant Thomas S. Williams, one of the brethren of the Mormon Battalion who had overtaken the pioneers on the Green River, should return to meet Capt. James Brown and the Battalion company from Pueblo, accompanied by Samuel Brannan, and inasmuch as they had neither received their discharge, nor full pay, Bro. Brannan should tender them his services as pilot to conduct them to California and to aid them in getting their discharges and back pay.*

To Brannan, it all could not have worked out better. He was more than glad to offer his services to guide Brown's company of well over 100 via the Great Salt Desert south of the lake and down the Humboldt to its sink. From there they would then move onward, in far more clement conditions than the Donner Party had encountered, over the Sierras to join with the newly discharged Mormons of General Kearny's command. Once this was accomplished, Young directed, they could then make their way to San Francisco or Sutters Fort together and if they wished to remain there for the autumn and winter and not start back for Salt Lake until the following spring or summer, Young had agreed that was all right, too.

Sam Brannan had no difficulty at all convincing himself that once the Mormons saw the area where President Young planned to establish the new Zion, then compared it to the beauty and bounty of New Hope in the San Joaquín Valley, it was likely that *all* the Saints would elect to remain in California at a Zion that was far more closely aligned to what they had for so long imagined.

So, without further delay, Sam Brannan and Sgt. Thomas S. Williams set off at once toward Pueblo, heading back eastward across the Wasatch Range again, past Fort Bridger and over South Pass. And at last, today, July 15, they had successfully intercepted the remainder of Captain Brown's command on its march toward California.

The grand plan Samuel Brannan had conceived back at Green River was now cleverly launched and he was certain it would prove of great benefit—not to the Mormon detachment of sick and not to the Mormon companies being discharged after a year of active duty, nor even to Brigham Young and the Mormon cause in general. Though no one knew it yet, nor would they for however long he could maintain his covert purposes, Sam Brannan's grand plan was geared to benefit only one person in particular: Samuel Brannan.

*[July 15, 1847 • Thursday • 6:00 p.m.]*

General Kearny, his escort and his entourage had harbored high hopes that upon arrival at Fort Hall, they would be able to purchase whatever additional supplies of food they might need for the remainder of the trip back to Fort Leavenworth, but they had been disappointed. They had arrived at the post just after noon and found it virtually destitute of the supplies they had planned on procuring, so they had simply moved on, gloomily accepting the prospect of having to live on harsh rations dominated by horse meat for some time.

As they continued, moving southward now toward the Greenwoods Cut-off that would take them back to the main trail leading to the Continental Divide at South Pass, General Kearny reviewed the notations he had made in his ledger of matters of specific importance since their departure from the grisly scene of the Donner Party tragedy just a couple of days over three weeks ago, on June 22.

The first notation dealt with a sad and needless occurrence early the following day when Pvt. Robert Quigley accidentally shot himself. Quigley, who had marched to California with Company C of the First Dragoons as their bugler in Lt. Col. Cooke's command ever since leaving Santa Fe, had been guilty of carelessly mishandling a weapon. It abruptly discharged and sent its heavy lead slug into Quigley's high left chest just below the collarbone and, though it passed through his body without breaking any bones and exited midway down his back, it was nevertheless a serious wound that slowed them considerably. That evening they had camped on the bank of the Truckee River, which was badly swollen and "running a perfect torrent."

In the morning they had followed the river a short distance before coming to where a tall pine had fallen and partially bridged the stream. A discharged soldier riding with them pointed out another pine on the opposite bank which, if felled properly, would interlock with the one from their side and offered to swim across and cut it down for that purpose, if made worth his while. With no other choice available, Kearny agreed to pay him $10 to do so. With a double-bitted axe strapped to his back, the soldier swam his horse across with considerable difficulty and then expertly felled the big pine perfectly. The men then formed a line across the makeshift bridge and passed their weapons and packs from hand to hand without incident until everything had been brought across. Then, as Pvt. Nathaniel V. Jones put it in his diary in camp that night:

> ...*after many efforts our animals, who were very reluctant to take to the water, all crossed safely by about three o'clock, at which time we started and came over twenty miles over a rough road. Left Col. Fremont at the crossing of the Truckee.*

To avoid the more than two dozen repeated dangerous crossings of the river, General Kearny took the party northward and eastward around the big stream's twisting canyon, traveling twenty-five miles as opposed to the twelve by following and so-often crossing the river, but did so without losses of either men or equipment.[233]

The night's camp was established on the evening of June 26 after a very difficult day's travel. As Pvt. Jones noted it in his diary:

> ...*Very rough all the way. We camped by an Indian village (if it would be proper to call it such) for there were no signs of it except some brush which had been cut and stuck in the ground. There were about two hundred [Digger] Indians in number, some ran to the mountains and others laid in the brush. Some of them came out after we had been there a short time. Men and women alike go naked.*

The following day, June 27, they came to the area where, just over a year earlier, Mountain Man Jim Clyman had lost his dog, Buck, in a boiling pool. Jones wrote:

> *Sunday, June 27. Started very early in the morning, came twenty-five miles across a barren desolate sand plain. Then we came to the hot spring. It was a curiosity. It was some two or three miles from the mountain to our right, on a small rise of ground. The water was thrown out by steam in a solid column four feet high*

*and sometimes higher. The steam could be seen close to three or four miles off. It would discharge one barrel in one minute. The ground all around there seemed to be hollow underneath, and it was hot for half a mile around. There was a mule broke through a half mile or more from the spring. The stream came up very hot. I have no doubt, from the present appearance of things that two hundred feet from the surface, is a mass of liquid fire. The rock and sand for miles around and the ashes that we saw all look as if they had undergone the action of fire.*[234] *We came twenty miles from there and camped, making in all forty-five miles, all without wood, water or grass. The place where we camped is called Mary's River* [sic].[235] *It is a sunken river. It sinks in the sand where we struck it. No wood and but very little grass. It seems as though the curse of God rested upon this country. It is all a barren, unfruitful waste.*[236] *Some of our mules and horses gave out today.*

William Graves, traveling with the party, was a bit more graphic in his description of the natural wonder and the loss of their mule, as he wrote in his diary:

*...a very singular cavern was revealed to us by the instantaneous disappearance of a mule in the Company, which fortunately had on him neither rider nor baggage. On examination it was found that the crust of the earth thro' which the mule disappeared was but a few inches in thickness. The cavern was sounded forty feet without bottom bing found and, but for aught the party knew, its depth might be five thousand feet. The earth for a considerable distance around the hole sounded hollow...*

Sgt. Tyler added a bit more to that description with his own notation about the geologic phenomenon:

*...after traveling a considerable distance over a sandy desert, a hot spring was reached, which threw up a column of boiling water from four to six feet high. The water boiled up and ran off at the rate of about one barrel per minute. The ground underneath seemed to be hollow, and the sound of the water was as if poured upon red-hot rocks; it could be heard for a considerable distance. The ground was*

more or less heated for about half a mile from the spring in each direction. A mule broke through the surface, nearly a half mile from the spring, and steam immediately issued forth from the hole made. The rocks and sand for miles around, as well as the ashes, all looked as though they had undergone the action of fire. After leaving these springs, great scarcity of good water, feed for the animals, and wood, was experienced. Most of the water found was either salty or bitter, and much of the country was a barren waste. Some of the mules gave out from hunger, thirst and fatigue.

Conditions became much better the farther upstream General Kearny's party traveled, so long as they stayed close to the river. Often, on the other side of the river or far in the distance, they could see rising plumes of steam from other boiling pools and geysers. Even though still early in the season, the country became unbearably hot during the day and so the party, at Kearny's direction, adopted a pattern of beginning their march in the predawn hours, resting from about 11 a.m. until about 4 p.m., then traveling again until dark.

On July 8 four of the party's pack horses were stolen at night by a party of Shoshone Indians called the White Knives from the Tosowich Band, who were very troublesome. As Fremont's group, which had delayed somewhat, overtook Kearny's about the same time, the General allowed Fremont and his group to rejoin the main party so they could travel together thereafter for the better security of both. A detachment sent by Kearny to attempt to overtake the party and recover the horses, however, finally lost them altogether in a tract of low mountains.

On July 9 the party reached the cut-off which would have taken them over the Great Salt Desert along the southern shore of Great Salt Lake but, only too cognizant of what had occurred to the Donner Party, apparently as a result of using that route, General Kearny turned his party up the well established trail over the western and northern regions of the lake to Fort Hall. On July 14, as they neared Fort Hall and were now decidedly on the Oregon Trail they quickly passed two wagon trains, one of twenty-three wagons, one of forty-three.

Finally, earlier today—Thursday, July 15—after riding fifteen miles, they had reached Fort Hall, where they had been able to purchase some bacon, but little else, at the same time learning of the passage of the small Samuel Brannan Party, six day earlier. Their concern over being reduced to eating horse meat, however, did not occur. After leaving Fort Hall in the afternoon, they encountered increased numbers of wagon trains, some as few as a dozen wagons, some approaching 100, all with food supplies abundant enough that they were delighted to sell some to the Kearny Party at considerable profit to themselves.

With the reassurance that there would be a steady stream of wagon trains from this point on, the Kearny Party continued eastward on a much better trail than previously.

# Chapter 14

◆

*[July 20, 1847 • Tuesday]*

Henry Bigler, no longer a private, now that the Mormon Battalion had finally been discharged, was among those of his former unit who were not entirely clear about where they should go and what they should do. The overriding joy that had infected them all at being finally discharged from service in the United States Army had finally begun becoming more subdued now and no one seemed entirely sure what should be done next.

Considering the keen pitch of anticipation that had engulfed virtually the entire Battalion over the previous weeks, the actual entire discharging ceremony that had occurred on Friday, July 16, was, more than anything else, best described as anticlimactic. All the Mormon soldiers, from their various post of duty in southern California, had finally gathered together in their five companies as a complete Mormon battalion one final time on July 15 at Fort Moore, just outside the limits of Los Angeles. It was the first time the full unit had been reunited since Company B had been detached to San Diego from San Luis Rey four months earlier. A strong but subdued sense of excitement prevailed among them all and throughout the day and then into the evening and the night, every soldier wondered what the final ceremony would prove itself to be. Filled as they were with the anticipation of discharge, few among them got any sleep at all that night of the fifteenth.

Most of the men simply lolled about in loose formations as July 16 dawned—some dozing as the lack of sleep overcame them, others continuing to be keyed up with high anticipation—a sense of growing impatience filling them all as the morning hours ticked away. Then the afternoon was upon them and still the delay continued. Not until 3 p.m. did anything concrete occur. At last, then, Lt. Andrew Jackson Smith emerged from the headquarters building, followed by a young enlisted man. A dozen yards from the building they paused and Lt. Smith nodded to the private, who raised a bugle to his lips and sounded the clarion call of assembly, exactly one year to the day after they had been mustered into service at Council Bluffs, Iowa.

With alacrity the waiting Saints shook off their lethargy and efficiently formed into their five company units, a few paces between each, Company A in front and Company E in the rear, nearly filling the entire parade ground. There were no marching bands, no speeches, no military pomp and ceremony. Lt. Smith, with his usual officious expression, stared at the assembled 300 men for a long moment and then simply strode past each company in turn before returning to the front. There he stopped, faced them smartly and then spoke in a voice so low in tone it was barely audible to those in the rear: "You men of the Mormon Battalion, are now discharged from service in the United States Army."

Except for receiving their final pay, which occurred over the next three days, such was the mustering-out ceremony of those who had marched afoot across half a continent in service of their country and their religion; yet, far from taking offense at the brevity of it, the low-key discharge rather pleased them. The men let loose then with three rousing cheers and broke from ranks, private citizens once again for the first time in a year.

Now, almost immediately, came the formation of the group of eighty-two discharged Saints who were already calling themselves the Mormon Volunteers, plus three former civilian aides to officers; men who had agreed to remain behind and serve as a new unit, to re-garrison San Diego until they would be formally discharged a year from this date, in March of 1848. All the two hundred twenty others assembled in a short time at a previously agreed-upon rendezvous three miles distant along the San Pedro River.

The rendezvous was important because, while excited and relieved to be finally discharged from their obligation to the United States Army, there still remained more than a thousand miles of wilderness—mountains and deserts—to cross before they could be reunited with their loved ones and the fact of the matter was, they really had no good idea where they would find those families. They certainly were no longer at

Nauvoo, nor even at their Winter Quarters along the west bank of the Missouri River, but only at some as yet unspecified location in the vast expanse of the Great Basin.

Fortunately for the brethren, stock and provisions were cheap enough here and now that they had received their mustering-out pay they could afford to buy the supplies and provisions they would need to carry them through on their return—but their return to where? No one was quite certain. Nevertheless, the majority quickly formed themselves into organized companies for traveling according to the custom of the ancient Israelites—in companies of hundreds, fifties and tens, with an elected captain presiding over each and Daniel C. Davis, former captain of Co. E, now elected as top commander of the various companies.[237] To their great joy, the majority of the men being discharged were finally paid over the 17th, 18th and 19th of June. Some of the Brethren, for varied reasons, elected to stay and settle in southern California.

Now others, in their variously-sized groups and having received their final pay for their services, started at once to seek out their Church and their people. A handful decided to drop off at Samuel Brannan's settlement of New Hope in the San Joaquín Valley, but the majority simply started off toward the northeast, optimistically hopeful of learning, as they traveled, exactly where they were going. Most had a notion they would simply intercept their families and the majority of Latter-day Saints sometime, someplace during their journey. As William Wood wrote to his parents of this exodus, he hoped to find them

> ...somewhere to the east of us, perhaps about 500 miles from here near the Great Salt Lake.

Henry Bigler clearly underlined the fundamental uncertainty of by far the greater majority of the men as he wrote in his diary this evening:

> Jun 20th. We began to gather, to organize and prepare for a general move for Bear River Valley (as we call it) where we expect to meet or find our people of the Church. Most of the boys have already bought animals to pack and ride and have everything ready for a move, except a few who have sailed up the coast to San Francisco. Ten are chosen, including myself, to act as pioneers, one of whom is to act as the Captain over the nine. That is Elisha Everett. We

*hardly know what way to strike out, for we have no guide, except an old California map with very few rivers or anything else marked on it, and a paper pretending to give the route, that somebody had given to some of our men. Still, great uncertainty prevails amongst us about which way to go. The men only understand that they are going home (and where that is, no one in camp knows.) Despite all this, we feel like birds let out of a cage.*

No matter how one looked at the situation, it was hardly an auspicious beginning for what promised to be a very long trek.

[July 21, 1847 • Wednesday]

James Marshall was on the verge of beginning his establishment of what he was, in his own mind, already referring to as the Marshall-Sutter Sawmill. With so many newcomers now coming into the Sacramento Valley, he knew that John Sutter was every bit as eager as he to get the sawmill built and the lumber business firmly established. Once that was accomplished, the agreed-upon full partnership would kick in and he and Sutter would share equally in a business that could very well make them both quite wealthy.

The two men had traveled to the proposed sawmill site on horseback from Sutters Fort, accompanied by Marshall's Indian companion, Nerio, who was on foot. Marshall was quite uncharacteristically bubbling over with enthusiasm as he guided Sutter along the forty-five-mile trail he and Nerio had personally blazed; a trail that he had no doubt would quite soon become their wagon road for the shipment of sawn lumber from here to the forty-mile-distant fort. When, at Marshall's signal, they finally drew their mounts to a halt on the high level ground of the left bank of the stream, Sutter said nothing at first, his sharp gaze fastening upon each aspect of the site momentarily before moving along to the next, then eventually coming back and weighing them all again with even greater care. It was obvious where the lumber mill could best be located and where the race would be dug to divert and channel the current into a new path, swift and strong enough to turn the great saw blade with unfailing speed and power. The local Indians called the place Coloma, meaning "beautiful vale" and with justification, as the area was very scenic. But, as Marshall knew full well, scenery was not the criterion they sought. Was the timber abundant enough to be harvested in quantity?

Was it timber of good quality? Could it be shipped with relative ease by rafting or wagons to Sutters Fort? To Marshall, the answers were positive from the very instant he first laid eyes on the place and nothing about it during his further weeks of inspection and planning since then had changed his mind.

The great hill directly across the river was only one of several such in the area, plunging steeply down to the river's edge, the entire slope dense with virgin timber of oak, pine and balsam mutely crying to be cut; even the valleys were abundant with extensive stands of sugar pine. The river itself was broad enough and deep enough to accommodate whole flotillas of logs if need be or, better yet, shallow-drafted rafts loaded with sawn planking to be floated without difficulty directly to a lumber holding yard adjacent to Sutters Fort; the terrain south and west of the left bank gently rolling and ideal for construction of the lumber road directly to the fort, upon which wagonloads of sawn lumber could, with strong teams, reach the fort and its customers in as short a time as two days, perhaps even less. There was ample room for the construction of cabins from the very timber being cut and for the building of sheds and barns and corrals.

A few times as he looked, John Sutter let little pleased grunts escape his lips; lips that widened into broad smiles as new aspects of the terrain and its possibilities impacted him. Finally, after long minutes he released a great exhalation, as if he had been holding a breath for too long, and shook his head wonderingly. "I don't see, Mr. Marshall," he said approvingly, "how the site could be any better. It has everything... and well within our reach. Now all we have to do is hire the men and build the mill. I commend you on a job well done!"

*[July 24, 1847 • Saturday]*

As sick and feverish as he was, and infinitely weary from the rugged journey through the Wasatch Mountains, Brigham Young nonetheless smiled broadly at the site before him and absolutely *knew* with undeniable conviction that he had finally found the Zion he had been seeking for his followers for so long a time. The valley was lush and green and the river flowing through it he likened to the River Jordan. In the distance to the northwest stretched the shimmering expanse of a great inland sea, which he likened as well to the Biblical Dead Sea, and rightly so, since this was the Great Salt Lake.

The wagons of the others in his advance party crowded up behind him and the whole assemblage became infected with the same sense of jubilation and gratification at what they saw. Here was the place they had sought so diligently, so lengthily; this was the Zion that Joseph Smith and his brother, Hyrum, had sought but which had been denied them; the site free of unjustified prejudices where the Saints could at last sink their roots permanently and be free of the persecution that had followed them so doggedly through the eastern states.

For seventeen years, through such tormented sites as Fayette and Kirtland, Clay County and Jackson County, Nauvoo, across the span of Iowa and Missouri, the Nebraska lands and the Wyoming Territory, through endless seasons of persecution and want and desperation, through the loss of their religion's founder and his family and the hundreds who had died clinging through the years to his beliefs that a Zion awaited them somewhere, the Saints had sought but never really found what now finally stretched out before their eyes.

Still standing in his wagon, Young raised his arms high and the babble of voices from his followers hushed. He looked over the throng for a long moment in silence, thought as well of the fifteen thousand or more others still coming behind and experienced a surge of gratification such as few men in history have ever known. His voice, when at last he spoke, trembled with the emotion that had risen in him, yet it carried well to all the listening ears.

"We have arrived!" he told them. "This is the place! We have at last reached our Zion. We are on the spot where we will build a great city; a city from which we will never be driven. The Lord has led us to this place and here we will plant our crops and build our homes and erect our temples to His greater glory. This is the place I have long seen in my vision. I know it. I have no doubt of it, nor should you. This is our great Zion, our Canaan in the midst of a surrounding desert and I call this land the State of Deseret—Land of the Honey Bee...and here we will plant and nurture our crops and the city we will build here in sight of the Great Salt Lake we shall call Salt Lake City and it shall forever after be the home and the haven and the headquarters of the Church of Jesus Christ of Latter-day Saints."[238]

*[July 30, 1847 · Friday]*
General Stephen Watts Kearny's party, with its escort of thirteen

mounted Mormon soldierss, breathed a collective sigh of relief, since now the Rocky Mountains were finally behind them. Their spirits had elevated considerably with such ease of travel through the Great Plains and they marveled at the enormous herds of buffalo, since they had not seen these huge animals on the Santa Fe Trail a year ago.

The journey thus far had been very rugged, though with occasional highlights of interest. They had encountered a number of wagon trains already, most of them heading for the Oregon Territory. They met, as well, the mountain man named Charles Smith, who until recently had been traveling with Samuel Brannan. They camped together for one night and Smith regaled them with tales of his experiences in the mountains. What interested them most, however, was the valuable information gleaned from him in regard to the emigrating Mormons, who were now beginning to collect along the eastern edge of the Great Basin at the southeastern rim of Great Salt Lake; Mormons who were evidently establishing their new headquarters there. Kearny's escort had become excited, knowing now, for the first time with certainty, where they would be heading once they were discharged from Kearny's service and from the Army itself.

While traveling along the Bear River after passing Fort Hall they encountered the phenomenon called Soda Pool, a large lake whose waters were as bubbly and as healthful to drink as the bicarbonate powders some of the men carried in tins. Six miles beyond that they reached Soda Spring, which was even more bubbly and with a very strong flow of water.[239]

At a Shoshone Indian camp encountered as they followed Hams Fork, they met the old mountain man known as "Black" Harris, who told them of a better and nearer route to take eastward than the trail they were following, which would take them to Fort Bridger. The newer trail, he said, was called Greenwood's Cut-off and it easily cut off days of difficult travel. Grateful for the information, General Kearny hired him to guide his party at least through the remainder of the mountains. Harris also told them of having encountered the trail of Brigham Young's westbound party of Mormons on June 27 near South Pass, but his own party's taking of Greenwood's Cut-off had prevented them from overtaking the large party of Mormons, which was journeying west via Fort Bridger and the Wasatch Mountains.

Continuing eastward, once Kearny's Party connected with the

# The Infinite Dream

main Oregon Trail again, they met an almost continuous flow of Mormon wagon trains heading westward, following their leader's trail.

Over the next few days, averaging about thirty miles per day, the party followed the Sweetwater a considerable distance and came to areas where the sage brush was more scattered and grasses becoming more abundant and, with them, far more frequent sightings of antelope and buffalo. After passing through the Rocky Buttes and camping at a place they called Rose Camp, the following night they camped almost in the shade of Independence Rock and then, the following evening, Capt. Henry Turner wrote in his journal:

> 28th. Camped at Willow Spring where we met the rear-most party of Emigrants, who seemed to despair of getting farther than Fort Hall this season. Missed counting many of the Mormon emigrants who went through Fort Bridger, as we took the [Greenwood's] Cut-off, but of those we saw I counted 1,336 men, 789 women, 1,384 children under sixteen, and 941 wagons on the trail—numbers for the Oregon and California emigration of 1847 that may be relied on.

Finally, today, General Kearny's Party had reached the North Platte River and followed it downstream some thirty miles before camping for the night on Deer Creek, a mile and a half from its mouth, the mountains now clearly behind them and vast expanses of prairie grasses ahead, liberally dotted with the shapes of thousands of grazing buffalo. In the dimness behind, the Rocky mountains were gradually fading from view and the great journey back to Fort Leavenworth was finally nearing its end.

*[August 7, 1847 · Saturday]*

The months of virtual military lethargy had been affecting General Winfield Scott far more than anyone realized. Replacement of troops whose enlistment had expired had gradually been occurring, but only with excruciating slowness and an aura of exasperation seemed to enshroud the commander of the Army of the West.

Since May, when he had moved the remnants of his army from Jalapa and Perote to where they were now encamped at Puebla, practically nothing of military importance was occurring. Roving spy patrols sent out at intervals returned dejected and with little of any substance to report: a gradual build-up of General Santa Ana's troops in Mexico City; a more concentrated effort among the Mexican officers to better train and equip the growing number of volunteers and those being impressed into service; the sense of fatalistic knowledge that a decisive confrontation between the Mexican and American armies would almost surely occur before long, but no one had any solid idea of where this would take place or, equally important, when. It was as if one massive siesta had overtaken all the participants and no one was inclined to awaken and get things moving again.

No one except, of course, General Scott.

The only action of any consequence that had occurred during this three-month interval had occurred in July with the appearance of General George Cadwalader, who landed at Vera Cruz with a small force of recruits and regular officers. As soon as the landing was accomplished and the men had drawn their supplies, uniforms and weapons, General Cadwalader had marched them out to join with Scott's remnant force. They had a bit of trouble en route, however, when they encountered resistance as they reached the National Bridge. With that overcome, the unit had quickly joined Scott.

Now, no longer content to sit and do nothing, the commanding general left a small garrison at Puebla to protect his hospital there and then marched his army out, moving southward over the final range of mountains and then down onto the great central plateau of Mexico. It was time for *something* to happen!

[August 7, 1847 • Saturday]

The affront Sam Brannan had received from Brigham Young over the past eleven days was one he would neither forgive nor forget, though no one but Brannan himself was aware of it. Not yet, at any rate. The anger that seethed within him for what Young had already done, and what he planned for the future of the thousands of Saints converging to join him, rankled Brannan as few things ever had in his life before now. It was, however, a definite comfort to him to know that when the Mormon president eventually became aware of Brannan's rage, it would be too late for him to do anything of a concrete nature about it except to excommunicate him...and so far as Samuel was concerned, his own self-excommunication had already begun.

It was hardly what Brannan had in mind when he finally, in mid-

July, intercepted the body of just over three hundred detached Saints from the Mormon Battalion, who, deemed ill and unfit, had been separated from General Kearny's group so many months before and had over-wintered at Pueblo in the Colorado country. Captain James Brown was still in charge of that detachment and was in the process of marching them to California for their discharge when Brannan and Sgt. Thomas S. Williams intercepted them only a short distance eastward from South Pass. Brannan had at once agreed to guide them back to California, but explained that a stop-off was planned at Great Salt Lake to confer with Brigham Young, who was evidently still paused there with his own advance party of Mormons from Winter Quarters.

Brannan, Williams and Brown, leading that "unfit" detachment of Mormon Battalion members, had finally arrived at the southeastern corner of Great Salt Lake hardly a week later and Brannan was more than a little dismayed to find Young had already begun laying out what he said would be called Salt Lake City—and what he emphatically announced was to be the new and final headquarters of the Church of Jesus Christ of Latter-day Saints. They were, in fact, he added, already making preparations to sow their first crop.

The invalid Saints in Captain Brown's Company, Young declared, would not have to return to California for discharge, but could be discharged right here by Captain Brown and only Brown himself, with a small escort, need return to California. There, as their senior officer and attorney, he would secure their formal discharge from the army and their final pay from the government and return with it to Salt Lake City. Joyful though the Brown detachment was at being reunited with their own people here and not having to march all the way back to California as all had believed would occur, Brannan did not share in the general jubilation. He was silently aghast at how swiftly Brigham Young was moving things along.

Reluctantly, but nonetheless with some small degree of optimism still flaring within him, Brannan accepted Young's invitation to ride along with him in a carriage to more fully inspect this site that the Saints were already calling home, hopeful that he could convince the Mormon president during the tour that Young's own future and that of the Church of Jesus Christ of Latter-day Saints would prosper much more grandly in California than here. The word pictures that he painted, however, of California and its fine rivers and extensive growing season and admirable climate moved the Church's leader not at all. Young simply shook his head and his words were icicle stabs in Brannan's heart.

"We Latter-day Saints have all too often in the past felt the whip and the gunfire of those who misunderstand our way of life. A land as desirable as California must be," he added softly, "will, just as surely as syrup draws flies, draw other men who will covet what it offers and there is no hope that in such a place the Saints will find peace and isolation.

"Samuel," he continued after a brief pause, "God's kingdom and the kingdom of the world can never grow side by side in harmony. Even in these arid valleys you say you detest so much, the Saints must fight to live—and because we must turn everlastingly to God for help, we *will* survive. The ease you speak of that is evident in California would mean, for us, spiritual and physical death, can't you see that? Only by our taking that which no other man wants can we be free from human rapacity and be reasonably certain of building and strengthening the Mormon pattern of life unmolested."

The brief carriage ride left Brannan frustrated in defeat and the black anger in his soul darker than ever. He quickly made preparations for his return to California with Captain Brown, but not before making one last effort to convince Brigham Young how terribly wrong he was and how he had no right to make such a decision on behalf of all the Mormons, most of whom were not yet here and had not yet experienced the severity of this land. His effort turned into a bitter quarrel, from which Brigham Young emerged with a newborn distrust of Samuel and an implacable decision not to change his mind under any circumstance.

Now, with Brown making hasty preparations for leaving Salt Lake City and returning to the Mormon community in California, the final affront was delivered to Brannan when Young entirely ignored the fact of Brannan's leadership in California's Mormon events and, instead, entrusted Captain Brown with the responsibility of safely delivering and reading aloud to the Saints at New Hope the contents of the Council's letter of instructions, a letter which said:

*Camp of Israel, Valley of the Great Salt Lake*
*August 7, 1847*
*To Capt. Jefferson Hunt & the officers and soldiers of the Mormon Battalion:*
*Brethren: As Capt. Brown and escort is about to leave this place for [army] headquarters in California, we improve the opportunity*

*of saying to you, that hitherto hath the Lord God of Israel blessed us and brought us to a goodly land, where we design to build a house unto his name and a city, which shall be a meeting place unto his saints.*

*In the former part of April we left your families and friends at Winter Quarters (and vicinity), a city which we built last fall on the west bank of the Missouri river, nearly opposite the Liberty pole of your enlistment, consisting of more than 700 houses; and some of your families occupied some of the first that were built, and your families were better supplied with houses, fuel and provisions than the families with us generally, and we say this to you at this time to comfort your hearts and not to boast of what we have done. We will let our boasting be till another day.*

*The pioneer company with us number 143 men. We arrived here in this valley of the Great Salt Lake on the 22nd (and 24th) of July and the detachments of the "Mormon Battalion" from Pueblo arrived here on the 29th, together with a company of saints from the Mississippi, and now we number about 450. Before leaving Winter Quarters we made every arrangement possible for our tents and wagons, and all those within our influence, to be sent on with your families as soon as the season would permit, and come to the place of our location. We have heard that they started in June and have sent back our messengers to pilot them to this place, and we expect them here in a few weeks. We do not know that every one of your families will come in this company; it is hardly to be expected; but if the brethren do as we have done, and we anticipate they will do, a great many of them will be here. Therefore, when you receive this and learn of this location, it will be wisdom for all, if you have got your discharge as we suppose, to come directly to this place, where you will learn particularly who is here, who not. If there are any men who have not families among number who desire to stop in California for a season, we do not feel to object; yet we do feel it will be better for them to come directly to this place, for here will be our head quarters for the present, and our dwelling place as quick as we can go and bring up our families, which we left behind this season for the purpose of bringing on yours, that you might meet them here; and we want to see you, even all of you, and talk with you, and throw our arms around you, and kill the fatted calf, and make* merry; yes, brethren, we want to rejoice with you once more. Come then and see us and we will do you good, and we will show you a location which cannot be beat upon the Pacific Ocean, and you shall have an inheritance in this goodly land. We do not suppose that you want any urging to come here, but we speak out of the fulness [sic] of our hearts.

We are making every exertion to prepare for the families that we expect immediately here, and will spend but little time in writing to you now, as Capt. Brown can tell you a great deal more than can be written. Some few have passed by a new route to California called the Hastings cut-off by the south border of the Salt Lake, but it is not a safe route on account of the long drive without water, and it is not wisdom for you to come that way. Brethren, cultivate the spirit of kindness and assistance towards another, and do each other all the good you can, and be humble and prayerful, and show yourselves men of God wherever you may be, and God will bless you.

Should this meet you in the southern part of California, or should any circumstance prevent your returning previous to the approach of cold weather, do not attempt to come by the north route, but come on the southern route.

Your arms, equipments, camp equipage, etc., you will retain and bring with you, for you will need them all at this place.

We remain your brethren in behalf of the Council,<br>
Willard Richards, clerk<br>
Brigham Young, President

Almost an afterthought, over the signature of Brigham Young, clerk Willard Richards also wrote this day a brief letter officially appointing Samuel Brannan "President of the Saints in California," which Brannan accepted more as a sop to his ego than anything else; the title was one he had worn unofficially ever since leaving New York. From this point on, Brannan resolved, without exception, to put himself first in all matters.

[August 20, 1847 • Friday • 1:00 p.m.]

In the Hudsons Bay Company's post of Fort Hall, Richard Grant was showing the first signs of unease at having so large a force of "malcontents" as the Mormons settling so near to him. As he wrote today to his own superior, Sir George Simpson, he allowed his trepidation to surface slightly:

> *A party of 300 "Mormons," composed of all nations, propose to take up their quarters for the winter at Great Salt Lake, where it is supposed they intend to form a permanent settlement for persons possessing their peculiar opinions. They have the character of being a knavish set, and I fear they will give me trouble before long; however, I think that the Indians of this place will be a sufficient protection against violence, should any attempt be made upon the establishment...*[240]

[August 20, 1847 • Friday • 6:30 p.m.]

The hope that had risen strongly in General Richard Scott's mind that a final peaceful settlement could be made with Mexico without further conflict was now thoroughly shattered, as the events of this past week had so clearly proven. The army's advance had been fairly much without resistance of any sort until it reached the area of Ayotla but then, just beyond that town, the army encountered the fortified hill called El Penon, which blocked direct access to Mexico City. Several risky reconnaissance missions revealed that there was a passable road that would take them southward around Lake Chalco and so, while General Twiggs held the attention of the enemy by demonstrating against El Penon, the majority of the army successfully took the trail under the cover of darkness and arrived without opposition at San Augustin, some eight miles south of Mexico City, on August 17.

General Santa Ana became aware of the maneuver far too late in its progress and moved his force quickly to meet the advance, but his delay had cost him an advantage and the Battle of Contreras began on August 19.

The bloody conflict continued throughout the remainder of August 19 and well into August 20, but an American victory seemed foreordained, even though with frightful losses. General Santa Ana had fully intended to defend the principal approaches to Mexico City at San Angel and San Antonio, but his insubordinate General Gabriel Valencia, in direct violation of command orders. moved forward to the isolated hill position called Contreras. His disobedience was followed by an even graver error on the part of the Americans, when General Pillow made his

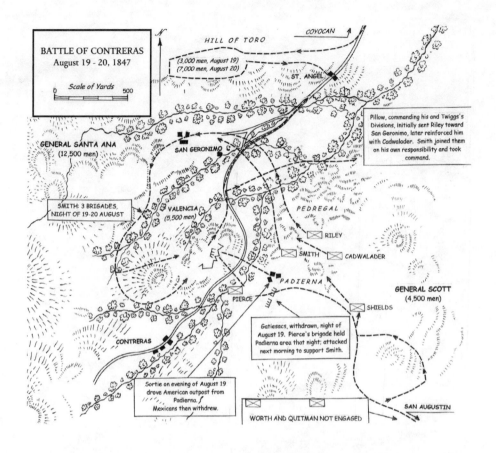

unauthorized attack on General Valencia's position with the divisions under his and Twigg's command; an attack which utterly failed due to the heavier, well-placed Mexican artillery and the exceedingly rough terrain leading to it. Fortunately, the day was saved for the Americans when a gully was discovered that led to the rear of Valencia's position. Along that gully the brigades under Generals Persifor F. Smith and Brigadier General George Cadwalader advanced under cover of darkness and at dawn they attacked the enemy position from the rear while the force under Brigadier General Franklin Pierce attacked the front. Under such an onslaught, General Valencia's defenses collapsed and the withdrawal of his force became a rout, which was met by the dismayed General Santa Ana as he moved his 7,000-man force forward. Quite abruptly, the whole Mexican contingent suddenly fell into retreat.

Later, that same day, as the Mexican force withdrew northward

# The Infinite Dream

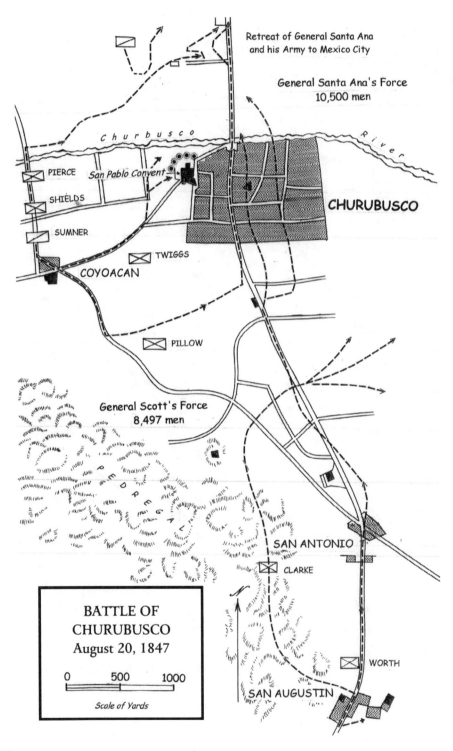

to Mexico City, the American advance followed steadily and an equally bloody struggle—judged as among the fiercest of the entire war—occurred in the Battle of Cherubusco, which brought the American force to the very gates of the capital. This was another bloody battle that came close to being lost by the Americans due to the ineptness of General Pillow, who unfathomably exposed his entire force to defeat. General Santa Ana then ordered all his Mexican troops to concentrate along the inner defenses of the city.

Retiring in obedience to Santa Ana's order, the San Antonio garrison was struck in its flank by one of Worth's brigades and the Mexicans panicked and scattered. In hot pursuit of the Mexican force, the American force converged in a direct attack against Cherubusco's fortified bridgehead—a position which General Santa Ana had ordered should be held at all costs. A single Mexican defending artillery battalion fought their approach with amazing ferocity and justifiably so, since that defending artillery battalion was composed almost entirely of American deserters who were only too well aware they could expect no mercy from the Americans. In the fight that followed—some of the fiercest fighting of the entire war—repeated American attacks were beaten back with significant losses, but the Mexican force simply was unable to halt the American advance. After the initial repulses, Pierce and Shields got their troops across the river, as did some of Worth's troops, who attacked the bridgehead from the rear. It was at that point that all Mexican resistance collapsed, except for that at the San Pablo Convent where the garrison held on desperately for some while. Shields and Pierce struck the retreating forces in their flanks and the dragoons pursued them right to the city proper.

It was the brilliant maneuvering of Robert E. Lee, directed by General Scott himself, that saved the day for the Americans, overcoming the gross failings of General Pillow and the mediocrity of General Pierce. A first class American army engaged a first class Mexican army and for a time it was touch and go as to who would prevail, but the Mexican generals proved they lacked the staying power and guts to hold their ground and this became their downfall.

Lee and Persifor Smith, ably supported by Twiggs, Worth and Quitman, more than made up for the potentially disastrous bumblings of Pillow and Pierce and, with military brilliance that was stunning, Scott's force emerged victorious.[241] However, even though victory was his, General Scott was very much opposed to allowing any further American lives to be lost, so he sent an envoy—Nicholas Trist—to meet with the Mexican commissioners and propose terms of a peace treaty. The commanding general of the Mexican army agreed with alacrity, but this turned out to be nothing more than an attempt on his part to buy time.[242]

For perhaps the first time in his illustrious—and often notorious—career, General Santa Ana seemed to realize time was running out.

*[August 22, 1847 • 10:00 a.m.]*

The long journey of General Stephen Watts Kearny was at last completed.

In the midst of the forenoon today, the General and his escort arrived at Fort Leavenworth—ironically, perhaps, exactly one year to the day when the man who had mustered the Saints into service in the U.S. Army, Lt. Col. James Allen, had died. They had come a long way from their return trip's starting point in Monterey—2,152 miles in just eighty-three days. The last 1,905 miles, begun at Sutters Fort, had been covered in sixty-six days, without the procession having laid by for a single day of rest.

The advance squad of four Mormon Battalion Saints had arrived here late last night, but their news of the approach of the Kearny detachment spread quickly and galvanized into activity both the military at the fort and the civilians in the area surrounding it. The next day, as one newspapers reported it:

> *...The old General was welcomed back by friends, and a salute of 13 guns was fired in honor of his return.... He is a great soldier, one who knows no fear, and minds not fatigue.*

No time was lost in separating the Mormon Battalion members from their service. Because their enlistments had been extended beyond the July 16 expiration date due to this special duty, the men of the escort were immediately paid $8.60 each for their additional service, after which they turned in their mules and other public property to the proper officers and were quickly discharged from the Army in a brief, simple ceremony during which General Kearny personally thanked the men and shook the hand of each in gratitude and farewell. The discharged soldiers headed immediately for Council Bluffs, Iowa, for the long anticipated reunion with their families.²⁴³

There remained one final matter for General Kearney to take care of and he sent a runner with a summons for Lt. Col. John Charles Fremont to report to him at once. It was not a moment the general was looking forward to, despite his grim anticipation for this moment to come, ever since leaving Monterey.

Exactly three weeks ago, as Pvt. Jones recorded it in his diary, the detachment:

> ...moved camp early, crossed the Platte and went down [the] left hand side of the river. Came fifteen miles and camped. I have seen more timber in the last few days than I have seen this side of the California mountains. Started at one [p.m.], crossed the river on the right hand side of the river again. Came twenty two miles and camped on the Horse Shoe Fork of the Platte. Hail and rain tonight. Came forty miles...

The following day they started very early and rode twelve miles before finally stopping to cook breakfast and rest. When a small war party of Lakotah Sioux warriors unexpectedly approached and were seemingly prepared for an engagement, the general immediately held a brief council with them and, lest they contemplated mischief, delivered a stern warning: "Your Great Father far to the east has warriors as numerous as the sands upon the shores of this river. You would be very unwise to provoke his wrath."

Apparently they took him at his word and without speaking further, though evidently angry, they rode stiffly off upstream and not a warrior in their party looked back while they remained in view. It was ominous in portent and General Kearny commented aloud, though more to himself than to anyone else: "There'll come a time—and not in the too-distance future!—when these Indians will become a very real problem to everyone on the Oregon Trail."

He was not far wrong because almost immediately this same band of Lakotahs joined other bands from the same tribe and targeted the emigrating Mormons not far to the east for their depredations, sweeping in with wild cries and robbing them of a goodly number of their horses before disappearing just as rapidly.

At noon General Kearny's party started out again, following a crooked road along the right bank of the Platte and by dusk they had covered a total of thirty-seven miles for the day. They camped that evening of August 2 at the Laramie Fork of the Platte, three miles above the fort itself. That was when the advance unit reported in with news that the main body of the Mormon emigrants was camped at that moment only a day's journey down the North Platte. Pvt. Jones and two companions immediately asked for—and received—permission to visit the Mormon encampment in the sudden hope their own families would be part of the group.

It took until mid-day on August 4 for them to reach the encampment and it was much larger than they expected; more than ten times the size of the initial party led by Brigham Young himself, which had gone via Fort Bridger, which they'd missed by taking the Greenwoods Cut-off. Captain Henry Turner made a statistical count as they passed the Mormons and tallied 800 men, 750 women, 1,556 children under sixteen years of age, as well as 4,350 head of cattle being herded, plus 142 horses and mules, 344 sheep and a total of 685 wagons; and this was only the second of successive waves of Mormon wagon trains on the move.[244]

Pvt. Jones' expectation of encountering his wife, Rebecca, however, was dashed; she was not with them, but at least the group had a letter for him from her—a letter written fully two months earlier in Iowa on June 6, but it was the first word he had received from her for over a year and he was overjoyed to receive it. He and his two companions found many of their former acquaintances with this present group and had a very happy time with them for several hours before the General's party arrived and joined them. Then they all camped together for this one night alone.

A great deal of information was exchanged and for the first time the Battalion members learned unequivocally that the Mormon emigration was not heading to California; but by Brigham Young's decree newly received, The Promised Land—the new Zion for the Mormons—had turned out to be at Great Salt Lake, where they were already rapidly digging in and anticipating this second wave of Saints to join and help them as swiftly as possible. Lt. Sylvester Hulett's family was among this group of Mormons and General Kearny, being especially gracious, gave the lieutenant permission to drop out of the escort and accompany them the remainder of their journey to Salt Lake. It was here, too, that Pvt.

Amos Cox sadly learned of the death of his daughter, Loenza, which had occurred the previous winter at the Mormon Winter Quarters.

That they had crossed over to the south side of the river before camping turned out to be a very fortunate circumstance, since by morning the river had swollen considerably and had become easily a half-mile wide. That day, August 7, they traveled forty miles and camped for the night at Ash Hollow, at which point their bugler, Pvt. Robert Quigley became ill and unable to ride. By the General's order, he was left behind with three privates—Matthew Caldwell of Co. E, Charles Y. Webb of Co. A, and hospital steward William W. Spencer—to remain with him and see him safely to Ft. Leavenworth when he was able to travel again.[245] They were left with their rations, one horse each and two packs.

On August 8 they broke camp at sunrise and struck off southward across the plain, leaving the North Platte and, in twenty miles, camped along the South Platte, which Pvt. Jones described as being "...*larger than the North Platte and discharges as much again water as the North Platte. It is three fourths of a mile wide.*" They went twelve miles further down the South Platte, crossed over and camped. By this time buffalo were becoming plentiful and three were killed during the day for food.

On August 10 they reached the confluence of the North and South Platte rivers and continued down the south shore of the main Platte. Here Pvt. Jones marveled at how innumerable the buffalo were and how they were able to subsist in such vast herds. Thomas Swords estimated that over a million animals could be seen in one view. They traveled forty miles that day over a landscape that had, as Jones put it: "...*considerable timber and plenty of grass, through as beautiful a country as I ever saw. We camped on the Big Platte.*"[246]

On August 12 they found the river had enlarged considerably and was described as being "...*from two and a half to three miles wide...*" and, after covering forty-two miles during the day, they stopped for that night at an old abandoned Pawnee Indian encampment. Two days later, General Kearny having taken a cut-off route, they camped for the night at another old Indian site on Little Blue Creek some fifty miles from the Platte. In two days they left the Blue and struck off across the prairie and at the end of forty miles on August 16, camped along Sandy Creek. They reached the Big Blue at noon two days later and didn't stop until after nightfall, having covered a solid forty-five miles for the day.

General Kearny's advance, having eaten the last of their food early in the morning yesterday, August 21, finally reached Fort Leavenworth after nightfall, wholly exhausted, while the General and his escort reached the fort today in midmorning and received the thirteen-gun salute honoring his arrival. Colonel Fremont, who had been bad-mouthing General Kearny almost without pause since leaving California, was summoned immediately and the General for once minced no words with him.

"You, Sir," he told Fremont, motioning to a guard standing ready nearby with shackles to bind the colonel, "are now under close arrest and as of today you will remain in irons until our arrival in Washington, D.C., where you will stand court-martial on charges of insubordination and mutiny."[247]

*[August 22, 1847 • Sunday • 2:30 p.m.]*

The army-discharged Saints, in their scattered and somewhat disorganized companies, were today only a single day's march away from Sutters Fort and still very much uncertain as to what lay in the immediate future for them. There were those among them who wanted to push ahead at all speed to cross the Sierra Nevada range and reach the desert flats of the Great Basin before the possibility of becoming snowed in on the heights became an actuality. Others, fearful because of what they had heard frightening tales of what occurred to the Donner Party, gloomily advocated waiting until next spring before even making the attempt. Some suggested perhaps joining the Mormons they had heard were in their New Hope settlement and wintering with them in the San Joaquín Valley.

At this point—as it had been since they left the Los Angeles area—it was pretty much a toss-up.

The journey thus far, from the coastal foot of California up to somewhat beyond its mid-point, had been of interest to all. There were those who were intensely curious about Monterey and San Francisco, about which they'd heard so much, and who wished to visit—perhaps even become a part of—the burgeoning life there. Others opted for the same type of visit at Sutters Fort where, so they'd heard, John Sutter was offering good employment to any outsiders who came by, either temporarily or with permanent residence in mind. The majority, however, had families and returning to them as expeditiously as possible seemed the only valid course to follow.

The Saints had argued the relative merits of these three principal plans ever since their journey began, shortly after their honorable discharge from the Army, but no real decision had as yet been made; all of them only too keenly aware of the hazards that they might well encounter in the Sierras, as had the Donner party. They hoped a pause at Sutters Fort and meeting with John Sutter himself would help provide the answer they sought. One thing was already clear to all: winter was rapidly approaching and they still had perhaps a thousand miles or more to travel before they could be reunited with their families somewhere in the Rocky Mountains or Great Basin. And that was definitely part of the problem: no one knew positively where such a reunion might take place, or just how much of a burden they might themselves be upon reaching The Promised Land. The hope was strong that Captain Sutter could give them the benefit of his knowledge and insight.

By July 21, the majority of the discharged Mormons were on their way generally northward, opting to follow the base of the Sierras northward, as this would take them to Sutters Fort in about 600 miles, as opposed to 700 had they chosen to follow the Pacific coastal path. As Henry Bigler commented about it in his diary:

> *On the twenty-first day of July we made a move for home, it Being just one year since we took up our line of march at Council Bluffs. We hardly know what way to strike out, for we have no guide, except an old California map with very few rivers or anything else marked on it, and a paper pretending to give the route. Our course was up the San Pedro* [Los Angeles] *River, the pioneers heading out. Made this day about ten miles and made an early encampment on the bank of the river.*[248]

They veered from the coastal route quickly and for the next several days traveled generally northeast until they encountered the San Joaquín Valley, which they followed northward. At one point they stopped at the ranch of Andrés Pico at the Mission San Fernando where, as Bigler put it:

> *...we bought some fine pears and also took a little wine for our stomach's sake. The owner, General Andrés Pico, who had beaten General Kearny at San Pasqual last January, is a fine specimen of humanity, well dressed, wearing a red silk sash around his*

body. He bore in his hand a lance and showed us how it was used, maneuvering it as if in action with an enemy.

They then stopped at the 48,600-acre Rancho San Francisco and visited with its owner and *alcalde*, Antonio del Valle and purchased from him forty-five saddle-broken three-year-old horses at $2.00 apiece, as well as fifty head of cattle to drive along with them. They soon found, however, the cattle too wild to drive well and much too dangerous, as they would charge any horseman who got in their way. After losing fifteen steers in the heights, they decided to kill the rest and dry the meat to take along with them, which they did during the last two days of July.

By August 3 they had reached a powerful river and followed it upstream for twelve miles, seeking a safe place to cross. The men generally referred to it as the Tulare River, but Bigler strongly doubted this, writing in his diary:

> 3d I think this lake is Kern Lake and this river Kern River. The river runs swift and seems to abound with plenty of fish. Elk and antelope seem to be very plentiful along here.[249]
>
> 4th We traveled up the river some six or eight miles and crossed by swimming our animals, and we made a raft and ferried the most of our baggage over. Some waded and carried their things on their heads.

The country continued to be rough traveling, with some of the hills extremely steep and in some cases the pitch was easily forty-five degrees. Nevertheless, they continue to travel between ten and sixteen miles per day. On August 11 their twenty-eight-mile journey across a hot, dry plain very nearly did some of them in; two men gave out and could no longer travel and others flagged so badly that it seemed all would perish. Those in the lead finally managed to reach a river and drank deeply, then filled their canteens and returned to revive their comrades. Though a close call, all finally recovered enough to reach their camp.[250]

Finally, on August 16, after days of perilously low water reserves, they reached a beautiful stream with a strong current and about a hundred yards wide, which turned out to be the San Joaquín River and followed its course northward for a while, but left it when it turned northwest. They continued due north for eighteen miles without water along a trail that

*The* Infinite Dream

was said to be Fremont's route. At nightfall of August 18 they reached a beautiful stream and encountered a lone Indian who spoke some Spanish and from him discovered they were at the Merced River and only three days' journey south of reaching Sutters Fort on the Sacramento.

They slogged on, still following Fremont's trail and within ten miles crossed a stream flowing west which turned out to be the Calaveras River. And now, Sunday afternoon, August 22, they made camp on the side of a beautiful watercourse flowing out of the mountains to the east and discovered from a native that this was the Mokelumne River and they were now less than a day's journey from Sutters Fort as well as the trail that would lead them over the Sierras and back, at last, to their fellow Saints...wherever they happened to be by now.

[August 30, 1847 • Monday]

The construction being overseen by James Marshall at the sawmill site on the South Fork American River was coming along quite well. The initial crew having been selected, and their accommodations built, everything was ready for construction of the actual sawmill to begin. The past several weeks of preparation had been busy days indeed and it had only been due to the fortuitous return of the Saints, who had turned back from their push over the Sierras, that had allowed Marshall to reach this present state of preparedness. The current state of progress had its commencement when John Sutter hired three discharged Mormon Battalion men who suddenly appeared and applied for work. Sutter took them on as helpers in his flour mill construction just a few miles upstream on the American River from the fort.

Another four Mormons arrived at Sutters Fort on August 23 and these, too, were hired to work at the flour mill, as Sutter prepared for a greater influx of emigrants. This same day Charles Smith arrived from the east and reported that he had encountered 1,500 wagons of emigrants en route to Oregon and another 500 who were bound for Salt Lake to join with the Saints already there under Brigham Young, who was establishing a rapidly growing town being called Salt Lake City.

Former Sgt. Daniel Tyler and his group of Saints reached Sutters Fort the next day—August 24—and he was delighted at encountering a largely American settlement. As he wrote of it in his journal this evening:

*24th. we reached a settlement of white people, and were almost*

565

> *overjoyed to see a colony of Americans, the first we had seen since leaving Fort Leavenworth, about a year previous. But the best of all was the news brought by a man named Smith, who said he had accompanied Samuel Brannan to meet the Mormon Church leader, Brigham Young, and who informed us the Saints were settling in the Great Salt Lake Valley. He added that more than five hundred wagons of Mormons were on the way there. This was our first intelligence of the movements of the Church since the news brought by Lieutenant Pace and Brothers Lee and Egan, at the Arkansas Crossing. One must have our previous sad experience to appreciate our feelings on this occasion.*[251]

This same day was a banner one for both Marshall and Sutter and marked the beginning of their true partnership in the lumber enterprise. It was on this day that Marshall returned to the fort and enthusiastically reported to Sutter that he had found the ideal location for the erection of a sawmill, some forty-five miles distant up the South Fork of the American River, five miles downstream from the Coloma Indians' village. Sutter immediately began gathering the men and equipment to be transported there by Marshall and the erection of the sawmill and its camp begun. On Wednesday, August 25, Captain Sutter wrote in his logbook:

> *Capt. Hunt of the Mormons arrived with a good Many of his Men, Quartermaster, Clerk, Mr. [Isaac] Harrison, Messrs. [Gilman] Gordon, [James] Davis, & Chs. Heath arrived...They had orders for Govt. Horses, which I delivered to them, (War Horses) not paid for yet. They bought provisions and got blacksmith work done. I employed about Eighty Men of them, some as Mechanics, some as laborers, on the flour Mill and Millraise [mill race] at Brighton; some as laborers for the Sawmill at Columa [sic]...The majority, however, pushed hurriedly on into the Sierras.*

The Saints themselves were every bit as enthusiastic at finding work at Sutters Fort as Sutter himself was at having the opportunity of getting American workers. As Daniel Tyler wrote of it in his journal:

> *The following day, we rested and held meeting in the evening, as we had frequently done since our discharge. Some, having but a poor*

*fit-out, wished to remain here and labor until spring, wages being good and labor in demand; besides, a settlement of New York Saints was within a few miles. President Levi W. Hancock made some appropriate remarks on the union that had been and was among us, and thought that a few might remain and labor until spring and all would be all right. He then asked the company if, in case any felt to remain, they should have our prayers and blessings. All voted in the affirmative. Good remarks were also made by others on the same subject. A few remained. Wages were said to be from twenty-five to sixty dollars per month, and hands hard to get at any price, as there were so few in the country.*

On this same day, another segment of the former Mormon Battalion reached the Cosumnes River south of Sutters Fort and another member of their group, unidentified, wrote in a notebook:

*25 [August 1847] day[.] this day rested on Causumey [Cosumnes] river or Creek while our pilots went on to fort sooters [Sutters Fort] and while here a Mr John P Roads [Rhoades] came to our camp and told us the horable [horrible] tales of those men and women who eat each other[.] he states that one Mr Keesburg [sic] of the Doner Party was a most horable [horrible] canable [cannibal] and the tale he states is the most shocking account I ever read or hered [heard] of in my life[.] this man ses [says] that there was more hands and feet than one man could carry which this Dutchman eat[.] he must have murdered many[.] he had two tin buckets of blood dryed [sic] and human bodys [sic] all around[.] one mans [sic] privats [sic] with the lower part of his belly lay on the ground before the fire beside of his child[.] he states that he had a man and women [sic] boxed up and says he would cut of[f] the head of a man and split it open and he ate the brains and when he saw one woman after he got through he told her that he would like to eat her she looked so good[.] he knew she would eat well[.]*[252]

Henry Bigler's group encamped this same day on the north side of the American River and as he wrote in his diary this night:

*August 25. This morning we got a few bushels [of] wheat for one*

> dollar per bushel. The Spanish phrase and price was two dollars per fanega. Our course today was northwest across a large plain for twenty miles and we encamped on the north side of the American River about one mile and a half from [above] Sutters Fort.

The next day—August 26—he added:

> August 26th. Laid by while some visited the Fort, where there was a blacksmith shop, and got their animals shod, as some of them were tender-footed. The price of shoeing was one dollar for each shoe made and nailed on. We learned here was plenty of grain and unbolted flour and peas to be had. Unbolted flour (which is all the kind in California these days) is worth eight dollars per sack, peas one dollar and half per bushel. Captain Sutter seems to have plenty of everything in the shape of cattle, horses and mules, grain, etc. Several of our boys concluded to stop here and go to work for Sutter, as he was wanting to hire and was offering pretty fair wages, as the boys thought, and fit themselves up and come on [to Salt Lake City] the next spring. Depending on skills, Sutter offers twenty-five to forty dollars a month.

While the majority of Bigler's group—about eighty men—remained at Sutters Fort to get their horses shod, Bigler himself and the Pioneers group of about thirty others pushed on without further delay, advancing about eighteen miles up the Sacramento until reaching the mouth of the Yuba River, where they turned upstream eastward toward Emigration Pass.

For Sutter and Marshall, this was an important day. Having inspected, early in August, the site chosen by Marshall as ideal for the lumber mill site—and fully in accord with Marshall's evaluation of it as an excellent location—the two men returned to the fort and today, August 27, they formally entered into their partnership in the lumber business—Sutter to provide foodstuffs, equipment and wages, Marshall to undertake establishment of the mill itself, its raceway, its crew quarters and its timber needs, as well as transporting the cut timber to Sutters Fort and the two men to share in the proceeds equally.[253] As Marshall wrote in his diary on the 27th:

> You may be sure Mr. Sutter was pleased when I reported my

success. We entered into partnership; I was to build the mill, and he was to find provisions, teams, tools, and to pay a portion of the men's wages. I believe I am, at this time, the only millwright in the whole country.

Having already selected a crew of men, including twenty Indian workers and about a half-dozen Mormons—along with the Peter Wimmer family, including his wife, Eliza Jane "Jennie" Wimmer as cook for the white workers—Marshall set off for the site the next day, August 28, with a half-dozen ox teams and wagonloads of tools and provisions, and driving a flock of sheep for food, his plan being to first erect two cabins and then get construction of the Marshall-Sutter Sawmill begun without further delay.

Sutter himself wrote in his *New Helvetia Diary* Sutter Log on this day:

*Friday Aug. 27th 1847 A good Many of the Mormons here, to get some Blacksmith work done, & to buy some provisions. Made a contract and entered in partnership with Marshall for a sawmill to be built on the Amer. fork.*[254]

Marshall and his men set out for the mill site and, on arrival there, the first task was to build a double cabin—they called it a dog-run cabin—where two separate cabins are joined by a covered porch-way. One portion was constructed to house the mill workers, the other to serve as a dining area for the whites as well as accommodations for the Wimmers—Peter, his wife, Jennie, as cook, and their seven children from different marriages. About forty local Coloma Indians were immediately engaged to excavate the millrace and to build the diversion dam, while the more skilled white men set to felling trees and whipsawing them into timbers for the mill.

Where the river swung widely around a bar, Marshall began at once erecting a log-and-brush dam and a head-gate. Then, across the base of this peninsula-like bar, past a double pine tree that was to be the landmark of the site, construction of a dry channel was begun, which would be deepened and formed into the race through which the river's flow would be diverted. The mill building, built of hewn and hand-sawn timbers, was planned to straddle the upper end of the race, with its timbers prepared on the site, along with the huge wooden-pegged flutter-wheel, twelve feet wide and twelve feet in diameter. The axle, crank and pitman irons for this project were forged at Sutters Fort. The task of excavating and forming the raceway was difficult, but the work was attacked with oxen, plows, scrapers and blasting powder and the project moved along with surprising rapidity. As James Marshall himself put it:

> *Our first business was to put up log houses, we intended remaining here all winter.*

[September 8, 1847 · Wednesday]

It was as Samuel Brannan was on his way back to San Francisco, while passing through the high Tahoe Basin in the Sierras, that he encountered first thing the day before yesterday the advance group of discharged Mormons who were en route to rejoin their families somewhere in the Great Salt Lake area and then, early yesterday morning, the larger main contingent of Mormons heading in the same direction.

The Mormons had left Captain Johnson's ranch on August 28 and, as Henry Bigler had written about Johnson in his diary that evening:

> *On the 28th we made about the same distance and camped on Bear River. Here at this easternmost outpost of northern California were a few families—an American, a German and two Frenchmen— one by the name of Johnson. This man had Indians laboring for him, who were entirely naked. I noticed one large man, probably six feet in height, come and stand by the door, an unabashed picture of nature unadorned. He was apparently waiting for the young woman of the house—the captain's wife—to give him something to eat. Captain Johnson passed in and out of the house while the savage stood by the door, without taking any exceptions to his nude appearance, from which we inferred that he was used to seeing the Indians in such condition. Indeed, we were informed that those he hired, went without clothing, and the Indian we saw there was probably one of his employees.*[255]
>
> *Captain Johnson was said to have been one of Fremont's Battalion, and his young wife was one of the survivors of the ill-fated company who had been snowed in at the foot* [height, actually] *of the Sierras,*

*already alluded to. Her mother, Mrs, Murray [Murphy], who was a Latter-day Saint, was among the number who perished in that horrible scene of death. The circumstances under which she became a member of that company were explained to us by her daughter, Mrs. Johnson.*

The Mormon Advance, of which Bigler was a member, was commanded by Elisha Everett, former musician of the Mormon Battalion's Co. A, who had now been elected as Captain of their group. While the remainder of his party rested and waited for him on September 2, Captain Everett and a few men went ahead to examine the trail. In the interval, Henry Bigler took his gun and left the camp to hunt for a few hours, but quickly gave up the notion, as Bigler noted in his diary:

*...in consequence of its being so hard traveling over rocks. I seated myself on a high rock at the north end of the valley, where I had a full view of a mountain, still north of me about half a mile distant to me. It was a sight to look upon. I think the mountain must have been a mile high and appeared to be a solid mass of rocks, with here and there a few scattered pines. It looked grand and yet lonesome and dismal.... We were now surrounded with high mountains covered with a heavy forest of pine and balsam timber. The land looked dark and dreary, and I thought if there were any witches and hobgoblins in the world, they must live in these mountains.*

It was on September 5 that the group in which Bigler was traveling reached the final summit atop what General Kearny had renamed Donner Pass. As Bigler commented about it in his diary:

*September 5....We ascended the mountain passing over snow three feet deep. We now had gained the summit and main chain of the great Sierra Nevada Mountains, and on the east side at the top was a windlass, where emigrants had to haul up their wagons over a very steep ascent in order to gain the summit of the great Sierra Nevada. Passing down the mountain to the head of Truckee River some six or eight miles, we came to a shanty built last winter, and about this cabin we found the skeletons of several human beings.[256] I discovered a hand. It was nearly entire. It had been partly burned* to a crisp. The little finger was not burnt. The flesh seemed to be a little dried. I judged it to be the hand of a woman. I do not believe the wolves disturbed them. The place had the appearance that they had been burned after death.... I noticed the timber about this shanty that had been cut down; the stumps were ten or twelve feet high. This showed how deep the snow was at the time it was cut. After leaving this painful looking place about three miles, we camped in a handsome little valley by a creek, where good water and grass were plenty.

It was the following day—September 6—that had become momentous for the Mormon party in which Henry Bigler was traveling, as this was the day they encountered Sam Brannan riding alone and heading for San Francisco. As Bigler described it in his diary:

*September 6. Soon after leaving camp this morning, we met Sam Brannan, who had been up to Salt Lake to meet our emigration. He informed us that Captain Brown with his detachment from the Pueblo country on the Arkansas was just behind on his way to Monterey to get their discharge, and that the Captain had a package of letters and also an epistle from Brigham Young and the Twelve to the Battalion boys. As part of our company was still behind and had not as yet overtaken the pioneers since leaving the settlements, we concluded to turn back to our last camping place and there await the arrival of Captain Brown, and also for the rear part of our company, where all might be together and all hear the news together. After we had returned to camp, Brannan stopped an hour or so to let his animal feed and to eat a bite himself and talk with the boys etc. He was traveling alone. He and Captain Brown had had a quarrel that morning (as I understood), and so sharp had words and threats been made that Brannan left the Captain and his crowd to travel without his company.*

At the time of their actual meeting, Brannan had been especially cordial. "I have just come from your brethren," he announced, after identifying himself as the leader of the Saints who had established the New Hope settlement in the San Joaquín Valley. "I have been in conference there with our president, Brigham Young, where he has established a new temporary Zion for our people, which he is calling Salt Lake City." He emphasized the word "temporary," explaining confidently that the true Zion would undoubtedly be established in California and quite probably where his own flock was now located at New Hope.

The brother Saints he met, which included Henry W. Bigler and Azariah Smith, were eager to learn all they could of the eastern contingent's overland migration and were especially eager for news of their own family members. The men visited together for a couple of hours, plying each other with questions. What Brannan did not reveal in the slightest, however, was his vast disappointment that his meeting with Brigham Young had not in the least altered the Mormon president's determination to make his new site there the permanent—and final— headquarters of the Church of Jesus Christ of Latter-day Saints.

Brannan's long and difficult journey had been one of great sacrifice on his part and certainly involved grave personal risk, yet he had felt it worthwhile if there was the remotest possibility of convincing the Mormon president that his choice for locating the permanent Zion of his people was, in fact, an error and that such Zion should be established in California, which was, as Brannan put it, the true Goshen of modern-day Israel.

In his "inspection" with Brigham Young of what the latter termed their "new Zion," Brannan had looked aghast at what was revealed to him. Not only had Young halted the western march of his followers in a hostile and frightening wilderness, he had actually marked out a large community he was already calling Salt Lake City. Brannan was appalled at the sight of sun-baked earth that been flooded by creek diversion and then plowed and planted. He groaned at the sight of the fort and dwellings already under construction and at the streets and town plats that had been laid out as "inheritances" to be dealt out to the faithful. For public meetings, an open-air "bowery" had already been established and even a substantial plot had been selected for the erection of the new Mormon temple.

It was impossible for Brannan to accept Young's vision of the new Zion; in comparison to the gentleness of climate, fertility of soil, safety of movement and myriad other factors, California was, in his opinion, infinitely more desirable as a home base for the Latter-day Saints than any other place they had ever tried to settle. How, he wondered, could anyone forego the benefits California offered over the brutal heat and harshness of the Great Salt Lake area, with its sparse creeks that quickly dried up and disappeared, its wickedly cold winters and its blistering winds? The very thought of it all was so depressing that he literally begged Brigham Young to change his thinking and settle the Church instead in California where the manifold blessings were so abundant and so available.

The Mormon President could not be swayed and his words to Brannan had been like the closing of an impenetrable iron door: "It is not my choice that we have come here, Samuel," he explained calmly. "It is God who has dictated this place for us; the purpose and wisdom are His, not ours. The Latter-day Saints have too often in the past faced the guns and felt the lash of those who misunderstand our religion and our way of life. A land so desirable as you describe, Samuel, will draw men as surely as syrup draws flies and there would be no hope for Mormon peace and isolation contained therein. God's kingdom and the kingdom of man's world can never grow harmoniously side-by-side. In these arid settings you so detest, the Saints will have to fight in order merely to live. Because they will everlastingly have to turn to God for help, they *will* survive, they *will* live. Don't you see, Samuel, that ease means both spiritual and physical death? Only by our taking that which no other man could possibly want can we ever be freed of human rapacity; only in such a place as this, which no one else wants, can we be reasonably certain of establishing and building the Mormon pattern of life unmolested."

That he had failed utterly in his mission to convince Young of the greater benefits of California was a bitter disappointment to Brannan, yet one that, for the time being, he was keeping to himself. Unquestionably, he was strongly opposed to Young's stance in establishing the new heart of the Church in the rim of land east of the barren Great Salt Desert and at the western foot of the treacherous Wasatch Range of the Rocky mountains. Yet, even though he quarreled bitterly with Young, Brannan allowed no hint of the apostasy that was so strong in his thinking by this time to show through. So far as anyone else needed to know, he was still the leader of the Saints on the West Coast and he meant to maintain this posture for however long it would benefit him.

Though for the most part he was successful in hiding from the Church's president how rankled he was over Brigham Young's adamant stance as to where the new Mormon Zion should be, as well as the Young's cavalier treatment of him, Brannan was not entirely successful at masking his feelings from others. Well before he and Captain James Brown and the rest of their little party of horsemen had reached the eastern fringe of the Sierras, bitter argument had risen between Brown and himself. This was the result both of the injured feelings Brannan was nursing and the anger he was experiencing at Brigham Young's shoddy treatment of him. Brannan considered himself spiritual leader of all the West Coast Saints and to have Young so abruptly and inexplicably ignore him and entrust the epistles of comfort and counsel for the California Saints to Brown was a decided slap in the face. Though Brown was himself not responsible for Young's action, he became the focus of Brannan's fomenting wrath. The upshot was that the pair had argued violently; to such degree, in fact, that Brannan had abandoned the procession and went on alone, leaving Brown to lead his party as best he could over the Sierras and to Sutters Fort on his own.

None of this strife came through in his conversation with the advance party of Saints just encountered, however, although the word-picture he painted of Salt Lake City was hardly one to create anticipation. At the same time he impressed upon them the instructions Young had given him to relay to them.

"President Young has instructed me to inform you," he told them, "that if you wish to continue this journey of yours to Salt Lake City, you will be welcomed by all, but you must be informed that conditions there are still very crude and difficult. He gives you, if you wish to take advantage of it, permission to remain over the winter months in California, accept work there and earn what you can, then join them at Salt Lake City next year when passage over the Sierras becomes less hazardous. The choice is yours."

That Brannan's carefully chosen words had a significant impact on the eastward bound Mormons was clearly evident in Dan Tyler's journal entry last evening, as he wrote:

> ...*We learned from him* [Brannan] *that the pioneers had reached Salt Lake Valley in safety, but his description of the valley and its facilities was anything but encouraging. Among other things, Brother Brannan said the Saints could not possibly subsist in the Great Salt Lake Valley, as, according to the testimony of the mountaineers, it froze there every month of the year, and the ground*

*was too dry to sprout seeds without irrigation, and if irrigated with the cold mountain stream, the seeds would be chilled and prevented from growing, or, if they did grow, they would be sickly and fail to mature. He considered it no place for an agricultural people, and expressed his confidence that the Saints would emigrate to California the next Spring. On being asked if he had given his views to President Brigham Young, he answered that he had. On further inquiry as to how his views were received, he said, in substance, that the President laughed and made some rather insignificant remark; "but," said Brannan, "when he has fairly tried it, he will find that I was right and he was wrong."*

*He thought all except those whose families were known to be at Salt Lake had better turn back (to California) and labor until spring, when in all probability the Church would come to them; or, if not, they could take means to their families. We camped overnight with Brannan, and after he left us the following morning, Captain James Brown of the Pueblo detachment, which arrived in Salt Lake on the 27th of July, came up with a small party. He brought a goodly number of letters from the families of the soldiers, also an epistle from the Twelve Apostles, advising those who had not means of subsistence to remain in California and labor, and bring their earnings with them in the spring.*

It had now become a time of agonizing decision for the Mormons and they split in their conclusion; some so eager to be back with their families that no argument could have dissuaded them from the effort. This morning, after Brannan's departure westward, they continued their own journey eastward and downward into the Great Basin.

A sizable portion of the Saints, however, remembered very clearly John Sutter's invitation for them to stay over the winter in California and accept employment at good wages at either his new gristmill or the lumber mill about to be established. They decided that their best interests lay in doing just that. Included among the latter group were Azariah Smith and Henry Bigler, who set out immediately on Brannan's trail and, as Bigler wrote in his diary this evening:

*September 8. This morning myself and some thirty others gave our brethren the parting hand, but not till after we had divided our provisions with them, barely keeping enough to last us back to the first settlement, about one hundred fifty miles. It was hard to part but we knew the Council of the President and the Twelve was wise and we would be safe in obeying it.*

[September 11, 1846 • Friday • 3:00 p.m.]

By September 11 the accommodations being constructed at the site James Marshall had selected for the Marshall-Sutter Sawmill along the left bank of the South Fork American River had begun to take shape. The grub cabin , as it was already being called, where the workers would eat their meals, was also the quarters of Peter Wimmer and his wife, Jennie, along with their seven children. The connecting "worker's cabin" was occupied by the seven white men who were originally sent out to the Coloma mill site at the end of August, including Marshall himself, along with Henry W. Bigler, Azariah Smith, James S. Brown, Alexander Stephens, William Scott, and W. Johnson. That number was quickly increased by another contingent from Sutters Fort the following day, consisting of five more Mormons—Ebenezer Persons, Roswell Stevens, Samuel L. Brown, William W. Willis and his brother, Ira Willis, plus three non-Mormons, including the brothers Cam and Heiman Heuge, and Charles Seyti, who brought with them from Sutter twenty head of sheep and a sturdy wagon drawn by three yoke of oxen.

The majority of the Mormons who had returned from the Sierra Nevada after their discussions with Sam Brannan had agreed to the terms of employment offered them by Sutter at the gristmill, where they were already occupied with installation of the new millstones and spindle Sutter had just received and rigging it to be bolstered by horsepower to supplement the power generated by the millrace current on the big wheel. On September 4 Sutter reported in his *New Helvetia Logbook* that Gingery had returned from the sawmill with the big wagon and three of his Indian helpers, Charles, Gutche, and Kong. On the evening after that, all arrived at Sutters Fort for an hour's private conference with Sutter, but rode out on his return early in the morning on September 6 and was followed an hour later by Charles and Kong driving a two-yoke wagon loaded with further tools and provisions for the sawmill. Three days later a trio of former Mormon Battalion privates working at the gristmill—Lysander Woodworth, Thomas Frazier, and Jim Douglas—were sent by Sutter up to Coloma to aid in the work on digging the race for the lumber mill.

That there would quickly be serious trouble brewing between Jennie Wimmer and the mill workers was almost immediately apparent. It took Henry Bigler and his cabin-mates very little time after their arrival to discover that Mrs. Wimmer, as she positively insisted upon being referred to, was a very short-tempered, sharp-tongued woman whom no one could please, including her husband. All the Mormons and even the Indian laborers quickly discovered that the abuse, nagging and berating from her was little short of intolerable and they very quickly came to dread having to assemble for meals at the big table in the Wimmer cabin on the tight schedule she dictatorially established. Even though Bigler was easily the most tolerant of all the mill's male employees, he finally shook his head and gloomily uttered the words all of the men considered as being prophetic:

"Either she goes or we go," he said, adding, "…which I hope will happen soon, before one of us actually kills her!"

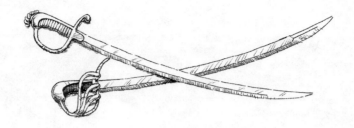

# Chapter 15

◆

[*September 11, 1846 · Friday · 10:00 p.m.*]

Major General Winfield Scott scrawled his signature at the bottom of the battle report he had just concluded writing for Secretary of War William L. Marcy in Washington, D.C. and, as usual upon completing the chore he most detested, now sat back to read what he had written as a final check for possible errors, though he knew quite well there would be none; at least none that were not deliberately conceived.

"It's history now," he murmured to himself in the cramped adobe at Tacubaya where he had established his temporary headquarters. He shook his head and sighed, took up the pages he had just completed writing and read his own account of the Battle of El Molino Del Rey:

*Headquarters of the army, Tacubaya, near Mexico*
*September 11, 1847*

*Sir:—I have heretofore reported that I had, on August 24, concluded an armistice with President Santa Anna [sic], which was promptly followed by [a] meeting between Mr. Trist and Mexican commissioners appointed to treat of peace.*

*Negotiations were actively continued, with, as we understood, some prospect of a successful result up to the 2nd instant, when our fair commissioner handed in his ultimatum, (on boundaries,) and the negotiators adjourned to meet again on the 6th.*

*Some infractions of the truce, in respect to our supplies from the city, were earlier committed, followed by apologies, on the part of the enemy. Those vexations I was willing to put down to the imbecility of the government, and waived pointed demands of reparation while*

# The Infinite Dream

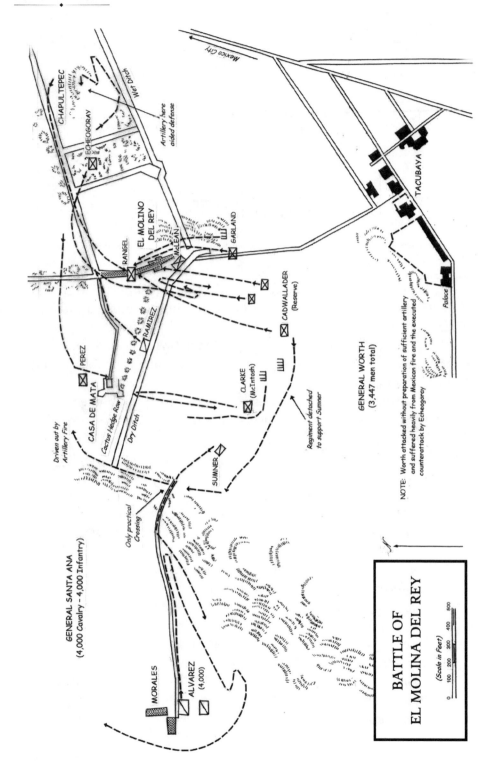

any hope remained of a satisfactory termination of the war. But on the 5th, and more fully on the 6th, I learned that as soon as the ultimatum had been considered in a general council of ministers and others, President Santa Anna [sic], on the 4th or 5th, without giving me the slightest notice, actively recommended strengthening the military defenses of the city, in gross violation of the 3rd article of the armistice.

On that information, which has since received the fullest verification, I addressed to him my note of the 6th. His reply, dated the same day, received the next morning, was absolutely and notoriously false, both in recrimination and explanation. I enclose copies of both papers, and have had no subsequent correspondence with the enemy.

Being delayed by the terms of the armistice more than two weeks, we had now, late on the 7th, to begin to reconnoiter the different approaches to the city, within our reach, before I could lay down any definitive plan of attack.

The same afternoon a large body of the enemy was discovered hovering about the Molino del Rey, within a mile and a third of this village, where I am quartered with the general staff of Worth's division.

It might have been supposed that an attack upon us was intended; but knowing the great value to the enemy of these mills, (Molinos del Rey,) containing a cannon foundry, with a large deposite [sic] of powder in Casa Mata near them; and having heard, two days before, that many church bells had been sent out to be cast into guns, the enemy's movement was easily understood, and I resolved, at once, to drive him early the next morning, to seize the powder, and to destroy the foundry.

Another motive for this decision—leaving the general plan of attack upon the city for full reconnaissance—was, that we knew our recent captures had left the enemy not a fourth of the guns necessary to arm, all at the same time, the strong works of each of the eight city gates; and we could not cut the communication between the foundry and the capital without first taking the formidable castle on the heights of Chapultepec, which overlooked both and stood between.

For this difficult operation, we were not entirely ready and *moreover we might altogether neglect the castle, if as we then hoped, our reconnaissance should prove that the distant southern approaches to the city were more eligible than this southwestern approach.*

*Hence the decision promptly taken, the execution of which was assigned to Brevet Major General Worth, whose division was reinforced with Cadwallader's brigade of Pillow's division, three squadrons of dragoons under Major Sumner, and some heavy guns of the siege train under Captain Huger of the ordnance, and Capt. Drum of the 4th artiller—two officers of the highest merit.*

*For the decisive and brilliant results, I beg to refer the report of the immediate commander—Major General Worth—in whose commendations of the officers and men—dead and living—I heartily concur; having witnessed, but with little interference, their noble devotion to fame and to country.*

*The enemy having several times reinforced his line and the action soon becoming much more general than I had expected, I called up, from the distance of three miles, first Major General Pillow, with his remaining brigade (Pierce's,) and next Riley's brigade of Twigg's Division—leaving his other brigade (Smith's) in observation at San Angel. These corps approached with zeal and rapidity, but the battle was won just as Brigadier General Pierce reached the ground, and had interposed his corps between Garland's brigade (Worth's division) and the retreating enemy.*

*The accompanying report mentions, with just commendation, two of my volunteer aids—Major Kirby, paymaster, and Major Gaines, of the Kentucky volunteers, I also had the valuable services, on the same field, of several other officers of my staff, general and personal—Lieut. Col. Hitchcock, acting inspector general; Captain R.E. Lee, engineer; Capt. Irwin, chief quartermaster; Captain Grayson, chief commissary, Capt. H.L. Scott, acting assistant adjutant general; Lieut. Williams, aid de camp, and Lieut. Lay, military secretary.*

*I have the honor to be, sir, with high respect,*
*Your most obedient servant,*
*WINFIELD SCOTT.*

What General Scott glossed over in his account was that General

Santa Ana had duped him into agreeing to an armistice for peace negotiation, which the Mexican general had no intention of considering, merely to give himself time to reorganize his forces; since he did not dare risk his own standing in the Mexican government by acknowledging how grave the situation was in the face of Scott's advance with troops far more disciplined and skilled than his own. Major General Winfield Scott and the principal U.S. peace negotiator, Nicholas Trist, had enemies much more deadly to them than Santa Ana and, though both were as yet unaware of it, they had now been thoroughly discredited in Washington D.C. Malicious lies and dirty politics, bolstered by profoundly poor communications, had convinced President Polk of exactly what he had long wished to be convinced about—that Winfield Scott and Nicholas Trist were decidedly out of sympathy with the chief executive, which, insofar as President Polk was concerned, unequivocally made them traitors.

It was of no benefit to Scott whatsoever that the principal objective in this costly two-hour battle just fought had entirely failed to materialize, as what he believed to be a cannon foundry there in El Molino del Rey was not such at all and a great many lives in Major General Worth's division were lost to no truly worthwhile purpose. General Santa Ana's detachment was simply forced to retreat to the great hill guarding the approach to the gates of Mexico City—a hill called Chapultepec, where the Mexican commander now had 30,000 troops awaiting the American advance.

[September 14, 1847 · Tuesday · 1:00 p.m.]

While Samuel Brannan's stopover at Sutters Fort today was very brief, it neatly cemented certain odds and ends that the dapper young entrepreneur had put into motion before his trip to see Brigham Young at Salt Lake City; odds and ends that would almost surely result in both Brannan and his junior partner, Charles Smith, becoming immensely wealthy.

Agreeing to a partnership weighted in Brannan's favor, in which they would establish a mercantile business, the pair approached John Sutter this morning and leased from him a large, one-room adobe just east of the fort's walls. Far downstream, San Francisco had now grown to over four hundred fifty permanent residents and since Brannan already had his own business there, called Samuel Brannan & Company, he thought it best that this newest enterprise be called C.C. Smith & Co. With no competition whatever anywhere nearby, the partners were confident they were founding a mercantile monopoly that would bring to each of them a fortune.

The new name did not fool the Sutters Fort residents at all. The emporium might officially be called C.C. Smith & Co., but even before the new sign was hung over the front door, the Yankee settlers in and around the fort were now referring to the rapidly growing town simply as Sacramento, and to the new business as Brannan's Shirt-Tail Store. And quite as Samuel Brannan had anticipated, the customers flocked in to buy whatever the store had to sell, even at the sharply jacked-up prices he charged for everything.

*[September 14, 1847 • Tuesday • 11:45 p.m.]*

For all intents and purposes, the War with Mexico ended today as Major General Winfield Scott's troops raised the American Flag over the National Palace in Mexico City. True, there were mop-up skirmishes still to be faced, but the Mexican Army under General Santa Ana had fled the Mexican capital city and was in complete disarray. Top Mexican officials, more political than military, had met this afternoon with General Scott and unconditionally surrendered both the capital city and the entire Mexican government to the American Army and, while terms of the surrender remained yet to be hammered out—a process estimated to take about a third of a year—the actual war itself was finally over.

The final victory had not been at all easily won and General Scott, just now completing his comprehensive report of the tumultuous events of the past three days in his full accounting to Secretary of War William L. Marcy in Washington, D.C. was as wearied mentally from the many hours of writing his report as he was physically from the devastating final conflict that had ended in victory, but at great cost to the United States Army.

It had all centered about the Mexican capital's protective hill called Chapultepec.

The odds that had faced the Americans were staggering: with fewer than 6,000 men they struggled upward to take a fortified hill defended by no less than twenty-one thousand of the enemy and perhaps as many as 30,000, who were not only well-armed individually but with numerous formidable artillery batteries in place to wreak the greatest possible

The Infinite Dream

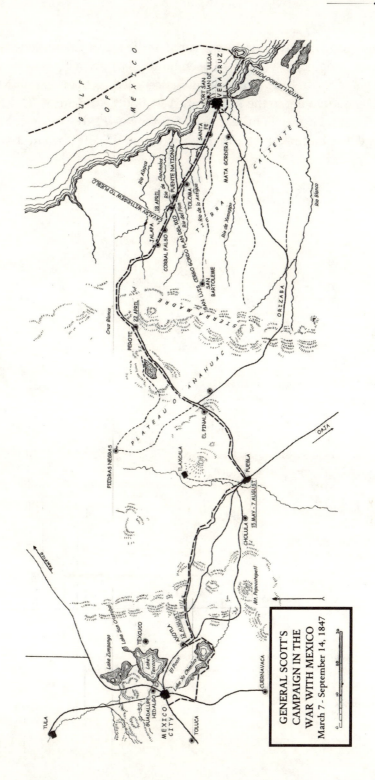

# The Infinite Dream

havoc among the attacking Americans. At the top of Chapultepec was an immense stone palace that had been built as a summer residence for the viceroys of Spain but which was now occupied by the Mexican Military College, equivalent to the American West Point Academy.

Throughout the entire day on September 12 the Mexican Military College was battered by barrages from General Scott's heaviest artillery,

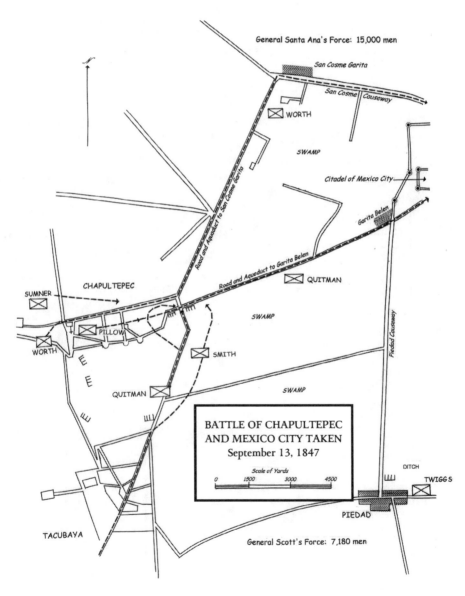

but the prolonged cannonading had inflicted very little damage of any substance. Scott conferred earnestly with his chief strategists in an effort to ascertain how best to proceed against Mexico City. The options were limited: either the heavily defended stone causeway crossing the swamps and leading into the city from the south could be stormed, or he could attack the causeway that led into the city from the west, which was more lightly held but stronger because it was under the protection of the Chapultepec batteries. Captain Robert E. Lee was one of those strategists Scott consulted, but for once Lee's advice was disregarded and the strategy of Pierre Beauregard adopted. Scott chose to attack Chapultapec itself, doing so on September 13.

Seasoned assault parties from the divisions of Generals Worth and Twigg set out to storm the bastion, clawing and shooting their way up a hill nearly vertical in the midst of a punishing return fire of musketry. Amazingly, the Americans managed to climb the palace walls with scaling ladders and actually drove the defenders out—including the young cadets at the Mexican Military College, who stayed even after Santa Ana had ordered them to be relieved. The resultant capture of Chapultepec and its fortress effectively opened a way into the city itself. Hoping to mollify his innumerable grievances through allowing him to finish the job, General Worth was permitted to work his way down one causeway. It was the one Santa Ana himself was bitterly defending, yet Worth was able to penetrate that defense and get a little way into the city proper before finally digging in for the night. The same held true for General Quitman, who fought his way down another causeway just as stubbornly defended as the first.

To draw as many as possible of the Mexican troops away from the defense of Chapultepec, Twiggs feinted against the San Antonio *garita*—a stone structure pre- viously used to house the police and a customs station. At daybreak on the fourteenth, Quitman's Division, with support from Smith's brigade, attacked northward from Tacubaya and pushed his force on into the center of the city while Hitchcock, Worth and Scott talked terms with civilians who were wanting to surrender. General Pillow then, supported by Worth and with aid from Quitman's advance, attacked and captured Chapultepec in the face of gallant resistance, whereupon Quitman proceeded up the Belen Road and seized the *garita* Belen. Worth passed through Pillow's troops and, in a heavy action, took control of San Cosme Garita. There, at 7 a.m. in the Plaza de Armas,

# The Infinite Dream

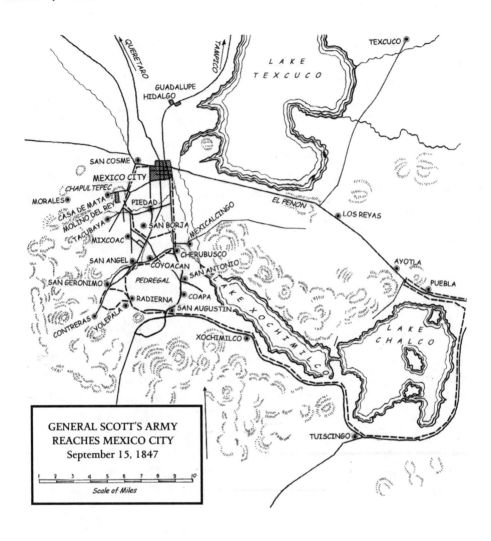

atop the Palace of the Montezumas, Quitman raised the American flag to thundering cheers from the Americans—the first American flag ever to fly above the capital of a conquered nation. They discovered that Santa Ana and his troops had fled the city during the night. But before leaving, Santa Ana freed and armed all the convicts in city jail and they, with the local criminal element, fired upon the Americans, causing stern measures to be taken to suppress them. Two hours later, General Scott himself entered the National Palace—having closed the book on a classic feat of generalship pulled off against all but impossible odds and one that at last put an end to formal military opposition in Mexico.

So now, in his headquarters, only mere minutes before the end of this highly eventful day, Major General Winfield Scott wearily completed writing his official report to the War Department and, for once, was well pleased with what he was finally able to write—an accounting of the tumultuous events that had brought to a close, at last, the War with Mexico.[257]

[*September 19, 1847 • Sunday*]

The military government's occupation of Sutters Fort had finally come to an end after, so far as John Sutter was concerned, much too long an interval. The government launch had arrived at mid-day, an Army lieutenant aboard, with orders to permanently remove the U.S. garrison to Sonoma and return possession and control of the installation back to its owner. As much as Sutter had yearned for this day to come, his diary entry concerning it was extremely brief and unemotional:

*Sunday Septr 19th 1847*
  *The garrison was removed, Lieu't Per Lee took her down to San francisco* [sic].

[*September 23, 1847 • Thursday*]

General Stephen W. Kearny's letter to Adjutant General Roger Jones composed on Monday last—written from his temporary quarters in Washington, D.C., after a personal visit with President Polk –was typical of the type of caring commander he continued to be:

*Washington Sept. 20, 1847*
Sir
  *I have to call the attention of the Hon. Secy. Of War & thru' him that of the Presdt of the U.S. to the Services rendered by Major Cooke, 2d Dragoons—Capt Turner 1st Dragoons, & Lieut Emory of the Top*[ographical] *Engrs., all serving under me in the Expedition from Missouri to California, & I have most respectfully to recommend that the first named officer be honored with the Brevt Rank of Lieut Col., & the other two with that of Major.*
  *Major Cooke was assigned by me in October 1846 to the Command of the Mormon Battn., (5 Comps. of Infy.) with the Rank, Pay &c. of Lieut Col, & took command of that Battn. At Santa fe*

[sic]—*marched it over to the Pacific, where he arrived in January 1847 having left the Del Norte about 250 miles below Santa fe* [sic] *carrying his Baggage Waggons* [sic] *with him, the whole distance, & over a Country where Waggons* [sic] *had never before passed thus solving the Problem of the possibility of their doing so, which is to be a subject of much importance to the U.S. Maj. Cooke at the head of his Battn., marched on a portion of the frontier of Sonora, passing thru' Tueson* [sic], *from which place he drove off a considerable Mexican force which was collected to oppose his progress—He is highly talented, a most efficient Soldier & Disciplinarian, educated at West Point & has been in the Army since 1827...*

Brig. Genl. R. Jones            *Very Resp'y Your Ob. Servt*
Adjt. Gen'l., U.S.A                  *S.W. Kearny*
                                                 *Brig. Gen'l*

Though he had not anticipated any particular honor to himself for the services he had performed, General Kearny was more than pleased when today a site was officially selected by Lieutenant William Woodbury along the Platte River for a new Western post on the Oregon Trail; a new permanent installation, to be named Fort Kearny. The fort was to be built from scratch and was being established to replace the similarly named temporary post erected in 1846 on the Missouri River near the mouth of Table Creek. As Lieutenant Woodbury wrote:

*...I have located the post opposite a group of wooded islands in the Platte River, three hundred seventeen miles from Independence, Missouri, and three miles from the head of the group of islands called Grand Island....*[258]

[September 29, 1847 · Wednesday]

The work on the new grist mill at the Brighton site, five miles upstream from Sutters Fort and near Natoma, was already nearing completion and John Sutter was well pleased. Similarly, he was content that the sawmill under construction some thirty miles farther upstream, near Coloma, was also moving along well. In the latter case, while it would still be a considerable while before it was a fully-fledged lumber-producing operation, the mill itself was shaping up nicely under the skilled carpentry of James Marshall. Eight Indians had been hired and brought from Sutters Fort to do much of the heavier work of digging the mill race under close supervision of one of Marshall's foremen, Peter Wimmer. The crew of whites—almost all of them veterans of the Mormon Battalion—were working well together and, for the most part, very cheerful except on those occasions when it became necessary for them to associate with Jennie Wimmer.[259] The days of digging and building were long and tiring, but the crew worked with a generally pervasive aura of companionship and there was a customary sense of humor that was shared by all. Except, of course, for the fact that Jennie Wimmer continued to be the single thorn in a bed of roses.

Most of the white men hired as laborers by John Sutter were discharged Saints from the Mormon Battalion. They had been working at the gristmill just upstream from Sutter's where the mill structure itself was complete and all hands were laboring on the tailrace, broadening its width and gradually deepening it to effect an adequate water current through its entire length. As Henry Bigler wrote in his diary on September 17:

> ...all hands were on the ditch with spades, plows, picks, shovels, and a few scrapers, Sutter furnishing all the tools. Our teams to work on the race are oxen—Spanish cattle that we have gotten from Sutter as part pay. Some of them are not very well broken, and some have never seen a yoke nor anything else.... However, the boys soon got to manage them with very little trouble.

Ten days later, however, on September 27, Bigler wrote of a considerable change that had occurred for him and several others who were working with him at the grist-mill:

> ...when a man dressed in buckskin came to our quarters while we were at dinner, informing us that Captain Sutter wanted four men from our crowd to go with him (the man in buckskin) up the American fork into the mountains about thirty miles, to work and help build a sawmill. This man, whom we were to accompany, was James W. Marshall, an entire stranger to us, but proved to be a gentleman nevertheless. He told us that he had been up in the mountains with a few hands only a short time; but as some of them were going to leave soon he wished to get a few more. We learned

that he and Sutter were together in co-partnership in building the sawmill. So, late in the afternoon myself and three others set out with Mr. Marshall, accompanied by a Charles Bennett, late from Oregon and a former Dragoon under General Kearny, all taking at the same time an ox team and wagon loaded with provisions and a few tools.

The other three men selected were former Mormon Battalion members Israel Evans, William Johnson and Azariah Smith—the latter having long been a close companion of Bigler's in the Battalion. They stopped and camped overnight along the way and arrived at the proposed sawmill site near Coloma on September 29, where Bigler wrote in his diary:

Here I found several of the Battalion boys at work who had remained at Sutter's at the time our company passed there in August. Four, however, soon left and returned to the Fort and went to work on Sutter's flouring mill. The country around this new mill site looks wild and lonesome. Surrounded by high mountains on the south side of the river, the mountains are densely covered with pine, balsam, pinon pine, redwood, white oak and, low down, the live oak, while on the north side there is not so much timber; the mountains are more abrupt and rocky, covered in places with patches of chamisal and greasewood. This country is infested by wolves, grizzly bears, and Indians. The work now to be done is to get out mill timbers, dig out a mill site, put in a dam, and cut a tail race forty or fifty rods long. They have already built a nice double log cabin with a hall or entry between. The building is built of nice pine logs and covered with pine clapboards, riven out with a frow—bastard-fashion, as they call it.

The house is built by a spring gulch on the side of the mountain about one-fourth, or nearly so, of a mile from the mill site. Here the family of Peter L. Wimmer (including his wife [and] their seven children by former marriages) lives in the west end, while we others are using the east-end cabin to sleep in. Wimmer's wife, called "Jennie," the only white woman here, will do the cooking for the mill hands while Wimmer himself, who is 36, oversees the Indians (eight in number), showing them how to work.

# The Infinite Dream

The new foursome recruited from the grist mill immediately got to work at what their boss was openly referring to as the Marshall-Sutter Saw-mill, alongside those already employed there: Henry Bigler was quickly occupied with drilling at the head of the race, while William Scott and Charles Bennett, neither of them Mormons, were occupied doing bench work. William Barger and Alexander Stephens were utilized as axe men, hewing timber, along with Azariah Smith and William Johnson, while James S. Brown was engrossed in teaching one of the Indians the elements of whip-sawing. The brothers Ira and William Willis, along with William Kountz had just returned to the grist mill to aid Sutter in erecting a dam across the American River and Ezekiel Persons had returned to Sutters Fort due to ill health.

On October 3 those at the sawmill became alarmed when their "tame" Indians aroused them during the night to report that there were bad Indians sneaking around nearby, who would not reply when spoken to or tell what they wanted. This alarmed the whites, who became even further concerned last night, October 4, when the entire camp was disturbed and aroused again by calls of *"Malo hinty! Malo hinty!"*—Bad Indians!—from their own workers. As Bigler commented about it in his diary today:

> *We could see nothing but we could hear them walk. Our Indians said they saw some of them, and some of our party caught a glimpse of an Indian. We still could not get them to talk. They kept at a proper distance in the dark among the pine timber. Up to this time we had not thought of much danger, and we began to think we had been rather careless. There were ten white men and only four guns. We (the Mormon boys) had left our muskets below, and for the guns present there were scarcely any balls. All was in a bustle. Some commenced forthwith to molding bullets, others to cleaning and putting in order the guns, for some of them were in poor trim for an action. For the first time we set out a guard, and we will keep it up, too, for some time to come. The intruders, however, seem to have left entirely, finding out perhaps that we have something besides bows and arrows for them.*
>
> *Our grub here will be mainly unbolted flour, pork, mutton, salmon, peas, tea, coffee, and sugar. If Sutter should fail to send up supplies and we become short of meat, Mr. Marshall has chosen me*

to be his hunter and plans to frequently send me out with his rifle (and he has a good one) to kill a deer, as they are plenty, and [with] an Indian to carry it in. This kind of labor I have no objection to and will not grumble in the least if Marshall continues to keep it up.

As much as Henry Bigler enjoyed hunting—and as skilled as he was at it—this suited him just fine, especially since his wages for hunting remained the same as if he were working at manual labor along with the others.

[October 19, 1847 · Tuesday]

Now that he was no longer hampered by any real sense of devotion to the Church of Jesus Christ of Latter-day Saints, at least in his own mind if not yet openly, Samuel Brannan was a much happier individual and moved swiftly to preserve and expand his already substantial holdings. His own newspaper, the *California Star*, had just been delivered to the front door of his spacious San Francisco home and he settled down with it in his favorite chair to make sure his editor had placed the advertisement exactly where he had specified he wanted it.

The long and arduous journey he had taken on horseback to the Great Salt Lake and back had hardened him considerably, both physically and in spirit. The chiding he had received from Brigham Young in regard to where he felt the new seat of the Church should be established and his own role in it had most definitely changed him; not, however, as Young surmised, to the better service of God, but to the better service of the Lord God Brannan. Now that he had returned, though he clad himself just as meticulously as always and maintained the same debonair aura of dapper insouciance as before, there was somehow a greater sharpness in his mien, a more penetrating alertness than had been there previously, a much greater sharpening of his proclivity to take the fullest possible personal advantage of whatever situation confronted him. There were, he was learning, opportunities galore for expanding his own wealth and position in San Francisco and elsewhere and he was determined to let no opportunity pass him by for doing just that.

He still regularly collected tithes from the Saints still under his jurisdiction but now with a significant difference; the funds outwardly appearing to be for use to the betterment of God and God's flock but in reality finding their way quite conveniently into the coffers of one

Samuel Brannan. His clothes were the finest that could be purchased here or elsewhere, his home indisputably the most sumptuous mansion in San Francisco and being invited to the entertaining he did therein quickly became one of the hallmarks for getting ahead in the western world. The Brannan house indisputably was already the most popular gathering place for every person of power, wealth or influence on the Pacific shore; the accepted gathering place where those entertained included governors, important military officers and, most certainly, the more influential and wealthy land barons among the Spanish Californios. Rarely, however, were any of the Saints invited to enter his door, as he considered the majority to be much too "unpolished" in their demeanor.

Impressively sharp in business dealings, Brannan not only made an immediately favorable impression upon the more astute in San Francisco and elsewhere, he unhesitatingly took instant advantage of any business or profit opportunities that opened toward him, not only in the rapidly growing bayside town but equally in Monterey and at Sutters Fort, wjich was becoming better known by its new name of Sacramento. In short order he was the owner of numerous businesses and dabbled very heavily in real estate, owning at any given time scores of residences and lots. His success in such matters, abetted by his popularity among the gentiles and his outstanding success in money-making ventures, greatly distressed many of the Saints in his flock. The feeling was especially aggravated since he clearly had no intention of sharing his good fortune with them, which was, to their way of thinking, at cross-purposes to the precepts established aboard the *Brooklyn* before it left New York City's harbor, in which they and their leader had bound themselves to hold all things in common. A few others of the Saints were prospering, too— though none so spectacularly as Brannan—and it was the most destitute among his flock who were the most anxious to preserve the original precepts of Samuel Brannan & Company, where all would share equally. Not unexpectedly, increasing business opportunities, however selfishly engaged in, almost wholly undermined the original exalted premise by which they had bound themselves.

Once the reality of the situation sank in, the majority of Saints at New Hope lost little time in abandoning the pollyannic precepts under which their community had been established and many acquired farms of their own or, less willing to work so hard, became involved with business enterprises in the burgeoning city of San Francisco. Brannan lost no time in setting wheels in motion that would eventually allow him, under the purview of his office, to appropriate even the improvements and farm that had initially been earmarked for the Twelve.

Just two days ago, still maintaining his façade of devotion to the LDS, he had written enthusiastically to President Young and the Twelve:

> ...The friendly feeling and confidence of the people and government of this country still continues to grow stronger and stronger in our favor. Since my return home the subscription list of the Star has increased nearly double. I forward you full files to this date. My reception since my return by all classes has been with the warmest and kindest feelings.... The Star takes a bold stand and a straightforward course, cutting to the line and at the same time meeting with universal approbation. On my return home I deemed it most prudent to dissolve our company association from the fact that a great many were idle and indolent and would try to live upon the earnings of the few, and at the same time it would leave me less incumbered [sic] to perform the duties involved upon me in sustaining the interest of the cause of Zion.
>
> I hope, brethren, that you will not suffer your minds to be prejudiced or doubt my loyalty from any rumors or reports that may be put in circulation by brethren or others.... I want your confidence, faith and prayers, feeling that I will discharge my duties under all circumstances, and then I am happy. No undertaking will then be too great or any burden too heavy. I hope it may be counted wisdom by your council for one of your number to visit us next fall.... My whole soul, might and strength is bent on laboring for you night and day. I look upon no one as being judges [sic] of the fruits of my labor except your honorable body. To you I stand ready at any moment to render an account of my stewardship...
>
> About twenty of the Battalion are working here in town and are doing well. About the same number are at Captain Sutter's and many more scattered about different parts of the Bay, and as far as I can learn, they are doing well.

That same day Brannan's advertisement had appeared in the *Star* and neatly initiated the liquidation of the assets of Samuel Brannan & Company and commenced the ultimate dissolution of that institution:

> *The subscribers offer for sale, on reasonable terms, the following effects of the late firm of Samuel Brannan & Co., as follows:*
>
> *A large quantity of wheat; American cattle, horses and mules; A large quantity of a good breed of pigs; A valuable lot, situated on the corner of Kearny and Pacific Streets; a lot and farm house, cor. of Clay and Stockton Streets; school books; Harper's Family Library, 169 volumes; A medium chest; The launch,* Comet; *Wagons, chairs, yokes; Two drums, muskets, swords, powder, etc.; Linen thread, wicking; one hat block, matches, and twine; Castor oil, mustard, soap, eight hundred barrels salt, empty hogsheads, etc. etc.*

However much of the above listing that could be sold, Brannan was willing to share the proceeds with the Saints in his flock, but those items that could not be immediately sold, Brannan was determined to claim for himself.[260]

### [October 28, 1847 • Thursday]

John Sutter was well pleased with the work thus far accomplished in the establishment of the new lumber mill being erected by James Marshall and his helpers near Coloma. He hoped—and felt assured—that the mill-race would be dug and the mill itself completed toward the end of December or, if not, then surely no later than mid-January, at which time the much-needed enterprise could go into full operation. The fact that that arbitrary date was already a couple of days past did not bother him as much as he had anticipated it might. Certainly by the beginning of February all the preparations would be finished and he was content with that projection. More than ever he eagerly anticipated completion of the construction and the benefits that would accrue equally to himself and Marshall with the lumber sales that would result. The mill, he thought, would almost certainly become every bit as productive and profitable as the new flour mill, just upstream from the fort, was already proving itself to be.

Marshall, accompanied by former Mormon Battalion captain James Brown, had arrived on horseback here at the fort yesterday to report on what progress had thus far been made and Sutter was delighted that, despite his initial projections, which were admittedly very optimistic, the work was actually progressing even faster than he had more realistically anticipated. He was glad that his early assessment of Marshall's skills and energy had proven out thus far without reservation.

Only moments ago Marshall and Brown had headed back to the saw-mill, Brown now having been appointed, with Sutter's hearty approval, Marshall's second-in-command at the operation, where the white workers were concerned. Now, however, before adding today's comments to his New Helvetia Logbook, Sutter took the time to page back through his log entries over the past fortnight to review, briefly, what he'd written on matters regarding the operation under Marshall's control:

> *Tuesday, Septr 28th 1847—...started Ezekiah [Azariah] [sic] Smith, Henry Bigler, William Johnson and Israel Evans, for the sawmill seat. Mr. Gingery started with Sidney Willis, Brouet & Wm. Kelley, to build two large flat boats, to build the Dam. Allen, Thomas, Dun [Thomas J Dunn] & 3 other Men left for the Mountains to make Shingels [sic], Clapboards and getting more timber out for the Mill. Despatched [sic] a Wagon for the Sawmill seat.*

Sutter paused momentarily in his reading to reflect on recent happenings here at the fort. A great many new emigrants had continued showing up here, mainly from other locations in California and Sutter somehow always found work for all of them to do at fair recompense. That his aims to establish something of an empire in the Sacramento Valley involved his hiring of native Indians almost on a slave-labor basis seemed to bother him not at all. The natives were, for the most part, entirely satisfied with the manner in which he paid them, which was primarily in trade goods rather than cash money. He very easily snared them into a credit-and-debt set-up which, once begun, it was almost impossible for them to break free and he had the benefit of their virtually unpaid labor in regard to his various forms of farming and livestock raising, the tanning of cow hides in his leather-making operations, large-scale manufacturing of adobe bricks and other similar manual labors requiring brawn but very little thinking, including various types of housework, the digging of drainage ditches, milling of grain into flour, gardening, and the butchering of sheep and cattle for meat and various by-products. One day, he was sure, they would come to him and demand more in payment, but until such time arrived, he was quite content to maintain the status quo.

Lighting his pipe with a burning twig from the fireplace, Sutter now continued to scan through his own words as he had written about the continuing efforts to get the saw-mill up and running. Actually, little had occurred of moment during the remainder of October and November except for a continuation of the work of actually erecting the saw-mill. Sutter's failure to follow through speedily in sending along necessary provisions, however, made it very difficult for Marshall and the workers there. Had it not been for the hunting skills of Henry Bigler, the food situation at the mill site could have caused severe problems. Bigler's acceptance by the others as principal hunter for the group was not unexpected but nevertheless gratifying and, as he wrote in his diary:

> *Nov. 6th. I rested from my work today and went out with my gun to look for my horse, found him and also found a large blacktailed deer within reach of my bullet. An Indian with me carried it to the camp.*
>
> *Nov. 15th. I have spent much of my time in hunting, for which Marshall pays the same wages as for work at the mill, and he sends an Indian with me to carry home my deer. Sutter had neglected to send provisions and we should have been on short allowance but for my game.*

Sutter's negligence in sending the promised provisions when needed was not a deliberate oversight; simply the result of his having so many irons in so many fires that occasionally he simply forgot. Now, however, he had seen to the problem and was gratified to write as today's logbook entry:

> *Saturday Novmbr 20th The 5 Wagon loads of provisions that I had finally gotten off to the sawmill have, according to Mr. Marshall, arrived there safely and before the rainy season set it* [in]. *Those supplies should serve them well until Spring.*

Sutter blotted the page, set the log aside and sighed, vaguely wishing the saw-mill was in operation now and regretting the revenue being missed, since realistically it would still probably be close to six weeks more before it could be up and running.

*[November 22, 1847 • Monday]*

Despite definitive peace talks being engaged in and preliminary documents approved and signed, the War with Mexico was not yet over and heated fighting was intensifying in the western regions of Mexico, though thus far still to American benefit.

Commodore William B. Shubrick had landed a week ago with his U.S. Marines to occupy San José del Cabo, a farming center at the southern tip of the Baja Peninsula. Since then he had consolidated the American foothold there, despite the fact that a Mexican scratch force raised by Capt. Manuel Pinada attacked the little command of Lt. Col. Henry S. Burton that had been sent ahead as an advance by Shubrick. Fortunately, Burton's New Yorkers, though outnumbered, had been able to fight them off. However, since Captain Shubrick had immediately thereafter sailed on to capture Mazatlan on Mexico's west coast, this forced Governor Mason to weaken his own command in California by sending a company of his men to reinforce Burton near Cabo San Lucas at the southern tip of the Baja.

No, the war was not over. Not yet.

# Chapter 16

◆

*[December 21, 1847 • Tuesday]*

John Sutter was pleased with the word just received by express messenger from his lumber enterprise partner that the work on the lumber mill near Coloma was moving along much faster than anticipated. The message from James Marshall was characteristically to the point:

*Millwork ahead of schedule. Mill-iron models are being sent to you today shd [sic] arrive tomorrow and be cast at once in duplicate to complete the set, with spares of each on hand in case of cracking or breakage due to iron fatigue ocuring [sic] God forbid. Deversion [sic] dam near ready now and Millrace digging shd [sic] be all done and test ready in about one month.*

Gratified that matters were moving along well, Sutter was pleased with the quality and thoroughness of Marshall's work thus far and commended himself for agreeing to the partnership, which he remained convinced would turn out to be of considerable benefit to them both. The mill road construction was already nearing completion between them and the new roadbed was holding itself well despite the rainy season underway. Since his own initial tardiness in shipping provisions to the mill site, Sutter had been quite on time with all the necessaries and planned to continue punctually. He had even accepted—slightly less than graciously—his partner's naming of the operation as the Marshall-Sutter Sawmill and remained a bit rankled that his own name did not come first. It as not, however, a matter important enough to create a stir.

On October 30 the beautifully sunny autumn weather had changed quite drastically, with a biting wind from the north and overnight the Sierra peaks to the east had become snow-covered. Numerous flights of geese en route southward from Oregon Territory split the skies with their V-wedges and distant honkings. The following day, however, it warmed a bit and became densely overcast, causing Sutter to write in his log during the next two days:

> *Sunday October 31th [sic] 1847 A strong wind from the South, threatening to rain, called the people in to work and get done with cleaning Wheat, but they are coming very slow...in the Night very heavy rains.*
>
> *Monday Novbr 1st 1847 Getting with a great deal of trouble and with breaking wagons the four Runs of Millstones to the Mill Site (Brighton) from the Mountains.*

The following day it rained heavily at intervals and on November 3 rain pelted down throughout the entire night. It continued sporadically day after day and when word was received that four pairs of millstones had been received at Nemshaw, Sutter took steps to get them to their destination swiftly and safely, writing in his logbook:

> *Friday Novr 12th 1847 Despatched [sic] Wittmer [sic, should be Wimmer] with four of the best Wagons the best drivers & 12 Yoke of Oxen, and Ajeas & Achilles, to get two of the four pairs of Millstones...A good Many of the Working hands here from the Mill & Millrace...*
>
> *Saturday, Novr 13th 1847 Wm Stevens arrived from the Sawmill seat and brought a letter from Marshall. Visiting the Mill, Millrace & Dam.*

The letter from Marshall was nothing more than a simple work report to keep Sutter advised on conditions and progress; the men had been laboring in the business of felling trees, constructing the brush dam across the South Fork and daily deepening the channel for the mill site race by the expedient of turning in the water by night to carry off sand and debris and then utilizing the men by day to remove accumulated stones and obstructions and continue digging. For the next two days, Sutter wrote:

> *Started 5 Wagons with provisions…principally to the Sawmill Site. Two white men, Frazier & Woodworth, went with the Wagon's* [sic] *Stevens & Dun*[n] *left likewise…. In the night the Millstone Expedition arrived with Wittmer &* [John] *Mouet, only 3 Stones arrived, one Wagon brocke right on the Spot with a rock. Rain.*
>
> *Wednesday Novr 17th 1847 Despatched* [sic] *Millstones to The Mill.*

Little of note occurred during the remainder of the month apart from the continuing work on erection of the grist mill—which was one of several such flour mills he had in the region—and on the digging of its extensive race. Sutter was gratified at the progress being made and on the final day of the month wrote in his log:

> *Tuesday Novr 30th 1847 …Went to Natomo* [Natoma] *to see how they are raising the fram* [sic] *of the* [grist-] *Mill. 34 hands has been employed on it, and all was going on well and no accident happened.*

Work continued apace and on December 3 Sutter was able to dispatch an additional four wagons to the forty-mile-distant saw-mill site with provisions. Two days later he hired another experienced carpenter—a newcomer named Tom Scott—and sent him at once to the saw-mill to assist Marshall. Nothing more of consequence occurred until mid-month when a large number of the hands at the grist mill were given a couple of days time-off from work, preparatory to commencement of scraping the millrace, so they could come to Sutters Fort for a rest and to replenish their own personal supplies at his store. On December 18, Marshall himself arrived from the more distant saw-mill site to inform Captain Sutter that some unfamiliar Indians had shown up at there and killed one of his working bullocks for no apparent reason except mischief. Sutter had immediately dispatched a posse of his own guard force of Indians to attempt to apprehend those tribesmen responsible, but a sudden rainstorm destroyed the traces of where they had gone and the posse returned.

Then, the day before yesterday, Sutter had ten yoke of oxen delivered with their yokes to the men at work on the American River grist mill race, loaning them, as Sutter wrote:

*...Chaines* [sic], *Scrapers, ploughs, etc.... and the wagon from the Sawmill returned.*

Yesterday, even more activity occurred, about which Sutter wrote:

*Monday December 20th 1847 Sending provisions to the grist Mill race. Getting firewood and hauling logs for the Coalpit. Repairing Wagons. Commencing on the Mill-irons for the Saw mill...*

Throughout all, James Marshall continued diligently readying the Marshall-Sutter Sawmill site. While his company of white men refined the carpentry and fitting work being done on the saw-mill itself and the Indians, working under Marshall's personal instruction, relayed through his assistant, Peter Wimmer, labored daily on the mill race that would eventually channel the river's main current through the great paddle-wheel, Marshall himself continued making the models for the mill-irons that would be needed. As these models were completed, Marshall shipped them off to Sutters Fort, where foundryman Levi Fifield was already at work casting them. In another fortnight, Sutter thought, Marshall should have everything ready for final installation and inspection and full lumber production could begin.

[December 31, 1847 • Friday]

His curiosity finally getting the better of him, Richard Grant had at last resolved to see for himself what it was the Mormons were doing who were attempting to establish themselves in what they called their new Zion at the southeastern rim of Great Salt Lake. As head of the Hudson's Bay Company's western headquarters at Fort Hall in the Idaho country, Grant had noted with interest the greater number of emigrants from the east heading onward to Oregon but, at the same time, an influx of Mormon men moving southeastward from his post as they were en route from California to the new Mormon headquarters they were grandiosely calling Salt Lake City.

Those men were almost all former soldiers of the now defunct Mormon Battalion and their service for the U.S. Army completed, they had been discharged and were now traveling as private citizens to be reunited with their families where they had apparently gathered to settle at the southeastern rim of the Great Salt Lake. Grant could hardly imagine a less hospitable region in which to attempt to establish a settlement. That thousands of the Saints were already there and settling in, with perhaps tens of thousands more poised to join them from what they called Winter Quarters along the Missouri River simply boggled his imagination and he had to see for himself.

Joining with one group of returning Saints of the Mormon Battalion traveling under command of their former lieutenant, James Pace, they had arrived at Salt Lake City on October 16 and Richard Grant was privileged to share in the great joy experienced both by those returning and those who had already arrived from Winter Quarters on the Missouri River and assembled at the new Zion and waited. Some of the former Battalion members found, much to their relief and joy, their families, friends and relatives living in a fort of sorts, consisting of a row of buildings running at right angles around a block fully enclosing ten acres. These adjoining buildings all had rooms that opened into the enclosure and, on the outer side, had portholes for both ventilation and defense.

The entrance to this large enclosure was through a huge gate situated in the center of the eastern row of buildings—a gate opened during the daytime but firmly locked at night to ward against possible attack by hostile Indians or, even more likely, hostile Missourians.[261]

Grant noted that many of the returning former Mormon Battalion members were all but destitute of adequate clothing and what they wore was little more than rags remaining of their former uniforms or what little had been supplemented by buckskins. Almost immediately, however, community leaders at Salt Lake City—led by President John Taylor and presiding Bishop Edward Hunter—made a collection of whatever clothing could be donated by the families already in residence and this clothing was liberally doled out to the returned "Battalion boys," who accepted it gratefully. Nothing that had been donated was considered unfit, as anything that would cover their nakedness was entirely acceptable. Need and comfort were the keynotes, not style, but the result turned out to be a ludicrous assemblage of men clad in a wide variety of garb. Not all of the former Battalion members returning were in dire straits in regard to their clothing, of course. A few returned very well fitted out, but hardly having the appearance of the Saints who had marched away more than a year before. Their encounter with the Mexican culture had created a jarring impact upon them which, for many,

# The Infinite Dream

influenced the way they were clad when they reached Salt Lake City. Most were coming back in the form of seasoned frontiersmen, which was often reflected in their garb. As John Steele wrote:

> *Our men that looked natural enough when they left Council Bluffs, now look like mountaineers, sunburned and weather beaten, mostly dressed in buckskin with fringes and porcupine quills, moccasins, Spanish saddles and spurs, Spanish bridles and jinglers at them, and long beards, so that if I looked in the glass for the young man who left the Bluffs a year ago, I would not have known myself. Went away afoot, came home riding a fine horse.*

On their march through the Southwest, all these former members of the Mormon Battalion had greatly broadened their own experience, well beyond what might possibly have occurred had they remained with their families. Among other new things, they had gained firsthand knowledge of a Mexican culture that was almost entirely Catholic and they were further influenced by their encounters with Indians, both civilized and wild. The very experience they had gained through the adventures they endured had conferred upon them a confidence and courage they would otherwise not have experienced and imbued with a rather striking sort of resilience and independence. As James S. Brown put it so well, "We became accustomed to pioneer life."

The "giving" done for the benefit of the returning former soldiers had not been all one-sided, sine many of the Battalion boys had returned with cuttings of fruit trees and seeds of various vegetables that might do well in the climate of the Great Salt lake basin; seeds and cuttings that were a greater godsend to those already in residence than anyone had actually anticipated. Foremost among these were the agricultural products brought along by both Lt. James Pace and Sgt. Dan Tyler; the former with a plentiful supply of the seeds of club-head wheat, which some came to believe was developed by God for growth in the Great Salt Lake Valley, since it took hold so splendidly; the latter with numerous containers of dried California peas which did extremely well and quickly became known as the field pea of Utah. A secondary variety of wheat, known as the *taos* grain, was brought by the detached Battalion members who arrived almost simultaneously from Pueblo in the Colorado country near the headwaters of the Arkansas River. Cuttings of apples and peaches, apricots and pears also sprang into beneficial life almost immediately upon planting. As much as anything else, the potatoes brought along thrived well and instantly became a major crop in the area.

Despite how well they did, none of the seeds, tubers or cuttings were sufficient to sustain the Saints through this first winter at Great Salt Lake, but the emigrants were by now well accustomed to deprivation and they possessed the will and determination to see through the lean times until next year and the years following, when all the crops would begin producing well. As Tyler wrote in his continuing journal:

> ...I left six quarts of the California peas with Brother Seely Owens, who proposed to raise them on shares, giving me one-half of the proceeds on my arrival the next year [and] on my arrival in the fall of 1847, with my family, Brother Owens delivered to me half a bushel of dry peas, stating that while they were the best and most prolific peas he ever saw, these were all he had saved.

Some of the peas had been ready for use as fresh green peas as early as the previous June, but Owens and his family, with their provisions all but exhausted, had subsisted mainly upon them until the late heavy frosts of last fall had stopped their bearing.

"Up until that time," Owens declared, "the crops were successive and a new crop came in just as fast as the first crop was picked off. I will make compensation for what I have used over what portion was due me, but I would like a few for seeding if you can spare them. I definitely do not want to be out of them as seeds of such a prolific and tasty variety."

Tyler nodded. "I'll be glad to take a half of what is left," he said, "and consider the matter satisfactorily settled. I still want to give a couple of quarts of the seeds to others, but that will still leave me about six quarts for next spring's planting."[262]

Through all this, Brigham Young was absent in person, though not in spirit. He had returned to Winter Quarters on the right bank of the Missouri in order to lead back to the new Zion those Saints still amassing from the march across Iowa. These emigrants—still upwards of 10,000 of them—were being prepared by Young to resume the westward march as soon as the weather permitted next spring and he vowed he would lead them all again to their new Zion, where they would assemble "as God's own children in God's own mansion" by next fall.

Among the returning Mormon Battalion members was former Lt. William Hyde, another journal-keeper, who faithfully documented his own arrival at the new Zion in October:

*Reached the camp of the saints in Salt Lake Valley on the 12th of October. The reception with which we met gladened [sic] our hearts and revived our spirits. A small portion of the company found their families here, and consequently had got home. The Presidency [sic] and some of the pioneers had returned to Winter Quarters. The saints that were remaining felt very well pleased with the situation of the Valley, and my conclusions were that it was a place of retreat, or a hiding place which God had, in his wisdom, prepared for his people.*

Many of the returnees, however, became immediately dissatisfied with what they found at the new Zion, the Great Salt Lake Valley not living up to their expectations of what it should be. Some of the men of such reasoning decided to return to California immediately, others to continue eastward and into Iowa to settle. Many, however—probably most—elected to cast their lots with those of their Brethren already settling in the Salt Lake Valley and were quite determined to remain loyal to Mormonism for the remainder of their lives.

The men who returned now to the anchor of the church more or less split into three factions: those few who had found their families already awaiting them at the new Zion and who needed to go no farther; those who did not truly wish to stay but were forced into doing so because of illness or fatigue, and those who preferred to remain in the Great Salt Valley and prepare a home for their families who would eventually leave Winter Quarters and join them here. There were, however, thirty-two of their number who were so eager to be reunited with their wives and children that they simply could not wait and so did not hesitate to continue the journey, even though it meant an additional thousand-mile march eastward at a time of year when sudden storms and deep snows could quite probably cause them great difficulties, perhaps even their lives.

Those inclined toward such a journey were informed that plenty of flour could be obtained at Fort Bridger, 115 miles distant, and so, relying on that prospect, they had left the Great Salt Lake Valley on October 18 and started the hazardous journey eastward in high spirits, each man supplied with about ten pounds of flour. Their spirits were dampened considerably, however, when just as they arrived at Fort Bridger, the first major snowstorm of the season struck and they learned, to their chagrin, that the stock of flour that had been on hand there for sale had all been purchased by previously passing emigrants bound for Oregon or California and none remained.

"Hell's bells," Jim Bridger remarked, "not only is the flour all gone, we didn't even think to reserve some for our *own* needs. Now we're stuck with eatin' only meat 'til somehow we k'n git replenished. Since you fellers're headin' east though, I 'spect ya'll k'n git whatever ye need on fairly reasonable terms at Laramie."

So they had purchased a small amount of dried beef there to hold them until they could bring down some game, and pushed on. It was a tough march and, as Tyler wrote about it in his journal:

> *We killed two buffalo bulls before reaching Laramie, and jerked the best of the meat. We had an occasional cake until we reached the upper crossing of the Platte, 100 miles above the fort. There we baked our last cake on the 4th of November, having made our 10 pounds of flour, each, last sixteen days. Of course, during that time we had eaten considerable buffalo and other beef and occasionally had some small game, including one elk killed by Wm. Maxwell.*

All this was information imparted to Richard Grant shortly after he arrived at Salt Lake City and now he had, in fact, seen with his own eyes the unbelievable activity occurring at the site and had been deeply impressed by it all, despite the fact that he had been primed by many passing travelers, especially those from Missouri, to be wary of the Mormons, who were, as it was put to him, "so different."

Because such an occurrence could not help to be of interest to the governing board of the Hudson's Bay Company, Grant, now back at his own desk in the Fort Hall post, was taking the opportunity to write to his company's chairman of the board of directors, Sir George Simpson:

> *In this Wild Mountainous Country great changes are daily taking place, between here and the Great Salt Lake, a distance of about two hundred miles, we now see several Mormon Farmers settled down to begin farming and grazing operations. At the Great Salt Lake is*

> already a population of principally—I would say all—Mormons, exceeding 3,000 souls, the work they have done there since their arrival in July last, is scarcely to be credited without seeing. They have already built up of their present residences about 600 Adouby [adobe] or sunburnt brick houses, besides three or four mills under way, with a wall enclosing the place about 1-1/4 miles square. From what I have seen and the dealings I have had with a number of those people I have found them the reverse of what they are generally represented, particularly by the Folks of the western States. They appear to be what I found them: a moral good set of people polite in their demands and ready to pay for what they get.

It was an assessment that more and more gentiles were acknowledging, once they experienced first-hand association with the Mormons and knew they could no longer trust the tales they had been told by the detractors of the Saints.

*[January 8, 1848 • Saturday]*

At last the Mexican commissioners, in conference with U.S. negotiators at Guadalupe Hidalgo were making advances toward the establishment of a peace treaty between themselves and the United States. February 2 had now been tentatively scheduled as the date when Mr. Trist, on behalf of the United States, along with the Mexican peace negotiators, would formally sign the final peace treaty between the two nations at the little town of Guadalupe Hidalgo, west of Mexico City.

President Polk was being strongly urged, now that Mexico was, in fact, defeated and its army in total disarray, to simply annex the entire country of Mexico to the United States, but he absolutely refused to consider such a proposal and, instead, instructed his negotiators to give the Mexican people terms very nearly as liberal as those that had been offered to them before General Scott had stormed Chapultepec. This, in essence, meant that all the many lives that had been lost on both sides in the fierce battle had, in essence, been pointlessly sacrificed.

It all made little sense to the American public, but the die was now cast.

*[January 9, 1848 • Sunday]*

There was, in John Sutter's temperament lately, a sense of

growing excitement over the saw-mill near Coloma finally approaching completion. In the latest dispatch from James Marshall, work was progressing "steadily and well," though still with a substantial amount of friction existing between the white mill-hands and the camp's designated cook, Jennie Wimmer. It was a problem in which Sutter was clearly disinclined to become involved, yet he admitted to himself that it was growing so intense he would undoubtedly soon have to step in and settle the matter one way or another. Not yet, however; the saw-mill was still a low-priority matter and only one among numerous others vying for his attention.

John Sutter's empire was branching out in numerous directions and 1848 bore promise of becoming a banner year for him in numerous enterprises—agricultural projects, dairy concerns, beef production and butchering, sheep production with its resultant shearing, baling and shipping of the wool; horse breeding and breaking; hog raising and butchering; land development and its sales and rentals to the growing influx of emigrants; flour milling for the entire surrounding region and the baking of breads to fill the growing needs and, most certainly, firearm production.

Indians by the hundreds were on hand to be recruited and instructed in the proper means of preparing the land, sowing the wheat and oats and barley and corn and subsequently reaping the grains when they matured; milling the dried grains into fine flours and meals; planting and pruning and tending the extensive orchards and vineyards and pressing and barreling the grapes for wines; processing the meat from growing herds of cattle to be butchered; tanning and working into fine leather the multitude of cowhides; making the shoes and boots and moccasins needed by all; managing the corps of trappers headquartered here and grading, tanning, baling and shipping the furs and elk hides they harvested; training the Indians to plant and tend and harvest the steadily increasing acreages of vegetable crops; managing and training the corps of native fishermen in seasonal spearing and netting of the vast schools of salmon and sturgeon that migrated up the Sacramento and processing their roe into fine caviar, mainly to be shipped abroad; maintaining and operating the distillery; firing the forge and smelting and blacksmithing and producing sturdy tools; ferrying passengers to and from San Francisco in the launch. Thus, the gradually shaping sawmill was, for Sutter, a matter of keen interest but still not yet fully

# The Infinite Dream

imbued with the priority of other endeavors already established here and in full operation.

Edwin Bryant spent some quality time at the fort just as the year turned and his description of what he found painted a broad and comprehensive word picture:

> *A garden of eight or ten acres is attached to the fort, laid out with taste and skill, where flourishes all kinds of vegetables, grapes, apples, peaches, pears, olives, figs and almonds. Horses, cattle, and sheep cover the surrounding plains; boats lie at the embarcardero.*
>
> *The fort is a parallelogram of adobe walls, 500 feet long by 150 in breadth, with loop-holes and bastions at the angles, mounted with a dozen cannon that sweep the curtains. Within is a collection of granaries and warehouses, shops and stores, dwellings and outhouses, extending near and along the walls 'round the central building occupied by the Swiss potentate, who holds sway as patriarch and priest, judge and father. The interior of the houses is rough, with rafters [exposed] and unpainted walls, with benches and deal-tables, the exception being the audience-room and private apartments of the owner, who has obtained from the Russians a clumsy set of California furniture; the first made in the country, he says, and strikingly superior to the crude furniture of the Californios, with rawhide and bullock-head chairs and bed-stretchers. The dining room has merely benches and a deal-table, yet displays silver spoons and China bowls, the latter serving for dishes as well as cups. In front of the main building, on the small square, is a brass gun, guarded by the sentinel, whose measured tramp, lost in the hum of day, marks the stillness of the night, and stops alone beneath the belfry-post to chime the passing hour.*
>
> *Throughout the day the enclosure presents an animated scene of work and trafficking, by bustling laborers, diligent mechanics, and eager traders, all to the chorus clang of the smithy and reverberating strokes of the carpenters. Horsemen dash to and fro at the bidding of duty and pleasure, and an occasional wagon creaks along upon the gravelly road-bed, sure to pause for recuperating purposes before the trading store kept by Smith and Brannan. Prices are $1 a foot for horse-shoeing, $1 a bushel for wheat, peas $1.50, unbolted flour $8 a 100-lbs. Here confused voices mingle with laughter and sometimes*

*the discordant strains of drunken singers. Such is the capital of the vast interior valley, pregnant with approaching importance.*

*At the close of last month Sutter reported a white population of 289 in the district, with 16 half-breeds, Hawaiians, and negroes, 479 tame Indians, and a large number of gentiles, estimated with not very good precision at 21,873 for the valley, including the region above the Buttes. There are 60 houses in or near the fort, and six [grist] mills and one tannery in the district; 14,000 fanegas of wheat were raised during the season, and 40,000 expected during the following year, besides other crops. Sutter owns 12,000 cattle, 2,000 horses and mules, from 10,000 to 15,000 sheep, and 1,000 hogs. There are 30 ploughs in operation. John Sinclair figures as alcalde, and George McKinstry [sic, but should be McKinistry] as sheriff.*

*The greater portion of people round the fort depend upon Sutter as permanent or temporary employees, the latter embracing immigrants preparing to settle, and Mormons intent on presently proceeding to Great Salt Lake. As a class they present a hardy, backwoods type of rough exterior, relieved here and there by bits of Hispano-Californian attire, in bright sashes, wide sombreros, and jingling spurs. The natives appear probably to better advantage here than elsewhere in California, in the body of half a hundred well-clothed soldiers trained by Sutter, and among his staff of steady servants and helpers, who have acquired both skill and neatness. A horde of subdued savages, engaged as herders, tillers, and laborers, are conspicuous by their half-naked, swarthy bodies; and others may be seen moving about, bent on gossip or trade, stalking along, shrouded in the all-shielding blanket, which the winter chill has obliged them to put on. Head and neck, however, bear evidence to their love of finery, in gaudy kerchiefs, strings of beads, and other ornaments.*

Through all that was occurring as the old year ended and the new commenced, Sutter maintained his daily log and the progress with sawmill related matters was duly recorded. For the final two days of 1847 he had written:

*Friday December 31st 1847 Sending two large teames [sic] to*

> the Coal pit, getting Coals here.... Working on the Sawmill irons.... Dispatched a wagon with provisions to the [saw]Mill, upper house and Dam.
>
> Saturday January 1th [sic] 1848 All hands worked on the [saw-]Mill dam, which is built of brush.

The latter entry was sketchy in the extreme, considering the near-tragedy that had occurred and it was only in Bigler's diary that a more complete idea of the jeopardy they had faced became apparent, as he wrote:

> By New Year's we had the mill frame up and the fore bay in and ditch dug for the tail race, but it was found not to be deep enough and we had already struck the base rock (a rotten granite). This was rather a drawback as it was now going to be a slow job to cut it out deep enough. In order to economize labor, a dry channel was selected 40 or 50 rods long, which had to be deepened and widened. This involved some blasting at the upper end; but elsewhere it was found necessary merely to have the Indians loosen the earth in the bed by day, throwing out the larger stones, and let the water during the night pass through the sluice-gate to wash away the debris. The dam was nearly completed. We had built it of brush laid in with the butts downstream, but it commenced to rain and continued for several days. The river rose, a flood resulted that threatened to sweep away the whole structure and fears were entertained that all our work would be lost. Marshall directed us as we worked in the rain almost night and day to save the dam and mill. We did save it.

Marshall remained almost constantly on hand now, directing the Indian workers during the daytime hours, then opening the sluice-gate at night and patrolling the ditch to make certain it drained well throughout the night, sweeping along with it whatever dirt the Indians had loosened. At Sutters Fort, John Sutter continued writing his sketchy entries:

> Monday January 3th [sic] 1848 Mr. Robert Pixton arrived from the Sawpits in the Mountains to get provisions, as they are out. Commenced to rain at 3 OClock in the Morning and continued nearly the whole day.

*Tuesday January 4th 1848 Robt Pixton left with Wittmer* [sic, but should be Wimmer] *with provisions to the Mountains.*

*Thursday January 6th 1848 Started 4 teams to the Mountains, under Command of Charles. Woodworth arrived with the team from the sawmill—Wittmer returned likewise.*

*Friday January 7th 1848 Today the Sawmill Crank has been commenced and will be finished to morrow* [sic] *as the iron is good, this the heaviest kind of Blacksmith work which ever has been done here, and* [I] *give Fifield great Credit as a good workman.*

*Saturday January 8th 1848 Despatched* [sic] *two Wagons more to the Mountains under Command of Jacob Wittmer, to get lumber to the Mill. Finishing the Sawmill Crank. A good many people of the Neighbourhood* [sic] *here. At 10 OClock in the Night the four Wagons under Comand* [sic] *of Charles returned here, after having made the trip in 3 days,—the lumber they have discharged at the Mill at Natoma.—Left 1 Yoke of Oxen behind.*

*Sunday January 9th 1848 The last Night we had some heavy showers of rain which continue this Morning. In the evening Wittmer returned with the boys and Oxen, leaving the Wagons at Leidsdorffs, on account the continual rains.*

So, while the matters concerning the sawmill were not yet a number one priority, it was clear they were definitely not forgotten. John Sutter was certain they would be taking on much greater importance by the end of the next fortnight.

He was quite correct, but hardly for the reason Sutter expected.

*[January 12, 1848 · Wednesday · 11:00 a.m.]*

Abraham Lincoln made few friends today when he stood up in Congress to explain the resolutions he had proposed and which were presently tabled. Nor did it improve his standing with the administration when he attacked President James Knox Polk. His voice ringing with outrage, Lincoln challenged Polk to locate geographically for the nation the first bloodshed that occurred between Mexico and the United States.

"If President Polk can show," he thundered, "that the soil was ours where the first blood of the war was shed—that it was not within an inhabited country or, if within such, that the inhabitants had submitted themselves to the civil authority of Texas or of the United States, and that the same is true of Fort Brown near the mouth of the Rio Grande—then I am with him for his justification."

President Polk, of course, had no defensible response to the accusation, but despite his current unpopularity, reaction from the public dealt a blow to Lincoln who was, in their estimation, gratuitously offending his own Seventh District, many of whose constituents had lost sons, husbands, lovers and friends in the war. It was decidedly an object lesson for Abraham Lincoln, who vowed to hereafter recognize the wisdom of not being too hasty—and vociferous—in straying from his own party's record.

[January 16, 1848 · Sunday]

Despite his own personal vow to make the daily entries in his New Helvetia Logbook more detailed and with data more extensive, John Sutter continued to write his entries with a lack of elaboration only he could appreciate. Increasingly these days, as the Marshall-Sutter Sawmill neared completion and he received reports from Marshall or his workers in reference to what was occurring, all too often he noted matters with disconcerting brevity:

*Tuesday January 11th 1848 The whole past night heavy rains. Sending provisions to the Mill race. The Amer: fork rose about 8 feet. Appearance of clearing up, but rain again in the evening till Night.*

*Wednesday January 12th 1848 The whole past Night continual heavy rains which continues [sic] this Morning. Afternoon clearing a little up and this evening stopped raining and had the appearance of good Weather again.*

*Thursday January 13th 1848 This Morning the Water very high, the Amer: fork rose last Night so that we had a rapid running stream behind the fort, a thick fog, but at 11 OClock the Sun appeared and made it pleasant. Gingery, Sidney Willis and others, reporting that the high water injured nothing, only entered into the [grist-mill] race and washed a little sand away.*

*Friday January 14th 1848 Despatched [sic] Woodworth with a Wagon 2 boys & 3 yokes of Oxen with the Mill irons to the Sawmill. Mr. Marshall left likewise. The water fell a good deal last night.*

*Sunday January 16 1848 A very cold morning and fog. Started*

*Valentin, Gutche & Justino* [Indian workers] *with 37 Sheep to the Sawmill. The four boys* [Indians] *Com, Seity, Heimin & Heimin junr arrived from the Sawmill, stating that all is well there and nothing injured by the high water. The wagon sent last friday* [sic] *is only half ways. Sent provisions to the Mill race. Mr. Johnson arrived from the Sawmill.*[263]

### [January 23, 1848 · Sunday]

The trouble with Jennie Wimmer that was being experienced by the saw-mill hands, who were erecting the mill near Coloma and digging the race it required, had not eased at all and had, in fact, worsened. So austere and vociferously domineering had her behavior become that four of the Mormon workers—Henry Bigler, Azariah Smith, James Brown and William Johnson—agreed among themselves that they could not—*would not*—tolerate such any longer.

The dispute, which had all come to a head this past Christmas morning, had been fomenting for a long while before that, stemming from the white workers' initial occupation of one of the dual cabins, which had no cooking facilities and forced them to take their meals in the Wimmer cabin, where Jennie Wimmer reigned with dictatorial supremacy. Part of the problem was her taking uncommonly extreme offense if the men did not arrive almost instantly at her Christmas mid-morning breakfast call, with which they could not comply without first cleaning themselves of the mud in which they had been working. Equally aggravating to the men, it became clear that Jennie Wimmer was being very partial in her distribution of food and obviously was giving her two eldest sons far more to eat than was offered to anyone else.

The friction created stretched into the new year and only became worse. Every act occurring seeming to cause greater ire to rise between them, often creating mountainous resentment over molehills of irritation: complaints about Mrs. Wimmer's cooking and her distribution of food; her almost uncontrollable anger when the men were late in answering her breakfast call; Henry Bigler's Christmas morning sermon, with which she took sharp issue; the "disappearance" of six bottles of brandy that had been consigned to the Wimmers; even the occasional tensions that arose between Marshall and his crew, since he was a man of little humor and took offense easily at their jocular jibings.

Thus, in the new little cabin that the seven white men had built for themselves, where they could do their own cooking when it pleased them to do so, they found far greater contentment than they had previously experienced under Mrs. Wimmer's dictatorial demeanor and an uneasy truce of sorts prevailed. Of course, it didn't help the relationship they had with her very much at all, except to tickle the funny-bones of his six room-mates, when Henry Bigler sat down one evening and, with some degree of difficulty, composed a humorous little verse which, with an uncharacteristic lack of chivalry and a distinct flaring of impish irreverence, he entitled:

> ***That Willfully Wicked Wimmer Woman***
> *On Christmas Morn in bed she swore*
> *That she would cook for us no more,*
> *Unless we'd come at her first call,*
> *"For I am mistress of you all!"*[264]

Despite the minor frictions that arose here and there among the men, the prevailing atmosphere reflected a fundamentally contented workforce. Bennett and Scott worked compatibly at the bench.[265] Stephens was occupied almost entirely at hewing timbers. Brown and Barger worked variously at chopping, scoring or cutting down timber and sometimes they whip-sawed together. Occasionally it was Brown and one of the Indians who worked together, sawing, the latter eager to learn all he could. As Bigler wrote in regard to the latter:

> ...When we told him we were making a mill that would saw by itself, he did not believe it. Said it was a damned lie, [that] such a thing in his estimation could not be done. Wimmer had charge of some Indians cutting the race a little deeper. I was drilling into some boulders near where the water wheel was to be, while Marshall superintended the whole affair. He was in the habit of visiting Wimmer and the Indians every afternoon to see how they were making it in the granite, which proved the most of it to be soft and rotten.

On January 17, even though the machinery of the mill was not yet fully installed, but with the head-race, dam and tub wheel all readied, Marshall ordered the head-gate opened for the first time and watched expectantly as the water from the river gushed in. Suddenly, however, the water was definitely not running with the result Marshall anticipated. The wheel had been set too low and the downward pitch from head-race to tail-race was simply not quite enough. The water, instead of flowing through steadily in a firm stream, tended to slow down and eddy, resulting in a current not strong enough to fill the mill-wheel paddles and cause a resultant continuous revolution of the big wheel.

Angered at the situation he knew at once would delay their completion date substantially, Marshall ordered that a broad, deepening channel be dug down the center of the race so that the pitch from head-race to tail-race became acute enough to permit a constant, heavy flow. It was no easy job and all hands—Indians and whites alike—were put to the task. With the head-gate closed and the water diverted, the chore was begun.

Marshall oversaw the work almost constantly now and was gratified to see that the biggest problem was going to be able to be resolved more swiftly than he had at first estimated. The greatest blockage of current flow was the first score of feet or so where the base rock was granite, but a close examination showed the rock pan itself to be so rotten that it was easily broken up by the picks the men wielded. By the first day's end, enough of a new channel had been formed to allow the water, once the larger rocks were removed and tossed aside, to push through with a stronger current and begin scouring away the looser soils and debris farther down the race.

Marshall now estimated that with the entire crew put to the chore, the men digging during the daylight working hours and the head-gate opened to allow the water to flow through the race during the night, the obstacle could be cleared in about a week. He selected two of his brawniest young men—Henry Bigler and Azariah Smith—to open the head-gate each evening when the day's digging was completed and to close it at dawn so the digging and rock-breaking could be continued throughout the day.

Marshall decided that, as much as possible, he would himself inspect the race each morning as soon as the gate was closed and determine to his own satisfaction when a strong enough current could be maintained through the race to turn the big mill wheel with the consistent power required for the giant saw blade to produce a steady supply of lumber. For the Marshall-Sutter Sawmill, the ending of construction was now in

# The Infinite Dream

sight and James Marshall, in his customary meticulous way, was intent on making sure nothing else occurred to slow its progress. It became necessary, however, for him to make a quick trip to Sutters Fort and he was gone for several days, returning yesterday, January 22, in the late afternoon. He hadn't slept much, he told his men, and needed a good night's rest, which he intended commencing as soon as he conferred with James Brown, who was temporarily in charge of the Indian crew during Peter Wimmer's absence to Sutter's. As Brown stated it:

*January 23, 1848 (Sunday):*

*It has been customary to hoist the gates of the fore-bay when we quit work in the evening, letting the water through the race to wash away the loosened sand and gravel, then close them down early in the morning, and a gang of Digger Indians have been employed to dig and cast out the cable rock, such as was not moved by the water. I, having picked up sufficient of the Indians dialect to direct the Indians in that labor, was set to look after that work, and as all hands were getting out timber so near the race, I had stepped away from them and was with the white men when Mr. Marshall came down to look after the work in general. Having talked a few moments, he stepped away to the head of the race where it entered from the river. He discovered a bed of rock that had been exposed to view by the water the night before; the rock that was in sight was in the bottom of the race and was from three to six feet wide and fifteen to twenty feet long. It appeared to be granite, but so soft that it might be scaled up with a pick, yet too solid to be carried away by the water. I, being an all-around worker, sometimes called from one thing to another, and the Indians did not require my whole attention, Mr. Marshall called me to come to him. I went, and found him there examining the bed-rock. He said, "This is curious rock. I am afraid that it will give us trouble," and, as he probed a little further, he said "I believe that it contains minerals of some kind, and I believe that there is gold in these hills." Said I to him, "What makes you think so?" He said that he had seen what he called "the blossom of gold," and I asked what that was, and he told me that it was the white quartz scattered over the hills. I, being no better informed, asked what quartz was. He answered that it was the white flint-like rock that was so plentiful on the hills. I told him that it was flint-rock, but he said no, that it was called quartz in some book that he read, and that it was an indication of gold. He then sent me to the cabin to bring a pan so that we could wash some of the sand and gravel to see what we could find. (It is well to say here that Alexander Stephens, H.W. Bigler, James Berger, Azariah Smith, W. Johnson and the writer had built a cabin near the site of the mill and were doing our own cooking, and it was to this cabin I was sent.) On my return we washed some of the sand and gravel, separating thereby as much of the dust as a ten-cent piece would hold, and also some of the bed rock that we scaled up with a pick. As we had no idea of the appearance of gold in its natural state, our search was unsuccessful. Then he said, "Well, we will hoist the gates and turn in all the water that we can to-night, and tomorrow morning we will shut it off and come down here, and I believe we will find gold or some kind of mineral here;" then he went about his business, stopping a while to ponder on the matter. As he was rather a notional kind of man, I had but little thought of what he said: do not think I even mentioned it to the other men. We each went our way.*[266]

*[January 24, 1848 • Monday]*

As soon as the sun cleared the mountains to the east, James Marshall left his quarters at the lumber mill site and sauntered down to the race near its fore-bay gate. He was pleased to see that the all-night water flow which had been permitted had already, in accordance with his instructions, been turned off by the closing of the main intake gate to the tailrace, which he presumed had been done shortly after daybreak by Henry Bigler and Azariah Smith.

The water in the race had largely drained away and Marshall was pleased to see the drainage was not only more complete than previously, the current created throughout the night, abetted by a heavy rainfall for an hour or so, had swept away a large portion of the sand and small pebbles that had accumulated. A number of substantial, newly exposed rocks remained in the channel and these, he knew, would be cleared away by the Indian work crews today under Peter Wimmer's supervision. By day's end, he thought, with a fresh flow of water through the race, the mill's large water-wheel would be turning steadily and with the power requisite for maintaining a steady and consistent revolution of the giant saw blade. It was still, Marshall knew, nine days until the peace negotiations between Mexican and American officials became finalized at Guadalupe Hidalgo, at which juncture California and much of the West would officially and irrevocably become part of the United States. He was gratified that this new enterprise of his would unquestionably be in a fully American possession.

As he walked down the race, he followed the newly opened and more clearly defined downward sloping of the channel as created by the work crews yesterday. He was some two hundred feet below the head-gate and mill, still passing the decomposing granite base rock that had been newly broken up to allow greater freedom of water passage, when he began to notice sand, granules of material and tiny pebbles that had been washed into and caught in cracks of the granite bedrock no more than six inches below the surface of the water.

Marshall had previously entertained the idea that there might be some unusual minerals present, this probability perhaps bolstered by the recent discovery of an uncommonly rich deposit of mercury—which most were calling quicksilver—in an extensive deposit presently being mined not many miles northeast of Monterey Bay at a place called New Almaden. He had, in fact, only the other day, mentioned in an offhand way to Henry Bigler that there might be "interesting" minerals to be found in the excavations they were making here in the mill-race, but, Bigler, at that time, had only "laughed at such an idea and dismissed the notion."

Now, however, on closer inspection, Marshall's breath suddenly caught as he noted that the trapped debris, caught in cracks of the granite some six inches beneath the surface of the clear water, included a glittering, golden-colored pebble slightly bigger, perhaps, than half the size and shape of a large garden pea. He stooped and carefully picked it up on his knife-point, then transferred it into the palm of his free hand. It seemed uncommonly heavy for its size and he judged its weight to be close to an ounce.

"Pyrite," he muttered to himself, initially concluding that this was merely a larger piece of the residue of fine, sand-size or smaller iron pyrite deposits that were not especially uncommon in stream beds in the area and that the diggers had been encountering ever since excavation of the race had begun. This piece, however, because of its size, was somewhat unusual and when he brought it closer to his eye his breath suddenly caught. Pyrite—Fool's Gold—he was familiar with in his own rudimentary studies and he had always been amused by those unfamiliar with mineral deposits who mistook pyrite for a precious material. But this...this *piece* did not exhibit the characteristics he associated with pyrite, having neither sharp nor broken edges; in this piece, those areas were fairly smoothly rounded, evidently from the wear of being tumbled along the bottom by the current. Further, the color did not seem quite as he'd seen it in the pyrite specimens he'd encountered and examined in the past, lacking the hard, bright *brassiness* that was expected and exhibiting more of a warmer deep yellow, more of a truly golden hue.

Unwilling to allow himself to become unduly excited, he still felt his own heart beating a little faster as he removed his old white hat and tilted his palm so the specimen rolled into the crown.[267] Then he reached in and, between finger and thumb, plucked up the piece. He held it up and turned about so the sunlight struck it from different directions and he studied it more closely, but it told him nothing more. He quickly decided it had to be one of several possible substances he'd been reading about in his geology book: pyrite, mica, sulphuret of copper or gold. Mica he ruled out at once because of its heaviness; the specimen seeming to Marshall to weigh about an ounce. Pyrite remained likely but to test this, he bent over one of the remaining larger emergent rocks and carefully set the piece on top of it. With the tip of his hunting knife he put pressure on it, fully expecting it to flake or break as pyrite normally would.

It didn't break. Neither did it flake or crack. Instead, the knife tip scored the smooth surface, ruling out, as nearly as he could recall, both pyrite and sulphuret of copper. To be sure, he picked up a smooth, fist-size granite rock and banged it down on the piece. It clearly flattened and bent somewhat, exhibiting a malleability that suggested to him one thing only.

*Gold!*

The thought struck with almost physical impact and he sucked in a deep, shuddering breath. He touched his tongue to it but detected no taste, nor was there any of the suspicious "smell" he associated with sulphuret of copper. Though he thought at first it was warm, he quickly chided himself for an overly active imagination. But the fact of the material was there, right before his eyes. Could it possibly be? What else might conceivably react like this? Nothing he knew of, unless this were some form of pyrite or copper he'd never before encountered, which he very much doubted; pyrite was iron and a knife blade could not score it so easily, if at all. But what, then? Copper? No! Definitely not; wrong color and no bitter, coppery taste, no vestige of a scent. He fumed at his own ignorance of what else it might possibly be.

Carefully, very carefully now, he picked up the piece—no, he corrected his own thought, the *nugget*—and dropped it into the indented crown of his hat. His legs suddenly felt very weak and he squinted his eyes for a moment against the sunlight and steadied himself. He then began moving along parallel to the newly opened channel, far more closely studying every crack and behind every small projection, pausing now and again to gouge out other, similar pieces with the knife-tip and placing them inside the hat with the first. Before much longer he had a number of such pieces and he noted with wry amusement that he was trembling.[268]

At the end of another ten minutes of searching, he carefully climbed out of the race excavation and, his hat clasped purse-like, with the opening closed, made his way to the nearby small cabin where his white workers were now quartering themselves. He heard voices from within and he tapped on the door with his free hand and stepped inside. All the men were sitting around a rough central table, drinking coffee and eating stick-bread someone had just baked.

Their voices fell away as he approached and they noted on his face the strangest expression they had ever seen him wear. They watched, curious, as Marshall strode to the crude table, cleared a spot in the center of it and placed his hat in the brightest spot of lamplight. He opened the gap to the crown then and exposed a dozen small rounded nuggets.[269] His voice was trembling and a little croaky as he spoke:

"Boys, by God, I believe I have found a gold mine!"

# Specific Sources

◆

## Prologue

**AAH** – 21. **ACHC** – VI-132. **AHOI** – II-66. **AOI** – 17-20, 24, 26, 31, 69, 71, 74, 113f14, 132, 162, 337, 382, 401, 453f85. **ARJO** – 87-101. **BCW** – 7-15, 25, 51, 54, 70. **BOSF** – 348-357. **CC** – 22. **CGC** – 151, 308. **CHMB** – 157, 164. **CJS** – Dec., 1890. **CPMN** – in BYU *Studies*, 32:I, (Winter 1992), 195-222. **DJAS** – 1-6, 8-11, appdx. **DPC** – 11, 19, 84. **FASH** – 2-4. **HOC4** – 16, 16f36, 19, 20, 67, 199, 221f, 238f28, 498, 708. **HOC6** – 4, 6, 11-11f15, 12, 15-16, 16f29, 16f34, 17-17f43, 19-20, 27-27f3, 28, 28f3, 31-32, 67, 121-122, 122f21,164-165, 488, 498, 506, 531-533, 559-560. **JHLDS** – March 7, 1835. **JOF** – 7-22. **JSRA** – 5, 30, 32, 32f1, 34-69, 79-123, 134-137, 140-162, 167-199, 218, 246. **KF** 2-7. **LAJM** – vii-viii, 3-5, 5f1, 6-7, 8-8f2, 9, 52, 102-107. **LCBGD** – LXI, No. 2, Dec. 1890. **MBATT** – 308. **MCSF** – Vol XLI, No. 2, Dec 1890. **MML** – 352. **NHD** – v-xix, xxii-xxiii, 4-5, 8-9, 11-12, 25-30, 34. **OST** – 62. **SBCM** – 19-22, 26-27, 31-34, 37, 135. **SBEE** – 18 Jan 98, 2 Mar 98. **SFC** 26 Jul 96. **TCOM** – 71-71ff. **TPA** – 266-267. **TPC** – 366, 369-372, 374, 376-377, 379, 383, 385, 390, 392, 397-399, 402, 405-406, 408, 414-415, 417, 425, 428, 430-431, 436, 438, 440-441, 443, 445-447, 449, 451-452, 454. **USMW** – 2, 6, documents. **WBD** – 558, 1375, 1568. **WISC** – 242-245. **YOD** 5-9, 11-18, 20-24, 38-40, 44-65, 68-74, 76-87, 89-92, 96, 107-108, 110, 167-168, 168f80, 194, 204, 215, 230, 235-236, 236f3, 255, 265, 267, 300, 331, 351, 362, 413, 415, 440-441, 443, 445-446.

## Chapter 1

**AAH** – 21. **ACHC** – VI-132. **AOI** – 17-22, 24, 31, 44f9, 69, 71, 74, 113f14, 132, 162, 190, 337, 382, 401-402. **AHOI** – II-66. **BCW** – 7-16, 25, 51, 54, 56, 58, 75f4. **BOSF** – 348-357. **CC** – 22. **CGC** – 151. **CHMB** – 110-111, 157, 164. **CJS** – Dec., 1890. **CPMN** – in BYU *Studies*, 32:I (Winter 1992), 195-222. **DJAS** – 1-2, 8-11, appdx. **DPC** – 19, 51. **FASH** – 2-4. **GRC** – 1. **HOC4** – 16, 199, 221f, 238f28, 498. **HOC6** – 4, 6, 11-11f15, 12, 15-15f28, 16, 16f29, 17-17f43, 19-20, 67, 127, 164-165, 488, 506. **JHLDS** – March 7, 1835. **JOF** – 7-18. **JSRA** 5, 30, 32, 32f1, 34-69, 79-120, 122, 134-137, 140-162, 167-199, 200-218, 246. **KF** 2-7. **LAJM** – 8-8f2, 9, 102-107. **LCBDG** – LXI, No. 2, Dec. 1890. **MBATT** – 308. **MML** – 352. **NHD** – v-vii, xii-xix, xxii-xxiii, 1-25. **OST** – 62. **SBCM** – 19-26, 29-31, 37-38, 83-84. **SBEE** – 18 Jan 98. **TCOM** – 71-71ff. **TPA** – 266-267. **TPC** – 366, 370-372, 374, 376-377, 379, 383, 385, 390, 392, 397-399, 402, 405-406, 408, 414, 417, 428, 430-431, 436, 438, 440-441, 443, 445-447, 449, 451, 453-454. **USMW** – 2, documents. **WBD** – 558, 1375, 1568. **WISC** – 242-245. **WPA** – map 13 text. **YOD** 5-29, 38-44, 52-65, 67-68, 72-73, 76-86, 88-89, 105, 114, 167-168, 192-195, 214-215, 236, 255, 267, 300, 319, 362-364, 415, 418, 440, 446.
 **INTERNET SOURCES:** http://www.dunwy.org/mexwar/intro.htm.

## Chapter 2

AAH – 19. AOI – 35-36. BCW – 15-16, 58. CGRH – XLI-No. 4, Feb, 1891, 22. CHMB – 111-112. DJAS 11. DPC – 11, 37-41, 54-57, 65, 83, 145. GRC – 1. HOC-6 – 15, 18. ISGR – 61. KF – 28. LAJM – 9-13. LFLO – 3 Dec 1846. NHD – 25-37. SBCM – 33-37. TPC – 453-454. UEN – 23-25. USMW – 2-3, 6, 9, Documents. WPA – 13-14, 14A-Map, 14-inset. YOD 49-52, 70, 74-76, 86-87, 89-92, 96, 103-118, 121-131, 137-140, 149, 165-166, 166f17, 183-197, 227-229, 237-238, 245, 265, 300, 412

INTERNET SOURCES: http://www.
gi.grolier.com/presidents/ea/bios/12ptayl.html;
indirect.com/www.crockett/Brooklyn.html;
sfmuseum.org/hist6/fremont.html;
sfmuseum.org/hist6/muzzy.html.

## Chapter 3

AOI – 20-22, 31-44, 190. APS – 27 May 1846 (T.L. Kane to Elisha K. Kane), 3 Jul 1846 (T.L. Kane to Mother). ATGM – 27. BCW – 15-16, 58-59. CHMB – 112, 114-115. CIMM-1 – Vol. XLI, No. 4, Feb, 1891. DONN – 1-10, 12-25, 68-70, 89. DPC – 37, 39-40, 42-53, 58-60, 62-84, 115. DJAS – 12-14, 32-34. EDOSF – 79-80. GDCHS – Vol. XIX, 35-36. GRC – 1. HOC 5 – 160-164. JHLDS – 6 Jul 1846. JSRA – 220. LAJM – 7, 9-13, 15-29, 140f7-8. MBAHA – 1974. NHD – xx-xxi, June 9-10, 1846, 37-44. RILDS – 2:204-13. SBCM – 36-40, 84-87. SBEE – 18 Jan 1988. SJP – Apr 23, 1846. SOCAL -195-196. TPC – 454, 457. USMW – Chrono. Documents. 3, 6. WPA – 13-13-map,14-14A. WTY – 42, 356. YOD – 21-25, 53, 83, 98, 118, 121-122, 131, 140-162, 166-181, 187-188, 192-193, 197-203, 207-208, 211-212, 218-227, 229-230, 232-235, 238-240, 243, 246, 250-251, 256, 277, 300, 318, 360-361, 364, 411, 413

INTERNET SOURCES: http://www.
alcovespring.html;
indirect.com/www/crockett/Brooklyn.html;
over-land.com /westfort.html;
sfmuseum.org/bio/geary.html;
sfmuseum.org/hist/chron1.html;
sfmuseum.org/hist6/fremont.html;
sfmuseum.org/ hist6/impact.html;
sfmuseum.org/hist6/muzzey.html;
sfsu.edu/~gbpabst/Bernal.html.

## Chapter 4

AAH – 190-191. AOI – 21-22, 31-44, 190. BCW – 15-16, 58-59. CALIN – 26 Sep 1846. CIMM – XLI, No. 4, Feb., 1891. DJAS – 12-14. DPC – 40, 42-53, 58-60, 62-84, 115. GRC – 1. HOC5 – 160-164. JSRA – 220. LAJM – 7, 9-13, 15-29; 140f6-8. LDS – Little to Polk, June 1, 1846, July 6, 1846. MHOBY – Jan. 26, 1846, June 1, 1846. NHD – xx, 37-44; June 9-10, 1846. OVMO – "Patty Reed" in Jan-June, 1917. PSQ – Bancroft Library, VI, No. 1, p.26. SBEE – Jan 18, 1998. SBCM – 36-39, 84-87 SOCAL – 195-196. SPRO – July 30, 1846. TGG – 22. TOT – Alcovespring.html. TPC – 454, 457. UHQ-1974 – W.R. Luce in *"The Mormon Battalion: A Historical Accident?"*. USMW – Chrono, Documents, 3, 6, 17. WISC – May 17 23, 25, 30 1846; June 6, 12, 15. WPA – 13-map-13, 14-14A. WTY – 356. YOD – 53, 83, 98, 118, 131, 140-147, 149-162, 166-181,187-188, 192-193, 197-203, 207-208, 211-212, 218-227, 229-230, 232-235, 238-240, 243, 246, 250-251, 256, 277, 300, 318, 360-361, 364, 411, 413.

INTERNET SOURCES: http://www.
alcovespring.html;
dmwv.org/mexwar/intro.htm;
indirect.co/www/crockett /Brooklyn.html;
notfrisco.com/calmem/goldrush/farnham.html;
over-land.com/westfort.html;
sfmuseum.org/bio/geary.html;
sfmuseum.org/hist/chron1.html;
sfmuseum.org/hist6/fremont.html;
sfmuseum.org/hist6 /impact.html;

sfmuseum.org/hist6/muzzey.html;
sfmuseum.org/hist6/toddflag.html;
sfmuseum.org/hist10/cowan.html;
userwww.sfsu.edu/~gbpabst/Bernal.html.

## Chapter 5

**AAH** – 77. **AMHIR** – XIV: 744, 759-760. **AOI** – 17-18, 23-24, 44-49, 51-52, 54-63, 73-78, 93, 168f80. **APS** – T.L. Kane to Elisha, 16 May and 17 May, 1846; same, undated, 18 May 46; T.L. Kane to Mother, 3 July 1846. **BCW** – 17-19, 59, 96. **CHMB** – 113-115, 117-135, 201, 256, 344, 351-355. **CIMM** – XLI-4, Feb., 1891. **DJAS** – 14. **DPC** – 52, 75, 83, 86-104, 112-114, 116, 119, 121. **GRC** – 1, 1846-1849. **HOC-4** – 19-20, 260-261-261f12, 708. **HOC-5** – 16, 498. **HOC-6** – II - 17, 118, 256-258. **JLDS** – 80-81. **JSRA** – 221-223, 234. **LAJM** – 25-32, 32f10-33, 40-46, 140-141-141f9. **LDSA** – G.W.Taggart to F.P.Taggart, July 8, 1846; A. Smith Journal, July 2, 1846; T.L.Kane to parents, 18-22 July 1846; J.F.Allen Autobio-graphical Sketch, c. 1846. **LDS** – Vol. I: 188-189, July 1, 1846; July 16, 1846; July 18, 1846; July 21, 1846; Diary of Robt W. Whitworth: *A Large Camp of Little White Tents*, Aug 1, 1846; C.T. Stanton to S. Stanton, July 19, 1846. **MATM** – 262f98. **MOB** – 279-290. **MORM** – 80, 166-167. **NHD** – xix-xxii; 44. **PCOTS** – July 29, 1847. **PSQ** – Bancroft Library, VI, No. 1, p.26. **TPC** – 454-455. **USMW** – 5-6; Documents, July 7, 1846; Chronology, July 21, 1846; Chronology, July 30, 1846. **WISC** – July 4, 1846. **WPA** – 13, map. **WTS** – 21. **YOD** – 31, 53-54, 129, 153-154, 162-165, 176-177, 181-182, 204-205, 209-210, 215, 224-225, 230-231, 235, 239-241, 243-250, 254-258, 263,-264, 272, 274-282, 287-288, 293, 295-302, 304-308, 310, 331, 333, 365, 433.

**INTERNET SOURCES:** http://www.
asusd.edu/~ross/brannan.html;
ccnet.com/~aplaza/cal-ist5.htm;
huntel.com/~artpike/fort4.htm;
indirect.com /www/crockett /Brooklyn.html;
notfrisco.com/calmem/goldrush/Sherman.html;
notfrisco.com/calmem/Stockton.html;
nps.gov/ olachrono.htm;
over-land.com/westfort.html;
sfmuseum.org/hist/steamer.html;
sfmuseum.org hist1/early.html;
sfmuseum.org/hist6/Fremont.html;
sfmuseum.org/hist6/impact.html;
sfmuseum.org/hist6/muzzey.html;
sfmus-umorg/hist6/sherm40s.html;
sfmuseum.org/hist6 /sherman2.html .

## Chapter 6

**AAH** – 18-22. **AOI** – 28-29, 44, 47f11, 64-65,69-71, 78-96, 101-114, 117-119, 131, 128f49, 144-147, 168f80. **ATYV** – yod-269-270. **BCW** – 9,19, 22-25. **BHAND** – yod-265-266. **BOTW** – 647. **CALST** – 13 Feb 47. **CHMB** – 42, 118, 128, 138-139, 141-144, 147-161, 165-166. **CIEFS** – opp. 54. **DJAS** – 11. **DOTMB** – 17-27 Sep 46. **DPC** – 99, 101, 103, 105, 108-109, 114, 116, 118-122, 124-125, 128, 130-136, 138-140, 142, 144-146, 148, 150, 154, 156. **GDJAS** – 29-32. **GRC** – 1, 1846-1849. **HOC-4** – 20, 260-261f12. **HOC-6** – 26f1, 255. **JHBJ** – yod-433. **JJDL** – 52. **JOAS** – A. Smith, 1846. **JOF** – 22. **JRB** – 69. **JSWC** – 5. **LAJM** – 27, 32-46. **LDS** – see also under specific code designations, **Letters** (individual): Clark, Bulah (stet) A., to Young, Brigham; 19 Aug 46 in **AOI**-82-84; Compton, Mary Betts, to Compton, Allen (Pvt.) in **LDS** Archives, 26 Aug 46; Gully, Samuel, Qtrmstr, to Young, Brigham in Brigham Young Collection, **LDS** Archives, 22 Aug 46; Hunsaker, Eliza, to Hunsaker, Abraham in **LDS** Archives, 24 Aug '46, *Mormon Battalion Correspondence Collection*; Hunt, Jefferson, Capt., and Hunter, Jesse D., Capt., to Young, Brigham, 17 Oct 46, in **AOI**-98-99; Long, T. Pope, to ?, from Ft. Bridger, 19 Jul 46 in **DPC**-103; Medill, William, to Young, Brigham, 2 Sep 46 in **AOI** 64-65; Rawson, Maria, to Rawson, Daniel, *Mormon Battalion Correspondence Collection* in **LDS** Archives, 23 Sep 1846 and **AOI**-82-84; Reed, James F., to ?, from Ft. Bridger, 31 Jul 46 in **DPC**-105; Reed, James

F., to *Illinois Journal*, 9 Dec 46 in **DONN**-48; Sanderson, George B., to Young, Brigham, 22 Aug 46 in **CHMB**-153; Scott, Margaret, to Scott, James Allen, (Cpl.), 30 Aug 46 in **AOI**-66-68; Smith, Andrew Jackson (Col.) to Jones, R., Adj. Gen., in *S.W. Kearny Selected Papers*, MIC-139, National Archives and **AOI**-94-95; Smith, Andrew Jackson (Col.) to Mason, R. B. (Col.), 26 Jul 1847, in *S.W. Kearny Selected Papers, 1846-1847 in* Utah State Historical Society; Smith, Andrew Jackson (Col.), to Young, Brigham, 23 Aug 1846 in **CHMB**-154; Young, Brigham, to Hunt, Jefferson (Capt.) "and the Captains, Officers, and Soldiers of the Mormon Battalion", 19 Aug 46 in **CHMB**-144-147; Young, Brigham, to Smith, Andrew Jackson (Col), 27 Aug '46 in **CHMB**-155; Young, Brigham, to Sanderson, George B., Surgeon, **MBATT**, 27 Aug 46 in **MIC**-139, National Archives; Young, Brigham, to Polk, James K., 9 Aug '46, seeking establishment of "State of Deseret" bounded on the north by Canada, on the south by Mexico, east by Rocky Mtns., west by Cascade Mtns. in **LDS** Archives and **AOI**-69-71; Young, Brigham, to Mormon Battalion, Aug, 20, 1846 in **AOI**-78; Young, Brigham, to Gully, Samuel, Qtrmstr., 27 Aug 46 in **AOI**-95-96 and **CHMB**-155-156. **MATM** – 116, 122, 128, 283-284. **MHOBY** – 221, 261-262. **MMB** – 150-171. **NHD** – xxi. **OJHST** – 3-18. **PCOS** – 106. **RESPS** – Map: 12 Sep 46. **RRF** – 221. **SBCM** – 34-35, 89-93, 98-99, 112. **SFC** – 1900. **SFPMB** – 53-54, 61. **TOT** – 402-403. **TSOD** – 13; **TPC** – 454. **UEN** – 4-16, (DPC)-125. **US GOVT** - 29th Congress, 2nd Session, House Exec Doc 4. **USHS** – 19-20. **USMW** – 5-6, July 31, 1846, chrono., 16 Aug 06. **WBD** – 558. **WPA** – Map 13. **YOD** – 66-68, 75-77, 92-94, 104-105, 108-110, 123-127, 130-131, 167, 211, 215-217, 235-236, 240-242, 258-261, 263-276, 279-280, 286-292, 299-301, 303-304, 308, 311-327, 330-337, 350, 359-367, 413, 433, 467,474

**INTERNET SOURCES:** http://www.indirect.com/www-/crockett/-Brooklyn.html (15 Apr 46);
*Kansas Forts,* University of Kansas,993,history.cc-ukans.edu/heritage/research/-Kansfort.html(KF);
memory.loc.gov/cgibin/query;
notfrisco.com/-almanac/timeline/goldrush.html(**CCHGR**);
notfrisco"GoldRush,The,1848to1869" –in *Chronology of California History;*
notfrisco.com/calmem.stockton.html;
*OregonTrail,The.isu.edu/~trin-mich/*(**TOT**);
sfmuseum.org/hist/chron1.html;
sfmuseum.org/hist6/Fremont.html (**CIMM**);
sfmuseum.org/hist6/muzzey.html;
sfmuseum.org/hist6/toddflag.html;
sfskydeck.com/timeline/1848.html (**GORU**).

## Chapter 7

**AAH** – 36-38, 77, 1912. **ADHMW** – 202. **AOI** – 17-18, 23-24, 47f11, 44-49, 51-52, 54-63, 73-78, 84-86, 91-93, 95f59, 98-99, 103, 105-107, 119-123, 127-136, 136f57, 136f69, 137, 143, 145-147, 168f80. 172-173, 409. **BCW** – 22-26, 59. **BOSF** – 348-357. **BOTW** – 645. **CALIN** – vol 1, no. 7, 26 Sep 1846. **CBFR** - 2 Sep 1849. **CHMB** – 113, 115, 117-136, 141-142, 158, 161-166, 201, 256, 344, 351-355. **CIEFS** – 52-55. **CIMM** – XLI-4, Feb., 1891. **DJAS** – 14. **DPC** – 144, 158, 160, 162, 164, 166, 168-169, 170, 172, 174, 176, 178, 359-361. **EST** – 69. **GRC** – 1, 1846-1849. **HOC-4** – 19-20, 260-261-261f12, 708. **HOC-5** – 16, 498. **HOC-6** – 11-11fl6, 17, 118, 256-259. **JHBJ** – 1. **JSRA** - 221-223, 234. **LAJM** - 25-32, 32f10-33, 40-46, 140-141-141f9. **LDS** – G.W.Taggart to F.P.Taggart, July 8, 1846; A. Smith Journal, July 2, 1846; T.L. Kane to parents, 18-22 July 1846; J.F. Allen Autobiographical Sketch, c. 1846, Vol. I: 188-189, July 1, 1846; July 16, 1846; July 18, 1846; July 21, 1846; Diary of Robt W. Whitworth: *A Large Camp of Little White Tents*, Aug 1, 1846; C.T. Stanton to S.Stanton, July 19, 1846. **MATM** – 262f98. **MORM** – 80, 166-167. **NHD** – xix-xxii; 44. **NOPS** – Aug, 1847. **OJHST** – 3 Oct 1846. **PCOS** – 106. **RFGF** – 35. **SBCM** – 39-41, 43-50, 86-95, 97-98, 112. **SJP** – 23 Jun 1877. **TOT** – 402-403. **TPC** – 454-455. **TYC** – 41-42, 47. **USGOVT** - 29th Congress, 2nd Session, House Exec Doc 4; Senate Document 2 (31-Spec. Sess.), 1848, Serial 547. **USMW** – 5-6; Documents, July 7, 1846; Chronology, July 21, 1846; Chronology, July 30, 1846. **WCMB** – 504. **WISC** – July 4, 1846. **WPA** – 13-13(map),14-14a-14b(map). **WTS** – 21. **YOD** – 31, 53-54, 77, 124, 129-130, 153-154, 162-165, 176-177, 181-182, 204-205, 209-210, 215, 224-225, 230-232, 235, 239-241, 243-250, 254-258, 263,-264, 272-289, 293, 295-302, 304-308, 310, 318-320, 327, 331, 333, 336-341, 349-351, 353-355, 365, 368-369, 376-377, 379, 433. **ZTB** – Taylor Bio.

INTERNET SOURCES: http://www.
asusd.edu/~ross/brannan.html;
ccnet.com/~aplaza/cal-ist5.htm;
dunwy.org/mexwar/intro.htm;
gi.grolier.com/presidents/ea/bios/ptayl.html;
huntel.com/~artpike/fort4.htm;
gi.grolier.com/presidents/ea/bios/12ptayl.html;
indirect.com/www/crockett/Brooklyn.html;
notfrisco.com/calmem/Stockton.html;
notfrisco.com/calmem/goldrush/Sherman.html;
notfrisco.com/calmem/Stockton.html;
nps.gov/ olachrono.htm;
over-land.com/westfort.html;
sfmuseum.org/bio/Vallejo.html;
sfmuseum.org/hist/chron1.html;
sfmuseum.org hist1/early.html;
sfmuseum.org/hist6/Fremont.html;
sfmuseum.org/hist/impact.html;
sfmuseum.org/hist6/muzzey.html;
sfmuseum.org/hist6/sherman2.html;
sfmuseum.org/hist/steamer.html;
sfmuseum.org/hist6/sherm40s.html;
sfmuseum.org /hist6 /sherman2.html;
sfmuseum.org/hist6/toddflag.html;
sfmuseum.org/hist10/cowan.html.

## Chapter 8

**AAH** – 14-21. **ADHMW** - 202. **AOI** – 22-24, 47f11, 91, 95f59, 98-101, 103, 105-107, 120-121, 127-137, 137f75, 138-143, 145-151, 151f24, 152-153, 168f80, 172-175. **BCW** – 22-28, 59. **BOSF** – 348-357. **BOTW** - 645. **CALIN** – Vol. 1, No. 7 (Monterey) Sep. 26, 1846; Vol. 2, by Theodore H. Hittell, San Francisco, 1897; Vol. 7, 753, 755-756. **CHMB** – 141-141, 158, 164-170, 173-175, 177-191, 202-205. **CIEFS** – 52-55. **CIMM** – Feb., 1891,Vol. XLI, No. 4, 347, 396-397, 399-400, 402, 443. **DPC** – 172, 174, 176, 178, 180-181, 184, 186, 188, 192-196, 198, 200, 202, 206, 252. **EST** – 69. **GRC** – 1, 848. **HED** – Doc. 4. **HOC-6** – II – 11f16, 258-259. **JHBJ** – 1. **JJS** – 10. **JSRA** – 232. **LAJM** – 40-46. **NHD** – xix, xxi, xxiii-xxv. **SBCM** – 46-50, 91-104, 112. **SJP** – June 23, 1877. **TOT** – 402-403. **TPC** – 454, 457. **USMW** – Chrono; Documents; 5-6. **WCMB** – 504. **WPA** – map-13, 13-14, 14A. **YOD** – 77, 124, 130, 231-232, 245, 274-275, 279-280, 282-286, 289, 318-320, 327, 336, 339-346, 351-356, 368-369, 377-381, 414. **ZTB** – 1-12.

INTERNET SOURCES: http://www.
gi.grolier.com/presidents/ea/bios-/12ptay1.html;
score.rims.k12.ca.us/activity/suttersfort/sutter.html;
sfmuseum.org/bio/Vallejo.html;
sfmuseum.org/hist/chron1.html;
sfmuseum.org/hist6/chron1.html;
sfmuseum.org/hist6/Fremont.html;
sfmuseum. org/hist6/muzzey.html;
sfmuseum.org/hist10/cowan.html.

## Chapter 9

**AOI** – 153-158, 167f75, 175-178, 190, 191f4. **ATGM** – 27. **BCW** – 28-32. **CHMB** – 175-177, 205-223, 256-260. **CIMM** – Feb. 1891, Vol. XLI, No. 4. **DPC** – 208, 210, 212, 214, 216-221, 222-224, 226, 228. **SBCM** – 112. **SBEE** – 16 Feb 1998. **TPC** – 454. **USMW** – 6, chrono. **WPA** – Map 13-14, Map 14-A. **YOD** – 50, 88, 226, 345-347, 352-353, 355-359, 367-371, 377-380, 388-389, 408, 413, 415-416, 431-433, 441, 455, 457.

**INTERNET SOURCES:** http://www.
acusd.edu/~jross/goldrush.html;
ceres.ca/geo_area/counties/;
notfrisco.com /calmem/stockton.html;
sfmuseum.org/hist/chron1.html;
sfmuseum.org/hist6/fremont.html;
sfmuseum.org/hist6/indian.html;
sfmuseum.org/hist6/muzzy.html;
sfmuseum.org/hist6/sherm40s.html;
sfmuseum.org/hist10/cowan.html .

## Chapter 10

**AOI** – 123-127, 160-164, 178-180, 423-424. **BCW** – 27-28, 34-38. **CHMB** – 171-173, 191-196, 199-200, 210, 230-238. **CIEFS** – 52-55. **DPC** – 230, 232, 234, 237-238, 240. **SBCM** – 102, 104-106. **USMW** – chron-0. **WPA** – 13-14, 14A. **YOD** – 94-98, 213-214, 338, 347, 379-394, 408, 434-437, 468-470, 476.
**INTERNET SOURCES:** http://www.
huntel.com/~artpike/fort4.html;
notfrisco.com/calmem/goldrush/sherman.html;
sfmuseum.org/hist2/rancho2.html;
sfmuseum.org/sfmuseum.org/hist6/fremont.html;
sfmuseum.org/hist6/muzzey.html.

## Chapter 11

**AAD** -27 Jan 1847. **AOI** – 25-26, 164-171, 180-182, 184, 202f22, 221f76. **BCW** – 38-48, 51-52, 57, 59-60. **CHMB** – 194, 196, 238-255, 260-263, 293-296. **CJ** – 15 Jan, 17-18 Oct 1846, 1, 4-5, 9, 23 Jan 1847. **DPC** – 244, 246, 248, 250-252, 254, 256, 258, 260-261, 263, 266, 268, 270 **HOC-4** – 260-261, 261f12. **HOC-5** – 444-451. **HOC-6** – II – 165, 259-260. **JOAS** – 11 Jan 1847. **JSRA** – 233, 235. **LAJM** – 13-14, 46-49, 49f13. **NHD** – 44. **SBCM** – 48-49, 56, 102-107, 109-112. **TPC** – 454, 457. **USMW** – 5-6, chrono. **WPA** – 15. **YOD** – 89, 368-369, 371-374, 392, 394-395, 408-412, 416, 437-441, 455-458, 477.
**INTERNET SOURCES:** http://www.
acusd.edu/~jross/goldrush.html;
acusd.edu/~jross/yerba.html;
ccnet.com/~laplaza/calhist5.htm;
cc.utexas.edu/~scring/timeline.html;
notfrisco.com/calmem/goldrush/sherman.html;
notfrisco.com/calmem/stockton.html;
sfmuseum.org/bio/vallejo.html;
sfmuseum.org/bio/sherman.html;
sfmuseum.org/hist/steamer.html;
sfmuseum.org/hist1/early.html;
sfmuseum.org.hist6/fremont.html.

## Chapter 12

**AOI** – 170-186, 190-193, 193f6, 194-199, 222, 222f81. **BCW** – 48-50, 52. **CHMB** – 196, 263-268. **DPC** – 202, 204, 217, 253, 262, 264, 272-275, 277-278, 280-284, 286-287, 289, 291, 293-295. **HOC-4** – 260, 261f12. **HOC-6** – II – 260-261. **LAJM** – 13-14. **SBCM** – 56, 109-115. **USMW** – Chrono, 6. **WBD** – 558. **WPA** – 13, map-13, 14, 14a. 14c. **YOD** – 88, 345, 367, 395, 401, 411-421, 456-458, 470-471.
**INTERNET SOURCES:** http://www.
ccnet.com/~laplaza/calhist5.htm;
gi.grolier.com/presidents/ea/bios/12ptayl.html;
notfrisco.com/calmem/goldrush/Sherman.html;
score.rims.k12.ca.us/activity/suttersfort/sutter.html;
sfmuseum.org/bio/Sherman. html;
sfmuseum.org/hist6/muzzey.html;
sfmuseum.org/hist6/sherm40s.html.

## Chapter 13

**AOI** – 186-187, 190, 192, 195-202, 217-218, 234, 234f32. **BCW** – 50-51, 55. **CHMB** – 196, 200. 267-274, 283-284. **CIMM** – XLI-4, Feb., 1891. **DPC** – 206-207, 296-299, 300-311, 313-316, 318, 320-321, 324-325, 328, 330, 332, 334, 336-338, 340-343, 347. **GRC** – 1 Mar 1847. **HHRD** – I-324. **USMW** – Chrono; Documents, 4 Mar 1847. **WPA** – 13, 14A, 15. **YOD** – 395-403, 419-430, 441, 458-460, 471-472, 475.

**INTERNET SOURCES:** http://www.
sfmuseum.org/hist6/Fremont.html;
sfmuseum.org/hist6/sherm40s.html.

## Chapter 14

**AAD** – 15 Aug 1847, 7 Mar 1848. **AOI** – 26-27, 187, 201-203, 203f25, 204-207-214, 214f55, 215, 215f57, 216-217, 219, 219f67, 220,-239, 221f77, 223f83, 224, 243, 253-258-264, 286, 356, 381-382, 402. **BCW** – 52-57, 60-62, 73-74, 74f28, 75-76, 92f8, 110f16. **CHMB** – 196-199, 201, 273, 277-278, 280-294, 296-297, 299-302, 306-308. **DJAS** – 14-15. **DPC** – 307, 321-323, 326, 329, 344, 347-349. **HOC-6** – 15, 26-27, 26f1, 28-29, 128, 260-261, 261f12. **IJ-** 16 Dec 1847. **JHBJ** – 2-12. **JOF** – 22-24, 66-67. **JSRA** – 233-237. **LAJM** – viii, 49-54, 131-132. **NHD** – xxv. 45-55. **SBCM** – 50-65, 111-117. **SBEE** – Jan 18, 1998. **SCT** – 203-205, 221. **TPC** – New York City, 1979, 443, 457. **USMW** – chrono, document, 6-7. **WPA** – 13, 15-15A. **YOD** – 214, 245-246, 374-375, 400-401, 403-406, 425, 428, 430, 432, 441-450, 460-462, 472-473.

**INTERNET SOURCES:** http://www.
asusd.edu/~jross/goldrush.html;
ccnet.com/~laplaza/calhist5.htm;
notfrisco.com/calmem/goldrush/sherman.html;
nps.gov/fola/chrono.htm;
sfmuseum.org/hist6/impact.html;
sfmuseum.org/hist6/muzzey.html;
sfmuseum.org/hist6/sherm40s.html;
sfmuseum.org/hist6/sherm40s.html.

## Chapter 15

**AAD** – 15 Aug 1847, 7 Mar 1848. **AOI** – 26, 187, 216-217, 220, 220f71, 224, 229, 229f14, 230, 236, 238-252, 264-276, 333-360, 366-367, 381-382, 394-396, 407-409, 421. **AUAJO** – 69. **BCW** – 61-82, 96f15, 123f1. **BICH** – 61-62, 73. **BOTW** – 710-711. **BSSH** – 2, 5. **CHMB** – 201-202, 204, 290, 297-298, 302-317, 326-329, 332. **CIEFS** – 9-10. **DHWB** – 241-245. **DJAS** – 15-16. **EJCF** – map. **ELSJ** – 5. **ESVG** – 83-84. **FKSL** – 151-152. **FRON** – 53, 55, 58, 102, 108. **FYAM** – 175-179, 182, 189. **GDJAS** – 101-102. **HED** – 17 (31-1), 1850, 336, Serial 573. **HISTO** – 111-112. **HOC-2-XIL** – 49-51. **HOC-5** – 580. **HOC-6** – II – 17, 17f46, 28-31, 49, 128, 260. **ICHBC** – 20 Sep 1847. **JDP** – 80, 86. **JHBJ** – 11-14. **JHLDS** - 26 Jan 1846; 3 Oct 1847, 9. **JOF** – 23. **JRB** – 114, 120-128. **JRNL** – 24 Aug 1847. **JSRA** – 239-244. **JSWC** – 56-58. **JSWW** – 20. **KEPAP** – 20 Sep 1847. **LAJM** – 51-55, 131-133. **LDS** – II – 11-12, 30, 58-60, 69, 368-369. **MBA** – 11-12. **MBATT** – 201, 308, 315-316. **MEJO** – 100. **MFNP** - 144-145, 164. **NHD** – 55-81. **OPH**-II – 381. **OPH**-XVII – 89, 96-97. **OTMF** – I – 272. **OTMF**-II – 112, 444f. **OVCA** – 34, 40. **SBCM** – 65-73, 77-78, 116-119. **SBEE** – 18 Jan 1998. **SBGF** - 1944. **SCT** – 203-205, 215-221. **SED** – 18 (31-1) Serial 557, 318-322. **SLHIS** – 11-12. **SWK** – 332-334. **TCALT** – 190-192. **TFWO** – 2-3. **TPC** – 457, 459. **TPL** – 241, 248. **TTJ** – 132-133. **USGSD2** – 343-344. **USMW** – Chrono; Documents; 7. **WBD** – 558. **WPA** – 13, map 13, 15; map 15A, 16. **WQ** – 172. **YOD** – 88, 442-443, 450-454, 462-464, 471, 473-474, 477-478.

**INTERNET SOURCES:** http://www.
2getgold,com/folklore/history_pg1.htm;
glittering.com/gallery/sutters_fort.html;
malakoff.com/grp.htm;
notfrisco.com/calmem/goldrush/bidwell.html;
notfrisco.com/calmem/goldrush/marshall.html;
notfrisco.com/calmem/goldrush/sherman.html;
pbs.org/goldrush/discovery.html;

sandi.net/kearny/history/swk/fk.htm;
score.rims.k12.ca.us/activity/suttersfort/sutter.html;
sfmuseum.org/hist6/grush.html;
sfmuseum.org/hist6/impact.html;
sfmuseum.org/hist6/muzzey.html.

## Chapter 16

**AOI** – 23, 27, 243, 273-274, 361-364-380, 382-384, 394, 409-411, 418-422, 426-427, 444, 446-448. **AUAJO** – 61-62. **AWLH** – 99. **BCW** – 81-89, 93-98. **BICH** – 88f. **CGC** – 77-78. **CHMB** – 317-334. **CIES** – 11-12, 14-18, 21, 24-25, 28-31, 33-34. **COTW** – 88. **DJAS** – 16-17. **DOMC** – 48-49. **DPC** – 188. **EEAB** – 5-6. **EEGW** – 19 Oct 1847. **ELD**-I- 73. **FKSL** – 159-160. **FRON** – 177, 181, 247-248. **GDJAS** – 21 Nov 1847, 106, 108. **GHJ** – I – 189, -IV – 754. **GOLDR** – I, 113-114, 263. **GSOCT** – 80-81. **HOC**-5 – 2. **HOC**-6 – II – 1-4, 6-12, 15-16, 16f32, 16f35, 17-21, 27, 29-30, 32-33, 128-129, 260-262, 465, 473, 562. **ICHBC** – 31 Dec 1847. **ISGR** – 50. **JHLDS** – 16-17 Oct 1847, 16 Nov 1847, 23 Feb 1849. **JJS** – 17. **JMCL** – 58-59. **JODL**– I – 96 **JOF** – 23-25. **JRB** – 125. **JWM** – 421-428. **LAJM** – viii-ix, 54-55, 132-133. **LAJM** – ix-x, 56-57, 137. **LOAP** – 107. **MBA** – 14. **MORM** – 101. **MXM** – Winter, 1999, 178. **NHD** – xx, xxv-xxvi, 83-105, 107-112. **NOPR**–III – 186. **OPH**-VIII – 534. **OPR** – 169-174. **OTMF**–I – 290-291, II – 343. **PAWM** – 301-310. **PCOTS** – 34, 76. **SBCM** – 73-76, 119-120. **SBEE** – 18 Jan 1858. **SMGM** – 49. **TOPH** –V – 307-310. **TPC** – 457, 460. **TYC** – 266. **USHS** – 5-6. **USMW** – chrono. **WPA** – 13, 14A, 16. **YOD** – 129, 131, 354, 442, 464-467, 477, 483-484.

**INTERNET SOURCES:** http://www.
2getgold.com/folklore/history_pg2.htm;
acusd.edu/~jross/goldrush.html;
ceres.ca.gov/ceres/calweb/geology/goldrush.html;
ccnet.com/~laplaza/calhist5.htm;
lib.berkeley.edu/BANC/Exhibits/Goldrush/discovery.html;
glittering.com/gallery/Sutters_fort.html; malakoff.com/grp.htm;
malakoff.com/grpsutter.htm;
malakoff.com/tcgcintr.htm;
mercurycenter.com/goldrush/goldrush_story1.shtml;
mercurycenter.com/goldrush/goldrush_story13.shtml;
notfrisco.com/almanac/timeline/goldrush.html;
notfrisco.com/calmem/goldrush/marshall.html;
notfrisco.com/calmem/goldrush/sherman.html;
pbs.org/goldrush/discovery.html;
pbs.org//sanfran.html;
score.rims.k12.ca.us/activity/suttersfort/sutter.html;
sfmuseum.org/hist1/early.html; sfmuseum.org/hist6/grush.html;
sfmuseum.org/hist6/impact.html; sfmuseum.org/hist6/muzzey.html;
sfskydeck.com/timeline/1848.html; utexas.edu/~scring/timeline.html.

# Bibliography Source Codes

◆

NOTE: To view full publication data keyed to the following source codes, simply check the author's name (or publication)—listed here following alphabetized code entries—in the fully alphabetized Bibliography section, which follows this section.

| | | | |
|---|---|---|---|
| AAD | Boyle | AWE | Wexler, Alan |
| AAH | Muzzy, David Saville | BAPW | Johnson, Kristin |
| ACHC | Roberts, B. H. | BCR | Johnson, Kristin |
| ACHN | Kemble, Edward C. [Bretnor, H., ed.] | BCW | Bigler, Henry W. [Gudde, Erwin G. ed] |
| ADHMW | Butler, Steven R. | BECON | Johnson, Kristin |
| ADP | Hardesty, Donald L. | BHAND | Hafen, LeRoy R. [with Ghent, W. J.] |
| AEC | Kelly, William | BICH | Bigler, Henry W. |
| AHCEH | Guinn, J.M. (notfrisco.com/calmem/goldrush.placerita.html | BIOB | *San José Pioneer,* "Biographical Obituary: Samuel C. Young" 9 Nov 1878 |
| AHCN | McMurtrie, Douglas C. | BOSF | Eldredge, Zoeth Skinner |
| AHOI | Ford, Thomas | BOTW | Barry |
| AHR | *Santa Cruz Daily Sentinel.* "A Horror Revived", 31 Aug 1888, 3 | BRID | Alter, J. Cecil |
| | | BSDP | Johnson, Kristin |
| AHSI | Lyman, Chester S.. | BSSH | Cox |
| ALLS | Sherman, William Tecumseh | BSWI | Ide, Simeon |
| ALWH | Hancock, M. L. | BYC | Gully, Samuel, to Brigham Young |
| AOI | Bigler, Henry W. | C4688 | Harlan, Jacob W. |
| AOIM | Ricketts | CALAD | Rosales, Vicente Pérez [Morby, Edwin S., trans.] |
| AOSF | Soulé, Frank [with Gihon, John H. & Nisbet, James] | CALIF | Royce, Josiah |
| AOTP | Cardinell, Charles | CALIN | *Californian, The,* newspaper, Monterey. |
| APS | American Philosophical Society | CALMO | Patton, Annaleone D. |
| ARJO | Hafen, LeRoy R. | CALST | McKinstry, George |
| ASD | Smith, Azariah | CBFR | Bidwell, John |
| ASDC | Kelly, William | CC | Oaks, Dallin H., with Hill, Marvin S. |
| ATHOG | Larkin, Thomas O. & notfrisco.com/calmem/goldrush/larkin.html | CCHGR | notfrisco.com/almanac/timeline/goldrush.html |
| ATYV | Benton, Thomas Hart | CCNM | Cutts, James Ma |
| AUAJO | Pace, W. B. | CFSS | Askenazy, Hans |
| AUGS | Johnson, Kristin | CGAH | Brown, James S. |

| | | | |
|---|---|---|---|
| CGC | Gudde, Erwin G. | FOS | O'Day, Edward F. |
| CGRH | California Historical Society | FRON | Bagley, E. D. |
| CHAS | ccnet.com/~laplaza/calhist5.htm | FSLSF | Lienhard, Heinrich [Gudde, Erwin G. and Elisabeth K., trans./eds.] |
| CHMB | Tyler, Daniel | | |
| CHRC | Rydell, Raymond A. | FSP | Eberstadt, Edward |
| CIEFS | Stockton, Robert Field | FSS | Soulé, Fra |
| CIMM-1 | Century Illustrated Monthly Magazine | GDWR | Shaw, William |
| CIP | Bancroft, Hubert Howe | GABB | Turnbow, Samuel |
| CJS | *Century Illustrated Monthly Magazine* | GDASM | Brown, John, ed. |
| CNMC | Cooke, Philip St. George, Lt. Col. | GDCHS | Gasquet Documents |
| CNR | ceres.ca.gov/ceres/calweb/geology/goldrush.html | GDJAS | Smith, Azariah |
| | | GDSM | Brown, James S. |
| CPIF | Graves, William C. | GDUST | Morgan, William Ives [Muzzy, Flor- ence Emlyn (Downs) Muzzy, ed.] |
| CPIR | Bancroft, Hubert Howe | | |
| CPMN | Godfrey, Kenneth W. | GENOC | Browne, John Ross |
| CRUI | Browne, John Ross | GG | Riesenberg, Felix, Jr. |
| CTYT | Hill, William E. | GHJ | Jenson, Andrew |
| DGIC | Marshall, James Wilson | GORU | sfskydeck.com/timeline/1848.html |
| DHC | McKinstry, Byron N. | GRC | sfmuseum.org/hist/chron1.html |
| DHWB | Bigler, Henry W. [Hittell, John S., ed.] | GSOCT | Duffin & Brown |
| DJAS | Sutter, John A. | GZ | Stegner, Wallace |
| DMB | Westergaard, W., ed. | HCAP | Cleland, Robert Glass |
| DOGIC | Albertson, Dean | HED | Egan, Howard |
| DOMC | Bigler, Henry W. | HESSC | Power, John Carroll |
| DONM | Hall, Carroll D., ed. | HFOW | Wakeley, Darrel La Mar & ida.net/users/lamar/historicfort.html |
| DONN-2 | Rosen, Daniel M. & member.aol.com/DanMRosen/donner/apr46.htm | | |
| | | HHRD | Heitman |
| DOPA | Burns, Ric | HIOC | Hittell, Theodore H. |
| DOPB | Breen, Patrick | HISTO | Tullidge |
| DOTMB | Lee, John D. | HOC-4 | Bancroft, Hubert Howe |
| DPC | Donner, Frances | HOC-5 | Bancroft, Hubert Howe |
| DPC-G | Graves, William C. | HOC-6 | Bancroft, Hubert Howe |
| DPC-HL | Leinhard, Heinrich | HOCA | Eldredge, Zoeth Skinner |
| DPC-HL2 | Leinhard, Heinrich | HOTC | Smith |
| DPC-HL3 | Leinhard, Heinrich | HOU | Whitney, Orson F. |
| DPC-R | *Russian River Flag, The.* (Newspaper) | HSC | Wright, George F., ed. |
| DPRS | Steed, Jack | ICHBC | Simpson, George (Sir) |
| DTC | Pierce, Hiram D. | IJ | Illinois Journal, Springfield, IL. |
| EBY | Bourne, Ezra | ITNA | Swanton, John R. |
| EDOSF | Brown, John Henry | JAS | pwa.acusd.edu~jross/sutter.html |
| EEAB | Chamberlain | JBA | Brown, James S. |
| EGOC | Hastings, Lansford Warren [with bio by Carey, Charles Henry] | JCAF | Clyman, James. [Charles L. Camp, ed] |
| | | JDP | Pettegrew, David |
| EJCF | Spence & Jackson, eds. | JGS | Gregson, James |
| ELSJ | Jones, ed. | JHBJ | Brown, J. Henry |
| EST | Bieber, Ralph P. | JHLDS | Jenson, Andrew |
| ESVG | Stansbury | JHWB | Bigler, Henry W. |
| ETF | Bagley, Will | JJDL | Lee, John D. [Morgan, Dale L, & Kelly, Charles, eds.] |
| ETOC | French Government | | |
| FASH | Nebraska Game and Parks Commn. | JJS | Beckwith, ed. |
| FC | Curran, Harold | JMCL | Sampson |
| FCC | *Century Illustrated Monthly Magazine* | JMMB | Cooke, Philip St. George, Lt. Col. |
| FDGC | Brown, James S. | JMP | Lyman, George D. |
| FEGR | *San Francisco Chronicle,* 12 Sep 1925 | JNR | Johnson, George |
| FKSL | Little | JNVJ | Jones, Nathaniel V. |
| FKSP | sandi.net/Kearny/history/swk/fk.htm | JOAS | Smith, Albert |
| FN | White, Stewart Edward | JODL | Cleland, Robert Glass |

| | |
|---|---|
| JOF | Hafen, LeRoy R., [w/ Hafen, Ann W.] |
| JORA | Jordan, Rudolph |
| JOTC | Smith, Charles |
| JRB | Bliss, Robert S. [Alter, J. Cecil, ed.] |
| JRNL | Pace, James |
| JS | Evans, John Henry |
| JSRA | Wilbur, Marguerite Eyer |
| JSRB | Bliss, Robert S. [Alter, J. Cecil, ed.] |
| JSWC | Coray, William, Sgt. |
| JSWW | Owens, ed. |
| JWM | Gay, Theressa |
| JWMDG | Bekeart, Philip Baldwin |
| JWS | Hess, John W. |
| KBR | Johnson, Kristin |
| KEPAP | Kearny, Stephen Watts |
| KF | Chinn, Stephen, & history.cc.ukans. edu/ heritage/ research/ kansfort.html |
| LAJM | Parsons, George F. [Zane, G. Ezra, intro.] |
| LAR | Rotchev, Alexander [Cordes, Frederick C., ed./ trans.] |
| LAS | King, Joseph A. |
| LCBDG | *Century Illustrated Monthly Magazine* |
| LDS | Latter Day Saints |
| LDSEG | Clayton, William J. |
| **Letters (Individual)** | Clark, Bulah (stet) A., to Young, Brigham; 19 Aug 46 in AOI-82-84; Compton, Mary Betts, to Compton, Allen (Pvt.) in LDS Archives, 26 Aug 46; Gully, Samuel, Qtrmstr, to Young, B. in Brigham Young Collection, LDS Archives, 22 Aug 46; Hunsaker, Eliza, to Hunsaker, Abraham in LDS Archives, 24 Aug '46, *Mormon Battalion Correspondence Collection*; Hunt, Jefferson, Capt., and Hunter, Jesse D., Capt., to Young, Brigham, 17 Oct 46, in AOI- 98-99; Long, T. Pope, to ?, from Ft, Bridger, 19 Jul 46 in DPC-103; Medill, William, to Young, Brigham, 2 Sep 46 in AOI 64-65; Rawson, Maria, to Rawson, Daniel, *Mormon Battalion Correspondence Collection* in LDS Archives, 23 Sep 1846 and AOI-82-84; Reed, James F., to ?, from Ft. Bridger, 31 Jul 46 in DPC-105; Reed, James F., to *Illinois Journal*, 9 Dec 46 in DONN- 48; Sanderson, George B., to Young, Brigham, 22 Aug 46 in CHMB-153; Scott, Margaret, to Scott, James Allen, (Cpl.), 30 Aug 46 in AOI- 66-68; Smith, Andrew Jackson (Col.) to Jones, R., Adj. Gen., in *S. W. Kearny Selected Papers*, MIC-139, National Archives and AOI-94-95; Smith, Andrew Jackson (Col.) to Mason, R. B. (Col.), 26 Jul 1847, in *S. W. Kearny Selected Papers, 1846-1847 in* Utah State Historical Society; Smith, Andrew Jackson (Col.), to Young, Brigham, 23 Aug 1846 in CHMB-154; Young, Brigham, to Hunt, Jefferson (Capt.) "and the Captains, Officers, and Soldiers of the Mormon Battalion", 19 Aug 46 in CHMB-144-147; Young, Brigham, to Smith, Andrew Jackson (Col), 27 Aug '46 in CHMB- 155; Young, Brigham, to Sanderson, George B., Surgeon, MBATT, 27 Aug 46 in MIC-139, National Archives; Young, Brigham, to Polk, James K., 9 Aug '46, seeking establishment of "State of Deseret" bounded on the north by Canada, on the south by Mexico, east by Rocky Mtns., west by Cascade Mtns. in LDS Archives and AOI-69-71; Young, Brigham, to Mormon Battalion, Aug, 20, 1846 in AOI-78; Young, Brigham, to Gully, Samuel, Qtrmstr., 27 Aug 46 in AOI-95-96 and CHMB-155-156. |
| LFLO | Longfellow, Henry Wadsworth |
| LG | Wise, Henry Augustus |
| LH | Johnson, Kristin |
| LOAP | Brown, James S. |
| LOV | Scherer, James A. B. |
| LSGI | Sherman, William Tecumseh |
| LSJ | Stephens, L. Dow |
| LTF | Daingerfield, William P. |
| LWH | Bagley, Will |
| MAAC | Morefield, Richard H. |
| MATM | Bennett |
| MBA | Allred |
| MBAHA | Luce, W. Ray |
| MBATT | Roberts, B. H. |
| MBSF | Dana, Julian |
| MCSF | Vallejo, Mariano Guadalupe & sfmus eum.org/hist2/rancho.html |
| MEJO | Ricketts |
| MFNP | Morgan, ed. |
| MFTY | Paul, Almarin B. |
| MGD | notfrisco.com/calmem/goldrush/mar shall.html |
| MHOBY | Watson, ed. |
| MMB | Golder, Frank Alfred |
| MML | Fremont, John C |
| MOER | Jefferson, T. H. |
| MORM | Smart, ed. |
| MRD | Johnson, Kristin |
| MTOK | House Executive Document 60 (30-1), 1847-48, Serial 520 |
| MWS | Sherman, William Tecumseh |
| MXM | Matrix Magazine |
| NC | *Truckee Republican,* 24 Oct 1885 |
| NHD | Sutter, John A. |
| NMHR | *New Mexico Historical Review* |
| NOMR | Emory, W. H. |
| NOPR | White, ed. |
| NOPS | Bullock, Thomas |
| NVCCH | Upham, Samuel C. |
| NWC | Cronise, Titus F. |
| OIE | Morgan, Dale L. |
| OJHST | Turner, Henry S., Capt. |
| OLG | Kelly, Charles [with Howe, Maurice L] |
| OPH | Carter, ed. |
| OPR | Schindler |

| | | | |
|---|---|---|---|
| OST | Hafen, LeRoy R. | STC | Bieber, Ralph P. |
| OTMF | Lee, John D, ed. | SUT | Zollinger, James Peter |
| OTSP | Coues, Elliott | SWK | Clarke |
| OVCA | McMurtrie, Douglas C., ed. | SWM | McCutchen, William |
| PATR | Wagner, Henry Raup | SYC | Davis, William Heath |
| PAULC | Ryan, William R. | TBF | Burns, Norman |
| PAWM | Jenson, Andrew | TCALT | Stewart, George R. |
| PCOS | Bagley, Will, ed. | TCOM | DeVoto, Bernard |
| PFT | Hafen, LeRoy R. | TCOT | Parkman, Francis |
| PITW | Bolton, Herbert E. | TCSS | Osbun, Albert G. [Kemble, John Haskell, ed. |
| POC | Lewis, Donovan | TFW | Graydon, Charles K. |
| PRP-R | *Pacific Rural Express*, 25 Mar 1871 article: "Hastings Cut-off" | TFWO | Crayden |
| | | TGG2 | getgold.com/folklore/history_pg1.htm |
| PSC | Berthold, Victor M. | TLP | Larkin, Thomas O. [Hammond, George P., ed.] |
| PTW | Egan, Howard | | |
| RCH | Lamson, Joseph | TMAC | Clarke, A. B. |
| RCP | Abbott, Carlisle | TOCT | Altrocchi, Julia Cooley |
| RERM | Fremont, John C. | TOPH | Carter, ed. |
| RESPS | Jefferson, T. H. | TOT | Parkman, Francis, and isu.edu/~trin mi ch/ |
| RFGF | Long, John B. | TPA | Wallechinsky, David and Wallace, Irving |
| RIED | Brown, J. Henry | TPC | Trager, James |
| RILDS | Berrett and Burton | TPL | Carleton |
| RJC | Swords, Thomas | TSAC | Dana, Julian |
| RMS | Stenhouse, T. B. H. | TSAMC | Schaeffer, L. M. |
| ROC | King, Thomas Butler | TSM | Chever, Edward E. |
| RRF | Article: *Crossing the Plains in '46* | TSOD | Morgan, Dale L. |
| RTO | Ghent, W. J. | TSS | Spence, Thomas H. |
| SALAT | *Salt Lake Tribune*, "Rites Honor LDS Friend", 16 Sep 1977 | TTCAL | Potter, David M., ed. |
| | | TTJ | Turner [Clarke, ed.] |
| SBB | Stellman, Louis J. | TTMW | Willard, J. F., with Goodykoontz, C. B.] |
| SBCM | Bailey, Paul D. | TTP | DeLafosse, Peter H., ed. |
| SBEE | *Sacramento Bee* newspaper & calgold rush.com/part1/01.sacto.html | TYC | Colton, Walter |
| | | UEN | Johnson, Kristin |
| SBGF | Scott, Reva | USGB | gi.grolier.com/presidents/nbk/bios/18pgran.html |
| SCEDP | Norton, Henry K. | | |
| SCP | Boggs, William Montgomery | USGSD2 | United States Government, *Senate Document 2, 1848, Serial 547* |
| SCT | Bagley, Will | | |
| SDT | Kelly, Charles | USHS | Utah State Historical Society |
| SED | *Senate Executive Documents*, 18 (31-1), Serial 557 | USMW | dmwv.org/mexwar/intro.htm |
| | | WBD | Nielson, W. W., e.i.c. |
| SEFY | Little, John T. | WCJ | Clayton, William J. |
| SFPMB | Christiansen | WCMB | Carter, ed. |
| SFTC | Powell, H. M. T. | WFFB | Korns, J. Roderic, [with Morgan, Dale L.], eds. |
| SFYC | Davis, William Heath | WGF | Johnson, Kristin |
| SITW | Crockett, David R. | WISC | Bryant, Edwin |
| SJP | *San José Pioneer*, "Biographical Sketch of Sam Brannan", 23 Jan 1877 | WPA | Esposito, Vincent J., General, ed. |
| | | WPSGC | Young, Otis |
| SLHIS | Caldwell | WQ | Ward, ed. |
| SMW | Stanley, Reva H. | WTS | Sherman, William Tecumseh |
| SOCAL | Dana, Julian | WTY | Bieber, Ralph P. |
| SOS | Gudde, Erwin G. | WWCG | Schmidt, Jo Ann Brant |
| SOTM | Linn, William A.. | YOD | DeVoto, Bernard (includes *Wilmot Proviso*, 8 Aug 46) |
| SPR | Sutter, John A. | | |
| SPRO | Stockton, R. F., and notfrisco.com/almanac/timeline/goldrush.html | ZTB | gi.grolier.com/presidents/ca/bios/12ptayl.html |
| SPRO | Stockton, R. F. | | |
| SSB | Jacobson, Pauline | | |

# Bibliography

◆

The following listing represents the sources that were most frequently referred to by the author in the preparation of this volume, but by no means represents all the sources utilized, which were much too numerous to enumerate here in their entirety. NOTE: Bold letters in parentheses following each entry represent the source codes, which can be found on pages 633 - 636.

Abbott, Carlisle. *Recollections of a California Pioneer.* NYC, 1917. **(RCP)**
Albertson, Dean. "Discovery of Gold in California as Viewed by New York and London." *The Pacific Spectator,* III, No. 1, Winter, 1949. Internet: http://www.sfmuseum.org/hist5/albertson.html **(DOGIC)**
Alter, J. Cecil. *James Bridger.* Salt Lake City, 1925. **(BRID)**
Bailey, Paul D. *Sam Brannan and the California Mormons.* Los Angeles, 1959. **(SBCM)**
Bancroft, Hubert Howe. *California Inter Pocula.* San Francisco, 1888. **(CIP)**
_____. *History of California.* Vol. 6 of 7 vols. San Francisco, 1884 - 1890. **(HOC6)**
Bekeart, Philip Baldwin. "James Wilson Marshall, Discoverer of Gold." Society of California Pioneers *Quarterly,* I, No. 3. **(JWMDG)**
Berthold, Victor M. *Pioneer Steamer* California, *The, 1848 - 1849.* Boston, 1932. **(PSC)**
Bidwell, John. "Captain John Sutter." *Century Illustrated Monthly Magazine,* XLI, No. 2, December, 1890. **(CJS)**
_____. *Echoes of the Past.* Chicago, 1928. **(EOP)**
_____. "Fremont in the Conquest of California." *Century Illustrated Monthly Magazine.,* XLI, No. 4, February, 1891. **(FCC)**
_____. "Life in California Before the Gold Discovery." *ibid.,* XLI, No. 2, December, 1890. Internet: http://www.sfmuseum.org/hist5/bidwell.html **(LCBDG)**
Bieber, Ralph P. *Exploring Southwestern Trails, 1846 - 1854.* Glendale, 1938. **(EST)**
_____. *Southern Trails to California.* Glendale, 1937. **(STC)**
Bigler, David L. [with Will Bagley], eds. *Army of Israel: Mormon Battalion Narratives.* Spokane, 2000. **(AOI)**
Bigler, Henry W. "Diary of a Mormon in California." MS diary in Bancroft Library Collection. **(DOMC)**
Bliss, Robert S. "Journal of Robert S. Bliss, The, with the Mormon Battalion." *Utah Historical Quarterly,* IV, Nos. 3 and 4, and XXVII, No. 4. **(JRB)**
Boggs, William Montgomery. "Statement of Crossing the Plains, 1846." 18-page MS in Bancroft Library, University of California, Berkeley. **(SCP)**

Bolton, Herbert E. *Pageant in the Wilderness*. Utah State Historical Society *Publication*, Salt Lake City, 1950. **(PITW)**

Brooks, Sarah Meriam. *Across the Isthmus to California in '52*. San Francisco, 1894. **(AIC)**

Brown, J. Henry. *Reminiscences and Incidents of 'the Early Days' of San Francisco, 1845 - 1850*. San Francisco, 1886. **(RIED)**

_____. *J. Henry Brown Journal [Autobiography]* Works Progress Administration, L.C. Project, Washington, 1938. **(JHBJ)**

Brown, James S. *California Gold: An Authentic History of the First Find with the Names of Those Interested in the Discovery*. Salt Lake City, 1894. **(CGAH)**

_____. *First Discovery of Gold in California*. Salt Lake City, 1953. **(FDGC)**

_____. *Gold Discovery at Sutters Mill*. Salt Lake City, 1893. **(GDSM)**

_____. *James S. Brown's Account*, in Journals of Forty-niners [qv. JOF, 112 ff.], **(JBA)**

_____. *Life of a Pioneer, being the Autobiography ofg James S. Brown*. Salt Lake City, 1900. **(LOAP)**

Brown, John. *Autobiography of a Pioneer, John Brown*. Privately printed, Salt Lake City, 1941. **(APJB)**

Brown, John, ed. *Gold Discovery at Sutters Mill, The*. Unpublished 5-page MS in Bancroft Library, University of California, Berkeley, 1886.**(GDASM)**

Brown, John [with James Boyd]. *History of San Bernardino and Riverside Counties*. Chicago, 1922. **(HSBRC)**

Browne, John Ross. *Crusoe's Island*. NYC, 1859. **(CRUI)**

_____. *Genocide*. Internet: http://www.notfriscio.com/calmem/genocide.html [extract] **(CRUI)**

Bryant, Edwin. *What I Saw in California*. NYC, 1848. **(WISC)**

Burns, Norman. *Bigler Family, The*. Privately printed, Chicago, 1960. **(TBF)**

Cardinell, Charles. "Adventures of the Plains." California Historical Society *Quarterly*, I, 1922, 57 - 71. **(AOTP)**

*California History*. "California History: Achieving Statehood." *California History*, Internet: http://www.ccnet.com/~laplaza/calhist5.htm **(CHAS)**

*California Web Site*. "California's Natural Resources." Internet: http://www.ceres.ca.gov/ceres/calweb/geology/goldrush.html **(CNR)**

Chever, Edward E. "Through the Straits of Magellan in 1849." Society of California Pioneers *Quarterly*, IV, 1927, 137 - 163. **(TSM)**

Clarke, A.B. *Travels in Mexico and California*. Boston, 1852. **(TMAC)**

Clayton, William. *Latter-Day Saints' Emigrants' Guide, The*. St. Louis, 1848. **(LDSEG)**

_____. *William Clayton's Journal*. Salt Lake City, 1921. **(WCJ)**

Cleland, Robert Glass. *History of California: The American Period*. NYC, 1922. **(HCAP)**

Clyman, James. [ed. Charles L. Camp]. *James Clyman, Frontiersman: The Adventures of a Trapper and Covered Wagon Emigrant as Told in His Own Reminiscences and Diaries*. San Francisco, 1928. **(JCAF)**

Colton, Walter. *Three Years in California*. NYC, 1850. **(TYC)**

Cooke, Philip St. George. *Journal of the March of the Mormon Battalion*. Senate Document 2, Special Session, 30th Congress, Washington, 1847. **(JMMB)**

Cordes, Frederick C., ed./trans. "Letters of A. [Alexander] Rotchev, Last Commandant of Fort Ross." California Historical Society *Quarterly*, XXXIX, 97 ff. **(LAR)**

Cronise, Titus F. *Natural Wealth of California, The*. San Francisco, 1868. **(NWC)**

Cutts, James Madison. *Conquest of California and New Mexico, The*. Philadelphia, 1847. **(CCNM)**

Dana, Julian. *Man Who Built San Francisco, The*. NYC, 1936. **(MBSF)**

_____. *Sacramento, The*. NYC, 1939. **(TSAC)**

Davis, William Heath. *Seventy-five Years in California*. San Francisco, 1929. **(SFYC)**

_____. *Sixty Years in California: A History of Events and Life in California, 1848 - 1908*. San Francisco, 1889. **(SYC)**

DeVoto, Bernard. *Year of Decision, The: 1846*. Boston, 1943. **(YOD)**

dmwv.org. *U.S. Mexican War, The: A Concise History*. Internet: http://www.dmwv.org/mexwar/intro.htm **(USMW)**

Eberstadt, Edward. *A Transcript of the Fort Sutter Papers*. Eberstadt, n.p./n.d. **(FSP)**

Egan, Howard. *Howard Egan's Diary: From Fort Utah to California*. MS in Coe Collection, Yale University Library, 1917. **(HED)**

_____. *Pioneering the West, 1846 - 1878: Major Howard Egan's Diary*. Privately printed, 1917. **(PTW)**

Eldredge, Zoeth Skinner. *Beginnings of San Francisco, The: From the Expedition of Anza, 1774, to the City Charter of April 15, 1850; with Biographical and Other Notes.* San Francisco, 1912. **(BOSF)**
———. *History of California.* 5 vols. NYC, 1915. **(HOCA)**
Emory, W.H. *Notes of a Military Reconnaissance.* HR Executive Document No. 41, 30th Congress, 1st Session, Washington, 1847. **(NOMR)**
Esposito, Vincent J., General, ed. 2 vols. *West Point Atlas of American Wars, The.* NYC, 1959. **(WPA)**
Evans, John Henry. *Joseph Smith: An American Prophet.* NYC, 1933. **(JS)**
Fairchild, Lucius. *California Letters.* Historical Society of Wisconsin, Madison, 1931. **(CLET)**
Fremont, John C. *Memoirs of My Life.* Chicago, 1887. **(MML)**
———. *Report of an Exploring Expedition to the Rocky Mountains.* Washington, 1845. **(RERM)**
Gay, Theressa. *James W. Marshall, the Discoverer of Gold: A Biography.* Georgetown, CA, 1967. **(JWM)**
Ghent, W.J. *Road to Oregon, The.* NYC, 1929. **(RTO)**
Golder, Frank Alfred. *March of the Mormon Battalion from Council Bluffs to California.* NYC, 1928. **(MMB)**
Gregory, Joseph W. *Gregory's Guide for California Travellers.* NYC, 1850. **(GGCT)**
Gregson, James. *James Gregson Statement.* Unpublished 11-page MS
Grolier Online. *Ulysses S. Grant Biography: The American Presidency.* Internet: http://gi.grolier.com/presidents/nbk/bios/18pgran.html **(USGB)**
———. *Zachary Taylor Biography: The American Presidency.* Internet: http://gi.grolier.com/presidents/ca/bios/12ptayl.html **(ZTB)**
Gudde, Erwin G. *Bigler's Chronicle of the West: The Conquest of California, Discovery of Gold, and Mormon Settlement as Reflected in Henry William Bigler's Diaries.* Berkeley, 1962. **(BCW)**
———. *California Gold Camps: A Geographical and Historical Dictionary of Camps, Towns, and Localities Where Gold was Found and Mined: Wayside Stations and Trading Centers.* Berkeley, 1975. **(CGC)**
———. *Sutter's Own Story.* NYC, 1936. **(SOS)**
Guinn, J.M. *A History of California and an Extended History of Los Angeles.* Internet: http://www.notfrisco.com/calmem/goldrush.placerita.html **(AHCEH)**
Hafen, LeRoy R. *Armijo's Journal.* The Huntington Library *Quarterly,* November, 1947, 87 - 101. **(ARJO)**
———. [with Ann W. Hafen]. *Journals of Forty-Niners, Salt Lake to Los Angeles: With Diaries and Contemporary Records of Sheldon Young, James S. Brown, Jacob Y. Stover, Charles C. Rich, Addison Pratt, Howard Egan, Henry W. Bigler, and others.* Glendale, 1954. **(JOF)**
———. *Old Spanish Trail, The: Santa Fe to Los Angeles.* Glendale, 1954. **(OST)**
Harlan, Jacob W. *California, '46 to '88.* San Francisco, 1888. **(C4688)**
Hastings, Lansford Warren. *Emigrants' Guide, The, to Oregon and California...with Historical Note and Bibliography by Charles Henry Carey.* Princeton, 1932. **(EGOC)**
Hess, John W. "John W. Hess, with the Mormon Battalion." *Utah Historical Quarterly,* IV, 47ff. **(JWS)**
Hittell, Theodore H. *History of California.* 4 vols. San Francisco, 1885 - 1897. **(HIOC)**
Ide, Simeon. *Biographical Sketch of the Life of William B. Ide.* Claremont, NH, 1880. **(BSWI)**
Interactive Timeline. *1948: The Gold Rush: Gold Rush! The First Nugget.* Internet: http://www.sfskydeck.com/timeline/1848.html **(GORU)**
Internet: notfrisco. "Gold Rush, The, 1848 to 1869" in *Chronology of California History.* Internet: http://www.notfrisco.com/almanac/timeline/goldrush.html **(CCHGR)**
Internet: Oregon Trail, *Oregon Trail, The.* Internet: http://www.isu.edu/~trinmich/ **(TOT)**
Jacobson, Pauline.
———. "Story of Sam Brannan." *San Francisco Bulletin,* May 20, 1916. **(SSB)**
Jefferson, T.H. *Map of the Emigrant Road from Independence, Mo., to San Francisco, California.* MS map in Bancroft Library. **(MOER)**
Jenson, Andrew. "Goudy Hogan Journal Extract" in *Latter-Day Saint Biographical Encyclopedia,* IV, 593. Brigham Young University Library, Salt Lake City, n.d. **(GHJ)**
Johnson, George. *Notes, Reminiscences, etc., 1849 - 1942.* Unpublished 25-page MS with folder, 4 scrapbooks, in Bancroft Library, University of California, Berkeley. **(JNR)**
Jones, Nathaniel V. "Journal of Nathaniel V. Jones, The, with the Mormon Battalion." *Utah Historical Quarterly,* III, 6ff. **(JNVJ)**
Jordan, Rudolph. "Autobiography." *Society of California Pioneers Quarterly,* IV, 1927, 174 - 201. **(JORA)**

Kelly, Charles. *Salt Desert Trails*. Salt Lake City, 1930. **(SDT)**
Kelly, William. *A Stroll through the Diggings of California*. London, 1852. **(ASDC)**
_____. *An Excursion to California*. 2 vols. London, 1851. **(AEC)**
Kemble, Edward C. [ed., Helen Bretnor]. *A History of California Newspapers, 1846 - 1858*. Los Gatos, CA, 1962. **(ACHN)**
King, Thomas Butler. *HR Executive Document No. 59*, 31st Congress, 1st Session. Washington, 1850. **(ROC)**
Korns, J. Roderic. *West from Fort Bridger*. Salt Lake City, 1951. **(WFFB)**
Lamson, Joseph. *Round Cape Horn*. Bangor, Maine, 1878. **(RCH)**
Larkin, Thomas O. *A Thousand Hogs*. [Letter extract, August 29, 1848.] Internet: http://www.notfrisco.com/calmem/goldrush/larkin.html **(ATHOG)**
_____. [ed., George P. Hammond]. *Larkin Papers, The: Personal, Business, and Official Correspondence of Thomas Oliver Larkin, Merchant and United States Consul in California*. 10 vols. University of California, Berkeley, 1951 - 1964. **(TLP)**
Lee, John D. [ed. Charles Kelly]. *Journals of John D. Lee*. Salt Lake City, 1938. **(JJDL)**
Lienhard, Heinrich [trans./ed. Erwin G. and Elisabeth K. Gudde]. *From St. Louis to Sutters Fort*. Norman, 1961. **(FSLSF)**
Linn, William A. *Story of the Mormons*. NYC, 1902. **(SOTM)**
Little, John T. *Statement of Events in the First Years of American Occupation of California*. Unpublished 16-page MS in Bancroft Library, University of California, Berkeley. **(SEFY)**
Lyman, Chester S. *Around the Horn to the Sandwich Islands and California*. Yale University, New Haven, CN, 1924. **(AHSI)**
Lyman, George D. *John , Pioneer: The Life Story of a Trail Blazer on Six Frontiers*. NYC, 1931. **(JMP)**
Marshall, James Wilson. "Discovery of Gold in California, The." *Hutchings' California Magazine*, Vol. II November, 1857. **(DGIC)**
_____. *Marshall Gold Discovery (1848)*. Internet: http://www.notfrisco.com/calmem/goldrush/marshall.html **(MGD)**
McKinstry, Byron N.
_____. "Documents for the History of California, 1846 - 8." MS in Bancroft Library. **(DHC)**
McMurtrie, Douglas C. *A History of California Newspapers, 1846 - 1858*. The Sacramento *Daily Union*, December 25, 1858. **(AHCN)**
Morefield, Richard H. *Mexican Adaptation in American California, The: 1846 - 1875*. M.A. thesis in Bancroft Library, University of California, Berkeley. **(MAAC)**
Morgan, William Ives [ed., Florence Emlyn (Downs) Muzzy]. *Gold Dust: The Log of a Forty-niner, 1848, '50, '51, '52, '54*. Unedited MS diaries in Bancroft Library, University of California, Berkeley. **(GDUST)**
Museum of the City of San Francisco. *Gold Rush Chronology: 1846 - 1849*. Internet: http://www.sfmuseum.org/hist/chron1.html **(GRC-1)**
Muzzy, David Saville. *An American History*. Boston, 1911. **(AAH)**
Norton, Henry K. *Story of California from the Earliest Days to the Present, The*. Chicago, 1925 **(SCEDP)**
notfrisco.com. *Chronology of California History: The Gold Rush, 1848 - 1869*. Internet: http://www.notfrisco.com/almanac/timeline/goldrush.html **(CCHGR)**
_____. *Stockton's Proclamation*. Internet: http://www.notfrisco.com/almanac/timeline/goldrush.html **(SPRO)**
O'Day, Edward F. "Founding of San Francisco, The." in *San Francisco Water*, Vol. 4, No. 5, October, 1926. **(FOS)**
Osbun, Albert G. [ed., John Haskell Kemble]. *To California and the South Seas: The Diary of Albert G. Osbun, 1849 - 1851*. Hunting Library, San Marino, CA, 1966. **(TCSS)**
Parkman, Francis. *California and Oregon Trail, The*. NYC, 1849. **(TCOT)**
Parsons, George F. [Intro., G. Ezra Zane]. *Life and Adventures of James W. Marshall, The: The Discoverer of Gold in California*. Sacramento, 1870. **(LAJM)**
Patton, Annaleone D. *California Mormons*. Salt Lake City, 1961. **(CALMO)**
Paul, Almarin B. "My First Two Years in California." Society of California Pioneers *Quarterly*, IV, 1927. **(MFTY)**
Pierce, Hiram D. *Diary of a Trip to California and Return to New York, March 6, 1849 - January 8, 1851*. 113-page MS in Bancroft Library, University of California, Berkeley. **(DTC)**

Potter, David M., ed. *Trail to California: The Overland Journal of Vincent Geiger and Wakeman Bryarly.* New Haven, 1945. **(TTCAL)**
Powell, H.M.T. *Santa Fe Trail to California, The, 1849 - 1852.* San Francisco, 1931. **(SFTC)**
Power, John Carroll. *History of the Early Settlers of Sangamon County, Illinois.* Springfield, 1876. **(HESSC)**
pwa.acusd. *John Augustus Sutter.* Internet: http://pwa.acusd.edu~jross/sutter.html **(JAS)**
Riesenberg, Felix, Jr. *Golden Gate: The Story of San Francisco Harbor.* NYC, 1940. **(GG)**
Roberts, B.H. *Mormon Battalion, The.* Salt Lake City, 1919. **(MBATT)**
Rosales, Vicente Pérez. [trans. by Edwin S. Morby]. *California Adventure.* San Francisco, 1947. **(CALAD)**
Royce, Josiah. *California, from the Conquest in 1846 to the Second Vigilance Committee in San Francisco: A Study in American Character.* Boston, 1886. **(CALIF)**
Ryan, William R. *Personal Adventures in Upper and Lower California in 1848 - 49.* 2 vols. London, 1851. London, 1850. **(PAULC)**
Rydell, Raymond A. "Cape Horn Route to California, The, 1849." *Pacific Historical Review*, XVIII, 1948, 149 - 163. **(CHRC)**
*San Francisco News Letter.* "From the 1820s to the Gold Rush." September, 1925. **(FEGR)**
Sawyer, Lorenzo. *Way Sketches: Containing Incidents of Travel Across the Plains; with Letters Describing Life and Conditions in the Gold Region* NYC, 1926. **(WAYS)**
Schaeffer, L.M. *Sketches of Travels in South America, Mexico, and California.* NYC, 1860. **(TSAMC)**
Scott, Reva. *Samuel Brannan and the Golden Fleece.* NYC, 1944. **(SBGF)**
Sherman, William Tecumseh. *A Letter of Lieut. W.T. Sherman Reporting on Conditions in California in 1848.* Carmel, CA, 1947. **(ALLS)**
_____. *Memoirs of W.T. Sherman.* 2 vols. NYC, 1887. **(MWS)**
Smith, Azariah. "Diary." *Overland Monthly*, February, 1888. **(ASD)**
Smith, Charles. *Journal of a Trip to California.* NYC, 1920. **(JOTC)**
sonomavalley.com. *Lachryma Montis.* Brochure, Sonoma Valley Visitors Bureau. Internet: http://www.sonomavalley.com/home.html **(LMON)**
Soulé, Frank [with John H. Gihon and James Nisbet]. *Annals of San Francisco, The.* NYC, 1855. **(AOSF)**
_____. *Frank Soulé Statement to H.H. Bancroft.* Unpublished 4-page MS Statement in Bancroft Library, University of California, Berkeley. **(FSS)**
Spence, Thomas H. *Thomas Spence Statement to H.H. Bancroft.* Unpublished 12-page MS of 1878 in Bancroft Library, University of California, Berkeley. **(TSS)**
Stanley, Reva H. "Sutter's Mormon Workmen at Natoma and Coloma in 1848." *California Historical Society Quarterly*, XIV, 269 - 282. **(SMW)**
Stellman, Louis J. *Sam Brannan, Builder of San Francisco.* NYC, 1953. **(SBB)**
Stenhouse, T.B.H. *Rocky Mountain Saints.* NYC, 1873. **(RMS)**
Stockton, R.F. *Stockton's Proclamation*, 29th Congress, 2nd Session, HR Executive Document No. 4, Washington, August 17, 1846. Internet: http://www.notfrisco.com/calmem/stockton.html **(SPRO)**
Sutter, John A. *Diary of Johann Augustus Sutter, The.* San Francisco, 1932. **(DJAS)**
_____. *New Helvetia Diary: A Record of Events Kept by John A. Sutter and His Clerks.* San Francisco, 1939. **(NHD)**
_____. *Personal Reminiscences.* MS, Bancroft Library. **(SPR)**
Swanton, John R. *Indian Tribes of North America.* Smithsonian Institution Bureau of Ethnology Bulletin No. 145, Washington, 1952. **(ITNA)**
Swords, Thomas. *Report of a Journey from California by the South Pass to Fort Leavenworth in 1847.* 30th Congress, 2nd Session, HR Executive Document 1, 226 - 236, Washington, 1848. **(RJC)**
Tyler, Daniel. *A Concise History of the Mormon Battalion in the Mexican War, 1846 - 1847.* Salt Lake City, 1881. **(CHMB)**
Upham, Samuel C. *Notes of a Voyage to California via Cape Horn.* Philadelphia, 1878. **(NVCCH)**
Vallejo, Mariano Guagalupe. "Ranch and Mission Days in Alta California." *Century Magazine*, XLI, No. 2, December, 1890. Internet: http//sfmuseum.org/hist2/rancho.html **(MCSF)**
Wagner, Henry Raup. *Plains and the Rockies, The.* 2nd ed., enlarged. Charles L. Camp, San Francisco, 1937. **(PATR)**

Westergaard, W., ed. "Diary of Marcellus Bixby." Historical Society of Southern California *Publications*, XII, 1927, 317 - 333.**(DMB)**
Whitney, Orson F. *History of Utah*. 4 vols. Salt Lake City, 1892. **(HOU)**
Wilbur, Marguerite Eyer. *John Sutter: Rascal and Adventurer*. NYC, 1949. **(JSRA)**
Willard, J.F. [with C. B. Goodykoontz]. *Trans-Mississippi West, The*. Boulder, 1930. **(TTMW)**
Wise, Henry Augustus. *Los Gringos*. NYC, 1849. **(LG)**
Wright, George F., ed. *History of Sacramento County, California*. Oakland, 1880. **(HSC)**
Zollinger, James Peter. *Sutter: The Man and His Empire*. NYC, 1939. **(SUT)**

# Amplification Notes

♦

1 • Some accounts give Sutter's nationality as German, but this is incorrect. Kandern was located in Switzerland just south of the German border and eleven miles east of the city of Berne.
2 • Annette Dubeld's name is, in varied accounts, shown as Anna Dubeld or Anna "Nanette" Dubeld. Annette Dubeld seems to be the correct spelling.
3 • Sutter's children, in addition to his firstborn son, Johann Augustus Sutter were Anna Elisa (May 30, 1828), Emil Victor (January 16, 1830), William Alphonse (May 15, 1832) and Carl (December 26, 1833.) Carl, however, died during his first year of life.
4 • Shinnston (sometimes written as Shinnstown) is in Harrison County in present West Virginia, located 12 miles north of the county seat, Clarksburg.
5 • The two Mormon elders who met with the Biglers this day in Shinnston, VA (WV) have not been identified in any of the known documents chronicling this event.
6 • Although Henry Bigler had not yet at this time begun keeping the journal that became one of his crowning achievements, he was soon to do so. While in certain respects his prejudices were apparent, unlike so many other journalists or diarists of the time, he was unfailingly accurate in what he reported.
7 • While Westport no longer exists, it is believed that this community was subsequently absorbed into the larger and more permanent city of Independence, Jackson County, Missouri.
8 • The town (originally called a pueblo) of Sonoma, some ten miles north of San Pablo Bay in Sonoma County, CA, is located approximately midway between the present cities of Petaluma and Napa. It developed as an adjunct of the Mission San Francisco Solano established by the Franciscans.
9 • California at this time was known as Alta California—Upper California—by the Spaniards, as opposed to Lower California—the Baja Peninsula. California, Baja and Mexico were all parts of what was termed New Spain.
10 • Monterey, California was named by De Anza after the city of Monterrey in the present Mexican province of Nuevo Leon. Both cities will be referred to in this text but the difference will be noted in that the California Monterey is spelled with one "r" and the Mexican Monterrey with two.
11 • The Roman Catholic missionaries had been extremely successful in establishing an agricultural base all along the Pacific Coast, from the Baja—where Jesuits had been gardening successfully for more than one hundred years—to the Monterey peninsula. Vineyards and orchards developed quickly. Among the fruits grown in abundance were cherries, oranges, apples, figs, pears, pomegranates, peaches, apricots, melons and olives. In the southernmost areas, northward to San Diego, there were significant crops of bananas, plantains, cane sugar, citrons and dates. Vegetable crops grown in profusion included corn, carrots, varieties of squashes, cucumbers, potatoes, beets, beans, peas, lentils, onions and red peppers. Though not often exported, the tuna—fruit of the prickly pear cactus—was popular locally. Flowers, too, were grown in abundance; lilies, pinks, roses, nasturtiums, bougainvillea, sweet-peas, hollyhocks and many others.

12 • The Contra Costa River is a tributary of the San Joaquín River.
13 • Yerba Buena was, of course, the genesis of modern San Francisco. Mission Dolores was located on what is now Sixteenth Street and the hill that was called Loma Alto is today's Telegraph Hill. Just prior to secularization occurring, Mission Dolores had a population of some two thousand proselytized Indians living around its perimeter.
14 • In the Spanish/Mexican hierarchy, an *alcalde* is essentially equivalent to the American office of mayor, though with powers somewhat extended beyond those of the mayor of an American municipality.
15 • The Spanish measurement called a *vara* was just short of an American yard, actually measuring exactly thirty-three inches. Thus, Leese's lot of 100 *vara* was, in American measurement, 274 feet square. It was located at the corner of present Grant Avenue and Clay Street. At this time the waters of the bay came close to Montgomery Street.
16 • Although not himself a Mormon, Alexander Doniphan of Clay County was one of the few eminent Missourians sympathetic toward them. During the Mormons' earliest Missouri troubles in Jackson County, it was Doniphan who put a bill through the Legislature that set off the new counties of Caldwell and Daviess and arranged for the Mormons to occupy one. He had also acted as attorney for Joseph Smith in many of the lawsuits filed against him.
17 • At this juncture Lucas's force was joined by a large group of ruffians from the west, led by Cornelius Gilliam whose offer to help eliminate the Mormons was accepted. Gilliam painted himself with red spots and called himself The Delaware Chief and his men likewise painted themselves as Indians for the encounter. How much actual help they were is open to conjecture.
18 • The Liberty referred to by Doniphan was, along with Independence and Raytown, one of the more important communities in western Missouri at this time.
19 • Evidently this was another of General Lucas's orders that was not executed. Joseph Smith and the other Mormon prisoners remained in military custody throughout the winter until Lucas, apparently wanting this whole business to go away, arranged for the prisoners to escape.
20 • Sutter's young German aide is, unfortunately, never mentioned by name.
21 • Fort Vancouver, located on the north side of the Columbia River approximately 100 miles upstream from the Pacific and opposite Oregon's Willamette Valley, was in territory claimed by the British and was headquarters of Pacific operations of the Hudsons Bay Company.
22 • Fort Hall, a principal trading post of the Hudsons Bay Company and one of the most important emigrant stops on the Oregon Trail, was located at the site of present Fort Hall in the Fort Hall Blackfoot Indian Reservation nine miles north of present Pocatello, Idaho. It had initially been established by American settler Nathaniel Jarvis Wyeth in July, 1834 and was sold by him to the Hudsons Bay Company in August, 1837. It soon became the point at which the overland trail split, with the main Oregon Trail continuing to Oregon and the other segment heading into California. Early records of Fort Hall derive from the surviving records of the Columbia River Fishing and Trading Company, which operated that outpost.
23 • Several accounts have obliquely suggested that Sutter visited Fort Ross while en route between Sitka and San Francisco Bay, but this appears to be entirely supposition and no known documentation corroborates any such pause. The dates involved concerning his departure from Sitka and arrival at Yerba Buena fairly conclusively negate any likelihood of his having put into Bodega Bay on the voyage south.
24 • At least one account states there were two officers with this squad, but others are in accord with one officer.
25 • One account states that Leese had married a daughter of Mariano Guadalupe Vallejo and that this daughter had been born to them on April 15, 1838. That, however, could not be so, since Vallejo's eldest daughter was only five years old at this time. Since the child, when Sutter saw her, was in the care of an Indian woman who carried the little girl into the house, it is likely that the Indian woman was her mother.
26 • The old Spanish land measure of a square league was equal to 4,439 acres. Thus, the full scope of the eleven-square-league land grant bestowed upon John Sutter at this time encompassed a total of 48,829 acres.
27 • This encounter with Indians occurred approximately ten miles below present downtown Sacramento, evidently in the area of present Freeport.

28 • It is likely that this stream was the South Fork of Putah Creek, which was later diverted for construction of the Tule Canal and Sacramento Deep-water Ship Canal.
29 • Sutter was given the high civil office title of *Representante del Govierno en las fronteras del Norte, y Encargardo de la Justica,* meaning "Representative of the Government in the Northern Frontier and Commissioner of Justice." The prepared document was not officially recorded until June 18. 1841. Through it, Sutter was now endowed with full civil authority to administer local justice, to thwart robberies by adventurers from the United States, to repress hostile Indians, and to prevent illegal trapping by "the Company of the Columbia", meaning both Astor's Pacific Fur Company and the British operated Hudsons Bay Company.
30 • Joseph Nicollet, of Savoy, France, died in 1843 at age fifty-seven.
31 • For full details of the events resulting in both the Battle of Tippecanoe and the Battle of the Thames, see the author's *A Sorrow in Our Heart: The Life of Tecumseh* (Bantam, NYC, 1992).
32 • The order for the liquidation of Fort Ross had originally been written and dated in St. Petersburg on April 15, 1839 but was not immediately executed due to improved harvests of peltry and meat from the post at Bodega Bay.
33 • The sum of $30,000 today may seem insignificantly small for such an installation as Fort Ross and all its contents, but based on average income figures for the United States at the time, that sum was equivalent to well over $1.5 million in the year 2007
34 • Sutter seldom had fewer that 100 whites employed and often many more than 500 Indians.
35 • See John Bidwell's story in his article entitled "Life in California Before the Gold Discovery", in *Century Magazine,* Vol. XLI, No. 2, Dec., 1890.
36 • This area was located approximately three miles south of present Yuba City in present Sutter County.
37 • Sutters Fort was located at the site of present Sutters Fort State Historic Park bounded by 26th and 28th Streets and K and L Streets in Sacramento.
38 • In later years Sutter expressed deep regret that he had not, at the time of his purchasing Fort Ross, simply moved everything of his there instead of vice versa which, later, he thought, would have been financially much wiser.
39 • Ordination of Joseph Smith and Oliver Cowdery as first elders of The Church of Jesus Christ of the Latter-day Saints occurred in the Peter Whitmer house in Fayette, NY.
40 • Eliza—Anna Eliza Corwin—was also referred to as Ann Lisa Corwin. Eliza remained married to him for twenty-seven years before finally being granted a divorce in 1870.
41 • Joseph Smith's platform for the U.S. Presidency included a plank for the U.S. seizure of the West clear to the Pacific Ocean.
42 • Among many top echelon Mormon elders who pledged their support to Brigham Young were the brothers Parley and Orson Pratt, George Q. Cannon, Orson Hyde, Charles Coulson Rich, John Taylor, Wilford Woodruff, Willard Richards, Heber Kimball, Lorenzo Snow and Jedediah Grant.
43 • The Texas Rangers came into being at Waco, Texas, in 1837, with the establishment of Ft. Fisher by Anson Darnell, Starrett Smith and Jacob Gross.
44 • In 1841, Prussian gunsmith, Nikolas Dreyse, designed what he called the "needle-gun," which was the first successful breech-loader. A bolt-action rifle, it used a long, needle-like firing pin to penetrate through a black powder charge to detonate a primer positioned on the base of the bullet. However, it was seven years before the Prussian Army allowed the weapon to replace muzzle-loaders still in use by the army.
45 • Sutter reached Yerba Buena safely and found his schooner *Sacramento* almost on the point of embarking. He paid a courtesy call at the Customs House, boarded his little ship and weighed anchor. They were still within sight of the port when a rider arrived at the Customs House with General Castro's order for the arrest of Sutter and party if they should appear there, but by then it was too late.
46 • Following the Battle of San Jacinto, Texans defeated the much larger Mexican Army under General Antonio López de Santa Ana, President of Mexico. Santa Ana ordered his troops out of Texas and met with Texas leaders and secretly signed the Treaty of Velasco, which recognized Texas independence and that new republic's claim of the Rio Grande as its southern and southwestern boundary. Despite the treaty's later repudiation by the Mexican Congress, the Republic of Texas maintained its independence.

# The Infinite Dream

47 • The Oregon Territory in dispute at this time included the present states of Oregon and Washington and the Canadian Province of British Columbia. The forty-second parallel, where the Columbia River empties into the Pacific Ocean is the north border of present Oregon. The forty-ninth parallel was the already established Canadian/United States border from the Great Lakes to the Continental Divide in the Rocky Mountains.

48 • A.G. Benson, while a good talker and a man who could make things happen in political circles, was secondary to the intellectual Amos Kendall, a highly influential Democratic editor who was important in constructing the political program for the Jacksonian Democrats. His was a strong voice in Andrew Jackson's Kitchen Cabinet and he wrote numerous Jackson state papers. His claim of knowing everyone of importance in Washington, D.C. was not farfetched.

49 • The full U.S. Congress Joint Resolution outlining terms of annexation to the Republic of Texas was approved March 1, 1845 and stated: *"a State is to be formed out of the present Republic of Texas, with suitable extent and boundaries, and with two representatives in Congress, until the next apportionment of representation, shall be admitted into the Union, by virtue of this act, on an equal footing with the existing States, as soon as the terms and conditions of such admission and the cession of the remaining Texas territory to the United States shall be agreed upon by the Government of Texas and the United States: And that the sum of one hundred thousand dollars be, and the same is hereby, appropriated to defray the expenses of mission and negotiations, to agree upon the terms of said admission and cession, either by treaty to be submitted to the Senate, or by articles to be submitted to the two houses of Congress, as the President may direct."*

50 • Site of present Lambertville, Hope Township, Hunterdon County, New Jersey.

51 • Mosquito fever was a mild form of malaria, while ague was the ordinary term for what today is called influenza.

52 • Clyman did not go to the Sonoma area immediately as initially planned; instead he went to Monterey and met with American Consul Thomas Larkin, then to Yerba Buena where he spent a few months before heading into the Sierras to hunt grizzly bear.

53 • A letter of this acceptance by the Texas Convention was written to President Polk on July 12, 1845, by Anson Jones, President of the Republic of Texas, Washington on the Brazos, July 12, 1845.

54 • Much mystery still exists in regard to what these secret orders involved. Copies of same were in the frigate U.S.S. Congress, which immediately set sail for Monterey on the shipping route that would take it southward in the Atlantic, around the treacherous Cape Horn passage and then northward up the Pacific Coast of South America. Barring mishaps, however, the dispatches being hand-carried by Gillespie were expected to arrive first, which is what occurred.

55 • The orders to Fremont involved a high degree of secrecy in regard to their content. No copy of them is known to exist and President Polk did not mention them in his diary. Since that time it has been argued extensively among historians not only what the orders to Larkin included but, more importantly, what the secret instructions were to Fremont. In regard to Larkin, the matter was reasonably resolved three years later when the Senate passed a resolution demanding the letter be turned over to them that had been written in October, 1845, by Secretary of State Buchanan. A copy of the letter was produced and read, at which President Polk wrote in his diary on March 21, 1848:
*The letter was read. It was confidential and had for its object the protection of American interest and the prevention of Brittish [sic] and French interference in California. All [Cabinet] members agreed that the letter should not have been called for but, that it had been called for, a refusal to furnish it would lead to erroneous inferences, prejudicial to the administration. A false impression is being attempted by the administration in Congress, to be made, to the effect that this letter to Mr. Larkin contained instructions to produce a revolution in California before Mexico commenced the War against the U.S. & that Col. Fremont had the authority to make the revolution. The publication of the letter will prove the falsehood of such an inference.*

Buchanan's letter was, in fact, surrendered, as called for by the Senate. However, Polk's written orders to Larkin were not revealed, nor was there ever any clarification of content of whatever orders, written or verbal, that had been relayed to Fremont via Lieutenant Gillespie. It is probably reasonably safe to assume that Gillespie's urgent search for Fremont was not predicated merely on delivering the personal letters he carried for him from his wife, Jessie, and his father-in-law, Senator Thomas Hart Benton. It is likely—in light of Fremont's immediate peremptory actions after conferring with Gillespie, and in President Polk's personal efforts to protect Fremont in that

The Infinite Dream

officer's subsequent court-martial—that Polk's orders directed Fremont, in the event of Mexican/United States war being declared, to take the initiative and rally all Americans in California into a fighting force and to take whatever steps he deemed necessary to seize control of California for the U.S.

56 • This business of the contract Brannan signed, for transference of Mormon lands in exchange for political influence, was a fraud shrouded in mystery. Sketchy details of it rest primarily on comments by Brannan in his letters to Brigham Young. Exactly how Kendall and Benson hoped to swindle Mormons out of their future lands was never fully ascertained, but when the conniving Washington pair sent the contract to Young for his signature and those of the Mormon Council members, it was returned unsigned, with the notation that Elder Samuel Brannan had no authority to act in such manner on behalf of the Church. Benson and Kendall at that point apparently let the embryonic scheme die, as nothing further developed.

57 • There is nothing in Mormon documents to indicate that Brannan's plea was ever acted upon. The supposition is that when the time came to set sail for California, Brannan simply turned his back and walked away from whatever debts he had accrued in New York.

58 • Diverting emigrant settlers from the Oregon Trail to California was not difficult, since the Oregon Trail, especially from Fort Hall westward, had acquired an unsavory reputation due to its treacherous passage, which caused many deaths and heavy losses of equipment, supplies and wagons. Mountain Man Stephen Meek, acting as Elijah White's agent, undertook in 1845 to guide a party of some 200 wagons over a new route that would avoid the Blue Mountains and the extremely dangerous Columbia River descent. It was supposed to take them up the Malheur River and via suitable passes in the mountains to the southernmost reaches of the Willamette River Valley. However, they lost their way and the resultant panic and starvation took seventy-five lives. When this became known—and often grossly embellished—it was not difficult to convince emigrants to head for California instead of Oregon.

59 • A *fanega* is a Spanish dry measure equivalent to 1.58 bushels. Thus, the 800 *fanegas* of wheat Sutter was planning to plant was equivalent to 1,264 bushels, which would yield somewhere in the neighborhood of 21,000 bushels.

60 • Steamboats were not new to the Pacific Coast. The first, the *S.S. Beaver*, 101 feet in length, which was built in England in 1835, was first seen on her maiden voyage at Vancouver on May 16, 1836, and she ascended the Columbia and steamed into the mouth of the Willamette River fifteen days later. Earlier in the year, J.M. Shively, postmaster in Astoria at the mouth of the Columbia, officially proposed that the U.S. Government establish a line of mail steamships to ply the waters between Panama and Oregon on a regular schedule. Soon after the proposal was made, tensions increased between the U.S. and Great Britain in respect to Oregon's north boundary and Polk began giving the idea serious consideration and among those he selected to look into the matter was New York shipping magnate J.M. Woodward, whose careful investigations made him conclude that such a steamer mail proposal was not only feasible, with government assistance, but likely profitable as well. This was the beginning of the Pacific Mail Steamship Company. More explicit details of the first five years of that company's history can be found in the government document entitled: *Mails, Reports of the Secretary of the Navy and the Postmaster-general, communicating, in Compliance with a Resolution of the Senate, Information in Relation to the Contracts for the Transportation of the mails by Steamships between New York and California, March 23, 1852*. 32nd Congress, 1st Session, Senate Executive Document 50.

61 • Such claim was grandiose. Only once before, in 1841, had Texas claimed the Rio Grande represented her western and southern boundary. At that time they sent a combined force – diplomatic, military and marauding—toward the New Mexico capital, Santa Fe. It was a big mistake; the New Mexicans attacked the column, killing or imprisoning the majority. As a result of that episode, guerilla raids were still, as 1846 began, occurring between Texans and New Mexicans.

62 • The actual reason for Fremont's visit to Yerba Buena at this time with eight or nine of his men apparently remains a mystery. It may be that he was seeking support from Yerba Buena merchant traders for attacking and disrupting the shaky government of the Californios. That, however, remains only a conjecture unsupported by documentation.

63 • Where the $16,000 came from for the ship alterations has never been satisfactorily explained. Probably these were funds Brannan obtained from the Church, although this has not been

647

confirmed. Some accounts suggest it was Brannan's own money that paid for it. Considering the debts he had acquired in New York with his printing venture makes this explanation quite unlikely.

64 • The Truckee Pass route (later Donner Pass) north of Lake Tahoe, taken by Fremont's main force, turned out to be a much more difficult passage for both horses and men than the pass discovered by Walker's Detachment some thirty miles to the south, around the southern end of Lake Tahoe.

65 • Gavilan Peak was subsequently renamed to the designation it now bears: Fremont Peak.

66 • Later the name of Fort Texas was changed to Fort Brown, site of present Brownsville, Texas.

67 • As a matter of fact, whatever friendship existed between Pico and Castro rather dissolved at this point and never again regained its former warmth.

68 • An undisclosed number of others of Thornton's patrol were wounded, of which two later died. Among those captured was Thornton's second-in-command, Captain William J. Hardee.

69 • As nearly as can be determined, the *Brooklyn* was, at this point, approximately 100 miles south-southeast of the San Fernandez Islands and close to 400 miles southwest of Santiago.

70 • This was the island upon which explorer Alexander Selkirk had lived for five years (1704 - 1709) and which provided author Daniel Defoe with the inspiration to subsequently write his immortal novel, *Robinson Crusoe*, which many of the Saints had actually read.

71 • Later, when the city developed around the site, the name was changed a final time and became Brownsville, Texas.

72 • It was never revealed exactly what the secret orders were from President Polk that special messenger Archibald Gillespie, at the risk of his own life, took months to deliver to John Fremont. The question remains, why, when Gillespie was in danger of his life in Mexico on his way to find Fremont, he memorized and then destroyed the secret documents from President Polk to John Fremont, and finally delivered them—vocally—to Fremont, and Fremont only, the President's most secret orders? That question has never been answered and, quite probably, never will be.

73 • This, as it turns out, was the same day Gillespie arrived in a small boat at Sutters Fort to inquire after Fremont and was told by Sutter that Fremont was en route upstream on the Sacramento River to its headwaters, to continue mapping from there the trail leading northward over the mountains. Gillespie immediately pushed on in his boat and when he reached Lassen's he was told Fremont was just ahead, riding up the Sacramento with the view of continuing his surveying to the Willamette headwaters in the Oregon Territory. At that point Gillespie abandoned his boat, hired men and horses and pushed on as rapidly as possible.

74 • Polk, within two months of this occurrence, elevated John Kenzer Kane to the federal bench.

75 • The full text of President James Knox Polk's address to the joint session of Congress on May 11, 1846, requesting a Declaration of War against the Republic of Mexico may be found on the Internet by accessing the following address: http://www.dmwv.org/mexwar/intro.htm

76 • The full text of both reports can be found on the Internet under the title *The U.S-Mexican War: A Concise History*. See: http://www.dunwy.org/mexwar/intro.htm

77 • These buttes, later named the Marysville Buttes but presently designated as the Sutter Buttes, rise to a height of 2,117 feet rather spectacularly from relatively flat surrounding land with an elevation of 70 feet, 3/5 mile northeast of the mouth of Butte Creek. There are no other nearby prominences.

78 • John Bidwell set the number of horses at 150; Bernard DeVoto, however, usually the more reliable, sets the figure as "nearly 200."

79 • The entire saga of John C. Fremont's involvement, personally and militarily, is shrouded in more mystery and speculation than any other historical event the author has ever encountered. Much of what has been written in this segment is based on scattered bits and pieces of information that have been randomly found and fitted, as closely as possible into a scenario that has some basis in fact, but which, for the most part, simply cannot be entirely and irrefutably substantiated. As such, until and unless more revealing evidence can be unearthed at some future time, the reader is warned to take the matters in this segment involving President Polk, Lieutenant Gillespie, and—most particularly—John C. Fremont—as reconstructed history rather than a relation of absolutely verifiable history.

80 • While in no measure a significant skirmish, it had a good effect. Not only did the Mokelumnes fail in their horse-stealing attempt, but the death of their famed Chief Raphero caused them to abandon their plan to attack Sutters Fort in force and they withdrew into the distant hills.

81 • The flag created by William L. Todd (who was a nephew of Mary Todd Lincoln and who had been

raised in the Lincoln family) was retained by the Society of California Pioneers until 1906 when it was unfortunately burned beyond saving during the Great California Earthquake and Fire.

82 • The first writer to recognize the scope of this misunderstanding was W. Ray Luce, whose 1974 article in *Utah Historical Quarterly*, entitled *"The Mormon Battalion: A Historical Accident?"* clearly pointed out the remarkable misunderstanding of a Presidential directive that erroneously called for premature enlistment of the Mormons into the Army of the West immediately upon their arrival at Fort Leavenworth.

83 • Little to Polk, 1 June 1846, reprinted with Little's report and diary in Watson, ed., *Manuscript History of Brigham Young 1846 - 1847*, 216 - 217.

84 • For complete text of Secretary of State Marcy's letter to Colonel Kearny, see *Marcy to Kearny, House Executive Document 60 (30 - 1), 1847 - 48. Serial 520*, 153 - 155.

85 • The assessment written in 1891 by John Bidwell of the so-called "Bear Flag Revolt" is probably the most correct of any penned, considering how that episode in California history has, over the elapsed time, assumed so much greater importance than has truly been its due. Even though more details in regard to this incident have appeared over the years, little has changed to affect Bidwell's original assessment of the matter and the author, after intensive study in the matter, tends to agree with Bidwell's comments quoted in *"The California Bear Flag Revolt—1845"* by John Bidwell in *The Century Illustrated Monthly Magazine*, February, 1891, Vol. XLI, No. 4.

86 • Fremont was very well aware that Vallejo had become quite pro-American, had vociferously favored the U.S. annexation of California and had already offered his services in whatever move toward the takeover was projected. Thus, it became the cause of considerable bitterness among Merritt and his men, after the "capture" was effected, when Fremont loudly claimed credit for "ordering" the move on Sonora and the capture of the general and his guests. Merritt, on behalf of his men, later accused Fremont of "...wanting to hog the glory, after refusing to take the risk, if any." Nevertheless, it was Fremont who subsequently took over command from William Ide at Sonoma and generally received credit for the "coup".

87 • George F. Parsons in *The Life and Adventures of James W. Marshall: The Discoverer of Gold in California*, Sacramento, 1870 (code: **LAJM**), wrote, pp. 18 - 21: *"Fremont's course at this juncture is generally understood to have been something more than the result of momentary inspiration. His presence in the neighborhood of the outbreak at the critical moment was perhaps accidental, but there is every reason to believe that he had received instructions* [from President Polk] *to stay in California, and combat foreign influences as much as possible—which means that he was to pave the way for the absorption of California by the United States."* The author tends to concur fully with the conclusions drawn by George F. Parsons in this regard.

88 • The full text of Colonel Stephen W. Kearny's Special Order to Captain James Allen, can be found in *Kearny to Allen, Kearny Selected Papers*, MIC AI39, National Archives.

89 • The Golden Gate was named by Fremont in this manner and not, as so many came to believe, because of the gold deposits which were discovered in other areas of California a year and a half later, which so swiftly and profoundly altered the course of California's history [see *Internet: sfmuseum.org/hist/chron1.html*].

90 • Fremont had assessed with considerable accuracy what would occur when his report reached Washington and the information was released to the press. He became, even more than anticipated, and even more than General Taylor himself, the first great American hero in the Mexican-American War.

91 • False stories designed to mislead and create confusion abounded on the frontiers at this time, but none others quite so involved and deceptive as those that evolved in regard to the Mormons. Brigham Young much later, and long after Captain Allen's death, claimed that Captain James Allen's plan was to call for volunteers as part of a plot hatched by Missouri U.S. Senator Thomas H. Benton in conjunction with President James Polk's administration to exterminate the Mormons as they headed into the western wilderness. The supposed "conspirators" expected Young to reject the "tyrannical requisition", at which time President Polk would immediately call upon the governors of Missouri, Illinois, and Iowa for enough troops to massacre them all. Young, at that later time, claimed that he was able to "see through this wicked design" and undermined it "with a ringing show of patriotism." There is no element of truth in the story and the Mormons earned the respect of virtually all residents and transients on the frontier for their stalwart behavior in the face of deliberate falsehoods bandied about them and through an extremely difficult expedition.

92 · Captain John Allen quite some time afterward admitted that "I blame the Saints not at all for their resentment and had I been in the position of the Mormons at this time, I would not myself have enlisted under such circumstances, not even to save the government."

93 · All the men summoned by Brigham Young met with him as directed in the specific cottonwood grove designated; all having arrived at the location by 5:45 p.m. on July 18. Brooking no discussion, Young addressed them in a monologue that appeared to be well rehearsed. They were, he told them—those in particular who were chosen as captains—"…to be fathers of your companies and manage your affairs by the power and influence of your priesthood." He endowed them with the power to preserve their own lives and the lives of the men in their companies and enable them all to escape difficulties. He went on: "I am not afraid to pledge my right hand that every man will return alive, so long as they will perform their duties faithfully, without murmuring, and go in the name of the Lord. They must be humble and pray every morning and every evening in their tents. A private soldier is as honorable as an officer, if he behaves well. No one is distinguished as being better flesh and blood than another. Honor the calling of every man in his place."

94 · Commodore John D. Sloat's proclamation to the citizens of Monterey specifically and to Californians generally was issued on July 7, 1846. It stated: "*I declare to the inhabitants of California, that although I come in arms with a powerful force, I do not come among you as an enemy to California; on the contrary, I come as your best friend—as henceforward California will be a portion of the United States, and its peaceable inhabitants will enjoy the same rights and privileges they now enjoy; together with the privileges of choosing their own magistrates and other officers for the administration of justice among themselves, and the same protection will be extended to them as to any other State in the Union. They will also enjoy a permanent government under which life, property and the constitutional right and lawful security to worship the Creator in the way most congenial to each one's sense of duty will be secured, which unfortunately the central government of Mexico cannot afford them, destroyed as her resources are by internal factions and corrupt officers, who create constant revolutions to promote their own interests and to oppress the people. Under the flag of the United States California will be free from all such troubles and expense…*"

95 · Historian George F. Parsons in his book *The Life and Adventures of James W. Marshall, The Discoverer of Gold in California* [Sacramento, 1870, pp. 27 - 32] avers that a confrontation did occur and he quotes a substantial dialog alleged to have occurred between American Commodore Sloat and British Admiral Seymour at the time. The principal eyewitness account, however, penned by the Rev. Walter Colton in *Deck and Port*, NY, 1850, p. 393, who was aboard the *Savannah* at the time, mentions nothing of the kind and, in fact, Colton broadly remarks: "*It has often been stated by American writers that the Admiral [Seymour] intended to raise the English flag in California and would have done it had we not stolen the march on him. I believe nothing of the kind; the allegation is a mere assumption, unwarranted by a solitary fact.*"

96 · At approximately the same time as this American flag-raising was occurring at Yerba Buena (San Francisco), similar flag raisings were occurring at Los Angeles and Sonoma. The Yerba Buena flag-raising took place in what later came to be called Portsmouth Square, which for many years remained the central park of San Francisco. At present it is still a park of the same name located in Chinatown.

97 · What could possibly have prompted Fremont to name Major Ezekiel Merritt as quartermaster of the California Battalion has never been satisfactorily explained. Merritt, who almost always wore fringed buckskins that were filthy, could neither read nor write and he lived with an Indian squaw quite as dirty and illiterate as himself. He was an old trapper and mountain man who stammered badly, which wasn't helped any by the fact that he chewed tobacco, as Bidwell put it, "…to disgusting excess." He did have a reputation for great courage, although that may have evolved from his continual boasting of his own prowess as an Indian fighter and his alleged killing of many of them in hand-to-hand combat; the tomahawk that he carried in his belt had a handle in which almost a hundred notches had been scored , reportedly to record the number of Indian scalps he had taken. He was a very heavy drinker, whenever he could afford to imbibe and was frequently so inebriated he had difficulty walking. He also seemed to have an incredible ability to charm people virtually out of their senses, as occurred with Commodore Stockton.

98 · Actually, that was the last seen or heard of concerning that document, it having become invalid two days later, on July 7, when Commodore Sloat raised the American flag at Monterey that day and ordered it raised at other ports where American influence prevailed. [See *The California Bear Flag Revolt—1845* by John Bidwell in *The Century Illustrated Monthly Magazine*, 1891, Vol. XLI, No. 4.]

*The* Infinite Dream

99 • Having talked with the Potawatomi chiefs of the area, Brigham Young and James Allen received from them permission for the Mormon families to establish and over-winter camp on the west bank of the Missouri River. Though technically not empowered to make such an arrangement without approval of higher governmental authority, the exigencies of necessity prompted Allen to do so anyway and, to establish an official record of his debatable authority to do so, Allen wrote the following missive from his Council Bluffs, Iowa temporary headquarters:

*July 16, 1846*
*Head Quarters, Mormon Battalion Council Bluffs*
The Mormon people, now enroute to California, raised and furnished for the service of the United States a battalion of volunteers to serve with the army of the West in our present war with Mexico, and many of the men composing this Battalion having to leave their families in the Pottawatomie [sic] country, *the within permission to a portion of the Mormon people to reside for a time on the Pottawatomie lands, obtained from the Indians on my request, is fully approved by me, and such of the Mormon people as may desire to avail themselves of this privilege are hereby authorized to do so, during the pleasure of the United States.*

*James Allen Lt. Col. U.S.A.*
*Commanding Mormon Battalion*

100 • Jefferson Hunt, having been designated senior officer for the Mormon Battalion, chose to have his entire family accompany him on the march, including his first wife, Celia, and his second wife, Matilda. His two eldest sons, Gilbert and Marshall, promptly enlisted into their father's company. Others of Hunt's children brought along included four young sons and three daughters. Hunt was, at this time, one of a relatively few Mormon men who had adopted the Mormon policy of plural marriage, as it was revealed by Joseph Smith at Nauvoo, but which was not openly embraced by the LDS Church itself until 1852.

101 • It had initially been Brigham Young's plan to establish the Mormons' Winter Quarters on Grand Island in present Nebraska but, due to the slowness of the march, plus the fact learned that a sizeable contingent of Pawnee Indians each year wintered their horses on Grand Island and would not tolerate white interlopers and their cattle, Young changed his mind and applied for, and received, permission to establish Mormon Winter Quarters on the west bank of the Missouri River almost opposite Council Bluffs, Iowa. The site chosen, now a designated historical site, was located where Florence, Nebraska was once located but which eventually was absorbed within the limits of the present city of Omaha.

102 • Improbable as it seemed at the time Brigham Young uttered these predictions, all of them were, by and large, quite accurate.

103 • The rations and pay of the 500 men of the Mormon Battalion dates from July 16, 1846, the day the privates of the five companies were sworn in by their commanding officer, James Allen, at Council Bluffs, Iowa, and the date on which Allen assumed his rank of Lt. Col. At the time the oath was administered, not all of Company E had yet been assembled, but this gap was filled soon afterward. The complete composition of the role, as nearly as could be ascertained follows: **COMPANY A:** Jefferson Hunt *(senior captain and company captain)*; George W. Oman *(1st Lt.)*; Lorenzo Clark *(2nd Lt.)*; William W. Willis *(3rd Lt., 1st Sgt. at Mustering-in)*; James Ferguson *(Sgt. Major)*; Phinehas R. Wright *(1st Sgt. at Mustering-out)*; Ebenezer Brown *(2nd Sgt.)*; Reddick N. Allred *(3rd Sgt.)*; Alexander McCord *(4th Sgt.)*; Gilbert Hunt *(1st Cpl.)*; Lafayette N. Frost *(2nd Cpl.)*; Thomas Weir *(3rd Cpl., but private at Mustering-out)*; William S. Muir *(4th Cpl, private at Mustering-in, 1st Sgt. at Mustering out)*; Elisha Everett *(musician)*; Joseph W. Edwards *(musician, who died at Pueblo).* PRIVATES (alphabetically:) Rufus C. Allen; James R. Allred; James T.S. Allred; Reuben W. Allred; Albern Allen; James Bailey; Gordon S. Beckstead; Orin M. Beckstead; James Beran; John S. Briant; John Brown; Jacob K. Butterfield; Josiah Curtis; Henderson Cox; Hiram B. Chase; Alva C. Calkins; Edwin R. Calkins; James W. Calkins; Sylvanus Calkins; William W. Casper; Joseph Clark; Riley G. Clark; George Colman; Zechariah B. Decker; Joseph Dobson; Eli Dodson; James C. Earl; Robert C. Egbert; Henry Fairbanks; David Frederick; David Garner; James M. Glines *(Qtr.-Master Sgt. at Mustering-in, Pvt. at Mustering-out)*; Andrew Goodman; Gilman Gordon; James Hampton *(died at camp on Rio Grande)*; Benjamin Hawkins; Eli B. Hewett; William F. Hickenlooper; Elijah E. Holden; Henry P. Hoyt; Timothy S. Hoyt; Wilford Hudson; Schuyler Hulett; Martial (Marshall?) Hunt; Richard A. Ivy; Charles A. Jackson; Henry Johnson; Nicholas Kelley; William Kelley; James Kibly; Barnabas

651

Lake; James W. Lemon; Maxie Maxwell; Benjamin F. Mayfield; David Moss; Conrad Naile; Melcher Oyler; Henry Packard *(Mustering-out as Cpl.)*; Ebenezer Persons; John Ritter; Cariatat C. Roe; John Sessions; Richard Sessions; William B. Sessions; George Sexton; Lafayette Shepherd *(Mustering-out as Cpl.)*; George E. Steele; Isaiah C. Steele; Hamilton Swartout; Joseph Taylor; John Thompson; Adna Vrandenburg; Franklin Weaver; Miles Weaver; Charles Y. Webb; Merrill W. Wheeler; Joseph White; Samuel F. White; Jeremiah Willey; Alfred G. Wilson; Dennis Winn; Lysander Woodworth; Isaac N. Wriston; John P. Wriston. **COMPANY B:** Jesse D. Hunter *(captain, commanding)*; Luddington Elam *(1st Lt.)*; Barrus Ruel *(2nd Lt.)*; C. Merrill Philemon *(3rd. Lt.)*; William Coray *(1st Orderly Sgt.)*; William Hyde *(2nd Orderly Sgt.)*; Albert Smith *(3rd Orderly Sgt.)*; David P. Rainey *(1st Cpl.)*; Thomas Dunn *(2nd Cpl.)*; John D. Chase *(3rd Cpl.)*; William Hunter *(Musician)*; George W. Taggart *(Musician)*. PRIVATES (alphabetically:) Horace M. Alexander; Elijah Allen; Franklin Allen; George Allen; John Barrowman; Henry W. Bigler; Orson Billings; Erastus Bingham; Thomas Bingham; William Bird; Robert S. Bliss; Samuel Boley *(died along Missouri River)*; Benjamin B. Brackenberry; Francis Brown; Richard Bush; John Bybee; Thomas W. Callahan; J.G. Camp; P.J. Carter; R. Carter; Zacheus Chaney; Haden W. Church; George S. Clark; Philander Colton; Dorr P. Curtis; William J. Dayton; Henry S. Dolton; Albert Dunham; Thomas P. Dutcher; Marcus N. Eastman; Israel Evans; William Evans; Peter Fife; William A. Follett; Elijah N. Freeman; Phillip Garner; William A. Garner; Ephrain Green; George Haskell; Silas Harris; Nathan Hawk; William Hawk; Arza E. Hinkley *(Ezra on original)*; Jacob Hoffheins; Ephraim R. Hanks; Edward Hunter; Isaiah Huntsman; David H. Jones; Guy M. Keyser; John M. King; Thomas Kirk; John Lawson; Jesse B. Martin; Nelson McCarty; Samuel Miles; Thomas Morris; Hiram B. Mount; John R. Murdock; Price Murdock; Samuel Myers; Christian Noler; Robert Owens; James Park (1st); James Park (2nd); Ephraim Pearson; Harmon D. Persons; William Prouse; Peter F. Richards; Samuel H. Rogers; William A. Simmons; James C. Sly; Azariah Smith; Andrew J. Steers; Lyman Stephens; Dexter Stillman; Rufus Stoddard; David Study; William Walker; John Watts; John L. Wheeler; Francis T. Whitney; Edward Wilcox; Henry Wilcox; Ira Willis; W.S.S. Willis; Jacob Winters; Andrew J. Workman; Oliver G. Workman; Charles Wright; Jerome Zabriskie. **COMPANY C:** James Brown *(Captain, commanding)*; George W. Rosecrans *(1st Lt.)*; Robert Clift *(3rd Lt., promoted from Orderly Sgt.)*; Orson B. Adams *(2nd Sgt., 1st Sgt. at Mustering-in)*; Elmer Elijah *(1st Sgt., 2nd Sgt. at Mustering-in)*; Joel J. Terrill *(Pvt., 3rd Sgt. at Mustering-in)*; David Wilkin *(Pvt., 4th Sgt. at Mustering-in)*; Jabez Nowlin *(Pvt., 1st Cpl. at Mustering-in)*; Alexander Brown *(2nd Cpl.)*; Edward Martin *(2nd Sgt., 3rd Cpl. at Mustering-in)*; Daniel Tyler *(3rd Sgt., 4th Cpl. at Mustering-in)*; Russell G. Brownell, *(Cpl., Musician at Mustering-in)*; Richard D. Sprague (Musician). PRIVATES (alphabetically:) Wesley Adair; Addison Bailey; Jefferson Bailey; Walter Barney; Lorenzo Babcock; William E. Beckstead; Abner Blackburn; Henry G. Boyle *(Henry B. Miller on original)*; John Brimhall; Jesse J. Brown; William Burt; Henry G. Bybee; John Calvert; Isaac Carpenter; William H. Carpenter; George Catlin; James Clift; Jeptha Condit; John Q.A. Covil; Edward Dalton; Harry Dalton; Augustus E. Dodge; Neal Donald; James Dunn; Francillo Durphy; Hiram W. Fellows; John Fife; Levi Fifield; Lorin Forbush; Thomas Gibson; John C. Gould; Samuel Gould; John Green; Charles Hancock; George W. Hancock; Ebenezer Harmon; Lorenzo F. Harmon; Meltliah Hatch; Orin Hatch; James Hendrickson; Shadrach Holdaway; William Holt; Thomas C. Ivie; Jarvis Johnson; Jesse W. Johnston; William J. Johnston; Ebenezer Landers; Thurston Larson; Christopher Layton; Samuel Lewis; Benjamin Maggard; Levi H. McCullough; Orlando F. Mead; Calvin W. More; Harley Morley; John T. Mowrey; James Myler; Hiram Olmstead; Isaac Peck; Thorit Peck *(Cpl. at Mustering-out)*; David Perkins; John Perkins; Judson Persons; George Pickup; David Pulsipher; William Reynolds; Benjamin Richie; Benjamin Richmond; John J. Riser; William W. Rust; Joseph Shipley; Andrew J. Shupe; James Shupe; Milton Smith; Richard Smith; William Squires *(Cpl. at Mustering-out)*; Aurora Shumway; Elijah Thomas; Nathan T. Thomas; James L. Thompson; Solomon Tindell; Jacob M. Truman; Elanson Tuttle; Edward W. Wade; Moses Wade; Madison Welsh; Henry Wheeler; John J. White; Matthew Wilcox; William Wood. **COMPANY D:** Nelson Higgins *(Captain, commanding)*; George P. Dykes *(1st Lt.)*; Sylvester Hulett *(2nd Lt.)*; Cyrus C. Canfield *(3rd Lt.)*; Nathaniel V. Jones *(Pvt. at Mustering-out, 1st Sgt. at Mustering-in)*; Thomas Williams *(2nd Sgt.)*; Luther T. Tuttle *(3rd Sgt.)*; Alpheus P. Haws *(4th Sgt.)*; Arnold Stephens *(1st Cpl.)*; John Buchanan *(2nd Cpl.)*; William Coon *(3rd Cpl.)*; Lewis Lane *(Pvt. at Mustering-out, 4th Cpl. at Mustering-in)*; Henry W. Jackson *(Musician; as Henry J. on original)*. PRIVATES (alphabetically:) Joshua Abbott; Juthan Averett; William W. Barger; Samuel Badlam; Erastus Bingham; George W. Boyd; William

Boyd; Henry W. Brizzee; James Brown *(1st)*; *James S. Brown (2nd)*; Button, Montgomery; James Casto; William Casto; Abner Chase; John R. Clawson; James B. Cole; Robert H. Collins; Allen Compton; Amos Cox; Curtis, Foster; Eleazer Davis; Sterling Davis; James Davis; Douglas, James; Ralph Douglass; Ezra Fatoute; Thomas Finlay; Philander Fletcher; John Forsgreen; Thomas Frazier; William W. Gifford; John Gilbert; William Gribble; Thomas Hayward; William D. Hendricks; Daniel Henry; Alfred Higgins; James Hirons; Lucas Hoagland; Jonathan Holmes; Abraham Hunsaker *(1st Sgt. at Mustering-out)*; Dimick B. Huntington; Sanford Jacobs *(Cpl. at Mustering-out)*; Loren E. Kenney; Lisbon Lamb; David S. Laughlin; William Maxwell; Henry McArthur; Erastus Meacham; Peter J. Meeseck; Ferdinand Merrill; James Oakley; James Owen; Edwin M. Peck; Charles Perrin; James P. Pettegrew; Daniel B. Rawson; Almon P. Raymond; William Richmond; Benjamin Roberts; William Robinson; John Rollins; William Rowe; Levi Runyan; Henry W. Sanderson; Abel M. Sargent; Levi Savage; Albert Sharp; Norman Sharp; Sebert C. Shelton; John G. Smith; William W. Spencer; John Steele; Alexander Stephens; Benjamin Stewart; James Stewart; Robert B. Stewart; Clark Stillman; Nathan Swarthout; Myron Tanner; Henry Thompson; Miles Thompson; Thomas Treat; John Tippets; Thomas Treat; William Tubbs; Anciel Twichell; Edwin Walker; Almon Whiting; Edmond Whiting; Francis Woodward. **COMPANY E:** Daniel C. Davis *(Captain, commanding)*; James Pace *(1st Lt.)*; Andrew Lytle *(2nd Lt.)*; Samuel L. Gully *(3rd Lt.)*; Samuel L. Brown *(1st Sgt.)*; Richard Brazier *(2nd Sgt.)*; Ebenezer Hanks *(3rd Sgt.)*; Daniel Browett *(4th Sgt.)*; James A. Scott *(Cpl., died at Pueblo)*; Jesse Earl *(Musician)*; Levi W. Hancock *(Musician)*. PRIVATES (alphabetically:) George Allen; John Allen *(drummed out of service for being non-Mormon)*; William Beers; John Bentley; Daniel Brown; Newman Buckley; Edward Bunker; Matthew Caldwell; Jonathan Campbell; Samuel Campbell; James Cazier; John Cazier; Albert Clark; Samuel Clark; Samuel Chapin; John Cox; George Cummings; Abraham Day; Daniel Q. Dennett; Simon Dyke; Jacob Earl; Justice C. Earl; Martin F. Ewell; William Ewell; John Findlay; William T. Follett; Luther W, Glazier; Oliver N. Harmon; Robert Harris; Isaac Harrison; Israel Harrison; James S. Hart; John W. Hess; John Hickmot; Charles Hopkins; Henry Hoskins; T.C.D. Howell; William Howell; Bailey Jacobs; Charles Jimmerson; Hiram Judd; Zadock K. Judd; Thomas Karren; George Kelley; Albert Knapp; William Lance; Haslam McBride; William C. McClelland; Daniel Miller; Miles Miller; William A. Park; David Pettegrew; Alva Phelps *(died on the Arkansas River)*; Robert Pixton; Sanford Porter; Jonathan Pugmire, Jr.; L. Richards; Thomas Richardson; L. Roberts; Evart Rollins; Richard T. Sanders; James R. Scott; Leonard M. Scott; Joseph Skein; Richard Slater; David Smith; Elisha Smith; John Smith; Lot Smith; John Snyder; John Spidle; Stephen M. St. John; Roswell Stevens; Henry Standage; William Strong; Albert Tanner; Benjamin West; William Whitworth; James V. Williams; George Wilson; Thomas Woolsey.

The above listing was enumerated by Norma B. Ricketts in her book, *The Mormon Battalion*, Salt Lake City, 1902, pp. 279 - 290, where also are listings of servants to the officers and families who accompanied the Battalion.

104 • There is no recorded datum known that Mormon William L. McIntyre ever actually served in this appointment as assistant surgeon to the Mormon Battalion as indicated in Order No. 3. It may be that the Mormon antipathy for the appointed surgeon, Dr. George B. Sanderson was so great that McIntyre refused to serve beneath him.

105 • This was the large, well-known trading post established by Indian trader Peter A. Sarpy along the Missouri River within the present city limits of Council Bluffs, Iowa.

106 • In his manuscript prepared many years later, entitled *Autobiography of Zadock Knapp Judd*, and presently in the collection of the Utah State Historical Society, Salt Lake City, [pp. 19 - 20], Judd, an eighteen-year-old originally from Ontario, Canada, had suffered from weak ankles long before joining the Mormon Battalion with his brother, Hyrum, twenty-one, who were both assigned to Company E. Despite the malady, he enjoyed the more than 200-mile march from Council Bluffs, Iowa, to Fort Leavenworth and confidently wrote in his diary that *"the men were happy and cheerful, singing and dancing..."* but when these raw recruits were issued their equipment and arms, he quickly realized why the western Missouri Volunteers preferred riding horseback on the march west. Sergeant Albert Smith put it most succinctly when he complained that this equipment would make *"A hevy* [sic] *load for a mule!"* [*Journal of Albert Smith*, LDS Archives, Aug. 5, 1846] Judd never again complained publicly about his weak ankles after that, but he recalled vividly this moment in early August, 1846 when basic equipment, including muskets, were provided to the men of the

# The Infinite Dream

Mormon Battalion. He wrote: *"In due time we arrived at Fort Leavenworth. Here we were armed with flint lock musket.* [Note: According to firearms expert Charles Cresap, a descendant of Mormon gunsmith Jonathan Browning, the battalion received Springfield U.S. model 1821 flintlock muskets manufactured in 1826 and 1827. Tyler, in *A Concise History*,. p. 136, recalled that Companies A, B, and C " possessed a few cap-lock yaugers for sharpshooting and hunting." The Company A invoice of Ordnance in the Ricketts book, *The Mormon Battalion*, p. 38, indicates these "Jaegers" were actually half-stock Harpers Ferry 1803 Jaeger rifles of the type issued to the Lewis and Clark Expedition. *This rifle was reputed to carry an ounce ball one mile. Its weight was twelve or fifteen pounds. Its accoutrements were a large cartridge box with heavy leather belt two-and-one-fourth inches wide to carry over the left shoulder, a similar belt with bayonet and scabbard attached to carry over the right shoulder and then a waist belt correspondingly wide and heavy all white leather, and we were required to keep them clean.... Our muskets had to be cleaned often. Also a knap-sack in which to carry our clothing and other little necessities. It was so arranged that a strap came in front of each shoulder and under the arm with a long strap to reach around our bedding. With all these straps in front and the filled knap-sack behind, we were nearly covered from neck to waist. We were required to carry all these fixtures, our clothing and bedding and a few rounds of ammunition and then a canteen in which would hold three pints of water, and then a small cotton sack called a hover-sack, in which to carry our dinner and sometimes a day or two rations. These also were made to swing over our shoulders.... But to ease up on us a little the officers allowed each company to club together and buy a four mule team and wagon, in which to haul our knap-sacks and bedding, each man to bear an equal share of the expense. This was a great relief for a while, but when hard times came on, wagon broke down or teams gave out, we had to shoulder our knap-sacks and bedding.... Here in Fort Leavenworth we were given cooking utensils, a camp kettle, frying-pan and coffee pot. Here we drew our clothing money for the entire year, $42, which as I have said was mostly sent back to needy friends and relatives.... Here our commander, Colonel Allen, laid in a supply of provisions to last the Battalion one year, but by a mishap it was sent the wrong road.* [Note: Allen had sent the provisions over the Santa Fe Trail's Mountain Route, the road taken by Kearny, to Bents Fort on the Arkansas River, near present La Junta, Colorado. From this point the Mountain Route headed south over Raton Pass on the line now followed by Interstate-25 to Santa Fe. The battalion was ordered to take the Cimarron Route, a more direct trail, which left the Arkansas near present Ingalls, Kansas, and cut across the Oklahoma panhandle, while its supplies wound up at Bents Fort.] *After a few days rest and a little drilling and learning to use our guns and properly form ourselves into ranks and getting baggage wagons ready, we took up the line of march. Our Colonel being unwell at the time was not able to go with us, but it was expected he would overtake us in a few days.* [This letter can be seen in its entirety in *Army of Israel*, pp. 84 - 86]

107 • Despite the "official" name-change of Sutters Fort to Fort Sacramento, the local populace refused to accept the new designation and continued to refer to it as Sutters Fort, much to John Sutter's delight. Eventually the title of Fort Sacramento simply fell entirely into disuse and the installation remained as Sutters Fort until its eventual dismantling.

108 • Jonathan Trumbull Warner had first established his 49,000-acre land grant, called Warners Ranch, two years earlier, in 1844, which became as much an oasis to travelers on the Southern Emigrant Trail in California as Johnsons Ranch and Sutters Fort were to emigrants who arrived on the northern route. Warner, himself, had first come to California in 1831, at which time he had applied for and was granted Mexican citizenship and became one of that area's largest landowners. He had, when the need arose, become one of the earliest advocates of California's annexation by the United States and had very competently provided service as a special agent and confidential correspondent of Thomas Larkin, the American consul at Monterey. The ruins of the ranch buildings can still be seen today on San Diego County Road S2 less than one mile from its junction with State Highway 79, about thirteen miles north of present Santa Ysabel.

109 • This official document was created as the 29th Congress, 2nd Session, House Executive Document 4. It may also be viewed by computer on the Internet at: http://www.notfrisco.com/calmem/Stockton.html.

110 • The break-up of the Mexican Army and the continued flight of Governor-General Armijo before him toward Mexico caused the newly promoted Brigadier General Stephen Kearny to drastically alter his plans insofar as his continued march toward California was concerned. He immediately put the majority of his Army under command of acting Lieutenant Colonel Doniphan and Captain Philip St. George Cooke, with orders to hold the posts and cities already taken with part of the

force and Doniphan to lead the remainder of the "fit" soldiers to the south in pursuit of Armijo and, in whatever case, to place himself and his command under the direction of General Zachary Taylor for what conquest of Mexico remained to be accomplished. Reserving only a 100-man unit of dragoons for himself, Kearny prepared at once to move on toward California, fully expecting the 500 men of the Mormon Battalion to overtake and join him en route before the California border would be reached. Near Durango, Mexico, British Lieutenant George Frederick Ruxton of Her Majesty's 89th Regiment, making a pleasure trip through Mexico toward the "States", met Armijo and his small entourage accompanying the private freight wagons of Albert Speyer's Caravan and pleased himself by referring to the Mexican general as "...*that enormous mountain of fat...*" and, in fact, gave himself the further pleasure of calling Armijo, to his face, an "*arrant coward.*" Ruxton was, of course, quite correct. However, the Mexican lieutenant governor of the Spanish New Mexico Territory, Diego Archuleta—a brave patriot and an experienced Indian fighter—wanted nothing so much as to confront Kearny's force at the Rio Grande and prevent him from entering his domain, but the small handful of men left to him to command was simply insufficient to face such an enemy and was disbanded, much to the regret of many of his remaining men. The intimation by John Fremont's father-in-law, however, U.S. Senator Thomas Hart Benton in his book *A Thirty Years' View,* that General Armijo had been "bought-off" for a fee of $50,000 provided by the Administration in Washington, DC, has never been proven and is almost certainly untrue.

111 • James Allen became one of the first U.S. officers to be buried in the Fort Leavenworth National Cemetery, his headstone listing his rank as Captain, which was his regular army rank. In 1977, however, special services held at the Veterans Administration replaced the first headstone with one listing his rank as Lieutenant Colonel while commanding the Mormon Battalion. It should be noted that while some accounts list malaria as the cause of Allen's death, others list it as consumption, better know today as tuberculosis. Evidently it was an onslaught of both maladies simultaneously, exacerbated by alcoholism, that weakened him so he could not recover. See also Harold Schindler's article entitled *"Rites Honor LDS Friend"* in *Salt Lake Tribune,* Salt Lake City, September 16, 1977. General Kearny's adjutant general, Captain Henry S. Turner, described Allen as "...*a man of a few unfortunate habits which doubtless was the cause of his death.... There never breathed a man of a higher sense of honor; liberal to a fault, and just in all his opinions and dealing with men.*" It is also noted that the most common harmful habit of frontier officers was an addiction to alcohol; the implication being that both the malaria and consumption (tuberculosis) in Allen's case was exacerbated by his frequent heavy drinking. See also, Clarke, ed., *The Original Journals of Henry Smith Turner,* under date of Oct. 3, 1846.

112 • Several disparate sources list the name of the Fort Leavenworth post commander as "Major Horton", which is evidently an error. The commander at this time (August, 1846) was Lieutenant Colonel Clifton Wharton, as recorded in AOI, 91 - 93 for August 23, 1846.

113 • Gully to Young, Brigham Young Collection, LDS Archives, Salt Lake City, August 23, 1846.

114 • This letter by George B. Sanderson, entitled *The Death of Our Friend,* appears in Sanderson to Young, Brigham Young Collection, Latter-day Saints Archives, dated July 23, 1846. It should be noted that years later, during the Civil War and without known evidence beyond his own conclusions, Brigham Young was quoted as having said, regarding Lt. Col. Allen's death, "*I then believed, and do now, he was nursed, taken care of, and doctored to the silent tomb.*" This was recorded in *Journal of Discourses,* March 8, 1863, 10:104 in LDS Archives, Salt Lake City. In all fairness and despite the continued accusations by members of the Mormon Battalion of unfair and cruel treatment waged against them by Dr. Sanderson throughout their enforced association, the evidence indicates Sanderson was, in fact, appointed Battalion Surgeon by Lt. Colonel Allen in one of his final official acts (see General Order No. 4, Aug. 1, 1846, Allen to Mormon troops) and served them well enough, despite his acerbic language to and about them. Note: CHMB-135 - 136.

115 • Initially, Brigham Young had intended for the Mormon's Winter Quarters to be established on the gigantic island in the Platte River of Nebraska that was generally called Grand Isle. Two very good reasons caused him to withdraw that plan: The first, because he was informed by Bishop George Miller, whom he had sent ahead with a small party to check it out, that the island was where Pawnee Indians of the area traditionally corralled their horses over the winter and they would look most unfavorably on an invasion of whites making it their winter quarters; secondly, because the migration of the Mormons from Nauvoo was going so slowly, the majority could only reach, at best

# The Infinite Dream

by winter, the Missouri River. Fearful of attack by raiding Missourians if they remained at Council Bluffs on the Iowa side of the river, Young thereupon applied to the Omaha Sioux for permission to establish winter quarters, for this winter of 1846 only, on the west side of the Missouri in Nebraska Territory about a dozen miles upstream from Council Bluffs. This permission was granted. The site chosen was located at what later became the town of Florence, Nebraska, which subsequently became absorbed into the present limits of the city of Omaha. A plaque commemorating temporary Winter Quarters for the emigrating Mormons of 1846 can now be found on this site.

116 • This episode of the missing money became one of the bleakest episodes in Mormon history and has never been satisfactorily explained. Evidence seems to indicate that the men of the Mormon Battalion turned over to the official "collectors" of the Church a sum totaling at least $15,000 and perhaps even more. Historian Richard E. Bennett, in his book, *Mormons at the Missouri*, p. 116, and Historian W. Bagley, who edited *The Pioneer Camp of the Saints*, p. 106, both independently calculated that when Parley P. Pratt returned to Winter Quarters, he had with him as monies collected from soldiers of the Mormon Battalion, an exact total of $5,835…approximately $9,165 <u>less</u> than had reportedly been collected; and after his meeting with Brigham Young, the funds Pratt turned over to Bishop Newell K. Whitney amounted to only $4,375.19—a distinct disappearance of another $1,459.81. Who the recipient was of the missing total of $10,624.81 has never been incontrovertibly ascertained.

117 • What Bigler and others termed as Beaver Creek is today known as Dragoon Creek and the site of their camp was just west of present Burlingame, KS.

118 • Pennsylvanian Andrew Jackson Smith, thirty, had been graduated from the U.S. Military Academy at West Point, NY, in 1838. He became a major general during the Civil War and received citations for both gallantry and meritorious service in the Battles of Pleasant Hill, LA, Tupelo, MS, and Nashville, TN. Following the war, he served as the first colonel of the newly established Seventh Cavalry, until succeeded in that role by Samuel D. Sturgis. His unit rode to tragic fame in 1876 under its second in command, Lt. Col. George A. Custer, at the Battle of the Little Big Horn. At least one account states that the news of Lt. Col. Allen's death was delivered to the Mormon Battalion by Sergeant John Shelton.

119 • Howard Egan was one of the more feared of LDS "enforcers" and reputed to have established "Gestapo-like" tactics within the Church itself. He had gained for himself the appellation of "The Avenging Angel" from services as a policeman at Nauvoo. It is claimed that he brutally murdered his wife's lover. He earned more sedate and renowned fame later as an overland captain, Indian missionary and agent for the Pony Express.

120 • Bents Fort was located seven miles east of present La Junta, Colorado, on the north bank of the Arkansas River and was, from 1830 through 1849, one of the more important trading centers on a branch of the Santa Fe Trail.

121 • At this time a lengthy story swept through the Mormon encampment that the camp was aroused the preceding night by a star in the east moving up and down and sideways. Bigler admits he *"…could not see any thing of the sorts"*…but he nevertheless states it was about this time when the mob drove out the rest of the Mormons from Nauvoo. Cpl. Tyler was one of the many who saw the "dancing star" that night and he connected it with Phelps's "being physicked [sic] to death." That something very strange occurred in the night sky at this time became clear in the numerous diary and journal entries that made reference to the event. Scores of men saw and wrote about the "dancing lights" in the sky that flew both in formation and on individual traces for a considerable while before finally grouping together and heading eastward until they passed from the range of visibility. No reasonable explanation for this unusual UFO sighting witnessed by so many has ever been advanced.

122 • The other soldiers who were part of Captain Nelson Higgins' detachment as escort to Pueblo included Corporal Gilbert Hunt and Privates Dimick B. Huntington, Montgomery Button, S.C. Shelton, Nicholas Kelley, Thomas Woolsey, Harley Morey, Milton Kelley, James Brown, Norman Sharp, and John Tippets.

123 • While this written report of the alleged conversation between John D. Lee and Lt. Col. A.J. Smith was recorded in even greater detail by Lee himself to Brigham Young [Juanita Brooks, ed., *"Diary of the Mormon Battalion Mission, John D. Lee,"* 17 - 27 September, 1846, as appeared in the July-October issues of the *New Mexico Historical Review*] and dated at "Commancha [sic] Indians Desert

Encampment, Thurs., Sept. 17th, '46, it should be noted that Lt. Col. Smith's reputation for being extremely short-tempered makes it rather unlikely that he would have suffered himself to undergo such a tirade, especially from an individual, irrespective of how well placed in the Latter-day Saints hierarchy, with the nominal rank of Private.

124 • At this time, Edward Ruxton, lieutenant in the British Army, reported to his superiors, following a cautious tour of the American Southwest, that he found the Indians to be "...*possessed by a stoic mentality which issues from a conviction that their day is over and the white man cannot be stayed.*" That such "stoic mentality" did not encompass all the Indians of the American Southwest became evident, of course, in the severe Indian troubles that were eventually to erupt in this quarter. [See also VOD-124]

125 • *Jefferson Davis had, for three months in 1835, been General Taylor's son-in-law.*

126 • The Mexicans, in referring to this conflict, call it The Battle of Buena Vista for La Angostura. This battle could well have gone either way for the Americans, who were considerably outnumbered and more exposed. As it turned out, this was the single bloodiest battle in the War with Mexico. The Americans, hard pressed on all sides and fighting through some of the roughest terrain an army might encounter, were for a time in clear danger of losing. In the end, however, the Mexicans withdrew. This left Taylor with another victory and President Polk with an even stronger fear that Taylor was gaining far too much stature in his bid for the US Presidency in 1848.

127 • When the U.S. Land Commission confirmed Vallejo's grant of the enormous Rancho Nacional, the U.S. government carried the case to the district court, only to have it confirm the action of the Land Commission. Refusing to be thwarted, the U.S. authorities then appealed the case to the U.S. Supreme Court, which then rejected Vallejo's claims on grounds that "...while the Mexican government gave away its land in California to those who applied for it and then met the conditions imposed by such grant, it could not sell government land for food furnished to sustain its soldiers." Thus, in 1863, Congress, through special act, permitted the provisional holders of Vallejo land titles to buy their land at $1.25 per acre. Through such measure, Vallejo's great rancho called Petaluma—originally 10,000 square leagues, to which he added five leagues more through purchase—a total of 66,000 acres—was nibbled away until nothing remained but the little home farm and residence called *Lachryma Montis*—which is still owned by Vallejo's descendants. General Vallejo was somewhat careless and improvident when money was abundant and, while he realized considerable sums from the sale of lands and cattle, his later years were plagued by comparative poverty. The California town of Vallejo was named after him, as was a street in San Francisco. He sired sixteen children, of whom six died before reaching maturity. [**BOSF**-348 - 357]

128 • See *San José Pioneer* of June 23, 1877 for greater details of the Mormon agricultural and manufacturing program and promise.

129 • There is no record among the early documents of the Mormons in California that any of the proceeds received by Brannan ever became a part of the Mormon general fund and the assumption is strong that all such funds received were simply pocketed by Brannan. While almost certainly quite true, the assumption has never been judicially proven.

130 • Captain Philip St. George Cooke received this order from Kearny while at Fort Leavenworth and he hastened at once toward Santa Fe to assume control, as ordered, of the Mormon Battalion. He arrived there and took command on Oct. 13, 1846, which finally put an end to the rebellion of sorts over both the issuance of calomel to the troops and who would succeed Lt. Col. Allen. Cooke, captain of a Dragoon company, accepted this appointment, as Allen had, with the temporary rank of Lieutenant Colonel. A stern but fair disciplinarian, he left no doubt as to who was in command. Cooke, a 6'4" Virginian, had been one of West Point's youngest graduates. Now, at age thirty-seven, he had already served nineteen years in the frontier army and he understood full well that nature could be a deadlier threat to the Battalion's survival than hostile Indians.

131 • Lee notes at this point: "See *Psalms* 1:3, *Jeremiah* 17:8, and *Revelation* 22:1,2."

132 • Mormon Battalion Sergeant John Tyler, along with several other diarists, referred to the springs here as "Gold Springs," but Lee's entry as "Cold Springs" seems to have been correct.

133 • The campsite chosen, a rather scenic spot, was actually near present McNee's Crossing of Corrumpa Creek, which is a tributary of the North Canadian River. It was named after a young trader who was killed on the site, near present Seneca, NM, during a raid by Comanches on a trader caravan in 1828.

134 • The hills known as the Rabbit Ears or Rabbit Ear Mountains are a pair of large landmark buttes, plus several smaller ones, which can be seen for a considerable distance and are relatively distinctive for their isolation from other ranges. [AOI-121 - 123]
135 • Point of Rocks remains today a noted Santa Fe Trail landmark. It is a rock mound rising from the prairie, from which flows a clear spring of fresh water. It is located in present Colfax County, New Mexico.
136 • What the Mormon Battalion referred to in this instance as the Red River was, in actuality, the Canadian River.
137 • John D. Lee was with the Mormon advance party at this time. The Mora River, which he refers to as the Morough, is a tributary of the Canadian River. It was near this camp that the Cimarron Route, currently being followed by the Battalion, merged with the Mountain Route of the Santa Fe Trail, which was following the Arkansas River upstream on the approximate line of present U.S. Route 50. This route went on to Bents Fort, then headed south over Raton Pass to this present junction.
138 • This is the ruins of what today is known as the Pecos Pueblo, which was abandoned about 1838 and which is now a National Monument. According to the late historian Juanita Brooks, the term Lee uses—"Nephite building"—derives from *The Book of Mormon*, which mentions various ancient cities on the North American continent.
139 • Thomas Fitzpatrick, more commonly referred to as "Broken Hand," had been, along with Jedediah Smith, one of William Ashley's fur hunters. He later received an order from Gen. Kearny to claim the twenty-one best mules in Santa Fe for the general's advance party, which deprived Cooke's command of the finest animals. Fitzpatrick was subsequently replaced as guide by Pauline Weaver, Antoine Leroux, and Baptiste Charbonneau, the latter being the son of Sacagawea of Lewis and Clark fame.
140 • Actually, the individual referred to here was Private Maxie Maxwell of Company A, who was probably French-Canadian.
141 • Albern Allen, forty-four, and his nineteen-year-old son, Rufus Chester Allen, were privates in Company A. [AOI-136 - 137]
142 • The reference here is to Lee's adopted son, First Lt. Samuel Gully of Company E, who had been appointed assistant Quartermaster to the Battalion by James Allen at Fort Leavenworth. Gully served in this capacity until removed by Cooke at Santa Fe. Others among the Mormon officers later blamed his dismissal on Adjutant George P. Dykes. Gully died of cholera on his way to Utah in 1849.
143 • In this instance Lee apparently was referring to Cooke's appointment of Lt. Andrew Jackson Smith as commissary of subsistence and Dr. George B. Sanderson as battalion surgeon.
144 • Actually the reference here to Taos was incorrect, since the writer was actually referring to Pueblo, where the Mississippi Saints and the Battalion detachments were to spend the winter, and which occurred.
145 • See *The West of Philip St. George Cooke*, by Sheldon Young, p. 132.
146 • For greater details of this travesty meant to defraud the dependants of the absentee soldier/ Saints, see *Journal of John Steele*, p. 10, edited by Beckwith; *The Journal of Robert S. Bliss*, p. 76, edited by Cecil, p. 76; also *The Pioneer Camp of the Saints*, p. 106, edited by Bagley.
147 • A very recent West Point graduate, Lieutenant George Stoneman saw his first active duty assignment as part of the Army of the West. He served in Texas in the 1850s in Albert Sidney Johnston's elite Second Cavalry beside Lt. Col. Robert E. Lee. He was also companion to Major George Thomas, the future "Rock of Chickamauga." During the Civil War, Stoneman led a spectacular, though ineffective, attack on Richmond during the Battle of Chancellorsville. In 1883 he was elected fifteenth governor of California.
148 • Lee's unbending attitude here was quite characteristic of him. Years later, according to historian Juanita Brooks, Lee flatly refused to join in a dance that included men who had spoken disrespectfully of Brigham Young.
149 • The orders dictated by Lt. Col. Cooke on October 15 placed Capt. James Brown in command of the sick as well as the laundresses, who would be a great encumbrance to the expedition, and take them to winter near the source of the Arkansas River. The order continued:

> *The detachment will consist of Captain James Brown, three Sergeants, two Corporals, and sixteen privates of Company C; First Lieutenant E. Luddington and ten privates of company B; one Sergeant*

and Corporal and twenty-eight privates of company D; and one Sergeant and ten private of company E, and four laundresses from each company.

Captain Brown will without delay require the necessary transportation and draw rations for twenty-one days. Captain Brown will march on the 17th inst. He will be furnished with a descriptive list of the detachment. He will take with him and give receipts for a full proportion of camp equipments.

The commanding officer calls the particular attention of company commanders to the necessity of reducing the baggage as much as possible; transportation is deficient. The road most practicable is of deep sand and how soon we shall have to abandon the wagons it is impossible now to ascertain.

The generally bad health of the Battalion continued, however, after they marched out of Santa Fe and an epidemic of influenza soon caused Cooke to send back another "...*fifty-five of the sick and least efficient men.*" [See YOD-369]

150 • See *The Mormon Battalion* by Norma Ricketts, pp. 238 - 240.

151 • The sharpness of Lt. Col. Cooke in recognizing the talents of the men in his command and rewarding them for their abilities was here clearly apparent and a decided tribute to the commander. Ferguson, a native of Belfast, Ireland, had enlisted as a private in Company A but, over the next decade this extraordinary young man, who was both an accomplished actor and writer, served with distinction as adjutant general of the Nauvoo Legion of Utah's Territorial Militia. [See *The Autobiography of Sergeant Major James H. Glines*, p. 6]

152 • Those separated from the Battalion at this time as unfit for the remaining march to California and marched, instead, to Pueblo to over-winter at that location included the following officers and men: Abbott, Joshua, Co. D; Adams, Orson B., 1st Sgt., Co. C; Allen, Franklin, Co. B; Allred, James T.S., Co. A; Allred, Reuben W., Co. A; Averett, Jonathan, Co. D; Beckstead, William E., Co. C; Bingham, Erastus, Co. B; Bird, William, Co. B; Blanchard, Marvin S., Co. A; Brown, Alexander, 2nd Cpl., Co. C; Brown, Jesse J., Co. C; Calkins, James W., Co. A; Calvert, John, Co. C; Carpenter, Isaac, Co. C; Carpenter, William H., Co. C; Casto, William, Co. D; Chase, Abner (died), Co. D; Chase, John D., 3rd Cpl., Co. B; Clark, Samuel, Co. E; Cummings, George, Co. E; Davis, James, Co. D; Douglass, Ralph, Co. D; Durphy, Francillo, Co. C; Garner, David, Co. A; Garner, Philip, Co. B; Gifford, William B., Co. D; Glazier, Luther W., Co. E; Glines, James H., Co. A; Gould, John C., Co. C; Gould, Samuel, Co. C; Gribble, William, Co. D; Hanks, Ebenezer (3rd Sgt.), Co. E; Hess, John W., Co. E; Hirons, James, Co. D; Holden, Elijah E., Co. A; Hopkins, Charles, Co. E; Hulett, Schuyler, Co. A; Jackson, Charles A., Co. A; Jacobs, Bailey, Co. E; Johnson, Jarvis, Co. C; Karren, Thomas, Co. E; Kenney, Lorin E., Co. D; Lake, Barnabas, Co. A; Lamb, Lisbon, Co. D; Larson, Thurston, Co. C; Laughlin, David S., Co. D; Luddington, Elam, 1st Lt., Co. B; Mesech, Peter J., Co. D; Miller, Daniel, Co. E; Nowlan, Jabez (Cpl. at muster-in, Pvt. at muster-out), Co. C; Oakley, James, Co. D; Oyler, Melcher, Co. A; Park, William A., Co. E; Perkins, David, Co. C; Perkins, John, Co. C; Persons, Harmon D., Co. B; Persons, Judson A., Co. C; Pugmire, Jonathan, Jr., Co. E; Richards, Joseph W. (musician, died), Co. A; Roberts, Benjamin, Co. D; Roe, Caratat C., Co. A; Rowe, William, Co. D; Sanderson, Henry W., Co. D; Sargent, Abel M., Co. D; Sessions, John, Co. A; Sharp, Albert, Co. D; Shupe, Andrew J., Co. C; Shupe, James, Co. C; Smith, John G., Co. D; Smith, Milton (died), Co. C; Smith, Richard, Co. C; Steele, John, Co. D; Stephens, Arnold (1st Cpl.), Co. D; Stephens, Lyman, Co. B; Stevens, Roswell, Co. E; Stillman, Clark, Co. D; Stillman, Dexter, Co. B; Tanner, Myron, Co. D; Terrill, Joel J., Co. C; Tindell, Solomon, Co. C; Walker, William, Co. B; Whiting, Almon, Co. D; Whiting, Edmund, Co. D; Wilkin, David (Cpl at muster-in, Pvt at muster-out), Co. C; Williams, Thomas S. (2nd Sgt.), Co. D; Wright, Charles, Co. B; Wriston, John P., Co. A.

153 • The evening before—late on October 18—the old messes of the Mormon Battalion were all dissolved and new messes established comprised of ten men each.

154 • The first day's march carried them twenty-four miles, following present Galisteo Creek almost to the Rio Grande and they camped on the east bank opposite the tiny San Felipe Pueblo.

155 • It was only a matter of mere days—on October 20—when Lt. Col. Cooke placed the entire Mormon Battalion on rations, limiting each man daily to a quarter-pound of flour, three-quarter rations of sugar and coffee and a pound and a half of beef, with distribution of such rations strictly controlled on a company level by a non-commissioned officer appointed as Company Quartermaster.

156 • Albuquerque, at the time encountered by Cooke's troops, was 140 years old, having been established in 1706 by New Mexico's 28th Spanish governor, Don Francisco Cuervo y Valdez, who named the newly founded village after the 34th viceroy of New Spain, the Duque du Albequerque.

157 • The tiny village of La Jolla (sometimes spelled phonetically, as La Hoya) was located approximately

twenty miles north of present Socorro, New Mexico. It was here that the Saints first noted the Spanish practice called by John D. Lee "Spanish Rusty", wherein a man and a woman ride on the same horse, the woman straddling the mount ahead of the man. Some of the soldiers of the Mormon Battalion adopted this same practice when they returned to their families at Great Salt Lake, which infuriated Mormon leaders, who considered it obscene.

158 • Pvt. Rogers, a native of Portage County, OH, had left his family behind in Iowa to join the Battalion, as did so many others, at the request of Brigham Young through the order's spiritual leaders. His journal, faithfully kept throughout the arduous march from Fort Leavenworth across the northern provinces of Mexico to the Pacific Ocean, is now part of the Special Collections at the Brigham Young University Library.

159 • Socorro's name, sometimes appearing in older documents as "Succor", was first applied to the Indian pueblo that was situated at this site by Don Juan de Onate, first New Mexico colonizer, who, during his 1598 expedition, found relief here after traversing the waterless *Journada del Muerto*— Journey of the Dead Man.

160 • See Boyle, *Autobiography and Diary*, 24 - 31 October 1846.

161 • San Bernardino Spring, a famed watering place, was located at the abandoned San Bernardino Hacienda, some fifteen miles east of present Douglas, AZ.

162 • Kearny's force had left the Rio Grande several miles west of the present city of Truth or Consequences, NM, and headed directly west to reach the Gila River near present Silver City, NM, and the abandoned Santa Rita Copper Mine, then held by the Mimbres Apaches. This was where the historic Cooke's Wagon Road began and moved southward, running between the Rio Grande and the Pima Indian villages north of Tucson, on the Gila River.

163 • Included in the detachment of fifty-seven sick and feeble sent back to Pueblo from the Battalion on June 10, 1846, under command of Lt. W.W. Willis, were the following: Babcock, Lorenzo, Co. C; Bedlam, Samuel, Co. D; Bevan, James, Co. A; Bingham, Thomas, Co. B; Blackburn, Abner, Co. C; Brazier, Richard, Sgt., Co. E; Brimhall, John, Co. C; Brown, Daniel, Co. E; Burns, Thomas R., Co. E; Burt, William, Co. C; Bybee, John, Co. B; Calkins, Alva, Co. A; Camp, James, Co. B; Carl, James C., Co. A; Cazier, James, Co. E; Cazier, John, Co. E; Church, Hayden W., Co. B; Clark, George S., Co. B; Compton, Allen, Co. D; Curtis, Josiah, Co. A.; Dalton, Edward, Co. D; Dalton, Harry, Co. D; Dunn, James, Co. C; Eastman, Marcus, Co. B; Frederick, David, Co. A; Hewett, Eli B., Co. A; Higgins, Alfred, Co. D; Hinkley, Arza E., Co. B; Hoagland, Lucas, Co. D; Johnston, Jesse, Co. C; Maxwell, Maxey, Co. A; McClellan (or McLelland), William E., Co. E; Mecham, Erastus D., Co. D; Richardson, Thomas, Co. E; Richmond, Benjamin, Co. C; Rust, William W., Co. C; Sheen, Joseph, Co. E; Shipley, Joseph, Co. C; Squires, William, Cpl., Co. C; Stuart, Benjamin, Co. D; Stuart, James, Co. D; Thomas, Haywood, Co. D; Thomas, Nathan, Co. C; Tippetts, John H., Co. D; Tubbs, William R., Co. D; Welsh, Madison, Co. C; Wilson, George, Co. E; Woodworth, Lysander, Co. A; Woolsey, Thomas, Co. E; Wriston, Isaac N., Co. A

164 • Later, Lt. Willis, writing of these incidents, noted: *Active preparations now commenced to carry into effect the Colonel's orders, and by 4 o'clock of the same day we had collected of invalids fifty-six, one big government wagon, four yoke of poor cattle, five days' rations and two dressed sheep, as food for the sick. Our loading for the one wagon consisted of the clothing, blankets, cooking utensils, tents and tent poles, muskets, equipage, and provisions, and all invalids who were unable to walk. With some difficulty I obtained a spade or two and a shovel, but was provided with no medicines or other necessaries for the sick except the mutton before referred to, and only five days' rations, to travel near three hundred miles.... Thus armed and equipped we commenced our lonesome march, retracing our steps to Santa Fe. We marched the same day about two miles and were visited by Captain Hunt and others at night, who spoke words of comfort to us and blessed us, administering the Church ordinance to the sick, and bidding us God speed.*—[Cooke's Journal, 9 November 1846].

165 • Pvt Ephraim Knowlton Hanks was an ideal choice as one of the regular hunters for Co. B. This nineteen-year-old had already served three years at sea aboard the U.S. man-of-war *Columbus* and served his present company well by bringing in meat when no one else seemed able to do so. After his service in the Mormon Battalion, he became a rather legendary figure as a plainsman, Indian fighter and tavern operator at Mountain Dell, east of Salt Lake City.

166 • This stream is still known today as the Mimbres River, which rises in the Black Mountain Range west of the Rio Grande and flows southward toward Deming, NM.

167 • The river portrayed to Lt. Emory as the Sequoia River was evidently the river presently known as the Kern River and where the Mexicans claimed they had been rounding up wild horses was in the lush hill country in the then uninhabited region of the present Sequoia National Forest, between the present Greenhorn and Piute Mountain Ranges, probably reasonably close to the confluence of the present South Fork Kern River with the Kern River in the vicinity of present Isabella, Kern Co., CA.
168 • Stout's troubles were fairly exemplary of the majority of Saints who fled from Nauvoo, IL. One of his three wives died en route to Winter Quarters, as did his favorite little son, Hosea, after the priests had "cast out" the devil they determined was inhabiting his body. Another of his wives died in childbirth during that winter at Winter Quarters and his final surviving child died before the migration reached Salt Lake City. [YOD-431 - 432]
169 • At this time, Bonypart was the quite common spelling and pronunciation for Napoleon Bonaparte. [BCW-29]
170 • The Lawson referred to here was John Lawson, forty-one, of New York City, who was a private in Co. B. Lawson, a blacksmith, subsequently settled at New Harmony, Utah, where he died in 1844.
171 • Cooke's remarkable decision to head directly west became something of a witnessed miracle among the Saints. Pvt. Levi Hancock wrote, *"We would attend to prayers at night, that the Lord would keep us from the hands of our enemies and that the Colonel might be stopped by an angel before we should go to Sonora. Our prayers were answered. The Colonel called a halt and said he was not commanded to go that way, but to go west. Then spoke to our Lieutenant James Pace, who answered him to his satisfaction; when, it is said, he burst into tears to think the Mormon soldiers so readily obeyed his orders."* [Hancock to Daniel Tyler, Typescript, LDS Archives]
172 • The many thousands of goldseekers who subsequently followed Cooke's Road to California over Guadalupe Pass demonstrated quite convincingly that Cooke was correct in his astute assertion.
173 • The final total of Americans killed or mortally wounded at the Battle of San Pascual (which was fought near the present city of Escondido, CA) numbered twenty-one, as tallied by Sgt. Daniel Tyler. It was never accurately ascertained how many of the Californio lancers under Gen Andreas Pico were slain, but the number was believed to be slight, probably no more than five or six. [see AOI-167f25]
174 • The U.S. House Executive Document 4, 2nd Session, 29th Congress, states that "...the Californios lost two or three hundred soldiers..." which is, of course, a ridiculous assertion, since this was a greater number than the full force of the Californio lancers. [see Internet account at *http://www. notfrisco.com/calmem/stockton.html*] See also the estimate of enemy casualties by Sgt. Daniel Tyler in the immediately preceding Amplification Note.
175 • The three mountain men sent to Commodore Stockton at San Diego arrived there safely but Stockton, who had about 800 effectives in his command there, refused to send a reinforcement and returned the messengers with a note saying that "...for the time being" he could not help out. Exactly why he thought he could not send aid just then has never been ascertained. The three mountain men acting as messengers, including Alexis Godey, were captured on their return by the Californios, but were later released unharmed.
176 • Don Andreas Pico, despite being the commanding general of the Californios, earned the respect and admiration of the Americans who fought him in the Battle of San Pascual. In the report of this battle in the U.S. House Executive Document 4, 2nd Session, 29th Congress, he is described as being a leader *"...who was brave and honorable, displaying so much courage and coolness as to excite the admiration of the Americans. He never did an act beneath the dignity of an officer or contrary to the rules of war, and was humane and generous. If he saw one of the enemy wounded, he instantly called upon his men to spare the life of the wounded soldier. Kind and hospitable, Pico was held in great esteem by the Americans who knew him."*
177 • The attack of the Californio lancers under Gen. Andreas Pico was the bloodiest battle ever fought in California, before or since. For even greater details of the encounter, see the segment entitled "Justice" in *California in 1846*, pp. 52 - 55.
178 • The remains they found was the former San Bernardino Hacienda, which was the core of a ranch established in 1822 by Lt. Ignacio Perez as a buffer against the Apaches. This was on a land grant in excess of 73,000 acres. By the time the Mormon Battalion passed, the Apaches had driven out the Mexicans and made this spread and another (along the San Pedro River) into a hunting ground on which were about 100,000 head of cattle which, according to Cooke, *"support the Indians, just as*

buffalo on the plains." Prior to 1822 the scenic San Bernardino Spring, located now in Mexico just south of the border of Cochise County, AZ, had been a favored campground on the trail between Janos and Fronteras. The John Slaughter Ranch, which is now an historic site, lies across the international border from the original stopping place.

179 • Here occurs a most peculiar anomaly which, so far as the author can determine, has never been explained. All existing evidence clearly depicts Fremont at this time approaching Los Angeles at the head of his force of American volunteers. Yet, in his own journal for the date of December 3, 1846. poet Henry Wadsworth Longfellow, at his home in New England, notes that on this night he was delighted to host, as his guest of honor, Lt. Col. John Charles Fremont and that, following dinner, Fremont read to his host and other guests from his newly published book, *Fremont's Expedition to the Rocky Mountains—1842*, which Longfellow and guests found "...highly interesting and exciting. What a wild life, and what a fresh existence! But, ah, the discomforts!" [YOD-50]

180 • Beale's health was badly damaged for two years following this ordeal. His own remarks regarding this desperate night and following day were quoted in the biography *Edward Fitzgerald Beale* by Stephen Bonsal. Beale was regarded as a first-rate soldier and adventurer at this time and his later exploits were no less remarkable, picturesque and important. It was he who first suggested and then made famous the historic and quite successful experiment, under Secretary of War Jefferson Davis, of using camels in the deserts of the Southwestern United States.

181 • These were the ruins of the Santa Cruz de Terrenate Presidio, which had been constructed by the Spanish seventy years earlier to guard the road between Fronteras and Tucson. The installation had been abandoned in 1780 after the Apaches had slain two successive commanders of the post and many of their men stationed there. The ruins of this fortification are still visible just two miles north of where Arizona's State Highway 82 crosses the San Pedro River. [see Williams', THE PRESIDIO OF SANTA CRUZE DE TERRENATE: A FORGOTTEN FORTRESS OF SOUTHERN ARIZONA.]

182 • See Bigler, ed. *THE GOLD DISCOVERY JOURNAL OF AZARIAH SMITH*, p. 57.

183 • The Mormon Battalion left the San Pedro River close to the present city of Benson, AZ, and headed largely uphill for about eight miles on the line now followed by Interstate Route 10 toward Tucson, some fifty miles to the northwest.

184 • That "political chaos" was the principal reason why the United States was unable to provide any sensible form of government for Oregon until 1849, or for New Mexico, California and Deseret (Utah) until 1850.

185 • The campsite was located close to where the site of the present town of Mesilla, NM is situated.

186 • Present Cuidad Juarez.

187 • It should be noted, however, that irrespective of how much faith the Saints placed in their leader, Brigham Young, at this time, there were still lingering questions that tended to impugn the selflessness of Brigham Young at this time and, especially a little later, when the Saints became less unsettled in their search for Zion. Some of today's Mormons still tend to question what Young's motives and ambitions were at the time. These questions primarily involved how well—or, perhaps, how poorly –Young managed not only the Mormon Battalion's pay but, equally, his care – or perhaps, lack of it—during this very trying migrational period.

188 • Lt. Col. Cooke was here referring to the *Comancheros*, which were New Mexican traders from Taos and Santa Fe who, in disregard to the safety of the citizens, traded firearms and whiskey to the Comanches and Kiowas for the spoils of the raids those tribes made into Chihuahua and Sonora. Cooke had, of course, seen numerous examples of this illicit trade himself during his service in the frontier.

189 • Much later, while preparing his volume entitled *Conquest of New Mexico and California*, Lt. Col. Cooke wrote of this portion of his cross-country march and extolled some of the many benefits gained for the country by the Mormon Battalion's march across this then unknown territory: "*A new administration in which Southern interests prevailed, with the great problem of the practicability and best location of a Pacific Railroad under investigation, had the map of this wagon route before them...*" [the map prepared at this earlier time by Cooke himself] "*... with its continuance to the west, and perceived that it gave exactly the solution of it's unknown element, that a southern route would avoid both the Rocky Mountains and Sierra Nevada, with their snows, and would meet no obstacle in this great interval. The new 'Gadsden Treaty' was the result; it was signed December 30, 1853.*" [CHMB-233 - 234]

190 • A copy of the map of his travels in this area with the Mormon Battalion was rendered by Lt. Col.

Cooke and included in his letter to General Kearny. Map can be seen in *The Mormon Battalion*, p. 147, by B.H. Roberts, Salt Lake City, UT, 1919. [AOI-180]

191 • This was evidently the first information Lt. Col. Cooke received concerning Gen. Kearny's disastrous fight with the body of Mexican lancers at San Pascual on December 6. In response, Cooke dispatched his "useless guides," Charbonneau and Leroux and three others as express messengers to Kearny to inform the general of his approach and requested that fresh mules and beef cattle be forwarded to Warner's Ranch for his use when he arrived.

192 • These petroglyphs of animals, men and mystic figures were apparently rendered by some ancient tribe, possibly to denote a boundary area separating them from other tribes. Unfortunately, even though protected in recent times by the establishment of Painted Rocks Historic State Park, some 14 miles west of present Gila Bend, AZ (located between Interstate Route 8 and the river), many of these petroglyphs have, over the years, been defaced or destroyed by vandals.

193 • It is stated in *From the 1820s to the Gold Rush*, as prepared by the Museum of the City of San Francisco [see *sfmuseum.org/hist1/early.html*] that the first published edition of *The California Star* appeared on January 7, 1847, but this appears to be an error, since that date was a Thursday and the newspaper, from its onset, was a Saturday weekly. Other accounts, apparently correct, give the initial publication date as Saturday, January 9, 1847.

194 • The Capitulation was evidently misdated at its closing, as opposed to its opening date, which was correctly shown. The reactions of both Commodore Stockton and General Kearny to the Capitulation occurred on January 13, 1847, not January 16. Los Angeles capitulated on January 10 and General José Maria Flores immediately headed for Mexico, accompanied by José Castro, after relinquishing his command to General Andrés Maria Pico who, as noted, negotiated with Fremont the Treaty of Cahuenga on January 13, 1847.

195 • Although Major Cloud is not listed in the rosters assembled by either Tyler or Golder, Cloud, who was one of the Missouri Saints, was actually noted in the main roster as "additional paymaster". Later that same year—on August 4, 1847—while riding with John Sutter near Sutters Fort, Cloud was thrown from his horse and killed. [See NHD-181]

196 • While the exact location of this Alamo Mocha Well has never been accurately ascertained, it is believed to have been found in the Mexican portion of the Imperial Valley desert some six miles south of the present international boundary.

197 • Lt. George Stoneman, who is often mentioned in Cooke's Journal, later became general of a cavalry unit during the Civil War. He returned to the West when the war ended and subsequently was elected governor of California, a post he held from 1883 to 1887.

198 • The legislative council scheduled to convene in Los Angeles on March 1, 1847, never occurred, as matters regarding the legality of the select body were brought into question and only resolved at a later date.

199 • The 49,000-acre Warners Ranch in present San Diego County was established on a Mexican land grant in 1844 by Jonathan Trumbull Warner and was to emigrants the southern counterpart of what Johnson's Ranch in present Yuba County and Sutters Fort in present Sacramento County were to emigrants on the northern route. Warner, a New Englander from Massachusetts, had first arrived in California in 1831 and shortly thereafter took out Mexican citizenship, subsequently becoming one of California's largest landowners. He was among the first advocates of California annexation by the United States and served as a confidential correspondent to Consul Thomas Larkin at Monterey. The ruins of the ranch buildings are still visible today from San Diego County Road S2 just under a mile from its junction with State Highway 79, thirteen miles north of present Santa Ysabel. [AOI-168n]

200 • The reedy grass called *Carrizo* is common in numerous locations throughout southern California's Imperial and San Diego Counties. While hardy and digestible as fodder, it is not noted for its nutritional value for livestock. The Rogers Journal states they marched twenty-five miles by 1 p.m. this day which, while a large march, wasn't excessive. Henry Bigler, however, records in his journal that the day's march (which he says ended at 3 p.m., fourteen hours after beginning) was forty to forty-five miles long, which seems more likely considering the condition of the men and animals alike at its conclusion.

201 • Box Canyon is presently an historic site in the Anza-Borrego Desert State Park of California.

202 • The actual Ordinance changing the name of the city is as follows:

# The Infinite Dream

> AN ORDINANCE WHEREAS, the local name of Yerba Buena, as applied to the settlement or town of San Francisco, is unknown beyond the district, and has been applied from the local name of the cove, on which the town is built. Therefore, to prevent confusion and mistakes in public documents, and that the town may have the advantage of the name given on the public map;
>
> IT IS HEREBY ORDAINED, that the name of SAN FRANCISCO shall hereafter be used in all official communications and public documents, or records appertaining to the town.
>
> Washington Bartlett, Chief magistrate                                            January 30, 1847

Before the day's end, Samuel Brannan's newspaper, *The California Star*, changed its datelines to the new title of the city and published the text of Bartlett's ordinance of this date.

203 • The mission of San Luis Rey de Francis, named for Louis IX of France, was considered the premiere of California missions and was easily the largest throughout all of North America. It had been dedicated in 1798 as the eighteenth mission of those forming a sort of chain, each a day's journey apart, from San Diego to San Francisco Bay. Unfortunately, the mission at San Luis Rey had been looted by government officials and then occupied by local Indians after the wholesale secularization of the California missions in 1833. Presently restored to its former grandeur, this historic site can be seen today on Mission Avenue (State Route 76) some five miles east of present Oceanside in San Diego County.

204 • See Boyle, Henry G., *Autobiography and Diary*, 27 January 1847.

205 • The arrival at the Mission San Diego de Alcala marked the end of the great march of the Mormon Battalion—one of the most notable feats ever accomplished by any infantry unit in world history. The mission, justly described as the mother of California's Spanish missions, was, according to Cooke, "dilapidated and full of Indians and dirt." [*Cooke's Journal*, 29 Jan. 1847.] Recognition of the Mission San Diego de Alcala should not, however, go unrecognized for its importance. It was dedicated in 1760 by Father Junipero Serra, the renowned Franciscan. In 1765 it was moved to its present location some six miles up the San Diego River. At one point its congregation included some 1,500 Christian Indians and it had fine vineyards and grazing lands and included a school and fine gardens. As with some of the more important missions, it has been restored to a semblance of its former glory.

206 • In moving their force into the Spanish mission church at Taos, the resistance made a very serious error, not only in consolidating their leadership but by also entirely underestimating the power of the American mobile artillery. The ruins of this structure still stand on the grounds of this ancient pueblo as a memorial on the spot where the final action occurred in which an estimated one hundred of the enemy were killed, including nearly all of the top remaining leaders of the rebellion; those that were not killed were swiftly rounded up, tried on charges of treason, found guilty and executed. Only a relatively few minor incidents, never more than brief skirmishes, marred the peace which followed.

207 • The San Luis Rey Mission, originally founded in 1797, was located along the road between Los Angeles and San Diego, but about forty miles north of the latter city.

208 • See *The Conquest of New Mexico and California*, by Cooke, p. 289. Of those "contending" for the highest ranking office in California Territory, only General Stephen W. Kearny held the lawful authority to "occupy and establish civil government" in both New Mexico and California, this through his orders from Secretary of War W.L. Marcy dated June 3, 1846. His most serious contender was Commodore Robert Field Stockton, who possessed the military strength to take over such command but who had no official mandate to do so. Stockton, however, wealthy grandson of one of the signers of the Declaration of Independence, and distinctly eager to launch a political career of his own, stepped in swiftly to make the claim before Kearny had any opportunity to display his official orders in the matter. The Commodore handily occupied San Diego and Los Angeles with his sailors and marines and then quickly announced to the world that he had defeated the Mexican Army and restored peace, proclaiming himself, at that time, supreme commander and governor "by right of conquest"—afterward relinquishing those titles to his chief subordinate in those exploits, Lt. Col. John C. Fremont.

209 • On this same day, Feb. 5, 1847, Lt. Col. Philip St. George Cooke prepared his complete official report of the entire historic march of the Mormon Battalion during his time of his assuming command of that unit, from Oct. 2, 1846 at Santa Fe, NM, through Feb. 5, 1847 at San Luis Rey, CA, which he thereupon submitted to General Kearny. It was an official report that was little noted

publicly by historians when initially published by the U.S. Congress in 1848. Even in its second publication, by the *Utah Historical Quarterly* one hundred six years later, in 1954, little recognition was afforded it, though it compiles a wealth of well-presented information and is certainly by far the best accounting of the Mormon Battalion's very historic march. This report clearly depicts how strongly Cooke's unswerving discipline relied upon his own strong faith and self control. It clearly explains many of his decisions that certain individuals complained about at the time and expresses well the stresses undergone by his rigorous determination to carry out his difficult assignment while at the same time closely guarding the welfare of his men. In it Cooke, who would not allow his own private disappointment over his assignment to become revealed in his daily writings, finally reveals the frustrations he experienced while involved in "more humble labors" while his fellow officers were gleaning both fame and promotion on the battlefields of the War with Mexico. Cooke's official report is too lengthy to quote in its entirety here but, for those interested in following through on more detail and perhaps gaining a somewhat clearer insight into all that occurred during this historic march, the original report by Cooke may be found in Kearny Selected Papers, National Archives, MIC, A139, a copy of which is also on file at the Utah State Historical Society in Salt Lake City, UT. It is officially entitled: *Report of Lieut. Col. P. St. George Cooke of His March from Santa Fe, New Mexico, to San Diego, Upper California,* 5 February 1847, House Exec. Doc. 41 (30 - 1), Serial 517, 551 - 562. See also the excellent treatment provided by Hamilton Gardner in his account in *Utah Historical Quarterly XXII (January 1954),* pp. 15 - 40.

210 • Probably no other battle in the War with Mexico was so critical in the future of both Mexico and the United States than the Battle of Buena Vista. While General Zachary Taylor's report of it to the War Department was heavily biased to his own political benefit, it is nevertheless a document of immense importance in respect to that entire conflict, since it set the stage for the final actions in the war that resulted in Mexico's unconditional surrender to the United States and America's usurpation of the continent's western regions which ultimately became the contiguous western states of the United States in direct accordance to the visionary long-range plans held by President James Knox Polk to establish a United States of unbroken expanse from the Atlantic to the Pacific and from our present southern border at Mexico to our present northern border at Canada. Readers wishing to glean a clearer picture of the action that occurred in this Battle of Buena Vista are encouraged to read the official full report of the battle as submitted March 6, 1847 by General Zachary Taylor, written at Agua Nuevo, Mexico, to Secretary of War William L. Marcy at Washington, D.C.

211 • Colonel Alexander Doniphan's official report to Washington headquarters in regard to the very important Battle of Sacramento, Mexico, was submitted to Army Adjutant General Roger Jones on March 4, 1847. It is recommended reading for those who wish a clearer understanding of the events of the batlle and its future implications.

212 • See Kearny to Fremont, 1 March 1847, Kearny Papers, Missouri Historical Society.

213 • This was, of course, in reference to John C. Fremont's California Battalion, the poorly disciplined emigrant volunteers, most of whom refused to be mustered into the regular service and were thereafter discharged from their service a month later, in April.

214 • See Order No. 23, 6 March 1847, Records of the 10th Military Dept., 1846 - 1851.

215 • San Diego had, by this time, changed hands several times already. The original installation on the site, located on a low hilltop a quarter mile from the town proper had become known as the San Diego Presidio and had been constructed by digging a trench on the summit of the hill and surrounding it with a row of large logs against which was thrown up gravel and rock until a barricade was formed which was believed to be invulnerable. This installation fell into decay and was supplanted by a Mexican fortification constructed on its ruins. Within the barricade 17 cannon were arranged so as to command the town and entire surrounding area. In July, 1846, Captain Samuel F. Dupont, skipper of the sloop-of-war *U.S. Cyane,* captured the place and renamed it Fort Dupont. Soon afterwards, however, Californio insurgents recaptured it and held it until Commodore Robert Stockton, aboard the frigate *U.S. Congress* landed about 100 marines here on Sept, 31, 1846, once again took the place for the U.S. and renamed the fort after himself. Sgt. Albert Smith of Co. B states in his journal that *"...the U.S. marines and sailors still occupying the place reboarded their ship and left a few days after we came."* See *Albert Smith Journal,* 18 March 1847 [JOAS].

216 • This letter from Hunt to Kearny is missing from the correspondence of the 10th Military

Department, but it is referred to in a register of letters as having been received on 21 March 1847 and is summarized as follows: *"Capt. J. Hunt, Mormon Battln. Signifies the intention of the Mormon Battalion to settle near San Francisco, & wishes to work for the Government. San Luis Rey, March 17."*

217 • See Ames, ed., *A Doctor Comes to California: The Diary of John S. Griffin, Assistant Surgeon with Kearny's Dragoons, 1846 - 1847.*

218 • Turner to Cooke, Records of the 10th Military dept., 1846 - 1847, National Archives, Letters sent March 23, 1847 – July 8, 1851.

219 • This, of course was an indirect reference to Lt. Col. John Fremont and his subordinate officers.

220 • Stephen Watts Kearny was struck down in Mexico City, where he was serving as military governor, on 31 Oct 1848, but not by an enemy bullet. He was bitten by a mosquito carrying yellow fever and died of that cause.

221 • Major Cloud was, in the estimation of Col. Richard B. Mason, *"...a faithful officer, very attentive to his duties, and of sterling integrity."* Unfortunately, he was fatally injured three months later when thrown from his horse near Sutters Fort. [see Mason to Jones, 18 Sep 1847, in Senate Executive Documents 18 (31 - 1), 1849 - 50, Serial 557, 9:321 - 322]

222 • Considerable confusion reigns in regard to the actual number of escorts selected to accompany the Kearny procession. H.S. Turner reported there were 15 and his count included Pvts. Gilman Gordon and Thomas C. Ivie of Co. A and Pvt. Samuel G. Clark of Co. E. However, the dozen Saints definitely chosen to escort General Kearny eastward included Lt. Sylvester Hulett and Sgt. Nathaniel V. Jones, both of Company D, Pvts. Joseph Taylor, Charles Y. Webb and Jeremiah Willey of Co. A, Pvts. Ebenezer Landers, William F. Reynolds, Elanson Tuttle of Co. C, Pvts. John Binley, Amos Cox and William W. Spencer of Co. D, and Pvt. Matthew Caldwell of Co, E.

223 • The majority of the Saints in the Mormon Battalion were led northward from Los Angeles by Lieutenant William Tecumseh Sherman along the Pacific coastal path that was eventually to become the coastal highway now known as the El Camino Real. Simultaneously, Pvts Jeremiah Willey and Schuyler P.Hulett of Co. A, Pvt. Elanson Tuttle of Co. C and possibly Pvt. Ebenezer Landers, also of Co. C. accompanied General Kearny and Lt. Col. Cooke to Monterey by sea. Marshall, in his memoir, recalled that his journey up the Pacific coastal fringe *"...gave me the best kind of opportunity for seeing the country, which was very sparsely populated indeed, except by a few families at the various Missions. We had no wheeled vehicles, but packed food and clothing on mules driven ahead, and we slept on the ground in the open air."* [AOI-229 - 230]

224 • There remains great difficulty in attempting to ascertain the full identities of those making up this vanguard group led by Brigham Young. These were supposed to have been divided into groups of tens, but this did not always hold true, since some of the groups numbered as many as fourteen and a few comprised a member or two less than ten. Among them, usually uncounted, were included three Negro slaves—Oscar Crosby, Green Flake and Hark Lay—who, because of their race, were precluded by church doctrine from being bona fide members of the church, but who bore the surnames of their owners. There were also a handful of alleged "non-Mormon members in the party, who were evidently Mormons who had been lax in becoming re-baptized before the procession started but who were evidently Saints in good standing in all but acceptance of the formal covenants acquired at baptism and these were members who, as near as can be determined, were personally baptized by Brigham Young in the waters of Great Salt Lake upon the train's arrival in that area.

225 • The actual numbers of troops involved in the Battle of Buena Vista differed considerably from those reported to the Mormon Battalion, although the outcome was relatively similar, though somewhat more significant in view of the outnumbering Taylor's force faced. In the February 22 - 23 battle, Taylor had 4,800 able men against the Mexican force in excess of 20,000.

226 • American Naval warships were rated at this time by the quality and number of their armament. Ships of the line had more than one gun-deck and carried at least sixty-four guns; frigates were rated as 28, 32, 38 or forty-four-gun ships and the square-rigged sloops-of war, such as the *Lexington*, carried at least eighteen of the big guns. The *Columbus*, though rated as a seventy-four-gun ship, actually bristled with ninety-eight guns and was, in all characteristics, a top-of-the-line U.S. battleship.

227 • Philip St. George Cooke had been promoted to the rank of major in the regular army on February 16, 1847, and four days later was brevetted to the rank of Lieutenant Colonel *"...for meritorious*

*conduct in California."* [see Heitman's *Historical Register and Dictionary for the United States Army*, vol I, p. 324.]

228 • William Johnson's Ranch was located on Bear River three miles east of present Wheatland, CA.

229 • Whether or not General Kearny's utterance was responsible for the name changes that occurred there cannot be ascertained with any degree of certainly, but it seems likely to be so, since shortly after this time the principal landmarks in this area became known after the Donner Party, including Donner Pass, Donner Summit, Donner Lake and Donner Creek.

230 • Although the "clean-up" of remains delegated to Major Swords should have ended the matter, it did not. His detail's gathering up of the remains of the dead was poorly accomplished and many of the bones and body fragments were left scattered and remained visible to the horror of other individuals or groups that passed later. The cabin meant to be burned, where the bones were placed , did not burn in its entirety and the diaries of 'Forty-niners who passed en route to the gold fields two years later contain accounts of bones and skulls of humans being found in the vicinity and one of the cabins remained standing for some time afterward—the double cabin in which the Reed and Graves families had passed the winter. As late as the 1860s, a public house a mile or so from the lake was still exhibiting a pile of human bones, including a skull, identified (probably erroneously) as that of George Donner.

231 • It is very difficult to pinpoint either the exact date of the contract entered into between Sutter and Marshall in regard to establishment of the lumber mill, or precisely the terms that were involved. Both men—each in his own way—later claimed to be the instigator of the agreement entered into between them, beginning on April 26, 1847, in regard to exactly what the contract involved. There are several versions of the agreement, some of which disagree in fundamental concept and the responsibilities of the two principles. The fundamental version, which seems to be the most accurate stems from the verbal agreement entered into by the pair during their meeting on April 26, 1847. In his personal writing in his work entitled *New Helvetia Diary* [NHD-p. xxv] Sutter unequivocally states: *"In 1847 I began to build a grist-mill on the American River about four miles above the Fort. There I secured an adequate fall of water by going back and constructing a dam and digging a race four miles long. I had everything ready—four pairs of mill stones, wheels, a large building erected, and it would have all been in working order in six weeks if the discovery of gold could have been kept a secret that much longer. I had a man in my employ named James Wilson Marshall, a good mechanic who had made me looms, ploughs, spinning-wheels, and all such kindred material. In discussing a saw-mill with him, he said he thought he could build it. I was dubious about trusting him out of my sight with all his craziness, but the tools which one finds on a raw frontier are never stable enough to a builder's liking. I had no one else, so I must needs gamble on the man."* Existing evidence indicates that Siutter and Marshall were equal partners in ownership of the gold-producing properties.

232 • Marshall implies in his later writings that this site on the South Fork American River was located on his first search, but Sutter refutes that in his own notes, writing: *"He* [Marshall] *went out several times to look for a site. I was with him twice on these occasions. I was not with him when he determined the site of the Mill."* Sutter's comment appears to be correct. The site was not, however, reached by following the American River and its South Fork directly upstream. Instead, they followed the American upstream to its branch now known as Weber Creek and then, from that stream's upper waters, moved directly cross-country eastward to the valley of the South Fork, thus saving themselves many miles of meandering. The changing of the Indian village name from Culuma to Coloma, which it remains today, has been directly attributed to James Marshall who, in spelling the name phonetically, rendered it as Coloma, which spelling it has retained ever after. At least one sourc—[LAJM-53 - 54]—has used the spelling Culloomah, which is again a form of spelling derived from the phonic pronunciation.

233 • This lengthy but safe by-pass was accomplished just east of present Reno, NV.

234 • This was the same area of boiling springs which occurs about halfway across the Forty-Mile Desert on the Truckee River route—the same boiling pools where, fourteen months earlier, Mountain Man Jim Clyman had his spaniel, Buck, boiled to death when the dog plunged into one such pool. Many of the early travelers lost their dogs here but, so far as can be determined, General Kearny's party is the only one to have lost a mule in such manner. Presently drained by a geothermal food processing plant, the site is located today off Interstate Route 80 at Exit 65. [see "A Singular Cavern," in *The Illinois* Gazette, 16 Oct 1847.]

235 • Although the river that disappears here at the Humboldt Sink was originally called the St. Marys River, it was renamed—by Fremont during his first expedition here—after the renowned German scientist, Alexander von Humboldt and has been called the Humboldt River ever since.

236 • Although the Humboldt Sink's eastern and northern rim is now skirted by Interstate Route 80, it remains to this day quite as desolate and barren an area as it was when Jones first described it.

237 • It was on July 20, 1847, that the Brethren Saints who agreed to re-enlist assembled themselves into a new company calling itself "The Mormon Volunteers" and were mustered into the service of the United States Army by 1st Lt. A.J. Smith of the 1st Dragoons in a 5-point conditional enlistment specifically written out as follows:

> We, of the Mormon fraternity, whose names are herewith subscribed, purpose [sic] to enter the service of the United States as volunteers, on the following terms:
>
> 1st. That we enrol [sic] to serve under the government of the United States for one year, on condition that the authorized representatives of the government in California pledge themselves, if we require it, to discharge us on the first day of March, 1848.
>
> 2d. That we, during the period of our service, have the same privileges, pay and emoluments granted to us that other volunteers in the service enjoy.
>
> 3d. That, on our re-enlistment, we may have the privilege of garrisoning the town of San Diego, and not be sent lower down the coast than that post.
>
> 4th. That the authorities of California pledge themselves, on behalf of the government of the United States, at the [time] of our discharge, to furnish us with the rations and pay allowed by law to the Salt Lake, into which Bear river empties, or to the Bay of San Francisco, if preferred by us.
>
> 5th. That we shall all have the privilege of joining the battalion of Mormons, if there should be one raised.
>
> As far as I have the authority, I agree to the foregoing stipulations.
>
> J.D. STEVENSON,
> Col. Commanding Southern Mil. Dist. Of California.
> Ciudad de Los Angeles, July 20, 1847
> W.T. SHERMAN,
> 1st Lieut. 3d Art., A.A.A.G.

True copy

### Role of Officers and Men in Mormon Volunteers

OFFICERS:
Daniel C. Davis, *Capt.* Cyrus C. Canfield, *1st Lieut.* Ruel Barrus, *2nd Lieut.* Robert Clift, *3rd Lieut.* Edmund L. Brown, *1st Sergt.* Samuel Myers, *2nd Sergt.* Benjamin F. Mayfield, *3rd Sergt.* Henry Packard, *4th Sergt.* Thomas Peck, *1st. Corpl.* Isaac Harrison, *2nd Corpl.* Hiram B. Mount, *3rd Corpl.* Edwin Walker, *4th Corp.* Richard D, Sprague, *Musicn.* Henry W. Jackson, *Musicn.*

PRIVATES:

| | | | |
|---|---|---|---|
| Baily, Addison | Covil, John A. | Maggard, Benjamin | Smith, William |
| Baily, Jefferson | Dayton, Willard Y. | McBride, Harlem | Steel, George |
| Beckstead, Gordon S. | Donald, Neal | Morris, Thomas | Steel, Isaiah |
| Beckstead, Orin | Dutcher, Thomas P. | Mowry, James | Steers, Andrew |
| Bowing, Henry | Earl, Jacob | Mowry, John | Thompson, Miles |
| Boyle, Henry G. | Earl, Jessie | Neal, Conrad | Watts, John |
| Brass, Benjamin | Evans, William | Nowler, Christian | West, Benjamin |
| Brizzee, Henry | Fatout, Ezra | Park, James | Wheeler, Henry |
| Brown, William | Fellows, Hiram W. | Peck, Edwin M. | Wheeler, John L. |
| Bryant, John | Fletcher, Philander | Peck, Isaac | Williams, James V. |
| Calahan, Thomas | Harmon, Ebenezer | Richards, Peter F. | Winter, Jacob |
| Calkins, Edwin | Harmon, Lorenzo F. | Riser, John J. | Workman, Andrew J. |
| Carter, Philo I. | Harmon, Oliver | Riter, John | Workman, Oliver G. |
| Clark, Riley P. | Hart, James | Runyan, Levi | Young, Nathan |
| Clawson, John R. | Hickenlooper, William | Sexton, George S. | Zabriskie, Jerome |
| Clift, James | Kibbey, James | Shumway, Aurora | |
| Condit, Jeptha | Lance, William | Smith, Lot | |

238 • It was given to Orson Pratt, high priest of the Mormons, to offer up the prayer of thanksgiving at

the revelation of the site of Salt Lake City and he later wrote: "Here we called the camp together and it fell to my lot to offer up prayer and thanksgiving in behalf of our company, all of who [sic] had been preserved from the Missouri River to this point; and after dedicating ourselves and the land unto the Lord and imploring His blessings upon our labors, we appointed various committees to attend to different branches of business, preparatory to putting in crops, and in about two hours after our arrival we began to plow, and the same afternoon built a dam to irrigate the soil, which at the spot where we were ploughing was exceedingly dry." [YOD-451]

239 • The first "Soda Pool" spring the party encountered, located at today's Soda Springs in Idaho, is now submerged beneath the impoundment called Soda Point Reservoir. It is possible that the second soda spring encountered is the one that is now preserved within a Soda Springs, Idaho, city park.

240 • Sir George Simpson Incoming Correspondence, B.223/b/25, R3C 1T5, Hudson's Bay Co. Archives [AOI-243].

241 • So brilliantly conducted was General Scott's planning in the Battles of Contreras and Cherubusco that none less than Ulysses S. Grant, who was almost always highly critical of military maneuverings apart from his own, later declared the command generalship of the dual campaign to be "superbly executed" and General Scott's personal performance as commander "faultless." [YOD-473]

242 • Probably no better account could be presented of the Battles of Contreras and Churubusco, which heralded the beginning of the end of the Mexican War, than that which was prepared by General Winfield Scott himself in [see] his official report of August 28, 1847, to Secretary of War William L. Marcy in Washington, D.C.

243 • Of the discharged members of the Mormon Battalion, Col. Richard B. Mason, the new military commander of California, could only voice praise. As he remarked in regard to the service of the Mormons in his letter of September 18, 1847 to Adjutant General R. Jones in Washington, D.C.:

*...Of the services of this battalion, of their patience, subordination, and general good conduct, you have already heard; and I take great pleasure in adding, that, as a body of men, they have religiously respected the rights and feelings of these conquered people, and not a syllable of complaint has reached my ears of a single insult offered, or outrage done, by a Mormon volunteer.*

*So high an opinion did I entertain of the battalion, and of their especial fitness for the duties now performed by the garrison in this country, that I made strenuous efforts to engage their services for another year; but succeeded in engaging but one company, which, as before stated, is now at San Diego. Certain promises or pledges were made to this company, which you will find amongst the military correspondence sent to you by this same mail. Some few of the discharged Mormons are scattered throughout the country, but the great mass of them have gone to meet their families, supposed to be somewhere in the vicinity of the Great Salt Lake....* [Mason to Jones, Senate Exec. Doc. 18 (31-1), Serial 557, 318 - 322.]

244 • Captain Turner's close census, here and elsewhere, as revealed in the Clarke's editing of *The Turner Journal*, [TTJ-134] provides a fresh look at an oversight that has plagued the emigration's historians for many years: that the traditional Latter-day Saints' estimate that the single "Big Company" of following Mormons consisted of some 1,600 emigrants total when, in fact, the previous counts had actually failed to include a virtually equal number of children under sixteen years of age and, thus, increases the number of those included in the "Big Company" to approximately 3,200 individuals.

245 • Robert Quigley himself requested these three men, especially Spencer, who was the former Battalion assistant surgeon. When Quigley was finally well enough to travel, however, the foursome became lost. As Caldwell recalled: *"The men got lost and wandered around for three days and came upon our former camp ground. During this wandering we ran out of food. For seven days we had nothing but one little turkey hen about the size of a common hen. Talk about hunger! Who knows anything about it except those who have borne it."* Fortunately, Spencer met five soldiers on a bee hunt, who directed them properly to Fort Leavenworth. [Caldwell, *Short Life's History*, LDS Archives, p. 11]

246 • Immediately upon reaching Fort Leavenworth, Mormon Battalion Pvt. Nathaniel V. Jones, as part of General Kearny's escort, was given his discharge from the army and paid his severance of $75. Jones then headed back to his previous home in Missouri, where he located his wife in the town of Atchison, who, within the year, bore him a daughter, *"...a fine little girl in the image [of] Nathan."* Later in 1849 he emigrated to Utah and thereafter led a life dedicated to Mormonism. He became bishop of the fifteenth ward in Salt Lake City and during 1852 - 1855 served as president of the mission

# The Infinite Dream

to India. In 1856 he mined lead at Las Vegas and the following March he established a station for the Brigham Young Express at Deer Creek in what would subsequently become Wyoming. The sister of Mormon Battalion Pvt. William Coray claimed she married Jones that same year after having rejected the advances of Capt. James Brown. She wrote that Jones *"...was a very fine looking man...but he was well known to be a hard, cruel man,"* and that at one point she found a decapitated corpse in the butcher shop he established. [see Winch, ed., *Fifteen Years Among the Mormons: Being the Narrative of Mrs. Mary Ettie V. Smith*, pp 175 - 179, 182, 189.] Jones served in Echo Canyon as a Nauvoo Legion colonel during the Utah War, in which *"...he suffered many hardships and privations which told very much on his constitution."* [see Jones, ed., *Extracts from the Life Sketch of Nathaniel V. Jones*, p. 5] When Johnston's Army marched through the empty Mormon capital in 1858, Jones was one of the men selected to guard Salt Lake City. During 1859 - 1861 he served the Latter-day Saints as president of the British Mission. He died February 15, 1863, allegedly *"from overwork and exposure"* at the age of forty, having sired seventeen children with four wives, leaving them behind as his living widows. [*LDS Biographical Encyclopedia*, vol. 2, pp.368 - 369.]

247 • Taken in irons to the nation's capital, Fremont was tried by a military court-martial that began on November 2, 1847 in the nation's capital at the Washington Arsenal but did not end until many weeks later. He was brought to the court faced with three specific charges brought against him by General Stephen Kearny: the principal charge being (1) mutiny and the two subsidiary charges including (2) disobedience to the lawful command of a superior officer and (3) conduct to the prejudice of good order and military discipline. On the charge of mutiny, which was tried first, the court's decree was that Lt. Colonel John Charles Fremont was guilty, *"...and the court does therefore sentence the said Lieutenant Colonel Fremont, of the regiment of mounted riflemen, United States Army, to be dismissed from the service."* On the remaining two charges, each also tried individually, Fremont was found guilty as charged. For most officers who might be convicted of such military crimes the punishments were harsh and could well have led to Fremont being summarily executed or, at least, sentenced to life imprisonment...but such was not the result in Fremont's case, which became closely involved with high politics. This was not only because the Court itself recommended executive clemency, but primarily because Fremont was the son-in-law of one of the most powerful figures then in Congress, United States Senator Thomas Hart Benton, who was also serving as principal counsel for Fremont and Benton was himself being curried by the President for certain favors. In this situation, President James Knox Polk took it upon himself to arbitrarily throw out the Court's decree of guilty of mutiny, but, as a sop to the Court, he did sustain the decree of guilt on the lesser two charges, and approved the penalty leveled for them, which was dishonorable discharge from service in the United States Army...but then turned right around and remitted the sentence, dismissed the arrest charges formulated against Fremont and ordered him to report for duty. These, however, were decisions that took a considerable while to occur and the trial itself became almost farcical in what it conveyed. Benton was, in fact, a highly distinguished and honorable man, one of the most astute and admired of politicians and who had served America in exemplary manner for years. Because of his precise and bombastic rhetoric, he had long been known as "The Thunderer" and the causes he had won in the past had already had substantially beneficial effect upon the Republic. In this case, however, where his son-in-law was concerned—the husband of his beloved only daughter, Jessie—his steadfastness deserted him and he became dishonest, unjustly accusatory, puerile to the point of histrionics, in many respects downright silly and all too often coming perilously close to outright criminality. His attack on Fremont's accuser, General Kearny, was wholly devastating and entirely undeserved by one who had served his country for so long and so well. Among the many witnesses Benton called to establish and bolster Fremont's character on the American frontier were U.S. Naval Commander Robert Field Stockton, Edwin Bryant, Lieutenant Colonel Philip St. George Cooke, Willard Hall, Owl Russell and even General Kearny himself. Fremont was portrayed as the Great Conqueror and Intrepid Explorer who had, clad in buckskin and almost single-handedly, opened Western America to the American public. The officers who comprised the board of court martial for this trial clearly quailed before Benton's bombast and they unjustifiably allowed Benton and Fremont unprecedented leeway to deviate from legal procedure to such extent that it transformed an important military trial into a bombastic political circus. Senator Benton bestowed his son-in-law with the aura of a great public hero and, in doing so, created a martyr of almost Biblical proportion, portraying him as a man gifted with

such an abundance of providential forethought that the country itself would be the loser should he be too harshly punished; that his mutiny was statesmanship, his incompetence was courage, his self-centeredness admirable, his stupidity—portrayed as propensity for deep thought—qualifying him to lead armies and govern a nation; the whole emblazoning him as truly a mystical vessel of greatness with potential as yet not fully understood. Almost overnight Fremont became, to the American press—and, as a result, to the American public—a great champion whose value was underrated and whose achievements helped keep America itself from plunging into political chaos. At the same time Benton undermined General Kearny as a vindictively jealous incompetent. So gross a travesty to justice was it that it came perilously close to wrecking impartial judicial process in the Republic; so fierce Benton's attack upon Kearny that "The Thunderer" became virtually a demagogue of unprecedented scope in that courtroom or any other. And President Polk, in the process of all this, turned Benton against him at just the time when he needed him most; when the peace treaty with Mexico was being negotiated and coming up for ratification by Congress. In the midst of all this, Fremont himself settled matters by voluntarily resigning his military commis mitting himself, instead, to a political future. He led yet another expedition, this time in midwinter and into the Colorado Rockies where, as if patterned by the Donner Party, a dozen of his men died and others survived only through cannibalism. Next, he was off to California once again where he stabilized his Mariposa Grant, found a fortune in gold, became the new State of California's first Republican U.S. senator, and finally led a couple of hopelessly inept campaigns in the Civil War, his estimation of his own self as both martyr and great man unshaken to the end of his days. As for Senator Benton, his vitriol for General Kearny never diminished and, in fact, increased when a bill was introduced in Congress to confer upon Kearny the brevet rank of Major General. Kearny, after the trial, had become military governor of Vera Cruz and then governor of Mexico City itself and instrumental in bringing tranquility to a society far more turbulent than either New Mexico or California had been. Benton continued so virulently accusing Kearny of being a villain that it even inspired President Polk to write in his diary "Senator Benton is violent beyond what is usual, even for him." Kearny, even-tempered as always, held his own tongue and granted no interviews nor did he write any letters to newspapers or anyone else; his service, especially in 1846 - 47, was great and decisive, and he succeeded at everything he set out to do. He wrote no letters to politicians or the press, he conducted no intrigues and he was in no way involved in politics. Kearny admirably served the Republic without trying to serve himself as well. He was a man, a gentleman, and, most assuredly, an exemplary soldier. He died on October 11, 1848 of the effects of yellow fever, which he contracted during his military command service in Mexico.

248 • Some of the Mormons were already reasonably familiar with John Fremont's travels in the Central Valley and Henry Bigler's "old map" was undoubtedly a copy of the 1845 map made of Fremont's second expedition in early 1844 up the San Joaquín Valley, over Tehachapi Pass, and across the San Gabriel Mountains to the Mojave Desert. As soldiers, the Saints had heard only a very little about ways to cross the Sierra Nevada safely and, at this stage, were hoping to locate the pass that had been opened by Mountain Man Joe Walker in 1843. The Saints crossed the Tehachapi Mountains via Tejon Pass, along the present path of Interstate Route 5, then northward down the Central Valley basically a bit east of paralleling present U.S. Route 99—established trails that had been laid out initially by Francisco Garces in 1776, that had later been explored by Lt. Gabriel Morega in 1806 and used by Fremont in 1844 and 1845. Such route passed the southern end of the vast drainage today called Laguna Grande de Los Tulares—the presently vanished Tulare Lake—crossing the Central Valley to a trail heading northward along the Sierra Nevada western foothills. They missed Walker Pass entirely but as they passed through the heart of California they left a vivid record of the very wild country it then was. Especially valuable in this regard is the journal of Levi W. Hancock, former private and musician of Co. E of the Mormon Battalion. [see Bancroft's *History of California*, Vol. II, pp. 49 - 51.]

249 • Bigler was correct; it *was* the Kern River and was misidentified in both Huntington versions of the diary as well as the Bancroft version, as the Tulare River, which most researchers accept as accurate, though in this case it was not.

250 • The river encountered that saved their lives was the King River several miles east of today's city of Fresno in present Fresno County.

251 • Mormon Henry Bigler's party also encountered Americans on August 24, 1847, when his group

of Saints unexpectedly came upon a family of Americans living on the edge of the Mokelumne River—the family of Martin Murphy, Jr., which had arrived in California with the Stevens-Murphy-Townsend Party two years earlier. As Bigler wrote of it in his diary for this date: *"On the twenty-fourth traveled northwest some eighteen miles and encamped on a river. I think we called it the Macogamy. Here a few American families were living. I think their names were Murphys. Still, I am not sure. It did our eyes good to see them, the women and children, also chickens and milk cows, and the large piles of wheat already thrashed and cleaned for the sack. It was said there was over two thousand bushels. Here it was where we heard for the first time where the Church was. We were told that Brigham Young and the Twelves with three hundred pioneers had arrived at the Great Salt Lake and that five hundred wagons were close behind. Late in the evening Charles Lytle, who had left on the twenty-first returned, and reported that some of the people he visited* [at Sutters Fort] *were Mormons.*[BCW-69 - 70]

252 • This was John Pierce Rhoades, eldest son of Thomas Rhoades. John came to California in 1846 and was a member of both the First and Fourth Donner Party Relief teams. Louis Keseberg was, of course, the most infamous survivor of the Donner Party tragedy. Keseberg, in May, 1847, sued members of the Fourth Relief for defamation of character and won $1 in damages. Keseberg made and lost two fortunes; he managed a distillery for Samuel Brannan, and he ultimately convinced historian C.F. McGlashan of his innocence. Virtually all, however, who survived being marooned with him or who were involved in the various rescue parties, were entirely convinced of his guilt. Finally, penniless, Keseberg died many years later, unmourned and unattended by any family members.

253 • So much misinformation flooded California subsequent to the discovery of gold about who found it and when and under what circumstances of employment or partnership, that on January 7, 1870, to correct all the rumors and misinformation floating about, Samuel Kyburz, who was present at the time, twenty-two years earlier, made the following true declaration and statement of fact before Justice of the Peace Thomas Stephenson of Sacramento County, CA: *Affidavit of Samuel Kyburz. This is to certify that I, the undersigned, Samuel Kyburz, of the County of El Dorado, State of California, have been acquainted with James W. Marshall for many years. In the spring of 1847, while I was employed by Captain Sutter, as General Superintendent in the fort, said James W. Marshall, after his return from Southern California, did engage with Captain Sutter to work as wheelwright at the fort. They frequently conversed in my presence about building a sawmill together, Sutter furnishing all the iron work, provisions, etc., and Marshall to do all mechanical work, and have the general superintendence and management of the mill when built. Marshall, during the latter part of the Summer of 1847, at different times started out from the fort with Indian guides, to examine the country on the Cosumnes River, where it was Sutter's wish to have the mill built; but after thoroughly examining said river and vicinity, he reported to Captain Sutter the impracticability, and abandoned that locality, the distance from the fort being too great for carting the lumber. Marshall afterwards proceeded up the American River and selected the site where Coloma now is situated, and immediately thereafter Captain Sutter and Marshall entered into a written agreement of partnership, to which I was a subscribing witness, and Marshall proceeded with some half dozen of ox teams, some ten or twelve Mormons, and one family named Wemers* [sic], *the woman to do the cooking for the white laborers. He took also some twenty Indian laborers, for digging, etc., with about eight teams with tools, provisions, etc. When the mill was nearly completed, Marshall, thinking it would further advance the work on the mill race, let the water run through the race at night, and after shutting it off in the morning for the workmen to excavate again, he discovered some glittering particles at the bottom of the race, which on examination he concluded to be gold. Gathering a small phial full he brought it to the fort, and left it with Captain Sutter, who afterwards sold it to a man from Sonora for eighty dollars. Captain Sutter had never seen the place where Marshall discovered the gold, but on the day after Marshall's arrival at the fort he started for Coloma with his Indian guides. Marshall completed the mill subsequently, and delivered all the lumber of Sutter's flouring mill at Brighton. The amount I do not now recollect, but I do recollect that Marshall got pay for one-half the quantity received by Sutter. I have made the above statement because I have heard and read so many different and false statements, to the effect that Marshall was not the discoverer of gold at Coloma, and that he was not a partner with Sutter in the Coloma mill; and knowing all the facts, personally, I believe in rendering unto Caesar the things that belong to Caesar.* [signed:] *Samuel Kyburz.*

Samuel Kyburz personally appeared and made oath that the foregoing statement by him subscribed is true. [signed:] *Thomas Stephenson, Justice of the Peace, Natoma Township, Sacramento County, California. January 27th, 1870.*

254 • In *The Life and Adventures of James Marshall* (pp. 54 - 55) it is stated: "*...after many delays, caused principally by the attempts of others to interfere in the business, a partnership agreement was entered into between the two [Marshall and Sutter] on or about the 19th of August.... The formal articles of partnership were drawn by General John Bidwell, who was then acting as clerk in Sutter's store, and were witnessed by him and Samuel Kyburg, Sutter's business manager.*

255 • William Johnson was a sailor who had married Donner Party survivor Mary Murphy, whose family had lived in Nauvoo during 1841 - 1842. Reddick Allred stated Mary had been *"carried out over on the men's shoulders and thus her life was saved. She expressed regret that she was married and said that were she able she would mount a horse and go with us to the Church. We sympathized much with her for her husband appeared to be a heartless sailor."* [see Allred's *Mormon Battalion Experiences*, p. 12] Mary Murphy Johnson did, in fact, soon leave her sailor husband and had her marriage to him annulled. In 1850, the newly established city of Marysville at the confluence of the Yuba and Feather Rivers in present Sutter County was named for her.

256 • They had, in fact, come to the main lake camp of the Donner Party, where they found the two cabins that had not been burned, as General Kearny had directed they be...nor had the human remains been buried as Kearny had directed they be on June 22. As George R. Stewart wrote in *Ordeal by Hunger*, p. 277: *"Apparently Major Swords or his detail shirked the labor, so that many bones and fragments remained to the horror of later passers-by. They did not, moreover, burn all the cabins."*

257 • Because of the historic importance of the battles involved during the September 12 - 14 taking of the Mexican capital city and the ending of formal military opposition by the Mexican Army, it is recommended to interested readers to peruse the full report written by Commanding General Winfield Scott, preserved in War Department Records of 1847 under the following title:
   Major-General Winfield Scott, at Mexico City, to William L. Marcy, Secretary of War, at Washington, D.C.; Dispatch communicating Scott's report of the battles for, and occupation of, Mexico City, Head- Quarters of the Army, National Palace of Mexico, September 18, 1847

258 • The new Fort Kearny, however, was not immediately erected. By Christmas, 1847, Lt. Woodbury was back in Washington, D.C. and receiving orders from the battalion commander, Col. L.E. Powell, to secure organization of the new post. In a series of posts exchanged with General Totten, chief engineer, Powell requested an appropriation of $15,000 for materials and labor and, acting on Woodbury's request, he advocated hiring Mormons from Council Bluffs *"...to supply the new post and I urge the transfer of the large stockpile of lumber and millwork from present Fort Kearney [sic] to the new site..."* That site was where the post was erected along the right bank (south side) of the Platte Rive on the site of present Kearny, Nebraska. [Nebraska Game and Parks Commission and Nebraska State Historical Society; Fort Kearny State Historical Park. see http://www.sandi.net/Kearny/history/swk/fk.htm]

259 • The Wimmer name evidently was originally spelled Weimer, but because of its pronunciation it gradually evolved to Wimmer. The Henry Bigler diary most closely approached the correct spelling using Wemer.

260 • That Samuel Brannan followed through with this plan became evident later in a statement attested to by the Mormon Saint identified as William Glover, in which Glover wrote: *Samuel Brannan got the land, oxen, crops, house, tools and launch from New Hope; and the company, who did the work, got nothing.* [Glover unpaginated MSS, Bancroft Library]

261 • The site of that initial structuring was in the present Sixth Ward of Salt Lake City—and still referred to there as "the old fort," although the original walls have long since been removed and no trace remains except in the written words of those who built them and lived with them.

262 • The plan Tyler proposed worked very well and as he later wrote: *"The same result followed as the previous year. My provisions ran short and I had to fall back on the peas for my family's supply of food. Emigrants from the States for California came in hungry for vegetables, anxious to pay cash or other provisions for them. I picked and sold as well as used all we needed and gave some to my neighbors until almost winter, when the frost finally stopped their growth, after which I harvested three bushels. Of course, every family wanted some of the new variety. I found no difficulty in disposing of all I desired.... Provisions became more plentiful, and, instead of continuous crops of the California peas, when the first were matured the vines died, so that instead of a November harvest they ripened and began to shed from the dead vines towards the end of July and early in August, and this has been their history every since. Some argue that they must have been sown at some particular stage of the moon. That may have been so, but I can assure my friends*

that they were planted in the ground on our own little planet, and that while the moon may have looked complacently on, it was the same kind of Providence who said, 'It is my business to provide for my Saints in the last days,' that caused these unusual results. I may add, also, that many in those days of scarcity, testified that the flour increased in their boxes to their great joy and surprise."* [CHMB-318 - 320]

263 • John Sutter was at this time, just prior to the discovery of gold, at the peak of his power, influence and affluence. As he later wrote himself: *My greatest affluence were just before the gold discovery. Business increased to such a happy extent that I soon employed six hundred men in the harvest field; to feed them I had to kill from four to five oxen daily. I could raise forty thousand bushels of wheat then without inconvenience, reap the crop with sickles, thresh it out with horses, and winnow it in the wind. The Russians were my chief customers. I had twelve thousand head of cattle at the same time and fifteen thousand sheep. I had all the Indians at my call whom I could employ. There were thirty ploughs running with fresh oxen each morning. I had looms and taught the natives how to weave blankets and hats.* [NHD-xxv - xxvi]

264 • Quoted, sans title, from BCW-84 - 85.

265 • For reasons never clarified in any document known to the author, William Scott somewhat later committed suicide by slitting his own throat. [BCW-84]

266 • There has been a certain amount of dispute over the reliability of James S. Brown's account of his involvement in the initial discovery of gold, as appears in his book, *California Gold: An Authentic History of the First Find, with the Names of Those Interested in the Discovery*, Pacific Press Publishing Co., Oakland, California, 1894; also found on the internet at http://www.sfmuseum.org/hist6/grush.html. While Brown alleges he helped Marshall "pan" for gold on January 23, 1848, that appears to be false. That date is a Sunday and Brown's account leaves no doubt that it was a 'working day". In addition to being a Sunday, on which work was done only in an emergency (and none by the Mormons, of which Brown was one) this was the day when the Mormons Bigler, Brown, Barger, Johnson and Smith moved into their cabin which they had built after their altercation with Jennie Wimmer. Bigler himself wrote in his diary for this date: *"Clear. This day Myself and four others moved into a house that we had built last week."* Since Bigler has been shown to be scrupulously honest in his diary-keeping, it is reasonable to assume that Brown was less than truly honest in his reporting and somewhat falsified the facts in his own case to acquire greater fame to himself as participant in such a momentous discovery. [BCW-95 - 96; LAJM-132 - 133]

267 • One source [http://www.pbs.org/goldrush/discovery.html ] quotes Marshall later as saying at this point: *"I reached my hand down and picked it up; it made my heart thump, for I was certain it was gold. The piece was about half the size and shape of a pea. Then I saw another."*

268 • In one account [*The California Gold Rush Experience*, see http://www.lib.berkeley.edu/BANC/Exhibits/Goldrush/discovery.html] it is stated that Marshall sent the first nugget found back to the cookhouse, where Mrs. Wimmer boiled it in a pot of lye soap (a folk method for testing gold) and upon which she reported that it appeared to be genuine. Even after the material was tested by being bitten, hammered, compared to a $5 gold piece, and boiled in lye and still some continued to express their disbelief, Marshall gathered up the nuggets he was now entirely convinced were gold, still contended they were such and said, "I know it to be nothing else." [see *The California Gold Country* in http://www.malakoff.com/tcgcintr.htm. Immediately following that, Marshall gathered some other flakes and nuggets and personally took them to Sutters Fort, where they could be tested chemically, using information gained from an encyclopedia.

269 • The dozen nuggets were pure gold and ranged in value there from twenty-five cents to $5 each—a highly significant amount at a time when an average week's wages for workers back East was approximately $5. Thus, in monetary values of the year 2007, the nuggets found were equivalently worth roughly from $15.60 to $250.00 each.

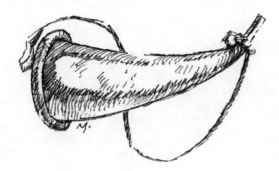

# Index

## A

Abbott, Joshua  652, 659
Abella, _____  36
Abert, J.W.  110
Adair, Wesley  652
Adams, John Quincy  245
Adams, Orson B.  652, 659
Alexander (Czar)  6
Alexander, _____, Capt.  490
Alexander, Horace M.  531, 652
Allen, Albern  651, 658
Allen, Elijah  240, 652
Allen, Franklin  652, 659
Allen, George  652, 653
Allen, James  200, 204, 213-216, 219-222, 236-241, 258-266, 272-273, 279, 303, 313-314, 443, 512, 558, 649-651, 654, 655, 657, 658
Allen, John  367, 653
Allen, Rufus Chester  651, 658
Allred, James R.  651
Allred, James T.S.  651, 659
Allred, Reddick N.  459, 651, 673
Allred, Reuben W.  651, 659
Almonte, _____  490
Alvarado, Juan Bautista  16, 21, 32, 34, 36-37, 39, 45, 47, 51, 54-55, 57-58, 65, 79, 82-86, 99, 427, 505-506
Alvarado, Martina Castro  18
Alviso, _____  192
Ames, _____  666
Ampudia, Pedro de  164, 289, 290, 292
Anashe, Chief  43
Anderson, _____  243
Anza, Juan Bautista de  13, 643
Archuleta, Diego  655
Arguello, Santiago  427
Arista, Mariano  164-165, 176, 178, 191, 289
Armijo, Manuel  224, 253, 254, 654, 655
Arrilaga, Paredes y  134

Artistan, Miguel  110
Ashley, William H.  658
Astor, John Jacob  16, 90, 645
Aulick, _____  485
Averett, Juthan  652, 659
Azua, Antonio  134

## B

Babcock, Lorenzo  652, 666
Badlam, Alexander  71-72
Badlam, Mary Ann Brannan  71, 72
Badlam, Samuel  652, 660
Bagley, W.  656
Bailey, _____  449
Bailey, Addison  652, 668
Bailey, James  651
Bailey, Jefferson  652, 668
Baldwin, _____  451
Bancroft, George  87, 110, 183-185, 187, 189, 269
Bandini, Juan  427
Barger, William W.  480, 593, 618, 652
Barnes, _____  320
Barney, Walter  366-367, 652
Barrowman, John  652
Bartlett, Washington Allen  231, 243, 276, 299-300, 435, 490
Baupista, Chief  436
Beale, Edward "Ned" Fitgerald  270, 357, 372
Bealieu, Rene  10-12
Beauregard, Gustave  463
Beauregard, Pierre  587
Beckstead, Gordon S.  651, 668
Beckstead, Orin M.  651, 668
Beckstead, William E.  652, 659
Bee, Harry  15
Beers, William  653
Belcher, _____  34
Bennett, Charles  592-593, 618

Bennett, Richard E.  656
Benson, A.G.  93-94, 113, 646-647
Bent, Charles  286
Bentley, John  653
Benton, Jessie  50, 181
Benton, Thomas Hart  49, 81, 105, 134, 140-141, 187, 189-190, 207, 304, 373, 383, 408, 447, 472, 646, 649, 655, 670, 671
Beran, James  651
Berger, James  621
Bernardo  47
Berryessa, Francisco  206
Berryessa, José de los Reyes  206
Berryessa, Ramón de Haro  206
Bevan, James  660
Biddle, James  507
Bidwell, John  60, 67, 83, 118, 126, 128-131, 142, 173, 233-236, 325, 471, 645, 648-650, 673
Bigler, Henry W.  8-10, 22-23, 25, 29-30, 64-65, 76, 78, 132-133, 215, 218-220, 222, 239, 261-262, 271, 273-275, 278-279, 317, 319, 326, 339, 347, 368-369, 371, 379, 391, 401, 424, 430, 432, 435-437, 430, 440, 457, 470, 477-479, 498-499, 532-533, 541, 543, 563-564, 567-568, 570-573, 576-578, 591-594, 598, 599, 614, 617-619, 621-622, 643, 652, 656, 662, 663, 671-673
Billings, Orson  652
Bingham, Erastus  652, 652, 659
Bingham, Thomas  652, 659
Binley, John  666
Bird, William  652, 659
Black, James  17, 140
Blackburn, Abner  652, 660
Blair, Frank  286
Blanchard, Marvin S.  659
Blinn, John  33, 34, 37, 38
Bliss, Robert S.  421, 652, 658
Boggs, Lillburn  24, 65, 73, 410
Boley, Samuel  239, 652, 660
Bonaparte, Napoleon  661
Bonneville, Benjamin Eulalie de  128
Bonsal, Stephen  662
Bowing, Henry  668
Boyd, George W.  652
Boyd, William  653
Boyle, Henry G.  364, 438, 652, 664, 668
Brackenberry, Benjamin B.  652
Brannan, Almira  73
Brannan, Harriet Hatch  73
Brannan, Mary Ann  71
Brannan, Samuel  71-76, 103-105, 112-115, 121, 136-138, 146, 148-149, 166-169, 174-175, 208-211, 227-228, 243-244, 247-248, 295-301, 409-411, 460, 511-512, 527-530, 533-536, 539, 543, 547, 459, 551, 553, 556, 570, 572-577, 583, 594-597, 647-648, 657, 664, 672, 673
Brannan, Samuel, Jr.  72

Brannan, Thomas  73
Brass, Benjamin  668
Brazier, Richard  653, 660
Briant, John S.  651
Bridger, James  126, 609
Brimhall, John  652, 660
Brizzee, Henry W.  653, 668
Brooks, Juanita  656, 658
Brouet, _____  659
Browett, Daniel  653
Brown, _____  177, 322, 572
Brown, Alexander  652, 659
Brown, Daniel  653, 659
Brown, Ebenezer  480, 651
Brown, Francis  652
Brown, Jacob  177, 179
Brown, James  237, 314, 318, 321, 534-535, 550-551, 575-576, 597, 598, 617-618, 620, 652-653, 656, 658, 659
Brown, James S.  577, 593, 606, 653, 670, 673
Brown, Jesse J.  652, 659
Brown, John  651
Brown, Samuel L.  577, 653
Brown, William  668
Brownell, Russell G.  652
Browning, Jonathan  654
Bryant, Edwin  384, 460, 511, 612, 670
Bryant, John  668
Buchanan, James  107, 139-140, 185-187, 646
Buchanan, John  652
Buckley, Newman  653
Bunker, Edward  653
Burgwin, John Henry K.  303, 329, 448
Burns, Thomas R.  660
Burt, William  652, 660
Burton, _____  510
Burton, Henry S.  600
Burton, John  15
Bush, Richard  652
Butler, Wm. O.  289
Butterfield, Jacob K.  651
Button, Montgomery  653, 656
Bybee, Henry G.  652
Bybee, John  652, 660

**C**

Cadwallader, George  549, 555
Calderon, Francisco  110
Caldwell, Matthew  561, 653, 666
Calhoun, John Caldwell  87, 140, 169, 382
Calkins, Alva C.  651, 660
Calkins, Edwin R.  651, 668
Calkins, James W.  651, 659
Calkins, Sylvanus  651
Callahan, Thomas W.  652, 668
Calvert, John, Pvt.  652, 659
Camp, James G.  652, 660
Campbell, Jonathan  653

Campbell, Samuel   653
Canalizo, _____   490
Canfield, Cyrus C.   442, 652
Cannon, George Q.   645
Carrillo, Francisca Benicia   17, 404
Carrillo, Joaquín   17, 37
Carrillo, José Antonio   417, 418
Carilló, Maria Ignacia López   17, 206
Carl, James C.   660
Carlos III   13
Carpenter, Isaac   652, 659
Carpenter, William C.   659
Carpenter, William H.   652
Carson, Christopher "Kit"   27, 68-70, 81, 83, 126, 128-129, 142-143, 155, 161-162, 179, 181-182, 191, 206, 243, 270, 303-304, 343-344, 356-358, 372-373
Carter, P. J.   652
Carter, Philo I.   668
Carter, Richard   652
Casper, William W.   651
Cass, Lewis   87
Castillero, Andres   120-121
Casto, James   653
Casto, William   659
Castro, José Emanuel Francisco Maria   16, 21, 55, 79, 83-86, 99-100, 120, 144, 156, 161, 163, 165, 170-171, 192-193, 195-196, 198, 204-205, 207, 235-236, 250, 269, 324, 344, 363, 384, 413, 648, 663
Castro, Manuel   55, 144-145
Catlin, George   652
Cavallada, Julio   83
Cazier, James   653, 660
Cazier, John   653
Chaney, Zacheus   652
Chapin, Samue   653
Chapman, William   453
Charbonneau, Baptiste   323, 324, 338, 349, 350, 431, 658, 663
Charles (Indian)   577, 615
Chase, Abner   653, 659
Chase, Hiram B.   651
Chase, John D.   652
Childs, _____   490
Church, Haden W.   652, 660
Clark, _____   314, 467
Clark, Albert   653
Clark, George S.   652, 660
Clark, Joseph   651
Clark, Riley G.   651
Clark, Riley P.   668
Clark, Samuel G.   653, 659
Clark, William   81, 88, 651, 654
Clawson, John R.   653, 668
Clay, Henry   74, 88, 90, 371
Clayton, William   527
Clift, James   652, 668

Clift, Robert   531, 652
Cloud, Jeremiah H.   370, 423, 503. 663
Clyman, James "Jim"   102, 103, 116, 179, 180, 537, 646
Cole, James B.   653
Cole, Tom   451
Collins, Robert H.   653
Colman, George   651
Colt, Samuel   81-82, 246
Colton, Philander   652
Colton, Walter   244, 247-248, 650
Com (Indian)   617
Comaduran, Antonio   396-398
Compton, Allen   653, 660
Conclin, George   93-94
Conde, Garcia   466, 469
Condit, Jeptha   652, 668
Conner, _____   247, 486
Cooke, Philip St. George   303-304, 313-319, 321-322, 323, 326, 329-331, 333-342, 347-348, 350-352, 366, 368, 370, 372, 375-379,389, 392, 396-402, 421-424, 430, 432-434, 436-438, 444, 446, 457, 458, 470, 472, 473, 475-480, 482-484, 495, 497, 499-501, 503, 508, 514-516, 536, 589, 590, 654, 657-666, 670
Coon, William   652
Coray, William   652, 670
Corwin, Ann Lisa   645
Corwin, Anna Eliza   73, 645
Corwin, Eliza   645
Corwin, Fanny   73
Covil, John A.   668
Covil, John Q.A.   652
Cowdery, Oliver   72, 645
Cowie, William   206
Cox, Amos   370, 561, 666
Cox, Amos D.   653
Cox, Henderson   651
Cox, John   653
Cox, Loenza   561
Cresap, Charles   654
Crosby, Oscar   666
Cross, Trueman   164
Crow, Robert   526
Cuevas, A.D. Luis G.   110
Cummings, George   653, 659
Curtis, Dorr P.   652
Curtis, Josiah   651, 660
Custer, George Armstrong   656
Custot, Octave   46

### D

Dallas, George M.   183, 184
Dalton, Edward   652, 660
Dalton, Harry   652, 660
D'Arce, Francisco   192-194, 204
Darnell, Anson   645
Davidson, _____   508

Davidson, J.W.   223, 356
Davis, _____   368
Davis, Daniel C.   237, 423, 442, 443, 500, 543, 653
Davis, Jefferson   290, 657
Davis, Sterling   653
Davis, Susan   423
Davis, William Heath   38, 44
Day, Abraham   653
Dayton, Willard Y.   668
Dayton, William J.   652
De Anza, Juan Bautista   643
De Camp, Samuel, Dr.   322
Decker, Zechariah B.   651
DeCourcy, _____   468
Defoe, Daniel   648
DeLeon, Ponce   387, 388
Dennett, Daniel Q.   653
Denny, _____   181, 182
Derby, _____   489
DeVoto, Bernard   648
Doak, Thomas W.   15
Dobson, Joseph   651
Dodge, Augustus E.   652
Dolton, Henry S.   652
Donald, Neal   652, 668
Doniphan, Alexander W.   24, 25, 200, 204, 224, 283, 286, 302, 303, 312, 313, 315, 322, 330, 384, 386-387-388, 403, 466-469, 495, 644, 654-655, 665
Donner, George   518, 667
Douglas, James   27-29, 43, 577, 653
Douglas, Stephen A.   92
Douglass, Ralph   653, 659
Doyle, Henry G.   332
Dreyse, Nikolas   645
Drum, _____   582, 603
Dubeld, Anna Nanette   7, 643
Dubeld, Annette   7, 643
Duncan, John   357
Dunham, Albert   652
Dunn, James   478, 652, 660
Dunn, Thomas   499, 598, 652
DuPont, _____   460
DuPont, Samuel F.   453, 665
Durphy, Francillo   652, 659
Dutcher, Thomas P.   652, 668
Dyke, Simon   653
Dykes, George P.   238, 262, 272, 311-313, 317, 319-321, 332, 334, 348, 443, 480, 481, 652, 658

E

Earl, Jacob   653, 668
Earl, James C.   651
Earl, Jesse   653, 668
Earl, Justice C.   653
Eastman, Marcus N.   652, 660

Edwards, Joseph W.   651
Egan, Howard   278, 314-315, 323, 566, 656
Egbert, Robert C.   651
Elam, Luddington   652
Elijah, Elmer   652
Emerson, Ralph Waldo   382
Emmons, Thomas   58
Emory, William H.   204, 223, 339, 342-344-345, 354, 357, 361, 403, 454. 497, 589, 661
Evans, Israel   592, 598, 652
Evans, William   652, 668
Everett, Elisha   543, 571, 651
Ewell, _____   489
Ewell, Martin F.   653

F

Fairbanks, Henry   651
Fallon, William O   517
Farqueson, R.   489
Fatoute, Ezra   653, 668
Fellom, Matthew   15
Fellows, Hiram W.   652, 668
Ferguson, James   322, 651
Fife, John   652
Fife, Peter   652
Fifield, Levi   604, 652
Findlay, John   653
Finlay, Thomas   653
Fitch, Henry Delano   531
Fitzpatrick, Thomas   81, 129, 286, 314, 658
Flake, Green   666
Fletcher, Philander   653, 668
Flores, José Maria   18, 356, 384, 413-414, 418-419
Flugge, William   66
Follett, William A.   652
Follett, William T.   652
Forbes, J.A.   15
Forbes, John Alexander   83
Forbush, Lorin   652
Ford, Henry L.   194, 206, 235
Ford, Thomas   30, 75, 91
Forsgreen, John   653
Forsythe, Jonathan   466
Fortuni, _____   36
Foster, _____ ( Dr.)   378
Foster, Curtis   653
Foster, Stephen C.   376-377
Fowler, William   206
Frazier, Thomas   577, 603, 653
Frederick, David   651, 660
Freeman, Elijah N.   652
Fremont, Jessie Benton   134, 646
Fremont, John Charles   49-50, 63, 69-70, 80-81, 88, 93, 96, 105-106, 112, 126, 129-131, 134, 141, 143-145, 155-156, 161-163, 179-182, 191-195, 199, 204-208, 216-218, 233-236, 242-243, 249-251, 269-270, 301, 303-304, 314,

363, 371-374, 384, 404, 412, 415-420, 427,
444, 447, 457, 459, 471-474, 481-484, 493,
495-497, 500-501, 505-509, 516, 519, 539,
559, 562, 565, 570, 646-650, 662-666, 670, 671
French, William   29, 31-32, 35, 37-38
Frost, Lafayette N.   651
Fuller, John   36

## G

Gaines, J.P.   582
Gales, _____   15
Galvez, José del   13
Gardner, Hamilton   665
Garland, _____   289
Garner, David   651, 659
Garner, Phillip   652, 659
Garner, William A.   652
Gibson, _____   362, 466
Gibson, Thomas   652
Gifford, William W.   653, 659
Gilbert, John   653
Gildea, W.B.   118, 130
Gillespie, Archibald H.   112, 134, 162-163,
   179, 181-182, 191-193, 216, 234-235, 249,
   270, 301, 356-358, 362-363, 415, 507, 646, 648
Gilliam, Cornelius   644
Gilpin. _____   386, 466, 488
Gilroy, James   15
Gingery, _____   598, 615
Glazier, Luther W.   653, 659
Glines, James H.   238, 322, 659
Glines, James M.   651
Glover, William   673
Godey, Alexis   361
Gomez, Dolores   452
Gomez, Joaquín   40, 67
Gomez, Salazar   344-345
Goodman, Andrew   651
Goodwin, Laur   174
Gordon, Gilman   566, 651, 666
Gould, John C.   652, 659
Gould, Samuel   652, 659
Grant, Jedediah   645
Grant, Richard   528, 553, 604-605, 609
Grant, Ulysses S.   178, 289, 291, 669
Graves, William "Uncle Billy"   517, 538
Gray, _____   373
Grayson, _____   582
Green, Ephraim   477, 652
Green, John   652
Greenwood, Caleb   116
Gribble, William   653, 659
Griffin, John   479, 508, 666
Grimes, Eliab   427
Gross, Jacob   645
Gully, Samuel L.   258-260, 265, 271, 323, 653,
   655, 658
Gulnac, Bill   15

Gutche (Indian)   577, 617
Gutierrez, _____   21

## H

Hale, W.P.   489
Hall, _____   431
Hall, Willlard   670
Hall, William Preble   516
Hammond, T.C.   223
Hammond, Thomas   357, 360
Hampton, James   333, 651
Hancock, Charles   652
Hancock, George W.   652
Hancock, Levi W.   326, 530, 567, 653, 671
Hanks, Ebenezer   653, 659
Hanks, Ephraim K.   338, 652, 660
Hardee, William J.   648
Hardin, John J.   92
Harmon, Ebenezer   652, 668
Harmon, Lorenzo F.   652, 668
Harmon, Oliver N.   653, 668
Harney, _____   490
Harris, Black   527, 547
Harris, Robert   653
Harris, Silas   652
Harris, William   299
Harrison _____   460
Harrison, Isaac   566 – 653
Harrison, Israel   653
Harrison, William Henry   50-51, 86
Hart, James S.   653, 668
Harvey, Thomas H.   267, 269
Haskell, George   489, 652
Hastings, Lansford W.   93-94, 96
Hatch, Harriet   73
Hatch, Meltliah   652
Hatch, Orin   652
Hawk, Nathan   652
Hawk, William   652
Hawkins, Benjamin   651
Hawkins, Edgar   177
Haws, Alpheus P.   652
Hays, John Coffee   82
Hayward, Thomas   653
Heath, Charles   566
Heimen (Indian)   617
Heimen, Jr.   617
Hendley, Israel   448
Hendricks, William D.   653
Hendrickson, James   293, 652
Henry, Daniel   653
Hensley, Samuel J.   235
Herrera, José Joaquín de   108, 110, 134
Hess, John W.   653, 659
Heuge, Cam   577
Heuge, Heiman   577
Hewett, Eli B.   651, 660
Hickenlooper, William F.   651, 668

679

Hickmot, John  653
Higgins, Alfred  653, 660
Higgins, Nelson  237, 280, 332, 652, 656
Hill, C.G.  489
Hinckley, William S.  20, 36, 38, 40, 47
Hinkley, Arza E.  652, 660
Hirons, James  653, 659
Hitchcock, _____  582
Hitchcock, Ethan Allen  165, 463
Hoagland, Lucas  653, 660
Hoffheins, Jacob  652
Holdaway, Shadrach  652
Holden, Elijah E.  651, 659
Holman, _____  530
Holmes, Jonathan  653
Holt, William  652
Hopkins, Charles  653, 659
Horton, _____  655
Hoskins, Henry  653
Howard, _____  460
Howell, T.C.D.  653
Howell, William  653
Hoyt, Henry P.  651
Hoyt, Timothy S.  651
Hudson, Wilford  651
Hugel, Frederick  40, 46
Huger, _____  582
Hulett, Schuyler  651, 659
Hulett, Sylvester  320, 560, 652
Humboldt, Alexander von  668
Hunsaker, _____  480
Hunsaker, Abraham  653
Hunt, Celia  651
Hunt, Gilbert  651, 656
Hunt, Jefferson  236, 241, 259, 262-263, 265, 272, 279, 281-282, 313-314, 320, 442, 478, 479, 498-500, 509, 551, 566, 651, 665, 666
Hunt, Marshall (Martial?)  651
Hunt, Matilda  651
Hunter, Edward  605, 652
Hunter, Jesse D.  236, 239, 314, 320, 326. 367, 442, 443, 478, 531, 533, 652
Hunter, William  652
Huntington, Dimick B.  653, 656
Huntsman, Isaiah  652
Hyde, George  511
Hyde, Orson  219, 645
Hyde, Stanley  299
Hyde, William  460, 531, 608, 652
Hyde, William A.  320, 333, 443

**I**

Ide, William B.  194, 198, 233, 234, 649
Ivie, Richard A.  651
Ivie, Thomas C.  652, 666

**J**

Jackson, Andrew  50, 87, 646
Jackson, Charles A.  651, 659
Jackson, Henry J.  652
Jackson, Henry W.  652
Jacobs, Bailey  653, 659
Jacobs, Sanford  480, 653
Jaggi, Samuel  6
Jarrero, _____  488
Jimmerson, Charles  653
Johnson, Cave  87
Johnson, Edward  158
Johnson, Henry  617, 651
Johnson, Jarvis  652, 659
Johnson, Mary Murphy  571
Johnson, W.  577, 621
Johnson, William  240, 592, 593, 598, 617, 667, 673
Johnston, Abraham R.  223, 358-362
Johnston, Albert S.  658
Johnston, Jesse W.  652, 660
Johnston, William J.  652
Jones, _____  460
Jones, Anson  646
Jones, Ap Catesby  230
Jones, David H.  652
Jones, John C.  29, 33
Jones, Nathaniel V.  480, 481, 516-517, 519, 537, 559-561, 652, 669
Jones, Roger  190, 273, 292, 357, 374, 411, 415, 419-420, 589, 669
Joseph II Emperor  6
Joyce, Caroline A.  174-176
Judd, Hiram [Hyrum]  653
Judd, Zadock Knapp  653
Justino (Indian)  617

**K**

Kamehameha III, King  32-33, 37
Kanaka Harry  33, 62
Kane, John Kenzer  183, 648
Kane, Thomas Leiper  183-184, 200 , 261, 265, 267
Karren, Thomas  653, 659
Kearny, Stephen Watts  111, 195, 199-203, 213-214, 216, 220, 223-224, 237, 240-241, 252-254, 259-261, 263-264, 266, 270, 272-273, 275, 281, 283-286, 302-306, 308, 311,. 313-314, 321-322, 325, 329-331, 334-336, 342-345, 348, 353-361, 363, 371-374, 384, 391, 398-402, 404, 411-416, 418-421, 424, 425, 432-434, 439, 441, 444, 447-450, 453-455, 457, 459, 460, 471-476, 478, 479, 481-483, 495-498, 500, 503-510, 515-518, 520, 534-537, 539, 546-548, 550, 558-563, 571, 589-590, 592, 649, 654-655, 657, 658, 660, 663-667, 670-673
Kelley, George  653
Kelley, Milton B.  656
Kelley, Nicholas  651, 656

Kelley, William  598
Kelly, William T.  651
Kendall, Amos  93-94, 113, 138, 184-185, 202, 646-647
Kenney, Loren E.  653, 659
Kern, Edward M.  242-243
Keseberg, Johann Ludwig Christian Louis  519, 567, 672
Keyser, Guy M.  652
Kibbey, James  668
Kibly, James  651
Kimball, Heber C.  221-222, 645
King, Henry  40, 46, 235
King, John M.  652
Kirby, _____  582
Kirk, Thomas  652
Kirker, Paul  466
Knapp, Albert  653
Kong (Indian)  577
Kotzebue, Otto Von  36
Kountz, William  593
Kouprianoff, _____  32-34, 40
Kyburz, Samuel  672, 673

**L**

La Salle, Robert Cavalier de  97
La Vega, _____  488
Ladd, Samuel  166
Lajeunesse, Basil  181, 182
Lake, Barnabas  651, 659
Lamb, Lisbon  653, 659
Lance, William  653, 668
Landero, _____  485
Landers, Ebenezer  652, 666
Lane, Lewis  480, 652
Larkin, Thomas O.  112, 116, 134, 143-144, 155, 163, 195, 207, 230, 294, 404, 427, 451, 505-506, 646, 654
Larson, Thurston  652, 659
Lassen, Peter  118, 179-180, 191-192
Laughlin, David S.  653, 659
Lawson, John  652, 661
Lay, Hark  582, 666
Layton, Christopher  652
Le Havre, France  6
Leavenworth, _____  460
Leavenworth, Thaddeus M.  511
Lee, _____  278-279, 566, 658
Lee, John D.  282, 305-306, 308, 311-312, 314-316, 323, 656, 660
Lee, Robert E.  463, 557, 582, 587, 658
Leese, Jacob P  20, 36, 52, 120, 205, 644
Leese, Rosalie  36
Leidesdorf, William A.  117
Lemon, James W.  652
Leonidas, _____  207
Leroux, Antoine  323-324, 347-348, 376, 425, 431, 658, 663

Lewis, Meriwether  81, 88, 654, 658
Lewis, Montgomery  453
Lewis, Samuel  652
Lincoln, Abraham  92, 615-616
Lincoln, Mary Todd  648
Little, Jesse C.  182-185, 200-202
Livermore, Bob  67
Llano, Manuel M.  293
Longfellow, Henry Wadsworth  662
Loring, _____  490
Lucas, William  24-25, 644
Luce, W. Ray  649
Luddington, Elam  659
Lyman, Andrew  653
Lytle, Charles  500, 531, 672

**M**

Macomb, _____  449
Maddox, _____  451
Madison, James  111
Maggard, Benjamin  652, 668
Magoffin, James  328
Manawitta  33, 62, 68, 119
Marcy, William L.  141, 145, 164, 203, 383-384, 485, 495-496, 579, 584, 649, 665, 673
Marsh, John  67, 83
Marshall, James Wilson  101-103 118, 143, 197-198, 211-212, 406, 413, 414, 493-494, 520-522, 544-545, 555-566, 568-570, 577, 590-592, 594, 597-599, 601-604, 611, 614, 616-624, 650, 666, 667, 672, 673
Marston, J.D.  511
Martin, Edward  652
Martin, Jesse B.  215, 652
Martinez, José  40
Martinez, Ygnacio  17, 40
Mason, Richard B.  410, 447, 460, 471, 473, 481, 500, 516, 669
Maxwell, Maxie  652, 660, 658
Maxwell, William  653
Mayfield, Benjamin F.  652
McArthur, Henry  653
McBride, Harlem  653, 668
McCarty, Nelson  652
McClane, Louis, Jr.  417
McClelland, William C.  653
McClelland, William E.  660
McCord, Alexander  651
McCullough, Levi H.  652
McDuffie, _____  140
McGlashan, C.F.  672
McIntyre, William L.  238, 653
McKinistry, George  613
McLane. Louis  418
McMahon, Green  102, 103
Mead, Orlando F.  652
Meade, George Gordon  226, 284, 288, 291, 463

681

Medill, William  267, 269
Meek, Joe
Meek, Stephen  647
Meseck, Peter J.  653, 659
Mejia, Francisco  157, 159, 164, 176-177
Merrill, Ferdinand  653
Merrill, Philemon C.  332, 377
Merritt, Ezekiel "Zeke"  192, 194, 205, 235, 363, 649-650
Mervine, William  330
Micheltorena, Manuel  55, 66, 78-80, 82-86, 99-101, 115, 135
Miles, Samuel  652
Miller, Daniel  653, 659
Miller, George  655
Miller, Henry B.  652
Miller, Miles  471, 653
Mitchell, _____  469
Montgomery, _____  460
Montgomery, John Berrien  192, 207, 211-213, 230-231, 275-276, 293, 296, 299-300, 430, 441
Moore, Ben  223
Moore, Benjamin D.  305, 360
More, Calvin W.  652
Morega, Gabriel  671
Morey, Harley  652, 656
Moroni, _____  72
Morris, Thomas  390, 652, 668
Morstein, Louis  40
Moss, David  652
Mouet, John  603
Mount, Hiram B.  652
Mowrey. John T.  652
Mowry, James  668
Mowry, John  668
Muir, William S.  651
Munchausen, Baron
Murdock, John R.  652
Murdock, Price  652
Murphy, Lavinia  519, 571
Murphy, Lemuel B.
Murphy, Martin  672
Murphy, Tim  17
Murray, H.F.  489
Myers, Samuel  652
Myler, James  652

**N**

Naile, Conrad  652, 668
Neal, Tom  162
Nelson, F.B.  489
Nevins, Joe  40, 43-44
Nicholas I, Czar  19
Nicholson, _____  449
Nicollet, Joseph  49, 645
Noler, Christian  652
Noriega, _____  488
Noriega, José  207

Nowler, Christian  668
Nowlin, Jabez  652, 659

**O**

Oakley, James  653, 659
Obando, _____  488
O'Dell, Jack  40, 43-44
O'Farrell, Jasper  460
Old Bullion  190
Olivera, Augustin  417-418
Olmstead, Hiram  652
Oman, George W.  306, 320, 424, 480, 500, 502, 651
Onate, Don Juan de  660
Ord, Edward Otho Cresap  451
Ortega, _____  293
O'Sullivan, John  108
Owen, James  653
Owens, _____  468, 481, 483, 501, 607
Owens, Robert  652
Oyler, Melcher  652, 659

**P**

Pace, James  258-259, 262-265, 271, 278, 320, 476-478, 500, 502, 531, 566, 605-606, 653
Packard, Henry  652
Pakenham, Richard  107
Paredes y Arrilaga  134, 246, 256, 257
Park, James (1)  652, 668
Park, James, (2)  652, 668
Park, William A.  653, 659
Parsons, George F.  649-650
Patterson, _____  490
Patton, _____  489
Pearson, Ephraim  652
Peck, Edwin M.  653, 668
Peck, Isaac  652, 668
Peck, Thorit  652
Pell, E. Ward  297
Pelly, George  29, 33
Peralta, Pedro de  316
Peralta, Vicente  207
Perez, Ignacio  661
Perkins, David  652, 659
Perkins, John  652
Perrin, Charles  653
Perry, _____  485, 486, 503
Persons, Ebenezer  577, 652
Persons, Ezekiel  593
Persons, Harmon D.  652, 659
Persons, Judson  652, 659
Pettegrew, David  347, 443, 458, 530, 653
Pettegrew, James P.  653
Phelps, Alva  280, 653
Phelps, John  217, 656
Philemon, C. Merrill  652
Pickering, _____  58
Pickup, George  652

Pico, Andres Maria  55, 353, 358, 362, 384, 414, 416-417, 563, 648, 661, 663
Pico, Pio  55, 79, 116, 119, 143-144, 161, 163, 164, 170-171, 192-193, 198, 207, 243, 250, 269-270, 324, 354, 358, 648
Pierce, Franklin  555, 557, 582
Pike, Gideon  87
Pillow, Gideon  464, 485, 486, 488-490, 557, 582, 587
Pinada, Manuel  600
Pinson, _____  488
Pitt, John  394
Pixton, Robert  614-615, 653
Plympton, _____  490
Polk, James Knox  74, 87-90, 93, 96-98, 106-108, 110-112, 123-125, 131-132, 139-141, 148, 150, 166, 169-170, 181, 184-188, 195, 199-203, 220-221, 227, 244-247, 255-257, 290, 303, 309-310, 330, 371, 380-384, 403, 407-408-409, 447-448, 464, 465, 471, 488, 439, 494-495, 512, 522, 583, 589, 610, 615-616, 646-649, 657, 665, 670, 671
Porter, Lucius  164
Porter, Sanford  370, 653
Powell, L.E.  673
Pratt, Addison  511
Pratt, Orson  112, 114, 150, 219, 645
Pratt, Parley P.  112, 114, 266, 645, 656
Price, Sterling  25, 279-280, 302, 313, 448
Prouse, William  652
Prudon, Victor  36, 120, 135, 205
Pryor, _____  508, 509
Pugmire, Jonathan, Jr.  653, 659
Pulsipher, David  652

## Q

Quigley, Robert  536, 561, 669
Quitman, John Anthony  290, 463, 557, 587

## R

Radford, William  517
Rainey, David Pinkney  320, 477, 652
Raphero (Chief)  196-198, 648
Rawson, Daniel B.  653
Raymond, Almon P.  653
Reading, Pierson B.  99, 118, 233-234-235, 418
Reid, _____  388
Reid, William  466, 468
Requena, _____  293
Reynolds, William F.  652, 666
Rhoades, John Pierce  567, 672
Rhoades, Thomas  672
Rich, Charles Coulson  645
Richards, Joseph W.  659
Richards, L.  653, 668
Richards, Levi  219
Richards, Peter F.  652
Richards, Willard  221, 237, 265, 553, 645
Richards, William  219
Richardson, Edward  114-115
Richardson, Thomas  653, 660
Richardson, William A.  17, 20-21, 36, 137, 146, 148, 166, 168-169, 173, 175, 210, 227-228, 297
Richie, Benjamin  652
Richmond, Benjamin  652, 660
Richmond, William  653
Ricketts, Norma B.  653, 659
Ridley, Robert  60, 118
Rigdon, Sidney  77
Ringgold, Robert  58
Riser, John J.  652, 668
Ridley, Robert  57
Riter, John  668
Ritter, John  652
Robbins, George Edward  167
Robbins, Georgiana Pacific  209
Robbins, John  209
Robbins, Phoebe  167, 209
Roberts, B.H.  663
Roberts, Benjamin  653, 659
Roberts, L.  653
Robinson, John  469
Robinson, William  653
Rockwell, O.P.  65
Rodgers, _____  660
Roe, Cariatat C.  652, 659
Rogers, Jacob  24
Rogers, Samuel H.  331, 334, 336, 351-352, 365, 389, 401, 478, 652
Rollins, Evart  653
Rollins, John  653
Romanov, Czar  34, 53, 56
Root, E.K.  246
Rosecrantz, George W.  320, 502, 652
Rotchev, Alexander  19, 34, 39-41, 53-54, 56
Rotchov, Helene de Gagarin  34, 39, 53
Rowan, _____  415
Rowe, William  653, 659
Ruel, Barrus  652
Runyan, Levi  653, 668
Russell, C.W.  299
Russell, William H. "Owl"  301, 371, 417-418, 427, 471, 472, 670
Rust, William W.  652, 660
Ruxton, George Frederick  655
Ruxton, Edward  657

## S

Sacagawea  658
Sanders, Richard T.  653
Sanderson, George B., Dr.  240, 258, 260-261, 263-264, 272-274, 278, 280-281, 283, 308, 317, 319, 321-322, 326, 333, 497, 517, 653, 655, 658
Sanderson, Henry W., Pvt.  653, 659

Santa Ana, Antonio López de   134, 246-247, 255, 257, 289, 309, 330, 380-382, 461, 462, 486, 488, 490, 499, 513-514, 522, 549, 554-555, 557-558, 579, 581, 583-584, 645
Sargent, Abel M.   653, 659
Sarpy, Peter A.   653
Savage, Levi   653
Schindler, Harold   655
Schnell, Carl   6
Scott, H.L.   582
Scott, James Allen   653
Scott, James R.   653
Scott, Leonard M.   653
Scott, Oliver   618
Scott, Richard   554
Scott, Tom   603
Scott, William   242, 577, 593, 673
Scott, Winfield   381-383, 403, 408, 409, 461, 463-465, 484-486, 488, 491, 494, 503, 522-523, 548-549, 557-558, 579, 582-584, 586-587-589, 610, 673
Seaton, _____   105
Seity (Indian)   617
Selkirk, Alexander   648
Semple, James   150, 151
Semple, Robert, Dr.   244, 247-248, 404
Serra, Junipero   664
Sessions, John   652, 659
Sessions, Richard   652
Sessions, William B.   652
Sexton, George S.   652, 668
Seymour, _____   230, 650
Seyti, Charles   577
Sharp, Albert   653, 659
Sharp, Norman   653, 656
Sheen, Joseph   660
Shelton, John   656
Shelton, Sebert C.   238, 653, 656
Shepherd, Lafayette   652
Sherman, William Tecumseh   232, 374-375, 448-451, 454, 481, 482, 506-509, 516, 666, 668
Shields, James   463, 486, 488-489, 557, 660
Shipley, Joseph   652
Shively, J.M.   647
Shubrick, William Branford   375, 447, 451-452, 453, 454, 459, 473, 474, 483, 484, 600
Shumway, Aurora   652, 668
Shupe, Andrew J.   652, 659
Shupe, James   652, 659
Sigler, Bill   180-181
Simmons, William A.   652
Simpson, George Sir   36, 52, 554, 669
Sinclair, John   517, 613
Skein. Joseph   653
Slater. Richard   653
Slaughter, John   662
Slidell, John   98, 110

Sloat, John Drake   110, 189, 206, 228-230, 248-249, 330, 441, 447, 650
Sly, James C.   532, 652
Smith, Albert   370, 424, 652, 653, 665
Smith, Andrew Jackson   258, 262-264, 272-275, 279-282, 306-308, 312-313, 315, 317, 319, 341, 446, 508, 542, 656-658
Smith, Azariah   377, 478, 479, 531, 573, 576-577, 592-593, 598, 617, 619, 621, 652
Smith, C.E.   484
Smith, C.F.   290, 490
Smith, Charlie   528, 547, 565, 583
Smith, David   653
Smith, Elisha   368, 653
Smith, George A.   219
Smith, Hyrum   24, 75-76, 91, 103, 546
Smith, Jedediah Strong   26, 658
Smith, John   653
Smith, John G.   653, 659
Smith, Joseph   9, 22-24, 64-65, 71-77, 91, 103-105, 123, 280, 394, 546, 644-645, 651
Smith, Lot   653, 668
Smith, Mary Ettie V.   670
Smith, Milton   652, 659
Smith, Persifer F.   404. 463, 490, 555
Smith, Richard   652, 659
Smith, Starrett   645
Smith, William   103-104, 122, 668
Snow, Eliza   154
Snow, Lorenzo   154, 645
Snyder, John   653
Sola, Ygnacio   16
Spear, Nathan   20, 36, 38, 40, 47
Spence, David   83-84, 86, 427
Spencer, William   370
Spencer, William W.   653, 666
Speyer, Albert   224, 655
Spidle, John   653
Sprague, Richard D.   652
Squires, William   652, 660
St. John, Stephen M.   653
Standage, Henry   370, 502, 653
Stanton, Charles   517
Steele, George E.   652, 668
Steele, Isaiah C.   652, 668
Steele, John   316, 319, 606, 653, 658, 659
Steers, Andrew J.   652, 668
Stephens, _____   618
Stephens, Alexander   577, 593, 621, 653
Stephens, Arnold   652, 659
Stephens, Lyman   652, 659
Stephnson, Thomas   672
Stevens, Roswell   323, 577, 653, 659
Stevens, William – 602, 603
Stevenson, Jonathan D.   441, 442, 444, 447, 495, 497, 504, 511, 530, 531, 533, 668
Stewart, Benjamin   653

Stewart, George R. 673
Stewart, James 653
Stewart, Robert B. 653
Stillman, Clark 653, 659
Stillman, Dexter 652, 659
Stockton, Robert Field 208, 210, 235, 247-252, 269, 270, 301, 304, 328, 330, 354, 356, 357, 361, 363, 371, 373, 374, 384, 402, 404, 410, 412-414, 416, 418, 420, 427, 444, 447, 450, 457, 478, 498, 506, 511, 650, 661, 663-665, 670
Stoddard, Rufus 652
Stokes, _____ 355
Stoneman, George 318, 424, 446, 476, 496, 499, 508, 530, 533, 658, 663
Stout, Hosea 152, 215, 345, 661
Strong, William 653
Stuart, Benjamin 660
Stuart, James 660
Study, David 652
Sturgis, Samuel D. 656
Summer, Avril 489
Sumner, Azinor 303, 305, 582
Sunol, Antonio 40, 67
Sutherland, G.T. 489
Sutter, Anna Elisa 643
Sutter, Annette Dubeld 6-7, 68
Sutter, Carl 643
Sutter, Clara 6
Sutter, Emil Victor 643
Sutter, Johann Augustus 5-6, 62, 68, 643
Sutter, John August 5-8, 10, 26-29, 31-37, 40-47, 51-52, 54, 56-58, 60, 62, 66-67, 69-70, 82-86, 99-101, 103, 115-121, 130-131, 135-136, 142-143, 162, 172-173, 179, 192-193, 196-198, 206-207, 242, 243, 324, 325, 404, 405, 491-494, 517, 520-522, 544, 545, 562-563, 565-566, 568-569, 576-577, 589-593, 596-599, 601, 603-604, 610-611, 613-616, 643-645, 648, 654, 667, 672-674
Sutter, William Alphonse 643
Swarthout, Nathan 653
Swartout, Hamilton 652
Swift, Granville P. 235
Swords, F. 454
Swords, Thomas 253, 476, 497, 518-519, 561, 667

T

Taggart, George W. 652
Talbot, _____ 270
Tanner, Myron 653, 659
Tanner, Albert 653
Taylor, John 219, 605, 645
Taylor, Joseph 652, 666
Taylor, Zachary 111, 141, 145-146, 157-160, 163-165, 176-179, 185-187, 190-191, 225-227, 232-233, 245, 287-288, 290-291-293, 301, 309-310, 330, 381, 383-385, 403, 408-409, 560, 461, 463, 499, 513, 522-523, 649, 655, 657, 661
Terrill, Joel J. 652, 659
Therlkill, George 526
Thomas, Elijah 652
Thomas, George 658
Thomas, Haywood 660
Thomas, Nathan T. 652, 660
Thompson, A.B. 36
Thompson, Henry 653
Thompson, James L. 652
Thompson, John 652
Thompson, Miles 653, 668
Thompson, Samuel 470, 479, 480, 500
Thornton, Seth 165, 186, 648
Thurneysen, Emanuel 6
Tindell, Solomon 652, 659
Tippets, John H. 653, 656, 660
Todd, William L. 198-199, 206, 648
Tompkins, _____ 454
Torre, Joaquín de la 194-195, 205-206
Torrejon, Anastasio 165
Totten, _____ 485, 673
Treador. _____ 520
Treat, Thomas 653
Trias, _____ 579
Tripps, David 26
Trist, Nicholas 558, 583
Truman, Jacob M. 652
Tubbs, William R. 653, 660
Tully, Tim 528
Turley, Theodore 123
Turner, _____ 369, 454, 478
Turner, Henry Smith 223, 402, 471, 483, 499, 518, 548, 560, 655, 666
Tuttle, Elanson 652, 666
Tuttle, Luther T. 652
Twichell, Anciel 653
Twigg, _____ 486, 488-490, 554-555, 587
Tyler, Daniel 307, 309, 319, 336-337, 339, 348, 351-352, 365, 366-367, 369, 378, 390, 422, 425, 428, 438, 440, 443, 458, 500, 503, 517-518, 530, 532, 538, 565-566, 575, 606-607, 609, 652, 654, 673
Tyler, John 50, 86, 97, 657

V

Valdez, Francisco Quervo 659
Valentin (Indian) 617
Valencia, Gabriel 554-555
Vallejo, José Juan 14
Vallejo, Mariano Guadalupe 12-14, 18, 20-21, 39, 45, 47, 51, 54-55, 59, 65, 78-80, 170-172, 205-206, 241-244, 270-271, 293-295, 404, 427, 460, 644, 657

685

Vallejo, Salvador 205
Vallejo, Ygnacio 14
Van Buren, Martin 50, 86-87
Vasquez, _____ 488
Vasquez, Louis 126
Victoria (Queen) 451
Vioget, _____ 85
Vrandenburg, Adna 652

## W

Wade, Edward W. 652
Wade, Moses 652
Walker, Edwin 653
Walker, Joseph Reddeford 128-129, 131, 142, 155-156, 162, 179, 648, 671
Walker, Samuel 245
Walker, William 652, 659
Warner, _____ 454,
Warner, Jonathan Trumbull 251, 362, 432-433, 654
Washington, George 64
Watts, John 652, 668
Weaver, Franklin 652
Weaver, Miles 652
Weaver, Pauline 323, 399, 658
Webb, Charles Y. 561, 652, 666
Weber, Charles 60
Webster, Daniel 49
Weeks, J.W. 15
Weightman, _____ 253, 467, 488
Weigart, Horace 177
Weir, Thomas 651
Welsh, Madison 652, 660
West, Benjamin 653, 668
Wharton, Clifton 258-259, 272, 655
Wheeler, Henry 652, 668
Wheeler, John L. 652, 668
Wheeler, Merrill W. 652
White, Elijah 93, 647
White, John J. 652
White, Joseph 652
White, Samuel F. 652
Whiting, Almon 653, 659
Whiting, Edmons 653, 659
Whitmer, Peter 645
Whitney, Francis T. 652
Whitney, Newell K. 266, 656
Whitworth, William 653
Wilcox, Edward 652
Wilcox, Henry 652
Wilcox, Matthew 652
Wilhelm, Frederick (King) 6
Wilkes, John 58, 195
Wilkin, David 652, 659
Willey, Jeremiah 652, 666
Williams, _____ 582
Williams, Abiather 122

Williams, James V. 653, 668
Williams, Thomas S. 150, 535, 550, 652, 659
Willis, Ira 577, 593, 652
Willis, Sidney 598, 615
Willis, W.S.S. 652
Willis, William W. 337, 577, 593, 660
Wilmot, David 255-257
Wilson, Alfred G. 652
Wilson, George 653, 660
Wimmer, "Jennie" 569, 577-578, 591-592, 611, 617-618
Wimmer, Peter 569, 577, 591-592, 602, 604, 615, 620-621
Winn, Dennis 652
Winters, Jacob 652, 668
Wise, Henry 450, 453
Wittmer, Jacob 615
Wood, William 543
Wood, William R. 652
Woodbury, William 673
Woodruff, Wilford 104, 215, 645
Woodward, Francis 653
Woodward, George W. 139
Woodward, J.M. 647
Woodworth, Lysander 577, 603, 652, 660
Woodworth, Samuel 615
Wool, John Ellis 284, 286, 302-303, 328, 347, 385, 403
Woolsey, Thomas 653, 656, 660
Workman, Andrew J. 652, 668
Workman, Oliver G. 652, 668
Worth, William J. 290, 292, 293, 310, 464, 485, 486, 489-490, 557, 581-583, 587
Wright, Charles 652, 659
Wright, Phinehas R. 651
Wright, Silas 87
Wriston, Isaac N. 652, 660
Wriston. John C. 652, 659
Wyeth, Nathaniel Jarvis 644

## Y

Yearwood, W. 489
Young, Brigham 65, 77-78, 91-92, 113, 121-123, 132-133, 138, 146, 149-151, 153-154, 182-184, 200, 210, 215-216, 219, 222, 236-237-238, 261-267, 278-279, 281, 298, 300, 305, 316, 319, 393, 395, 410, 479, 511-513, 524-529, 531-536, 545-547, 549-551, 553, 560, 565, 572-576, 583, 594, 607, 645, 647, 649-651, 655-656, 658, 660, 662, 666, 672
Young, Nathan 668
Young, Sheldon 658

## Z

Zabriskie, Jerome 652, 668
Zamorano, Augustin V. 248

# About the Author

◆

*[January 30, 1931 • July 7, 2011]*

Allan W. Eckert was an historian, naturalist, novelist, poet, screenwriter, and playwright. The author of forty published books prior to this one, he was nominated on seven separate occasions for the Pulitzer Prize in literature and, in 1985, was the recipient of an honorary Doctor of Humane Letters from Bowling Green State University in Ohio. In 1998 he received his second honorary doctorate, also in Humane Letters, this time from Wright State University in Dayton, Ohio. In addition to his books, he wrote and had published over 150 articles, essays, and short stories, as well as considerable poetry, a major outdoor drama, and screenplays for several movies.

Most noted for his historical and natural history books, Eckert's works have been translated into thirteen foreign languages around the world. A number of his books have been selections of *Reader's Digest Condensed Books* and several have been major book club selections. The seven of his books that have been nominated for the Pulitzer Prize in literature include *A Time of Terror: The Great Dayton Flood* (history), *Wild Season* (fiction), *The Silent Sky* (fiction), *The Frontiersmen* (history), *Wilderness Empire* (history), *The Conquerors* (history), and *A Sorrow in Our Heart: The Life of Tecumseh* (biography).

Eckert's varied writing includes over 225 performed half-hour television scripts which he wrote for the renowned *Mutual of Omaha's Wild Kingdom* series and for this writing he received, in 1970, an Emmy Award from the National Academy of Television Arts and Sciences in the category of Outstanding Program Achievement. He was playwright of the acclaimed Outdoor Drama entitled *Tecumseh!* which, in 2011, celebrated its 38th year of production at the multi-million-dollar Sugarloaf Mountain Amphitheater near Chillicothe, Ohio. It has been described as the finest outdoor theater production in America. Over that period, the production has been attended by upwards of three million people. For this drama and his other writings, he received from the Scioto Society, in 1987, the Second Annual Silver Arrow Humanitarian Award "for his contributions to the human spirit and knowledge as an author, novelist, playwright, naturalist, and historian."

Eckert's best known historical narrative, *The Frontiersmen*, from which he adapted his outdoor drama, *Tecumseh!*, won the Ohioana Library Association

Book-of-the-Year Award in 1968. He received, for his book *Incident at Hawk's Hill*, the Newbery Honor Book Award, the highest award for juvenile literature in America. Again for *Incident at Hawk's Hill*, in 1976 he accepted, in person in Vienna, the Austrian Juvenile Book-of-the-Year Award—the first time this prize was ever awarded to a non-Austrian. This same book brought him the Best Book of the Year Award from Claremont Colleges in California and it was also made into a two-part television movie by Walt Disney under the title *The Boy Who Talked to Badgers*. A quarter-century after that book's initial publication, Eckert wrote a sequel entitled *Return to Hawk's Hill*, which was published in May 1998.

His widely-acclaimed series of historical narratives entitled The Winning of America consists of six volumes, including *The Frontiersmen, Wilderness Empire, The Conquerors, The Wilderness War, Gateway to Empire,* and *Twilight of Empire*. For this series Eckert was presented the Americanism Award by the Daniel Boone Foundation in 1985, and the governor of Kentucky, late in 1987, bestowed upon him the status of honorary resident of that state and conferred upon him its highest honor, commissioning him a bona fide Kentucky Colonel. In 1995, his book *That Dark and Bloody River: Chronicles of the Ohio River Valley* was named runner-up for the Spur Award of the Western Writers of America. In 1997, Eckert was recipient of the Writer of the Year Award bestowed for his entire body of work by the National Popular Culture Association.

An esteemed American naturalist, Eckert specialized, in addition to historical writing, in writing about natural history subjects. He had a keen interest in the natural history subjects of geology, entomology, ornithology, herpetology, paleontology, archaeology, anthropology, mineralogy, and allied fields. Among his important natural history writings are his companion volumes, *The Owls of North America* and *The Wading Birds of North America*. He also wrote a series of four volumes, published in 1987 by Harper & Row Publishers, called *Earth Treasures*—a guide to over 5,000 sites in the contiguous United States where the amateur collector can find excellent minerals, rocks, and fossils. His major definitive work on the gemstone opal, entitled *The World of Opals* was published by John Wiley & Sons in October, 1997.

Allan Eckert was born in Buffalo, New York, raised in the Chicago area, graduated (1948) from Leyden Community High School in Franklin Park, Illinois, and, after four years in the United States Air Force, attended the University of Dayton (Ohio) and The Ohio State University.

In 1999, the Ohioana Library Association, in celebration of its 70th anniversary, invited all Ohioans to vote for their "all time favorite Ohio authors and their books." Ballots were sent to all public libraries in Ohio and many Ohio newspapers also participated in the event. Eckert's book *The Frontiersmen* was selected as Ohioans' favorite book "About Ohio or an Ohioan." Eckert was himself selected as Ohio's favorite author in the category of "About Ohio or an Ohioan," and in the principal category of "Overall Favorite Ohio Writer of All Time," the top honor resulted in a tie—shared by Toni Morrison and Eckert.

Allan and his wife, Joan, made their home in Corona, California.

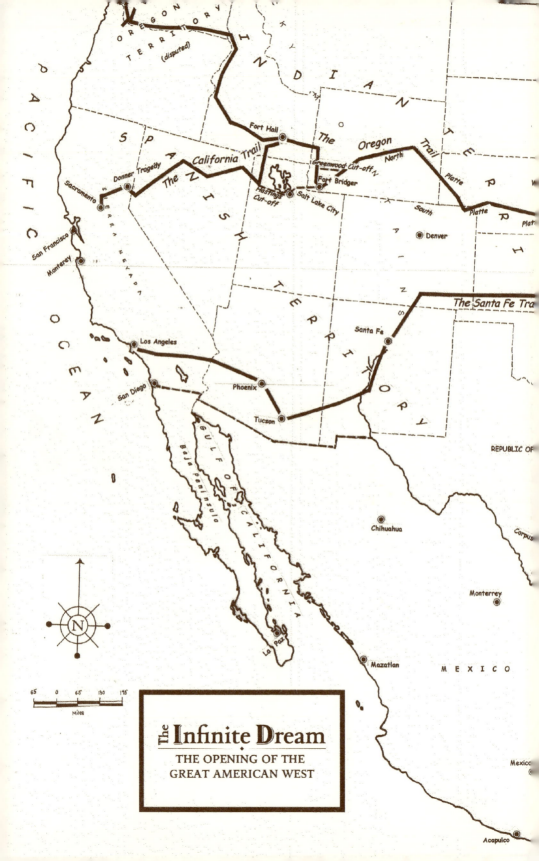